944'03 VERSAILLES : THE PASSIONS AND
BARRY, J POLITICS OF AN ERA.

Please renew/return this item by the last date shown.

So that your telephone call is charged at local rate,
please call the numbers as set out below:

	From Area codes 01923 or 0208:	From the rest of Herts:
Renewals:	01923 471373	01438 737373
Enquiries:	01923 471333	01438 737333
Minicom:	01923 471599	01438 737599

k

L32b

L32

D1333069

VERSAILLES

The Passions and Politics of an Era

VERSAILLES

The Passions and Politics
of an Era

JOSEPH BARRY

LONDON
VICTOR GOLLANCZ LTD
1972

Printed in Great Britain by
Lowe & Brydone (Printers) Ltd., London

To Liliane, Lola, and Alex
with love and gratitude

Contents

ACT TWO

ACT THREE

Contents

List of Illustrations

Note on Money

For sterling equivalents, it may be useful to think of the period's livre or franc as roughly approximating the shilling (5p). But one should also recall that the shilling was then worth £2, forty times that of today. All such conveniences, of course, have meaning only in terms of contemporary wages and prices. In 1666, for instance, a record shows a vineyard worker earning 12 sous a day. (There are 20 sous in a livre or franc, three livres in an écu, ten livres in a pistole and 20 livres in a louis d'or.) In 1762 a weaver (male) earned 20 sous a day, a weaver (female) ten sous and a weaver (child) five. In 1660 three steer (half today's size) sold for a total of 112 livres and in 1746 a cow sold for 50 livres. In 1712 a pair of wooden shoes cost a priest four sous. In 1749 the second-hand cloth coat of a defunct seigneur sold for 30 livres. In 1672 a peasant's house—one large room and a loft, two doors, two windows, and a fire-place—cost 20 livres. In 1725 one bedroom's furnishings for the Princesse de Condé were estimated at 10,000 livres. In 1774 in Troyes a weaver's family of four paid 32 livres as a year's rent. Other relevant information is offered in the text as the Revolution rumbles toward the palace of Versailles.

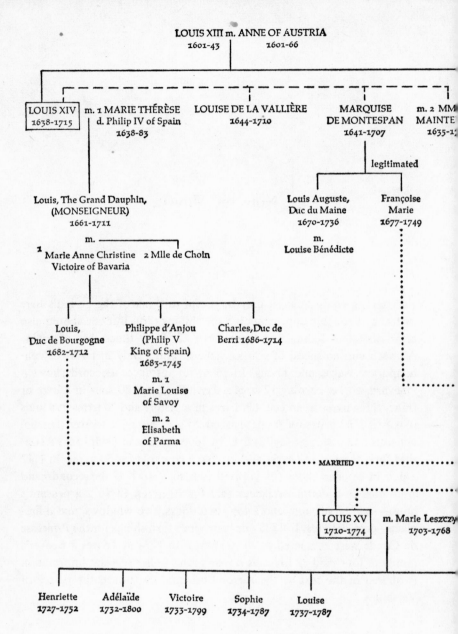

LOUIS XIII m. ANNE OF AUSTRIA
1601-43   1601-66

LOUIS XIV   m. 1 MARIE THÉRÈSE   LOUISE DE LA VALLIÈRE   MARQUISE   m. 2 MM
1638-1715   d. Philip IV of Spain   1644-1710   DE MONTESPAN   MAINTE
              1638-83   1641-1707   1635-1

                                                                    legitimated

Louis, The Grand Dauphin,   Louis Auguste,   Françoise
    (MONSEIGNEUR)   Duc du Maine   Marie
      1661-1711   1670-1736   1677-1749

         m.   m.
  1 Marie Anne Christine   2 Mlle de Choin   Louise Bénédicte
     Victoire of Bavaria

      Louis,   Philippe d'Anjou   Charles, Duc de
Duc de Bourgogne   (Philip V   Berri 1686-1714
   1682-1712   King of Spain)
                         1683-1745

                            m. 1
                         Marie Louise
                          of Savoy

                            m. 2
                          Elisabeth
                          of Parma

                                          MARRIED

                                    LOUIS XV   m. Marie Leszczy
                                    1710-1774   1703-1768

   Henriette   Adélaïde   Victoire   Sophie   Louise
  1727-1752   1732-1800   1733-1799   1734-1787   1737-1787

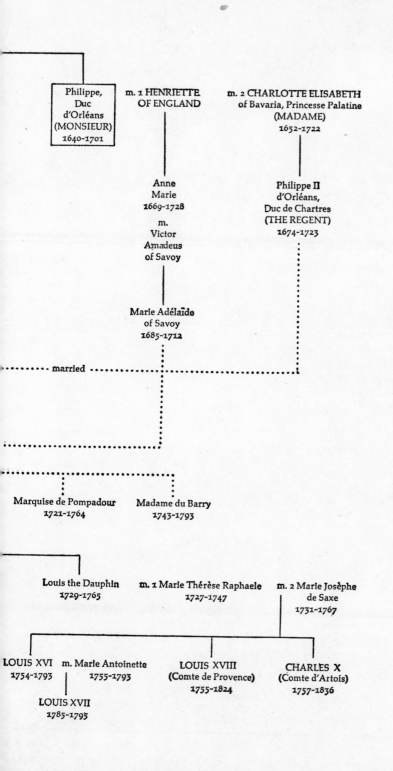

Philippe,
Duc
d'Orléans
(MONSIEUR)
1640-1701

m. 1 HENRIETTE
OF ENGLAND

m. 2 CHARLOTTE ELISABETH
of Bavaria, Princesse Palatine
(MADAME)
1652-1722

Anne
Marie
1669-1728
m.
Victor
Amadeus
of Savoy

Philippe II
d'Orléans,
Duc de Chartres
(THE REGENT)
1674-1723

Marie Adélaïde
of Savoy
1685-1712

····· married ·····

Marquise de Pompadour
1721-1764

Madame du Barry
1743-1793

Louis the Dauphin
1729-1765

m. 1 Marie Thérèse Raphaele
1727-1747

m. 2 Marie Josèphe
de Saxe
1731-1767

LOUIS XVI
1754-1793

m. Marie Antoinette
1755-1793

LOUIS XVIII
(Comte de Provence)
1755-1824

CHARLES X
(Comte d'Artois)
1757-1836

LOUIS XVII
1785-1795

Preview as Preface

Traditionally, visitors to the palace of Versailles arrive by way of the town and the huge cobbled courtyard forbiddingly called the Place d'Armes. Arrival is usually by the busload; one's first impression is that of a monumental and confusing pile. The dutiful, guided tour of the interior—largely emptied of its furniture and statuary by the Revolution, turned into a museum by Louis-Philippe—can be deadly and tiresome.

Instead, surprise the palace from the park, avoiding the town as much as possible. Detour around the château to the north and enter the gardens on the Trianon side. But don't be tempted by Mansart's sudden splendor of rose-marble columns. We shall come to this retirement palace in time, as did the Sun King in his twilight years. Rather, continue along the wide, tree-lined *allées,* or walks, washing the mind, preparing it for a past that slowly, as you walk, becomes the present.

The western gate is our goal. By the Basin of Apollo, whose chariot and horses of the sun rise from the waters, it opens to a great stretch of lawn called the Green Carpet. Step by step under the tall trees you approach the distant palace, the windows of its Hall of Mirrors stately dominating. Step by unhurried step, accompanied by human-scale statues of gods and goddesses, you reach the lovely Fountain of Latona. The palace by now has miraculously dropped from view, disappearing behind the vast terrace which is its platform. Then, sud-

denly, as you mount the stone staircase, there it is: beyond the reflecting pools, a serenely noble horizon of pale rhythmic stone.

Turn your back to it.

You are Louis XIV, standing where he loved to stand, admiring what he never ceased to admire: the sovereign view from the
lofty terrace to the Grand Canal and beyond to the remote paired poplars against the sky. It is a vista that makes a king of every man.

But for the historic beginnings of Versailles' palace, you must return
for the traditional approach on the town side.

By whatever avenue you arrive, you are led to it. All three avenues
converge on the Royal Grill—the medial Avenue de Paris like a
three-hundred-foot-wide shaft of a giant arrow—and they point across
the courtyard not to the Royal Chapel, but to the royal chamber.

That the Sun King should install his bedroom at the very center
of his palace, then the center of Europe and thus of Western civilization, is piquant enough. More to the point, he had installed it in the
little château, the hunting retreat, of his father, Louis XIII. The château
—the appealing, visible heart of the great palace of Versailles—can
be seen clearly by climbing the vast cobbled courtyard of the entrance:
it is a little castle of fairylike beauty with walls of faded brick and
white stone, poised above its own tiny courtyard of marble and
surrounded on three sides by the monumental wings and façades of
Le Vau and Mansart.

That "little castle of cards" was the beginning, for Versailles was
born not of Louis XIV, but of Louis XIII; not out of love for, but
a most un-Bourbon fear of, women.

ACT ONE

1. The Womanless Birth of Versailles

A French king lives and dies as he is born—in public.

To begin the birth of Versailles with the birth of Louis XIII, September 27, 1601, is not as arbitrary as it might seem.[1] His fishbowl life as infant, prince, and king opens the modern mind to what life will be like in the palace of Louis XIV.

The mother of Louis XIII was Marie de Médicis. (In the trip to France, everything Italian, from Renaissance style to proper names, became French.) She was the daughter of Francesco de' Medici, Grand Duke of Tuscany, and of Joanna, an Archduchess of Austria, and was thus part Habsburg. She felt the first labor pains of Versailles' future begetter at Fontainebleau. Feverishly—he was many times a father, but this was his first legitimate offspring—Henry IV sent for the midwife. He also sent for his cousins, the princes of the blood —Henry and Charles de Bourbon and François de Conti—to witness the birth. It was a custom and precaution that did not originate with the first Bourbon king. Questions of legitimacy could instigate civil or European war. In the case of Henry IV it was a particularly wise precaution. As a rollicking folk song of the period expressed it: he could drink, he could fight, and he could make love.[2]

Henry had married Maria in Florence on October 5, 1600—by proxy. On December 9 he met her for the first time in Lyons, bedded her that night, married her ceremonially the next day. But the forty-seven-year-old Henry (who, alas for the legend, looked older) found the twenty-seven-year-old Maria too heavy, haughty, and tall and went

off to twenty-one-year-old Henriette d'Entragues at the château of
Verneuil. Two sons were to be born almost simultaneously: Marie's in
late September, Henriette's in early October 1601. When Marie had
finally arrived in Paris (the previous February), Henry had presented
her Henriette, saying, "She has been my mistress. She would like to be
your personal servant."[3] She continued to be Henry's mistress, but she
never became Marie's servant. Rather, she was lodged in a palace of
her own near the Louvre, where she claimed to be the rightful Queen,
having fulfilled the King's condition for marriage by giving him a son.
Disdaining Marie de Médicis as "that *banquière*" (banker-woman),
she plotted from her palace to make her little Duc de Verneuil
Dauphin. Had the legitimacy of the future Louis XIII been in doubt,
there might have been another Louis XIV. Wherefore the princes of
the blood as witnesses in the royal bedroom on September 27, 1601.

The royal bed in the Queen's oval chamber was covered in crimson
velvet; so was the smaller bed next to it, in which she labored; and
the chair next to that, in which she gave birth. The midwife sat on
a smaller chair before her and received the baby. The King beckoned
the three princes closer. They bent and looked. The cord was cut,
the baby put into its crib. It moved feebly. The midwife called for
wine. Her hands were full; the King held a bottle to her lips. She
filled her mouth, then filled the child's from hers. It stirred more
strongly.

"*E maschio?*" the Queen asked twice, then rose to her feet to look.
The midwife uncovered the child for the King. "We have a beautiful son!" he cried, thanked God, and let the tears fall. The Queen,
too, cried and fainted.

The King threw open the doors to the antechamber. Two hundred
of the Court pressed in. The midwife protested. "This child," the
King replied, "belongs to everybody."[4]

He named Madame de Montglat, whose second husband was his
first steward, to be the Dauphin's governess.[5] She was tall, thin, and
domineering, "her character as sharp as her elbows." A week before
the King had appointed the remarkable Jean Héroard as the Dauphin's
personal physician. A man of about fifty, he had first served Henry
III. His meticulous journal of Louis XIII, beginning with the day of
his birth and ending with his own death some twenty-six years later,
fills six folio volumes of microscopic handwriting.[6] Kept day by day,
sometimes hour by hour, it may be the most faithful record of any

ruler in history, observing everything from food to evacuations, temper to temperature, conversations, love life—or rather, in Louis' instance, the relative lack of it.

The first days, Héroard notes, the Dauphin had difficulty sucking his milk, until an encumbering membrane was cut under his tongue. Then he needed two nurses (his father had sucked a legendary eight dry). But he was left the rest of his life with a speech defect that may early have turned him to music and away from court theatricals.

Within weeks of his birth, Louis was taken on tour for another public exposure. From Fontainebleau to Melun, Villeneuve-Saint-Georges to Paris, he was greeted at each town gate by trumpets and notables. Then, finally, after a stop at the Louvre and Tuileries palaces, the procession ended its public tour at the grim gray-stone château of Saint-Germain-en-Laye, fifteen miles west of Paris, chosen by Henry IV as the Dauphin's residence.

Throughout Louis' infancy affection came from his father, but it was not undivided. The King continued to distribute his energy among his affairs of state, his second wife (he had divorced Marguerite de Valois), his many mistresses (particularly Henriette d'Entragues), and his dozen or so other children. At one time there were nine children by five different mothers living at Saint-Germain; they were familiarly referred to throughout the land as *le troupeau* (the flock).[7] Characteristically Henry gave the name of Gabrielle, a defunct mistress, to the daughter of her successor, and would come to the Dauphin's room with the Queen and then return shortly afterward with Henriette. Louis, it might be noted, liked neither lady. Marie de Médicis may have been many things (particularly in Rubens' flattering portraits), but she was not a mother. The little Dauphin also took a pained view of mistresses. Before he was seven, the King had taken him for a walk in the gardens of Fontainebleau, pointed to the Comtesse de Moret, and said, "My son, I have given her a child. He will be your brother." The Dauphin had blushed, then stammeringly muttered, "He is no brother of mine."[8] And he turned his own affection to dogs and birds with such a ferocity that Louis XIII was to become the greatest killer of winged game in the history of that royal "sport." When eight, meeting a mongrel on the road, he insisted on its being taken along. "It's a poor dog," said the poor Dauphin, "looking for a master."

As a child, Louis was very neat, tidying up Héroard's room, to which he often crept, when he found it in disorder. And, yet a child, he was whipped by the King when he crushed the head of a live sparrow. He was frequently whipped by Madame de Montglat, who would sternly command, "You, Sir, bare your arse!" ("Whip him," the King had advised her. "There is nothing better for him . . . When I was his age, I was well beaten.") The language of his governess was even coarser than the period's and repeatedly shocked Louis.⁹

Before he was one, according to Héroard, it was decided that the Spanish Infanta would be his wife. At two he was asked if he would be as ribald as his father. "No," he said coldly. Not yet four he tried to strike his two-year-old sister. "I am afraid of her," he explained. "Why?" he was asked. "Because she is a girl." At seven he was teasingly asked if he were in love. "I flee from love," he answered solemnly. "And from the Infanta, monsieur?" asked Héroard. "No," he said, then: "Ha, yes. Yes!" He knew Héroard was noting down his remarks and would sometimes shout after one, "Write that down!"¹⁰

Still five, the Dauphin found himself staying at the château of Noisy-le-Roi, because of an epidemic at Saint-Germain. Seized by a sudden desire, he called his steward, Ventelet. "Tetay!" he cried. "Prepare the carriage and the birds. I want to go hunting!" That evening he returned from the nearby woods with a small hare run to earth by his hounds, and five or six quail and a brace of partridges taken by his hunting birds. At supper he talked of little else. It was his first hunt in his father's favorite woods—the woods of Versailles.

Louis was past seven when he was switched from the hard but feminine hands of his governess into those of his tutor, Monsieur de Souvré, put into a ruff and taught to shoot.* And he was not yet nine when he had dinner with the King on May 12, 1610. It hadn't happened often; it didn't happen again.

Two days afterward, before a shop with the sign of a crowned heart pierced by an arrow, Henry IV was stabbed to death by François Ravaillac. Hurriedly he was brought back to the Louvre, carried to his bedroom on the second floor, and laid out on the bed.

The Dauphin had been riding in another part of Paris. Hurriedly he too was brought back to the Louvre and taken to his father. "The

---

* Serious lessons began. At the age of seven in France, a child is assumed to have reached the age of reason.

King is dead," he heard from the Queen. "Your Majesty must excuse me," he heard the chancellor reply, "but kings never die in France. *Voilà,*" he pointed at Louis, "the living King, madame!"[11]

And the King cried like a baby.

Later that day he was again facing his public—the crowd that filed through the Louvre to stare at its new sovereign. Finally, exhausted, he went to bed, but he could not sleep. He rose, went to his tutor, said pathetically, "I am afraid of dreaming," and lay down beside him until almost midnight, when he was carried back to his own bed. There he slept with his half brother, Henriette's son, fetched by order of the Queen.

Never was a king mourned more widely in France than Henry IV. "The village poor," marvels an eyewitness, "massed on the highways, stunned, haggard, arms crossed, telling people passing of the disastrous news . . . finally disbanding like sheep without a shepherd."

For the French, the Vert Galant has remained the quintessence of the Frenchman. He had gaiety, courage, quickness of wit and movement, ruthlessness, a gift for diplomacy, a passion for pleasure, as easy a way with women as with power. He combined courtliness with vulgarity, pride with an uncondescending common touch, and tempered everything with self-mockery.

Louis' inheritance, in short, was the crushing legacy of a great father. "If only," he sighed to his nurse, "my father the King had lived another twenty years!"

A few days later the new King of France was spanked for obstinately refusing to say his prayers. "At least," he said to his tutor, "don't strike too hard." Afterward he went to see the Queen, now Regent, who had ordered the whipping. Marie de Médicis rose to make him the curtsy due him as King. "I would rather," he said wistfully, "not have so many curtsies and honors, and not be whipped."[12] On September 17, 1610, Louis XIII was again spanked, and on September 21 he signed a military alliance with England.

At ten Louis was writing verses and slaughtering game, traveling from castle to unfurnished castle, his carriages following or preceding him with his bed, furniture, linen, tapestries, and table service. But his hunting birds, organized like companies of soldiers, always accompanied him. So did a hundred falconers, dressed in the royal livery, and 150 hunting dogs. From the age of ten he was taming falcons, ultimately reaching the height of taming the great eagle, domesticating this wildest of birds to the point where it could be released into the air to strike down its prey and freely return to captivity. Louis was to hunt wild duck with falcons, quail with merlins, partridge with goshawks, hares with sakers, and train new teams of birds as if they were military commandos.[13] And he was to find a father figure in the ambitious courtier commanding his falconers, Charles de Luynes, twenty-three years his senior.

Rapidly Luynes became Louis' "favorite," his bedroom Louis' refuge. "Monsieur de Luynes," the English ambassador later observed in his memoirs, "gained much upon the King by making hawks fly at all little birds in his gardens, and by making some of those little birds again catch butterflies; and had the King used him for no other purpose, he might have been tolerated; but as, when the King came to a riper age, the government of public affairs was drawn chiefly from his counsels, not a few errors were committed."[14]

But that was to come later. Meanwhile Louis flew his birds, painted, danced, and composed, dreamed of—and wrote verses to—Luynes, cooked poached eggs, played the lute, and at the age of fourteen married the Spanish Infanta, who was five days older. She was blond and might have been pretty had it not been for her long Habsburg nose. Indeed, Anne of Austria (her mother was Margaret of Austria) looked remarkably like Louis, which in view of their Habsburg consanguinity was no coincidence.

They were married in Bordeaux on November 25, 1615. After the ceremony they returned from the cathedral, went to separate chambers in the archbishop's palace. Tired, the little King supped in bed while Messieurs de Guise and de Gramont and other cavaliers, notes Héroard, "regaled" him with coarse stories aimed at giving him "confidence." Toward eight in the evening Queen Mother Marie, still Regent, came to his chamber.[15]

"It is not enough, my son," she told him, "to be married. You must go to the Queen, your wife, who is awaiting you."

"Madame," said Louis, "I was but waiting your command. If it pleases you, I will go to her with you."

Ritually they handed him his bathrobe and small furred boots, and the little King went with the Queen Mother, two nurses (his and the little Queen's), Messieurs de Souvré and Héroard, the Marquis de Rambouillet, master of the wardrobe, and Monsieur de Beringhen, first *valet de chambre,* who lighted the way with a candle.

"My daughter," said the Queen Mother to the Queen, "I bring you your husband. Receive him well, I pray you."

Anne replied in Spanish that she had no other intention but to obey and please him, and Louis was put into bed beside her. Marie de Médicis whispered something to them in a low voice, then ordered all but the two nurses to leave.

Two hours later Louis called for his bathrobe and furred boots and returned to his bedroom. France was in the midst of civil war. But the rebellious nobility opposed to the marriage would now find it all but irrevocable. As for fourteen-year-old Louis, he was to recall that night with revulsion the rest of his life. It was three years before he could be brought to bed again with Anne; it was another twenty years before he became a father. But before either event could take place, there was Luynes to be removed as an inhibiting factor.

With this in mind, Marie de Médicis and the entire court connived to marry Luynes off to the pretty, charming, high-born—and rich—Marie de Rohan. They were successful, Luynes' marriage was successful, but subsequent approaches to Louis were not. Pressed by the Spanish ambassador and the papal nuncio to give France an heir, he resisted, pleading, "I am too young. It would be bad for my health." Then his half sister, Mademoiselle de Vendôme, daughter of Gabrielle d'Estrées, was married to the Duc d'Elbeuf, and efforts were redoubled.

"Sire," said the papal nuncio to Louis, now seventeen, "I do not believe you would want the shame of your sister having a son before Your Majesty had a Dauphin." Embarrassed, Louis allowed that he would not.

And it was not by chance that he was invited to the wedding chamber, encouraged to stay on as a spectator, the bride and groom lending themselves for a command performance. "Their act," the Venetian ambassador was to report, "was repeated more than once, to the great applause and particular pleasure of His Majesty. It is thought that this example has excited the King to do the same. It is also said that his half-sister encouraged him, saying, 'Sire, you do the same with the Queen, and you will be the better for it.'"

The King's pleasure and applause seem greatly to have been exaggerated. Five days later, at eleven in the night, Luynes himself had to go to Louis to coax him to the Queen's bed. Louis resisted. Luynes insisted. Annoyed, then anguished, Louis was carried weeping in

Luynes' arms down the corridor to Anne's chamber. And once again
Monsieur de Beringhen lighted the way with a candle. The two adoles-
cents were left together, except for Madame de Bellière, the Queen's
first *femme de chambre*. It was presumably she who provided Héroard
with the matter of the day. The King, he noted, *"s'efforce deux fois,
comme l'on dit"* (did his best twice, it is said). Louis returned to
his bedroom at two, slept unusually long (until nine o'clock).[16]

The public concern for so private an affair reached such an intensity
that not only the Pope (to whom the nuncio wrote on April 14, 1618
that the Huguenots were using Louis' chastity for their own purposes)
and the King of Spain (father of Queen Anne) felt legitimately
involved in Louis' love life, but the Duke of Savoy as well. An enemy
of Spain, he was told by *his* man at Court that the further the King
could be kept from the bed of the Queen, the closer he would be
to the House of Savoy. In a dispatch dated February 16, 1618, the
Savoyard ambassador related his own efforts in persuading the Duc
de Luynes to prevent the consummation. "'What wouldn't the Spanish do,'" he quoted himself as saying, "'of what would they not be
capable, once *their little Queen* had the person of the young King
in her arms every night?'"

The day following Louis' noble effort (on the night of January
25, 1619), Anne joyfully sent her master of ceremonies to the papal
nuncio and the Spanish envoy to tell them of it, and couriers were
booted for the ride to the capitals of Europe. On January 30 the
nuncio wrote Pope Paul V, "The King finally decided *conjungersi
colla Regina* . . . Since the first night except for one, their majesties
continue to come together . . . but for the sake of the King's health,
it will be seen to that His Majesty goes to the Queen at properly
spaced intervals." An interval of two weeks was recommended by
the court doctors as more likely to result in a Dauphin. In a second
dispatch the same day, the nuncio congratulated the Pope and himself
on the discomfiture of the Huguenots by news of the "conjugation,"
and added a good word for the persuasive efforts of Father Annoux,
the King's confessor.[17]

Politically, in the meantime, there remained the troublesome Concini to be dealt with. A Florentine adventurer, Concino Concini
was Marie de Médicis' long-time favorite, his wife, Leonora Galigaï,
her confidante. Together, since Henry IV's assassination, they had
been usurping power. One by one, by clever intrigue, they forced the

retirement of his ministers, replacing the disgraced Sully, emptying the French treasury he had so prudently accumulated, and patronizing the furious but thus far impotent Louis—who had been deliberately raised by Marie de Médicis, in the words of Tallemant, "to render him incapable of ever acting like a king."[18]

Were Concini and the Queen Mother lovers who had conspired in the murder of his father? Did Louis, Hamlet-like, add this likely suspicion to his plaint to Luynes? His two predecessors had been assassinated; it was a frequent enough form of politics. In any event, the young King ordered the arrest of Concini and perhaps his death as well. The Florentine was killed at the Louvre's Porte de Bourbon, his wife Leonora beheaded and burned as a witch, and Luynes made a duke and marshal in his place. It was then 1617; Louis was not yet sixteen.

Many of his father's ministers returned to power and influence, but Louis continued to have but one friend, the Duc de Luynes— and *he* died in 1621. Moreover, France was again in a fratricidal war. At this moment, as if waiting for it, Armand-Jean du Plessis de Richelieu reached the foot of the throne. Originally discovered by Concini, initially favored by Marie de Médicis—and therefore suspected by Louis—the Bishop of Luçon was a cardinal by 1622 and not long after the King's chief minister, eventually the ruler of his realm.

A kind of equilibrium was established. If it was not quite the glamorous time of Dumas' *Three Musketeers,* in which the dashing Duke of Buckingham publicly pleaded his love to the neglected Queen, Anne of Austria, life was plentiful enough, it seems, for all but the frustrated King. He had lost Luynes. He had Richelieu, but no intimate.

He had only Versailles, his dogs and his birds.

Increasingly, Louis escaped to the woods near the little village of Versailles-au-Val-de-Galie, a cluster of huts with four or five hundred inhabitants. It had a rude inn or two, a windmill, and twelfth-century church on the butte, the half-ruined château of the Gondi, and a little nearby stream, the Galie. It was a rendezvous for hunters, not a place to spend the night. It was a halt for carters and wagoners, their vehicles heavy with beef from Normandy for the markets of Paris.

But there were the douce woods of the Ile de France, full of game and grace. They were worth the long ride back after dark to Saint-Germain, eight miles distant. But why the ride back?

Modestly Louis planned a small château, no larger than a hunting lodge. Guardedly he budgeted it under *Menus Plaisirs* (we might say, Light Entertainment), rather than Bâtiments (Buildings). Discreetly he had it constructed, stopping by during his hunting, as on August 2, 1624, when he watched the battery of kitchen utensils installed.[19]

This very first Versailles structure was of brick and stone, in the style now called "Louis XIII." It was about eighty feet in all along the façade facing the small park, and only twenty feet in depth. As Baron de Bassompierre was to defend it before an assembly of notables in 1627, Louis' retreat was but a *"chetif château* [paltry country house] which any ordinary gentleman would not boast having built."[20]

There were three or four rooms for the King, a dozen or so for his suite: primarily the gentlemen of the hunt and officers of the company of a hundred musketeers, whom it amused the King to drill in the courtyard. Adjacent to Louis' rooms were the quarters of Claude de Saint-Simon, *premier gentilhomme,* briefly a "favorite" and future father of the great *mémorialiste.*

But there were no rooms for the Queen, the Queen Mother, or any of the ladies of the Court. They might be invited for a fête, as when the little château of Versailles was finished (Louis even served Anne the first dish and sat at her feet), or they might be allowed to join in a hunt (riding gentled palfreys, wearing large feathered hats against the sun), but they had no overnight privileges. This Versailles was to be a paradise reserved for men.

Meantime, on the political front, Louis confirmed Richelieu in power, if only to assure himself repose. Richelieu in return pledged to curb the power of the Protestants (crushing them at La Rochelle), the feudal princes (reducing their fortified castles), and the House of the Habsburgs (where he was only partly successful, their wings still encircling France from Austria to Holland, Italy, and Spain). Leagued against Richelieu at home were the King's only legitimate brother, Gaston d'Orléans, his wife, and his mother, the two queens of the "Spanish party," who were not above conspiring with their relatives among the enemy (Anne of Austria's brother was now Philip IV of Spain). And this struggle against the cardinal was to reach its climax at Versailles in the famous Day of Dupes.

Convalescing from an almost fatal illness, harassed by Marie de Médicis to dismiss his minister, Louis seemed to weaken and about to acquiesce. The critical conversation took place on November 10, 1630, in the Queen Mother's Luxembourg Palace. Unexpectedly, as it was ending, Richelieu appeared. Outraged, Marie de Médicis denounced and insulted him in a flowing mixture of Italian and French. He fell to his knees. He wept. Tears were part of Richelieu's superb equipment; these might have been real; out of office could have meant out of life. He begged pardon. He promised to do whatever the Queen Mother demanded. Louis paled, tried to interrupt. Haughtily, Marie asked him whether he preferred "a valet to his mother." Louis then ordered Richelieu to rise and leave the room. He himself soon took leave of Marie. It was late and he had to reach Versailles before it was too dark.

In the courtyard Richelieu desolately watched Louis depart without a look or sign. Inside the palace the cardinal's many enemies celebrated with Marie de Médicis. Returned to his own palace, Richelieu ordered silver and papers packed, and prepared for flight. Then word came from the King: Richelieu was to join him immediately at Versailles.

Away from Paris, the Court, and his mother, Louis recovered his composure in the late autumn serenity of Versailles. He went up to his cabinet and waited. Soon the cardinal came to him, fell at his feet, wept, offered his resignation—and allowed himself a refusal. He stayed that night in the château, in a room directly below the chamber of the King. The next morning, those who had gone to sleep in victory awoke to defeat. Richelieu had triumphed.[21]

Following that Day of Dupes, when Versailles first entered history Marie de Médicis was banished, eventually to die in exile in the Netherlands. The Maréchal de Marillac, who had aspired to Richelieu's office, was tortured and put to death; the Duc de Montmorency, a childhood playmate of Louis, was beheaded. (Refusing clemency, Louis had implacably remarked, "I should not be King, if I had the sentiments of private persons."[22]) And parcel by parcel, in forty-six separate purchases, the royal domain of Versailles was doubled; land and rights were bought from the Archbishop of Paris, Jean-François Gondy; and Louis' hunting lodge was remodeled.

It was enlarged (under the direction of architect Philibert Le Roy) but not enough to include rooms for the ladies. Femininity belonged strictly to the brightness of color, the gaiety of structure: red brick walls "chained" with white stone, balconies of finely wrought iron, roofs of blue-black slate and gilded terminals, tall white pinnacles and chimneys with decorative blue ornaments. The moat, too, was more decorative than defensive, and its stone balustrade out of a fairy tale. So was the marble courtyard we still see today.[23]

It was this "little castle of cards" (as Saint-Simon called it) that the Sun King, not yet born, was to discover in his adolescence and preserve in his maturity as the center of his own great palace, court, and power.

But it was here that Louis XIII came to escape his court and the cares of power, the intrigues of courtiers and their plots. Here in Versailles, Louis felt secure, free of women, less spied upon. When smallpox threatened Saint-Germain, he sent the Queen to Noisy, not to Versailles. "I fear," he explained to Richelieu, in one of his almost daily letters, "the great number of women who would spoil everything, if the Queen went there."[24]

Inevitably there were women as "mistresses." The son of the Vert Galant had perhaps no alternative but the keeping up of some semblance of appearances. There was the blond teen-age Marie de Hautefort, who, urged on by the Queen, terrified him. (He talked "only of dogs, birds and hunting," she complained to Madame de Motteville, *femme de chambre* of the Queen.) And there was the teen-age brunette, Louise de La Fayette, nudged forward by Richelieu, who may even have loved him, but when Louis said, in effect, "Come live with me at Versailles," she crossed herself and went to a convent in Paris.[25]

Before she departed, her confessor told the King that her decision could, at the least, be postponed. "Don't do it," he replied. "If I keep her from her call, I will regret it all my life." The relief in the renunciation is almost audible, though Louis wrote Richelieu a few nights later of his melancholy (the writing wavers, a tear drops, one still sees the traces).

Les adieus were made the morning of May 19, 1637. Louis wept, but by the time Louise reached her bedroom, she could see him across the courtyard in his carriage, on the way to the comfort of Versailles. "That day," reported the *Gazette de France, "la demoiselle de La Fayette,* one of the Queen's maids of honor, became a nun in the convent of the Visitandines, and was greatly regretted by the King, the Queen and the entire Court."

The pious, inhibited, possibly tormented King visited Louise, now Sister Angélique, several times that year—the first time for three hours, to the annoyance of Richelieu (as many others, Louis'had become his enemy). In November, Louis wrote his minister that he had just returned from the convent of Sainte-Marie (still standing near the Place de la Bastille), a visit "which brought back my health and increased my devotions." In the months intervening, the Queen had been discovered "in treacherous correspondence with the enemy" (Richelieu's words and discovery). La Porte, the Queen's intermediating *valet de chambre,* was imprisoned, the Queen, after abjectly asking pardon, was halfheartedly pardoned. Then Louis' last visit to Louise, early in December, was to bring an odd reconciliation.

As Louis and Sister Angélique talked—and talked—in the parlor, a storm rose of such violence that he could neither return to Versailles nor go on to Saint-Maur, where his bed, linen, and service had already preceded him. His apartment at the Louvre, a mile down the Seine, was not prepared for him. Guitaut, captain of the guard, now spoke up with his customary boldness. Since the Queen was at the Louvre, he pointed out, the King would find supper and lodging. Louis rejected the idea and said they would wait out the storm. They waited. The storm became even more violent. Again Guitaut proposed the Louvre. Louis replied that the Queen supped and went to bed too late for him. Guitaut said she would surely be glad to conform to his wishes. At last Louis agreed to the Louvre, and Guitaut galloped off to advise the Queen of his coming and his desires.

"They supped together. The King spent the night with the Queen, and nine months later Anne of Austria had a son, whose unexpected birth brought universal joy to the entire kingdom."

The account is that of Father Griffet,[26] an eighteenth-century historian, and it is told with such simple directness that it almost disarms one's suspicions. (The fatherhood of Louis XIV is still disputed.) And one could close this account of the birth of Versailles with the birth of its Sun King. Or one could—and perhaps should— close it with his father's last wish and leave out the unbecoming affair with the "beautiful Cinq-Mars." But if the affair is beyond the framework of Versailles' first château, it is still revelatory of the character of its begetter.

Always preferring that anyone close to the king be as close, politically, to himself, Richelieu had pushed forward the comely son of an old friend, and the young man had predictably caught the eye of the King. "Never," wrote Chavigny to Mazarin, "did the King have a more violent passion for anyone than for him." Cinq-Mars had arrived at seventeen, and his rise at court the next two years was truly meteoric—from a captain of the guards to grand master of the royal wardrobe to Monsieur le Grand, the grand equerry of the King, the Marquis de Cinq-Mars d'Effiat. "Not a bad beginning," Chavigny commented, "for a young man of nineteen."[27]

As Luynes had been thirty-nine to Louis' sixteen, so Louis now was thirty-nine to Cinq-Mars' nineteen. For Tallemant, who recounts tawdry tales concerning their intimacy, the relationship was quite clearly homosexual. On the other hand, it has never been proved* and Cinq-Mars' preference for Marion Delorme, the famous courtesan, has been established, if only by Louis' spies and his jealousy of her. That it was turbulent and passionate, however, is part of the official archives: Richelieu himself drew up peace treaties between King and favorite for their joint signature.[28]

Restlessly, Cinq-Mars overreached himself, turned enemy of Richelieu, joined the "Spanish plot" against him, alienated the King—and lost his head. At the hour of his scheduled decapitation, the King, according to one story, paused during a chess game, looked at his watch, and cynically remarked, "I would like to see the expression on Monsieur le Grand's face now." Poor Louis. "His loves," as Tallemant notes, "were strange loves, and he had nothing of the lover but jealousy." "He took no pleasure, as other men, in *la belle passion*," says Madame de Motteville. "Accustomed to bitterness, his *tendresse* was only that he might feel pain and suffering the more."[29]

Yet the legacy Louis XIII left France, if only the accomplishments of his minister, was considerable: the founding of the French Academy, the patronage of Corneille, a "certain idea" of France—of glory and grandeur—a sense of state and administration, and a minister, Mazarin, trained to continue Richelieu's mission. All this, of course, was Riche-

---

* Historically "proof" has consisted in an unconcealed homosexual promiscuity, as Henry III's, and a quasi-transvestite flamboyance, as in the case of the powdered and painted brother of Louis XIV, Monsieur. Neither of these characteristics was true of Louis XIII, nor did the times demand their concealment (nor does either of the last statements disprove the probability).

lieu's work, as indeed was the beginning of modern, centralized France, and his death, to no one's surprise, was swiftly followed by the King's.

Long ailing, Louis was not long dying, thanks to his doctors. In a single year Bouvard bled him forty-seven times, gave him 215 enemas and 212 different drugs. Before dying, the King accused him bitterly of his death.[30]

But before that he had confided his last life wish to his confessor. Should God give him back his health, Louis said—he was, after all, only forty-one—he would, "As soon as I see my son able to ride and of the age of majority [thirteen] . . . put him in my place and . . . retire to Versailles with four of your priests, there to discuss holy matters, and to think no longer about anything but my soul and my salvation."[31]

One month later, on May 14, 1643, Louis XIII was dead.

2. The Making of a Sun King

As if a fantasy fulfilled, the first political memory of Louis XIV may have been the dreamlike image of his mother, the Queen, coming from the deathbed of his father, to kneel before him in the nursery, hailing him as her king.

Pre-Freud historians prefer a slightly earlier anecdote, but the mask of Oedipus is even more apparent. On April 21, 1643, the Dauphin had returned from his baptism to his sick father's bedside. (His godparents had been the Princesse de Condé, for whose favors Henry IV had almost plunged Europe into war, and the astute Jules Mazarin, Richelieu's successor.) The Dauphin had been given the name Louis le Dieudonné, Louis the God-given, as if, it was inevitably remarked, Louis XIII had needed divine assistance in becoming a father.

"What is your name, Monsieur mon fils?" asked the dying King.

"Louis the Fourteenth, Monsieur," said the Dauphin, four years and seven months old.

"Not yet, not yet," said Louis the Thirteenth.

He said it sadly or bitterly, according to the historian,[1] for in three weeks it was so.

The ambiguities had begun well before Louis XIV's birth. As the Queen, in her late thirties, lay groaning in labor with her first child, Louis XIII had beguiled himself in an adjoining room reading stories of happily widowed kings[2]; and afterwards he had to be coaxed to Anne of Austria's bed by Madame de Motteville to give her a congratulatory kiss. Two years later, the Queen's lady-in-waiting recalls in her memoirs, the King was more cheerful about his second child, "having feared never having any."[3] But he was to complain his few remaining years to Richelieu that Anne was raising the Dauphin to dislike him,* and continually threatened to take both sons from her. (Dead, Louis XIII was not to be mentioned in Anne's presence and only once—apropos his death—was he referred to in passing by Louis XIV in the six volumes of his *Works*.)

His father's was the only jarring note in the general adulation. The birth of the God-given Louis had brought thunder from the Bastille cannon and fire from the capital's muskets in celebration. Had Louis XIII died childless, they would have erupted in civil war (as, indeed, they did a decade later). Huge barrels of wine were rolled onto the streets, "the drinks," according to the *Gazette,* "paid for with only a *Vive le Roi.*" Astrologer Campanella, convenient to the Queen's chamber at Saint-Germain, declared that even the sun had swung closer to the earth "to share in the great event," and in Rome there was a three-day fête for the "eldest son of the Church."[4]

The future Sun King was a large (nine-pound) baby with a large appetite, painfully complicated—for the succession of seven peasant women called on to feed him—by the two sharp teeth he was born with. Such was his "ardent temperament," the Swedish ambassador dispatched homeward, "that he tore the teats of his nurses." And he added: "Let the neighbors of France beware of so precocious a rapacity."[5]

But the French rejoiced. It proved the new Dauphin more Bourbon than Habsburg. And they showed their pleasure en masse on the death of Louis XIII, when they cheered the little King as he rode from Saint-Germain to the fortified Louvre—while the late King went on to Saint-Denis and the royal cemetery. He who was to be the most famous of French kings, however, was in fact as Spanish as French, as much the grandson of Philip III as he was of Henry IV.†

* "Whenever he sees me, he cries," Louis XIII wrote his minister, September 9, 1640, "as if he saw the devil."
† See Ernest Lavisse's masterful essay in his monumental *Histoire de France.*[6] To detail Louis XIV's ancestry (Nancy Mitford finds traces of Jewish and Moorish "blood"[7]) is to deal in eighths, sixteenths, thirty-seconds, sixty-fourths, etc., so tangled were the royal "blood lines" even in the seventeenth century. In broad national terms, the Sun King was one quarter French, three eighths Austrian, one eighth Italian and one quarter Spanish. (Peasants, not nobles, were fixed to their native soil.)

B

More immediately, Louis XIV was the son of the Spanish Infanta, now Regent of France during his minority by proclamation of Parlement. France, as Voltaire observed, would allow its queens the regency but never the crown; but Anne was to safeguard the power that would be eventually her son's.

Mother and son, theirs was the ideal relationship. She raised him to be King, and he, born to her after more than two decades of despised womanhood, had made her no longer a foreign intriguer, as in the time of his father, but a French regent and mother of a French king.[8] Unlike Marie de Médicis, who neglected the young Louis XIII, Anne of Austria would not be separated from Louis XIV, playing with him, praying with him, promenading him in the gardens. And unlike Queen Mother Marie, whose intimates were the bullying Concini, Anne's mainstay, probable lover, possible husband, was Mazarin, who proved himself a discreet, concerned, and uncompetitive godfather—that is, one who played Prime Minister but never King. "He loved me," Louis was to write, "and I loved him."[9]

The popular view, which won Saint-Simon's powerful support and thus posterity's (though the gifted *mémorialiste* came on the scene of Versailles thirty years *after* Mazarin's death), was otherwise: Mazarin played the Queen's lover for his own ambitious purposes. Satirical, scurrilous *mazarinades* mocked him as another Italian adventurer who arrived penniless in France to make his fortune. Born Giulio Mazarini, son of the Sicilian major-domo of the Colonna household of Rome, he gave many outward appearances of an opportunistic rise as master of his year-older French mistress. He lived in conspicuous luxury, but with as much taste and wit as wealth. La Princesse Palatine, the second wife of Louis XIV's brother, tells of Mazarin's confiscating *mazarinades,* then secretly selling them for ten thousand écus, laughing at the whole affair. "The French," she reports his saying (La Palatine arrived at Versailles ten years after his death), "are a very likeable people. I let them sing and write, and they let me do what I want."[10]

Mazarin was courtly and courteous. Madame de Motteville, contrasting him to Richelieu, found him "full of gentleness." He was cultivated: he introduced opera to Paris, art to Louis. He was clever, perhaps too clever by half. The Spanish don with whom he was to negotiate Louis' marriage was to comment: "He has one great defect in politics. He is continually trying to deceive."[11] It was a comment that delighted Voltaire, no admirer of Mazarin, but a quality that Richelieu had found useful. He made Mazarin, whom he persuaded the Pope to send to Paris as nuncio, his secretary, then minister and cardinal, though Mazarin, as Richelieu, had never been ordained a priest. Anne, in turn, as Regent, had passed over Monsieur, Louis XIII's brother; the Prince de Condé, whose twenty-two-year-old son had just brilliantly defeated the Spanish at Rocroi; the Duc de Vendôme, Henry IV's bastard; and the *beau* Beaufort, the duke's son; and chose Mazarin to rule beside her. Outraged, the snubbed formed the *cabale des importants* against the foreigner, particularly when she made Mazarin superintendent of Louis' education, thus prime minister of his mind. For he who possessed the person of the King possessed France—and there was to be more than one battle for that possession.

Louis was a beautiful, graceful boy and, seeing it reflected in every eye about him, was so to regard himself as a man. He was a solemn little boy, when, not yet five, he became Louis XIV, already impressing the Venetian ambassador with his "air of grandeur," as he sat with remarkable poise in the royal ride by coach to the Louvre. And when the young King reached his sixth birthday, the envoy confirmed his first impression in a fuller report: "His Majesty has a lively spirit and the beauty of his nature gives promise of virtue. His body is robust, his [hazel] eyes animated and rather severe, but of a severity full of charm. He laughs rarely, even at play. He insists on respect and obedience from his brother, the Duc d'Anjou, aged three. He knows he is King and wants to be treated as such. Sometimes when the Queen Mother reproves him, he replies that one day he will be the master.* When the ambassadors speak to the Regent, he does not listen. But when they address him, he is very attentive, and later asks that their speeches be repeated to him. In short, if life and education do not lack him, he promises to be a great king."[12]

He was to have the life and the education.

As a child, Louis played soldier with a miniature army of silver figures and was to play soldier as well in his maturity. ("I loved war too much," he said remorsefully on his deathbed.) He was also to play King, and for that he was more solidly trained, for no one has ever played it better.

Instruction began seriously at the age of seven. He was dressed

* His first confessor, on the other hand, described him as being "as gentle and docile as a lamb," and a governess, as too meek and submissive.

in a boy's breeches, instead of long skirts, taken from his governess and formally turned over to men. His memorable—and memoir-writing—valets were Dubois and the valorous La Porte, who replaced Beringhen as the first *valet de chambre,* paying for the position with money from the Queen. She thus repaid La Porte for his loyalty and silence while in the Bastille. Louis himself, it should be noted, was not loath to remain in the hands of women. He preferred their blandishments, their fairy tales, such as the Cinderella-like *Peau d'Ane,* to the schooling he was about to undergo.[13]

But the "discipline" was generally deferential. His guardian, the Duc de Villeroi, was so ready with a *Yes, Sire,* that he was nicknamed *Ouisire* by the scornful Louis. His writing master set him the task of copying a line that was to be inerasable: "Homage is due to kings. They act as they please." The six copies, each signed with a large *Louis,* are his first preserved writings. Headmaster Hardouin de Péréfixe, historian and abbé, taught him the royal catechism.

Abbé: "What does His Majesty mean when he says God created him and brought him into the world?"

Louis: "I mean that he made me from nothing and brought me forth from the nothingness in which I was to give me my being, my life, kingdom and all the advantages I possess."[14]

There were nine other masters (the Saint-Simon legend of Louis' underschooling—"the King was barely taught to read and write, and remained in the gross ignorance in which he was carefully raised"[15]—sinks under their number), with Mazarin himself weighing in heavily at unexpected moments. In descending order of their pay and consequently, perhaps, their importance, they respectively taught Louis mathematics, arms, dancing, drawing, Spanish and Italian (by the same tutor), reading, riding, guitar, and lute. By now the royal family had removed from the Louvre to the more comfortable, neighboring Palais Royal. There a large map in Louis' study, labeled *l'Europe française,* indicated French influence, if not domain, extending to Constantinople and Jerusalem. And there was more playing soldier in the palace gardens, where Mazarin had a small-scale fort erected with small, blank-firing cannon.

Politically, the mirror in which Louis was expected to model himself—and which was daily held up before him by Péréfixe—was his great predecessor and grandfather, Henry IV. (Louis' father, Louis XIII, was always passed over in silence or in haste.) Page by page, while still in progress, the abbé would read to Louis the work specially written for him, *l'Histoire de Henri le Grand*. It was the endless lesson, or rather, admonition, about do-nothing kings (*rois fainéants*) and the contrasting example of Henry IV, and it was never forgotten. "From childhood itself," Louis began his *Instructions to the Dauphin*, "just hearing the names of *les rois fainéants* and *maires du palais* [prime ministers acting for them] would upset me."[16] Encouraged by the Queen, La Porte never failed to stir him from indolence to anger by suggesting he might become another Louis V, the Do-Nothing King, if he didn't apply himself to his studies.

All his life Louis was to be preoccupied with the *métier de roi*—the profession or business of being king—and was to write about it as such: *"Le métier de roi est grand, noble, délicieux."* He would always add that "work is indispensable for ruling." It echoes, probably consciously, a key passage of Péréfixe's *Henri le Grand:*

"Royalty is not the *métier* of a do-nothing. It consists above all in action. The King must take delight in duty, pleasure in reigning, but he must realize that to reign is to put his hand to the task before him, to hold the helm of state himself, that there is neither glory nor honor to the title of prince, if he does not fulfill its highest functions. So it was with your illustrious grandfather, the most active and hard-working of kings, who, more than all others, devoted himself to the careful management of his affairs."[17]

In early imitation of Henry IV, at the age of twelve Louis surprised his preceptor with his own translation of several chapters of Caesar's *Commentaries*. (The version published is an honorable one, though likely revised by Péréfixe. However, the memoirs of his maturity, accepted as Louis' own, have won praise from no less a critic than Sainte-Beuve.) Education was offered in diverse forms: history was dramatized in skits and made into a game of cards, the pack specially designed to drive home Péréfixe's lesson. The cards, according to the instructions of their designer, Jean Desmarets, were "to be divided, on one side, by the good and the illustrious kings, and on the other, by the do-nothings and the wicked, with points for the first and penalties for the second. I can promise you," he stressed, "that a young prince passing his time playing this game will find printed forever on his soul an extreme desire to imitate the former and a great horror for the faults of the others." There were, as well, cards for the queens, the chaste and the unchaste, the saintly and less saintly—Anne of Austria, for instance, was a saintly Queen of Clubs.[18]

The Duc de Saint-Simon's legend of Louis XIV's ignorance could easily derive from his distaste for a king who so little valued dukes and also from Louis' own self-deprecating remarks. "I am an ignorant fellow," he told the schoolgirls of Saint Cyr in 1694, and to the Dauphin he often described himself as largely a self-made, self-taught king.[19] It is a claim so characteristic of signally successful men, in its exaggeration and its own kind of truth, that it requires no comment other than Anne of Austria's. Kings, she observed, had little need to study history, since they lived it; or, she might have added, made it. (Is that not, to be generous, what Henry Ford had back of his mind when he remarked, "History is bunk"?) In time, Mazarin's own example would be a lesson in pragmatism.

In the meantime, there was the religious example of his mother. Though he was to manifest it only many mistresses later, the youthful Louis was impressed from childhood by the austere Spanish piety of the Queen. Twice a day she heard mass, spent hours on her knees in prayer, tirelessly visited churches, often with the young King. Normally indulgent, she once sent him to his room for two days for a round oath; as a man he would use them rarely, if at all. She spanked him, if not lightly, at least with love. Less whipped than Louis XIII, he would employ prison as punishment for his enemies rather than his father's headman's ax.[20] Clemency, too, was Mazarin's exemplary practice.

Whenever he could, La Porte complained, the young King would escape to the apartments of the Queen, "where everyone praised him and no one corrected him." But the protesting *valet de chambre* understood. Louis, he says in his memoirs, "had a great deal of affection for the Queen, and she had much more for him than children of his condition were accustomed to receiving from their mothers." The towering confidence, the impregnable security, of the Sun King was built on this cornerstone.

Mindful of the intrigues and rivalry of the late King's brother, Gaston d'Orléans, the Queen Mother went to extraordinary lengths to reduce, if not eliminate, Louis XIV's sibling problems, both emotional and political. She clearly ordered his younger brother to defer in all things to him; she may have deliberately dressed him as a girl beyond the age of seven (as he was to dress himself on occasion the rest of his life). Indeed, historian Philippe Erlanger, in a biography of Monsieur, Louis XIV's brother, finds Anne of Austria largely responsible for his flamboyant homosexuality.[21]

Meanwhile La Porte, stubbornly suspicious of Mazarin, tried to pass on his aversion for the minister to Louis, "when I was not being observed." (Mazarin, not without reason, had spies' everywhere, including the schoolroom.) Mistakenly La Porte thought himself successful, gleefully noting that Louis once referred to His Eminence, as he passed with his great suite, as *le Grand Turc.* Several pages later, in two paragraphs, La Porte lays the ground for another continuing accusation: that luxury-loving Mazarin, who accumulated an immense private fortune (and was even said to perfume a pet monkey), so neglected the necessities of Louis' life that his feet poked through holes in his bed sheets and his worn, outgrown bathrobe hiked to his knees. Furthermore, La Porte says, when he told the King he could not possibly go out in his coach, it was so dilapidated, "that night the King complained to the Queen, to His Eminence and to Monsieur de Maisons, then Surintendant des Finances, and forthwith had five new carriages." The contradiction of the conclusion seems to have escaped the sturdy valet, and, astonishingly, the excellent W. H. Lewis; he repeats the accusation in *The Splendid Century*—"What was unpardonable in Mazarin's conduct was the sordid poverty in which he kept his sovereign . . ."—but does *not* add the conclusion—five new carriages.

Of such is history made—and once again the aging Louis contributed to his own accumulating legends, in this instance what might be called, "The Sun King as Barefoot Boy." Madame de Maintenon was his confidant. "The King always surprises me," she related (in *Entretiens sur l'éducation des filles*), "when he talks of his childhood. His governesses, he says, played all day and left him to their chambermaids . . . He ate anything he could get his hands on, without anyone paying attention to whether it was good for him. He and Monsieur, his brother, would snatch part of an omelette [on its way elsewhere] and gulp it down in a corner." The King, she says, also told her that his constant companion in those days was a peasant girl, "daughter of the servant of his mother's servants, whom he called Queen Marie," because in their make-believe games together she played Queen and Louis her valet and footman.

It may have happened—Louis XIV was always to feel particularly comfortable with his servants (what public figure does not?) and to be reproached by the courtiers for his familiarity with his valets—but not with regularity. Here, too, is the self-conscious myth-making —with the model of Henry IV before him—of one so high he must claim low companions. As a matter of fact, the young King's companions were carefully chosen from the children of the Comte Loménie de Brienne, the Marquis de la Châtre, the Duc de Mortemart and similar old, aristocratic families. As for Louis' "impoverished youth," the memoirs of his second *valet de chambre,* Dubois, reveal another, already regal Louis at the age of nine. Admiring a soldier's dexterous swordplay outside his window, he told his tutor, Villeroi, to reward the man with a coin. Villeroi called for a half pistole. Louis said it was not enough. Villeroi demurred, saying it was. "For that soldier," Louis replied, "it is enough, and for you, too, if you were giving it. But for me, it must be a whole pistole."[22]

However, there undoubtedly was an honest confusion in Louis', if not La Porte's, memory of the childhood years with the truly difficult years of his adolescence during the Fronde, the civil war that lasted from 1648 to 1653.

It was not the first civil war of the century; it was the ninth in less than four decades, a time, in Voltaire's stinging words, "when more French gentlemen were killed by fellow gentlemen than by the enemy." But it was Louis' first (and last) civil war, and it was to create, or rather re-create, Versailles.

The initial Fronde* was the revolt of the Paris Parlement—not to be identified with the English Parliament, concurrently holding Charles I prisoner. The French Parlement was neither elective nor representative. Its seats were bought (for as much as a hundred thousand livres) and it was hereditary. Nor was it legislative. Its members (almost entirely magistrates) registered the King's acts, or taxes, and made them law. Or refused, as in 1648—and prepared to spend more in revolt than demanded in taxes.

Mazarin, engaged in war with the Spanish, counseled compromise. Anne, swallowing her Spanish pride, agreed. Then the new Prince de Condé, hero of Rocroi, defeated the Spanish at Lens in the last important battle of the Thirty Years' War. "Parlement," said Louis, not yet ten, "will be very sorry when it hears this." Promptly Anne

* Deriving from *la fronde,* or sling, used by French gamins for stoning each other—and others—frequently in the dry moats outside the walls of Paris.

ordered the arrest of the three principal rebel leaders, white-haired Pierre Broussel, "Father of the people," among them. The colorful Paul de Gondi, future Cardinal de Retz,* urged Broussel's release. "I'd sooner strangle him with these two hands," cried Anne, waving them in Gondi's face.[23] Two hundred barricades sprang up in Paris, some a hundred yards from the palace Again Mazarin counseled compromise. Anne released Broussel, but the tension remained, more barricades went up, and Mazarin had himself booted, ready for flight. "Little Monsieur," says Dubois of Louis' seven-year-old brother, "was seized with fright. The King did his best to encourage him, brandishing his little sword, which he did with an admirable grace . . . cheering him with the air of a great general."

Mazarin and the Queen Mother called on the Prince de Condé to defend the crown from Parlement. A Prince of the Blood with the proud name of Louis de Bourbon, at twenty-seven the Grand Condé was the finest general of France and his arrogant eagle's face reflected it. As contemptuous of Parlement as of Mazarin, whom he thought to replace Condé agreed. The mobs cried, "Death to Mazarin! Long live the King, the King alone!" and Parlement pressed for more reforms. "If I yielded to you," Anne told its magistrates, "my son would be no more than a playing card king."[24] And again Mazarin counseled compromise until the Treaty of Westphalia was completed with Spain. But it came too late to be effective. On January 6, 1649, the royal family fled Paris for Saint-Germain, and the Court slept on straw. Parlement decreed Mazarin an outlaw to be hunted down as a criminal. This was the time Louis' "impoverishment," when the Queen had to pawn the crown jewels, chamber pages were sent away for lack of food, and Henriette of England stayed in bed (one day) for lack of fuel.

The first Fronde itself is "worth recording only in comic verse"— the words are Condé's, who also called it a "war of the chamber pots."[25] Nobles joined Parlement to win back the privileges lost under Richelieu; their ladies charmed their lovers into joining them, such as Condé's own sister, the Duchesse de Longueville, who took the future Duc de La Rochefoucauld into the rebel camp. Thus Condé found himself opposed not only to his sister and his brother-in-law, the Duc de Longueville, but to his younger, malformed, jealous brother,

* "The first bishop of France to make civil war without having religion as a pretext" (Voltaire).

B*

the Prince de Conti, who led the Parlementary forces. Their own
capriciousness defeated them. Seeking Spanish help, they stirred a
patriotism among the people and even in Parlement which they,
feeling above it, could not have anticipated. That plus several defeats
in the field and the beheading of Charles I in England brought
moderates to power in Parlement and temporary peace to France.
All was officially forgiven, but nothing was forgotten, and nothing was
learned. The first Fronde ended; the second was about to begin (without
the Parlement).

Condé despised the court which he had just defended and brought
back victorious to Paris, haughtily quarreled with Mazarin, joined the
cabala of his enemies—and suddenly found himself imprisoned along
with Conti and Longueville on January 18, 1650.

At this point, the Duchesse de Longueville virtually took command.
(In France, Mazarin once commented, unlike Spain, "a woman cannot go to sleep until she has discussed State affairs with her lover or
her husband. She wants to manage everything."[26] Have women in
your private life, Louis was to admonish the Dauphin, but never in
your public affairs. It was one of the Fronde's lessons.) The duchess
raised a rebellion in her husband's province of Normandy, disturbances in Poitou with her lover, La Rochefoucauld, then persuaded a
new lover, the Maréchal de Turenne,* to join an old enemy, Spain,
for a march on Paris. There, a day's further march from the city's
walls, they met defeat from, of all men, Mazarin. But the Prime
Minister was not as successful off the battlefield, and the royal family
was frustratedly penned by an angry public in the Palais Royal.
Gambling, Mazarin personally unlocked the three princes from their
prison, and lost his wager that it would appease either them or the
public. Condé joined the *frondeurs* in Paris and Mazarin fled to
Brühl in Germany, continuing to direct Anne by coded letters. "Condé,"
he wrote her, "thanks to his pride and impulsiveness, will soon
antagonize his followers," and he advised patience.

Patience was not among Anne of Austria's qualities, but she hung

---

* Second only to Condé as a general. Thus the French once again witnessed
the spectacle of such Frenchmen as Conti and Turenne leading the Spanish
enemy (as the Grand Condé himself was soon to do) against France, while a
Sicilian (Mazarin) was the leader of France's defenders. (True, the *frondeurs*
thought of themselves as fighting against Mazarin "for the release of the King,"
not against France, as three centuries later, a Louis de Condé was to participate in
an assassination attempt against de Gaulle, in order to keep Algeria French.)

on with all her tenacity and Mazarin's wits for the few months left before Louis' thirteenth birthday, September 5, 1651, when he would be of an age to rule. On that day, during the *lit de justice** before Parlement, Louis conducted himself, Mazarin was informed by a loyal courtier, "as if he were a man of twenty-five." "Messieurs," he said, in a manner foreshadowing the Sun King's, "I have come to my Parlement to tell you that in accordance with the law of the land, I intend to take the government myself." Anne resigned her eight-year-old regency and was immediately named chief councilor by her son.

Offered conciliation, Condé refused it. At odds with everyone, he sulked for awhile in his château at Chantilly, then flew down to Bordeaux, still seeking revenge, planning to establish a separate kingdom with Spanish help and recognition. Fellow *frondeurs* stirred up the provinces and the revolt spread. But this time the young King personally rode out to inspire opposition to it. By November he felt strong enough to recall Mazarin, who warmly joined him at Poitiers. Turenne, meantime, re-turned his coat and was once again with the royal troops. And another of France's famous women appeared on its battlefields.

In March 1652, the city of Orléans dispatched a message to its duke—Monsieur, Gaston d'Orléans—to help defend it from his nephew's advancing army. Since he was Monsieur (as brother of the late King), his wife was Madame and his daugher Mademoiselle. Tall, strong, the richest princess of Europe, Mademoiselle de Montpensier has ridden through history as *La Grande Mademoiselle*— and it was she who rode down to Orléans in place of her weak, ever-wavering father, to close its gates to her cousin's forces.

It was the first of the blows to her own ambition to marry Louis. When he was still in the cradle, Mademoiselle, a good eleven years older, called him, "my little husband." Anne of Austria, she says in her memoirs, while yet pregnant called her, "my daughter-in-law."[27] In time, La Grande Mademoiselle was to seek—or reject—in marriage not only Louis XIV, but the King of Spain, the Emperor Ferdinand, the Emperor's brother, the Emperor's son, Charles II, the Grand Condé, the King of Portugal, and was finally, fatally, to fall in love

---

* A symbolic "bed of justice," in which French kings once actually reclined, imposing their will on Parlement while a few of the grander officials stood and all others knelt. It was a bed, Talleyrand quotes writer Fontenelle as saying, in which justice went to sleep.

with the younger Comte de Lauzun when she was forty-three and marry him when she was fifty-four.* But in the meantime, she was to fire another shot at her first ambition.

Condé, risking all, drove directly to Paris. Attacked near Montmartre, he sent at dawn to Monsieur for help. Monsieur replied that he was ill. Informed, Mademoiselle hurried to her father, found him fully dressed. "I thought I would find you in bed," she told him. "I'm not sick enough for bed," he replied, "but I'm too ill to go out." She then advised him to go to bed and at least pretend to be ill, and persuaded him to give her a paper with his signature authorizing her to act in his name. Armed with it, she went to the Hôtel de Ville,† talked the city authorities into opening the gates of Paris to Condé and his troops, should they need it, hastened closer to the fighting in the Saint-Antoine suburbs, established her headquarters next to the Bastille. On the streets, among the dead and wounded, she saw La Rochefoucauld, blinded with blood, riding a horse led by his son. "I stopped to talk to him, but he didn't reply." (It is one of the most harrowing pages of her memoirs.) Told of her arrival, Condé, "the dust two fingers thick on his face, his collar and shirt bloody," rushed into Paris to talk to her. "You see a man in despair," he cried. "All my friends have been killed!" And he rushed out to resume the madness.

It may have been the last medieval battle of France. Waving banners of royal fleurs-de-lis at each other, five thousand of Condé's men against twelve thousand of Turenne's troops, they fought on in the stifling July heat for seven or eight hours, the two great captains of France themselves in pistol-to-pistol combat. And the Parisians looked down from the city walls as if at a circus (in which one out of three were left dead on the ground). Meanwhile Mademoiselle had gone to the Bastille, mounted one of its towers, looked on with a telescope and sent reports to Condé about what she spied.

Slowly Condé's men were being cut to pieces, their retreat to Paris threatened by a cavalry charge. Seeing it, Mademoiselle ordered the Bastille cannons loaded, turned, aimed, and fired at her cousin Louis' men. From the nearby hill of Charonne, surrounded by the Court, Louis was looking on. At first he thought the Bastille was loyally firing at the rebels, but shot after shot brought down the

* After he had spent ten years in Louis' prisons.
† Paris' City Hall.

royal riders, Mazarin's nephew, Paul Mancini, among them. Told
that it was Mademoiselle directing the fire, Mazarin declared, "She
has killed her husband," that is, her last chance to marry Louis.[28] And
while the gates of Paris opened to succor Condé and his men, the
King and his Court had to seek shelter for the night at Saint-Denis—
and again the idea of Versailles, a royal residence securely distant
from riotous Parisians, was seeded.

Within two days, as Mazarin had predicted, Condé was quarreling
with the municipal authorities who had opened Paris to him, inciting
a mob to set fire to the Hôtel de Ville, killing several of its officials.
By October he had to decamp from Paris for Bordeaux. Louis returned
to a cheering capital, not to the Palais Royal, but to the fortified Louvre.
By early 1653, Mazarin was fully re-established, Mademoiselle banished, the last of the Fronde finished, but Paris, for Louis XIV, never to
be forgiven.

For more than four impressionable years, from the age of ten to
fourteen, Louis had felt the impact of the worst of wars—civil war.
Unforgettable was the flight to Saint-Germain in the winter of
1649, unassuaged by the return to a Paris so fickle it now fought
for the privilege of touching his garments. Unforgettable was the
counsel of Mazarin, between Frondes, that he humor the Grand Condé;
unforgettable the insolence and revolt of the nobles. Unforgettable
was the state of France during the fighting, when "the King saw
masses of sick and crippled soldiers stumbling after him, asking for
money to help them in their misery, and he had nothing to give
them."[29] He had wept with rage during the siege of Bordeaux in
1650. "I will not always be a child," he had cried to his companion,
Loménie de Brienne. "Those Bordelais knaves won't lay down the
law for me much longer! But hush, keep quiet about my crying.
I don't want anyone to know." "He would hide his feelings," Brienne
recalled, "from me as from everyone."[30] ("Know how to dissimulate," Mazarin had taught Louis.)

Again and again he was to experience what the person of the King
meant to the people—nothing less, Madame de Motteville informs
us, than France itself, and she describes the mob that had stood guard
outside the Palais Royal in February 1651 to prevent his being
spirited away. When a rumor spread that it had already happened,
as in fact was being prepared, Captain des Ouches of the Fronde
insisted on confirming the young King's presence. The Queen had

him brought to Louis' bedroom. There he drew aside the curtain and held a candle to his face, as the boy feigned sleep.

Returning to the mob, des Ouches tried to reassure it that the King was still in the palace. Suspicious, the mob broke through the gates, some pushing to the palace, shouting, "Show us the King!" "Immediately," says Madame de Motteville, "the Queen ordered the palace doors opened, the people taken to the King's chamber. They were delighted with this frankness. They crowded around the King's bed, its curtain drawn back for them. Their old feeling of love returned and they gave him a thousand blessings. For a long time they watched him sleeping, and could not admire him enough. The sight of him made them respectful. They wanted more than ever not to lose him, but they showed it now by signs of loyalty. Their anger ceased. They had entered full of fury, but they left as faithful subjects, praying God with all their heart to save the young King, whose presence had so charmed them."

There was flattery for the young Louis in such adoration, but there was frustration too. "It all ended," as Madame de Motteville says, "in a kind of prison to which the King and the Queen were confined for more than a month, unable to leave the Palais Royal."

Free at last, a note in the *Gazette* for April 18, 1651, tells us, twelve-year-old Louis XIV went hunting, for the first time, at Versailles.

For eight years the small red-brick château of his father had slumbered under caretakers as a *dépendance* of Saint-Germain. The Queen had had little reason to remember it with pleasure, and Louis none. Now did the Paris prison of the Palais Royal make Versailles look a royal paradise in comparison? In any event, Louis and his suite dined there, the *Gazette* reports, "all extraordinarily satisfied." And the King was to return twice in June and every year thereafter with his brother or the Cardinal.

But in the summer of 1651, a short month or two before his thirteenth birthday, there were other glimmerings of the future Sun King. "We rode seven or eight times together," La Grande Mademoiselle records, "with Madame de Frontenac," her lady-in-waiting, "following. The King seemed to take such great pleasure in being with us that the Queen thought him in love with Madame de Frontenac, and thereupon put an end to our rides, which extremely irritated the King. Since he was not told the reason, he offered the Queen one hundred pistoles for the poor every time he rode* . . . Seeing she refused his offer, he said, 'When I am master, I'll go where I want—and that will be soon!' The Queen cried; the King too; then they were reconciled." The real reason for the forbidden rides, Mademoiselle adds confidently, was the Queen's fear that Louis would fall in love with *her* and discover that "I was the best *parti* that could possibly be offered him, except for the Infanta of Spain."

It was two more years before the delayed coronation of Louis in the cathedral of Rheims took place—and rarely has the cult of the king ever had a more persuasive ceremony. For Louis—and his subjects—*le sacre* at Rheims confirmed his God-given birth by consecrating him King by divine right. It coincided with Anne's own Spanish view of royalty and the person of the king as a mystical blend of absolute power. It coincided with Parlement's own conception of the King. "For us," Advocate General Omer Talon had told the four-and-a-half-year-old Louis at his first *lit de justice,* "the seat of your Majesty represents the throne of the living God."[31] (Parlement was antitaxes and anti-Mazarin but not anticrown.) It coincided with the juridical view of the day. Grotius' *De Jure belli ac pacis,* scorning the notion that sovereignty resided in the people, was dedicated to Louis' father. And it coincided with the popular feeling. "The cry to be heard from the people," Péréfixe had read to Louis from his *Henri le Grand,* "was *'Govern us!'"* After the frightful years of the Fronde, the princely pillaging of the provinces, the cry was once again heard from the people.

Regarded as Godlike ("France," wrote an Englishman who had witnessed Louis' reception by Paris in 1652, "is the only nation of Europe which worships its sovereign"), how could Louis XIV regard himself as anything less? As everything had prepared France for viewing the future Sun King as the very image of the King, so everything had prepared Louis to be that King. But there were still six more years in the making, despite the sacred ceremony at Rheims, despite the growing impatience of a crowned, adored, sixteen-year-old-King.

The training, supervised by Mazarin, continued. A typical day, described by Dubois, has become the historical source:

"Waking [the valet writes] the King recited his prayers and told

* Was this the poor little King of La Porte's memoirs?

his beads. That done, Péréfixe entered and read to him from the Bible or from his history. That done, he rose from bed and we entered. Then he sat on his *chaise percée* [toilet chair], which was in the same *chambre de l'alcôve* in which he slept, staying on it for half an hour, more or less. Afterwards, he went into his *grande chambre,* where the princes and *grands seigneurs* were waiting to attend his *lever* [formal rising]. He was dressed in his bathrobe, and went directly to them, speaking to them so familiarly, one after the other, that they were delighted. Afterwards, he sat in his chair and washed his hands, his mouth and his face [with scented alcohol spirits]. After being dried, he removed the bonnet which was tied around his head because of the [abundant chestnut] hair beneath. He prayed to God in the ruelle of his bed with his almoners: everyone kneeling, no one daring to remain standing, to speak or to make a sound. The usher would have had them put out. The King's prayer over, he returned to his chair, where he was combed and dressed simply in light, serge trousers and a Dutch linen shirt, and he went to the large room behind his antechamber, where he did his exercises. He vaulted, but with admirable agility. He had the wooden horse raised to its highest, then leapt on it like a bird, landing on the saddle as softly as if on a pillow. Afterwards, he practised with weapons and the pike and returned to his *chambre de l'alcôve,* where he danced [under the direction of a professional ballet dancer] and returned to his *grande chambre,* where he changed and breakfasted. Afterwards, he left his bedroom, always crossing himself, and went up to M. le cardinal de Mazarin, who was his Prime Minister and who lived in private above his bedroom, where he had a Secretary of State come every day to make reports, by means of which, as well as by more secret reports, the King was instructed about his affairs for an hour or an hour and a half.

"That done, the King went down to say good morning to the Queen, and from there to the manege to ride until the Queen his mother went to Mass and he accompanied her. Mass heard, he reconducted her to her apartments with a great deal of deference and respect. The King went back up to his bedroom and changed, either for the hunt or for the palace. If he went hunting, it was an ordinary suit, but if for the palace, though modest, somewhat better, with little ceremony and no affectation. He was easy to dress and he often dressed himself. His body was so marvelously well made that it could not have been better. If dressed, he dined, often with the Queen. If, after dinner, there was an audience with ambassadors, he could not have been more attentive to them. After their speeches, he chatted with them for a quarter of an hour with great familiarity about the things cherished by their sovereigns or their people, their long-standing alliances and relationships, houses and reigns . . ."

There are such "admirable things in the King," Dubois continues, "that they merit a Queen of Sheba coming to see him and to hear what God has poured into this chosen vessel . . . He is a Saint Louis in piety, a Caesar in goodness. After dinner, the King goes to his studies, or talks in passing to people of quality. His studies over, he goes to the council meeting,* if it is the day for it. Often there is a serious play. The play finished . . . Their Majesties have supper, after which the King dances [in a ballet], his *petits violons* playing, with the Queen's maids of honor and others. That done, they play some games, such as *stories:* they sit in a circle; then one begins a story and continues until it is too difficult to go on, then the one who is next picks up the story and continues it, thus one after the other the adventures, often very amusing, are unfolded. When midnight approaches, the King says good night to the Queen and goes to his bedroom and prays to God and undresses in the presence of those who are there and chats charmingly with them. Afterwards, he bids them good night and retires to his *chambre de l'alcôve,* where he sleeps. Entering it, he sits on his *chaise percée,* where those most familiar, such as the first gentlemen of the chamber and a few others who have the right to enter, chat with him."[32]

Such was a day in March 1655—something of a mélange of several— when Louis XIV was sixteen. It was a decorous day in a significant year. A month later, April 13, Louis was hunting at Vincennes, the great, fortified estate of Mazarin slightly east of Paris, stocked by the cardinal with wild boar and deer. They were riding together that morning when a messenger brought news of an unauthorized meeting of all chambers of Parlement at the Palais de Justice, to reconsider the seventeen edicts just signed by the King for financing the resumed war with Spain. It was an incipient Fronde. With a decisiveness

---

* "Don't worry about the King," Mazarin told a tutor who complained of Louis' lack of application, "when he comes to a council meeting, he asks me a hundred questions about whatever is being discussed."

that must have been his own, since it was so uncharacteristic of
Mazarin, Louis immediately galloped off to Paris and the Palais de
Justice. There, dressed for the hunt, riding crop in hand, Louis took
the chair reserved for him and faced down the scarlet-robed magistrates. He may not have cracked his whip, as legend would have
it, or have snapped the words, *"L'Etat, c'est moi!"* But the recorded
statement will serve:

"Everyone knows"—Louis' authoritarian tone stunned them—"how
much trouble your meetings have stirred in my State, and how many
dangerous results they have had. I have learned that you intend
to continue them on the pretext of debating the edicts which were
just published and read in my presence. I have come here to forbid
it expressly. I now do so absolutely, and forbid you, Monsieur le
Premier Président, to permit or tolerate it."[33]

Louis strode out of a speechless Parlement, returned to the hunt at
Vincennes. Parlement soon recovered its speech and Mazarin the occasion for his customary compromise. Had he not, Louis' gesture might
have come down in history as more foolish than prophetic. The cardinal persuaded Turenne to go before the leaders of Parlement and
plead the military necessity of the new taxes. Then, when Monsieur
le Premier Président, Pomponne de Bellièvre, added his own persuasive voice, Mazarin gave him three hundred thousand livres, as undoubtedly agreed in advance. The tax bills became law, Louis' "I am
the State" became history.[34]

School texts, however, leave unmentioned a more private matter.
Early in May of the same memorable year, 1655, the sixteen-year-old
King suffered a malaise publicly attributed to his activity in the
Spanish campaign. For his doctors it was a more delicate affair which,
contemporaries agree, was nothing other than a confrontation with the
gonococcus.[35]

Having inherited the constitution of his mother rather than that of
his father, Louis was successfully to resist the treatments of his corps
of doctors for almost eight decades. His only childhood disease, for
instance, was smallpox at the age of nine, for which he was bled four
times by a physician who had paid twenty thousand écus for such
privileges. The young King was hailed for his stoicism. Seven years
later, the sentiment expressed in that extraordinary document, the medical diary of Louis XIV, kept by his doctors, was one of embarrassment

—an embarrassment which arose not only from the nature of the disease noted, but also from the fact that the diarist—then Vallot—well knew the King would read it.[36] So, the disagreeable discharge identified with the lesser of the two diseases of Venus was attributed in the diary to the King's vaulting and riding too much, since, Vallot writes, "I had no doubt about the purity and chastity of his life." Pomades and liniments were prescribed, the carbonated waters of Forges, and various essences taken, all very discreetly, "because I received the express command to tell no one about an affair of such consequence." By the end of the year, thanks largely to the self-limiting character of his difficulty, the King was cured. But he continued to ride as usual during treatments, to Vallot's despair, and was to remain, in Saint-Simon's lilting phrase, "all his life a lover."

Was the first in a very long line Catherine de Beauvais, his mother's personal maid, who "waylaid him as he was coming from his bath?"[37] A widow in her forties, for forty more years she was to live on the prestige of the event. Was it Olympe Mancini? "Anything looked good to him," La Palatine, who liked, perhaps loved, her brother-in-law,* says, "so long as it was a woman: peasant women, daughters of the gardeners, chambermaids or women of quality. They had only to pretend to love him."[38] On the other hand, virtually every woman at Court, servant or noblewoman, prodded by husband and parent, thrust herself upon Louis and considered being brought to bed by the King a personal honor as well as a guarantee of her family's advancement. Taste, not resistance, was expected of Louis.

Olympe Mancini . . .

Mazarin, having made his fortune, set about securing his family's. He sent for his nephews, his widowed sister, his nieces—all Mancini, they were promptly and appropriately tagged *les Mazarinettes*. Olympe first caught the eye of Louis, perhaps more. There is an insistence on the part of historians that the relationship was platonic (until some time later, after marriage to the complaisant Comte de Soissons, when Olympe gave Louis a little girl). Quick and bright, she was "the Snipe" to the Court, "the serpent of the Mazarins" to the Queen. The danger, however, came from a more innocent Marie, the tall, dark, convent-trained younger sister (whose teeth alone Madame de Motteville allowed

* Elizabeth Charlotte (Liselotte) of the Palatinate (Bavaria), she married Monsieur, Louis' brother, in 1671.

her admiration). She was sixteen, Louis seventeen. Romantically she read to him in Italian from Ariosto, romantically he played to her on his guitar—meanwhile running around with a rakish group, *Les Endormis* (the sleepy ones), destined soon to be broken up by the watchful Mazarin. (Louis was to become master of the double—and triple—life.) Concerned about his courtship of Marie, the Queen sent for the banished Grande Mademoiselle. She came, Mazarin embraced her knees. For twelve nights Louis danced with her, but there were almost twelve years of age between them. Moreover, when they didn't dance, they discussed her favorite topic—military affairs. It helped defeat her own campaign, and finally she left. Louis returned to Marie. Moved by Marie's solicitude when he was stricken with fever in 1658, Louis felt the sensation of falling in love. If an illusion, it was as effective as reality, for he soon made it known to Mazarin that he loved and would marry his niece.

That the cardinal discussed the idea with the Queen is most likely. That he proposed it, as Madame de Motteville relates (adding that the Queen instantly flamed up, crying she would personally lead a new Fronde to prevent it), is less likely. Their relations were too intimate, too daily, for that. But something obviously had to be done, not only about Louis' growing passion, but eventual peace with Spain. The solution seemed inevitable: marriage to the Spanish Infanta, daughter of Anne's brother, Philip IV.

As usual Mazarin's approach was by ricochet. Since the Spanish King hesitated, Louis' marriage to Marguerite of Savoy, a granddaughter of Henry IV, was rumored as imminent. The entire Court went down to Lyons—Louis' and Marie's riding together tolerated by Mazarin, for it showed a young King in no hurry for any arranged marriage—for formal discussions with Marguerite's mother, the garrulous, widowed Duchess of Savoy. Days and nights passed; finally Philip sent the envoy Mazarin awaited, proposing the Infanta as Louis' bride. And Louis, who had just told his mother that he found Marguerite, also at Lyons, quite acceptable, consented. Only the duchess behaved badly, until Mazarin gave her a small fortune in jewels.

Yet, during the long, careful negotiations of so important a matter as peace and marriage between France and Spain, Louis and Marie continued to see each other, Louis wavering as Mazarin watched. He sent for his niece. He told her she must leave Paris for Brouage. She told Louis. He went to the cardinal, who was with the Queen, implored them to change their minds. Anne weakened, Mazarin remained firm. The risk of a resumed war with Spain was too great. Once again Louis accepted the voice of reason.* The lovers' adieus were exchanged in the Louvre courtyard. Louis wept. "You love me, you are King," Marie said, "you cry, and I go!" That line, which has sprung tears in the eyes of French schoolgirls for generations, may be La Palatine's, a superb letter writer, but the separation was to inspire Racine as well. And Louis was to pay a price for it, other than the nine-strand necklace of pearls he bought for Marie, with money from Mazarin. "His Majesty," Vallot noted not long afterward, "has fever, suffers insomnia and a considerable loss of weight."[39]

Daily Louis sent Marie love letters by special courier. Almost as frequently Mazarin counseled him from the Spanish frontier, where he was conducting the final negotiations. "Remember," he wrote, "what I had the honor to tell you when you asked me what must be done to become a great king: that one must begin by dominating one's passions, because when one feels passion, whatever one's good intentions, one is in no state to do what one must."[40] And he wisely appealed to what was to be Louis' consuming passion: *gloire* and *grandeur* (to which his relationship may be described as erotic). "Love of glory," the Sun King wrote the Dauphin, "surely preceded all in my spirit," and with astonishing insight, he compared it to physical love: "It has the same *délicatesses,* and, if I dare say so, the same *timidités* as the most tender passions, for as great as my ardor for distinction has been my fear of failing . . . I have felt myself equally pushed forward and held back by my desire for glory."

Meanwhile, down on the Spanish border, Mazarin was driving a hard bargain with a destitute Spain, demanding a dowry of half a million écus or, failing payment (as he expected and hoped would happen), maintenance of the Infanta's rights (as to the Spanish Netherlands) on the death of Philip. The marriage contract was signed in November 1659, one of its conditions the pardon of the Grand Condé, who had led Spanish troops to the bitter finale. The wedding was held in the little church of St.-Jean-de-Luz on June 9, 1660.

Louis and Marie-Thérèse, as France was to know her, were each twenty-one, each curious about the other. She found him, as she told his brother, "very handsome and very nice." He found her démodé

---

* "Louis XIV," wrote Sainte-Beuve, "had nothing but good sense, but he had a great deal of it."

in the Spanish fashion, smaller than he (always welcome to a man of average height*), anxious to please, and he told the Prince de Conti that he thought it possible to love her. Impatiently, after the wedding supper, he bid the company good night. "But it is too early!" said the bride, then reconsidered, and went to her rooms. "Hurry, hurry!" she said to her maids as they undressed her. "The King is waiting for me!"[41] Undoubtedly recalling her own disastrous wedding night, the Queen Mother embraced and blessed the young couple, drew the curtain tight around their bed. The next morning Louis showed no sign of displeasure, but their first meal was taken separately—and the Court spoke of it. They had little in common and what they had they could scarcely communicate; she had no French, he little Spanish. More than two distinct cultures, theirs were two worlds apart. Ignorant, simple-minded, Marie-Thérèse was to share Louis' bed (and clap her hands on rising so the Court would know that the only exchange available to them had actually taken place), but never his crown or his concerns. On the long voyage to Paris, they conspicuously slept together, but Louis detoured through Brouage for a sentimental stopover, accompanied only by Marie Mancini's brother and two other gentlemen, and rejoined his honeymoon suite the next day. (Marie herself, no longer at Brouage, would soon marry Prince Colonna, in whose household Mazarin's father had once been a servant.) The entry into Paris on August 26 was ceremonious and popular. Mazarin, ailing and close to death, looked on from a balcony of Madame de Beauvais' new manor house in the Marais. So did the Queen Mother, the Henriettes of England, mother and daughter, ladies of the Court and their companions, such as Madame Scarron.† Passing, Louis reined in his horse, removed his plumed hat and saluted Mazarin and his mother. He owed much to both, his debt to Mazarin mounting even higher in the remaining six months.

Suffering from gout, stones, and dropsy of the lungs, sensing death, Louis' godfather, mentor, and prime minister prepared him for the

---

* Louis XIV has been described as tall *and* short, sometimes by the same person, as La Palatine. His height inevitably varied from youth to old age, and so do the descriptions of it. The parish priest of Versailles said he was "a very tall man and very well-proportioned, six feet tall or so, with broad shoulders and well-shaped legs." Saint-Simon said he was short. It is likely that Louis was closer to five foot five than to six, as were most men of his time, looking taller because of his high red heels and, more important, because he looked a king.
† Who was to become Madame de Maintenon.

kingship, as he prepared himself for death. In Louis' youth, he had had him attend council meetings when the agenda was not too complicated. Later Mazarin's lessons became daily and "at the councils he held almost every day with Fouquet, Lionne and the Secretaries of State, he wanted none to talk about the affairs of state without the King being present."[42] "While the Cardinal still lived," confirms Colbert, "nothing of consequence was done without the King being informed." In short, "Mazarin had styled his master in the art of ruling."[43] (Mazarin himself repeatedly told Louis, "A king not capable of ruling is not worthy of reigning." That he exposed Louis to Machiavelli, reducing *The Prince* to instant maxims, was a typical anti-Mazarin story. That he taught him patience and political pragmatism was soon to be seen.)

Batista Nani, the Venetian ambassador, describes the Louis of this time as interested primarily in military exercises, such as drilling his musketeers. "As for the rest, hunting, dancing, *jeu de paume* [tennis], and card playing, to which he gives himself more than moderately, are his favorite pastimes." But "he is well informed about affairs, though he considers himself still too young and in-experienced to direct them." No one, Nani continues, "has ever seen the King lose his temper, complain or lie, even in pleasantry. He affects a complete impartiality towards everyone, so that none among his familiars can boast of any special sign of favor or confidence. This quality, rarely met in a prince, is astonishing in a monarch in the prime of his life. . . .

"The young King reveres his mother . . . He is extremely taken by his wife. He is fond of his brother, but all his affection seems to go to the Cardinal . . . One must acknowledge that there is a profound sympathy between them, a voluntary submission of spirit and intelligence, which moves so great a prince to depend on the genius of a private subject . . . He sees him several times a day. As soon as he is dressed, he goes to the cardinal . . . The visits are made without any ceremony and in complete familiarity. The cardinal does not come out or reaccompany him. If he is occupied, the King waits in the antechamber . . . Generally their meeting lasts several hours, during which the Cardinal posts him on everything, instructs and forms him. Thus His Majesty knows about everything from a good source."[44]

It is rather moving to record that the last theatrical experience Louis and Mazarin were to have together was at a Court production of Molière's *Les Précieuses ridicules,* since it was Mazarin who introduced

Louis to dramatic spectacles, thus godfathering not only the future Sun King, but the pleasures of his future palace. And together they gave Molière three thousand livres.

Mazarin, fifty-nine had a few more months to live—and knew it from his first physician. A sudden fire in the Louvre on February 6, 1661, obliged the cardinal to move in the middle of the night to his château at Vincennes. It was a premature separation from his beloved Titians and Correggios, his library and treasures. Much has been made of his accumulated fortune, but none made more of it than Mazarin himself. Offering it to Louis, it is said, with relief he heard the offer rejected; his family would inherit. But so too would Louis, when Colbert told him on Mazarin's death where much of it was hidden. (Was this Mazarin's devious way of leaving it to his king, since it was unseemly for him to accept a private subject's fortune?) During the last days they were almost inseparable, and Louis was to dictate from memory Mazarin's deathbed advice:

To support the Church, but oversee the hierarchy; to keep the magistrates within the bounds of their duty; to lighten taxes; to punish anyone who exercised political initiative without his express knowledge; to suffer neither impiety nor scandal at court; to regard the nobles of the sword as his right arm but to name none to his council; to prevent division among the French; to persuade all that the King was the sole master—that is, to be his own prime minister.[45]

History has Mazarin whispering in his last breath as well: "Leaving you Colbert, I discharge all my debts. But beware of Fouquet"—the ambitious, powerful, forty-five-year-old superintendent of finances.

Mazarin died during the night of March 9, 1661. Wakened at the Louvre, Louis wept, and went to Vincennes. There he ordered the Court to wear black, an honor reserved for death in the royal family, and called his first council meeting. It lasted a perfunctory two hours. He summoned a second for seven the next morning at the Louvre.

"Monsieur," said Louis that morning to the chancellor, "I have had you assemble with my Ministers and my Secretaries of State to inform you that until now I have chosen to have my affairs managed by the late cardinal. I will now manage them by myself, and you will aid me with your counsels, when I ask you for them." Nothing, Louis went on, was to be signed or sealed without his consent—not even a passport—and he instructed Fouquet to use the services of Colbert.

Later the same day, the Archbishop of Rouen came to the young

King and asked to whom he should address himself concerning the clergy now that the cardinal was dead.

"To me," replied Louis.[46]

Twenty-two years old in 1661, Louis XIV was to give his name to an entire century. He was to be its Sun King, the image of God on earth. But perhaps Taine came closer to the truth when he wrote in 1861: "God in the 17th century was a kind of Louis XIV."

3. Pyramids and Early Pleasures

With Louis XIV at the summit ruling with a "Pharaonic pride"[1] if not yet power, one might describe seventeenth-century France as a social pyramid of cascading wealth, privileges, and scorn. One might describe it in the same descending order, but one more profitably plunges directly to the pyramid's base—the peasants. They produced at least three quarters of what we now call the gross national product, though only a fraction filtered back to them. It would be hardly necessary to note in passing that this four fifths of the population owned less than half of the land were it not that their counterparts across the Channel or the Rhine could claim even less.[2]

The very bulk of the young King's pyramid may have been, initially, its most impressive feature. The France of Louis XIV had eighteen million to twenty million people, almost *twice* that of Tsarist Russia, which had not yet displaced Sweden on the eastern Baltic shore and whose boundary with an expansive Poland was but a few days' march from Moscow.

Figures for Spain and England at that time run loosely from five million to not quite eight million for each. (Considering the period, it should cause no surprise. Today's estimates of China vary by one hundred million.) In any case, Louis XIV's most sorely underestimated rival, the Dutch Republic, had a greater power than indicated by its some two million. As for the more conspicuous contender, the Holy Roman Empire, generally referred to as the Empire, though ten times as populated as Holland, it was perhaps two hundred times as divided, consisting of over three hundred sovereign states with their own rulers, armies, currencies, and laws, jostling each other in Germany, Austria, Bohemia, Hungary, and other parts. Germany alone was a "republic of princes" divided by religion, the Emperor possessing "not even a single village by virtue of being Emperor."[3]

Thus, concentrated France, with more workers and peasants, could field more soldiers, supply and arm them with more tax money—when its millions worked and taxes were collected. The masses were likely miserable, though less than others on the Continent—Holland excepted. Largely illiterate, they were called *sottes,* or stupid, by the worldly Madame de Sévigné, for whose class, on the whole, they were the invisible eight tenths of the pyramid. But they were also called *les peuplades sauvages* by the saintly Vincent de Paul, who came from among them. Yet, in the paintings of the brothers Le Nain, the peasants disclose a rude, robust dignity, and we prefer calling these portraits realistic.

Of one hundred born, twenty-five would die in the first year, twenty-five before their twentieth year, another twenty-five between the ages of twenty and forty-five.[4] Ten might reach sixty or more; peasants and artisans, safely past infancy, usually outlived members of the Court, probably because they could not afford the doctors of the day. Women were rapidly used up—there were forty births per year per thousand*—and widowers rapidly took another wife. Infant deaths were accepted—or so we are told, and so it may have been—with the fatalism of grazing animals singled out by a pride of lions. Death came from the triple scourge: famine, as in 1661, war, and plague. Taxes too were triple, collected by the crown, the clergy, and the seigneur. Yet this was the France which produced the first people and, when crops didn't fail, much of the food of Europe.

Richer peasants, become landowners, generally ruled the village along with the seigneur (the equality of village life is a romantic myth) or in his name when he was absent at Court, as increasingly occurred under Louis XIV. Ordinary peasants simply tried to survive. If after the year's taxes—the land and income tax, or *taille;* the oppressive salt tax, or *gabelle* (extorted by the forced buying of an excessive quantity of bad government salt at inflated prices); the *dîmes* (tithes or tenths, which in practice were often less) for the

---

* Parents of ten children received one thousand livres, parents of twelve, including seigneurs, two thousand.

clergy; the *aides,* or indirect tax on drink; and the seigneurial dues—
the peasant could keep half his labor's product, he could consider
himself fortunate. It was more than his counterpart on the Continent
(one needs only think of the Spanish peasant or the Russian serf)
ever retained.

Admittedly our frames of reference are few, our experience of
peasant life limited or nil; the peasants of the period were subjects
of the King, not of the period's memoir writers. The pretty "peasant"
met late in Louis' reign by Madame de Sévigné and described by her
in a letter could not have been typical: she owed the literary lady
eight thousand francs (or about twenty-eight thousand dollars).[5] In fact
we know more about Louis XIV than we do about the peasant.

More familiar might have been the slumlike condition of the urban
workers, one twentieth the number of peasants. Landless, propertyless
(they rented their dark spaces), theirs was wage serfdom. For work
done at home they were paid in kind, usually a shoddy kind—
selvages of fabric, falsely measured flour—or dubious coin. It was a
tyranny tempered by a fellowship much later termed corporative. As
often as not dominated by the *patrons,* the corporations, or trade
guilds, were not the powerful workers' protectives we have since
made of them, but they did provide some mutual succor, some form
of pressure on employers. Best of all for the urban worker, he paid
few taxes; if only because he had little that was seizable.

Unfortunately for the social historian, Molière's Monsieur Jourdain
has so frozen the image of the French bourgeois *gentilhomme* it is
difficult to present him except as a figure of fun. That he was more
force than farce, however, would become evident, even to the Court
snob, as French society spun its way toward its revolutionary fall. In
the interim, those of bourgeois origin were to be Louis' first choice as
ministers—Colbert, who was a draper's son, Le Tellier, who came from
a family of lawyers, and Lionne, who rose on his own merits as a
diplomat.* And the bourgeoisie were to industrialize France, frequently
becoming landowners and seigneurs in the process.

French nobility at the beginning of Louis' reign was not yet so

---

* *"Le règne de la vile bourgeoisie,"* Saint-Simon was to scorn the celebrated
triade of Louis' inner council.

  "It was not to my interest," Louis himself explained to the Dauphin, "to
choose more eminent subjects. . . . My intention was not to share my authority
with them." Moreover, entirely dependent on him, they would not aspire to anything higher than the honors he gave them, unlike "those born of a high rank."[6]

rigidly split between the *noblesse de la cour* (of the Court) and the *noblesse campagnarde* (of the country) that they might be called two classes. (Recruited from the dukes, the domesticated *frondeurs,* and other noblemen, the former will come to flower in the gardens of Versailles—and we to them in time.) The country nobleman lived on and from the land in a manner more Chekhovian, the courtly memoirs would have us conclude, than lordly: his provincial château was beastly uncomfortable, his food badly cooked and badly served, his conversation a series of silences, in short, his social life a bore.

But the country nobleman's shrinking returns from the land were a less risible matter, for it affected all titled landowners, absentee courtiers above all. Income no longer flowed in with feudal regularity and abundance. The transitional period—from feudalism to early modern times—found the local seigneur as confused and bewildered as any student, three centuries later, trying to make sense out of the dusty dossiers of customs, regulations, and duties varying from region to region and recorded on barely decipherable texts.

If energetic, the seigneur might manage his land directly. More usually, he would form a quasi-partnership with a *métayer,* providing him capital for a percentage of the crops. Or he would let out the land in perpetuity to peasants at a fixed rent and face a steadily declining return from his estate as money declined in value. Contracts inherited from his ancestors would have already halved his real income. But one must not blink at the burden, exploitation, and humiliation of the peasant-seigneur relationship; the French Revolution is there to remind us of its reality. The peasant's grain could be ground only in the seigneur's mill, baked only in the seigneur's oven, and every sixteenth loaf, a record shows, given to him.[7] The game and the fish were the lord's, and it has been said with as much truth as irony that the Revolution was fought to give the ordinary Frenchman a right to today's popular sport: hunting. Formerly only the nobleman had the privilege and he rode roughly across cultivated fields in pursuit of it.

And there was the Church, its highest orders sharing the heights of the wealth and power pyramid of France. Distinct from the other two estates—the nobility and the bourgeoisie—the clergy was not completely separate from them, for the former frequently "colonized" the Church's hierarchy and its richer convents with their younger sons and unmarried daughters. Church largesse, if not for an eternity, was thus at least assured for a lifetime. Possessor of vast productive lands, beneficiary of wealthy benefactors, the Church laid up treasure on earth, and its princes and princesses lived accordingly. In fact, the Church was a pyramid unto itself.

At *its* base was the village curé, or priest, next in importance to the seigneur. He was assisted by a *marguillier*—churchwarden or treasurer—but it was the King's Intendant who supervised collection of the peasant's tithe, solid sign of the Church and the crown as one and the same, thus faced with the same fate in the peasant's revolts. At the top of the hierarchical pyramid were the archbishops and cardinals, fully enjoying its power and privileges. Gallican, or France-centered, as they generally were, they nevertheless played Rome against Paris when it suited them—as, indeed, Louis XIV was to play their Gallicanism against the Vatican.

Throughout his long reign, Louis was to be involved with internal Church dispute, particularly the Jansenist controversy. And to all such controversies he applied one standard: did it strengthen or weaken the Crown's position? "No one," says La Palatine, "could have been more ignorant in religious matters than the King." Her explanation follows: "His confessors had so frightened the King with hell that he believed that all those who had not been educated by the Jesuits were damned, and he was afraid of being damned as well by frequenting them. It was enough to tell him that someone was a Huguenot or Jansenist for him to be lost. My son wanted to take into his houshold a *gentilhomme* whose mother was a declared Jansenist. The King sent for him and said, 'Nephew, what can you be thinking about to take a Jansenist into your service?' Laughing, my son replied, 'I can assure Your Majesty that he is not. It is even more to be feared that he does not believe in God,' 'Oh,' said the King, 'if that is all, and if you can assure me he is not a Jansenist, you may take him.'"[8]

The Jansenists, unjustly called Calvinist by their Jesuit opponents for their stress on austerity and predestination, were condemned from the beginning to clash with the crown, merely from having formed an opposition, however theological, to the established order. Richelieu's initial, inevitable blows against them had not been mortal; typically Mazarin had temporized (as Pascal ably supported them with his *Provincial Letters*); and it was not until the end of Louis XIV's reign that the sanctum of Jansenism on the edge of Paris, the sad, still-haunting Port-Royal convent, was leveled and plowed under—to send up sprouts later in the eighteenth century.

But we are still considering the France of 1661.

Economically it was stagnant, the King's treasury empty. The royal debt was twice the royal revenue, and the revenues for the next two and a half years were already spent. The best roads—the rivers—were impassable six months of the year, the others much of the time, and the number of local tolls has not yet been tallied. A few hundred French ships floundered in the wake of Holland's eight to nine thousand, which was half the world's fleet (China excluded). Traffic between French possessions was conducted by costly courtesy of the Dutch. French iron was poor; cannons, balls, and powder were bought abroad from the Danes—and the Dutch. Copper came from Sweden and Japan—by way of Amsterdam. The best fabrics were English— and Dutch. The best farming was English—and Dutch. The great East India trading companies were Dutch. They were the most enterprising and prosperous people on the Continent.

Yet France had won its foreign wars. Louis could think of himself as the first king of Europe. Wherein lay his power? In the French people, their overwhelming number, ingenuity, endurance, productivity and capacity to pay taxes. With modern foresight, Louis progressively reduced the *taille* by 10 per cent and in time doubled his revenue. He also cut state expenses, kept personal control over all expenditures, worked eight hours a day with Colbert and his inner Council— Lionne, Le Tellier, and, for the moment, Fouquet—and by 1667 accumulated a surplus in the royal budget.

But the unity of France, the absolutism attributed to Louis XIV, was still to be accomplished. "Disorder reigned everywhere," he described the year 1661 to his son. "A traveler in France," Voltaire tells us, "changed laws as often as he changed horses."

Towns and provinces had their own rule and regulations; "Every village," Richelieu had complained, "is a center of power." They were linked to the crown by ancient agreements that as often limited the King as themselves, defining not only their obligations but their privileges. Brittany and Provence, for instance, had their own *parlements,* military and fiscal arrangements. Paris and Rouen were exempt from the *taille.* Frequently the links were feudal—fief to lord to king. But the King "was not equally king everywhere in his kingdom,"[9] and he sent out his intendants to deal as best they could with the officials he had inherited. (It was not until a decade later that the

Code Louis was established, uniformly governing France until the Code Napoleon of a century and a half later.)

Abroad, where Louis yearned to win *"la gloire et la grandeur"*— the phrase resounds in his memoirs—there was not the same disorder. Spain was not quite "put in its place" behind the Pyrenees, nor yet removed from the north of today's France, but it was held peacefully at a distance. The Rhine states provided a neutral buffer to the empire; moreover the Habsburgs had full-time troubles with the Turks. And if France had not yet reached the frontiers nationalists call natural, such as the Rhine, the Alps, the length of the English Channel, she was not too far from them. Lorraine would be bought from its duke in 1662 and Dunkirk from the English in the same year. The annexation of all Alsace would be more complicated, the conquest of Franche-Comté from the Spanish came much later, and Savoy to the southeast would have to await the French Revolution before it became a French province.

France was to be first, protocol meant French priority, and few monarchs ever insisted on it more fiercely than Louis XIV. Would the Genoan ambassadors enter the Louvre, along with French ambassadors, to the sound of drums (as instructed by Genoa)? They would not. Genoa had once been ruled by a French king. Enough of that "mad pretension," Louis told the Genoese Republic and was pleased to make it "tremble with fear." After a bloody dispute between the suites of the French and Spanish ambassadors to the Court of St. James, Louis coldly warned Spain to prepare for war unless its representative apologized. And so he did, before all London's ambassadors. In the project of a treaty of alliance with Austria against the Turks, Louis forced the Emperor to delete reference to himself as "Chief of the Christian People." The title was for Louis. He was to deal with kings only as the king of kings.[10]

But that, too, was to take a decade. Meanwhile . . .

It is still 1661. A month after Mazarin's death, Philippe d'Orléans, Monsieur to the Court since the death of Gaston, was married by his brother Louis to cousin Henriette, daughter of Queen Henrietta of England. She was a desirable match now that *her* brother, Charles II, had been restored to the English throne. The honeymoon lasted exactly a fortnight, as the horrified husband discovered that his young male friends praised Henriette's looks more often than his own.* They were, according to the difficult Madame de Motteville, not much: at most a good complexion, "small but gentle, shining eyes." Henriette herself tall and extremely thin.

Bored with his own wife, the dull, dwarfish, soggily religious Marie-Thérèse, twenty-two-year-old Louis found his sixteen-year-old cousin, whom he had once misprized as a skinny little girl with the "frail bones of the Holy Innocents," suddenly to his taste. Henriette liked theater and music, as did he, and could brighten a conversation with spirit and the unexpected. So, as his brother returned to his "beautiful as an angel" Chevalier de Lorraine[11] (*and* the Comte de Guiche), Louis entertained his brother's wife, who, if not as beautiful, had the even greater "gift of knowing how to please."[12]

Fontainebleau, loveliest of the royal sites until the re-creation of Versailles, was their favorite playground. Swimming parties, supper parties, balls, ballets, Molière's *School for Husbands* (an unwitting Marie-Thérèse looking on), coach rides in the dark woods ending at two or three in the morning (Marie-Thérèse usually retiring before nine in the evening), the young King luxuriated in his first Mazarin-less months. But there was still the Queen Mother.

Though his own pleasures were conspicuously elsewhere, Monsieur's pride brought him complaining to Queen Mother Anne, who, Henriette informed Louis, was forwarding his complaints to England, to Henriette's mother. They would have to camouflage their affair, pretend Louis was infatuated by one of Henriette's maids of honor, wherefore his presence in her apartments. But which one? Choosing the maid she thought least attractive (having learned nothing from her own experience), Henriette proposed thin little La Vallière (and established the precedent of Louis' ladies almost invariably introducing him to their successors).[13]

Louise de La Baume Le Blanc, Demoiselle de La Vallière—it has the lilt of Mallory's *Elaine the fair, Elaine the lovable, Elaine the lily maid of Astolat*—was seventeen, a silvery blonde with a low, sweet voice and a slight, appealing limp. She was shy and vulnerable, "a violet,"[14] and Louis took her. They met in June; by July she was his first *official* mistress, and he, most likely, her first love. The fête he gave at Fontainebleau—Louis dancing the leading role in

---

* Widowed, Monsieur was to go on to a second wife, whom we have quoted so frequently—La Princesse Palatine. Specified in their marriage contract was the clause that only he might wear Henriette's jewels.

C

the ballet *Impatience,* with his usual dash and shapely grace—was his way of announcing it as fact. But he was faithful, too, in his own fashion, to the Queen. He treated her courteously and Marie-Thérèse could count on him once every fortnight to make her a wife and, by November, a mother. Meantime Madame, as we should now call Henriette, outraged by the result of her own strategy, took up with one of her husband's favorites, the versatile Comte de Guiche, and made him her lover. As for the Court, it seemed quite content again to have a king who healthily exercised his prerogatives. And so the summer ended well, as the Marquis de la Fare comments in his memoirs, with the King's auspicious choice of a proper mistress, and everyone playing, more or less properly, by the rules of the royal game.[15]

In the fall of 1661, with Louise by his side, Louis saw the woods of Versailles in the special light of autumn and love. And seeing his father's small château in that light, he may, for the second time in but a few weeks, have foreseen his own great palace and park. For it was during the summer, a short month after Louise had become his mistress in a little room lent by his first gentleman of the chamber, that Louis went, one fateful day in August on Fouquet's brash invitation, to a fête at Vaux-le-Vicomte—"Versailles antici-pated."[16]

4. A Day in August

Nicolas Fouquet is a name little known outside France, yet he might have been a second Richelieu or Mazarin who would have reduced Louis XIV to the impotence of his father, Louis XIII. Had he succeeded, there would have been no Sun King, no great palace at Versailles.[1]

Fouquet was the superintendent of finances, thus master of the treasury at a time when France was a plutocracy and the young king's goal was an absolute monarchy. There was scarcely a courtier or ambassador who did not expect him to be named Prime Minister, to rule France while Louis devoted himself to La Vallière.

Fouquet, too, thought the young King's interest in governing would be brief, misreading Louis as Colbert did not. More than twice Louis' twenty-two, he rather looked forward to the softening uses of love and a royal succession of mistresses, misunderstanding completely Louis' abiding love of power, his Henry IV capacity for not only a simultaneity of mistresses, but of mistresses *and* power.

The young King was a poor man compared to the great financiers and moneylenders of France—and Fouquet was the first among them. When Queen Christina of Sweden had observed Anne of Austria's difficulties finishing some of her buildings, she suggested that the Queen Mother become superintendent of finances for a while and recoup her fortunes. While Mazarin still lived, Voltaire relates, "the King sometimes asked Fouquet for money. 'Sire,' he would reply, 'there is no money in Your Majesty's coffers, but Monsieur le Cardinal will lend you some.'"[2] It was money garnered for the cardinal by Fouquet, who reaped his own rich harvest from it.

And on the death of Mazarin, foreign ambassadors were reporting home that Fouquet would take his place as Prime Minister and wield an even greater power, since he was financially shrewder and even Mazarin had depended on his money-magic.

Portraits of Nicolas Fouquet at forty-five show him as dark, lean, and not particularly attractive, though his success with high-born women reminds one as well of Sainte-Beuve's remark, "Fouquet was not handsome, but a superintendent of finances is never ugly."[3] The two greatest beauties of the Court, according to the young Racine, were his mistresses. Fouquet himself was born (1615) high enough to climb higher. His family device was the squirrel (*fouquet* in Breton), its slogan, *Quo non ascendet?* To what heights will he not ascend? His father was a counselor to the Paris Parlement, his mother belonged to the *noblesse de robe* (nobility of the gown, i.e., the robed magistrates), his grandfather was a former comptroller general of finances. Educated by Jesuits in Paris (more sophisticated than the provincial Jesuits who had raised Colbert), Fouquet at sixteen was a lawyer at the Paris Parlement, at nineteen a counselor to the Parlement of Metz, and at twenty, favorably noticed by Richelieu, back in Paris as a *maître des requêtes* (state inspector). From 1642 to 1650, he was *intendant* (chief administrative officer) of several armies, including Mazarin's, and remained faithful to him during the Fronde. As a reward, in 1650 Mazarin permitted Fouquet, then thirty-five, to buy the important post of attorney general of the Paris Parlement. Here, too, he remained loyal during the second Fronde, counseling the exiled cardinal, protecting his interests and possessions, and, as attorney general, virtually legalizing his return. This time the recompense was the office of superintendent of finances in 1653, shared for six years with Abel Servien, whom Fouquet relegated to the department of payments while he took charge of receipts, a more enriching department and experience.

Fouquet's mission, to put it most simply, was to find money, a position for which, having money, he was well prepared. At twenty-five he had married a fortune; widowed at twenty-six, he had married another. And his appointment was popular with moneylenders for the same reason. Fouquet had personally to guarantee loans to the King, a dubious client. Further, as attorney general, he could help financiers with their judicial problems and cut off parliamentary investigations.

He was both minister and creditor of the King, lending the crown money and ensuring himself a high return. Thus the finances of Fouquet and the state were in a state of confusion, which greatly benefited Fouquet's finances. As for "normal" state revenue, of eighty-five million francs in taxes, only thirty million reached the treasury, such was the staggering cost of the many outstretched hands of the collection system.[4]*

In the early days of Louis' reign, the demands were always urgent and heavy, Fouquet's response generally improvised and sometimes adequate. In 1656, after the royal army's defeat at Valenciennes, Fouquet had literally sent wagon loads of silver, collected from family and friends, to the beleaguered crown. It was the occasion for conspicuous gratitude and Mazarin rose to the occasion. He thanked his superintendent, writing that he had spoken to Their Majesties, "who are both agreed of their great fortune in having you as a friend."[5]

Fouquet had his own friends, whom he favored with gifts, allowances, tax rebates, positions, and privileges. He would buy up the paper debts of the government at a fraction of their face value and have them reimbursed in full for himself and the favored few. He would balance accounts with fictitious expenses, exploiting a system which, in the words of Colbert, "had been deliberately entangled over the past forty years by the cleverest men of the kingdom so as to make the system comprehensible only to themselves, and themselves indispensable to it."[6]

Mazarin was neither innocent nor unaware and cautiously initiated an inquiry into Fouquet's handling of state funds, which, if pursued, would have found Mazarin as culpable. Indebted to Fouquet, he detested his debtor but did not dare let him go. Instead he alerted Colbert. Taking alarm, Fouquet bought the island of Belle Ile, just off the Brittany coast, and fortified it with cannon, just in case. Toward the end of his life, Mazarin dropped the inquiry, but before he died, he warned the King and "gave" him Colbert.

Every afternoon, Fouquet would bring Louis the accounts, every evening Colbert and the King would check them, slowly accumulating

* Indirect taxes, for instance, were collected by general farmers (or, to be more descriptive, tax-farmer generals), who were some sixty bankers to whom the profitable rights were "farmed out" by the crown on payment of an advance to the state treasury. Thousands of private collectors were under their control.

evidence of Fouquet's fraud. But Louis, with a dissimulation which was a lifetime trait, displayed a remarkable patience for one so young and Fouquet an unaccountable blindness for one who had gone to the school of Richelieu and Mazarin. In part it was blindness to the nature of the young King, seemingly absorbed in La Vallière, in part a sense of almost unchallengeable power, now that Mazarin was gone. In truth, the power was real enough to make the older man careless, as it compelled the younger to patience.

Fouquet possessed not only fortified Belle Ile—and possible British allies near at hand—but disposed in person, or through relations, of Calais and Amiens, Le Havre, Guingamp, Mont St. Michel, and other strong points. Through the Marquis de Gesvres he had access to the Royal Guards, through Admiral de Neuchèse to the Atlantic fleet, through Maréchal de Créquy to that of the Mediterranean. Most financiers were beholden to him; so were some of the King's own ministers. His brothers were an archbishop, a royal chancellor, a grand equerry of the royal stables. He himself was viceroy of America, controlled a whaling fleet of twenty-five armed vessels to which he had added six warships purchased from the Dutch. Above all, he was still attorney general of Parlement, thus effectively immune from arrest and in any case subject to trial only by his peers, who were his friends.

Fouquet had friends in every part of the land, in every corner of the court, including Louis' inner Council—particularly Hugues de Lionne, acting secretary of foreign affairs who owed him money. He not only paid Anne's maids of honor—making one both his mistress and his court spy—but the confessors of both Their Majesties. He prefigured the Sun King himself with his dazzling patronage of the arts and artists, sciences and writers. He "protected" Pierre Scarron, Madame de Maintenon's sickly, witty, first husband (who relieved her of her martyrdom by dying in 1660), novelist Mademoiselle de Scudéry, poet Paul Pellisson, who was his clerk before he became Louis' secretary and polished Louis' memoirs, Charles Perrault, who wrote "Cinderella," "Little Red Riding Hood," and more serious cultural essays. La Fontaine was his poet laureate, the young Madame de Sévigné his presumed mistress. He brought Corneille back to the theater, presented him with an allowance of two thousand livres, and the playwright hailed Fouquet for being as much "Superintendent of Belles-Lettres as of Finances, whose house is as open to people of intelligence as to those of affairs."[7]

Fouquet collected art and artists like a Renaissance prince. Lavish in public, privately he carefully noted the 48,301 livres 15 sols 6 deniers, the wheat, wood, salt, pig ("fat"), and 12 chickens brought him yearly from his peasants at Vaux. But he had a library beyond pretension. It contained Bibles, Korans, and Talmuds, diplomatic papers, ambassadorial reports and rare manuscripts, medical treatises, scientific theses and curiosa—38,544 volumes according to the 1665 inventory. Fouquet had great ambitions—his friends called him "The Future," Scarron more pointedly "The Boss"—but he was not a great man.[8]

Nevertheless Fouquet was not easily to be disposed of. Finally taking warning of Louis' intentions, he dared turn to the Queen Mother to remind her of her indebtedness. In his arrogance, however, he forgot her pride, and she dismissed him. From one blunder he went to another, or rather sent his procuress, Madame Duplessis-Bellière, to none other than Louis' devoted La Vallière. His proposition was vague, her reply was not.

"I am still furious," Madame Duplessis-Bellière wrote to Fouquet,* "when I think of the contempt with which that little demoiselle de La Vallière treated me. To capture her good will, I had complimented her on her beauty, which is actually very slight. Then, having told her you would always see that she lacked for nothing and had put aside 20,-000 pistoles† for her, she flared up, saying that 200,000 wouldn't make her take a false step, and she repeated it so fiercely, though I did everything to mollify her before taking my leave, that I am afraid she will talk of it to the King, which means we must take some precautions. Don't you think it might be advisable to anticipate her by telling the King she had asked you for money, and that you had refused her? That would make all her complaints seem suspicious."[9]

Fouquet, however, meeting Louise de La Vallière in Madame's antechamber, thought to make amends by speaking to her directly, exaggerating his admiration for her lord and master, the King. Astonished, he saw her face harden. She turned on her heel, quit the room, and that evening complained to the King of Fouquet's conduct. But again Louis bided his time. More, when Fouquet at last confessed to "minor" irregularities in his accounts, deriving, he ex-

---

* Authentic or forged (only a copy remains), the extraordinary letter does not contradict what is known to have followed Fouquet's tactless approach.
† See Note on Money p. vi.

plained, from the careless days of Mazarin, which, he promised, would not recur, the King listened with such tolerance and feigned friendliness that Fouquet assumed complete forgiveness. It made all the easier Louis' astute opening move: persuading Fouquet to sell his post of attorney general as a preliminary step toward his replacing Séguier as Louis' chancellor and eventually becoming prime minister. Envisaging himself in charge of both the royal seal and the royal treasury, Fouquet sold his parliamentary post—the 1,400,000 livres going as a present to the King. "All goes well," Louis exulted to Colbert, "he has taken the bait."[10]

But at the time Fouquet's sentiment was one of triumph and foolishly he celebrated by inviting the King and the Court to a fête at Vaux-le-Vicomte. There have been few such fêtes in French history— and the Sun King's were to be inspired by it—but, more to our purpose, Fouquet's new château and park, about to burst on the world, were no less, as we have noted, than "Versailles itself anticipated."[11]

Besides his Paris house, Fouquet possessed a great manor at Saint-Mandé, convenient in its day to Mazarin's castle at Vincennes. But, even as a young man, he had planned a château at Vaux, which would be more convenient to the Court when it came to Fontainebleau. Moreover, the great estate he purchased had the title of *vicomte* attached to it.

From 1641 to 1655, Fouquet had amassed the funds for Vaux and by the time park and château were finished, three villages had been razed to make room for them and eighteen million francs spent. But Fouquet's most remarkable feat, in the retrospect of time, was to bring three remarkable men together: Le Nôtre, Le Vau, and Le Brun.

François Mansart was the grand old man of architecture, but forty-four-year-old Louis Le Vau was the fashionable, adaptable man of the moment, and Fouquet sent for him. (Even at this late date one is tempted to regret the choice and compare the elder Mansart's cubist masterpiece at Maisons, built five years earlier, with the château at Vaux. However, there will be the occasion to consider it when the younger Mansart, François' grandnephew, will take Le Vau's "envelope" at Versailles and make *it* a masterpiece.*) Characteristically, Fouquet worked closely with Le Vau. When the latter indicated a combination of brick and stone, Fouquet had insisted on all stone,

* See below, "The Remaking of a Palace," p. 75.

since brick had become bourgeois and common—and so brick was used for the outbuildings, the *communs*. The façade was to be over seventy meters long, the area covered more than two thousand square meters. But even with these dimensions, the massive central dome is vastly overscaled.[12]

Construction went swiftly; at one time eighteen thousand men were employed; and as the château reached termination, painter Charles Le Brun (forty) was called in to perform, it developed, the greater part: decoration, furnishing, and adornment of such unprecedented unity and taste that *le style Louis XIV* might be said to have been created at Vaux before Louis XIV himself had found his own style. Sculptors, painters, ceramists, cabinetmakers, metalworkers, weavers —a special factory for tapestries was set up at nearby Maincy, also a hospital for the thousands of workers—labored under Le Brun's directions, generally to his designs. Handsomely installed in his own apartment at Vaux, Le Brun himself presented Fouquet with all the honors of Mount Olympus: huge allegorical paintings for ceilings and wall panels, such as the *Apotheosis of Hercules,* that is, "the Boss," which were so much to Fouquet's and Le Brun's, and very shortly Louis', fancy.[13]

Came August 17, 1661, the King, the Queen Mother—the Queen was pregnant and indisposed—Madame, Monsieur, the Grand Condé, and the rest of the Court. And one would like to imply, as so many have, to heighten the drama of that day in August, that this was Louis' first visit to Vaux. However, the *Gazette* records an earlier visit the year before on the way to, and possibly from, the wedding in St.-Jean-de-Luz; and all one might hazard is that, without the perfect finish—workers had scarcely removed the scaffolding in time for *this* royal visit—and the splendid fête, magnificently designed and stage-managed by Le Brun, neither Vaux nor a previous stopover could have been as shattering to a young King's pride.[14]

The Court had left Fontainebleau at three in the afternoon, had arrived at six, crossed a moat to the Vaux courtyard and received Fouquet's welcome. It was a hot day; Their Majesties rested in the royal apartments. Then Louis was escorted to the dining room, shown a portrait of himself by Le Brun. It is yours, said Fouquet grandly, but he did not offer the house. It may have been one of his last mistakes. Not the painting, but the paintings, clambering with Fouquet's ambitious squirrels, the fantastically rich furnishings and fabrics, the gold cloth,

C*

silver vases and mirrors, Persian carpets, tables of marble and porphyry—the post-arrest inventory of Vaux was to read like a page out
of *A Thousand and One Nights*—were the more dangerously impressive.

Or was it the walk in Le Nôtre's garden?

It was still daylight. The courtiers had already descended, their
ribbons and plumes brightening the paths along the pools and the
parterres of flowers. (The French Court, unlike the Spanish Court at the
bleak Escorial, was forbidden black.) Pausing on the terrace, Louis took
in the park. He had never seen anything like it in France, nor, for that
matter, had anyone in Italy. Elegant and orderly, it was as if Descartes
had written on the landscape with a giant, sensitive hand.* *Les jardins
de l'intelligence,* La Bruyère would describe them, the gardens of intelligence. Here in the garden of Vaux was the grandeur Louis had dreamed
of: a great vista along a *grande allée* leading to the dimly visible statue
of Hercules two miles distant.

And here one would like to add to La Fontaine's fables of Vaux
the legend of Louis' first meeting, or at least first walk, with André Le
Nôtre that day in August.[16] Was Le Brun, too, at Vaux, to explain
his allegorical paintings, and Le Vau his architecture? It is unlikely
any of the three was unknown to Louis. Le Vau was the first architect
of the King, Le Brun had just painted a ceiling at the Louvre, and
Le Nôtre was the gardener at the Tuileries. The startling fact was that
the King saw, and for the first time could fully appreciate at Vaux,
their creative work as a team—an event which proved a turning point,
for it pointed to Versailles.

Together, then, if only symbolically, Louis XIV and Le Nôtre descended the stairs to the garden and strolled the entire two miles from
the palace to the gilded, glistening statue at the far end of the great
park. The courtiers, if not Fouquet, followed discreetly behind, the
Queen Mother in a light, two-wheeled calèche. Distinct on his high
red-heeled shoes, the young King brandished a long, gold-headed cane.
Somber in brown, the much older (forty-eight) Le Nôtre pointed
from time to time with his strong gardener's hand. Down the *grande
allée* they went, between two hundred *jets d'eau* flinging two walls
of water thirty-five feet tall, past the flowered *parterres de broderie*
rolled out, on both sides, like great Oriental rugs, to the grotto, the

---

* "The visible world," said Descartes, "would be more perfect if lands and seas
had more ordered shapes . . . if the rains were more regular."[15]

cascades, the amphitheater and the grand canal. Louis missed nothing in the astonishing park, neither the statues of Anguier nor the termini of Poussin (for they were eventually to be removed to Versailles).

Did the King and the gardener talk of Versailles? Likely not. Louis was otherwise occupied with the problem of Fouquet, whose blunders multiplied.

At the dinner following the walk, the royal family ate from gold plates, the Court from silver. Fouquet had a gold and silver service for almost seven thousand people; Louis, as he knew too well, did not. Twenty-four violins played Lully's music. Vatel was Fouquet's steward—the famous Vatel who, serving the Grand Condé ten years later, was to stab himself to death at Chantilly because the fish had arrived too late for a dinner at which Louis XIV was the guest.* At Vaux, the young King, whose appetite was not yet Gargantuan, may have felt Fouquet's pheasants, quail, ortolans, and partridge stick in his throat. "Madame," he said to the Queen Mother, "shall we make these people disgorge?" And he suggested arresting Fouquet on the spot. It was not, Anne replied, the proper behavior for a guest.[18]

Outdoors in the garden, at the end of an *allée* of firs, Molière and his troupe waited in the gathering dark. Two weeks before Fouquet had asked for a new play and production, in two weeks it was written, rehearsed, and ready to be performed: *Les Fâcheux*, the Bores, some of Fouquet's best friends. Molière was one of Louis' court entertainers. Between acts there were ballets with music by Lully, and Lully was one of Louis' own composers. Increasingly the entire entertainment became a kind of deliberate lese majesty. He already knew from Colbert that the wood used in building Vaux had come free from the royal forests of Fontainebleau, the kilometers of lead pipes for the fountains free of duty from England.

Fouquet's fête ended with a giant mechanical whale belching fire and smoke in the grand canal, and thousands of fireworks, some loosed from the château's massive dome (possibly lightening it momentarily), tracing huge, interlaced *L*'s (for an unentranced Louis) in the sky. They covered him with a vault of fire (two of Anne's carriage horses reared and fell back into the moat) as he returned to the château for

---

* Madame de Sévigné to her daughter, Madame de Grignan, April 26, 1671: "Poor Vatel had gone up to his room, put his sword against the door and thrust it through his heart, but only at the third attempt . . . Meanwhile the fish was arriving from everywhere . . . The King said he had delayed coming to Chantilly for five years, because he realized all the trouble it would cause."[17]

supper and more violins, before the drive back to Fontainebleau for arrival at dawn.[19]

Rather, Fouquet's fête ended three weeks later with the arrest of the host.[20]

Whether as a touch of bravado or perfect dissimulation, Louis chose to strike in the heart of Brittany, Fouquet's own strong point. At the end of August accordingly, he went to Nantes to preside over the local parliament. There Fouquet joined the King, along with other members of the Council. So, more discreetly, did d'Artagnan, captain of the Royal Musketeers, hero of Dumas' novel, and, more pertinently, in debt to Colbert. He was told to arrest Fouquet the following morning without arousing his suspicions beforehand. Belle Ile was but seventy-five miles from Nantes, and Fouquet, warned by friends, had a boat readied and waiting. Not taking it was his last mistake. At six in the morning of September 5, d'Artagnan assembled his men outside the castle of Nantes. After a council meeting, Louis delayed Fouquet's departure until he confirmed from a window that d'Artagnan was in place. Within minutes, Fouquet was encaged in a royal carriage, within days in a succession of prisons.

The trial itself dragged on before a special court for over three years. As time passed, as the paradox of a guilty man, defended by honest men, proved guilty by dishonest means, slowly unfolded before the French public, Fouquet rose in popularity. Charges of treason were not substantiated, malversation of finances was, but only nine of the twenty-two judges, despite the King's pressures, voted the death penalty. Instead, Fouquet's sentence was banishment for life, which Louis commuted to confinement until the end of his days in the most distant prison under French command, the Piedmontese fortress of Pignerol, just below Turin. The former superintendent knew too much, Louis himself was to write, to be left at large, even abroad.[21]

At Pignerol, Fouquet was carefully isolated, allowed no ink, pens, or paper. Ingeniously he dissolved soot in wine, plucked the feather of a chicken he had dined on, penned a letter on a handkerchief, vainly trying to reach his friends. Thereafter, even the linings of his clothes had to be black. Until virtually the end, Fouquet's only relieving contact was with a fellow prisoner, the Comte de Lauzun, the reluctant lover and eventual husband of La Grande Mademoiselle, who had managed to penetrate Fouquet's rooms, possibly by way of the chimney, from his own below, and went on to court Fouquet's daughter before marrying Louis' strong-minded cousin. In the meantime, after fifteen years at Pignerol, Fouquet died.

Throughout his trial, Fouquet's literary protégés had remained faithful, as the artists, on the whole, had not, and the letters of Madame de Sévigné have permanently colored his portrait for posterity. Down to our own day, readers and writers—how could a patron so generous to writers and artists be a complete scoundrel?—have been prejudiced by her, allowing Fouquet only one major flaw, a lack of hypocrisy. As for artists, a very few, such as sculptor Puget, remained loyal, and paid for their fidelity with Colbert's unremitting enmity. Le Brun, on the other hand, the day after Fouquet's arrest, gave Madame Colbert a drawing as a gift—and within a year was ennobled by the King.[22]

Artists and artisans, creators of Vaux, they easily shifted their allegiance to one who was truly royal, for only a Sun King could employ them so grandly—in the creation of Versailles. And only by putting down Fouquet and becoming master of his own treasury and kingdom could the Sun King have arisen—and Versailles been created.

5. The Fairy Tale of a Fairyland

Of all the Sun King's galaxy of creative men, André Le Nôtre the gardener was first summoned to perform in the miracle of Versailles.[1]

"It is impossible to build a great palace on this site," Colbert had noted solemnly for the young King: the little château of Louis XIII sat on a narrow butte; its park was hemmed in by "the village, the church and the swamp"; the land sloping to the west "permitted no expansion without turning everything upside down at prodigious expense. . . . A suitable terrace was impossible."[2]

But Versailles, "that most dismal and thankless of sites, without vistas, woods or water,"[3]* was transformed into a pagan paradise— and that was the miracle. Titanlike, Le Nôtre leveled hills, scooped out basins and lakes, moved a mountain of earth—at a cost, to Colbert's despair, of more than five hundred thousand écus the first two years—to create a platform for Le Vau's, and later Mansart's, pleasure domes.

For almost four decades Louis and Le Nôtre were to work together. "Send me news of the smallest project," the King demanded of Colbert from the battlefield. Back in Versailles, he would put aside the red-heeled pumps and put on boots, so he might tramp alongside Le Nôtre. He would borrow a pair of his gardener's shears to help trim a bush, suggest another outdoor ballroom with walls of pleached, living trees, turn on the spigots of yet another fountain. If, as Louis re-

* Saint-Simon exaggerates. There were lovely woods, if not large trees. But the site *was* bad and there was only a small local stream.

marked, "there is grandeur in Le Nôtre," there was also a gardener in Louis. He did not wish to create, the King records in his memoirs, but to "understand everything."[4]

Their audacity still beggars description. From horizon to horizon Le Nôtre was to tame and humanize the landscape, convert it into a French garden "readable" at a glance. And no one, it is said, who has not stood on Le Nôtre's terrace at Versailles can understand the French spirit. Its vista is the world made visible and rational, as clarified as a Poussin painting. "The pleasures of the intelligence," said Poussin, "are primary." Man is most man, said Pascal, when he reasons. Le Nôtre ordered every foot—every tree, bush, vase, and statue—of the three-mile vista: from the lofty terrace with its palace and reflecting pools, to the fountains of Latona, the immense lawn of the *allée royale* rolling down to the Basin of Apollo and the Grand Canal, whose mile-long waters lift the eye to the paired, lonely poplars on the horizon.

But Versailles, over the years, was to have intimacy as well as infinity, small inviting bypaths leading to bosky shadows as well as broad sun-lit and tree-lined *allées*. So strict was Le Nôtre's formality there was room for every fantasy—from grottoes to triumphal arches. From the very start the young King wanted everything. As the Petit Parc was being planned, a story goes, Louis and Le Nôtre stepped out of the château, in the full confusion of remodeling, onto the muddy terrace. Here, on a plank, Le Nôtre unrolled the first of his plans. Pleased, the King cried, "For this I will give you twenty thousand livres." Le Nôtre spread out a second. "For this, too," said the King, "I will give you twenty thousand livres." Le Nôtre spread out a third. "Another twenty thousand livres!" cried the King, wanting to see more. But Le Nôtre stopped and smilingly said, "Sire, you will not see any more, for otherwise I should ruin you."[5] Apocryphal or not, as the story may be, Colbert would not have been amused, for in a letter to Louis XIV, he warned that Le Nôtre and Le Vau might indeed ruin him.[6]

The official *Comptes des bâtiments du roi*[7] may confirm Colbert, though the greatest expenses were to come later. As the King was too impatient to wait for his woods to grow tall, Le Nôtre sent for mature trees, transported them in specially designed carts, transplanted them in great lines as if they were so many peonies in the Grand Parc. Three quarters died? They were promptly replaced. "Six thousand elms from Flanders," the records read, "4,040,000 feet of hornbeam from Normandy." Thousands of more evergreens from the northern

Vosges, oaks from southern Dauphiné were to follow. "Swaying like seesaws on ox-drawn wagons," wrote Madame de Sévigné, were "entire leafy forests being ferried to Versailles."[8]

"Nine thousand bulbs each of narcissi, hyacinths, heliotrope, jonquils and tuberoses" were a consignment from Constantinople. More came from the Low Countries. Royal nurseries were established along the Mediterranean, others closer—in Paris and Versailles. From one near the Tuileries, millions of tulips were to arrive several times a year. And from Spain—for the palace and the Orangerie—groves of tubbed jasmin and orange trees to join the five hundred that once belonged to Fouquet.

Rapidly the number of men working on the grounds rose from hundreds to thousands, until whole regiments were pressed into service. So it was with the Swiss Guards, who dug the 2250-foot ornamental lake to the south named after them, hundreds dying from malaria. Many more were to die bringing water to Versailles.

For Louis, as for Le Nôtre, basins, lakes, and pools (*parterres d'eau*) were the marriage of the earth and sky, their reflections of trees, statuary, and the palace, as in the two great parterres on the terrace, splendor redoubled. For them water in motion was the life of a garden, and they added fountain to fountain until finally there were fourteen hundred *jets d'eau* to be fed—or, rather, watered. Even today, with less than half the jets remaining, almost a million gallons of water are flung skyward every hour—but only for a few minutes. One goes, according to a plan, on the days of *les Grandes Eaux* at Versailles, from one fountain to another. So, too, the fountains played in sequence as the King promenaded—but *he* wanted them playing all the time.

Only rain water and the little stream of Galie were the available sources, and they had to do for the first years. The Galie's waters were dammed up in a pond, lifted by a horse-driven pump to a reservoir near the palace, with the aid of three windmills, then pumped and repumped into the air. The ingenious if insufficient system was that of the Italian Francini brothers, who worked with Le Nôtre. As the fountains multiplied and the reservoirs emptied, they tapped the Seine five miles away. Since its waters were well over three hundred feet *below* Versailles, they had to be raised by the famous *"machine de Marly"*—fourteen hydraulic wheels, each forty feet in diameter, and

259 pumps—to a hill from which they might flow by gravity to the Versailles gardens.[9]

Nor was this enough. The amount of water needed never caught up with the mounting number of fountains, and finally, reaching for more grandeur—the story of the later years—the Grand Monarch overreached himself. Rising one August morning in 1684, he announced the mad scheme of diverting to Versailles the waters of the river Eure, fifty miles to the west.

This venture was turned over to Maréchal de Vauban and the French Army. Its engineers ambitiously planned two gigantic aqueducts with some arches twice the height of Notre Dame's towers. One may still visit their Roman-like ruins at Maintenon, thirty-four miles from Versailles, for the stupendous project reached thus far, and no farther. But before it stopped, thirty thousand soldiers were to labor on the scheme night and day for three years, and thousands were to die from malaria. Louis himself barely escaped the contagion; his chief military adviser, Louvois, caught it. Over eight million livres were spent, but not until war itself summoned the soldiers elsewhere did Louis call off the Eure misadventure.[10]

Happily for our "fairy tale," which risks at many points becoming heavily Grimm (the human, and other, costs of Versailles will be explored, the reader is promised), Le Nôtre was only incidentally involved; these events were offstage and invisible at Versailles. For Versailles was above all a stage set, and so, superbly playing King, Louis would employ it. For each mistress he would decree a fête, filling the air from twilight until dawn with the sounds of gaiety, feasting, and fireworks. Candlelight and torches would twinkle along the paths and glow along the Grand Canal, lighting the way for gondoliers and lovers.

It is Le Nôtre who made this fairyland of Versailles. It is Le Nôtre who lulls the most skeptical chronicler into a fairytale mood. Not a story not an anecdote, in the scandalous memoirs of these scurrilous times stains his memory—an extraordinary accomplishment for a man who had so much success and left, on his death, so much money.

The guilelessness of the gardener even affected the waspish Duc de Saint-Simon. "Le Nôtre died about this time," he wrote of the year 1700, "after having lived in perfect health for eighty-eight [actually eighty-seven] years, retaining his good sense, excellent taste and abilities to the end. He was celebrated for having first designed

the fine gardens that adorn France and so effaced the reputation
of those of Italy—which are really nothing in comparison—that the
most famous Italian masters in this field come here to study and
admire.

"Le Nôtre was honest, honorable and plain-spoken, a man everybody loved and respected. He never stepped out of his place
[making him particularly endearing to the protocol-conscious duke]
nor forgot it, and was always perfectly disinterested. He worked for
private persons as for the King with the same care, seeking only to
aid nature and reveal its beauty at the lowest possible cost. He had a
guilelessness and candor that charmed everyone."[11]

The story of Le Nôtre's life, from the few facts that can be
gathered—the humble gardener who became the consort of the Sun
King and embraced a pope, whose genius was to reach from the
banks of the Seine to those of the Potomac and the Neva—is, for a
gardener, strangely unearthly.

Of all the King's men, Le Nôtre left the most enduring imprint
on Versailles, though few of the people who walk in its gardens even
know his name. In an age of flaunted arrogance, he remained a
remarkably modest man. He left no memoirs, no manuals, few records
except his work. He had, as Jacques des Gachons admirably put it,
no "posthumous conceit."

André Le Nôtre was born on March 12, 1613, on Rue St. Honoré. His father was the chief gardener of Louis XIII at the Louvre,
his father's father chief gardener of Marie de Médicis at the Luxembourg. His birthplace was a few steps across the fields from his father's
Tuileries gardens.

With a gift for drawing, young André first dreamed of painting.
Patiently, or possibly considering it in any case the first of the disci-
plines, his father gave him what he wanted—lessons with Louis XIII's
court painter, Simon Vouet, whose studio was in the palace. Instructor of
the King, and later of Le Brun, the baroque artist had traveled along
the Bosporus, bringing back drawings of Byzantine gardens whose
broken curves were to reappear in Le Nôtre's. From Madame Vouet,
a painter originally Italian, he learned Italian art and design as
well.[12]

Perhaps because he realized it was the second discipline for the
gardener—and this, not painting, was to be his profession—André
next studied architecture, possibly under the talented, difficult François

Mansart. But at twenty-two he laid aside the brush and (temporarily) the triangle for his father's tools, the spade and the hoe. Hereafter his palette was to be flowers, his architecture of the landscape, each tree like a brush stroke on canvas. "Even the air of Versailles," La Fontaine was later to marvel, "was painted with a hundred colors."

Le Nôtre's first spadework was in the flowered parterres of his father's gardens, their intricate patterns transcribed directly from books on embroidery. (His interests were to be larger. *Parterres de broderie,* he was to say, were for nursemaids, tied to their charges, to look at from upper stories.) The flowers he planted were the few then available—tulips, hyacinths, asters, tuberoses. Between the low-cut box hedge, he spread crushed red brick, black iron filings, varicolored sands and pebbles.* His tutor at the Tuileries was Claude Mollet, member of another of France's famous families of gardeners. Solemnly he was warned never to plant apple or pear trees in the light of the full moon, or to use manure as a fertilizer. "For who would want to eat its fruit?" the older man might demand.[13]

At twenty-three Le Nôtre was assured his father's position by Louis XIII and assumed it on his father's death when he was forty-two and Louis XIV was seventeen). In the meantime he had his own apartment at the Louvre. A fair horseman at twenty-six, a lively wit and spirit brightening a fine, strong face, Le Nôtre was popular with courtiers, fellow workers, and at least one young lady. At twenty-seven he married his childhood garden playmate, blond, blue-eyed Françoise Langlois, daughter of the Louvre's governor of pages at the royal stables. Cheerfully courtiers and gardeners joined in wishing the young couple well at the local parish church of St. Roch (where Le Nôtre was eventually to be buried and the Revolution to scatter his bones, along with royalty's).

The ceremony over, the comely couple were accompanied to their new home in the Tuileries. Here in a two-story house—no longer standing—in the northwest corner of the gardens, the pair lived happily and increasingly prosperously. All his long life, Le Nôtre was a man who loved his family, even—at a time when such faithfulness was not exactly fashionable—his wife. When early in their marriage they lost their three children, Le Nôtre fathered his nephews and made them

---

* " 'Where are the flowers?' Parisians would complain," says Jean Dieumegard, today's Tuileries gardener, "if we ever returned to the original austerity."

his successors, as he had succeeded his father and his father, *his* father.

While he was yet in his twenties, Le Nôtre's skill became known. Monsieur, Louis XIII's brother, solicited his advice for the Luxembourg gardens, soon after other notables called on him for theirs. At thirty he designed a small, ingenious park for the Bishop of Meaux with a meditation walk which still delights.

François Mansart sought Le Nôtre for the gardens at Maisons. Here were the first signs of Le Nôtre's mature work: the long, tree-lined walk, or *grande allée,* with a view to the horizon; the spacious circle carved out of the woods, or *rond point,* with other walks radiating from it in a *patte d'oie,* or "goose foot."

But the turning point, as we have seen, came for Le Nôtre in his forties with the garden at Vaux. Here was born the Versailles of Louis XIV—not only the palace and the park, but the new French capital.

With the genius he showed in ordering the landscape Le Nôtre laid out the new Versailles community. Courtiers were given land, but had to build according to plan: nothing higher than the palace, nothing disturbing the Grand Scheme. Roads and residences were spaced and arranged with the precision of the parterres and *allées.*

The three principal avenues converge on the palace, the central Avenue de Paris pointing to the royal bedroom at its center. If continued, it would cut through the very bed of the King to the terrace, joining the *allée royale* and the Grand Canal in a giant axis, as if following a line drawn by the sun as it rose in the east and set in the west.

Versailles' similarity to Washington, D.C., was to be no accident. Pierre L'Enfant drew the plan for the American capital, but the plan he drew on was Le Nôtre's. The great Mall stretches to the Potomac exactly as the *allée royale* to the Grand Canal. The star burst of avenues comes straight from Versailles. So did L'Enfant. His father was painter to the King in the Court of Louis XV, and the son had spent his youth there before joining General Washington.[14]

In Leningrad, the impressive Nevsky Prospekt was laid out by Alexandre Le Blond, who designed the Peterhof garden, St. Petersburg's Versailles-by-the-Sea. Le Blond had been a disciple of Le Nôtre, and that is why Peter the Great sought him. Scarcely had Charles II been restored to the English throne when he called on Louis XIV for

Le Nôtre's services. With Versailles, the scepter of art passed from Italy to France, and stayed there. Le Nôtre opened the Renaissance garden to the horizon, as Gothic architecture, a French style, had lifted the Romanesque arch to new heights. The kings and princes of Europe, who wanted the sweep—or reassurance—of a royal vista, surrounded themselves with Le Nôtre gardens.

Louis' Versailles had become the center, envy, and model of the Continent, his gardener one of the most sought after men. But the King was ever loath to see Le Nôtre go. Even at the siege of Cambrai, he kept him close by, lodging him with the Grand Condé, lending him a stallion from his own stables. Together they toured the embattled city on horseback; side by side they received its surrender. And always as the guns thundered, they talked of the King's gardens.[15] Mistresses came and went, but Le Nôtre remained, designing gardens for each as one succeeded the other.*

Ennobled by the King at sixty-two, Le Nôtre, according to legend, was asked his choice of a coat of arms. "Three snails crowned with a head of cabbage," he replied, then added, "But how can I forget my spade? Do I not owe it all your honors?"

Four years later Louis granted Le Nôtre his wish to visit Rome and his nephew.

It was a spring morning in 1679.[16]

The Sun King had risen with the customary ceremony and good humor. Privileged courtiers had followed the chief doctor and the chief surgeon to wish him good health and a good day. One extended His Majesty a slightly warmed shirt in an envelope of silk.

"What news from Rome of our good friend, Le Nôtre?" the King asked Bontemps, his first *valet de chambre*.

Bontemps replied that he had just received a letter from him and requested permission to read it aloud.

Courteously Louis XIV turned to his courtiers and asked their consent. Warmly they granted it. They knew the affection of Louis for his gardener, and they shared it.

While in Rome, Le Nôtre wrote, "the Holy Father asked to see me. So I went to him with my nephew, Claude Desgots, a student here at

---

* Le Nôtre's favorite gardens were for the Grand Condé at Chantilly, where there was a river of water at his disposal. And Louis' envy was so obvious when he saw it that the Prince de Condé diplomatically told him to consider the garden his and himself "your concierge."

the French Academy who speaks Italian. I kneeled before His Holiness, who promptly had me rise and immediately show him the plans of Versailles. He had heard so much about them, he said.

"I can't describe how astonished he was when I told him there was no river at Versailles, that we had to bring in the water for all the ponds, canals, fountains and cascades he kindly admired. I was so overjoyed by his pleasure in all that I showed him that I said, 'Now I can die in peace. I have seen the two greatest men of the world: Your Holiness and the King, my master.'

"'But what a difference,' said the Pope. 'The King is a victorious Prince, whereas I am a poor priest. He is young. I am old.'

"'Oh, no!' I cried. 'You look wonderful! You will bury the whole Sacred College!'

"He was very moved by what I said, and I, more and more charmed, couldn't help embracing him."

At this point, the Duc de Créquy interrupted Bontemps' reading of Le Nôtre's letter. "Embrace the Pope?" he exclaimed. "What a tale! I'll wager a thousand *louis* Le Nôtre would never dare."

"Don't make that wager, monsieur le duc," said the King quickly. "You'll lose it. Whenever I return from the country, Le Nôtre embraces me. He could well have embraced the Pope."

In his late seventies, as alert and lively as ever, Le Nôtre designed a garden for the aging Louis and Madame de Maintenon at the Trianon Palace. On the far northwest edge of the Versailles park, it was a new departure for Le Nôtre, somewhat anticipating the English garden of much later. It had more cover and shade and rambling paths. (One risked sunstroke on the "vast, scorching expanse" of Versailles proper, Saint-Simon complains.)

It was at the Trianon that Le Nôtre astonished even the blasé Louis. Entering the palace one day, the King had observed one kind of flower garden. Emerging a few hours later, he was surprised by an entirely new one. Le Nôtre had turned the trick with a complete change of flowerpots, the pots themselves buried in the ground. There were two million available for such "tricks" at the Trianon.

But finally even Le Nôtre, in the late evening of his long life, asked permission to retire. Reluctantly Louis consented after receiving a promise of frequent visits. To make it more convenient, Le Nôtre was given his own apartment at Versailles, though noblemen were clamoring for even an attic room.

Home for Le Nôtre, however, continued to be the small house in the gardens of the Louvre. Here he lived on with his wife, his nephews, his laurel and orange trees, his chickens and his collections. Even in his grand old age he would shop and poke about for curios. Neatly dressed in his dark brown jerkin with its bright gold buttons, he was a familiar figure in the flea markets and artists' studios of Paris.

Among connoisseurs, it was common knowledge that whenever Le Nôtre went out he would leave the house key hanging on a nail. Thus any might enter and look at his remarkable collection of paintings, lacquers, porcelains, and medallions, which Le Nôtre sometimes accepted as payment for his gardens. And never, Tallemant tells us, did he miss anything.[17]

The King himself, according to a contemporary story, used to sit and admire Le Nôtre's medallions. And whenever he came across those struck abroad in commemoration of his defeats, Le Nôtre would sweetly say, "Sire, here is one which is *against* us!"[18]

Eight months before he died—at four in the morning of September 15, 1700, at the age of eighty-seven—Le Nôtre drove to a notary and dictated his will. First, he gave thanks to God and money to the poor. Then he left legacies to his cousins, nephews, grand nephews, and servants. Finally he left most of all to the faithful Françoise.

"Said wife," Le Nôtre dictated with a touching wit, "had kept such a careful hand over his affairs, since the testator himself had always been inclined to spend money for his collections without thought of cost," that without her there would have been nothing to leave to her. In fact, Le Nôtre left his wife a handsome fortune of one hundred thousand livres plus an annual income of some twenty thousand more.[19]

Rarely—outside of fairy tales—has virtue been so richly rewarded. But perhaps most revealing was Le Nôtre's collection of art. His trained and gifted eye led him to the finest painters of the age: Poussin, whom he knew in his youth, and Claude Lorrain. Several of their canvases, which he presented to the King, are fittingly in the Louvre, for outside is one of the Louvre's greatest treasures: Le Nôtre's gardens.

"A month before Le Nôtre died," writes Saint-Simon, "the King, who greatly enjoyed seeing and conversing with him, once again took him through the park. Because of his old age, he had him sit in a chair, which a footman wheeled alongside his own, whereupon Le

Nôtre exclaimed, 'Alas, if only my father had lived to see this poor gardener, his son, riding in a chair beside the greatest King on earth, how complete would have been his happiness!' "[20]

Surely afterward, before they parted, Louis and Le Nôtre, as so many times before, went up to that noble terrace at twilight to look at their work for the last time together: the wondrous park, its fountains and pools and flower beds, its long graceful view to the trees on the horizon, as if to the gates of heaven.

6. The Remaking of a Palace

On that terrace, not yet Le Nôtre's (we are moving backwards in time) was the little château of Louis XIII, not yet Louis XIV's. The royal palace for a monarchical utopia was still to be constructed, French dukes to be reduced to domestics, the effrontery of the Fronde not simply to be forgoten, but potential *frondeurs* to be contained in a golden cage. Eventually Versailles was to be the physical embodiment of France predominant, but the early years were the impecunious years, and the palace, like the gardens, which expanded parcel by purchased parcel, village by displaced village, was to grow by stages, two of them under Le Vau, the third under Mansart.

In modern terms France was having a building boom, but the King was more badly housed than many of his courtiers. Nothing lacked in the great houses of the financiers, Colbert complained, "but the King's were often left unfinished and unfurnished for lack of money, without even a pair of silver fire dogs for the Royal chamber."[1]

Louis, that is, was "badly housed" in the royal residences of Saint-Germain, the Louvre, and Fontainebleau, and while work was going on at Versailles, it went on in the other palaces, as if the King had not quite made up his mind as to which would signify *his* France, *his* regime. Even after Versailles emerged victorious, there were the other residences to be maintained and, in many cases, completed. (Between 1664 and 1679, over 10,600,000 livres were spent on the Louvre and the Tuileries.)[2]

In all these enterprises, Louis Le Vau, the King's first architect

since 1654, was to have a directing if not, as is now soundly suspected,*
a primary designing hand. Before Vaux, he had been Mazarin's
architect at Vincennes, and before Versailles, he had redone the
Queen's apartment at the Louvre.

The first work at Versailles was in the garden, the terrace determin-
ing the ultimate château. In that sense the first architect was Le
Nôtre. But Le Vau, too, was to begin, if more modestly, almost
immediately. There was, for this womanless château of Louis XIII,
an apartment to be found and decorated—by painters Errard and
Coypel—for the Dauphin, born to Marie-Thérèse on November 1,
1661, and for his mother. In the forecourt, the smaller dependencies
were demolished to make room for larger ones and two long wings
were built with habitable pavilions. The left wing, contained stables
for fifty-four horses, the right wing the kitchen.³†

The château itself remained the gold, white, and rose brick and
stone palace of Louis XIII, but with additions: an encircling balcony
of forged iron, mansard dormer-windows instead of skylights, statues
set on corbels in the façade overlooking the marble courtyard. Before
the entry court, other stone and brick buildings went up for several
of the courtiers—the beginning of the new great community.

On the park side, Le Vau erected an Orangerie under the southern
terrace. At the same time, the touch of fantasy that marked the first
years appeared in Le Vau's Ménagerie on the southwest edge of the
gardens. Courtyards for "exotic" animals—pigeons and pelicans, geese
and gazelles, ground hogs and elephants—spread spokelike from a
miniature château, whose principal room was an octagonal salon.
Here two pumps were installed for fountain effects in the various
courtyards, and the King himself tested and regulated the flow.

Rapidly Versailles was becoming Louis' favorite, if only because
building in process appealed so greatly to him. Pleased, Louis Le Vau's
brother and collaborator, François Le Vau, wrote Colbert of the King's
visits and particularly his satisfaction with progress at the Orangerie.
Not at all pleased, Colbert, who considered Versailles an unnecessary
extravagance, since Saint-Germain was but eight miles away, penned
a famous letter to his young monarch, dated September 28, 1663 by
some historians:

* And will be further discussed.
† The still-existent stable wing is mistakenly called *aile Louis XIII*.

Your Majesty just returned from Versailles. I beg him to permit me to repeat a few thoughtful words which I have offered to him before and which he will, if it please him, pardon as deriving from my zeal. This mansion is concerned far more with the pleasures and diversions of Your Majesty than with his glory, and since he has made it clear to the world how much more highly he regards the latter than the former, there being no doubt that this indeed is the true feeling in his heart, so that one may safely speak freely to Your Majesty upon this matter without the risk of displeasing him, I would think myself as betraying the loyalty I owe him if I did not tell him that, while it is entirely right that after the great and constant application he is pleased to give to affairs of State, with the admiration of the entire world, he should grant some time to his pleasures and diversions, nevertheless great care must be taken that these do not become prejudicial to his glory.

However, if Your Majesty desires to discover where in Versailles are the more than 500,000 écus spent there in two years,* he will have great difficulty in finding them. Will he also deign to reflect that the accounts of the royal buildings will always record the evidence that, during the time he spent such vast sums on this mansion, he has neglected the Louvre, which is assuredly the most superb palace in the world and the one worthiest of Your Majesty's greatness? And God forbid that those many occasions which may require him to go to war, thus depriving him of the financial means to complete this superb building, should give him lasting regret for having lost the time and opportunity.

Your Majesty knows that, apart from brilliant feats of war, nothing marks so advantageously the greatness and genius of princes than buildings, and all posterity measures them by the yardstick of these superb edifices which they have erected during their lifetime. *Oh what a pity were the greatest and most virtuous of kings,* of that real virtue which makes the greatest of princes, *to be measured by the yardstick of Versailles!* And yet, there is reason to fear it. [Emphasis added.]

As for myself, I confess to Your Majesty that, notwithstanding his reluctance to increase the cash payments, had I been able to foresee that this expenditure of money would have become so high, I would have preferred it in cash warrants so as to eliminate knowledge of the expenditure.

Your Majesty will also observe, if it pleases him, that he is in the hands of two men† who know him primarily at Versailles, that is, in his pleasures and diversions, and not at all in his love of glory, from wherever it might come; that their understanding, which derives from

---

* Primarily on the gardens.
† Le Nôtre and Le Vau.

their position, their separate, particular interests, the idea that they should court Your Majesty, and from the patronage they already enjoy, will result in their leading Your Majesty from one design to another to ensure immortality for their work—if he is not on guard against them.

In order to reconcile everything, that is, render to Your Majesty's glory all that is its due, and the same to his diversions, he might promptly terminate the Versailles accounts and decide on a fixed sum to be employed there annually. It might even be advisable to separate it entirely from the other building funds and concentrate on completing the Louvre; and if peace continues, erect public monuments that will carry the glory and grandeur of Your Majesty's name further than any built by the ancient Romans.[4]

Louis' reply is not on record. That he accepted the "miserable measure" of Versailles as his own is evident, for the building of Versailles went on. In 1664 Colbert was named superintendent of buildings—Charles Perrault a *contrôleur* under him—and thereafter offered the expected, loyal services.

Devoting himself eight hours a day to the pursuit of glory, Louis gave at least equal time to the pursuit of "pleasures and diversions," principal, though not sole, among them Louise de La Vallière. Frequently they hunted together at Versailles—Louise was an excellent shot—and the first park may be thought of as hers. Originally Madame and the Comtesse de Soissons (Olympe Mancini) had favored Louis' affair with Louise, for it masked their own with Louis, lifting the burden of the Queen's sad bitterness from what might loosely be called their consciences.* Later, "no longer able to please the King by herself, seeking to conserve his favor by all other means" (Motteville), Olympe encouraged his passion for yet another maid of honor. It was at this time that Louis was adventuring along the roofs of Saint-Germain trying to reach the maids' rooms only to find the great chimneys grilled against his passage by the Duchesse de Navailles, who was in charge of the ladies. When the young King sent Le Tellier to tell her not to interfere, she replied, according to Motteville, that he should

* Once, as La Vallière passed through her bedroom on the way to supper with the Comtesse de Soissons, Marie-Thérèse said in Spanish to Madame de Motteville, "That girl with the diamond earrings is the one the King loves." The Queen Mother's lady in waiting tried to comfort her. All husbands are unfaithful, she said, or pretend to be, so as not to look foolish at Court. But the Queen, she adds in her memoirs, "remained sad."[5]

look for his girls "elsewhere than in the house of the Queen, which was also his own, since it seemed he had already chosen one there in the person of Demoiselle de La Vallière." Not long afterward the duchess and her husband were expelled from the Court.

In December 1663, Louise de La Vallière gave birth in great secrecy to a son (who would die less than three years later). In May 1664, Louis gave Louise a fête at Versailles, though it was ostensibly in honor of the two queens. It celebrated love, Louise and Le Nôtre, and helped efface Fouquet, then still on trial. It was Versailles—or rather its gardens —that now burst on the world. The seven-day fête, entitled *Les Plaisirs de l'isle enchantée,** announced the Sun King and the beginning of his century.

Louis himself had chosen the romantic theme from Ariosto's *Orlando Furioso*—the story of Roger and his companions, captivated by the enchantress Alcina, finally released from witchcraft by the ring of Angelica, "lovingly" slipped onto Roger's finger. On the opening day, Louis as Roger, dressed in Greek armor, led the mounted procession of Ariosto's knights around the *grand rondeau* basin, the Court and six hundred guests looking on from a great amphitheater. The sun chariot of Apollo, followed, driven by Time and escorted by the Hours. Then came the tilting at a ring at full gallop down the *allée royale*. After a fine, admired run, Louis yielded to the other knights, and Louise's brother, the Marquis de La Vallière, carried off the first prize, a sword of gold encrusted with diamonds, presented by the Queen Mother.

At nightfall a myriad of tree-hung chandeliers, each with twenty-four candles, and two hundred tapers, held by an equal number of men in masks, lighted the arena of the *grand rondeau*. Lully's violins played as the Seasons entered: Spring on a great Spanish horse, Summer on an elephant, Autumn on a camel, Winter on a bear. Diana and Pan appeared, their attendants offered meats, and the Court sat down to supper.

On the second night, Molière and his company performed a specially written play in an open-air theater, designed by Le Vau for a central *rond* of the *allée royale*. On the third, the most spectacular of Vigarani's†

---

* Preserved, on Louis' orders, in a book of nine engravings by Israel Silvestre, the recording artist of the period.

† Carlo Vigarani, "a gentleman from Modena," *machiniste extraordinaire,* was shortly afterward appointed the King's engineer in charge of Versailles fêtes.

entertainment "machines" worked its awaited effects. On the smooth
expanse of water in the *grand rondeau,* he had erected the "rocky" isle
and castle of the enchantress Alcina. On its stage were Lully's musicians, on the bank opposite the seated Court. Suddenly from behind a
great "rock" Alcina emerged on a barge which was drawn toward the
bank by a "marine monster." Attended by two nymphs of Molière's
troupe—the one, Racine's future mistress, the other, Molière's wife—she
addressed complimentary verses to the Queen Mother, then turned
back to the enchanted isle. She waved her wand, the castle walls
opened, revealing, among its wonders, a ballet of dancing, bewitched
giants. With the last of the ballets, Roger—no longer Louis—appeared,
received the magic ring from the fair Angelica, and with it broke the
spell binding his companions. Thunder clapped, the palace sank in
splendid flames, and fireworks streaked the sky.

The formal pleasures of the enchanted isle were over, but Louis
prolonged the fête several days more. On the fourth, there was the
game of "head-hunting" in the dry moat of the château: racing, mounted
courtiers tried to impale the wooden heads of a Turk, a Moor, and
Medusa successively on a lance, an épée, and a javelin while the Court
looked down from the balcony. On the fifth day, there was a visit to the
new Ménagerie; that evening, a performance of *Les Fâcheux* in its
salon. On the sixth, a lottery and a "head-hunting" duel between two
noblemen; in the evening, the first three acts of Molière's new play,
Tartuffe, at which the aging Queen Mother was visibly upset.* On the
next, another "head-hunting" competition in the moats, another Molière
play, and on May 14, the Court left Versailles for Fontainebleau—*most
of its courtiers with relief.*

The fête had been unforgettable, the entertainment a triumph,
but the château was dismally inadequate and the few inns of the
village of Versailles fit only for passing carters and tradesmen. In
his *Journal,* Olivier d'Ormesson interrupts his account of the Fouquet
trial, at which he was the King's unco-operative *rapporteur,* to remark,
"Mme de Sévigné told us about the entertainments at Versailles, which
lasted from Wednesday to Sunday, of the tilting at the ring, ballets,
plays, fireworks and other fine inventions; and told us that all the
courtiers were furious, because the King had not taken care of any

---

* *Tartuffe,* the tale of a religious hypocrite, so offended the Church that it
obliged the King to forbid it public performance in Paris, though he displayed
his favor for Molière by having the first acts performed at Versailles.

of them, and Mm. de Guise and d'Elbeuf had hardly a hole in which to take shelter."

This, it would seem likely, spurred Louis' announcement that he would pull down his father's château and put up a more adequate palace. He opened a competition for it among the leading architects. It may have been a reflection on Le Vau's remodeling; it may have been the caution of a still youthful Louis. The same hesitation occurred in deciding the important eastern façade of the Louvre, though Le Vau had impressively designed the Grand Carré to which it acceded. (True, he had deliberately designed it in keeping with the older style of Lescot and Lemercier, that is, of François I and Louis XIIII, and that may well be why Louis XIV opened a competition to find something closer to his own burgeoning style.)

Even Bernini, the Italian baroque master, had been sent for by Colbert for his ideas for the Louvre. And before him, Louis' minister had consulted France's own grand old man, François Mansart.

Typically the elder Mansart had brought no less than fifteen incomplete plans, refused to decide on any of them, telling Colbert he must feel free to do better, even in mid-construction. (A perfectionist perfectly capable of pulling down a half-built building if an improved design occurred to him, Mansart had been replaced two decades earlier by the Queen Mother, fearful of the mounting cost, at the still unfinished Val-de-Grâce Church, commissioned in celebration of Louis XIV's "miraculous" birth.) "If it were for me," Colbert told Mansart, "it would be all right to pull down the Louvre eight or ten times, but it is for the King, and it is the Louvre." "Each," concludes Charles Perrault, who recounts the affair in his *Hommes illustres,* "persisted in this manner and so the matter rested."

Cavaliero Bernini was to fare no better, though far more expensively. He came, presented various projects—too baroque, too Italian for even the Italianate Louis—and was sent home after the formal laying of a cornerstone for a façade never to be built. He left with a compensatory *pension* and the commission for an equestrian statue of the French King, which Louis so disliked when Le Nôtre had brought it back with him from Rome that he had it exiled to the far end of the Lac des Suisses, where it is today barely visible from the terrace.

And instead of Mansart, instead of Le Vau, physician Claude Perrault, whose architectural qualification may have been brother

Charles Perrault's most imaginative creation, was mysteriously chosen. (Translator and annotator of Vetruvius, he had never before designed a building, though he *had* dissected camels.) Rather, a royal commission had the amateur architect modify a plan originally submitted by the Le Vau office, most likely drawn by its modest, unobtrusive designer, François d'Orbay,[6] though almost universally attributed to Perrault. The modified plan of paired columns for the Louvre façade had the right touch of Roman majesty and restrained French classicism for the emerging Louis XIV style.

A façade, however, is not a palace, and it was Le Vau's—or d'Orbay's—plan, not Perrault's, which was finally selected for Versailles. It was the famous "envelope"—the surrounding of the old château on three sides with new wings and a park-side façade (whose paired columns are strikingly, but not surprisingly, similar to those of the Louvre, since d'Orbay most likely designed both). And this choice, in turn, gave birth to the myth which has become part of the folklore of Versailles, namely, that Louis XIV so venerated his father he would not have his little château demolished, but rather made it the very center of his own. Such proved to be Louis' decision, but not for the reasons of sentimentality offered posterity by Charles Perrault.

Piqued, it would seem, by his brother's failure at Versailles, Charles Perrault rendered an explanation in his memoirs, written some thirty years after the event, that would be a fine example of a writer having the last word, were he the last writer. Describing Le Vau's first remodeling, Perrault blandly asserts that the new pavilions and dependencies accorded so badly with the old structure "that Colbert and almost all the Court . . . tried to persuade the King to demolish the little château and complete the palace in the style of what had been newly built.

"My brother was ordered to make a design for such a building. He drew a plan and an elevation which were very favorably viewed not only by the King, but by his Council, to which he had summoned all the Princes, several Ducs and Marshals of France. But as always the King insisted on preserving the little château. It did little good to tell him it was falling into ruins and buckling at several points. He was suspicious of the remarks and said in a loud voice, moved by anger, 'Do what you will, but if you pull it down, I will have it rebuilt as it is without a change!' These words reaffirmed the château and made its foundations thereafter unshakable."[7] And obviously led to

Louis' choosing Le Vau's makeshift "envelope" instead of Claude Perrault's "magnificent plan," according to brother Charles Perrault.

Colbert's fascinating memorandum of 1665, however, records a contradictory fact. "The great, public declaration of the King," he notes toward the end, "that he would raze the little château, committed him irrevocably to said act." It follows a lengthy discussion of possibilities for enlarging Versailles' accommodations, repeating Colbert's theme that the cost would be better and "more gloriously" spent on the Louvre. But, alas, it was clear "the King would not take that decision." So, one must decide whether "everything should be torn down or what has been built anew be conserved."

There was a third choice—Colbert's own—"to keep to the decision taken the year before to allow the little château to remain and to continue the envelope already begun. . . . Everyone will see that the King had this little pleasure house and simply added buildings for his and the Court's shelter." It was here that Colbert adds that unfortunately the King's "great, public declaration that he would raze the little château committed him irrevocably to said act."

Provoked, as Colbert apparently intended, Louis clearly decided that what he had declared he could undeclare, for the little château was preserved, not out of sentimentality for his father, but because of Colbert's false sense of economy. If the King were to neglect the Louvre in favor of Versailles, then, Colbert's memorandum reasons, let it be a minor, diversionary exercise involving the least possible remodeling (a far more costly solution in the long run). Not only for appearance's sake at a time of penury, but in the expressed hope, as Colbert concludes his memorandum, "that the whole building will come down after the King's pleasure in it is sated."

Le Vau's plan was not so much chosen as allowed to proceed, Colbert commenting on it to the King that at least "it preserved what already existed." And, once preserved, the little château persisted—if only out of a bad building habit. Louis' sentiments were not for his father, but for the established order.

We owe to another amateur in architecture, who, as compared to Claude Perrault, was to prove beyond cavil his authentic gift, a curious description of "what already existed" and what was currently going on in French building. In the early summer of 1665, while the plague raged in London, thirty-two-year-old Christopher Wren "took a journey

D

to Paris," his grandson Stephen recounts, and wrote home to a friend in Oxford:

"The Louvre for a while was my daily Object, where no less than a thousand Hands are constantly employed on the Works; some in laying mighty Foundations, some in raising the Stories, Columns, Entablements, etc., with vast Stones, by great and useful Engines; others in carving, inlaying of Marbles, Plaistering, Gilding, etc., which altogether make a school of Architecture the best probably at this Day in Europe. . . .

"The Palace, or, if you please, the Cabinet of Versailles, call'd me twice to view it; the Mixtures of Brick and Stone, blue Tile and Gold make it look like a rich Livery; not an Inch within but is crowded with little Curiosities of Ornament: the Women, as they make here the Language and Fashions and meddle in Politicks and Philosophy, so also in Architecture; Works of Filgrand and little Knacks are in great Vogue; but Building certainly ought to have the Attributes of eternal, and therefore the only Thing uncapable of new Fashions."[8]

Christopher Wren's Anglo-Saxon judgments reflect more justly on Louis XIII than on Frenchwomen, so far as the "femininity" of Versailles at the time is concerned. The missing "masculinity," if that means majesty, was to appear with Louis XIV—that is, with Le Vau and Mansart.

Along the shorter, northern and southern sides of the old château, Le Vau erected two large all-stone pavilions, and on the west, facing the park, a great, ground-floor salon with an open terrace on its roof extending between the two pavilions. On the court, or entry side, the old, brick and stone château and its marble courtyard remained picturesquely if anachronistically exposed—as it is down to our own day.

The moats were filled in, the stable and kitchen wings joined to the château, other *communs* built, and the pitched roof flattened. The last-mentioned, Italianate effect was without precedent in France and much criticized for the upkeep required in a climate of rain-filled skies. Where did the idea come from? Again François d'Orbay is indicated.[9] Apprenticed to Le Vau at fourteen, he had spent the years 1659 and 1660, while in his mid-twenties, in Rome, studying its architecture. His hand as chief designer for the Le Vau office can be discerned in most of the drawings for Versailles: the stately, colonnaded façade on the park side, the flat Mediterranean roof and attic cornices decorated by balustrades, sculpture, and vases, the terrace with its heavy, arcaded supporting wall. Neither Vaux nor any other building of Le Vau—who had never visited Italy—had had these characteristics.

One might add, without prejudice, that Le Nôtre's terrace, park, and vast perspectives virtually impelled the flat roof and horizontal design for which d'Orbay was so well prepared. But at the death of Le Vau in 1670, in the six years before the younger Mansart took over, d'Orbay was to stand alone at Versailles, bringing the "Le Vau" phase to its completion, including the superb Staircase of the Ambassadors leading to the state apartments.

The years of each additional structure are not certain. The accounts (one trusts) are: in 1664, 3,222,365 livres, five million in 1669, and over seven million in 1671.[10] In the meantime Louis XIV was approaching the maturity and confidence of thirty and the attendant change of mistress, marked by the great fête of 1668.

Death had come two years earlier to the Queen Mother, and though he seems undoubtedly to have loved her, there was surely an element of release in Louis' grief. Sixtyish, suffering from cancer, Anne of Austria had become a gray, heavy presence in an increasingly colorful and amoral court. In October of the same year, Louise de La Vallière had given clandestine birth, as usual, to a third child and, during the convalescence and the King's visits, had engaged her wittiest friend, Athénais de Montespan, to help amuse him. A month later, La Montespan fully succeeded, but not yet officially.

Dark, blue-eyed, rounded where Louise was not, Madame de Montespan had one disadvantage—her husband, the Marquis de Montespan. But during the first years, he was largely away from Court on his own affairs. As for Louise, in May 1667 she was made a duchess—as if, she said, it were a present to a retiring domestic—and was left behind when the King went off to lead his army against the Dutch, quaintly accompanied by the Queen, the Court, and the new favorite. Nightly in the house of the accommodating Madame de Montausier, near the Netherlands border, Louis visited Madame de Montespan before joining the Queen. "Last night," complained Marie-Thérèse to La Grande Mademoiselle after one such occasion, "it was four o'clock and almost dawn before the King came to bed. I don't understand what he can have been doing." Overhearing, Louis hastily explained, "Reading dispatches and writing replies."[11]

On July 18, 1668, two and a half months after the Peace of Aix-la-

Chapelle brought a pause, if not peace, to the indecisive war with
Protestant England, Holland, and Sweden, Louis gave one of his
grandest Versailles fêtes. It lasted one night, cost over one hundred
thousand livres, and was officially engraved *ten years later* by Le
Pautre, such was the impression it left. Louise and the Queen were
honored, but the ballet, the Court well knew, celebrated the unabashed
Triumph of Bacchus—and La Montespan.

Again. Louis decided the entertainment and the garden sites (in-
tersecting *ronds* of the principal *allées* and the *allée royale*), displayed
the new sparkling waters and fountains (cooling the air for dancing)
and the beginning of the great cruciform Grand Canal, where but a
few years earlier had been marshland. Again Lully and Molière were
the entertainers, Vigarani in charge of the spectacular effects.

In the late afternoon, Louis, the Queen, and the Court emerged
from a collation in the château—only the royal family and a few
ladies were provided rooms for repose—and joined some three thousand
guests on the great terrace and in the gardens. They strolled northward
to the Grotto of Thétis,* admired its arcades, hydraulic organ, shell-
like décor, its fountains and water jets suddenly wetting visitors at the
entrance (such was the "playfulness" of the period). Then they went
down to the Basin of the Dragon with its new, gilded-lead figures, on
to the Bosquet de l'Etoile, the junction of five *allées,* along each of which
a long buffet had been ranged. Pears, apricots, peaches, Dutch goose-
berries and Portuguese oranges—preserved and fresh—hung from the
trees. There was a mountain of meats, a castle of marzipan and sugar,
whose leveling by the hungry public following, after the King and Court
had feasted, was a considerable part of the pleasure—not only for the
public.

The King in his calèche, the Queen, pregnant with the Duc d'Anjou,
in her sedan chair, the courtiers in their carriages—all rode around
the *grand rondeau* (the future Basin of Apollo) to Vigarani's theater.
Refreshments were served, Molière's *George Dandin* performed and
over a hundred danced Lully's *Triumph of Bacchus* on the enormous
stage. On then to another *rond* of park paths (today's Fountain of
Flora) and supper. Here a domed pavilion of foliage displayed a
Mount Parnassus tumbling with water and studded with statues of
Apollo—Louis XIV was now the Sun King acknowledged[12]—the

* Conceived for La Vallière, it was completed for La Montespan and disappeared
with Madame de Maintenon.

Muses, and Pegasus. In an arbor opposite, the King and the more privileged were served a banquet of five courses, each of fifty-six dishes; throughout the park were laden tables for the others. As the official mistress, Louise shared the King's table, and Madame de Montespan a table with Mademoiselle de Scudéry and Madame Scarron, who would be *her* successor. After supper, Le Vau's marble and porphyry ballroom—"No palace in the world," exclaimed Scudéry, "could boast a room so fine, so large, so high and so superb!"—in which the best of the King's sculptors had worked, with the permanency of snow, in plaster and papier-mâché. Water flowed from the pedestals, formed a stream along the length of the great room which was lighted by chandeliers, and the sound of the water mingled with that of the violins.

As the King and Court emerged from the ballroom in the darkness before dawn, suddenly all was as brilliant as high noon. The château, in Mademoiselle de Scudéry's words, had become a "Palace of the Sun, everywhere illuminated, its windows filled with what seemed the most beautiful statues of antiquity, alight with color. . . . The balustrades and terraces of the gardens, ordinarily edged with porcelain, flower-filled vases were now lined with vases blazing with flames which lit the furthest corners. And there were also rows of glowing termini, colossi, statuary and caducei interlaced with fire . . . And then, as if it were not sufficient to charm the eyes with so many luminous objects, the thunder of a thousand mortars was suddenly heard, followed by a thousand jets of fire rising from the basins, the fountains, the parterres, the leafy woods—a hundred different places!"[13]

Fire and water, continues André Félibien, historiographer to the King, "were so mingled it was impossible to distinguish them. . . . When a thousand flames were seen rising from everywhere in the gardens, it seemed there were as many canals supplying fire that night as water during the day. . . . Everyone, thinking that this marvel of fireworks must be the end of the fête, returned to the palace, when suddenly the sky was filled with bursting flashes and the air with a crash that seemed to shake the earth. Everyone stood near the Grotto and watched innumerable giant rockets shoot from the water tower. . . . There were even some that traced the royal monogram as they turned and twisted, writing double L's against the dark sky in vivid, brilliant light. . . . And then day, as if jealous of so brilliant a night, began to appear."[14]

But once again, as the sun climbed higher, the King and Court had to go elsewhere—to Saint-Germain this time. The château of Versailles was still undergoing Le Vau's transformations, and even these would be inadequate. The formal moving of Louis' court and government to Versailles would have to await another day and another architect.

In the fall the Court went to Chambord, where La Montespan and Louise—resigned to half an aloof Louis—had adjoining rooms. The following summer Monsieur de Montespan arrived in Paris, boxed his wife's ears in Saint-Germain, plotted—together with a fellow Gascon and our recurring friend, the Comte de Lauzun—to carry her off to Spain, had his men beat up a bailiff for interfering with a love affair in Perpignan, and for *that* was banished to his estates by the King.[15] Meanwhile Louise faded with Louis' interest, fell ill in 1670, fled to a convent, returned on Louis' request, sought nunship for a third time in 1674, this time asking permission, this time receiving it, and lived the rest of a long life as Sister Louise de la Miséricorde.[16]

By 1674, Le Vau's envelope was completed around the little château. The Queen had her apartments in the south wing, the King in the north, Madame de Montespan nearby. Resting from the reconquest of Franche-Comté, Louis spent his longest period of residence until then at Versailles and leisurely spaced six days of fête through the months of July and August.

Madame de Montespan and her legitimized children by now were openly pre-eminent, and as if to mark it, the first day of the fête, July 4, 1674, opened in the afternoon in a bosquet whose central feature—a bronze tree with tin leaves and metal reeds spouting water —had been *her* idea.* After a collation, toward six all removed to the marble courtyard of the old château, which had been transformed into a theater for Quinault's *Alceste*—Molière had died the year before, stricken on stage while performing *Le Malade imaginaire*—with music by the enduring Lully. Toward midnight all retired to the interior for supper.

Entertainment a week later, for the second day of the fête, was entirely at the Trianon de Porcelaine. Designed by Le Vau (or

---

* Le Nôtre having tactfully—and tastefully—delayed executing it, Colbert had taken it on, knowing it would please the King to please his mistress.

d'Orbay), its pagoda-like roof, its walls of blue and white faïence suggest the *chinoiserie* of its taste. The village of Trianon had been leveled, its cemetery exhumed, for this pleasure dome à la Montespan, which fortunately gave way, a decade and a half later, to Mansart's Trianon de Marbre.

The third day of the fête began at the Ménagerie and continued on the Grand Canal. Six months before, Venice had sent two exquisitely finished gondolas to Louis XIV—the first of the extraordinary Versailles flotilla—together with four gondoliers, and "for an hour the King tasted the freshness of evening," Félibien tells us, on the waters of the canal, before going on by calèche to the Grotto of Thétis for Molière's *Le Malade imaginaire,* without Molière. On the fourth day, there were fireworks and ballets, on the fifth, Racine's *Iphigénie* in the Orangerie, "received by the Court with its usual high esteem for this author," on the sixth, three weeks later, the final *fête de nuit.*

That night the great parterres, the *allée royale,* the Grand Canal were outlined in flame, the canal itself ornamented with luminous figures of giant fish, termini, pyramids, and palaces of fire. At dark the King and the Court went out among them. "In the deep silence of night," Félibien relates, "were heard the violins which followed his Majesty's vessel in another. The sound of the instruments seemed to give life to the figures, whose light, in exchange, lent a charm to the music it would not have had in complete darkness. As the boats passed, one could see the water whiten about them, the oars softly striking the dark surface of the canal with measured strokes, streaking it with silver."

The Sun King's historiographer adds a rhapsodic note. "The great expanses of water," he writes, "lighted only by the luminous figures, resembled long galleries and salons enriched and adorned by architecture and statuary of a beauty never before known and beyond anything the mind of man can conceive."[17]

So ended the fête of 1674 with La Montespan's dominance of the Versailles scene. And as she reached the high-water point of her career as the King's mistress-in-residence, Jules Hardouin-Mansart began the racing, meteoric climb toward his own eminence.

In 1674, to the woman who had everything, Louis gave the immensely costly Château de Clagny, a short stone's throw from his own at Versailles. Or rather, he gave the order for its design to the twenty-eight-year-old architect who was to make a *chef-d'œuvre* of Le Vau's envelope, creating the palace that Le Nôtre's terrace demanded.

But before Mansart, Molière . . . *in memoriam.*

7. The Entertainers

He had asked for a priest, but none came from his parish. Dead, he was refused burial in Church ground: he had not renounced his profession.* So ruled the Archbishop of Paris, and Armande went to Louis XIV at Versailles and threw herself at his feet. "If my husband was a criminal," she cried, "it was Your Majesty himself who approved his crimes!" Louis paused, then continued down the Grande Galerie, his courtiers glacially following. Quietly the next day he arranged with the archbishop for a discreet religious burial.

Whether or not Armande's words were quite so memorable,[1] her appeal dramatized the actor's lot. Excommunicated since the Synod of Elvira, ca. 305—which aimed at the mimes and *histrionici* of the declining Roman Empire—*comédiens* were subject to the capricious protection of sovereigns and nobles. Socially ostracized—the solid citizen registering his suspicion of the vagrant and rootless—the actors wandered, their condition in France varying from parish to parish, see to see, time to time. The two cardinals of our chronicle—Richelieu and Mazarin—had patronized the players and arranged special performances at Court. Louis XIII, on Richelieu's advice, had supported the royal troupe eventually settling in Paris at the Hôtel de Bourgogne; Mazarin had brought to France Tiberio Fiorelli, who, as Scaramouche, had been Louis' delight at the age of two and continued to be when Louis was XIV. But actors and actresses, whether or not under protective wings, could not be married or buried by the Church unless,

* "Molière died," says playwright Jean Anouilh, "one of us."

in the first instance, they characterized themselves as something else, usually musicians, or, in the second, repented, renounced their calling, and were absolved.

Molière might have avoided all this. He was born (1622) Jean-Baptiste Poquelin, child of a respectable bourgeois family of upholsterers and decorators. Indeed, when he was nine, his father was named *valet tapissier de chambre du roi* with the privilege he could bequeath his son of arranging the royal furniture, making the bottom half of the royal bed, and living, the three months of his yearly attendance, in the royal household and receiving an annual allowance of three hundred livres. Meanwhile Jean-Baptiste was sent to the Jesuit Collège de Clermont, where for five years he studied Latin and philosophy, partook in school ballets and dramatics—a school device for learning literature and declamation—before going on to philosopher-scientist Pierre Gassendi, law studies and, somewhere along the line, a loss of faith. At twenty, Jean-Baptiste may have traveled with Louis XIII in his ailing father's stead, as *valet tapissier de chambre,* but the same year he met red-haired actress Madeleine Béjart, signed away his right as the royal bedmaker for 630 livres, and formed the Illustre Théâtre with the Béjart family. Imprisoned for debt when it failed, he was freed from debt by his father, reorganized the Illustre Théâtre, and for a dozen years toured the provinces, forevermore to be known as Molière.

Traveling like a circus, by horse, mule, and lumbering cart, transforming tennis courts and fair grounds into make-shift theaters, the troupe played Toulouse, Bordeaux, Narbonne, Lyons. As did Shakespeare, Molière learned the art, tricks, and devices of holding a rough audience without losing himself. He acted, directed, mimed, managed and buffooned, and relatively late (at thirty-three) wrote his first play, *L'Etourdi* (The Scatterbrain). The Prince de Conti, persuaded by his secretary, who fancied actress Mademoiselle du Parc, provocative wife of one of the players,* had undertaken to support the troupe with his money and name in Languedoc. But within a few years, suddenly become pious, the Prince had a *crise de conscience* and discarded Molière's company. (In his *Traitè de la comédie,* written ten years later, he was to accuse Molière, in their youth a fellow student at the Collège de Clermont, of leading a new school of atheism.) Prince-

---

* The title Madame was reserved for noblewomen and royalty.

less, Molière resumed touring the provinces—Nîmes, Orange, Avignon, Grenoble, Lyons, Rouen—and from Rouen discreetly prepared his return to Paris.

"After several secret journeys thither, he was fortunate enough to secure the patronage of Monsieur, the King's only brother, who granted him his protection, and permitted the company to take his name, presenting them as his servants to the King and the Queen Mother."[2]

In the capital there were the jealousy of rival playwrights, the ruthless, would-be monopoly of the Paris stage by the King's *comédiens* at the Hôtel de Bourgogne and the private company at the Théâtre du Marais. Molière did not fear the competition but needed Monsieur's patronage. The presentation to the King took place in a theater arranged in the guardroom of the Louvre, and here the thirty-six-year-old Molière and his troupe, who would brighten Versailles' fêtes, met the twenty-year-old Louis XIV for the first time. It was almost a failure. Aspiring to tragedy—then as now considered the "nobler" form —Molière put his company through Corneille's *Nicomède*. Sensing the failure at its close, he came forward and asked the King's permission to put on "one of the little pieces with which he had regaled the provinces," *Le Docteur amoureux*. A dubious farce, it apparently pleased the younger, less critical Louis, for the next day he had Molière's troupe installed in the Salle du Petit Bourbon, which adjoined the Louvre, and here it alternated with Scaramouche and his Italian players.

Henceforth comedy was indicated. Molière's talent and appearance —a broad face with a broad, flaring nose, a wide-spread mouth, widely spread eyes (is their touch of melancholy one's own addition?), and heavy, "elevatable" eyebrows—dictated the direction, escape it as he might try. Moreover, Voltaire informs us,[3] he had a "kind of hiccough that unfitted him for serious roles," but made "his comedy the more enjoyable." The first hit at the Petit Bourbon, according to La Grange,* Molière's devoted associate, was *L'Etourdi*. But the first play to give more than an inkling of Molière's satiric dimensions was undoubtedly *Les*

---

* Faithfully he had noted the receipts, performances, and daily activities of Molière's company from its arrival in Paris in October 1658 to the end of August 1685. The yellowed, parchment-bound record is kept in a strongbox at the Comédie Française, but a published version is available: La Grange (Charles Varlet). *Registre*. Paris, Claye, 1876.

Précieuses ridicules (The Ridiculous Exquisites), often called the first comedy of manners. Until then, the exquisites were the untouchables. Afterward, one frequenter of the Marquise de Rambouillet's famous salon was heard saying as he left the theater, "Yesterday we admired all the absurdities which have been so delicately and sensibly criticized; but in the words of St. Remy to Clovis, we must now burn what we have adored, and adore what we have burned."[4]

To the *chambre bleue* of the Hôtel de Rambouillet—where the Italian-born marquise received in bed (wrapped not against the cold but the heat) and made it fashionable—had come the Grand Condé and the Grande Mademoiselle, La Rochefoucauld, Mesdames de La Fayette and de Sévigné, and the wits and exquisites of the time. We know the *précieuses* of her salon-court—or would, were it not so unreadable—through Mademoiselle de Scudéry's novel, *Le Grand Cyrus,* or decorous love in ten volumes. We know them in fact—or rather prefer thinking we do—through Molière's looking-glass, which, even an admirer must admit, is also a distorting mirror. The civilizing of Louis XIII's society, the creation of Louis XIV's, began in the French salon and if the French sexes are companionate, it is thanks to the salon conversation then developing into the art of exchange, in which all might be said, if said civilly, wittily, and well.

Exquisitely the Marquise de Rambouillet replied to Molière's satire by inviting him to perform it for the special benefit of her Blue Room. Gallantly he pointed out in a later preface that the mirror he held up reflected her provincial imitators, not her friends, and so he had plotted his play. Briefly, two *précieuses* from the country protest being hastened into marriage before a romantic courtship. "Matrimony," says Magdalon, sensibly enough, "should never be brought about till after other adventures. A lover, to be agreeable, must understand how to utter fine sentiments, to express the soft, the tender, the passionate, and all according to the rules." But the rules of the game played by the *précieuses* included the priggish absurdities of Scudéry's romances, pushed to the extreme in Molière's satire by Cathos, the other country cousin. "For myself," she says, "marriage is a shocking thing! How can one endure even the thought of lying next to a man who is . . . who is . . . naked!" And the two rejected suitors costume their already pretentious valets in their clothes and have them court the two cousins according to the rules, before stripping them of their plumage and exposing them to the ridiculed pair.

Soon after returning to Paris in the summer of 1660, Louis took his new young Queen and the Court to see *Les Précieuses*. He was familiar with it, having read a copy sent him by Molière in St.-Jean-de-Luz the previous winter, when "a *précieux* of quality had its further performance prohibited."[5] Louis had quickly granted permission for the play to continue at the Petit Bourbon and, five days after seeing it in Paris, commanded a performance for Mazarin, standing throughout behind the dying minister's chair. In the fall the Louvre underwent alterations, the Petit Bourbon was demolished, and Molière was installed in a *salle* of Richelieu's Palais Royal. Again he tried tragedy, again he failed. *L'Ecole des maris* (School for Husbands), or how to train young women to be faithful wives of older men, was predictably more successful. But Molière's own problem, at thirty-nine, with comedienne Armande Béjart, less than half his age, can be all too painfully read between the lines. True, it ends happily—Léonor, eighteen, marries the gentle Ariste, the sixty-year-old guardian, and presumably remains faithful forever after—but life for Molière was to be no comedy.

That he was gentle and loved La Grange testifies. Despite the lures of the two rival companies, his troupe remained intact. "All the actors," says La Grange, "loved their chief, who united his extraordinary genius with an honorable character and charming manner, compelling them to protest that they would never leave him, but always share his fortunes." It was at this time they put on *Les Fâcheux* at the Vaux-le-Vicomte fête, whose finale was Fouquet's misfortune as, six months later, Molière's marriage to Armande was his own.

Armande was the sister—some said the daughter—of Madeleine Béjart, still active in the troupe; as Madeleine had been Molière's mistress, he was accused by his enemies of being Armande's father. Montfleury, leader of the increasingly bitter royal company at the Hôtel de Bourgogne, wrote to the King himself in 1663, as we know from a letter of Jean Racine to Abbé Le Vasseur: "Montfleury has prepared a brief against Molière and given it to the King. He accuses him of having married the daughter after having slept with the mother. But Montfleury has no audience at Court."

Was Armande Madeleine's daughter? She could have been, with the Comte de Modène her father, as he was of a previous child of Madeleine, whom he recognized as his. Several contemporary records, however, indicate Armande as the daughter of Marie Hervé Béjart,

Madeleine's mother.[6] But Marie Hervé being some fifty years old when Armande was born, and Joseph Béjart, her husband, having died shortly before, it has been assumed by several, such as Michelet, that she was accepting Madeleine's child as her own. All possible but unproved. Both Madeleine and Marie Hervé were alive; it is scarcely credible they would have condoned the marriage if Molière, and not Joseph Béjart or the Comte de Modène, were the father. But one must assume the stories haunted and taunted Molière.

Further, would Louis XIV have replied to Montfleury's accusation by standing as godfather a year later to Molière's first born, with Madame as godmother, if he did not firmly believe it untrue?* Hardly likely. He had his police; they had their sources. Fond as Louis XIV may have been of his playwright and *comédien,* he was his pious mother's son—and she, too, was still alive. Immoral, or amoral, as one may consider the King, he was not irreligious; incest, the most mortal of sins, was punishable by burning at the stake.

Armande was punishment enough. No Léonor, she frolicked and flirted and was quickly unfaithful to the man who had doted on her as a child, made her an actress and his wife. Married in February, by December Molière was brooding in *L'Ecole des femmes* (School for Wives) about the infidelity of young, much-courted women and the jealousy of the confused, much-older men who would marry them. Thus Arnolphe, played by Molière, raises his ward Agnès in complete innocence, hoping to keep her that way as his wife. However, she falls in love with the young, handsome Horace and runs off with him, only to be retaken by Arnolphe. About to strike her, Arnolphe-Molière stops and reflects, with Armande, surely, on his mind: "How strange to be in love! that men should be subject to such weakness for such traitresses! . . . Their mind is wicked and their spirit is weak. Nothing is more feeble, more imbecilic, more unfaithful. And yet, for all that, in this world we do everything for these animals." Agnès marries Horace; a friend consoles Arnolphe by saying only in that way can he be really sure of not becoming a deceived husband.

Birth by way of the ear, ribald *double-entendres,* rough, blunt dia-

---

* The Duc de Créquy, the King's first gentleman, and Madame's first lady-in-waiting, actually stood in their stead at the baptism of Louis Molière. It should also be noted that Mazarin and the Queen Mother had been the godparents of Scaramouche's second child, at the same church of Saint-Germain-l'Auxerrois.

logue—it was too much for many of the Court and most of the Church. The Prince de Conti came out flatly against Molière's play. Bossuet condemned it from the royal pulpit.* The Hôtel de Bourgogne mocked its "vulgarities." Molière responded with a stinging skit, *The Critique of the School for Wives,* in which he satirized his critics, especially posturing ladies and gentlemen of the Court. The Hôtel de Bourgogne riposted with *The Countercritic.* It was fair play. ("Admirable," said Molière, who attended a performance.) Another incident was more revealing of the time and explains some of the bitterness in Molière's *L'Impromptu de Versailles* a few months later. The Duc de La Feuillade, identifying himself with a particularly idiotic marquis in Molière's *Critique,* met the actor-playwright on the street and, feigning friendliness, beckoned him closer. Molière approached, bowed, La Feuillade seized him and rubbed his face against the diamond-pointed buttons of his coat until the blood ran. Louis XIV berated La Feuillade for it, but his act remains. (And the only reason his name is even mentioned here is that contact with Molière.)

The King further showed his favor by calling Molière to Versailles, where he put on *L'Impromptu,* wittily, mercilessly parodying the actors of the Hôtel de Bourgogne, Molière himself mimicking Montfleury. Their attacks had reached him, despite his "admirable." But what touches one today is not the play's historicism, but its *tristesse,* its sadness at the actor's and the playwright's fate: to make courtiers laugh, Molière remarks from the Versailles stage, "who laugh only when they care to," to write plays that must please the patron, for whom "it is wiser to write badly, but in time, than too late. And if one is ashamed for having failed, one can always have the glory of having quickly met the command."

Fouquet, the King must have felt, was the target, not himself. (*Les Fâcheux,* Molière was reminding everyone, was commissioned, written, and performed in fifteen days.) In the midst of the row over

---

* Son of a family of Dijon lawyers, Jacques Bénigne Bossuet early brought attention to himself at the age of sixteen, when, challenged, he delivered a brilliant sermon in the salon of the Hôtel de Rambouillet on a subject spontaneously chosen. Later, an abbé in Metz, he attracted the attention of the Queen Mother, who summoned him to Paris out of concern for Louis' growing attachment to La Vallière. A decade later, Bossuet was to annoy Louis by encouraging Louise to retire to a convent, but Louis, ever the admirer of talent, retained Bossuet for the drama of his performance on the royal pulpit, most markedly on the occasion of deaths in the royal family.

The School for Wives, he accorded Molière an annual allowance of a thousand livres, not as a *comédien,* but as an *"excellent poète comique."* There were forty-four other Frenchmen, and fifteen foreigners, on the fascinating list of Louis' protégés, among them, the Dutch physicist Huyghens, the Italian mathematician Viviani, the two Corneilles, Racine, Quinault, Charles Perrault. The last-mentioned recalls in his memoirs that the first year the royal coins were delivered to each domicile in gold embroidered purses, the second year in purses of horsehair and "thereafter one had to go to the treasurer in person, the years stretching into fifteen and sixteen months." (But no sovereign in history may have been so generous a patron. Boileau, as poet and arbiter of literary taste, was to live grandly on his allowance, Racine, as royal historian, on his.) The following January, dressed *"en égyptien,"* Louis danced in the second act of Molière's *Le Mariage forcé* to music by Lully and in February godfathered Molière's child, who died before December.

But intervening was the famous Versailles fête of 1664, *Les Plaisirs de l'isle enchantée,* scene of La Vallière's triumph and Armande's escapades, setting for *Tartuffe* and a sea of troubles.

Tartuffe, tale of a religious scoundrel, was a strange choice of theme for a festival of love, but a courageous act for a playwright already in difficulty with the Compagnie du Saint Sacrament, the lay fraternity of the fanatical known as the Cabale des Dévots.* Tradition has Louis XIV encouraging Molière in writing *Tartuffe,* perhaps because the *dévots* were agitating public opinion against his liaison with La Vallière, perhaps because he thought Tartuffe was a satirized Jansenist heretic of the Port Royal school and convent, with which he was then in conflict, perhaps simply because he had given Molière a free hand in organizing the theatricals for the Versailles festival.

The opening nights, at least, were pure festivity: the parade of the Seasons, Pan and Diana (Molière and his young wife), reciting verses to the Queens on the first evening, and, on the second, Molière's *Princesse d'Elide,* hastily written and quickly forgotten—were it not for Armande. She appeared, as the princess, for the first time since her pregnancy, revealing her available charms to the *galants* of the Court. Their applause, her success, the soft spring nights, the royal

* La Bruyère: "A *dévot* [bigot] is one who, under an atheistic king, would be an atheist."

example, the heady sensuality of the fête, the handy groves of Versailles, Armande was vulnerable and Molière was betrayed.

But he was the busy actor-manager of a troupe with *Tartuffe,* one of his greatest plays, to perform. The story line, as usual, is a tangled one. Orgon, a rich bourgeois, first meets Tartuffe in church, where "the fervency with which he sent up his prayers to Heaven attracted the eyes of the whole congregation," and Orgon takes "the poor pious creature" home with him to his wife and children. Tartuffe's hypocrisy is exposed when he tries to seduce the wife, though promised the daughter and given the house. God and conscience, he says to Orgon's resisting wife, can always be managed. Outraged, the hidden Orgon emerges and orders Tartuffe from his home. The house, Tartuffe reminds Orgon, is now his. The King's men then suddenly enter, in a typical Molière denouement, declare Tartuffe a long-sought criminal and take him away. The curtain falls with a long tribute to the justice of the King. Clumsy as playwriting, the tribute is understandable: only Louis could make possible the performance of *Tartuffe.*

But what the young King permitted himself at Versailles in private performance he was not yet ready to risk in public, in open confrontation with the Church, which now objected to a performance in Paris. Prudently he withheld permission for *Tartuffe* to be staged at the Palais Royal—and withheld it for three years. Meanwhile it was read privately—to a group at Court that even included a representative of the Pope, who raised no objection—and privately performed—before Monsieur and Madame, Molière's warmest supporter at Versailles. He badly needed her. A pamphlet published in Paris in 1664 by Pierre Roullé, vicar of St. Barthélemy, called on the King, "as a foretaste of the fires of hell," to order the burning of Molière, "that demon in the flesh, the most impious creature and libertine that ever lived." The pamphlet was suppressed, the vicar was rebuked, the King increased Molière's allowance and made his troupe his own (until then it was Monsieur's), but one feels the violence of the period.

Two years passed. Molière revised *Tartuffe,* read it to the King, received unwritten permission to stage it. So he did, while the King was off to war in Flanders, and the following morning the playwright found his theater closed by decree of the President of the Paris Parlement, in charge of public order in the King's absence. Molière's good friend,

Boileau, took him to the official. "You are a comic genius, M. de
Molière," Président Lamoignon told him. "You are an honor and a
glory to France, but it is not the theater's business to dabble in
religion."[7]

The King was petitioned; returning to Paris, he counseled patience.
In 1669, *Tartuffe* was again performed and has been performed
again and again ever since—more often than any other play in the
almost three centuries of the Comédie Française's existence. "*Tartuffe*
will live," Voltaire has written, "so long as there is good taste and a
hypocrite in France." "It is a masterpiece," said Napoleon at Sainte
Hélène, "but if it had been written in my time, I would have forbidden
its performance."[8]

It was an astonishing period of masterpieces for Molière, which
saw his three greatest plays—*Tartuffe, Don Juan,* and *Le Misanthrope*—appear in three successive years. (One needn't count two
others dealing with the doctors of the time; Molière's war with them was
to continue to his death.) *Don Juan* was the most daring, the Don
challenging even God in his pursuit of pleasure and the seduction of
—1003 his valet calculates—women. It was not, however, the Don's
love making which infuriated the *dévots,* but his atheism, not the seduction scenes, but the scene with a religious mendicant.

He prayed daily, a beggar says to Don Juan, for those who gave
him charity. Don Juan: "A man who prays every day must be a rich
man." Beggar: "Most of the time I don't even have a morsel of
bread to put between my teeth." Don Juan offers him a louis d'or,
if he will blaspheme. The beggar hesitates, then refuses. "Take it then,"
says Don Juan, "in the name of humanity."

"Nothing more impious ever appeared," wrote a member of the
Paris Parlement, "even in pagan times." But the King once again
backed Molière and raised the royal subsidy for his company. In a
few months, however, *Don Juan* disappeared from the repertory, to
reappear after Molière's death in a bowdlerized version but not until
the nineteenth century in its present complete form.

Part cause of Molière's creative outburst was his separation in
1665 from Armande. They were to meet only on the stage, most
memorably, for our purposes, with Molière as Alceste in the title role of
Le Misanthrope and Armande as Célimène, authoress of his mis-
anthropy. Alceste, as morally demanding of himself as of others, loves

Célimène, who is far less selective in *her* loves, or rather suitors. "Can I help it," she tells him, "if people find me lovable?" She might, says Alceste, be less impressed by their absurd courtship and language. Philinthe, philosopher and friend, advises compromise with the ways of the world. "I take people with great calm," he says, "just as they are. I train myself to endure what they do. I believe that at Court, as in the world outside it, my phlegm is as good a philosopher as your bile." Alceste, however, uncompromisingly renounces the world and the Court and retires to solitude.

Shortly before *Le Misanthrope,* perhaps while he was writing it and perhaps also part cause of it, Molière had an unpleasant encounter with another entertainer (who would wince at the description) seventeen years his junior.

Born in 1639 of upper-middle-class parents, who died before he was three, Jean Racine was raised by his grandparents. The family, technically noble, had as its arms a punning combination of a rat and a swan (*rat-cygne,* pronounced ra-cínya) which Racine, as a courtier, rid of the rat. It was not so easy to eliminate the Jansenism with which he was brought up. His aunt was a nun, eventually an abbess, at the Port Royal convent to whose school he was sent as a youth. From there he went to a *collège* in Paris, where he discovered women and the theater. Still a youth, he submitted a play to Molière. Impressed, Molière encouraged him with money but didn't produce the play. Alarmed, the family recalled Racine for proper religious studies under an uncle who was a canon and could promise him a career in the Church. When his uncle fell into difficulty and his religious career became uncertain, Racine returned to Paris. At nineteen, Racine wrote an ode celebrating Louis' entry into Paris in 1660 with the young Queen; he showed it to Perrault and Chapelain, who suggested changes, and rewrote it. Read to the King, it was rewarded with a hundred louis. Launched, Racine wrote another play, which Molière produced—for four performances. Then his aunt wrote him from Port Royal: "I have learned with sorrow that you frequent, more than ever, people whose names are an abomination to all people of piety, and rightly, for they are forbidden access to the Church or its sacraments."[9] And movingly she abjured Racine to renounce the theater. Instead, he wrote *Alexandre,* and Molière put it on at the Palais Royal on December 4, 1665. On December 18, to Molière's surprise, he dis-

covered that Racine's play was being performed at the Hôtel du Bourgogne. Racine had not liked the way of Molière's troupe with tragedy
and had taken his, without a word, to the rival company—and along with
it very shortly his mistress, Mademoiselle du Parc, of Molière's company. Breaking with Port Royal* and his family, Racine was to go on
from success to success. Molière recovered, was to call Racine friend,
but in 1665 the experience, in some measure at least, contributed to
Le Misanthrope.

Molière, unlike Alceste, did not quite renounce the world, but
he did withdraw a few kilometers from Paris to a house by the Seine
in Auteuil. Nor did he cease writing, acting, or managing his theater,
though Boileau, who saw him often, urged him to reduce his activities
for the sake of his disquieting health. La Fontaine, poet Chapelle, Lully
("Make us laugh, Baptiste!" Molière would greet him), and on occasion Armande with a courtier, or a comrade from the theater, would
join him at Auteuil. There is a particular wryness in a famous line of
Amphitryon, which Molière wrote at this time for Louis XIV and the
reigning mistress. Jupiter, having brought his wife to bed, tells Amphitryon, *"Un partage avec Jupiter n'a rien du tout qui déshonore"*
(To share with Jupiter is not at all dishonorable). Good friend Boileau
detested the play.

George Dandin, more down to earth and a greater play, was
performed the same year at the Versailles fête of 1668, but again the
story of a deceived husband's torments reveals Molière's own. "When
a man has married a wicked woman, as have I," Dandin says just
before the final curtain, "the best thing he can do is to go off and
throw himself into the water." But Lully's sumptuous ballet intervals
and the *bacchanale* which followed made the program a prodigious
success for Louis and his three thousand guests. *Dandin* and the
sparkling ballets were performed in a vast theater created by Vigarani
for the festive occasion. Erected in the *allée royale,* on the *rondeau*
that would be the future Basin of Apollo, it was decorated with foliage

---

* Racine's teacher at Port Royal, Nicole, issued a virtual communiqué, declaring
that "novelists and dramatists are public poisoners who destroy not men's
bodies, but their souls." Corneille and Molière separately replied. So did
Racine. "What do novelists and dramatists have to do with Jansenism?" he
scornfully wrote his former teacher. "We are not at all surprised at your
damning poets: you damn so many people. . . . Content yourself, Monsieur,
with ordering things in the other world, not in this one." Later in life at
Versailles, Racine was to regret his letter.

on the outside and hung with tapestries and lighted by chandeliers within. Gaily, singing actors pushed Molière's poor hero about, as Vigarani's intricate stage machinery put on its own entertaining show. Performed starkly by itself at the Palais Royal, *Dandin* became a tragicomedy, its hero a tragic figure—and the audience squirmed uncomfortably.

Molière's bitterness was to reappear in *L'Avare* (The Miser), a play not immediately popular, though loyally Boileau supported it with his laughter, and disappear three plays later in *Le Bourgeois gentilhomme.** In the interim, *Tartuffe* had finally been given full public performance and Madame, the gay Henriette of England, to whom Molière had so often gone at Versailles for encouragement, had died two weeks after her twenty-sixth birthday, crying to her confessor that she had been poisoned. "Oh disastrous night, oh dreadful night," intoned Bossuet in his most touching funeral oration, "in which resounded like a thunder clap the terrible news: Madame is dying, Madame is dead!" The Court mourned for four months (Monsieur married the Princesse Palatine in less than a year) and Louis ordered a new entertainment from Lully and Molière—*Le Bourgeois gentilhomme*. Almost as much music as language, richly costumed and orchestrated, the entertainment cost the King fifty thousand livres. He had asked for a comedy-ballet making sport of an absurd Turkish emissary who had visited Versailles not long before. Molière had obliged, but made it a minor part of a larger satire on the middle class and its aping the manners and ways of the aristocracy. To this effect, Monsieur Jourdain, the bourgeois *gentilhomme,* hires a music master, a dancing master, a fencing master, and a philosophy master—from whom, the world's school children well know, he learns that "he had been speaking prose all his life without knowing it." Molière played Monsieur Jourdain, Lully the Mufti. It was a small role in a ballet sequence, but Lully was as excellent a mimic as a musician and his success was greater than Molière's.

Three months later, Lully was the dominant figure in an entertainment involving not only Molière but also Corneille and Quinault, who wrote most of the verses for a new-style tragic ballet, *Psyché*. It was to be the beginning of French opera, but the beginning of the end for Molière. By now Lully had become Louis' favorite Court

* Louis was to have danced in one of the three plays, *Les Amants magnifiques,* but Racine's cutting lines about applause-seeking rulers in his play *Britannicus* made him renounce it, and the stage, for the rest of his life.

entertainer—a long climb from the kitchen of the Grande Mademoiselle, where he had begun as a scullery boy.

Lully was born Giovanni Battista Lulli in Florence, in 1632. He was the son of a miller, but later no one would dare remind him of it. In his marriage contract, his father would be described as Laurent de Lulli, Florentine *gentilhomme*. Music in Italy offering the quickest road upward, Battista was early taught to sing, dance, and play the guitar and violin. When he was fourteen, the Duc de Guise came upon him playing and dancing during intermission at a theater and brought him back to France for his cousin, the Grande Mademoiselle. Nineteen and then living at the Tuileries, she had asked for an Italian lad to help her with conversational Italian. It seems, however, he helped with the dishes, for he was rediscovered by the Comte de Nogent. Hearing music coming from the kitchen, he had investigated and found the small, dark, lively Lulli playing the violin and entertaining the servants. "You have an Orpheus in your kitchen," the count told Mademoiselle. She sent for Lulli and asked him to play. Beguiled, she paid for his music lessons, which included composition. Somewhat later, one summer evening, while taking the evening air in the garden of the Tuileries, she had noticed a statueless plinth in one corner. Strolling by the same corner the next night with two ladies of the Court, she was surprised to see a new statue of a naked shepherd boy playing a flute. She approached to admire it. The statue leapt to the ground, dropped the flute, and fled through the trees. It was Lulli.[10]

During the Fronde, Italians were so unpopular (because of Mazarin) that Lulli was almost lynched on the streets, but at Mademoiselle's receptions he entertained with his own music, ballets, and violinists. The Fronde defeated, Mademoiselle and her household were banished to the provinces, where they all languished. All but Lulli. Twenty, he promptly left for Paris on a borrowed horse with a violin and fifteen écus. He sought service with the King, found it as a dancer, and one day, visiting a rehearsal, the King found Lulli. He was miming, playing the violin, redirecting the dancers, improvising a ballet number, and in less than an hour Lulli had the fourteen-year-old Louis in the palm of his hand. Dancing was then the young King's delight, and he asked Lulli to dance beside him in the next Court ballet. Skillfully Lulli helped him through his five *entrées* so cleverly that Louis' performance looked flawless, and Louis was very appreciative. *"Jeunesse de prince, source de belles fortunes,"* La Bruyère has written; he who is fortunate enough to be the companion of a king in his youth will make his fortune; and so it was with Lulli. He became the young King's dance and music adviser and, not yet twenty-one, his composer. Resented by the royal group *les vingt-quatre* (twenty-four) *violons,* Lulli, with Louis' authorization, formed his own group of violinists, thereafter called *les petits violons de Lulli,* and it was *they* who went down to Saint-Jean-de-Luz for the King's marriage. Counseled by Colbert, Lulli had nothing to do with Fouquet and the Vaux fête. Shortly afterward, Lulli petitioned Louis for naturalization as a Frenchman and became Jean-Baptiste Lully,* and in 1662, he was named superintendent of music. One by one, Colbert collaborating, he eliminated competitive composers, mostly Italian, from the Court. Lully was now French, but so (it is not irony) was his music. In his hands it became lively and more danceable; he imposed a new rhythm for ballet and new instruments, such as the beautiful, difficult French horn, in the orchestra. (Today nothing brings the Sun King's period dancing to life like Lully's music.) To say he continued to be disliked by French musicians at Court is to say little: everyone disliked him, save the King (which sufficed). He was as homosexual as Monsieur, but more careful. He married in 1662, gave his wife six children in six years, then devoted himself to men and boys. Louis knew it, didn't like it, but Lully was indispensable in the royal *divertissements.* More so than Molière, who was only fifty—*but who was dying.*

After five years of separation, Molière had returned to Armande and a house near the theater. He gave up his milk diet and gave himself to her. Tubercular, exhausted, Molière nonetheless felt—perhaps with Armande's pregnancy—a new spurt of life. Sadly, his old friend, Madeleine Béjart, had died (making Armande her heiress), but his new play, *Les Femmes savantes,* gave him pleasure; it ticked off with great success his favorite targets—the pretentious and the *précieux;* and he was encouraged to meet Lully's challenge. It was the challenge direct. By early 1672, by purchase and blackmail, Lully achieved a monopoly of music not only at Court but in all French theaters. He bought the title to the Paris Opéra from Pierre Perrin, who was then in the Bastille for debts, and literally black-

* Though the street in Paris is spelled Lulli.

mailed Louis into confirming the title and control over all musical performance by threatening to return to Italy if he did not. La Fontaine scarcely exaggerates his description of Lully in *Le Florentin:*

> C'est un paillard, c'est un mâtin
>   Qui tout dévore,
> Happe tout, serre tout; il a triple gosier.
> Donnez-luy, fourrez-luy, le glout demande encore;
> Le Roy même peine à le rassassier.

(He's a lecher, an all-devouring, all-grabbing, all-hoarding mongrel with a triple gullet. Give him anything, stuff him with it, the glutton asks for more; the King himself would have trouble appeasing him.)

And indeed Louis could not refuse Lully, as he confessed to Colbert, because he could not do without him for his entertainment. (Colbert, too, continued to support Lully, publicly declaring, "I would like to see him earn a million livres composing operas, so as to set an example for other musicians." To this a musician named Mollier risked the reply that if there were two such Baptistes in France at the same time, "one would die of hunger.") No vocal work might now be performed without written permission of Sieur de Lully. Moreover, a few days later Lully had Louis forbid any French theater from employing more than six singers and a dozen musicians, a decree that struck directly at Molière's company. Molière responded with a revival of *Le Mariage forcé,* replacing Lully's score by one of Charpentier. Lully countered by having the King issue yet another decree: that he had exclusive control not only of his own airs but of all words for which he had ever written music. Molière defied the decree that winter by performing *Psyché* with the original number of singers, dancers, and instrumentalists and with Lully's own score. But it was an inconclusive clash. Molière's heart was no longer in it. The child born to him in September had been buried in October.* His cough racked him mercilessly.

On February 17, 1673, deadly sick, Molière insisted on going on as usual in his latest play, *Le Malade imaginaire.* Armande and his young protégé, Baron, begged him to remain home this one time. "What would you want me to do?" he replied. "There are fifty poor workmen who have only their day's wages to live on. What will they

* One child, a daughter, survived him.

do if there is no play? I would reproach myself for having failed to give them even one day's bread, if I possibly could."[11]

Rising from his bed, he went to the theater and prepared for the four-o'clock curtain. He had the title role: he was the imaginary invalid. He went on stage. Shaken throughout with convulsive coughs, he converted them—to the audience's delight—into his customary comical hiccups and managed to finish before he collapsed. He was carried home and cared for by two nuns. He asked for a parish priest, but none would come. Night fell, he coughed more violently, burst a blood vessel, choked on the blood, and died. The abbé who finally arrived came too late.

Since there had been no last rites, no dying renunciation of his actor's profession, the Archbishop of Paris refused him a church burial. Armande, as we have noted, went to the King, who promised nothing but sent word to the archbishop, who yielded. There would be no church ceremony and burial would have to be after sunset, so that it would be little remarked, but it would be religious and in church ground. A great crowd, however, followed Molière's coffin to the cemetery.

Three days later Molière's troupe performed *Le Misanthrope,* a week later *Le Malade imaginaire,* which Louis had them perform at the Versailles fête of the following year. In the meantime, Lully had taken the Palais Royal theater for his own; Armande and La Grange had to move the troupe elsewhere. But in 1680 Louis XIV united the companies of Molière and the Hôtel de Bourgogne, creating the Comédie Française. In 1687 Lully, beating time during a rehearsal with his cane, struck his little toe and died of gangrene.* Ten years earlier Racine had renounced the theater, becoming, with Boileau, the royal historiographer at Versailles.

"Who," the aging Sun King asked Boileau, "would you consider the finest of the great writers honoring France during my reign?"

"Molière, Your Majesty," came the reply.

"I would not have thought so," Louis said reflectively, "but you know more about such things than I."

The story is told by Racine's son.[12]

---

* In 1693, Louis XIV, who would outlast them all, watched twenty-five-year-old François Couperin triumph in a competition at the organ in the Royal Chapel, to become his court organist.

8. The Builder and the Decorator

Returning to Jules Hardouin-Mansart, after the tragic-noncomic interlude of Molière, is to return to another fairy tale, an eighteenth-century account by Abbé Lambert.

Strolling in the *allée royale* at Versailles (it relates), his hand decorously on Mansart's shoulder, Louis XIV told his architect to put on his hat against the sun. Observing ("nothing escaped him") the startled resentment of his courtiers, uncovered, as custom required, in the presence of the King, "he turned to them and said, '*Messieurs*, this is a man I must preserve. I can make twenty dukes and peers in a quarter of an hour, but not in centuries a Mansart.' "[1]

Two of Jules Hardouin-Mansart's grandchildren, also architects, grandly gave themselves eight centuries of architectural antecedents, going back to a mythical Michaëlo Mansarto in the tenth century. Grandly and unnecessarily. Jules Hardouin's granduncle, François Mansart, whom their own generation considered "the god of architecture,"[2] sufficed.

François Mansart and Jules Hardouin-Mansart—even the French confuse them, uncertain as to which created what. Historically, however, the confusion suggests what actually happened: the joint creation of French classicism (the finest French style since another that had gone around the Western world: Gothic). Characterized by balance, harmony, and rhythm, measure, restraint elegance, and scale, it meant the domestication of Italian Renaissance, the taming of Italian Baroque. Thus the appropriation of eight centuries of architectural ancestors by the Mansart descendants was not wholly inappropriate. Behind François Mansart, born in Paris in 1598, were centuries of schooled French architects, artisans, and builders. French masons were the best in Europe, their stonework unequaled (in Italy materials took second place to theatrical effect). From father to son to cousin, in a pony express of tradition, they passed on their skills.

François' father was Absalon Mansart, carpenter to the king, his uncle was Jehan, the sculptor. He spent his first orphaned years under his brother-in-law, an architect, then served his apprenticeship under Salomon de Brosse, the architect of the Luxembourg Palace. His own beginnings were baroque, but his passage from mannerism to classicism was early marked by the great wing he designed for Gaston d'Orléans, Louis XIII's brother, in the château at Blois. The elevations are almost modern-flat, the forms massive, solid, and satisfying. The roof line is unprecedentedly continuous, but not yet mansard.* The old and new wings are a still-intriguing marriage of the Late Flamboyant Gothic of Francis I, which was a kind of French Renaissance, with the cool classicism of François Mansart, who, of course, wanted to redo the entire château.

At Maisons, Mansart stands strongly alone. In René de Longueil he had found his ideal client (and was never to find him again): an enormously wealthy *grand bourgeois* who permitted, or at least did not prevent, the execution of a complete plan. The result is a cubist masterpiece of massed, balanced forms.

In Paris, Mansart added two wings and galleries to Mazarin's palace (now, in part, the Bibliothèque Nationale) and was presumably recommended by the Cardinal to the Queen Mother for the Val-de-Grâce Church. A perfectionist, Mansart had become in his last years even more perfectionist, presenting, as we have noted, no less than *fifteen* possible plans for the Louvre's eastern façade in 1665, refusing to choose among them. *La Mansarade,* a hostile contemporary pamphlet, scores him again and again for his costly habit of changing his mind in mid-construction, wittily advising potential clients to "prepare two purses: one to pay the builders, the other to pay the demolitioners."

* The mansard roof was not invented by François, but he was to bring it to perfection, cutting off the useless Gothic top and providing more usable inner space with an ingenious scheme of two differently sloping roofs, one of which becomes a wall.

In 1666, François Mansart died. The man who was to work with Colbert and the King to *their* perfection was now twenty, and he had spent most of his last formative years with his granduncle.

Jules Hardouin was born, not yet Mansart, of Raphaël Hardouin, painter to the king, and Marie Gautier, daughter of François Mansart's older sister. He may have studied painting with his father, but the scanty record indicates only drawing lessons from an artist named Poërson.[3] Art, in any case, as for Le Nôtre, was the primary, indispensable discipline. At fifteen, Jules Hardouin entered the office formed some years before by François Mansart and Jacques I Gabriel.* Here Jules Hardouin began by cutting stone and became a master mason. Lacking work, his granduncle sent him on to Libéral Bruant, then busy with plans for the Hôtel des Invalides in Paris. At nineteen, Jules married Anne Bodin, daughter of an affluent notary, and *her* sister was to marry an architect—a very fine one—Robert de Cotte. At twenty, Jules fell heir to the unmarried Mansart's office on the condition that he add the Mansart name to his own and wear his granduncle's livery.

Jules Hardouin-Mansart, says the Duc de Saint-Simon, who saw much of him at Court in the late years, "was a tall, well-built, comely man, who came from the lowliest people, but who had a great deal of natural wit, which he used to ingratiate himself with his betters, though he never purged himself of the vulgarity of his origins."

Since the little duke so disliked him, because of the King's favoring—and eventually ennobling—one so "low-born," we can assume the comeliness and quick wit. When, however, he suggests that Jules Hardouin was François Mansart's bastard claiming to be his nephew, "in order to become known more quickly" he adds the calumny often disfiguring his vivid portraits. "Step by step he climbed," Saint-Simon continues, "until he caught the King's eye."

Abbé Lambert's eighteenth-century account places that encounter at the Hôtel Vendôme (not, as written, Place Vendôme). Young Mansart was cutting stone for another Bruant building (thus he must have been under twenty, though the abbé talks loosely of twenty-two)

---

* The Mansarts and the Gabriels between them account for the two dominant centuries of French architecture. Jules' first cousin on the Mansart side married Jacques IV Gabriel. Their grandson, Jacques-Ange Gabriel, was to design the Petit Trianon, the Versailles Opéra, the Place de la Concorde, returning aesthetically to François Mansart, whom he greatly admired, thus closing a circle of French architecture.

when chance brought the King on a visit. Attracted by his dexterity and fine figure, the King stopped, "discovered he was the nephew of the celebrated François Mansart," and spoke to him kindly. "At the same time, His Majesty asked for a drawing of the section that was being built. Young Mansart, seeing that the architect the King addressed was not responding quickly enough, drew a sketch with a pencil, then quickly erased it for fear of arousing the envy of his companions and perhaps the jealousy of the architect under whom he was working. This adroitness and diplomacy did not escape the penetrating eye of Louis XIV and predisposed him in young Mansart's favor."

The truth is fairy tale enough. Probably due to the office he had inherited, though at this point it strangely fades from the story, Mansart (we might as well drop the Hardouin) had worked with Le Nôtre at Chantilly and with his younger brother on a Paris *hôtel,* or mansion, when the Duc de Créquy had turned to him for his grand *hôtel* in Versailles. An instant success, at twenty-five Mansart was not simply launched, but had already arrived. Le Vau dead, in two years Mansart was doing some work at the Versailles palace. In three he was redoing a Henry IV hunting lodge at Saint-Germain. In four he was replacing Le Pautre as the architect for reigning mistress Montespan's Clagny Château.

Demolished a century later, Clagny was not finished before Madame de Montespan fell out of favor, but even as it rose, it was regarded as nothing less than sensational, and Mansart's own rise no less. For thirty years he was at the Sun King's side, a position and period with few parallels in architectural history. Never has there been such a burst of royal building with one architect in effective command. And if, in his passion for building—but, far more importantly, for war—Louis XIV was to drain the French treasury, he was, one can put it quite unsentimentally, to endow France with some of its greatest treasures.

Unsentimentally and unblindly.

During July 1668—the same month as the Montespan fête—Olivier d'Ormesson noted in his *Journal:* "Two important incidents have just taken place. A woman who had lost her son when he fell [from a scaffold] while working at Versailles, but who was taxed by a court of justice, beside herself with grief, presented a blank petition to call attention to her case. When, laughingly, the officials asked her what she was claiming, she began hurling insults at the King, calling him a whoremonger, a tyrant and a thousand other stupidities and extravagances, astonishing the King, who demanded if she was referring to him. She replied 'yes' and continued her vituperations. She was seized and condemned on the spot to be whipped. . . . Many found fault with the severe punishment and said she should have been treated as mad and put in the Petites Maisons and thus public indignation would not have been so provoked.

"A few days later, a man of sixty, who expressed similar feelings of outrage, was accused of having said that the King was a tyrant and that there were still Ravaillacs and men of courage and virtue. This man . . . was condemned to have his tongue cut out and to be sent to the galleys. . . . Even blasphemers have only their tongues pierced."[4]

On October 12, 1678—the year work began in earnest on the Mansart wings—the Marquise de Sévigné wrote to her cousin Bussy-Rabutin, a former *frondeur* and no friend of Louis: "The King wishes to go on Saturday to Versailles, but it seems God wills otherwise, because of the impossibility of having the buildings in condition to receive him, and because of the enormous mortality among the workmen, of whom every night, as if from the Hôtel-Dieu [Hospital], wagonloads of the dead are carried away. These sad processions are hidden from the other workmen so as not to alarm them."

It might, in fairness, be noted that Versailles suffered a slight epidemic in 1678; that Madame de Sévigné was still writing indignantly about Fouquet's imprisonment and Ormesson was still affected by the injustices of Fouquet's trial; that in 1672 one hundred livres had been given to a widow whose son had fallen to his death from a scaffold; that as work progressed at Versailles a system of compensation had been devised: forty livres for a broken arm or rib, sixty for the loss of an eye, forty to one hundred to a widow for the loss of a husband (the sum varying, it seems, according to the number of dependents).[5]

There were no security measures (there would be few for workers until our own time). The influx was so great Versailles was suddenly crowded with workmen and, later, their families, packed into shabby inns and wooden barracks, specially erected in the great square in front of the palace. The aspect was that of a bustling frontier town on the edge of a gold field. There were more deaths from fever than from accidents, which averaged about one hundred a year.[6]

As for the prickly, never satisfactorily answered question: what was the cost of Versailles—buildings (including the Trianons), gardens, and land—over the half century of its different constructions? The estimates vary, from less than eighty million to more than one hundred million livres, and vary even more when it comes to the equivalent in today's currencies: from two hundred million dollars to five hundred million dollars.[7] No more than the price of an old-fashioned airplane carrier, says Philippe Erlanger. The cost of one year of the Algerian War, comments Pierre Verlet. The cost of four or five days of the war in Vietnam, an American might add. And, indeed, Louis' wars were costing France vastly more than his building. In 1683, thirty-eight million livres were spent for war out of a total expenditure of one hundred nine millions, and only six millions—less than half of it for Versailles—for the King's residences. There were several years, such as 1685, when Versailles represented more, but from 1664 to 1715 it averaged perhaps 5 per cent of the royal budget. Emotionally, however, in the next century, "Versailles" was to mean not so much the palace, the park, and the Trianons, but the courtly excesses and extravagances, the hidden world of the masters, the heavy purses to their mistresses.*

But we have not yet reached that point. In the meantime Mansart was incessantly to perfect Versailles—in the peak year of 1685, over thirty-six thousand men and six thousand horses were at work—and the sound of hammering, day and often night, was not to cease in his lifetime.

Boldly, barely thirty, Mansart had taken over the incredible constructions at Versailles in its final, Madame de Maintenon phase. He turned Le Vau's envelope around Louis XIII's hunting lodge into a stately governmental palace. He extended its wings north and south for almost half a mile. He converted its terrace into a great Hall of Mirrors.† He unified the façade, harmonized the structure, so that the palace and all its parts became architecture and not a collection of historical footnotes. He added the Grand Commun, so Versailles might house up to ten thousand, for on May 6, 1682, the King

* Finally, the estimated *value* of Versailles today? This question was put to André Malraux, then minister of culture, by the present writer. His answer was: "Priceless." He may not have been thinking of the tourist revenue of millions of yearly visitors (though in the final accounting of profits and costs for France of Versailles, one legitimately must).
† Called more commonly the Grande Galerie by the Court than the Galerie des Glaces.

formally moved Court, government, and all his ministries to Versailles. From then until the Revolution, still four generations away, it was to be the center of France, when France was the center of Europe.

Versailles was "a dove with the wings of an eagle" to Peter the Great. A modern visitor might think of Mansart's palace as the first horizontal skyscraper, with the most disciplined of Mies van der Rohe's in mind. For it did become an international style, little Versailles springing up everywhere from Peterhof to Potsdam. Mansart was undoubtedly the most influential architect since the Renaissance down to our own century, when Mies and Le Corbusier set new patterns for the world's building. And if these references seem shockingly contemporary, when but a few pages before we were in the serene presence of the Sun King, one can only reply that Mansart's Versailles provokes them. Le Vau's disappeared by dilution and all that is left of Le Roy's is the thickness of the walls. Mansart's is magnificently here and now.

At Versailles, too, Mansart created the frequently, and badly, imitated Grand Trianon, a retirement palace for the twilight years of Louis XIV. Its play of peristyle against sky, rose marble against greenery, volume against volume seems to resolve once and for all the iron alternative of "romanticism vs. classicism." But if the beauty of the Trianon needs little comment, the grandeur of Mansart's Orangerie, which replaced Le Vau's, has long escaped general notice.*

Facing south under Le Nôtre's terrace, thus protected from the north, the Orangerie is sheltered as well on the east and west by two great flights of stone stairs called the Hundred Steps, over which Rilke has rhapsodized:

> Even so this flight of steps ascends in lonely
> pomp between pillars bowing eternally;
> slowly and by the Grace of God and only
> to Heaven and nowhere intermediately.[8]

Within is the equivalent of a Roman temple for the thousands of tubbed palms and orange trees that winter there. For theirs is a noble, vaulted space so vast the *Mercure Galant* commented, in 1686, when it was completed, "it would be possible to perform operas in it,

---

* Requiring a special pass, except on rare occasions, relatively few visit this purest of Versailles' architecture.

and in several parts of the building at once without the performers inconveniencing each other. It was this," it continued, "that made the Siamese ambassador [on a famous visit] say the magnificence of the King must indeed be great, seeing that he had raised so superb a palace for his orange trees."

And there are Mansart's stables, once sheltering 2500 horses and 200 carriages. Their curved stone walls form a sweeping baroque space with that of the palace courtyard. And the Royal Chapel, to which we will return—best viewed from the upper, royal pew, for which it was designed.

Mansart's Clagny is gone. Mansart's Marly is gone. But Versailles is still there—the most colossal architectural organization of a court, society, and civilization one could imagine, only one king could have dared, and perhaps one architect have conceived.

But even the completion of Versailles was not the whole of Mansart's activities. There is his Paris masterpiece, if not the masterpiece of Paris: the Invalides dome. It may be the most perfect expression of domical architecture. (Not domed. At the Invalides, the dome *is* the church; it is not an addition to it.) Derived from a never-executed plan of François Mansart, its elegance, *mesure,* and delicate scale make it the quintessence of the French spirit in architecture.* Here, God speaks French: religion is rational, human reason elevated to an art form, divinity a kind of French aristocracy. And—again we race ahead—it is rather fitting that the last work of Mansart at Versailles (finished by his brother-in-law and successor, Robert de Cotte) was the Royal Chapel in the north wing. White and radiant, its vaulted ceiling by Antoine Coypel, almost alone in the palace, it recalls the Sun King in a still-felt splendor.

In Paris, too, is Mansart's Place Vendôme, a great square enclosed by a colonnaded façade, behind which individuals bought plots and built as they wished—so long as what they built remained invisible from the square and left the façade unchanged. The result is a classical mask accommodating everything from the Hôtel Ritz to the Ministry of Justice and the IBM offices.

Lyons, Dijon, Arles, Tours, and Marseilles similarly asked Mansart for public squares, city halls, arches of triumph, bridges (there is one

---

* As contrasted with Christopher Wren's dome for St. Paul's Cathedral, or Michelangelo's for St. Peter's. Each has its own virtue: structural vigor in the first, drama in the second. Neither can be mistaken for Mansart's.

in Paris). Meanwhile his architectural practice, for courtiers as for the King, continued: at Chantilly for the Prince de Condé, at Dampierre for the Duc de Luynes, at Saint-Cloud for Louis' brother, at Rouen for Colbert's son.

How did he manage? (It has bothered modern critics as much as his own contemporaries.) Quite simply, according to Saint-Simon: "Mansart did not know his business, and de Cotte, his brother-in-law, whom he made his head architect, didn't know it any better. They took all their plans, drawings, and inspirations from a designer named L'Assurance [Pierre Cailleteau], whom they kept as much as possible under lock and key."

Cailleteau, was about eighteen when he worked in the Mansart office the year Mansart, twenty-eight, designed the Clagny Château. Moreover, his career thereafter was generally undistinguished. The accusation nonetheless goes on with one name or another substituted for Mansart's. Anyone who had ever been associated with him has been mentioned, for almost everyone in French architecture at that time and for years afterward had been with him: d'Aviler, d'Orbay, Le Pautre, Gittard, Boffrand, the Gabriels, de Cotte, Cailleteau. The Mansart office, in fact, was the seedbed for a century of French architecture.

But the question—how did Jules Hardouin-Mansart manage?—has not been answered by any substitution, however plausible. The answer is to be found in the organization he created, and none of his detractors deny him *that* genius. Mansart's was probably the first modern architectural practice—with all that is implied of corporative efficiency —before planes, trains, telephones, dictating and duplicating machines. It was, moreover, a family organization with tight family loyalties.

Robert de Cotte, brother-in-law, was made administrative head, specially responsible for the royal plans, estimates, and execution. Jacques Gabriel, cousin, assisted him. Desjardins, nephew by marriage, was in charge of waterworks and surveying. Two secretaries (possibly not relatives) followed Mansart everywhere, jotting down his comments on separate slips of paper as he visited his projects, consulted his clients, or traveled the fifteen carriage miles between Paris and Versailles, and they would deliver them, usually the same day, to de Cotte for distribution. Mansart's own sketches were generally rough and passed on to a draftsman, such as Cailleteau, for finishing (wherefore Saint-Simon's accusations). The Mansart office, by now, was in a state building at Versailles, the staff state-supported, and Mansart immensely rich. As an architect, he could not be his own contractor or entrepreneur, but his cousins could be, and were.

Superintendent of royal buildings, the first professional holding that supreme office, Mansart made order out of the previous chaos, and 60,886 livres from his first year in office (1699). He had ready entree to the King. Even at war, Louis would ask for details by courier and pencil remarks or corrections on the drawings. Daily Mansart checked the royal *Registre des ordres*. A chimney smoked? Mansart promised instant attention, later adds that it has been taken care of. He was responsible for the repair, upkeep, and improvement of every royal building in France. He kept dossiers on everything and audited them closely.

He solved most problems by correspondence. For projects of higher importance, he sent his assistants: de Cotte to Lyons, Boffrand to Lunéville, Le Maistre to Moulins. Asked by Madame de Maintenon for additions to her school at Saint-Cyr, he went himself. As he had worked with painter-decorator Le Brun on the interiors of Versailles, so he worked with engineer Vauban on the aqueducts for the Eure, with another on the Pont Royal for Paris. Carefully and diplomatically, he consulted fellow architects at the Royal Academy on structural problems and costs.

But Mansart's was the final responsibility. Why not, then, the achievement? He created his organization and dictated its operation. He chose his subordinates—none of whom did better on their own— and oversaw their work. He decided the final plans, and there is no conclusive evidence that he did not initiate them. He saw to their prompt and near-perfect execution. He solved the enormous problems posed by a Sun King and gave him the architectural setting for a *gloire et grandeur* which still endure.

Before going on to the decorator of that great stage set, one last note on Mansart's end:

He was rich, ennobled, landed, an intimate collaborator of the King. Nothing stood between him and further riches, honors, and activity, when suddenly on May 11, 1708, a month after his sixty-second birthday, Mansart was dead. Fagon, the King's surgeon, summoned to help as he lay seized with stomach cramps, declared "quite gaily," Saint-Simon tells us, that there was no remedy, that Mansart "had died of a dinner of ices and peas and other new vegetables from the King's gardens, having royally feasted on them before even the King." The body was puffed, poison was suspected, fingers pointed at a group of tax farmers whom Mansart was about to denounce to the King. That may have been the case, says Saint-Simon coolly, or it might have been a severe attack following the King's refusal to grant Mansart more money for building. But the little duke has the decency to add that nothing was found among Mansart's papers—sealed by the King on his death—"to tarnish his memory." Indeed, the Invalides dome, the Place Vendôme, the Grand Trianon, and above all Versailles are still with us to testify to its brilliance.

THE DECORATOR

As Mansart, Charles Le Brun was a remarkable administrator, and that is what Colbert, who had a state to run, sought for the King in the arts, as in government and the economy. All activities, he believed, must be efficiently organized for the effective service of France, thus the establishment of state factories and royal academies, each with a strict hierarchy and an accepted dogma. The pyramid of Louis' own power—and glory—depended on their smooth, heresy-free functioning. From Bossuet, who found in the system a divine order, to the parish priest, from the greatest duke, who may once have been a *frondeur,* to the lowliest peasant, few seem to have questioned it—and, unquestioned, it worked.

As Mansart, Le Brun had to satisfy the demands of a Sun King, meeting them not only with patience but dispatch. Too many, almost too much, for one man, it meant the talent of directing the talented, organizing not one but multiple schools of executants, the capacity of being able oneself to do everything one wanted done. Le Brun's range was phenomenal. At Versailles, as at Vaux—Colbert and the King noted—he was the supreme *décorateur,* in the full theatrical sense of décor. He designed keyholes and furniture, the moldings of a mirror, the details of a staircase, the paneled sweep of stately rooms complete with his murals, tapestries, furnishings, and paintings. The many sculptures in the Versailles gardens, signed Girardon, Desjardins, Tuby, Coysevox, were done from Le Brun's drawings. The Gobelins tapestries for which he elaborated cartoons with exact colors would cover more than two acres if laid out together.

Art historians, impatient to get to Watteau, brush by Le Brun, the painter, pausing only to consider the aesthetic dictator of the Versailles decades. What, then, of the Versailles décor? The greatest artist of his time—Henri Focillon, when he first said it, was only half jesting—was Louis XIV. In that sense, Le Brun was his instrument and executant. Or, as Anthony Blunt has expressed it, Le Brun "produced no single work one is tempted to study, linger over, analyse*—but in creating an ensemble such as the decoration of Versailles he was a master."[9]

Le Brun was a little master shortly after birth, the son of a modest sculptor, in February 1619. He drew praise for his sketches before he could even write. When he died in February 1690 he was "Monsieur Le Brun, equerry, Sieur de Thionville, First Painter to the King, Director of Royal Manufactures of the Furnishings of the Crown at Gobelins, Director, Chancellor and Rector of the Royal Academy of Painting and Sculpture."[10]

Preparing to direct sculptors, he sculpted in wood at nine. At thirteen he was studying with Vouet; as his assistant, he impressed the future chancellor of France, Séguier, with his astonishing precocity. Not yet nineteen, already specializing in allegorical painting, with a predilection for Hercules and Olympian heroes, he did murals for Richelieu and became painter to the king. Twenty-three, he was taken by Poussin to Rome, where, supported by Séguier, he studied— or rather adapted—Raphael, Caravaggio, Romano and Cortona in the development of his own ornamental style. In 1646 he returned to France; in 1648 he was one of the twelve founding members of the Royal Academy.

Alertly following Le Brun's work in the Hôtel Lambert in Paris, Fouquet hired him as decorator and co-ordinator at Vaux. Interrupting his activities at Vaux, Le Brun went on command to Fontainebleau to paint frescoes from the story of Alexander for the King. Daily Louis would watch him at work. Once he asked Le Brun to paint in a figure, which Le Brun did on the spot—and Louis saw a man who could do what he wanted as quickly as he wanted it. Similarly, for the entry of the King and the Queen into Paris in 1660 (a recurring event in the story of the writers and artists of this period), Le Brun had decorated the Place Dauphine with a grandiose architectural

---

* Compare, for instance, the superb portraits of Richelieu and the Port Royal nuns by Philippe de Champaigne, Le Brun's contemporary.

Arc de Triomphe, crowned by a giant obelisk, which had carried away the honors of the occasion. In 1661, Le Brun did the décor for the new Galerie d'Apollon at the Louvre; in 1662, following the Vaux fête, he was ennobled and given an allowance of twelve thousand livres a year by the King, or exactly what he had been receiving from Fouquet; in 1663, he was made director of royal manufactures at Gobelins, to which Colbert had removed Fouquet's tapestry works at Maincy, entire with workmen.

Here—as at the Royal Academy—Le Brun was to exercise his "dictatorship" over French art and artisanry for the next two decades. He supervised the teaching of art students and the training of apprentices. He directed and designed for not only tapestry weavers but scores of other craftsmen (250 in all): painters and sculptors, goldsmiths, silversmiths, and cabinetmakers, ironworkers, woodworkers, marble workers and mosaicists. From the Gobelins factory came the silver basins, inlaid tables, wall decorations, endless furniture, and *objets d'art* to the display rooms of Versailles. So Louis himself conceived the public rooms of his palace, reached by the spectacular Ambassadors' Staircase. So Mansart and Le Brun designed and decorated the *grands appartements*. Here in the showcase of Versailles the Sun King and Colbert were quite literally selling the Sun King and France to the Continent—their grandeur, glory, and manufactures. Once this is realized, the key role of Le Brun becomes clearer, his importance to Colbert and the King firmly grasped.

From this view, too, the great Hall of Mirrors, 240 feet in length and thirty-four in width, with its forty-three-foot-high ceiling paintings vaunting the King of France and his conquests, can best be understood if not appreciated. The overarching propaganda of France, in the person of an Apollonian Louis XIV, supreme in war and peace, wisdom and commerce, is literally underlined by legends written by Racine and Boileau: "The King commands a simultaneous attack on four Dutch fortresses, 1672" (one of his greatest mistakes), "The Franche-Comté conquered for the second time, 1674" (a more lasting conquest). Some, mercifully, are dusty and unreadable, and Le Brun's ceiling, fortunately, also has been blurred by time and forgotten allegory into almost abstract pools of color.

But beyond historical apology and memory (here a German empire would be proclaimed, the Treaty of Versailles signed) is the superb harmony of Mansart's architecture and Le Brun's decoration.

Seventeen tall, arcaded windows are mirrored the great length of the Galerie des Glaces in seventeen tall arcades of Venetian glass* framed between marble pilasters. Golden capitals carry the eye to the colorful vaulted ceiling; sculpted cornices, festoons of gilded metal punctuate the marbled walls. Missing are the fourteen crystal and silver chandeliers that hung from the ceiling, "so heavy, though well-suspended, that the strongest and most robust of men had to use all their strength and weight to raise or lower them."[11] Missing are the curtains of white damask that covered the windows, the great expanse of Savonnerie carpets that covered the parquet floor. Missing are the furnishings of a scarcely imaginable luxury and splendor: silver tables, large and small; silver benches, chairs, and stools; silver braziers, candelabra and girandoles; silver figures and statues; silver tubs for the orange trees that stood along the marble walls; silver cups, clocks, vases, and bowls. All of delicately chased silver, "all done at the Gobelins," reported the *Mercure Galant* in December 1682, "and executed according to the designs of M. Le Brun," and all melted down a year before his death in 1690, to help pay for the wars celebrated in his paintings in the Galerie des Glaces.

But even in 1682, when the *Mercure Galant* was singing his praises, Le Brun was falling out of favor, his influence declining with Colbert's. The first of the King's ministers, though he never had that title, could no longer defend the King's treasury against the King and the war minister's encouragement of his foreign adventures. The critical shift will be discussed later, but the death of Colbert in 1683 and his succession by War Minister Louvois were to prove mortal for Le Brun. Pierre Mignard was Louvois' choice for directing the Gobelins works (and the Royal Academy), and although Le Brun retained his positions, he lost his power. As Louis looked on neutrally, he who had been so active fell into a fatal inactivity.

Pathetically Le Brun wrote to the Maréchal de Créquy, asking him to intercede with Louvois, ending his letter, "I am used to favorable treatment. It is what gives life and sustenance to men of genius, and if I could just render myself agreeable to Mgr. de Louvois by faith-

---

* The glass of Saint-Gobain was apparently not yet good enough, though many of its workers had been recruited (bribed, said the Venetian Republic) by Colbert's agents from the island of Murano to give the new French industry Venetian quality. Venice had branded the workers traitors, sending its own agents and spies to persuade them to return, poisoning an unknown number of those who refused.

fully executing one of his commands, the happiness of it would give me new strength, and I would regard it as the fulfillment of my most ardent desires and the summit of the highest glory to which I could hope to aspire . . . You will be better able than I to explain this and add to it what you think best."

Instead, Créquy handed the letter itself to Louvois, who reproached Le Brun, when he met him at Versailles, for writing it, and also for his absences from Gobelins. Le Brun no longer had the heart—or the health—to go there. In his last years, he turned to religious paintings, offering them to the King (who accepted them) and to Louvois (who refused them). Not long before, Louis had said to the Dauphine, "After the death of Monsieur Le Brun, his paintings will be greatly valued." Observing that Le Brun had overheard his remarks, he had said to him, "But don't let yourself die for that. I value them highly already."

Sick, Le Brun was taken to the Gobelins—the workrooms were empty, the machines idle; only the war was still going on—and died.

9. The Poisoned Years

There was a long moment in Louis' reign when the "natural" boundary of France was considered sufficiently north to include, by manifest destiny, the multiple, prosperous mouth of the Rhine River.* Rather, had Louis succeeded in reaching it, it would now be called the natural French frontier. But on the road to it—as on the trade routes to the Indies, East and West—was the stumbling block of the Protestant, thus irreverent, and irrepressible Dutch. Why not incorporate them in a greater France? Even Colbert, at odds with Louvois, was initially seduced by the idea.

"If the King were to subjugate the United Provinces of the Low Countries," he wrote his monarch in a famous memorandum, July 8, 1672, "their commerce would become the commerce of his Majesty's subjects, and nothing more could be desired." In an even more famous phrase of La Fontaine, Colbert was selling the bear's skin before the bear had been bagged, though the bear, at this time, was on the run.

Earlier on the glory road to the North Sea, Louis XIV had seized part of the Spanish Netherlands (today's Belgium) as counterpart for Marie-Thérèse's unpaid dowry. He had humbled Spain but alarmed Europe, particularly the Dutch. Together with England and Sweden

---

* And its recital will take Louis XIV and the reader on a rapid, occasionally bloody, gallop through a few pages of compressed history.

E*

they formed the Triple Alliance, which "mediated" the compromise Treaty of Aix-la-Chapelle in 1668, obliging Louis to return the Franche-Comté to Spain but allowing him his conquests in Flanders. For this, too, the Dutch were unforgiven and to be taught a lesson, once separated diplomatically from their allies. (Louis was a superb diplomatic tactician with illusions of military genius nourished by his generals.*)

The German states were equally disturbed by Louis' ambitions, and a diversionary proposal was outlined for Paris by Leibnitz, a young philosopher then counselor at Mainz: the French should direct their destiny as the leading Christian, therefore civilizing, power not in Europe, where it was less needed, but in North Africa and the Near East, even to the extent of digging a Suez Canal. But Louis would not be diverted. From the time of the peace treaty, he and Louvois prepared for war. Tirelessly, ruthlessly Le Tellier's son, Louvois, secretary of war since 1666, when he was only twenty-five, fashioned the first of modern armies from the feudal one he had found. Not yet a citizen army (that would have to await the Revolution), the French Army became a well-drilled, disciplined force of about 120,000 men, the largest in Europe since the Roman Empire. The Dutch, intimidated, offered "any satisfaction His Majesty might reasonably consider his due."[1] But Louis disdained to reply or even to declare war. He simply posted his intentions on April 6, 1672, and proceeded with invasion. The English, now on his side, thanks to a subsidy to Charles II, had opened more formal hostilities on the sea in March.

Posing for history—Paul Pellisson, Fouquet's former secretary, was his official historian†; Van der Meulen, his official painter—Louis joined his troops at Rocroi, announced he would lead a simultaneous attack, "in person," on four strongly fortified places on the Rhine— and then took them as announced. On June 12 he crossed the Rhine— on a bridge of boats. The crossing, if not the boats, has since become a legend, and it seems to have taken William of Orange, defending Amsterdam, by surprise. Indeed, the Grand Condé, after Utrecht too was taken, urged the King to press on immediately to Amsterdam and

---

* For an almost convincing counterview, see John B. Wolf's scholarly *Louis XIV*, New York, Norton, 1968.

† Racine and Boileau were appointed in 1677, one year before the war's end. The truth, Racine was to discover, was easier to write about than to find. Boileau, unable to justify the Dutch invasion, lost interest in writing the war's history.

a conclusive victory. But Louvois and the King preferred laying classical sieges to other fortified towns. Desperately buying time, the Dutch
opened the dikes at Muiden. In five days the land was flooded and
Amsterdam was an island in the Zuider Zee. For many Frenchmen,
Louis' hesitancy was his greatest mistake; for modern historians, such
as Pierre Goubert,[2] the war was that. Voltaire, who loved Amsterdam
and admired Louis XIV, thought it would have been a tragedy had
the French King followed Condé's advice and taken Amsterdam. "That
storehouse and market of Europe, where two hundred thousand men
cultivate commerce and the arts, would soon have become a vast
marshland." France, he wrote, would have been unable, or unwilling,
to maintain the cost of the dikes, "and the neighboring lands would
at last have been submerged, leaving to Louis XIV nothing but the
lamentable glory of having destroyed the most beautiful and remarkable monument ever raised by human industry."[3]

Briefly the Dutch rivals—Jan de Witt and a subordinate William of
Orange—worked together in the time so dearly bought. Louis, who still
held Holland's principal strong points, was offered enormous concessions for the sake of peace. Wanting more, he spurned them. Furious,
the Dutch revolted, butchered the brothers de Witt as symbols of
appeasement, called on William of Orange, twenty-two, to lead them.
Hubris had created Nemesis. In William, Louis had forged a lifelong
enemy, a man temperamentally "his exact opposite," plodding, stubborn and phlegmatic, "knowing neither the pleasures of greatness nor
those of ordinary humanity" (Voltaire). More dikes were opened
against the French, but Louis returned to Versailles; what was left
to be captured, in his words, was "not worthy of his presence."

William counterattacked and reached as far as Charleroi, captured
by France in 1668. Condé, who had been wounded at the Rhine
crossing, was back in action but pessimistic. (Philosophically he sent
for Spinoza to chat with him in Utrecht, then was kept from his own
rendezvous by the war.) In 1673 Louis returned to Flanders with the
Court, the Queen, La Vallière, and a pregnant Montespan. (Louvois
to his intendant at Dunkirk: "Lodge Mme de Montespan in the bedroom marked L, and have a second door made connecting it to the
King's apartments. Madame la Duchesse de La Vallière will lodge in the
bedroom marked V, where the same will be done."[4])

Louis participated, in cinematic fashion, in the siege of Maastricht,
actually masterminded by a military engineer of genius, Sébastien de

Vauban. That, too, entered French legend and painting. Other acts entered Dutch schoolbooks and memories. Entire villages were razed on Louvois' orders, their populations with them. Men bought their lives with money, when they could, but as early as 1673, Intendant Robert wrote his war minister regretfully that he "could no longer extract money, no matter how many exemplary executions he ordered, there was so much poverty." In the burning of Swammerdam, Louvois coldly reported, "not a single Hollander was allowed to leave his house." France, defeated, adds Lavisse, would have been similarly devastated. The armies it faced were composed of equally barbarous mercenaries,* but no other nation at that time, the French historian objectively remarks, could have applied so systematic a scorched earth—and people—policy as the France of Louvois and Louis XIV.

In self-defense, Europe again formed a coalition against France: Spain joined the Empire, Denmark, Lorraine, and several German states on the side of the Low Countries. One of Louis' demands on the Dutch—equality of worship for Catholics (an equality he was shortly to deprive the Huguenots)—particularly disturbed the English, who feared their country's becoming papist again under the Catholic Duke of York, next in line to the throne. They signed a separate peace with Holland; Cologne and Münster followed. Louis turned eastward, took Franche-Comté from Spain for the second time, returned to Versailles for the last of the great fêtes, and began to talk peace. But less than ever were William of Orange and the Allies willing to accept Louis' terms. Moreover, the Dutch florin was paradoxically flourishing—Dutch trade was *increasing* on the high seas— while the louis d'or and the livre were disappearing or in flight to the banks of Amsterdam.

Twelve years of French growth reached their apogee in 1672. Taxes went up to pay for the war, but, industry and farming down, revenue declined; the treasury was in deficit and Colbert back to the time of Fouquet. He was spending money borrowed against future tax receipts. Two years before the Dutch invasion he had written the King, "Your Majesty thinks ten times as much about war as about his finances." But he had been complicit in *this* war and was probably reminded of it. In 1675, Louis wrote Colbert, "You know I have

---

* The French forces included two infantry regiments of Irish, one each of Scots, Germans, and Spanish, 3000 Southern Italians, 2000 Swiss, 1200 Genoans, three regiments furnished by Savoy. Part of their payment was the right of pillage—and the blinking at rape.

great confidence in your succeeding in difficult matters. That is why I believe you will somehow find the funds needed." Later he was to play Vauban against Colbert, complaining about the cost of building at Versailles, saying that Vauban's fortresses cost less. He uses soldiers, Colbert would reply. Louvois, the King commented, gets things done more quickly. To this Colbert had only a grieved silence to offer.

The response in the countryside was more violent. The war, dragging on, lost its popularity. There were uprisings in Brittany and Bordeaux. Turenne, Louis' finest commander, had been killed on the battlefield, leaving the tiring Condé to carry on. That winter the troops were quartered in the rebellious provinces and after hanging several thousand of his subjects, Louis moved his troops back to the front. Three more years the war dragged on, but not yet to French defeat. The French army was still the best in the field and Louis, still the shrewdest diplomatic maneuverer, drove diplomatic wedges between the Allies. Indeed, by 1678 and the Treaty of Nijmegen, he emerged, for all appearances, as the master of Europe. He kept Franche-Comté and added half of Flanders to his kingdom. Not since Charlemagne had France, or its ruler, looked grander, and Louis, the treaty signed, reached for more: Strasbourg and ten other cities of Alsace. Further, he had Algiers shelled into submission by the new French mortar-carrying boats and repeated it at Genoa three years later for the republic's lese majesty of building galleys for the King of Spain. The Doge of Genoa had to come in person to Versailles to beg Louis' pardon.

AT HOME

It was 1685.* On the surface, Louis was at his height. In fact, like the French economy, he was in a long, slow decline that had begun in 1672 with the Dutch invasion and the poisonous years that immediately followed . . . *if they did not literally precede.*

---

* In three years La Bruyère would publish his classical, unforgettable description of the French peasant (in *Les Caractères*): "One sees certain wild animals, male and female, spread across the countryside—black, livid, and all scorched by the sun—lashed to the earth they dig and turn with such indomitable stubbornness. They have a kind of articulate voice, and when they rise to their feet, they show a human face. They are, in fact, men. And at night they slink back to their holes, to their black bread, water and roots."

"From 1667," according to a report by La Reynie, Louis' remarkable police chief of Paris, "Madame de Montespan had been in the hands of La Voisin."⁵ And La Voisin, or Catherine Monvoisin, was to be burned alive in 1680 for witchcraft involving abortions, child slaughter, Black Masses, and poison.

L'affaire des poisons, an affair of horrors, was the most scandalous of the century, but it may have begun innocently enough for Athénaïs (born Françoise; she changed it to the more precious form) de Montespan. Few were prouder or came from an older family—the Mortemarts. Yet she had gone to the middle-aged, middle-class, monstrous, though matronly looking, Monvoisin in the house near Saint-Denis for help in winning the King's affections: rather, to be as blunt as the period, for powder to stir his desires. She was not alone. "Most of the ladies of Paris," Primi Visconti tells us, "seem to have visited La Voisin. . . . The Duchesse de Foix had asked the means of enlarging her breasts, Mme de Vassé her hips; many wanted the secret of making men love them, some the place of Mme de Montespan [in the King's bed]."⁶

But La Montespan had not yet reached that royal spot when she initially went to La Voisin for the means to get there. She had been at Court for some time; two children and four years of marriage had made her impatient. Then La Voisin's potions—powdered moles, dried blood, various obscenities—seemed to work: the King took her as his mistress during the first Flanders campaign and celebrated it a year later in the Versailles fête of 1668. However, La Vallière was still the official favorite and shared the official favors. It was then that Montespan may have graduated from love philters to Black Masses. In La Voisin's employ were two renegade priests, Mariette and Lesage, who were to testify under torture that early in 1668 they had sprinkled holy water, recited the Gospel of the Kings over Madame de Montespan's body, burned incense while she chanted an incantation for the Dauphin's friendship, the Queen's sterility, the King's love, and La Vallière's "disappearance."

But we are a decade ahead, anticipating La Reynie's police work and an older Louis' disenchantment. In the meantime, the thirty-year-old King was enjoying two mistresses; though the one was fading, the other was in full bloom (the aphrodisiacs she was stealthily feeding him did not yet produce the headaches that later bothered him). But the double adultery required a mask, however transparent. The

Marquis de Montespan was very much alive and of another mind; so was the Church. The mask, too, was doubled. Louis paid the flimsiest possible homage to virtue by passing through Louise's bedroom on his way to La Montespan's. The hurt to one who still loved him was another matter, somewhat like the "regrettable" sacrifice of the Dutch who stood on the way to what should have been manifest as his destiny.

The other mask seems to have been worn with more gaiety as the Comte de Lauzun, on Louis' "request," pretended to court a yielding Montespan. It was a year or more before his affair with La Grande Mademoiselle and its price in the Pignerol prison. Lauzun was still one of Louis' favorite pranksters, though already pushing his luck. Promised the post of grand master of the artillery, he had talked prematurely about it and Louvois had intervened to prevent it. What followed is so incredible that Saint-Simon, who recounts the story, could scarcely himself credit it. Lauzun, he says, "went off in search of Madame de Montespan to ask her to help him. She promised him miracles and kept him content that way for several days. He tired of the shilly-shallying . . . and decided on a course of action that would be unbelievable if it had not been attested to by everyone then at Court." In effect, Lauzun seduced Montespan's first *femme de chambre* and, knowing the King's habits, had her hide him under Montespan's bed shortly before the King was due. (Saint-Simon: "Throughout all his love affairs, the King never failed to end the night by sleeping with the Queen, though it was sometimes very late. To be more at ease, therefore, he joined his mistresses in bed after dinner.") Here, under the bed, Lauzun heard Louis' criticisms of him and Montespan's additions to them. A cough would have betrayed him, but "Lauzun was luckier than he was wise and he was not discovered." The King and his mistress shortly rose from bed, each to prepare for a ballet performance, "at which the King and Queen and the entire Court would attend." In cold rage, the Comte de Lauzun went directly from under the bed to the door of Montespan's dressing room and waited for her to emerge. When she did, he asked "in honeyed and respectful tones" if she had put in a good word for him. Yes, she said. "He then approached her ear, called her a liar, a piece of baggage, a jade and a dog's whore, and repeated word for word the entire conversation between her and the King." Montespan was so thunderstruck she could barely make her way to the ballet and fainted when she reached her seat. "Alarmed, the King went to her and had trouble restoring her to consciousness." That evening she told him what Lauzun had said, "convinced the Devil himself had informed him." (She herself was then bargaining away her soul to the same gentleman from the lower depths.)

Meeting the King a few days later at the *grande entrée,* Lauzun persisted in asking him to keep his promise. Louis replied that Lauzun had broken his pledge of secrecy, releasing him from his promise. The Count turned his back on the King, drew and broke his sword, swearing he would never serve a monarch who had broken his word. "The King," says Saint-Simon with unusual praise, "beside himself with anger, made perhaps the finest gesture of his life: he turned away, opened the window, threw his cane out of it, said he would have been sorry to strike a man of quality, and walked on.

"The next morning . . . Lauzun was taken to the Bastille."

But it was for a brief sojourn, and he was shortly back at Court, still a source of amusement and service to the King. One service was to follow Louise de La Vallière on one of her flights and try to persuade her to return. (It finally took Colbert.) Another involved him with her two successors. (Once, when all three were together—La Vallière, Montespan, and Madame Scarron—a Court wit referred to them as "the past, present and future.")

Early in the morning of April 1, 1670, muffled in a concealing cloak, Lauzun had carried the newborn child of Louis XIV and the Marquise de Montespan to a waiting carriage, Madame Scarron hidden inside. It was the future Duc du Maine, wrapped in a napkin—such was the haste to get him away before the marquis might claim the child as his own. The carriage drove off in the darkness to one of several secret nurseries in the suburbs of Paris. The year before a little girl, the first of Montespan's seven with the King, had been similarly spirited away. (Four were to live full lives; only one of the Queen's six, the Grand Dauphin, was to live beyond infancy.)

From nursery to nursery, Madame Scarron would go at night. Only nurses were allowed inside and she had to do all the work, "the nurses," as she has written, "refusing to put their hands to anything for fear of tiring themselves and spoiling their milk."[7] But in 1673 the children were legitimized and brought together in a single house under Madame Scarron; a year later they lived openly at Court. By then there were four. The first had died, cared for, worried over, and grieved by Madame Scarron, more mother than the children's own.

Once again Louis' mistress had presented him with her successor. During her earliest pregnancy, it was Madame de Montespan who had suggested her old acquaintance, the widow Scarron, as the governess for the children. It was Louis who had objected. He thought her too devout at this period in his life, the sort of woman who wore somber clothes when the Court was in color. She seemed a *femme savante,* if not a *précieuse,* a woman of reputed wit, when Madame de Montespan may already have been offering him as much wit as he cared for. She was called beautiful, but no contemporary portrait is convincing and Louis' hesitancy rather confirms our doubts.* Moreover, at the last minute, when he had finally agreed, the widow Scarron had offered objections and had gone to her confessor for advice. If the King asked her, he said, thus acknowledging the children, she should accept.

Madame Scarron, the future Madame de Maintenon, was born—three years before Louis, and in prison—Françoise d'Aubigné. Her father, then a prisoner for an unknown reason, had married the prison governor's daughter. Baptized a Catholic, Françoise was raised by a great aunt as a Calvinist until the age of ten, when her father reunited the family and took it to Martinique. There he died and the family returned to France, Françoise to her great aunt and Calvinism. Indignant, her mother's Catholic family petitioned Anne of Austria herself for control of Françoise's religious education—against Françoise's own very Protestant feelings. But at the age of fifteen, sent to a convent in Paris, she was reconverted to Catholicism. In Paris, too, she met Paul Scarron—burst into tears and married him.

Nothing Françoise had been told about the famous forty-one-year-old writer—his picaresque and satiric *Roman comique* was just appearing—had prepared her for the sight of him, and no wonder. "Reader," Scarron has described himself, "I am going to tell you as nearly as possible what I am like. My figure was well-made, though small. My malady has shortened it by a good foot. My head is rather large for my body. My face is rather full, but my body is that of a skeleton. My sight is fairly good, but my eyes protrude, and one

* The writer must confess that virtually all the "celebrated beauties" of the time, from La Vallière to Madame de Maintenon, seem betrayed by their portraits. Either the style of portraiture or our taste in beauty has so changed that it seems preferable to imagine Louis' mistresses as portrayed by the more literary memoirists. Mademoiselle de Scudéry, for instance—perhaps significantly —spoke mostly of Madame Scarron's eyes: "They were the most beautiful in the world, black, brilliant, sweet, passionate and full of spirit."

of them is lower than the other. . . . My legs and thighs formed at first an obtuse, then a right, and finally an acute, angle; my thighs and body form another; and with my head bent down on my stomach I resemble not badly the letter Z. My arms have shrunk as well as my legs, and my fingers as well as my arms. In brief, I am a condensation of human misery."[8]

Syphilis? Rheumatoid arthritis? Probably both. Like Racine, Scarron had spent his nights as a young dog with ladies of the evening, but with less good fortune—and it ran out when he was thirty. But it is a tribute to his unaffected mind and spirit that the famous—Scudéry, Sévigné, Ninon de Lenclos, the Duc de Gramont—came to his table and even paid for their dinners when his debts, despite Anne of Austria's allowance, made him demand it of them. The tribute is to them as well, another indication of the pre-eminence of a witty tongue, which alone moved freely in Scarron's paralyzed body, in French society.

The paralyzed body could only have appealed to the sense of duty in a devout, convent-trained sixteen-year-old. Scarron, realizing it, paternally offered Françoise money for her board and room at the convent (thus relieving her of the necessity of taking the veil) or, if she preferred, as a dowry for a husband. She refused it and he offered marriage. She accepted, served him as a nurse, secretary, and hostess but never, as he had warned her from the first instance, as a wife. And when he died in 1660, the widow Scarron was a worldly if virginal twenty-five, dependent on the Queen Mother's pension and on friends, to whom she made herself useful—as, in 1669, to Madame de Montespan, the King's mistress.

Devotion—she was to spell *devoir* with a capital D in her letters—was now to the King's bastards, particularly the sickly, brightly precocious, permanently lame Duc du Maine, his preferred child. (The lumpish Dauphin knew of his father's preference, kept out of his father's way, and was to go, indefatigably, hunting.) In 1674, disguised as the Marquise de Surgères traveling with her invalid child, she took the infant duke to an Antwerp doctor for a cure. More quack than physician, he failed, and "mother and child" were soon back at Versailles. In gratitude for her devotion, Louis gave her the money to buy the Maintenon estate and Madame Scarron became Madame, soon Marquise, de Maintenon. When, a year later, undisguised, she and the little duke went down for the waters of Barèges, in the

Pyrenees, they were greeted everywhere (she wrote) "as if we were the King himself . . . infinite crowds shouting Vive le Roi."*

Unexpectedly early, they returned to Versailles, and the King, "when he saw M. le Duc du Maine enter his room, led by the hand by Madame de Maintenon, was transported by joy" (Madame de Sévigné). It was a joy slowly transferring from the mother to the governess of his son, but meanwhile he was experiencing other transports. It was the period of his most Bourbon behavior involving the Dutch war and other, domestic conquests. La Montespan ever pregnant, Louis fathered a child with her maid, Mademoiselle des Oeillets, in the antechamber. He fathered another with the Princesse de Soubise. Intermittently there was Athénaïs' sister, Madame de Thianges. Madame de Ludres followed, until La Montespan "wittily" cut her down with the remark to Louis that the scurf covering her body was the result of poison given to her when she was a young girl. (Louis did not seem to have asked how she knew such things.) Then Marie-Angélique de Fontanges, "beautiful as an angel and stupid as a basket,"[9] succeeded her, until, having given birth to a stillborn child, she fell ill, was bundled off to the Port Royal convent, and died.

From poison?

La Montespan had become unforgivably fat—"I had a glimpse of one of her legs," notes Primi Visconti, "and it was as broad as my body"—and she had begun wearing the strong perfume of stout, aging women, which Louis sharply told her made him ill. The perfume, like the powders, may have come from La Voisin's "beauty parlor," and Louis was receiving La Reynie's reports (judiciously sent via Louvois). Montespan, already under suspicion, would shortly be in purdah.

It was Colbert who had discovered Gabriel-Nicolas de La Reynie in 1667 and appointed him first lieutenant of police for the City of Paris—a particularly distinguished choice. But it was Louvois, in opposition to Colbert, who wanted to press the hideous *affaire des poisons*. In 1679, taking it out of the hands of Parlement, the King

* When moralizing (anachronistically?) about the Sun King's conduct, it is well to recall this hailing of the illegitimate son of his most notorious mistress by the French people as if he were as noble a prince as the Dauphin; also, the occasion in 1667 when the King, Queen, Montespan, and La Vallière had traveled in the same coach to Flanders and the crowds happily cheered "the three Queens" of France.

created a special commission, the Chambre Ardente,* to conduct an investigation of it.

Scarcely a court in Europe was without the stench of poison, but at Versailles it had reached the proportions of a popular scandal. When Henriette of England, the first wife of Monsieur, had suddenly died in 1670 in her mid-twenties, poison was so generally suspected Louis took immediate measures to disprove it. Promptly Foreign Minister Lionne informed the French ambassador in London of them: "The King and Monsieur ordered that her body be opened in the presence of our most famous doctors, and that the English ambassador should attend and bring anyone he might wish. Said ambassador brought an English physician and a surgeon of the King of England, and the dissection was done in the presence of these gentlemen and of more than a hundred other persons who were in the room. As each part was examined—stomach, liver, heart, lungs, spleen, intestines, etc.—its condition was recorded." The subsequent report of no poisoning was signed by the experts present, Lionne emphasized, "notably the two English physicians."[10] The Duke of Savoy's representative also reported "no formal signs of poison,"[11] but for Saint-Simon, over twenty years later, there was no doubt: Monsieur's mignon, the Chevalier de Lorraine, had arranged Madame's death. (Henriette, it is thought today, died from acute peritonitis.)

A clear case of poisoning, however, brought the Marquise de Brinvilliers to the headman's ax in 1676. She had procured *her* poison from an apothecary to the King, who had also served Fouquet, and had coolly tested it on her servants and hospital patients, to whom she brought "charitable" baskets of food. Assured by the results, she proceeded to poison her father and two brothers and was working on her husband when she was apprehended. With the marquis, however, she was experiencing ambivalent results: as she administered poison, her lover and accomplice gave him a counterpoison. "The lover," Madame de Sévigné explains, "didn't want to marry a woman as evil as himself." Subjected to torture by water—forced drinking of up to eight quarts—the marquise confessed. From the battlefield, Louis

* So called, according to the *Mercure Galant* of April 1679, because formerly "high-born criminals had been judged in a room . . . lit only by flaming torches." Thus the double play on the word *ardente* (flaming), indicating an incendiary affair with special treatment for the accused.

let it be known that he expected her judges "to do what good men should do." Her trial and execution were social events. Every window was full as her tumbril passed on the way to the scaffold. She was beheaded, her body burned, its ashes scattered to the winds, "so that we shall all inhale her, and by breathing her little spirits, become subject to a poisoning mood, which will surprise us all" (Madame de Sévigné). And in the same letter, such was the mixed mood of the period, the writer goes directly from the execution of the well-known Marquise de Brinvilliers to a few words about the siege of Maastricht.

The "little spirits" were indeed in the air and La Reynie had long since gotten a whiff of them. Priests had confided to him (from the King to the lowliest *clochard,* he inspired that kind of trust) that a frightening number of women were telling them in the confessional box of their use of poison. "Human life," La Reynie was to note,* "is virtually on sale. Poison is almost the only remedy for family problems." For some women it was the only available form of divorce, and arsenic, used for killing rats, was the "king of poisons." They would sometimes impregnate their husband's shirts with it; though it didn't kill them, the rash that developed would be diagnosed as syphilis by their doctors, gaining sympathy for the wives of such debauched husbands—the sole touch of "humor" in the entire story.

In the winter of 1677, Louis Vanens, an alchemist, was arrested with his band of poison traffickers and linked to La Voisin. The following year a Madame Vigoureux and a widow Bosse, fortune-teller and "cosmetician," were picked up, and they too led to La Voisin, whose turn finally came in 1679. Recognizing the dimensions the *affaire* was taking, La Reynie went to Louvois who went to the King. Louis assembled the Chambre Ardente, by-passing the Paris Parlement, in order to minimize publicity and hasten judgments. Members of Parlement, he decided, would be too slow to condemn their own kind—the highborn and the moneyed, who were the customers of the poison vendors. Swiftly the Chambre went into action: the vials and powders found in the Bosse house were analyzed. They contained arsenic, nitric acid, nail cuttings, powered Spanish fly, menstrual blood—poisons and supposed aphrodisiacs. Six days later

---

* On the death of La Reynie in 1709, Louis had his reports and documents dealing with the *affaire* burned, but La Reynie's personal police notes somehow escaped and are preserved at the Bibliothèque Nationale in Paris. Significant extracts appear in Mongrédien's *Madame de Montespan* (see Note 5).

La Voisin was interrogated. Lesage* joined her and the others at Vincennes. Confronted, each criminal denounced the other.

It looked as if the ugly *affaire* would be quickly wrapped up, as Louis wished. But increasingly noble names were now being mentioned, the grandest *dames* of the Court implicated: the Vicomtesse de Polignac, the Duchesse d'Angoulême, the Comtesse de Gramont, the Duchesse de Vivonne (Madame de Montespan's sister-in-law), the Comtesse de Soissons (Louis' youthful mistress, then Olympe Mancini). "The Vincennes and Bastille prisons," the Venetian ambassador wrote to his Doge, "are overflowing with the guilty, who are principally women of the nobility and the bourgeoisie." Primi Visconti later: "Besides the poisonings, the Chambre Ardente set up at the Arsenal investigated all superstitions and vices; it seemed a State inquisition of consciences. All France trembled, the more so on the sight of even princesses and marshals in flight, or in prison, simply on the basis of suspicion."

Lesage, possibly in desperation, told La Reynie that Madame de Montespan's own maid, Mademoiselle des Oeillets (her child by the King was fairly well known), presumably acting in her mistress's behalf, was one of La Voisin's customers. More, La Voisin herself was said to have taken not only love powders to Madame de Montespan, but a pair of poisoned gloves for Mademoiselle de Fontanges and a poisoned petition to be put into the hands of the King. This brought the *affaire* beyond the gates of Versailles to the very steps of the throne, and Louis XIV, disquieted, ordered further interrogation by La Reynie be kept discreet and reported to him via Louvois alone.

Put to the rack, La Voisin denied knowing either Madame de Montespan or her maid, and she died, burned alive as a witch, without changing her testimony. Her twenty-one-year-old daughter Marguerite, however, talked freely (perhaps imaginatively) to La Reynie about the philters, the poisoned gloves and petition, and her mother's relations with Montespan. For years, she said, whenever things went badly with the King, her mother would be consulted and she would offer or advise a remedy. Perhaps what had shocked the King even more than the story of the poisoned petition (he received La Reynie's reports to Louvois within the hour at Versailles) was Marguerite Monvoisin's description of a Black Mass in her mother's bedroom, conducted by one Abbé Guibourg over Madame de Montespan's

* The renegade priest in La Voisin's employ.

"naked body, stretched out on the mattress, her head hanging back on a pillow on an upturned chair, her legs dangling, a napkin on her belly, a cross on her stomach, and a chalice on the napkin."[12]

La Reynie, who took down this deposition, found *la fille* Voisin's testimony occasionally contradictory, but disturbingly similar in detail to Lesage's. (There could, of course, have been collusion; the prisoners often had access to each other and it may have become obvious that the deeper the King's mistress was implicated the less likely they would be brought to public trial. And such was to be the case.)

Lesage, too, had mentioned Guibourg, and not least in this odious affair is the likelihood that a proud Mortemart, companion of the King and mother of his children, had dealings with so ugly a scoundrel, the one-eyed, seventy-year-old Abbé Guibourg, apostate sacristan and vicar,[13] or with any of the repugnant band. Imprisoned with the rest, repeatedly tortured and questioned, Guibourg confessed to Black Masses for Montespan, the first in 1673, the second in 1675 (to dispose of Madame de Soubise's rivalry), others in the years following, as the King showed favor to other women. He described the Black Mass as held at night, secretly in a chapel whenever possible, otherwise in a suburban house or a Paris cellar. The altar was covered in black and black candles lit the naked woman lying on it, bartering her soul to the devil for the fulfillment of her wish—a child, the death of a husband or rival, the love of a loved one. There she lay as the apostate priest placed a chalice on her stomach and recited the true Mass backwards, desecrating a holy wafer. Sometimes a baby's blood would be dedicated to the devil and poured into the chalice, priest and woman partaking of the wafer and the blood.*

So foul were Guibourg's allegations Louis XIV brought the investigation concerning Madame de Montespan to a close and the Chambre Ardente to an end. Those who had accused her were chained in solitary confinement for life and beaten by the guards if they so much as breathed her name. But they escaped burning at the stake, which would have been their certain punishment had they been brought to trial.

Despite her disgrace in 1680, however, Madame de Montespan remained another decade at Versailles—she was the mother of the Duc du Maine and Louis was a master of appearances—but it is

---

* For La Reynie's fuller police notes, see Appendix I, p. 480.

doubtful that she ever remained alone with the King. She may have been innocent of everything but love philters and dangerous games distantly involving the devil,* but even the possibility of Black Masses and poison was too much. Was Louis finished with Montespan even before? Voltaire seems to think so. "The King," he wrote, "reproached himself for his attachment to a married woman and felt this scruple the more as he loved her less."

And the keeper of the King's conscience was Madame de Maintenon.

* So Mongrédien carefully concludes, quoting La Reynie to the effect that it was impossible to prove the accusations, but "equally impossible to disprove them."

10. A Twilight of Maintenon

It was a prolonged, premature twilight the Sun King was to spend with Madame de Maintenon, for it began not long after his high noon. He was still in his early thirties, she three years older, when they met. Montespan's children brought them together, and it is doubtful that a man of his temperament would not attempt to profit from the proximity, especially of a woman who resisted him. An early Maintenon letter suggests it, though, undated, it leaves the exact year of the essay unknown. "The Master," she wrote her cousin, "comes to see me sometimes at the house on Rue Vaugirard in spite of myself. He returns home without hopes but without feeling rejected. You can imagine that on his return home he finds someone to converse with. As for me, I am quite content knowing the propriety of my own behavior."[1]

Home was Madame de Montespan, with whom Louis still "conversed" but to whom he may have remarked on more than one return from Madame de Maintenon (then Madame Scarron) and her charges, "She knows how to love. It would be a great pleasure to be loved by her."

But there were to be a number of years, and mistresses to match, before it was an accomplished fact. In 1673 Madame de Sévigné noted his restlessness when Madame Scarron was absent; she noted as well Madame de Montespan's growing irritation at her presence. For a moment in 1675 (it was not very long), Louis seemed to resolve his dilemma by sending La Montespan to her home in Clagny as a gesture to the Church that he was renouncing double adultery, and then went off to war. The Queen and Bossuet came to Clagny to pay their respects; so did La Voisin, bringing black and white powders. When the King returned from war, Bossuet met him en route to ensure the renunciation. It was true, the King said, that Madame de Montespan would resume residence in her apartment at Versailles, but their relations would remain Christian and chaste. To prove it, they met in public, in the presence of the older ladies of the Court. They chatted, they withdrew to a window, they were seen to cry; the King led Montespan to the door of her bedroom, bowed to the ladies, and went in with her.

Madame de Maintenon, then in the Pyrenees with the Duc du Maine for its waters, returned to Versailles, to the King's revived delight. The women quarreled, made up, visited each other's château, quarreled again, made up once more; and Louis spent the rest of his thirties in his most public promiscuity, Mesdames and Mesdemoiselles des Oeillets, de Thianges, de Soubise, de Ludres, and de Fontanges tumbling into bed one after the other. But not yet, it would seem, Madame de Maintenon.

These were the difficult years of the Dutch War, of headaches, insomnia, and nightmares, when, according to the journal kept by his doctors, he would cry out in his sleep at night. By now the Grand Dauphin had reached the age of marriage and Louis looked north to Germany for a wife. The Princess of Bavaria had a bulbous nose, red hands, and bad teeth, and Louis probably regretted the royal arrangement when she arrived at Versailles. But the Dauphin took her—not, as Primi Visconti would have it, "as he took his lessons when he was a student . . . in fear," but, such was his taste in women—with pleasure. After two miscarriages, she delivered him a son and her father-in-law an heir, the Duc de Bourgogne. The line seemed assured. Louis XIV had a legitimate grandson; four years past forty, he was at last ready for a single woman in his life.

"I want to remain an enigma for posterity," that woman, Madame de Maintenon, told her secretary as she burned a great pile of letters written to her, many by the King. An enigma she remains, though Saint-Simon, who was her enemy, and La Palatine, who called her "an old witch," "an old bag," and worse, have left *their* legacy of vivid letters and memoirs which have weighed heavily against her. Saint-Simon was sixteen when he came to Versailles in 1691; Madame de Maintenon was then fifty-six. Fifty years later he was to recall her as a kind of "Tartuffe in petticoats" (W. H. Lewis), who manipulated the King as if he were a puppet. Yet he renders her "much wit . . . incomparable grace and an easy manner, measured and respectful . . . gentle, exact and well-phrased language, eloquent and brief." These, for an English historian, were the "lasting charms which men of sense . . . prize most highly in a female companion."* And Macaulay continues:

"A just understanding, an inexhaustible yet never redundant flow of rational, gentle, and sprightly conversation; a temper of which the serenity was never for a moment ruffled; a tact which surpassed the tact of her sex as much as the tact of her sex surpasses the tact of ours: such were the qualities which made the widow of a buffoon first the confidential friend, and then the spouse, of the proudest and most powerful of European kings."[2]

Their conversations lengthened, lasting "from six o'clock to ten" (Madame de Sévigné), and no period of that length at that time of the day with a woman would have failed to include the making of love by Louis—and so it came to Madame de Maintenon (by 1681, according to a careful biographer.)[3]

Guilt, conscience, or prudence—or the wise schooling of the King for husbandry—led Madame de Maintenon to persuade Louis to devote himself as well to the Queen. Poor Marie-Thérèse was so grateful she had her portrait painted as a gift to Madame de Maintenon. She was delighted when the Court joked about the King's attentions, and would laugh, wink, and rub her little hands. And so, gambling, praying, and hurrying to bed, she spent her last days in happiness. But not quite the last, July 30, 1683.

La Palatine: "Our Queen just died of an abscess under her arm. Instead of drawing it out, Fagon, unfortunately her physician, had her bled. That made the abscess burst inwardly. . . . After the bleeding, he gave her a strong dose of emetic and after that, the Queen left for another world. . . . That wicked old devil of a Fagon did

* Voltaire: "When a man is no longer young, he almost always needs the companionship of an easy-tempered woman; the weight of affairs makes such consolation especially necessary."
Louis himself once said to Madame de Maintenon, "A king is called Your Majesty, the Pope Your Holiness, and you, Madame, should be called Your Solidity."

it on purpose, so as to assure the good fortune of the old trollop"—
Madame de Maintenon.

Marie-Thérèse's heart was boxed in silver and placed in a chapel
near Anne of Austria's at the Val-de-Grâce church; her entrails were
embalmed and put into an urn; her body was taken to the Saint-
Denis basilica. And "in four days," wrote La Palatine, "the old
trollop found means to console him"—the King.

A few weeks later, that fall, completely eclipsed by Louvois, Colbert died of stone—and a broken heart. Scolded by the King for
the collapse of "a new apartment being built at Versailles," says
Spanheim, the Prussian ambassador, he had passed on his hurt to the
building contractors—and perhaps to Mansart—"worked himself into
a fever, fallen ill and died shortly afterwards." To be buried in the
secret of night, such was his unpopularity.

And that winter, according to Saint-Simon, Louis XIV married
Madame de Maintenon.

"It is certain and beyond doubt [he writes] that shortly after
the King returned from Fontainebleau in the middle of the winter
following the Queen's death—posterity will hardly believe it, though
it is perfectly true and established—Father de la Chaise, the King's
confessor, said Mass at midnight in one of the King's rooms at
Versailles. Bontemps, governor of Versailles and first *valet de chambre*
for that quarter of the year, and the most trusted of the four, served
the Mass at which the Monarch and La Maintenon were married
in the presence of Harlay, Archbishop of Paris, as diocesan, and
Louvois, who both extracted from the King his solemn word that he
would never declare the marriage."

Unofficial it remained, but the secrecy was dissipated in the whispers
and corridors of the Court, in phrases of Madame de Maintenon's
correspondence, in signs of not so much the King's intimacy as
his royal respect for her. Even beforehand, she wrote excitedly to her
brother, "The reason which prevents my seeing you is so valuable
and wonderful that it should fill you with joy." A week later she
assured her cousin that "the King has no love affairs" and he could
say so with certainty on her word. The Pope sent his blessing to Louis
and holy relics as a present to Madame de Maintenon. And the King,
who had referred to her as the Marquise de Maintenon, now called
her Madame, as he had the Queen.

Perversely, perhaps because she loved her brother-in-law, La Palatine for several years found the marriage "difficult to believe, so long as there is no declaration." If they were really married, she wrote the Duchess of Hanover, "their love would not continue to be so strong, judging by marriages in this country. Unless," she adds, "secrecy adds a spice missing in public marriages." Eventually even she accepted the morganatic marriage as fact, though she couldn't resist remarking in a later letter, "In the next world judgment will be made as to whether she belongs to the King or to the paralyzed Scarron; but when the King discovers the truth about her, there is no question that he will return her to Scarron."

The truth about the widow of the poet Scarron who had become the wife of the King of France involves the gravest question a chronicler of this period can pose: did she, the granddaughter of a Huguenot, play a major role in the Revocation of the Edict of Nantes —that is, in the persecution of the French Huguenot Protestants? Her conversion and reconversion, implying the zealousness of the overconverted, have burdened her with blame for Louis' act. But it is probably unfair. This saddest of stories of Louis' reign did not begin with Madame de Maintenon, but rather with his very early conception of absolute monarchy. The unity of France under one king had brought order at home and success on the battlefield. Why not, at last, one religion and one church at whose head would be the Most Christian King?* Why tolerate any longer a religious state within his state, potential *frondeurs* protected by the Edict of Nantes? One wonders, in retrospect, why its revocation had taken so long, particularly since it had the approval of almost all Frenchmen when it finally occurred. It may even have been Louis XIV's most popular act.

Earlier in his reign, as he recorded in the memoirs intended for the Dauphin, Louis believed in "reducing the Huguenots little by little," granting them what had already been accorded by Henry IV's edict of tolerance, but "obliging them now and then to reconsider" whether it wouldn't be to their advantage "to be like my other subjects." He may even have been sincere, preferring persuasion of one million or so Huguenots—one twentieth of his subjects—to force. (Turenne, his favorite field officer, was then a Huguenot.)

Former Huguenot Paul Pellisson, who helped Louis with his memoirs, proposed a conversion fund for Huguenots, a lump sum for changing religion. It worked to some extent, especially when freedom from taxes,

* Louis XIV: "One king, one faith, one law."

for a limited period, and occasionally a royal pension were added as inducements. Before that, Louis had offered reunion of both religions—under himself—with concessions on certain rites to the Huguenots. It came to naught and later in the '70s, as the Dutch War became unpopular and French unity a problem, Louis, moved as well by Louvois' prodding, became far less patient—and the Protestants suffered accordingly. War meant economic hardship, and the Huguenot, like the Calvinist, was a hard-working competitor; result, popular resentment. There were, too, the inevitable mutterings about a religious minority: its "heresy," by calling down God's wrath, was the cause of France's misfortunes; during the religious wars, wherever triumphant, Huguenots had "massacred" Catholics. Thus when the Crown swung the stick, there was no complaint, except among those stung. What was not specifically sanctioned by the Edict of Nantes was forbidden the heretical Huguenots, so they were barred from working as midwives, jewelers, printers, lawyers, tailors, and the like. Their pastors and teachers were restricted in number; mixed marriages were declared null and void, their offspring bastards.

Meanwhile, with more gentleness and permanence, Madame de Maintenon was pursuing her own conversion policy of persuasion with some effect—among friends and relatives and the peasants on her estate. She dared not, she told the Abbé de Fénelon, try directly to influence the King, for fear of being thought herself secretly Protestant in her feelings. In fact, Louis did have his doubts, but in turn did not interfere. Carrots were offered as well as sticks, bribery accompanied brutality. In Poitou, Intendant Marillac installed his own reign of terror, billeting his dragoons in Huguenot households, preferably among the wealthier. Such *dragonnades* were literally seasons for authorized rape, mayhem, and robbery, and only those Huguenots who renounced their faith might escape them.

It seems that Louis chided Louvois about Marillac's zeal and eventually had him dismissed. But the *dragonnades* continued and were effective: entire towns were converted by the "missionaries in boots." In 1681 Madame de Maintenon could write happily, or carefully, "If God preserves the King, in twenty years there will not be a Huguenot in the Kingdom." She may have been right. By 1685 there was about a quarter of their number left; conversion, emigration, and the galleys, in that order, had reduced them to that fraction;

the end of the century might have seen their own end. But Louis XIV pressed for a final solution with an impatience of Pharaonic consequence. ("The King my grandfather loved you," he once told a Huguenot nobleman, "the King my father feared you, but I neither fear nor love you."[4]) On October 18, 1685, "since the greater and better part of our subjects of the so-called Reformed Religion have embraced Catholicism," Louis signed the Revocation of the ("useless") Edict of Nantes. Protestant churches were to be destroyed, Protestant services to cease, Protestant schools closed down. Children born of Protestants were to be compulsorily baptized as Catholics. Pastors refusing conversion were given two weeks to leave the kingdom; members of their flock who tried to follow them but were caught at the border were sent to the galleys. ("Nothing," Madame de Sévigné said of Louis' Revocation of the Edict of Nantes, "is so beautiful.")

The seventeenth-century galley might be called the first, small, floating concentration camp with death by rowing the design. The long march of the *galériens* to the Mediterranean left a trail of blood, their life aboard the 140-foot galleys was so many "oars": they were no longer men.* Yet, to Louis' astonishment, two hundred thousand Huguenots fled France, preferring to risk the galleys rather than abjure their faith. They bribed guards or fought past them with swords. They took with them "their arts, their manufactures, their wealth"; they industrialized the north of Germany; "they populated a whole quarter of London with French silk-makers."[5] Holland gained hundreds of the finest French officers; William of Orange and the Duke of Savoy formed entire regiments from French refugees. Louis had reinforced his enemies with some of his best people. It was a high price for homogeneity.

There were no overt signs that Louis was aware of it; the façades of Versailles, inside and out, would have hidden them, in any event. If the Sun King's palace and park encompassed one world, it shut out the far greater other—and the forms of etiquette, the façades of Versailles were at least in part for that devised. It is a paradox easily explained that the low point in Louis' reign was reached simultaneously with the high point in its social forms and influences: the greatness of Versailles was in its creation, not in its court life.

* Pursuing them would take us too far from Versailles; the reader is urged to read the chapter of outrage about them in W. H. Lewis' *The Splendid Century*.

Louis XIV was not the first to fix the forms of court, nor his court the first to follow them. In 1585, Henry III signed the edict basically establishing the protocol and ritual of his entourage: who was to be admitted to his presence, how he was to be addressed, dressed, served, and undressed. (In Spain, Philip II's rules for court behavior were far more rigid.) Henry IV rode roughshod over the regulations but did not change them; Louis XIII applied them rigorously—to his courtiers—but left the supervision of them to his mother and to his wife.[6] Louis XIV polished them as if they were a silver mirror, in which the daily life, so often dull, shone like a pageant. In this contrived drama of court routine lies part of the explanation of why French nobles left their great estates for a small room at Versailles. Their influx carried, as well, its own contagion: obviously what was so sought by so many of one's class was eminently worth seeking.

But there was another factor more obvious to even today's Frenchman than to a foreigner of democratic bias: to be close to the King, to speak and be spoken to by him, to take precedence over others in closeness to him, was honor and ecstasy: the King was France incarnate. Madame de Sévigné, a *frondeuse,* felt it and Saint-Simon himself does not escape or even question it.* A day at Court was worth a month's income, to live at Court a lifetime of debts. Fortunes were spent on costumes; to be permitted a *justaucorps* like the King's was a summit of its own kind. So noblemen and their wives mortgaged their estates and hurried to Versailles.† They lived in town while hoping and scheming for an attic room at the palace. Their debts made them all the more beholden to the King for his favors, and so he encouraged their extravagances. His disapproval of an absent courtier is forever congealed in a famous remark: "That is a man I never see." The domestication of dukes and of an entire aristocracy, the centralization of power in the hands of a single sovereign, may never have received so perfected and *accepted* a framework of servility. The

* "Even a man as obsessed with rank as was Saint-Simon," wrote Harold Nicolson in *Kings, Courts and Monarchy,* "must sometimes have asked himself whether, amid war and famine, precedence was in fact so overwhelmingly important." The fact is Saint-Simon never did.

† "They ceased," says Mr. Nicholson in the book cited, "to execute the functions of their class"—that is, as the English country gentleman, bridge the dangerous gap between the country and the Crown. Had they in France as in England, the history of Versailles might have been different.

1. Hunting Lodge of Louis XIII at Versailles

2. ... became the palace of the Sun King, Louis XIV

3. Louis XIII

4. *Early view of fountains and Grand Canal*

5. *Modern view*

6. Louis XIV

7. Le Nôtre

8. *Jules-Hardouin Mansart*

9. Principal façade

10. Madame de Montespan

Marquis de Vardes, banished to his estates by Louis for an infraction, returned to Versailles twenty years later wearing the same clothes as when he had left. "When one is unfortunate enough to be far from your Majesty," he explained, "one is not only miserable but ridiculous."

The minor, lubricating forms of this tight little world were often understandable. For instance, one scratched on a door at Versailles with the little finger of the left hand, grown longer for the purpose: knocking would be too noisy, there were too many doors in the hotel-like palace. The pyramid of precedence had its own pyramid of privileged seating: at the bottom was the three-legged stool, or *tabouret;* above it the simple chair, or *chaise;* and, topping them all, the coveted armchair or *fauteuil.* Once, when one of Louis' lesser mistresses tiredly took an unauthorized seat, a courtier whispered in a loud aside, "Let her sit. She has earned it." In the King's or the Queen's presence, only the Dauphin and his family, the princesses (but not the princes) of the blood might ordinarily sit, and then on a *tabouret.* All others stood—except at the gaming tables, where all who could afford the stakes were allowed to sit with the King or Queen.

At the more informal Marly—where weekend invitations were another form of royal favor and a *pour* (for) added to one's name on the door the epitome of that favor—the rules were somewhat relaxed. But once when the wife of the foreign minister seated herself at the supper table above a duchess, Louis stared at the poor lady throughout the meal and later complained to Madame de Maintenon that the insolence had kept him from eating. The pecking order was especially inviolable; it indicated precedence. As Louis with his usual insight wrote for the Dauphin, "Nothing moves the well-bred so much as distinctions in rank. . . . It is one of the most visible signs of my power that I can give importance to a person who, in himself, has none." He would extend it to the less well born, tipping his hat even to a kitchen maid as she crossed in the courtyard. For ladies, he removed it entirely; for princes and dukes, he held it against his ear.

It was a charade, of course, but for a courtier suddenly to declare it foolishness would be to declare his own—even more than the King's —nakedness. The cult of closer-to-the-King-than-thou—one does not think solely of the black-velveted gentlemen of the chamber pot—was a mutual conspiracy between the King and the courtier. And if life at

F

Court did not wholly satisfy the latter, at least it kept him, as La Bruyère observed, "from being satisfied with anything else." The reason is implied in another lapidary remark of the Grand Condé's household tutor. "Society at Court," he wrote, "is like a house built of marble: it is constituted of very hard and very polished people"[7]—who were bored to death in any other society.

But boredom was to set in later, and one sensed its beginning in this period of the middle-aged Louis XIV and an older Madame de Maintenon. No longer was it the court of a young King and his young mistresses, great fêtes, ballets, gaiety, and Molière comedies. Louis had now begun to censure his court and more closely regulate its morals. The courtiers, conscious of the spies in every corner and corridor and among their servants—the mail itself was opened going and coming, as La Palatine well knew when she wrote things to inform or shock her royal brother-in-law—did not so much change their morals as mask them. Louis' own life was regulated to run like clockwork. A courtier acquainted with it, even on a desert, it was said, could tell what his King was doing at any hour of the day.

He was awakened at eight by the first *valet de chambre;* in the antechamber the courtiers were already assembled. Entered the first physician, the first surgeon, and his old nurse, who regularly kissed him, says Saint-Simon (whose long account is our source), every morning until she died in 1688. The others rubbed him down and usually changed his shirt, "for he was subject to sweating." Ritually at a quarter-past eight the grand chamberlain entered, along with other gentlemen, at which time they were permitted a private word with the King, a privilege they rarely exercised. They withdrew while he recited the *Office du Saint Esprit* and returned when he put on his dressing gown and a short wig. They were joined a few minutes later by lesser nobility for the *grand lever* as Louis slipped into his slippers —"all by himself"—and was helped through his toilet—washing with the spirits of wine. Solemnly they observed him shaved (every other morning) and changed from the short dressing wig (he was balding) into the first formal one of the day (there were wigs for every occasion). The first valet handed a silk shirt, warmed, if in the winter, to the senior nobleman present, and the honored man gravely offered it to the King. Dressed, the King prayed at the side of his bed, then went into his *cabinet,* or study, with his closest collaborators, Mansart often among them. Plans and orders for the day were decided and issued; Louis, followed by the Court which had been waiting for his passage in the Grande Galerie, went to the chapel for Mass—he bowing to the altar, the Court bowing to him—and from there to a Council meeting.

Dinner was at one—plentiful, ceremonious, and normally *au petit couvert*, i.e., restricted to Court attendance. The King sat alone at the table, talking little to those standing around him. (Once he offered his lingering brother a *tabouret* which was placed behind his own armchair.) If *au public,* the public, which had driven out from Paris for the spectacle, would file past Louis' table, the only requirement a decent appearance. Meantime the King's food made its own appearance in a ceremony approaching that of a High Mass. The *maître d'hôtel* would go for it to the kitchens in the Grand Commun, crossing the Rue de la Surintendance to reach the huge building. There he and the equerry of the kitchen tasted each of several dozen dishes and prepared for the most impressive ritual of all: the *cortège de la viande de Sa Majesté,* the procession of His Majesty's meat. From the kitchen, recrossing the Rue de la Surintendance on its long trip through corridors, galleries, and halls to the King's table, came the King's meat. It was preceded by two royal guards, an usher, the *maître d'hôtel* with his baton, the *gentilhomme-servant* of the pantry, the *contrôleur général,* the *contrôleur-clerc* of the pantry. Then came those carrying the King's meat, followed by the equerry of the kitchen, the *garde-vaisselle* and two others of the King's guards. (A courtier encountering the King's meat on the way to the King's table was obliged by a palace regulation to remove his hat and bow to it as to the King himself.)

After dinner, Louis would assemble another Council meeting or, if none were scheduled, toss his dogs a few biscuits and go hunting. "Insensible to cold or heat, or even rain" (Saint-Simon), he hunted stag, went shooting on foot in the park or walked in the gardens every day. He suffered indoor air badly, strong perfumes specially. Those who liked hunting accompanied him; those who didn't he preferred leaving behind, with no disfavor shown them. Returning, Louis worked a few hours in his study, received his bastards, had a word with Le Nôtre, went on to Madame de Maintenon's apartment, where, as he grew older, he would work with one or another minister, as she embroidered or read. In his middle years there was still three evenings a week, from seven to ten, the Versailles entertainment called the *appartement*. It meant a concert more often than a play, followed invariably by cards and billiards. The gambling was heavy; the stakes rose with the boredom (La Palatine found *l'appartement* "unendurable"). La Montespan lost and won 150,000 pistoles in a single evening; Dangeau, playing carefully, made his expenses at Versailles; so did others: when the Queen lived, Princess d'Elboeuf lived from Her Majesty's losses. His Majesty was not amused.

Supper was usually at ten, though sometimes closer to midnight—a spectacle reserved for the Court and the royal family. The spectacle, one suspects, was the King. His appetite was fabulous; he fed it with his fingers (among gentlefolk in Paris forks were already in general use). "I have often seen the King," La Palatine wrote home, "consume four plates of different soups, a whole pheasant, a partridge, a large plate of salad, two big slices of ham, a dish of mutton in garlic sauce, a plateful of pastries followed by fruit and hard-boiled eggs. The King and Monsieur greatly like hard-boiled eggs." Louis' post-mortem revealed a stomach twice normal size. La Palatine, one might add, found supper, at which her presence was expected, as dull as *l'appartement*. (Once, at Marly—never at Versailles—a playful Louis threw little balls of breadcrumbs at the ladies who threw them back.) Supper finished, Louis retired to his bedroom, bowed to the ladies at his door, spent a moment with his several families in a small private room, fed his dogs, and returned to his bedroom, where he prayed and was undressed with the same formality in a *coucher* that was a reverse image of the morning's *lever*. The last lucky courtier held the candle lighting the royal performance.

Louis XIV had begun suffering from bad teeth during the campaign of 1678; treatment, of course, made them worse. In 1685, his upper teeth were extracted, and his palate broken, so that food would sometimes dribble from his nose. Fourteen times in a single day the gaping hole had been cauterized with a hot wire, the operation, his doctors noted, exhausting the cauterizer more than the King (his endurance was indeed remarkable, and was soon to suffer a greater test). The sunken cheeks, the sucked-in upper lip of Benoist's portrait in wax* may have made their first abrupt appearance at this time,

---

* A profile in bas-relief, it was executed in 1706 and now hangs in a room at Versailles. Its faded, blue-gray wig may have been Louis' own, as well as the lace and velvet fragments at the neck and shoulders.

deepened a year later when the aging King underwent the harrowing, unanesthetized operation for an anal fistula.

For months beforehand his first surgeon, Félix, had practiced on patients—in Louvois' *hôtel* at Versailles—before undertaking the operation on Louis. "Some," says Father Hébert, the Versailles curé, "were cured."[8] Most died and were secretly buried. As for Louis' operation, no account can improve on d'Aquin's in the *Journal de la santé du roi:*

"At eight in the morning, M. Félix, in the presence of M. le Marquis de Louvois, myself and M. Fagon, aided by M. de Bessières, introduced a probe at the end of a specially designed bistoury into the entire length of the fistula as far as the bowel, which he reached with a finger on his right hand and, pulling it downward, opened the fistula quite easily, and having then introduced the scissors into the wound of the fundament, he cut the intestine just above the opening and the fibers holding the fistula to the intestine."

Madame de Maintenon, according to the Abbé de Choisy, sat by the bedside and embroidered as the King was scissored. And that day, he says, the King received "even the most minor courtiers" (and the next day the ambassadors—to show he was not dying). "He manifested no impatience during the scissor-cuts, saying only, 'Have you done, Gentlemen? Finish it and do not treat me like a king. I want to recover as if I were a peasant.'"[9]

Michelet in his personalized history of France divides Louis' reign into two major periods—before and after the fistula. One might. Fagon once said of the King, "Every time my client sneezes the fate of France is in doubt." For the conventional historian, William of Orange's forming of the more fateful League of Augsburg in opposition to Louis XIV falls neatly in the same year as the fistula operation (1686) and serves the same function, that is, it provides a turning point. From here on the direction was steadily downward.

In 1685, Louis had claimed the German Palatinate when its Elector had died childless; he had asserted his rights in the name of the Elector's sister, Princess Elizabeth Charlotte (our Liselotte or La Palatine), because she was his brother's wife. When he pressed his tenuous claim two years later with an invasion, the League of Augsburg's members—Spain, Sweden, the Habsburg Empire, and various German principalities—lined up in war against him. They were joined the following year by England, which now had William of Orange as its new King.* It would have taken a miracle to withstand them; France, for nine years, would fight virtually alone against the greatest powers of Europe.

Instead of first eliminating his principal enemy, Holland, Louis had struck at Germany, sending the twenty-seven-year-old Dauphin on ceremonial "command" of French troops. There were initial victories, but the atrocities accompanying them doubled the resistance of France's enemies. As in the Dutch War, Louvois had urged Louis toward a scorched earth policy depriving hostile forces their local supplies. Had Louis reluctantly agreed? According to Languet de Gergy[10] and Saint-Simon, when Louis heard of the order for the burning of Trier, he had gone after Louvois with a pair of fire tongs, and only Madame de Maintenon's intervention prevented him from using them. Nevertheless devastation of the Palatinate proceeded as planned. La Palatine herself, in whose name it was all presumably sanctioned, had pleaded with Louis to spare Heidelberg and Mannheim, at the very least. In vain. They were destroyed. And often, she wrote, she would awake shuddering from nightmares as she dreamed of the places of her youth. "Yet some people here," she adds bitterly, "take it badly that I am so upset!"

Voltaire in retrospect, so favorable in general to Louis XIV in his history of Louis' century, was aroused to one of his most eloquent denunciations:

"In February 1689, an order had gone down to the army from the King signed by Louvois to reduce everything to ashes. Accordingly, in the heart of winter, the French generals, who could but obey, announced to the citizens of all those flourishing and orderly towns, to the inhabitants of the villages and to the masters of more than fifty castles, that they must leave their homes, which were to be destroyed by sword and fire. Men, women, old people and children fled in haste. One group went wandering through the countryside, another sought refuge in neighboring countries, while soldiers . . . burned and sacked

---

* In a revolution called glorious, because relatively unbloody, William of Orange had replaced his father-in-law, James II, on the English throne, which he shared with his wife, Mary II. James II, meanwhile, was allowed to slip away to France to become Louis' guest at Saint-Germain and Versailles. In one brief attempt to reconquer his crown, the exiled Stuart King set off for Ireland in 1690; Louis had seen him off with the witticism, "The best thing I can wish you is never to see you here again." But after the defeat at the Battle of the Boyne, where French Huguenot officers had fought under William, James II was back again as Louis' guest for the rest of his life.

their own. The soldiers began with Mannheim and Heidelberg, seats of the Electors: their palaces were destroyed along with the homes of ordinary citizens; their tombs were opened by the rapacious soldiery, who thought to find treasures in them; their ashes were scattered. . . . The flames with which Turenne had burned two towns and twenty villages were but sparks in comparison with this second conflagration. Europe was struck with horror; the officers who executed the burning were ashamed to be the instruments of such harshness. They put the responsibility on the Marquis de Louvois, who had become more inhuman through the hardening of the heart produced by a lengthy ministry. He had indeed advised this policy, but Louis was sufficiently master not to adopt it. Had the King been a witness of the sight, he himself would have put out the flames. From deep inside his palace at Versailles, in the midst of pleasures, he had signed the destruction of an entire country; he had seen in that order nothing but his own power and the unfortunate prerogative of war; had he been an eye-witness, he could only have seen its horror. Nations which until then had only blamed his ambition now cried out against his harshness and condemned even his policy: for if his enemies were to invade his lands as he had invaded his enemies', they would similarly reduce his cities to ashes."[11]

Louis XIV was called a monster worse than any Turk, a tyrant who would enslave all Europe as he had his own "sighing France."[12] Everywhere cries of vengeance rose, and Louis replied by raising his army to almost half a million men. He sent the silver furniture of the Grande Galerie and the apartments of Versailles—including his own silver throne—to the Mint to help defray the costs. (Thus the first despoiling of Versailles was not the impulsive act of the Revolution, but the deliberate act of its creator.) There were more victories which Louis could less and less afford. When Louvois died in 1691, Louis appointed his son in his place and led in person the capture of Namur, in 1692, recaptured by William in 1694. But greater than that loss was the famine of the same year: there was no collapse, simply a sharper decline, as France was drained of its greatest treasure—its people.

"They are dying of hunger," The Abbé de Fénelon wrote in an anonymous letter intended for the King. "The cultivation of the land is almost abandoned; the towns and the countryside are being depopulated; all crafts and trades are languishing and can no longer support their workmen. All commerce has been crushed. You have consumed half the real strength of your State in order to defend vain conquests abroad. Instead of extracting money from your poor people, you should have succored and nourished them. All France is now a vast poorhouse, desolute and without provision."*13

The long, remarkable letter of François de Salignac de la Mothe Fénelon was probably intercepted on its way to the King by Madame de Maintenon. We know she sent it, or a copy, to Archbishop de Noailles in 1695, preferring, she wrote in an accompanying note, not to "irritate or discourage the King" with "such truths." We shall return to Fénelon, in his role as tutor to the Duc de Bourgogne, eldest of the Dauphin's three sons, but meanwhile we might consider the Dauphin himself. Lumpish, we have called him; lumpish he remained. Louis XIV, when he sent him to "command" in Germany, had cautioned him at the same time "not to endanger himself for the sake of the State, though for his particular glory it would be appropriate to fight." The caution prevailed and he increasingly withdrew not only from battle but from the Court. When his sad Bavarian wife died in 1690, he quietly married an inconspicuous Mademoiselle de Choin—inconspicuous, that is, except for "the largest breasts I ever saw"—La Palatine— "which enchanted the Dauphin, who would play on them as if they were drums"—and quietly they lived in the Dauphin's residence at Meudon. (Lully's two sons-in-law, co-directors of the Opéra, would on occasion supply him with a young girl from the ballet. Once an older, unattractive woman came along as chaperone, whom the Dauphin took, in his haste, into his apartment at Versailles without remarking his mistake.)

More anxious to please the King was Madame de Montespan's eldest son, the Duc du Maine. He too was sent to the front—to learn to command—and frequently wrote home, to Madame de Maintenon, about his "overflowing ambition." He now had his own estates, or rather those once belonging to the Grande Mademoiselle. (She had handed them over to him on the promise that her beloved Lauzun would be released from the Pignerol prison, a promise Louis finally kept.) The lame Duc du Maine acquitted himself fairly well at first: he "had a horse killed under him" at the battle of Fleurus, the *Gazette* reported, and he returned to Versailles in some triumph. He returned late in 1690, when the army went into its winter quarters; and he returned in time for his mother's own retirement from Versailles.

* For a more complete version, see Appendix II, p. 482.

Astonishingly, seven years after Louis' marriage to Madame de Maintenon, La Montespan was still lingering on at Court. (Nothing better points up the vastness of Versailles and its accommodations.) But there was a limit (even to Versailles' accommodations). The incident for Madame de Montespan's inspired departure was Louis' removing their youngest daughter, Mademoiselle de Blois, from her keeping and entrusting the pretty fourteen-year-old to a friend of Madame de Maintenon. Provoked—or provocatively—Montespan requested permission to retire to a Paris convent. To her chagrin, Louis immediately granted it. La Palatine's is a crueler tale. "The Duc du Maine [she writes] persuaded his mother to retire from the Court for awhile, so that the King might be brought to ask her to come back. She loved her son; she thought he meant her well. She went to Paris and wrote the King she would never return. The Duc du Maine forthwith had his mother's baggage sent to Paris without telling her beforehand. As for her furniture, he had it thrown out the windows [they were on the ground floor], so that she could no longer return to Versailles." And he moved into her apartment, as well as the Clagny château, as his sister moved into his.

Four years later, according to Saint-Simon, the Duc du Maine's cowardice on the battlefield* so upset Louis, when he heard of it from a *valet de chambre,* that he startled the Court later by flying into rage and caning a servant at the dinner table for pocketing a biscuit. But the King continued to favor the duke, albeit less blindly, turning now to the Duc de Bourgogne, and soon—in his sunset years— to the little princess who would shortly come up from Italy to marry his grandson.

* Disputed by W. H. Lewis. [14]

11. An Interlude of Love

He who was "all his life a lover," says Saint-Simon, never loved anyone more dearly. Did she recall Marie Mancini or La Vallière, or was it Henriette, her grandmother?

She was Marie Adélaïde of the Italian house of Savoy. She would travel to France at the age of ten to marry the Duc de Bourgogne and bring a separate peace between France and Savoy. (The Peace of Ryswick, finally ending the war, followed a year later.) She was the granddaughter of Louis' brother, Monsieur, and his first wife, the unforgotten Henriette of England.[1]

When the little princess arrived at Versailles, she brought a youth and gaiety to the aging Court and King unknown since the days of her grandmother. When she quit it as Dauphine, "darkness fell over the Court," her friend the Duc de Saint-Simon sadly recorded. Sorrow pierced the heart of the Sun King—"the only real sorrow he had ever known."*

Perhaps it is the very sadness of the ending that gives the story's beginning such poignancy that autumn day of 1696 in Montargis. Marie Adélaïde had been driven to the border town of Pont-de-Beauvoisin, where she stayed in a house on the Savoy side of the river, and then had been taken to the middle of the bridge. There her state coach stood, one half in France, the other in Savoy. She descended and walked to France; a Savoyard page, bursting into tears, handed her train over to a French page.

* Historian Michelet: "We still weep when we read the anguished pages."

While the princess and her new French household traveled toward Fontainebleau, the impatient Louis drove down as far as Montargis to meet her, arriving so early that he was at the door of her coach when it pulled up at six in the morning. He was charmed immediately. He would not, he told his brother, Monsieur, change anything in her, and dispatched a courier in haste to tell Madame de Maintenon of his delight.

"I went to receive her in her coach," Louis wrote as the little princess rested. "She waited for me to speak first, and then replied very well, but with a slight timidity that would have pleased you. I led her to her room through the crowd, allowing people to see her from time to time by illuminating her face by torchlight. This she endured with grace and modesty.

"Finally we reached her room, where there was a crowd and heat enough to kill one. I presented her from time to time to those who approached, and observed her from every vantage point in order to tell you what I thought. She has the most perfect grace and figure I have ever seen, dressed fit to be painted and her hair as well, eyes bright and beautiful, eyelashes black and admirable, complexion as smooth white and red as could be desired, the most beautiful black hair one could hope to see, and in abundance. She is thin, as is proper for her age, mouth very red, lips full, teeth white, long and irregular; hands well formed but the color of her age. She speaks little, at least so far as I have noticed, and is not embarrassed when she is looked at, as one accustomed to society. She curtsies badly, in the Italian manner, and she has something of the Italian in her face. But she pleases me, as well as others, as I could see in their eyes. . . . To speak to you as I always do, I find her exactly to my wish and should be very sorry if she were more beautiful. I repeat, everything pleases me, except her curtsy. I will tell you more after supper, for I shall notice many things that I have not yet been able to see. I forgot to tell you: she is small rather than tall for her age."

Touchingly, the Grand Monarch adds, "Until now I have conducted myself wonderfully. I hope I shall maintain the easy manner I have assumed until we reach Fontainebleau." After supper, Louis ended his letter: "The more I see the princess, the more satisfied I am. We had a conversation in public in which she said nothing, which tells us a great deal. I watched her undress; she has a beautiful figure, one might say perfect, and a modesty that will please you. . . ." And he closed:

"I send you a thousand good ———." (Madame de Maintenon scratched out the word but preserved the letter.)[2]

Ten miles below Fontainebleau, the Duc de Bourgogne, barely fourteen, met his bride to be, not yet eleven; both children were becomingly timid when the King presented them to each other. Scarcely taller, the solemn little duke bent to kiss her hand—twice—and the little princess blushed. Then they all rode to Fontainebleau, arriving at four in the afternoon. The entire Court was assembled on the great horseshoe staircase and a crowd stood below. "A magnificent sight," recalls Saint-Simon, to whom the petite princess, as the King escorted her, "seemed to be coming out of his pocket." Walking slowly along the terrace, introducing his charge to those who had the privilege, Louis led her to the late Queen Mother's apartment. Here in the princess's bedroom the Duchesse du Lude, henceforth her lady-in-waiting, had watchfully installed her own bed, as she was shortly to do at Versailles.

"Call me monsieur, not sire," Louis had told Marie Adélaïde, and ruled that she be called La Princesse, and that the Duc de Bourgogne be allowed to visit her only once every two weeks till the time of their marriage a full year later, and his two brothers only once a month. Soon, however, they were permitted a half hour together every Saturday, chaperoned by the Duchesse du Lude and the Duc de Beauvilliers, who had not long before replaced Fénelon as the Duc de Bourgogne's tutor.

Madame de Maintenon became *ma tante* (aunt) and Marie Adélaïde *ma mignonne* (my pretty) almost immediately at Fontainebleau; completely charmed, the former wrote the princess's mother: "She has a politeness which permits her to say nothing but what is pleasant. Yesterday I tried to stop her caressing me, saying I was too old. 'Oh, not so old as that!' she replied, and snuggled into my lap."

The little princess became even more familiar with the King. They played games together (he taught her how to play pall-mall). They drove together in the park (in a two-seat carriage he had specially made for her, himself handling the reins). She sat on his knee, said *"tu"* to him, tugged at his chin, mussed his wig—and made few enemies at Court. "Everybody," said La Palatine, "has become a child again."

Increasingly, remarks Saint-Simon, whose observations of his neighbors at Versailles had begun but a few years before, His Majesty delighted in the princess's spirit and precocity; he fixed the day of marriage for December 7, 1697, which fell immediately after her twelfth birthday. Though he had taken to dressing rather somberly those days—it was the brown decade—the King let it be known that he wished the Court to be resplendent for the wedding and ordered magnificent coats for himself. The Duc de Bourgogne was to wear a mantle lined with silver and embroidered in gold, his little bride a dress of silver so heavy with rubies and pearls she had to be supported by her first equerry in the wedding procession. "As for Madame de Saint-Simon and myself," says the ducal memorialist wryly, "between us it cost twenty thousand livres, and there were not enough workmen to have so many rich robes ready in time."

The exiled King and Queen of England, ordinarily at Saint-Germain-en-Laye, came for the wedding dinner, the Queen sitting between the two Kings. Afterwards, the ladies went to the *coucher* of the bride (the King sternly ordering all men to withdraw). While the Queen of England presented the nightgown to the new Duchesse de Bourgogne, the Duc de Bourgogne was undressing in the anteroom, attended by the King and the gentlemen of the Court, the English King presenting him *his* nightgown.

When the little duchess was in bed, the little duke was permitted to enter and join her. Then Louis (according to the *Mercure Galant*) called for the Ambassador of Savoy to enter the room so he could report to Turin that he had seen the married couple in bed together. Immediately afterwards, everyone left the nuptial chamber except the duke's father, the Grand Dauphin, and his tutor, who stood on the duke's side of the bed as the duchess's ladies and the Duchesse du Lude stood, dragonlike, on the other. The duke's father chatted for a while, then scandalized the Duchesse du Lude by telling his son to kiss the bride when he rose to depart. It turned out that she was right to object (says Saint-Simon), since the King, hearing of it, thought it indeed objectionable and said he did not want his grandson to kiss even the tip of his wife's little finger until they were really together. Meantime, the little duke dressed again in the anteroom and went to bed in his own bedroom. His twelve-year-old brother, the Duc de Berry, on the other hand, taunted him afterward about it and said that had it been he, *he* would have stayed in the duchess's bed.

In fact, the Duc de Bourgogne did—briefly—rebel at the arrangements. With the aid of a chambermaid, he hid in his little wife's closet and slipped into her bed when the Duchesse du Lude was asleep. But the latter woke and ordered him back to his room, complaining to the King the following morning about his behavior. Louis summoned his grandson. "I have learned, sir," he said, "that certain things have occurred which might be injurious to your health. I pray you see this does not happen again." "Sire," replied the Duke hurriedly, "I am very well." And the matter was not mentioned again.[3]

After the marriage, the King gave a great ball in the Grande Galerie, its mirrors reflecting the orange trees hung with sugar-coated fruit as, outside, fireworks fell from the skies. Fête followed fête, with the duke as Apollo and his young wife variably a muse, the Queen of Hearts, and a Chinese princess. Louis even gave her the menagerie at Versailles with its *fauves* and rare birds, cows, donkeys, and goats. Here Marie Adélaïde made cakes and played dairymaid à la Marie Antoinette of a century later, churning butter for the royal breakfast—and everyone exclaimed on its flavor to please the King.

Astonishingly, the teen-age princess did not lose her head as the flattery and jewels cascaded at her feet. No princess had been better prepared for a foreign court, few teachers had a more apt pupil (except, she would apologize to her grandmother in Savoy, for her handwriting). And where her French mother and grandmother (on her father's side) had left off, Madame de Maintenon happily carried on, sending Marie Adélaïde to her own select school at nearby Saint-Cyr.

Not even the great nobles might place their daughters in Madame de Maintenon's school, so strict were the King's requirements for admission (poverty was one, though ancestry was another).[4] But the rule was broken for the little princess, who entered at the bottom as "Mlle de Lastic," and wore the brown school uniform trimmed with the red ribbon of her class, so that she might acquire, said Madame de Maintenon, "dignity without pride." It was, of course, no disguise at all, since the schoolgirl brought her heavy silver wedding dress to school on her twelfth birthday to show her classmates.

Yet Marie Adélaïde won all hearts at Saint-Cyr as at Versailles; she mixed well and partook in all activities. They were many, and carefully Madame de Maintenon watched over them. Some years before, for instance, she had Racine's *Andromaque* put on by the students instead of the boring plays she had been forced to sit through. However, they performed its love scenes with such conviction that Madame de Maintenon wrote Racine, "Our little girls have just played *Andromaque,* and they acted it so well that they will not act it any more." And she asked Racine if he could not write something with a pious and moral subject, more suitable for young girls—but not dull. Racine hesitated; Boileau told him he thought the idea absurd. Not since the failure of *Phèdre* in 1677 had he written for the theater. He had returned to Jansenism, and his talents now went into notes for a history never to be completed. Moreover, he preferred the high society of Versailles to the "vulgar" stage.* Here, however, was an occasion for a religious play which would be a Court event, and he responded to it. He wrote *Esther* and later *Athalie* (the only two plays in his last twenty years). Since the good Esther was transparently Madame de Maintenon triumphing over Madame de Montespan ("the haughty Vasthi"), Madame de Maintenon was delighted and *Esther* was staged at Saint-Cyr. Louis, too, was delighted. He and the Court attended so frequently—the courtiers more often for the players than the play—that they turned the pretty little heads of the poor little gentlewomen, who promptly became inattentive and insubordinate in class, refusing even to sing Latin chants at Mass for fear of affecting their stage voices. Again Madame de Maintenon intervened, writing her directress to forbid the presence of any man, "even a saint, if there be one on earth." And by the time Marie Adélaïde joined Saint-Cyr, only decorous plays were once more permitted, though she loved acting in theatricals.

The Duc de Bourgogne seemed to shun such frivolities. Headstrong and vile-tempered as a child, he had been gentled by his Quietist tutor, the priestly Fénelon, into a studious, melancholy prince. It was Fénelon, too, who gave him the closest thing to a social conscience the age of Louis XIV could permit. "Each man," he told the boy, "owes infinitely more to the human race, which is the great country, than to the particular country in which he is born."[5] Such teachings, as well

---

* When the King observed Racine walking with the Marquis de Cavoye, he remarked, "I often see those two together and I am certain I understand why: Cavoye likes to think of himself as an intellectual, and Racine fancies himself as a courtier."

as his unsought advice to the King, contributed to his being exiled
to Cambrai as archbishop shortly after the princess appeared on the
scene.*

The duke adored his wife (they were allowed to live together two
years after the wedding) but abhorred the pleasures of the Court.
He disliked losing at cards; she lost often—the King looking on complacently. He disliked dancing; he had a slight limp from a twisted
back which a corset of iron, called his "iron cross," hadn't helped. She
enjoyed dancing enormously. ("She would as soon dance with a
comédien," Madame de Maintenon noticed, "as with a Prince of the
Blood," and carefully she limited the masked balls.) The princess had
more love from him than he from her, though she had been warned
to expect the contrary from a Bourbon.

"M. le Duc de Bourgogne," observed Monsieur's shrewd second
wife, "is so faithful that he cannot even look at another woman." And
La Palatine recounts a tale as revealing of Versailles as of the young
prince who was so out of tune with his times—and, at times, with his
princess:

One evening Marie Adélaïde thought it would be amusing to play a
joke on him, so she prevailed on Madame de La Vrillière to take her
place in bed and then made a great show of being tired. The prince,

---

* But at Cambrai, Fénelon continued his dispute with Bossuet, advocating the
mystical doctrine of Quietism which so affected Madame de Maintenon—the
achieving of unity with God through love and passivity of the soul—until the
Pope himself was invoked by the King to condemn it.

In *Télémaque*, published in 1699 while he was at Cambrai, Fénelon also continued to show his concern for public morality. "The whole race is one family,"
he wrote in this curious novel. "All men are brothers. Say not, O ye Kings, that
war is the path to glory. Whoever puts his own glory before the dictates of humanity is a monster of pride, not a man."

Saint-Simon's portrait brings him strikingly alive. "This prelate," he says of
Fénelon, "was tall and thin, well-proportioned, with a big nose, eyes from
which fire and intelligence poured like a torrent, and a face unlike any I ever
saw and which, once seen, could never be forgotten. It was full of contradictions,
yet they always harmonized. There were gallantry and gravity, earnestness and
gaiety; there were in equal proportions the teacher, the Bishop, and the Grand
Seigneur. His whole personality breathed thought, intelligence, grace, measure,
above all nobility. It was difficult to turn one's eyes away."

Two blots, however, may mar Fénelon's portrait for us: he approved the revocation of the Edict of Nantes and he participated in the persecution of the Jansenists.
He was ahead of his time, as Lord Acton has remarked, in seeing through
the majestic hypocrisy of the Court and foretelling that France was on the
road to ruin. But he was also of his time, and he died, fittingly enough, the
same year as the Sun King.

overjoyed that for once his wife wanted to go to bed early, hurried to undress. He entered their bedroom and cried, "Where are you?"

"Here I am!" came the voice, muffled by the bedcovers.

Quickly the prince took off his dressing gown and slipped into bed. Then he saw the princess approach, fully dressed. "What, sir, is this?" she exclaimed with mock indignation. "You play the saintly husband and here I find you with one of the prettiest women of France!"

Slipperless and half naked, La Vrillière fled as the prince reached for one of his own slippers.

And La Palatine adds a note so typical of Versailles: "Those who crowded in to see what was going on tried to calm him, but they were choking with laughter."

Yet the portrait Saint-Simon has sketched of Marie Adélaïde, who, like the King, was fond of Madame de Saint-Simon, remains that of a spritelike princess, scarcely touching the earth: ". . . light as a nymph, she was everywhere like a whirling breeze, bringing life and gaiety wherever she passed." For one familiar with the unsentimental duke, the affection is unexpected. But it is open-eyed:

"Normally she would be called ill-favored [he wrote of her later years]. She had sagging cheeks, a too prominent forehead, a nondescript nose, thick, mordant lips, but her chestnut hair and eyebrows were well defined and she had the most beautiful and eloquent eyes in the world. Her teeth were few and all decayed, but she was the first to mention and make fun of them."

One begins to admire the duke and understand the period, and when he continues, penetrating the surface plainness, he succeeds in explaining to us the princess's appeal:

"She had [however] a most beautiful complexion and a most beautiful skin, small but admirable breasts and a long neck with the suspicion of a goiter, which was not unbecoming to her. The carriage of her head was elegant, gracious and noble, and such too was her expression and her quick smile. . . . Whoever was with her was tempted to think her wholly and solely on his side."

Saint-Simon, one suspects, suspended his own ordinarily acid disbelief when he tells us the princess was as pleased to spend a quiet afternoon reading and embroidering, or conversing with her "serious ladies" (as she termed the older women of the palace), as playing cards or dancing. But at Versailles appearances were the ultimate reality and maintaining them the supreme achievement. Eventually that may have been what the declining Sun King, beleaguered by so many abroad, was to value most in his little duchess.

Though intimate with the King and Madame de Maintenon in a manner none of his children dared assume, in public Marie Adélaïde was modest, reserved, and respectful; her *"Auntie"* somehow combined the idea of Queen and Mother. But in private she chattered and skipped about, teetering on their knees or on the arm of their chair, hugging and kissing them, mischievously rummaging among their papers, unsealing their letters and, *when she saw it might amuse them,* reading one aloud with comments.

It was an intimacy that matured, rather than ended, with her own maturity, and it produced one of Saint-Simon's most curious anecdotes about private life at Versailles. "I would never tell the following story in such serious Memoirs [he begins apologetically], if it did not demonstrate better than any other to what point the princess felt free to say and do as she wished with them. . . .

"One evening there was a play at Versailles and she was chatting of various things when Madame de Maintenon's old *femme de chambre,* Nanon, entered the room. Immediately, dressed in her formal court gown and wearing her jewels, the princess went to the fireplace and stood with her back to it, leaning against a little screen between two tables. Nanon, who had one hand in her pocket, went behind her and dropped to her knees. The King, who was closest to them, noticed it and asked what they were doing there. The princess began to laugh and replied she was doing what he did on the days there was a play. The King persisted. 'Do you really want to know,' she said, 'because you haven't seen it for yourself? Well then, I am having an enema.'

" 'What?' cried the King, shaking with laughter, 'here, right now, you're having an enema?'

" '*Eh, oui,*' she said, 'I really am!'

" 'But how?' And all four laughed heartily.

"Nanon had brought the syringe, already prepared, under her petticoat, and had lifted the skirts of the princess (who held them up as if warming herself), and had inserted it. The skirts were then pulled down, Nanon took the syringe away under her own, and thus little was remarked. The King and Madame de Maintenon were either distracted or thought Nanon was rearranging some part of the princess's gown. The surprise was complete and they both found it highly amusing."

In truth, the princess was more comforter to the old King, now in his sixties, than companion to her young husband. The King seemed to need her more; he would sit unusually solemn and silent, even at his public suppers, when her pleasure parties, which he himself encouraged, took her from his side. As a result, she was careful not to mention them in his presence and made a point of seeing him before and after. If she returned too late, she would manage to be with him when he awoke, so as to cheer him with her little stories.

"The King wishes Mme la Duchesse de Bourgogne to do as she pleases from morning until night," the Marquis de Coulanges wrote Madame de Sévigné's daughter, "and it is enough for him to know she is happy. So life at Court is trips to Marly and Meudon, comings and goings to and from Paris for operas, balls, and masquerades, and the seigneurs, so to speak, are at dagger's point trying to attract the good graces of the princess."

That was on February 2, 1700. The century of Louis XIV was still to take a long time dying.

On the ninth of November the French monarch received an urgent message from his ambassador in Madrid: the Spanish King, Charles II, had died without an heir. Though a Habsburg, three weeks previously he had signed a will leaving his throne to the second of his great-nephews, the Duc d'Anjou, Louis' grandson and the Duc de Bourgogne's brother. For a week Louis hesitated. If he accepted, it would probably mean the revival of the war with the first Grand Alliance, which had barely ended. If not, Habsburg Austria would inherit the Spanish throne, France would be surrounded, and there would most likely be a war in any case.

Louis accepted. Four years of peace ended. Eleven years of the War of the Spanish Succession followed. England, Holland, and Austria formed the second Grand Alliance against France, joined by most of the German states; Portugal and Savoy sided with France and Spain, then shifted to the allies in 1703—and the princess's father was now at war with France.

These were the darkest days of Louis' reign. His need for the little duchess was never greater—not only for her relaxing ways but for her parties. Before Europe, appearances had to be brilliantly maintained. In war the serenity of the Sun King was worth battalions. Typically, after the shattering defeat at Blenheim, where thirty thousand of a French army of fifty thousand fell before Marlborough, Louis had

Marie-Adélaïde go to Paris to be seen, gay and undisturbed, at a great display of fireworks.

These were the years of forced growth—for the prince as for the princess. From Cambrai, Fénelon cautioned him not to sin by excess of piety. "A great prince," he wrote, "has not to serve God as a hermit." And Louis sent his grandson off to serve France in Flanders. (There, one of the officers said to the duke, "You will certainly win the Kingdom of Heaven, but as for winning the kingdom of this world, Marlborough and Prince Eugène [his ally],* go about it in a better way.")

It was the princess who now turned to prayer, writing her husband constantly, "her heart beating at the arrival of every courier, fearing for his life, for his reputation" (Madame de Maintenon), and defending him at Court. It was not easy for one whose father's family was at war with her husband's, and she paid, in addition to everything else, a posthumous price—an accusation, never proved, that she sent military secrets to her father's House of Savoy.†

There was another price the princess paid for her life and love with that complex man, the King of France. In 1704 she had given birth to a boy who died in less than a year. Two years later she gave birth to another who lived five years. And in 1710 she gave France its next King, Louis XV. In between, in 1708—but let Saint-Simon tell it:

"Mme la Duchesse de Bourgogne was pregnant and felt extremely ill. . . . The King wanted to go, as usual, to Marly. His granddaughter amused him and he would not go without her, though the moving about would be bad for her condition. Mme de Maintenon worried over it. Fagon quietly put in a word against it, which annoyed the King. He was not used to being denied anything and had been spoiled by his mistresses, who had always traveled with him, whether pregnant or just delivered of a child. . . . He would only concede twice postponing the trip for Low Monday, but did go on the Wednesday of the week following, despite all that could be done or said to stop him or gain permission for Madame la Duchesse de Bourgogne to remain at Versailles."

The result was a miscarriage. The news was broken to the King in the gardens in the presence of most of the Court.

* Son of the exiled Comtesse de Soissons, formerly Olympe Mancini.
† It was a story Voltaire considered and then dismissed as the kind always offered as an excuse for defeat by the defeated.

"M. de la Rochefoucauld exclaimed aloud that it was the greatest misfortune imaginable, since she had miscarried several times before and might not be able to bear children. 'And if that should happen,' the King interrupted with sudden anger, emerging from his silence, 'what difference will that make to me? Doesn't she already have a son? And if he were to die, is not the Duc de Berry of an age to marry and have children? Why should I care who succeeds me? Are they not all equally my grandsons?' Then, with sudden impatience, 'Thank God she has miscarried, since that was bound to be. Now I will not be crossed in my excursions and everything I want to do, by what doctors have to say, or midwives. I will go and come as it pleases me, and they will leave me in peace.' A silence in which you might have heard an ant walking followed this outburst. All lowered their eyes and scarcely dared to breathe. Everyone was stupefied; even the gardeners and the workmen stood still. The silence lasted a full quarter of an hour. The King, leaning on the balustrade, broke it, speaking of a carp. No one answered him. He then addressed his words to the workmen, who ordinarily were not included in his conversation, and he spoke to them only of carp."

It is a distasteful story and Saint-Simon congratulates himself "for having long ago decided that the King loved and esteemed only himself." But here, on fairer reflection, was also an upset old man with a sense of guilt, surely more than faint, ridding himself of it, trying to recover face. "The King," Madame de Maintenon was to write a friend, "rids himself of unhappy ideas as soon as he can."

Misfortunes were another matter, and the following year opened with the first of a formidable series. It froze. It froze for seventeen days. The Seine and the sea around the coast froze. The table wine at Versailles froze. Olive and orange trees froze. Grain, cows, goats, sheep, chickens, even rabbits, froze. It was a year of famine: eleven thousand Frenchmen died at Malplaquet.* The nobles turned in their silver plate. Stranger still, the people responded to Louis' appeal with recruits and valuables, and France somehow carried on. At his side was the princess, and the King found her "capable of difficult and important things." In her and his grandson he felt that the future, at least, was assured.

However . . . On the eighth of April 1711, Monseigneur (the Grand Dauphin) saw a priest carrying Communion to a dying man.

---

* "God," Louis said, "has forgotten all I have done for him."

He descended from his coach with the Duchesse de Bourgogne and knelt before the priest. A week later he was dead from smallpox. Louis went to Marly and wept in the dark. The next morning he named his grandson, not yet thirty, Dauphin. The duchess became the Dauphine. They now stood on the steps of the French throne.

The new Dauphin was suddenly a new man. Gone, as if overnight, were the shyness and timidity. He took his place at Court, attended all Council meetings, worked hard, won the respect of the King, and prepared for what seemed his destiny. When Louis offered him his father's monthly allowance of fifty thousand livres, he said he was content with his twelve thousand. He asked to be called Monsieur, not Monseigneur, and persuaded Louis to order an inquiry into the state of the nation. It filled forty-two folio volumes. "There can be no rest for a King," he noted, as he studied them. But he had never been happier.

"And all France expected from the Duc de Bourgogne a government such as the sages of old had dreamed, whose austerity would be tempered by the charms of the princess . . . the idol and model of the Court" (Voltaire).

She was the brightness in the King's gathering darkness—she and the young prince and their two boys.

On the eighteenth of January 1712, still in mourning, the seventy-three-year-old King took his Court to Marly. The Dauphine had arrived earlier, her face "hugely swollen," and immediately went to bed. At the King's request, however, she rose at seven to preside over the drawing room, her head swathed in a hood as she played cards. Then she returned to bed, where she ate supper.

The following day the Dauphin received a letter from his brother, the King of Spain, warning of poison. It greatly disturbed the twenty-six-year-old Dauphine. An Italian astrologer had foretold her death before twenty-seven, and frequently she recalled his words. "The time is approaching," she once told the prince. "Whom will you marry when I die?"

"No one," he said. "In a week I would follow you to the grave."

The next few days she felt better and on the first of February the Court returned to Versailles. On Friday the fifth, the Duc de Noailles gave her a beautiful snuffbox with fine Spanish snuff. She tried it, liked it, and put it aside. That evening she had a fever and felt pain, and implored the King not to enter her room. She was given opium and bled twice from the arm. She sent one of her ladies-in-waiting for the snuffbox. It had disappeared.

On the eighth the red spots that were the sign of measles spotted her body; the King came often to her bedside. On the tenth the Dauphin, who had never left her, was persuaded to go into the garden for fresh air; he came back almost immediately. Toward nightfall she became worse and spent a very bad night. The next day she was given the last sacraments. "Today a princess," she said resignedly, "tomorrow nothing." Seven doctors ordered her bled from the foot.

On the twelfth she was conscious only at intervals. Toward evening her servants became so distraught that many strangers were allowed into her room, even though the King was present. At eight o'clock she died.* The King, as custom demanded, left the death chamber a few moments before, and drove to Marly with Madame de Maintenon to be alone with his grief. He could not summon the strength to see or talk to the Dauphin.

As the end approached, he had been ordered by the King to keep away from his wife's bedroom, so that he might not catch the fatal fever. But on the fourteenth he looked so ill that Louis had the doctors take his pulse, and on the sixteenth the ominous spots appeared. "The sorrow of his loss," says Saint-Simon, "had shattered him." And Saint-Simon himself had been deeply shocked by the Dauphin's stricken look the day after the Dauphine's death. "One saw a man, torn by anguish, who somehow turned himself inside out to present a composed surface, and died from the struggle, his life cut prematurely short."

At eight-thirty in the evening, on the sixth day after his wife's death, the Dauphin died. "France," mourned Saint-Simon, "underwent her final chastisement: God showed her the prince she did not deserve."

And of the princess he wrote: "With her passing, all joy, all pleasures, entertainments and grace were eclipsed and darkness fell over the Court. She was its light. She filled every part of it. She was its center, its inner life, and if the Court continued to subsist after her death, it was only to languish for her. Never was a princess so regretted, never was one more worthy of it. Mourning for her has never ended, a

---

* "Doctor Chirac," wrote La Palatine bitterly, "assured everyone up to the very end that she would recover. In fact, if she had not been obliged to get up while she had the measles to be bled from the foot, she would still be alive." La Palatine, it must be said, tried to prevent it.

secret, involuntary taste of bitterness remains, a terrible emptiness which can not be diminished."

Nor was it ever diminished for the King. With her death, twilight became night, the war ended in exhaustion and compromise, and he prepared for his own death a few years later.

12. The Death of a King

Unrecovered from the death of his son, his grandson, his grandson's wife, Louis was suddenly confronted with the same deadly illness in his two great-grandsons, children of the Duc and Duchesse de Bourgogne: the fatal red spots had appeared on their bodies. More dangerously, Fagon had been called on to treat them. Consulting five Paris doctors, he prescribed what he would have prescribed in any case—bleeding, the cure that had just dispatched their parents. The older boy, now Dauphin, was duly bled, and duly he died. The younger was declared too small for bleeding by his governess, Madame de Ventadour, who snatched him from the royal quacks. Hurriedly she took him to her own room, had him breast fed, and saved his life.

Four deaths—three of them Dauphins—within a year, but the façade of Louis XIV showed no fissure: his was a sunset of terrible magnificence. Never, says Saint-Simon, had he so merited the title of Louis le Grand. Among members of the Court, however, the suspicion of poison hung heavily and it fell on Philippe, the Duc d'Orléans, the libertine son of Louis' brother. Ironically La Palatine, who cried poison after every death at Court, now had it cried after her own son. He not only had his own chemical laboratory but was widely—and wildly—accused of incestuous relations with his daughter, the Duchesse de Berri. At one point, Philippe's chemist, named Homberg, had gone to the Bastille to surrender himself, but since there was no order to receive him, he was refused admission. Philippe similarly asked the

King for a public trial; his mother likewise. But Louis defended rather than pursued his nephew, dislike him though he did. In any event, when the bodies were opened, no trace of poison was found.

Bleakly Louis returned to the last years of the war and to the general to whom they were now entrusted, the Maréchal de Villars.* The darkling mood of the Sun King has been movingly recorded by his general, who had arrived for an audience on April 16, 1712, preparatory to leaving for the front. "On that day," says Villars, "the self-control of the Monarch gave way to the feelings of the man. He shed a few tears and addressed me in a voice that shook, affecting me deeply. 'You see the state I am in, Monsieur le Maréchal. Few people have known, as I, what it is to lose within a few weeks a grandson, a granddaughter and their son, all of great promise and dearly cherished. God is punishing me and I deserve it. I shall suffer less in the world to come.

" 'But let us leave my personal misfortunes and rather consider what we can do to avert those of my kingdom. My confidence in you is well marked, since I have rendered you all the resources of the State and entrusted to you its safety. I know your zeal and the valor of my troops. But in the end fortune may desert you. If defeat should come to the army you command, what is your feeling about the part I should play?"

Astonished, Villars says, he remained silent as Louis continued: " 'Nearly all my courtiers want me to withdraw to Blois without waiting for the enemy to approach the gates of Paris, as they might well be able to do if my army were defeated. But I know that armies as strong as mine can never be so completely defeated that some elements could not retreat across the Somme. I know that river. It is very difficult to cross, but there are places which can be forded. My plan is to go to Péronne or Saint-Quentin, there rally my remaining troops and make one last effort with you, in which we would either perish together or preserve the State, for I will never consent to the enemy's approaching my capital.' "[1]

Three months later Villars captured the fortified town of Denain well to the north, defeating Prince Eugène in a brilliant engagement

---

* A *bon vivant* of boundless optimism, but with an ability to match, Villars had bought Vaux-le-Vicomte from Fouquet's widow. He changed its name to Vaux-Villars and installed himself in it with a pretty wife, thirty years younger, for whom his passion was a Court diversion.

(which Napoleon would describe as having saved France). Courtiers who had their trunks packed for flight to the Loire could now order them unpacked and Louis could negotiate a less than dishonorable peace at Utrecht in 1713. His Bourbon descendants were to keep the Spanish throne down to our own time and the kingdom of France its frontiers. And if the days of Louis' dominance were past, so at last was his pursuit of glory. The peace of resignation now entered his soul. There was a new humility in the Grand Monarch.

Also, a final loneliness tempered by Madame de Maintenon. Le Nôtre was long gone. So were Racine, in semidisgrace,* Boileau and Mansart, Vauban, Bossuet, and Father de La Chaise, who had been carried away by the year of the cold. Two years before, Madame de Montespan had died, her hair snow white, her mourner—in the privacy of her privy; the King would have none of it—Madame de Maintenon. Then in 1714, the Duc de Berri died from a fall from his horse, and that left as heirs to the French throne—renounced by Philip V of Spain—the delicate four-year-old Duc d'Anjou, the only surviving child of the Duc and Duchesse de Bourgogne, and his granduncle, the forty-year-old Duc d'Orléans.

---

* Racine, according to Saint-Simon, had remarked in the company of the King and Madame de Maintenon that the poor state of the theater was due to a lack of new authors, and as a consequence actors had to fall back on old authors and worthless plays. With typical absent-mindedness, he had named Scarron among them. "The silence which suddenly descended," says Saint-Simon, "awakened the wretched Racine"—but too late. He was never forgiven and died a few years later.

Saint-Simon may well have been indulging his dislike for Madame de Maintenon, but in the account of Racine's son, she also had a responsible hand. According to Louis Racine, Madame de Maintenon often discussed contemporary affairs with his father. Once, hearing him expatiate on the miseries of the peasants as a result of the war, she had persuaded him to write down his opinions. So Racine did, sending her a memorandum. "She was reading it," writes Louis Racine, "when the King entered her room, took it from her, read a few lines, then furiously asked who was the author." After some hesitation, she told him. " 'Because he knows how to write verses,' said the King, 'does he think he knows everything? And because he is a poet, does he now want to be a minister?' "

The result, in any case, was the same in both versions: Racine's disgrace, decline, and death. A Jansenist once again (for which he also fell from favor), Racine had left a wish that his body be buried at Port Royal—the monastery, it was said at Court, in which he had not been brave enough to be buried when he was alive. But even in burial Racine was not to rest in peace: ten years later, when Port Royal was leveled and its ground plowed under by order of the King, Racine's body was exhumed and taken to Paris for reburial.

It was Orléans who would normally be Regent, and Louis was not pleased with the prospect. Nor was Madame de Maintenon, concerned about her favorite, the Duc du Maine, who had, with the princess's death, regained the favor of the King. Louis' first move was to have Parlement declare his legitimitized children, the Duc du Maine first among them, eligible for the throne should the legitimate branch of the Bourbons die out. Then, prodded further by Madame de Maintenon, the old King added a codicil to his will that would have barred Orléans from full power as Regent. He appointed a Regency Council composed of fourteen noblemen, including the two sons of Montespan, the Duc du Maine and the Comte de Toulouse. Though Orléans would preside over it as Regent, decisions would be taken only by majority vote. Moreover, the care and education of Louis' successor, according to the will, would be entrusted to the Duc du Maine.

Sending for the officials of Parlement, Louis handed them his will, sealed with seven seals, and said: "Messieurs, this is my testament. The fate of the wills of my predecessors, and of the King my father, leaves me with no illusion as to what might happen to it. But *they* insisted, they pursued me and gave me no rest, no matter what I said. Now I have bought my peace. Here it is. Take it, come what may to it. At least now I shall have some peace and hear no more about it." (Or so reports Saint-Simon, an *orléaniste*.)

Nostalgically the old King returned to Molière's comedies. He continued to hunt, but drove a little calèche since he could no longer ride to the hounds. He may even have pressed on Madame de Maintenon "those painful occasions" about which she had once complained to her confessor.* But in May 1715, Englishmen were betting in London—"in the fashion of that country" (Voltaire)—that the French King would not outlive the month of September. The account was accidentally read to him by the Marquis de Torcy from a Dutch newspaper. Though he pretended to pay no attention to it, it rankled him. On June 18, a cataloguer at the Versailles royal library noted in his diary: "During supper His Majesty remarked, 'If I continue to eat with such good appetite, I will ruin a large number of Englishmen who have wagered large sums that I will die by September.'"[2]

Throughout spring, the ambassadors at Court had been reporting to

---

* Then in his early seventies, the "occasions" occurred, she wrote her confessor, as often as twice a day. To this Godet de Marais had reassuringly replied that at least thus she was keeping the King from immorality and scandal, and that soon, in any event, she would be safe and inviolable in heaven.

their capitals on Louis' falling appetite and failing health, his heavier walk and shrunken body. By mid-August the English gamblers seemed certain of winning. But for three weeks Louis was to face death like a king and, as throughout his life, virtually in public. Two of his modest gunbearers—the brothers Anthoine—have left a moving record of it.[3]

The long vigil began on August 10 with a pain in Louis' stomach and Fagon's unfailing malpractice, this time a dose of amber spirits. But Louis went out into the gardens at Marly in his three-wheeled chair, overlooked the placing of marble statues from Rome, and left that evening for Versailles. There he stayed in Madame de Maintenon's apartment, avoiding the crowd of courtiers, who had heard of his sickness at Marly. That night he suffered from insomnia and an unsatisfiable thirst.

On the eleventh Louis XIV rose as usual at eight-thirty but canceled his hunt and that night went to bed, "his face pale and drawn," and the courtiers talked of death. But he slept well and Fagon decided he might have his usual monthly purge, *"une grande évacuation"* resulting. He worked two hours with his finance minister and spent four hours with Madame de Maintenon. But during the night the "burning in his entrails" could not be quenched, however much he drank.

On the thirteenth the King ate well and ceremoniously received the Duc d'Orléans, the Prince de Conti, the Duc du Maine, the Comte de Toulouse, various other dukes, and several ministers. But at six in the evening he felt a sharp pain in his left leg and could barely walk; Madame de Maintenon sent for the first surgeon, Maréchal, who rubbed it with hot cloths. After supper, more pain sent Louis to bed and a restless night; doctors, surgeons, and valets slept in the royal bedroom or in the room next to it.

On the fourteenth the Paris doctors arrived, solemnly felt the King's pulse in order of their seniority, retired to an adjacent *cabinet* for consultation, returned, and prescribed ass's milk. A few hours later, after another consultation, they canceled it. Sitting up in bed, Louis held a Council meeting. For dinner he had boiled bread and butter and could barely swallow it. Madame de Maintenon, looking on, almost lost her self-control and hurried back to her apartment. All day the entire Court waited in the Grande Galerie, individuals entering the King's bedroom only when he called for them, and then leaving it quickly. All saw him at supper, when he was wheeled in to the table, and were distressed at what they saw.

On the fifteenth Louis XIV was carried from his white and gold bedroom to the white and gold chapel to hear Mass. He returned through the *galerie,* hearing *"Vive le roi"* from the courtiers; they pressed so thickly his chair bearers could scarcely make a passage through them. On the sixteenth he heard Mass in bed, but held a *Conseil d'Etat* afterwards. Orléans, Maine, and Toulouse, as usual, paid their respects. Seeing the last two dressed for the hunt, he sent them off, saying, "Don't lose any time, messieurs. It's too fine a day." That evening he was carried to Madame de Maintenon's room to listen to motets and Italian songs. It was his last visit to her apartment. He spent a bad night.

On the eighteenth he woke in pain but held his *grandes entrées* and worked all afternoon with his minister, Pelletier. Half a dozen huge glasses of water could not slake his thirst. He went early to bed but not to rest. At seven in the morning of the nineteenth Fagon and the rest of the doctors found that his fever had increased. They returned at ten. Maréchal noted a black spot on Louis' left leg—and rubbed it with hot cloths. It was a treatment, remark the Anthoines in their diary, "more likely to lessen the embarrassment of the doctors than to cure their patient." That night was Louis' worst. The following morning his leg was bathed for an hour in hot, aromatic wine held in a great silver basin. "Let all who wish enter," Louis said, and the room rapidly filled with courtiers.

On the twenty-first the King rose at nine to give orders and instructions to his state secretaries. Then the doctors entered, took his pulse according to their seniority, and left. At eleven, Louis entertained his Court and officials from Paris. He worked that afternoon with his war minister until pain in his leg stopped him. He slept badly. At nine the next morning ten doctors came from Paris, took his pulse in the order of their seniority, retired to an adjacent *cabinet,* took turns praising the wisdom and skill of the royal physicians and prescribed ass's milk. On Friday the twenty-third Louis' gangrenous leg was again bathed in aromatic wine and he was given a bowl of ass's milk to drink. Maine and Toulouse entered, dressed for riding, and again he sent them off to the hunt. Fagon brought in his troop of doctors, who took the King's pulse in the usual solemn order, and prescribed more ass's milk. Louis made out a second codicil to his will, then received the Court and called for his musicians and Italian songs.

After a particularly bad night for the King, Fagon and the doctors met, put the blame on the ass, "found nothing else to take her place," and bound Louis' leg with a cloth dipped in camphorated spirits, "to bring back the natural heat." At eleven Louis met with his finance minister and held a Council meeting. Maréchal unbound his leg in the presence of Villeroi. It was now completely black. The King said it no longer hurt him, "but those present, particularly Villeroi, saw it was incurable and Villeroi retired to his apartment, his eyes filled with tears." Louis knew then he was dying and called for his confessor, Le Tellier, to prepare him for death. The news spread, alarming the Court as well as the great crowd that had now gathered at Versailles.

On the twenty-fifth, Louis' saint's day and a national fête, the King had the drums and fifes played under his windows when he woke and his *vingt-quatre violons* played in the anteroom while he had dinner. In the evening Louis' body was anointed with holy oil, and he added a few lines to his will giving the Duc du Maine charge of the royal guards on his death. To Orléans he said, "My dear nephew, serve the Dauphin as faithfully and well as you served me." To Maine, Toulouse, and the princes of the blood he said, "Live in peace and unity." He slept for an hour and woke to find Madame de Maintenon beside his bed. He wept and gave instructions. His heart was to be taken to the Professed House of the Jesuits in Paris, the Dauphin removed to Vincennes, "where the air was better than at Versailles."

On the twenty-sixth the King sent for the Dauphin, who, as Louis XV, would inscribe the last words of the dying monarch on a plaque above his own bed—words copied down by Voltaire:

"You will soon be the King of a great kingdom. I urge you most strongly never to forget your obligations to God. Remember that you owe Him everything you are. Try to preserve peace with your neighbors. I have loved war too much; do not imitate me in that, or in the too great expenditures I indulged in.* Take counsel in all things and seek to know the best course so as always to follow it. Lighten the burden of your people as soon as you can and do what I have had the misfortune of not being able to do myself."[4]

On the twenty-seventh Maréchal cut into the King's leg. He felt nothing. His surgeon cut deeper. He cried out and asked if it was

---

* "Do not imitate my love of building nor my liking for war," reads Saint-Simon's version.

necessary to hurt him, since it was useless. Maréchal's eyes filled with tears and he discontinued. On the twenty-eighth Louis XIV "made an affectionate remark to Madame de Maintenon which she did not relish a bit and to which she did not respond. He told her that what consoled him in leaving her was the hope that at her age she would shortly rejoin him" (Saint-Simon).

On the twenty-ninth another hope stirred the dying King. A peasant named Brun somehow made his way to the royal bedroom, through the Duc d'Orléans, with a miracle liqueur. Further, he bullied Fagon ("who habitually bullied others"—Saint-Simon) into administering it to the King. At first Louis felt better and even ate some solid food ("Another mouthful," said Orléans, "and there will be no courtiers left in my apartment"), but the next morning he was worse. Threatened by the King's doctors with criminal charges, Brun disappeared.

By the thirty-first, gangrene had spread to the monarch's thigh. By eleven that night, prayers were recited for the dying. Louis responded, his voice heard above the others. *"Nunc et in hora mortis,"* he repeated several times, then cried, "Help, O God, help me—quickly!" He fell unconscious. At eight forty-five in the morning of September 1, 1715, "after a few short sighs and two gasps, without any agitation or convulsion," Louis XIV died. He was seventy-seven years of age less four days. He died in the seventy-third year of his reign. Two grooms of the royal chamber closed his eyes.

The night before, Madame de Maintenon had slipped away' to her bed at Saint-Cyr. The afternoon of the day Louis XIV's hearse departed for the basilica of Saint-Denis, the new, five-year-old King of France was driven, sitting on his governess's knee, to the castle at Vincennes—and the great palace of Versailles was left to a few caretakers.

On the roadway to Saint-Denis, along which the Sun King's body passed, a twenty-year-old youth, not yet known as Voltaire, remarked people "drinking, singing and laughing" in its wake.

ACT TWO

13. Between Palaces and Pleasures

The eighteenth century had at last arrived—fifteen years late and impatient. Even before Louis XIV's body was embalmed, his last will and testament, as he had predicted, was broken. Moving with a dispatch that surprised not only his enemy, the Duc du Maine, but his friend, Saint-Simon (who now had the "importance" he had always sought), the Duc d'Orléans had summoned Parlement and prepared for its coming. When the Duc du Maine and the robed magistrate, arrived at the Palais de Justice, they found its approaches guarded by over three thousand French and Swiss soldiers.[1] It was a precaution against a coup by the royal bastards.

The session opened with a tedious speech by Saint-Simon on ducal privileges—the famous *affaire du bonnet*.* Then it settled down to more important affairs of state—the reading of Louis XIV's will. With unexpected impressiveness and a stature beyond his short, plump self, Philippe d'Orléans rose to speak. The will, he said, was an affront to his birth and counter to the late King's real wishes; subject to a Regency Council, he would be a regent in name only. Speedily Parlement—as much to assert its own privileges as to render Philippe his—set aside the will. Then followed, as Philippe had proposed, discussion of the codicil naming the Duc du Maine superintendent

---

* Learning of the death of Louis XIV, Saint-Simon tells us in his memoirs, "I went to pay my respects to the new monarch . . . [and] went thence to M. le Duc d'Orléans to remind him of a promise he had given me, that he would permit the dukes to keep their hats on when their votes were asked for [in Parlement]." Such, for Saint-Simon, was the priority of priorities, now that Louis XIV was dead.

of Louis XV's education with command of the Household Guards. Again Philippe pointed out that no regent could rule when such royal power was elsewhere, and he demanded the codicil be revoked. Hurriedly the Duc du Maine replied: the King's education required that control of his person, which could be guaranteed only by the Household Guards. Besides, he said, the late King knew what he was doing when he made out the codicil. Here Philippe countered so warmly the debate was adjourned to another room to be continued *à deux* (save when Saint-Simon entered to whisper advice in the ear of an annoyed Philippe).

Reassembling after dinner, Parlement by acclamation set aside the codicil. Flustered, the Duc du Maine asked to be relieved of all responsibility other than the education of the child-king, and had no trouble in receiving acquiescence. Philippe had won. The Duc du Maine went home to his estate at Sceaux and to his terrifying wife, a Condé who had condescended to marry a bastard, albeit a royal one, and always reminded him of it. Doll-sized, she had a ferocious courage, ". . . certainly more than my husband," she once wrote Madame de Maintenon. "If it was necessary, I would kill the Duc d'Orléans with my own hands and drive a nail into his head." Unconfirmed but irresistible is the account of the Duc du Maine's reception that night at Sceaux (just south of Paris) by his Lady Macbeth-like wife:

"When Mme du Maine saw the Duc arrive, all sighs and silence, she suspected what had happened.

" 'Well, Monsieur,' she said severely, 'what has taken place?'

" 'The King's Will is ignored, repudiated, annulled. . . .'

" 'And you endured this, Monsieur?'

" 'What would you have me do, Madame? I was surrounded by swords, pistols, even cannon.'

" 'It were better never to return than to return dishonored.'

" 'What good would it be, pray, to get myself killed by the Orléans faction?'

" 'You are a coward, Monsieur; if I had been in your place I would not have given in so cheaply. Leave my presence, or my indignation may carry me to excesses which will dishonor us both.'

"She uttered the last words in a voice so charged, and with such a resolute gesture, that the Duc du Maine hobbled away, much put out of countenance."[2]

Philippe d'Orléans, Regent of France, had his victory, but it was not unshared. Two victors, in fact, emerged from the confrontation at the Palais de Justice—the Regent *and* Parlement. He had won the full powers of his regency by reaccording Parlement a right it had lost under Louis XIV, the "right of remonstrance" against royal edicts. It was a debt Parlement would attempt to collect down to the Revolution.

Within a fortnight, the five-year-old King arrived at the Palais de Justice for his first *lit de justice*. Carefully he repeated before Parlement the phrases taught him by his tutor, Maréchal de Villeroi. "Sir," he said to Philippe, "I wish to assure you of my affection," and to Parlement. "My Chancellor will tell you the rest." When the little King left the Palais, cannons thundered their salute from the Bastille, pieces of silver were thrown to the crowds and four hundred birds were let fly.[3]

The release was more than symbolic. The same day drawbridges were lowered at fortress prisons all over France releasing debtors and religious prisoners; Huguenots were relieved from the galleys. It was Philippe's doing, inaugurating a regency of such private depravity mixed with public virtue that one must step backward in time for some perspective.

Son of his father, the inverted Monsieur, but also of his mother, the energetic, extroverted Princesse Palatine, Philippe at twelve fell into the hands of Abbé Dubois, who both Saint-Simon and memorialist Duclos[4] agree was the sum of all the vices, some at second hand. His father had been a country pharmacist and from this background Dubois was to rise by way of an abbé's tonsure at thirteen and a Paris scholarship to cardinal power (abandoning a possible wife on the way). His portrait by Saint-Simon is a part portrait of the age:

"A little, pitiful, wizened, herring-gutted man in a flaxen wig, his weazel's face brightened by some intellect, in familiar terms, he was a scoundrel. All the vices fought within him for mastery, so that a continual uproar filled his mind. Avarice, debauchery, ambition were his gods; perfidy, flattery, bootlicking, his means; complete piety was his relaxation; and he maintained, as a fundamental principle, that all probity and honesty were but chimeras with which people adorned themselves, but which had no reality; therefore, for him, all means were good. He excelled in base intrigues and lived from them."

Thus "Dubois led M. le Duc d'Orleans"—a willing victim—"into debauchery." Saint-Simon is harsh: the abbé was a good scholar and an able diplomat. He formed the first *entente cordiale* with England when he became Philippe's chief minister (collecting a bribe from the British for what he wanted to do in any case) and gave France no major war during the Regency.

Of Philippe himself, Saint-Simon says, "He was born bored." It might stand as the slogan of the era. "Accustomed to debauchery, above all to the uproar of it, he could not do without it, and could only divert himself by dint of noise, tumult, and excess." But Philippe was intelligent and gifted; he painted, engraved, and played the lyre; he had (as we mentioned) his own chemical laboratory and was to collect art with discrimination (Poussin, Champaigne, Titian, Raphael, Veronese, del Sarto). He may have had a gift for power, but he had been deliberately untrained for it: brave as he was on the battlefield, he was always shunted aside by Louis XIV in favor of the Duc du Maine. *Divertissement* became his form of expression.[5] As for his later debauchery, one cannot forget (though one might exaggerate) the fact that at seventeen he was forced by Louis XIV to marry his bastard daughter, the Duchesse de Blois, sister of the Duc du Maine, "tearing" Philippe from Mademoiselle de Séry, the one woman, it seems, he ever loved. As for his wife, he was to call her with reason Madame Lucifer, and not at all to her displeasure. For the marriage, Philippe received a box on his ears from his mother and the Palais Royal from his uncle and father-in-law. (Louis even came to Paris from Versailles to see the redecorated palace, despite the memories of fleeing it four decades before.)

Regent at forty-one, fat, myopic, and unambitious, Philippe was to give France an almost complete epoch in eight years. Emotionally and politically it was a release, as, literally, for the prisoners, from the monolithic requirements of grandeur and the pietistic restraints of the last, Maintenon years. (Handsomely, Philippe visited Madame de Maintenon at Saint-Cyr and assured her she would want for nothing.) Hundreds who had been sent to prison by the *lettres de cachet* (sealed letters) of the previous regime, many for Jansenist non-conformity, were set free. But when Philippe intimated renewing the tolerant Edict of Nantes, Jansenists joined with Jesuits, and Dubois, to dissuade him. Philippe himself was an atheist, who as a young man read Rabelais, bound as a prayer book, at Mass in Versailles, and spent entire nights in the quarries of Vanves invoking the devil, eventually giving it up as a lost cause.[6] He disliked censorship and ordered Fénelon's *Télémaque* reprinted. (Fénelon himself, who died in 1715, was among Philippe's influences.) Once, when he was pilloried in a pamphlet, *Les Philippiques,* he had Saint-Simon fetch him a copy. It was sharp, it was cruel, but he smiled as he read it until he came to the passage implying a plot of *his* against the young King's life, and then he turned livid. However, when the author was found and brought to him, Philippe asked, "Do you believe what you wrote?"

"Yes, Monseigneur," said the pamphleteer.

"Then so much the better for you. Otherwise I would have had you hung."[7]

It is scarcely credible, but that it was even told indicates something about Philippe d'Orléans. Young Voltaire* *was* sent to the Bastille for his own lampoons of the Regency (he frequented the circle at Sceaux and lent his talent to the Duchesse du Maine's unslackened fury). But he was to write of Philippe himself that of all the Bourbons "he resembled Henry IV the most in his courage, goodness of heart, openness, gaiety, affability and freedom of access, and with a better cultivated understanding." Voltaire emerged from the Bastille with the name he had chosen for himself and a play, it was said, he had written in "prison" (where he had his own books, furniture, and linen and had dined frequently with its governor). The play shortly produced, in any case, was *Oedipus,* a daring enough venture for a twenty-four-year-old writer. The title itself suggested incest and someone drew a line through it, on a poster, substituting *Philippe.* But when it was performed at the Comédie Française, Molière's House, Voltaire was awarded an allowance of 1200 livres by the Regent. With a wit the world would soon recognize as unmistakably his, Voltaire thanked Philippe "for continuing to supply my board, but I would wish His Royal Highness would no longer supply my lodging."[8]

Perhaps the harshest and the finest thing one can say of Philippe is that he was more seduced by pleasure than by power. It was the Palais Royal in Paris, and not that at Versailles, which became the center of both. The young King and the greatly reduced Court—most of the courtiers had returned to their provincial castles—in the meantime had been moved from Vincennes to the Tuileries Palace.† And Philippe struck four hundred gardeners, a hundred gatemen and the gondoliers from the rolls of Marly and Versailles. Yet the latter had

* Still François Marie Arouet, and to whom we shall return.
† Destroyed during the Paris Commune of 1871.

its biweekly visits from the ambassadors and their entourage, and the fountains would play as if the moment were forever. The most colorful of Versailles' visitors during the interregnum was unquestionably Peter the Great, Tsar of Russia, whose visit had been repeatedly put off by Louis XIV.

On a tour of Western Europe, seeking a reversal of the French alliance with Sweden, which blocked Russia from the Baltic, the Tsar arrived with his suite of forty on May 7, 1717, in Paris. Six feet eight inches tall, turning forty-six, stooped but still powerful, Peter I intrigued the French Court with his tics, his epilepsy, his short brown wig, unbuttoned jerkin, and giant thirst. When he met the child-king, he swept him from his feet, lifted him high in the air and kissed him roundly in Russian fashion. "The King," says Saint-Simon with some pride, "young as he was, showed no fear." Characteristically, Peter the Great wanted to see workshops more often than palaces. At the Gobelins factory, he studied the tapestries minutely and watched the workers weaving them. Indeed, he embraced one of them, a gesture which struck Dubois de Saint-Gelais, who accompanied the Tsar. *We* may be more struck by another element in Saint-Gelais' story: the worker embraced by Peter the Great, he writes, was one of a group of weavers, "none of whom could have been older than seven."[9] Several days later, at the Hôtel des Invalides, the Tsar "tasted the soldiers' soup and wine, clapped them on the shoulder and called them comrades."[10]

There was a gust of visits, as well, to Saint-Cloud and the Luxembourg Palace, but Peter the Great obviously burned to see the palace and park of Louis le Grand.* Off he went with his suite on May 24 to walk every part of the gardens, boat on the Grand Canal, tour the Trianon and the Ménagerie. He was lodged in the château; so was most of his suite, the men thoughtfully bringing with them *demoiselles* from Paris, whom they bedded down in Madame de Maintenon's old apartment, next to the Tsar's. "Blouin, the old Governor of Versailles," says Saint-Simon, "was scandalized to see the very temple of prudery that he had known thus profaned." But it bothered Peter and his men not the slightest, and the next day he was off with them to Marly and its "machine," then to Fontainebleau and its environs.

---

* He had, even before the visit, created his own domain in their image. See p. 70.

He returned again to Versailles to see it at greater leisure, "it pleased him so much. . . ."

On Friday, June 11, Peter the Great went from Versailles to Saint-Cyr primarily out of curiosity. He wished to see Madame de Maintenon in retirement. He saw her in bed. "The tsar," she later wrote her cousin, the Marquise de Caylus, "came at seven in the evening. He sat at the foot of my bed. He asked me if I were ill. I said I was. He had me asked the nature of my illness. I answered, 'A great age.' He did not know what to say; his interpreter didn't seem to hear me. His visit was very short. . . . He had the curtains drawn back at the foot of my bed to see me. You can well imagine the sight was not a pretty one." (Two years later, aged eighty-three, Madame de Maintenon died.)

Peter I returned to Paris and, without the alliance he had sought, soon afterward left France. "Tranquilly" he continued his European tour, "not fearing a revolution in his country." This remark by his official historian[11] has a double irony. Before he left, the Russian Tsar had expressed surprise at the extravagance he had witnessed in France and warned his hosts that "sadly he foresaw luxury on this scale soon bringing their downfall."[12]

If Peter the Great was the first "modern Russian," Philippe, for Michelet, was the "first modern chief of state." He spread authority through some seventy councilors and ministers, replacing Louis XIV's tight handful of state secretaries. Had he thought himself other than a transitional figure, with a sense of fleeting power, he might have made France a great ruler. He had liberal inclinations—"Rise," he told a man kneeling before him, "I speak to no man in that position"—and often looked to England for his model. He worked conscientiously enough during the day, but night meant retirement to the rose-silk-upholstered private apartments of the Palais Royal. When the doors were closed, "even if Paris were on fire, there was no longer a Regent."[13]

Once, when his old concierge, who had known him as an infant, conducted Philippe as usual to the door of his night world, Philippe had mockingly invited him inside. "Monseigneur," the old man said, "my service ends here. I do not keep bad company and I am distressed to find you do." Philippe laughed and entered. Inside were his intimates, the companions he called his *roués* (men ordinarily broken on the *roue,* or wheel, for their blasphemous behavior). They were joined by their mistresses and teen-age dancers from the Opéra, by ladies of quality and ladies of the street. ("My son," said La Palatine, "is not difficult to please. So long as they are good humored, cheeky, eat and drink well, he doesn't mind.") But though he drank with the best of the *roués,* Philippe seems to have kept his head. Or did he pretend to drink the reputed half-dozen bottles, did he become more onlooker than participant as life leaked away and night after night repeated itself? Was it finally "the noise and tumult" of gaiety that "he could not do without"?

No holds (or embrace) were barred, nothing was sacred and everything permitted during the suppers and the subsequent orgies. No figure in the government or the Court was spared, and "M. le Duc d'Orléans had his say like the rest, though rarely did the stories make the slightest impression on him."[14] They remained locked in the night. He himself was remarkably discreet. On one occasion, when Madame de Sabran, whose magnificent body may have troubled even Saint-Simon (a most faithful husband), pressed for a state *confidence,* Philippe took her to one of the many mirrors and said, "Do you think one should talk about serious things to such a pretty face [*museau*]?"[15] But every time it thundered over Paris, La Palatine wrote, "I expected to see fire rain from the sky, as when it fell on Sodom and Gomorrah."

Philippe's daughters might have posed as muses of the Regency. His eldest and favorite, the Duchesse de Berry, when she lost her complaisant husband in 1714, had simply added to her lovers—and her weight. Father and daughter remained close, but one man finally separated them, a Captain Rion of the Luxembourg Palace guard. He was ugly, large-headed, and big-shouldered, a brute whom *les femmes débauchées,* says La Palatine, fought over, "La Polignac spending two days and two nights closed up with him." And "he treated the Duchesse de Berry," Saint-Simon adds, "as the Duc de Lauzun treated the Grande Mademoiselle." He gave her a daughter from whose birth she never recovered, and she died at twenty-four.

Mademoiselle de Chartres, second of Philippe's daughters, had become so infatuated with a singer at the Opéra that she was sent off to the convent at Chelles—and put in charge of it. As its new abbess, she promptly removed the convent from the world of prayer and made it a more worldly part of the Regency. "All Paris," said the

Duc de Richelieu,* "awaited the daily stories from Chelles"—only fifteen miles away. Seamstresses were brought in by the abbess, and soon nuns were turning out modish embroidered gowns with the requisite low neckline. There was also a sideline in skyrockets and other fireworks. The former Mademoiselle de Chartres herself "carried a pair of pistols on her, occasionally shooting them, frightening the entire household. Her talents included fine wig-making."[16]

A third daughter, Mademoiselle de Valois, was more the object than the subject of Regency society. At her debut, "everyone was struck by her beauty, not least of all the Duc de Richelieu."[17] Reaching her, despite the *gouvernante* and the guards at her door at the Palais Royal, obsessed the duke. Disguising himself successively as a merchant, a delivery boy, and a repairman, he managed and Mademoiselle de Valois yielded. Then, one evening, dressing himself in the borrowed clothes of her wardrobe mistress, he waited for her in the dressing room. There she joined him, spending so long a time her *gouvernante* became impatient. "Come, Princesse," she said, "you must go to bed. You can finish what you are doing tomorrow morning." To which the Regent's daughter replied, "I cannot, my dear, but I think in a moment I shall have finished."[18] Not yet satisfied, the Duc de Richelieu rented a room on Rue de Richelieu which abutted on the room of Mademoiselle de Valois and made a secret door in their common wall. While he was negotiating the passage nightly, the marriage of Philippe's daughter with the King of Sardinia was being discussed. The door was discovered; La Palatine could not resist writing about it; the King of Sardinia got wind of it; the marriage was off. In the meantime, the Duc de Richelieu was sent to the Bastille, but it was for another, more absurd, affair.

In December 1718 the indefatigable Duchesse du Maine had entered a Byzantine plot with Cellamare, the Spanish ambassador, Alberoni, the Spanish prime minister, and some French nobles, including Richelieu, to overthrow Philippe as Regent and install Philip V of Spain (Louis XIV's grandson) in his stead; the Duc du Maine, who seems to have known nothing about the plot, was to have been his prime minister. The plot was easily "discovered"—Dubois and Philippe knew of it all the time. The Duc and Duchesse du Maine were sent to

---

* Grandnephew of the cardinal and in his early twenties at this time, the duke eventually became a distinguished diplomat and general, figuring importantly throughout the eighteenth century. His *Mémoires,* though partly spurious in the original nine-volume edition (1790–93), are a rich source of lively material.

G*

prison—separate prisons, on the request of the duke. (They were released in 1721, to return to Sceaux and a few more intrigues.) For his minor role, Richelieu went to the Bastille. The price of his release, begged by Mademoiselle de Valois, was her reluctant consent to marry the Duke of Modena, a social comedown from the Sardinian King. (She may, according to La Palatine, have tried to kill herself on horseback not long after the marriage.)

If these three daughters of Philippe were the representative muses of the Regency, then Watteau, its greatest painter, remains its greatest mystery. Is his the poetry of the nonparticipant, the wistful view of the outsider, "that impossible or forbidden world which the mason's boy saw through the closed gateways of the enchanted garden" (Pater)? His was certainly not the world of the cynical memorialists we have been citing.

Antoine Watteau was born the son of a Flemish tilemaker (not a mason) and was apprenticed at fourteen with a local mediocre painter.[19,20] Penniless, he made his way to Paris in 1702 at the age of eighteen. Here he fell into a kind of factory for the production of souvenir religious paintings, and for his labor he received three francs and a child's ration of soup. Watteau's tuberculosis—he was the Keats of his time—may have dated from then. Nights and "spare time" he sketched. His sketches caught the eye of painter Claude Gillot, who hired him, then, jealous, fired him, and Watteau went on to the *atelier* of Claude Audran at the Luxembourg Palace. There he found Le Nôtre's garden, now grown to romantic fullness, and a great fellow Fleming, in Rubens' paintings of Marie de Médicis. Turning, in off hours, from the routine of ornamental design and decoration, Watteau painted the first of his own poignant tableaus, *The Departure of the Troops*. It was still the time of Louis XIV and the dreary War of the Spanish Succession. And it was now Claude Audran's turn to be jealous, and again Watteau was on his way.

A way station was the Royal Academy, the lovely *Embarkation for Cythera* the royal way. It marks the transition from the tired academicism of the late Le Brun to the period of the great romantics, indeed, to yesterday's Paris school of French painting. For over a century, in Will Durant's most felicitous phrase, it would be a "a memory of Watteau," his *fêtes galantes,* his preimpressionist, pre-Turner palette of warm, expressive color. It was a transition, too, as the Regency itself, from the ordered classicism of the seventeenth century to the humane enlightenment of the eighteenth, from one regime to another. The Regency, it is said, "still stands for elegant and corrupt cynicism."[21] If so, Watteau's art was its elegant retreat. Beauty always provides refuge; the beauty of Watteau's painting possessed the additional piquant touch of melancholy.

Appreciation of the *abstract* beauty of Watteau's work, one suspects, is for our own age. Regency rakes, more likely, saw only the pastoral scenes and characters—those graceful, exoskeletal creatures whose costumes seem their sole support. And if the ladies of the Regency could not aspire to their spirituality, they could at least affect their dress. Suddenly Watteau was the painter of Paris and Philippe appointed him painter to the king. Pierre Crozat, whose immense fortune was surpassed only by his brother Antoine's and his art collection by the Regent's, took Watteau in hand, installing him in his great *hôtel* on Place Vendôme. Here Watteau watched, without touching, more of the worldly world, worked as if he knew he had only four more years to live, and at thirty-six died.

The Regency had another year or so to live—in Regency style. Outwardly that style was baroque in the process of becoming rococo, a form as convoluted as the shellwork from which its name may derive. Furniture became curvilinear, aiming at comfort as well as form, and the love seat inevitably came into being. Private patrons, such as the brothers Crozat, now competed with royal patrons—all to the benefit of the painter. There were other collections being made, not only of women by men—and men, it must be noted, by women—but of *objets d'art,* which would shortly peak with Madame de Pompadour. Along with the Regent's sense of fleeting power, there was a general sense of fleeting time and fleeting affluence, the most powerful of stimulants for the collector of objects or sensations.

Regency affluence has its own fascinating story, which began with the death of Louis XIV and a state debt of three and a half *billion* livres.[22] Revenue for the next two years had been spent in advance and there was a confusion of currency, or what was left of it. Saint-Simon advised Philippe to declare state bankruptcy. The Duc de Noailles, head of the Conseil des Finances, objected and was upheld by the Regent. Noailles also proposed razing Versailles and removing it, presumably stone by stone, to Saint-Germain-en-Laye. Saint-Simon, at first speechless, replied, "Monsieur, when you have fairies and magic wands at your disposal, I will agree." Though he disliked Versailles, Saint-Simon, knowing the temptations of Paris for Philippe, counseled against moving the Court from Louis XIV's palace.

Other economic measures were taken—such as cuts in the army, the paring of expenses at Marly and Versailles—reforms in the tax system made—including the hanging of the most guilty tax evaders and rewarding those who informed on them. But bribery and corruption outbid rewards and defeated reforms, and net revenues were barely increased. At this point, or rather breach, a Scotsman named John Law re-entered the scene; he had first appeared in France in 1708 with a banking scheme which Louis XIV had not appreciated. This time he had his full hearing.

A twentieth-century financier born in Edinburgh in 1671, John Law is still dismissed in French schoolbooks as a "foreign adventurer" and a "cardsharp" who inflated the Mississippi Bubble until it burst.[23] He was all that, but he was also a man made internationalist by his enforced travels (he fled England after a fatal duel), who had studied the operations of the Bank of London, which had opened in 1694, and the Bank of Amsterdam, founded almost ninety years earlier, and who now proposed a similar Bank of France to the French Regent. Involved in his system were bank notes, bank credit, and bank balances, so familiar to us, but so foreign then to the French. Philippe, however, with his uninhibited intelligence, saw the possibilities in a paper money which, valued at several times the gold behind it, would immediately pump life into a moribund economy.

The beginnings were modest: a Banque Générale was established as a private concern run by John Law. It took in deposits, paid out interest, established credit, and issued bank notes whose stability proved greater than current coins (their weight was frequently changed by the state). Within a year the bank notes became acceptable as tax money. Two years later Law's private bank became the Banque Royale and the bank notes were legal tender. Law's system established a national source of credit for what looked like limitless expansion. Even the brothers Crozat yielded to him in their monopoly of Louisiana trade. To that Law joined the Mississippi and then the India companies, until he had a virtual monopoly of French foreign trade. The new conglomerate company required new capital, and confidently Law invited investors, promising fabulous returns. And so at first it was. Shares soared to forty times their original value. Philippe, who had received a gift of twenty-four thousand shares, appeared in person to distribute dividends. A dirty little street, Rue Quincampoix, became a Continental finance center. In the nearby Place Vendôme tents and wooden shanties sprang up as traders and gamblers poured in from all over Europe to get rich quick along with the Scotsman. Fortunes were made in a few hours: one banker, one hundred million livres in one day's span; an ordinary hotel waiter, thirty million in the same length of time. Duchesses queued with prostitutes to solicit John Law, who was busy with princes of the Court and Church.

The end was obvious—to a few. By now the paper value of shares in the Mississippi venture was eighty times the total value of all the gold and silver known to be in France. And a few cashed in before the fall—contributing, by their action, to it: the Duc de Bourbon, his shares for twenty million livres; the Prince de Conti, his for fourteen million more. Law could not refuse them. Three carts carried Conti's gold from the bank courtyard.[24] (Reproached by Philippe for disregarding the state's interest, the Duc de Bourbon replied, "I have a great love for money.") The panic began. Law drew on his own credit in an attempt to stop the hemorrhage, further ruining his great bank. The outflow reached tide proportions. The bubble burst. Murders and suicides occurred daily. A mob roared out of the "camp of the ruined" on the Place Vendôme, July 17, 1720, to lynch John Law.[25] He took shelter in the Palais Royal, fled, finally settled in Venice, where he died with only a diamond ring left of his fortune. And France? A phoenix all too frequent, it rose from the ashes of the burned, useless bank notes (redeemed at a fraction of their face value) and the Regency carried on as before (a central Banque de France to await Napoleon in the next century).

As if protected by a *cordon sanitaire,* neither the young King nor his palace at Versailles had been greatly affected by either the venture of Law or the adventures of Philippe. In the meantime, Louis XV was growing toward his majority in February 1723, at the age of thirteen. In anticipation, he had returned with the Court the previous June to Louis XIV's palace. Philippe was to return with him, but only to die (preceded by Dubois, whose last, half-mad years were spent trying to accrue every honor once earned by Cardinal Richeliu).*

* One should also say adieu to the Duc de Saint-Simon, who had pressed his advice on Philippe too often and was cold-shouldered into self-exile. He left the Court in 1723 and died, unremarked, thirty years later.

Our Parisian entr'acte, the Regency intermission between kings and palaces, thus draws to a close, as it began, at Versailles. On December 2, 1723, Philippe, now the King's prime minister, descended at the day's end to his apartment on the ground floor. He sank heavily into an armchair and called for his mistress, Madame de Falari. She sat near him. He caressed her hand. "Do you believe," he suddenly asked, "do you really believe in God, hell and paradise after this life?"

"Yes, my Prince," she said. "I really do."

"If so," he said, "you must be miserable leading this life."

"I hope God will have mercy on me," she said.

Depressed, Philippe drank a bit of cinnamon-flavored water, then fell forward in his chair. "Jésus Maria," cried his mistress, "have pity on me!" and she ran through empty corridors looking for help. Eventually she found a lackey who knew something about bleeding. But when he prepared to begin, he was stopped by Madame de Sabran. "My God," she said, "he has just been with a trollop! You'll kill him!"[26]

But Philippe had long since killèd himself, and death came a few hours later before he was fifty. With aesthetic appropriateness, he quit the stage together with his style.

14. The Unmaking of a Monarch

The twelve-year-old Louis XV, "as beautiful as Eros,"[1] had returned to Versailles on the arm of his Regent, so wrongly accused of wanting to poison him. The townspeople had known of his coming two months before. The great palace had been aired and made ready. On June 15, 1722, they lined the broad Avenue de Paris and cheered the young King and his consorts. He was to spend over half a century in his great-grandfather's palace, more years, indeed, than Louis XIV himself. He came with the Duc d'Orléans and the Duc de Bourbon, with his guardian, the old (seventy-eight) Maréchal de Villeroi, and his tutor, the aging (sixty-nine) Bishop of Fréjus, André Hercule de Fleury. Impetuously he led them through the gardens, down the paths and *allées,* past the fountains and parterres, like a child that had come home and raced to see his remembered treasures. Two hours they walked, the King dancing, until, tired, he returned to the palace and lay down on the floor of the Grande Galerie—not because he was tired, but the better to see Le Brun's ceiling.[2]

There may be no greater sense of kingdom for a little king—even the visitor feels it—than the enclosed kingdom of Versailles. But Louis XV was not quite King; that would await the sacred crowning at Rheims in October. The first scandal, though it scarcely touched him, could not, it seemed, wait even that long. Within the first month, nobles of the younger set, most of them under twenty and married, were discovered in the bosquets of the park sporting sexually with each other. Their wives, to whom their preferences were all too familiar, had taken lovers. The young men were the companions of the King; one was the grandson of Villeroi, his guardian. All but one, in fact, were banished from Versailles, their punishment capped by the forced accompaniment of their wives. A young marquis, who may have been the ringleader, was sent to the Bastille. (Neither boys nor men were to be Louis XV's problem, but he was so "pretty"—the word shocks, but the Rigaud portrait imposes it—it was thought best to remove unmanly influences.) When he asked about his missing companions, it was explained that they had been caught pulling up the palisades in the gardens and sent away. Thereafter, of course, they were referred to as *les arracheurs de palissades.*[3]

Villeroi, who loudly cried for his grandson's banishment,[4] was not long in following. Old and cranky, he had raised Louis XV to be suspicious of his uncle's "poisonous" schemes and the Regent "possibly" resented it.* Moreover, the ancient *maréchal,* after the move to Versailles, still tended to surround the King as if he were a bodyguard of one, asserting, as his guardian, that it was his royal duty to stay close to the King, even when he was closeted with the Regent. Thus one afternoon, the captain of the guards approached the old man, politely asked for his arm, saying, "I am to take you to a carriage and the carriage to Villeroi"—the *maréchal's* estate. Indignantly the old man refused. A *chaise à porteurs,* discreetly hidden, was now brought forward and he was bundled into it. The door was swiftly closed, the porters picked up the chair and "in the same twinkling of the eye" Villeroi was carried out a garden window, onto the terrace, down the great staircase of the Orangerie, and into a waiting coach.[5]

And his young charge? Louis tried to look brave when told about his guardian's induced departure, but that night in bed he burst into tears, as he had when his governess had been separated from him. Madame de Ventadour, who had snatched Louis as a baby from the royal quacks and saved his life, continued, as his governess, to care for him until, age seven, he was put into Villeroi's hands. He had been a delicate child and had become a sturdy, beautiful boy, shy, nervous, and petulant. Villeroi, who had the bearing of an old soldier, taught Louis how to carry himself as a king, but little else. He subjected him to endless parades, reviews, and receptions. If he did not create, he deepened, Louis XV's painful aversion for crowds, unfamiliars, and public appearances. He also had fatal political pre-

* Once he upset a *café à la crème* offered his charge by the Regent—Lavisse.

tensions. One feast day of St. Louis, he took the young King to a window of the Tuileries, pointed to the celebrating crowd outside and said, "Look, sire! All that multitude, all those people, are your subjects. They belong to you. You are their master."[6] He extended the same lesson in his advice on handling ministers. "Hold the chamber pot for them while they are in office," he told the boy, "but pour it over their heads when they are through."[7]

France and the King's ministers were more fortunate in the King's *précepteur*. Fleury, too, was an older man. He was in his seventieth year when the Court returned to Versailles, but he was to die in his ninetieth, the years in between marked by his influence. He had been almoner of Marie-Thérèse and Louis XIV, then Bishop of Fréjus when he was summoned to Court to become Louis XV's tutor. The promotion pleased him. ("Bishop of Fréjus," he used to sign his letters, "by divine indignation.") There was shrewdness in his tutorship. It may even have been true, as the Marquis d'Argenson tells us,* that Fleury brought a pack of cards, together with the Latin textbook, for Louis' lessons, the book often remaining open while they played cards. Melancholy plagued this prince, and his tutor, above all others, knew it. Diversions had to be mixed with lessons, but there are several hundred compositions and translations, written in the young King's rapid hand between the ages of seven and thirteen, available for Fleury's critics at the Bibliothèque Nationale. He preferred—what child would not?—his little printing press with which he put together—with unmentioned help—a seventy-two-page booklet on the rivers of Europe at the age of eight. There were also the dutifully copied maxims about being a hard-working rather than a do-nothing king with Saint Louis, in his case, designated as the model.

Approaching his majority, Louis was taught economy, political and domestic, by the Regent and Dubois. "The King," he was lectured, "can be only as rich as his subjects." The King had but to look around him when he left the Tuileries to see their poverty. He was loved, all historians agree, by the people. What prince, in his youthful promise, is not? Stories of a cruelty beyond that of most boys—shooting his tame doe,[8] tormenting to death the kittens of his cat[9]—had probably not yet reached the people and, if they had, were likely disbelieved, such was the charm of liquid eyes and long eyelashes, a

---

* René-Louis de Voyer, Marquis d'Argenson, future foreign minister and friend of Voltaire, his *Journal et Mémoires* offers many insights into the period.

budlike mouth, and being a prince. When, at eleven, Louis fell ill, the people wept; when he recovered, they rejoiced. The ladies of Les Halles, the central markets of Paris, rented carriages, loaded them with wine, and drove, drinking, to the Tuileries. "Long live the King!" they cried. "To the devil with the Regent!" Night after night Parisians took to the street (a dangerous habit) to celebrate.

They soon had another occasion. Negotiations with Spain had been completed: Louis XV was formally engaged to be married to the Infanta, María Ana Victoria, daughter of Philip V. (Informed, Louis wept.) She arrived six months later and Louis was taken outside the walls of Paris to meet her.

The Infanta descended from her carriage, Louis from his. She knelt before him, he raised her to her feet. "Madame," said the twelve-year-old king to his five-year-old fiancée, "I am delighted to find you have journeyed to France in excellent health."[10]

It was March 2, 1722. The next day the King gave the intended queen a doll. "Everyone," says Barbier, an observant, diary-keeping notary, "finds this marriage very original." Actually the marriage was not to take place before the Infanta was no longer such an infant— perhaps ten years thence. One can understand the uneasiness at Court during the affair of *les arracheurs de palissades* that July; few wanted the fine twig of their prince perversely bent.

That fall Louis was crowned King, that winter the Regent died. An odd pair replaced him as Louis' prime minister: the Duc de Bourbon, great-grandson of the Grand Condé, and his mistress, Madame de Prie. Even as Orléans lay dying—or was hardly dead—the Duc de Bourbon had scurried up the staircase to the King's apartments to press for the office. After a glance at his tutor and Fleury's apparent approval, Louis reluctantly nodded yes.[11] The Bourbon branch thus succeeded the rival Orléans faction. The Duc de Bourbon, according to La Palatine (an *orléaniste* of course), was grossly forbidding: "tall, bowed, thin as a splinter, with stork-like legs and spider-like body, two eyes so red you could not distinguish the good eye from the bad." More-over, neither his intelligence nor his integrity—we have remarked the fortune he made from John Law—matched his ambition. On the other hand, Madame de Prie, his mistress—she had originally tried for the Regent—may have had enough ability and charm for both. ("She possessed more than beauty; her whole person breathed seduction" —Duclos.)

Their two-and-a-half-year rule added to their fortune as it lessened the Infanta's and that of France. In 1725, when Louis fell ill, it was the Duc de Bourbon who became the more feverish. Should the young King die, the son of the former Regent would inherit the crown. A dozen times during the day, the duke looked in on the King and one night was seen going anxiously to him, dressed in his bonnet and dressing gown. "What will happen to me?" he was heard muttering. "Should he recover, he must be married."[12]

Louis was fifteen, the Infanta was eight. The duke and his mistress felt that they dare not delay. They decided to send her back to Spain and risk Spanish anger; it was the lesser risk. But they had to find another eligible princess. A secretary of state in the foreign ministry was set the task of preparing a list. Ninety-nine names were found for it, then narrowed down to seventeen. Carefully the pair studied them. There were, to begin with, the duke's own two sisters, but that would be too flagrant. There was the daughter of the Tsar, but neither she nor her father was considered completely sane or removed from barbarism. There was the daughter of the Prince of Wales, but she was Protestant. And there was Marie Leszczynska, daughter of a Polish nobleman who had sat briefly on the Polish throne. (Marie had never been distant from Madame de Prie's mind. At one time she had considered Marie as a possible, complaisant second wife for her lover, the Duc de Bourbon.) "The parents are not rich," read the remarks attached to her name, "and would doubtless want to settle in France—which would be inconvenient."[13]

Marie's father, Stanislas Leszczynski, was indeed living with the remnants of a court in Alsace on an allowance which arrived irregularly from France. Marie herself was pleasant and plain, and almost seven years older than Louis. But in Madame de Prie's eyes, the penniless princess would be forever beholden to her as Queen—and Marie Leszczynska was proposed to Louis XV. Disinterestedly he agreed, and a letter was dispatched to Wissembourg. Excitedly Stanislas called to Marie and told her to rejoice. Was he, she asked, recalled to the Polish throne?

"Oh no," he cried, choking with pleasure, "you are to be the Queen of France!"[14]

Stanislas promptly borrowed money and redeemed the family jewels from a Frankfurt pawnshop.

The Court at Versailles was not enchanted. Nor the people. "We have a Queen whose name ends in *ski*," mourned Mathieu Marais in his diary. And rumors flew that Marie was a freak with webbed toes and cold humors.[15] But the day after the wedding night, the Duc de Bourbon could write Stanislas a reassuring letter that went the rounds:

"I have the honor [he wrote] to announce that the King is enormously pleased with the Queen. The proof, if Your Majesty will permit, is that the King, after being entertained by a play and fireworks, retired to sleep with the Queen and gave her, during the night, seven proofs of his tenderness. It was the King himself who informed me through a mutual *confidant,* as soon as he rose, and then repeated it in person, elaborating on his satisfaction with the Queen."[16]

And the French Court was now relieved. It had a king, once again, who was interested in more than hunting—and it forgave him his first years of fidelity. Louis was to father ten children within less than ten years, and to be faithful for the first seven of them. It began with twin daughters in 1727 ("and they said I wasn't capable of even one child!" said the seventeen-year-old King) and continued with another daughter the next year (which he greeted with less delight), but a Dauphin was born in 1729, another boy in 1730, then a series of girls until the last in 1737, to be known as Madame Dernière. Six daughters and the Dauphin were to survive, and Louis, his duty done, looked elsewhere.

But the first years of his reign were not equally orderly. The Duc de Bourbon managed to displease, if not infuriate, every segment of the population. His financial advisers, the brothers Pâris, set the louis d'or and écu dancing up and down, and the price of bread, during the famine of 1725, tripled in six months. There were riots in Brittany and Normandy. Bakery shops were broken into and pillaged in Paris and there were disturbances in Versailles. The persecution of Protestants was foolishly resumed, and again whole provinces were empoverished by their flight. According to Narbonne, *commissaire de police* at Versailles, people believed it was the Duc de Bourbon's credo that "there were too many people in France and it was better that some died." Narbonne does note, as well, that "perhaps that rumor was without foundations."[17]

Fleury, who was a member of the State Council, kept the young King informed of the state of affairs—and the duke knew it. But when the duke attempted to discredit Louis' councilor, he hastened his own downfall. He solicited the Queen to draw the King to her apartment, so he might speak to him separately from Fleury. Louis, still in the flush of his first year of marriage, arrived and was surprised to find the duke, and was further surprised when he was handed a letter written by the Cardinal de Polignac full of accusations against the Bishop of Fréjus. He read it, then handed it back without a word. The duke asked him what he thought of the letter.

"Nothing."

"Your Majesty does not wish to give a command?"

"That things remain as they are."

"I have displeased Your Majesty?"

"Yes."

"Monsieur de Fréjus alone has Your Majesty's confidence?"

"Yes."

The duke reddened, the Queen paled. The duke kneeled and begged Louis' pardon. Louis granted it in a manner that held no promise, and left the room.[18]

Fleury himself, aware of the duke's stratagem, had gone to the Queen's apartment and found it locked against him. Immediately he quit Versailles, but he left a letter of fond farewell for Louis. "Reading it, the King broke into tears."[19] He was, one must remind oneself, only fifteen. He fretted, then sent for the duke and ordered him to write Fleury, asking him to return. The duke's days were now to number but a few months. One day in 1726 the King told his prime minister he expected him that evening at Rambouillet for supper, and departed. But that afternoon, before the duke left for the rendezvous, the order for his banishment to Chantilly was executed. At four the following morning, Madame de Prie was seen leaving Versailles for Normandy, accompanied only by her husband. A year later she was dead, "poisoned by her own hand."[20] As for the Queen, on the same day as the duke's banishment Fleury himself brought her a letter signed by the King. "I pray you, Madame," it read, "and if need be, command you, to do all the Bishop of Fréjus may require as if it came from me."[21]

Louis XV's devotion to Marie Leszczynska in the early years, so "movingly" described by contemporary memoirs, obviously had its Bourbon limits. Similarly, his dismissal of the duke, a popular measure, was immediately followed by a Bourbonic gesture. When his ministers asked him to whom they should now refer for instructions, he replied, in a faint echo of the Sun King, "To me." In truth, it was Fleury, seventy-three, who would exercise the power of prime minister—for seventeen years—without the title, but with the status of a cardinal (for precedence over the dukes in the State Council). He was a man who lived without luxury and would die without a penny, who chose his aides well and administered them effectively. He would keep France at peace until pushed otherwise and give French currency a stability that would last until the Revolution. He was the essence of *bon sens,* but his common sense—and behavior—proved too common for even so sensible a courtier as d'Argenson.

"One of the most ridiculous spectacles of the time," says the marquis, "is the *petit coucher* of Cardinal de Fleury. All France crowds his anteroom in attendance. His Eminence enters, goes into his cabinet, the door is opened to those waiting. You see this old priest take off his trousers, which he carefully folds. Then he is handed a shabby dressing gown and night shirt, and he combs his four white hairs." But d'Argenson describes Fleury elsewhere in his *Journal* as one who "loves the King and the State, and is honest and sincere."

Indeed all indications seemed favorable. "The King works admirably with his ministers," d'Argenson remarks in 1730, "and reaches just decisions. . . . People wonder if he will continue to work. . . . [but] we must remember that he is almost without passions or dominant tastes, and boredom leaves a void which has to be filled. . . . All this gives promise of a happy reign."

One must add to this portrait of Louis at twenty the observations of Barbier, who viewed the first half of his reign from the cooler perspective of Paris. April 1730: "Today the King went for six weeks to Fontainebleau to hunt stags, which is his only occupation." A year later: "His taste for hunting is unchanged, but people say it is less for the hunt itself than from an urge to move about from place to place."

France could afford Louis' restlessness because Fleury stayed in his place, wise, cautious, considerate, and gentle—to all but the Jansenists. It may have been his major fault and one of the fatal flaws of the *ancien régime.* If originally "Jansenism had been an aristocratic and doctrinal movement," it had since become "popular and sentimental."[22] In March 1730, Fleury thought to put an end to it once and for all by reviving the papal bull *Unigenitus,* condemning Jansenism in the last years of Louis XIV. The bull had been re-

sisted by a powerful group of seven bishops, supported by the Archbishop
of Paris and the Cardinal de Noailles; most of the religious orders,
jealous of the Jesuits, joined them in opposition to the bull; and so
did Parlement, sensing a popular issue. Consequently it refused to
register the March 1730 decree, signed by the King, and thus rendered
it inoperative. In April, Louis held a *lit de justice* overriding the
refusal. Parlement countered with a decree of its own. The decree
was then voided by the King's Council of State. After the interval of
summer's vacation, fifty members of Parlement drove in fourteen
carriages from Paris to the Court, then at Marly. They asked for
Fleury, the chancellor, or the King. None would receive them. Finally
they were informed that the King was "surprised" to hear of their
presence and expected them instantly to return to where they belonged.
Humiliated, they took the road back to Paris (as, one day, Parisians
would take the King back to where they thought *he* belonged). They
continued, nevertheless, to seek an audience. Exasperated, Louis summoned them to Versailles for the ultimate in a bed of justice.

When they arrived, they were told complete silence was expected
from them after the King had spoken. They were then taken into
the *chambre de parade* of Louis XIV for an imitation of the grand
manner by Louis XV. He all but brandished a riding crop as he told
them of his discontent (Fleury, of course, standing by). Chancellor
Daguesseau continued: all laws and their interpretations were the province of the King, not of Parlement. Theirs was but to execute them.
Those who refused would be considered "disobedient and rebel."

"Do not force me," said Louis, dismissing them, "to make you
know that I am your master."[23]

Unfortunately for Louis, Parlement had found a popularity it had
never before experienced. It was still a time of "miracles," and for
almost five years a simple tomb of a Jansenist "saint" in a Paris
cemetery had become the center of pilgrimages and demonstrations,
convulsions and cures (an abbé testified to them). Even the Princesse
de Conti had come (fruitlessly) for a cure for her blindness.[24]
The crowds increased, the hysteria likewise. Cures were recounted in
the clandestine *Nouvelles Ecclésiastiques;* hysteria became sedition.
On January 27, 1732, a royal decree closed the Saint-Medard cemetery, and three days later Barbier copied this graffito on its wall:
"De par le Roi, défense à Dieu/De faire miracle en ce lieu." By order
of the King, God is forbidden to work miracles in this place.

The "miracles" ceased, the hysteria subsided, leaders of Parlement were exiled, then appeased. But the cult did not disappear. In 1733, in the royal chapel at Versailles, a woman suddenly cried out to the King that he had a spell cast upon him, his marriage was nullified, and his children were not his. The King smiled, the woman was seized, taken to an asylum, then released.[25] The same year, if Abbé Proyart is to be believed, the King's second son, not yet three, was taken ill and surreptitiously treated by Jansenist cultists at Court hoping to curry the Queen's favor. They had him given pills made of dirt taken from the Saint-Medard tomb in Paris. The post-mortem revealed his intestines choked with earth.[26]

The year of 1733 was decidedly not the year of miracles, but it was memorable in its own way. It was the year of Louis XV's first war and first official mistress. The story of the first war is quickly told. Fleury had continued Dubois' policy of entente with England and got on well with Robert Walpole, who, preferring conquest by commerce, was equally pacific. However, in 1733, the pressures of prestige and bad advice led Fleury to support Stanislas' return to the vacant Polish throne; his daughter would then achieve her proper status and France its proper role in European affairs. French money bought the Polish electors, and Stanislas was again the Polish King. He even made gestures of becoming a strong king, at which point Russia and Austria intervened. The Russians took Warsaw and Stanislas took refuge in Danzig. Cautiously Fleury sent a token convoy of 1500 men to his rescue which was largely shot up on arrival. The Russians took Danzig, and Stanislas, disguised as a sailor, fled to France. Russia too distant, Louis declared war against Austria. Assailed by Spain and Sardinia as well, the Emperor eventually ceded. Stanislas was installed at Lunéville as "King of Lorraine" with the understanding among the powers that the province on his death would become part of France (as it did in 1766).

The tale of the first mistress is, justifiably, longer in the telling (Louis XV, unlike Louis XIV, increasingly gave his private life priority). It was a sad thing, old Maréchal de Villars said to him, to see a King of France, so young and lacking nothing, so bored. Why did he not add such diversions as music or the theater to his passion for hunting? Such things, replied Louis, were not to his taste, and he turned away.[27] For the Marquis d'Argenson, the cause of Louis' ennui was clearly the Queen. "She behaved like a prude." And the marquis quotes her tiredly saying, *"Toujours coucher, toujours grosse, toujours accoucher!"* Always being bedded, always pregnant, always having babies! So she swathed herself in bedclothes and feigned ill health (five years later it was to be true: she developed a scrofulous fistula, "and the King's ardor sought other channels").[28] She was superstitious and afraid of ghosts. At night a lady in waiting would hold her hand and tell her stories until she fell asleep, and that was the scene awaiting the King when he came "to render his conjugal duties."[29] There may be a masculine unfairness here; possibly the King's coldness had come first. But Marie was "always pregnant" and conceivably worn out from childbirth; in any case, she was a seven-year-older woman who had run to unappealing fat.[30] She turned her corner of Versailles (the south-facing apartments of the Queen) into a quasi-convent to which she withdrew together with her entourage, and there she ate, played at painting and cards, wove tapestry, chatted, and ate,[31]* often a dinner of twenty-nine dishes, exclusive of fruit.

Louis had not yet arranged *his* corner of the palace into a rakish bachelor's retreat. Shy, reserved, intimidated by the vast, public palace of his great-grandfather, he fled Versailles in his young manhood for the hunt and intimacy of other palaces. In 1730, for instance, according to Narbonne, he spent only 102 days at Versailles; in 1731, 126 days; the rest of the time he was at Marly, Fontainebleau, Compiègne, Rambouillet, or La Muette. "The King," Barbier noted, "does not like Versailles. He is always gay when he is away from it." One might add that custom required the Queen, when pregnant, to remain at Versailles.

When at Versailles, Louis often descended by an interior staircase from his northern corner to the ground-floor apartment of the Comtesse de Toulouse, just below. Here he found his own Court within the Court, a circle of intimates; the young men among them were called *les marmousets,* or urchins. Often, after a day's hunting at the Château de La Muette (on the edge of Paris' Bois de Boulogne), they would suddenly appear in the royal box at the Opéra, or at a masked ball, the King incognito in their midst. At Versailles, in

---

* "What should you do when you're bored?" she once rhetorically asked. "Give yourself indigestion. At least it is something to do!" (Lavisse).

the salon of the Comtesse de Toulouse, there was a Regency un-
restraint and the assurance of privacy; there were light conversation
and heavy gambling. And one of the games—with every woman present
expected to play it—was, Who would be Louis' first mistress?

The sister of the Duc de Bourbon, Mademoiselle de Charolais,
may have tried her hand and, failing (she was fifteen years older
than Louis), introduced him (with Fleury's blessing) to the one who
succeeded. Her Château de Madrid was a short carriage ride from
Louis' hunting lodge at La Muette; easily and gaily *les marmousets*
went back and forth between them. It was at La Muette that Louis
indicated that the game was drawing to a close. He lifted his champagne
glass and drank to "the unknown woman."[32] The unknown was not
long in becoming known: she was Louise de Nesle, the Comtesse de
Mailly and one of the Queen's own *dames du palais*. She was
exactly the same age as the King, with an ugliness that put him at
ease. Moreover, the Marquis d'Argenson enlightens us, she was "good-
natured, tractable and cheerful and by no means clever." When, later,
she became known as Louis' mistress, "her ugliness scandalized foreigners, who expect a King's mistress at least to have a pretty face."

The seduction scene (also according to the marquis) took place
in one of Louis' *cabinets* at Versailles, the young King more seduced
than seducing. Bachelier, the first *valet de chambre,* and Chauvelin,
keeper of the royal seals, had arranged it. "She emerged from behind
a screen. The King looked guilty and embarrassed. . . . She told
him her feet were cold and sat close to the fire. The King took her
pretty foot in his hand, then her leg, then her garter. As she had
been instructed not to show any resistance to such a shy man, she pos-
ingly said, 'Oh dear! If I had known Your Majesty had me come for
this, I should not have come!' Impulsively the King sprang to
embrace her." And she remained.

In the beginning there was discretion. For the Duc de Luynes, a
courtier close to the Queen, Madame de Mailly had become Louis'
mistress sometime in 1733, though it probably occurred a year earlier;
the Queen, informed, accepted it. But it would be five years before
it was official and Madame de Mailly installed in the remodeled
petits appartements of Louis' private world. She asked little and received it. The cardinal was content with so modest a mistress; she
attempted no intrigues and dreamed of no influence. She was smuggled
into the palace late in the evening for two hours with the King,

then smuggled out—until 1738, when the *petits appartements* were readied in the north wing and she became the *maîtresse en titre.**

Inevitably, then, Louise's successor could not be far off-stage. In fact, it was her sister, Félicité de Nesle, who replaced her. But not immediately. For a time they shared the King—with the Queen. Fresh from a convent, Félicité may have been the brightest of the family, but no more beautiful. According to her sister Hortense, "she had the face of a grenadier, the neck of a crane and the smell of a monkey."[33] She was *gigantesque,* brash, and ambitious. She had solicited older sister Louise's invitation to live with her at Versailles and had immediately set her cap toward becoming the Madame de Montespan of Louis XV's regime.[34]

It was Félicité's spirited brashness, says d'Argenson, that seems to have pleased the King. But it led her as well to displays of bad temper. After one such, Louis sharply rebuked her before the Court. "I know very well, Madame la Comtesse," he said bluntly, "what must be done to cure you of it. It would be to cut off your head. It would not even be too bad for you, since your neck is so long. Your blood would be drained and replaced by the blood of a lamb."[35] The story is by the Queen's confidant, the Duc de Luynes, thus possibly harsher than reality. The King seems to have loved Félicité within the limits of his capacity; it was he who made her pregnant and a countess (by arranging a marriage with the Comte de Vintimille).

But Louis' liaison with the second of the Nesle sisters was not long in duration. Pregnant again with his child, Félicité took to bed gravely ill. Forgivingly, sister Louise returned from the convent, to which she had withdrawn, to nurse Félicité back to health. The lying-in was painful and prolonged. Fever followed; death followed the fever. The countess died in the middle of the night in Louise's arms. (The son born would be called *demi-Louis* all his life, he so resembled his father.) The next day the King was "inconsolable"; and he left Versailles that night with Louise, but without a leave-taking from the Queen. (Louis XIV had a greater sense of the proprieties.) Then the inconsolable Louis was consoled by the eternally compliant Louise. She became his mistress again, or rather, in the interim, for she introduced him to the third sister. Fat, clever, and homely,

* Five of Louis' daughters were moved out of Versailles at this time. Madame Adélaïde, six, had thrown herself into Louis' arms, pleading to stay. She wept, he wept, she stayed.

Adélaïde de Nesle amused the King briefly, but a fourth, Hortense de Nesle, may have resisted him, since she became a friend of the Queen. But then there was a fifth sister.

Louis' carrousel of the sisters Nesle gave rise to the expectable Paris witticisms; the most popular was this verse of 1742:

> The first is forgotten, the second is dust;
> The third is ready, the fourth waiting
> To give way to a fifth.
> Is it infidelity or constancy
> To be faithful to an entire family?*

Marie-Anne de Nesle, prettiest of the sisters, was just twenty-four when she persuaded Louise to present her to the King. She had married the Marquis de La Tournelle at fifteen; he had died when she was twenty-three. Cleverer, more covetous than her sisters, she arranged the conditions of her surrender to the King through the Duc de Richelieu (our old friend, returned to the Court as a marshal and first gentleman of the royal bedchamber). And she became the acknowledged mistress of the King (with an apartment of her own above his) and the Duchesse de Châteauroux, with the estate's income of eighty thousand livres a year. Children born to them were to be legitimized and, coldest of her conditions, her sister Louise was to be exiled from Versailles. La Châteauroux boasted of this in a letter to Richelieu, away in Flanders, adding that the Queen was darting her the dirtiest of looks, "her right according to the rules of the game."[36]

Even the courtiers were shocked by the coldness. "One does not dare talk about it aloud," d'Argenson writes, "but all now worry about the character of the King"; and Versailles regretted Madame de Mailly's departure from his side. It was compared to La Vallière's, for Louise withdrew into piety, though she did not take the veil. Several years before she died, in 1751, she had gone, as usual, to the church near her father's place in Picardy. It was crowded as she entered, and she was led to her seat by the sexton. As he pushed his way past the worshipers, a man was heard loudly saying, "That's

---

* *La première en oubli, la seconde en poussière,*
La troisième est en pied, la quatrième attend
Et fera place à la dernière.
Choisir une famille entière
Est-ce être infidèle ou constant?

a lot of fuss for a whore!" Louise turned toward him. "Sir," she
said, "since you know my faults so well, pray God he will forgive
me."[37]

Meanwhile in the 1740's, Fleury, weakened with age, could no
longer resist the King's pressure to enter the War of the Austrian Succession, which had been brought on largely by Frederick II's ambition to
add Silesia to Prussia. It was Félicité de Nesle who had built the pressure in the King, when his mistress, to enter on the side of Frederick
and share a dismembered Austrian Empire with him. But within a
year of France's entrance Frederick was secretly negotiating a separate
truce with Austria; he was to acquire Silesia if he withdrew from the
war, which he proceeded to do.* French victories in Bohemia were
turned into a frightful retreat with which Fleury, in his ninetieth year
in 1743, could no longer cope. He died, ending, as Barbier remarks
and many felt, an era of relative tranquillity for France. There was no
reassurance when Louis XV once again at thirty-three, as at sixteen,
announced at the first Council of State after Fleury's death, *"Messieurs,
I am now the prime minister."*

It was a pose that must have struck the Marquis d'Argenson,
shortly to be appointed foreign minister, as particularly empty. Four
years earlier he had noted in his *Journal:* "The King rises at eleven
and leads a useless life. He steals from his frivolous occupations
one hour of work; the sessions with the ministers cannot be called
work, for he lets them do everything, merely listening or repeating
what they say like a parrot. He is still very much of a child."†

And a year later, more ominously, d'Argenson wrote: "With lack
of bread and rising prices in Paris, famine in the country and heavier
taxation, the Cardinal is at his wit's end and his resignation is expected
from day to day. When the King drove through the capital, he was
greeted with cries of *misère! du pain, du pain!* Bread! Bread! When
Fleury drove through Paris, women seized the bridle of his horses,
opened the door of his carriage and screamed *du pain, du pain,* we
are dying of hunger! He almost died of fright and threw coins to the
crowd."

After Fleury's death, Louis XV, his own prime minister, was sub-

---

* Wherefore the French expression, *travailler pour le roi de Prusse,* working
for the King of Prussia, as meaning pulling someone else's chestnuts out of the
fire.

† "I always felt," Louis XV wrote his uncle in Madrid on Fleury's death,
"that he had taken the place of my parents."

ject to the iron whim of the Duchesse de Châteauroux. Unhappily he
confided to her mother-in-law, the Duchesse de Brancas, who recounts
it in her *Mémoires,* that his mistress was pressing him to heroic action
on the battlefield. "I am desolate," he said. "Several times I told her
that she was killing me, and do you know what she replies? 'So much
the better, Sire. A King must be brought back to life.'"[38]

Reluctantly Louis took the traditional route to Flanders to join his
army and in the oldest of traditions the Duchesse de Châteauroux,
with sister Adélaïde, followed him. There were a few victories and
as many festivities, then the Austrians occupied Alsace and Lorraine,
and Stanislas had to flee from Lunéville. Louis hastened from Lille
to Metz, and there fell quite ill. It may have been no more than
sunstroke, but it provided the *dévots* of his Court, and particularly the
Bishop of Soissons, his almoner, with a heaven-sent opportunity to
demand the departure of Louis' mistress, who had come to "tend"
him. Death, the bishop told him, was imminent. He must reconcile
himself with God by sending away the duchess, for otherwise the
last rites could not be administered. Frightened, Louis yielded. "You
must go," he told his mistress, "I am dying." She left with her sister.
Wherever her carriage passed, on her way back to Paris, it was greeted
with jeers and pelted with rotten fruit; at La Férte-sous-Jouarre, where
it stopped for a change of horses, it was struck with stones.

Hurrying toward the King in the opposite direction, the cortege of
the Queen crossed the path of the King's mistress. There was no
greeting between them. Arriving at Metz, Marie went directly to Louis'
chamber. He embraced her and begged her pardon before members of
the Court. "God alone," she said, "has been offended." The Bishop
of Soissons imposed a full public confession. Fearing death and dam-
nation, again Louis yielded. Even the bourgeois of Metz came to hear
him ask forgiveness for his conduct, and his declaration, signed, was
sent by the bishop to every parish, to be read from every pulpit. The
Dauphin, despite the King's wishes, had been brought to Metz along
with the Queen, as if in preparation for a vacant throne.

Then "miraculously" Louis recovered. The people "rejoiced," a poet
lyrically referred to him as *le Bien-Aimé,* but Louis the Well-Beloved
was never to forgive those for whose forgiveness he had been forced
to beg. Briefly he rejoined his army, then returned to Versailles. He
banished the Bishop of Soissons and the *dévots* among his courtiers;
he recalled his mistress. But the triumph of the Duchesse de Châ-

teauroux was as ephemeral as Louis' mortal illness. "Barely," says the Duchesse de Brancas, "had she received the King's letter [calling her back to Versailles], when she felt unendurable pains in her eyes and head. Instead of going to him, she had to go to bed, and there she burned with fever. In two days she was dead."[39]

And Louis XV, thirty-four, awaited, as did his Court, his next mistress, the first other than the Nesle sisters.

But less than ever was there a sense of "the promise of a happy reign," expressed fourteen years before by the Marquis d'Argenson. The marquis himself became foreign minister at this time, to be dismissed four years later, completely disillusioned. He had believed, as he had written, that only an absolute monarchy could protect the people from oppression, but, observing Louis XV, the prince who had never grown up, he had become disenchanted. "Absolute monarchical government," he now confided to his *Journal*, "is excellent under a good king, but who will guarantee that we shall always have an Henry IV? Experience and nature prove that we shall get ten bad kings for every good one."

Louis himself may have agreed. However, heir to a system beyond him, his desires, or his pretensions, he said, "At least it will last my lifetime." Or, in the words of his next mistress, *"Après moi le déluge."*

Perhaps nothing symbolized this retirement from royal responsibility, this acceptance of being what Louis XIV had so abhorred, a *roi fainéant*, as Louis XV's play-acting of a *lever* and *coucher* before the Court. Morning and night, Louis XV would go through the motions of rising and going to bed in the great chamber of Louis XIV, then after the ceremony, if it were evening, slip out through the Council room to his own smaller (and better warmed) bedroom in the new *petits appartements*, to reverse the masquerade in the morning. The Sun King's bedroom, once the radiant center of the French monarchy, had indeed become a *chambre de parade* and his successor quite literally a *roi de parade*, a sovereign without substance.

But if Louis XV belittled the crown and palace of his great-grand-father, he provided the latter with a private world, a thing of bachelor beauty—the *petits appartements*.

15. Worlds Within Worlds

"It is the Versailles of Louis XV we see," says the poet who became its curator, Pierre de Nolhac.[1] And the loveliest of it is out of sight—a "delicious retreat" for the few who were privileged to enter it, a "rat's nest" for the many more who were not.

Slowly, with the hesitancy of indolence as much as respect, Louis XV converted his north corner of the great palace to his taste and life style. The taste, springing directly from the Regency, would be disparagingly called rococo; the life style had begun to take form with the first of the Nesle sisters as one, then the other, was successively, or simultaneously, installed above the *petits appartements*. Should one make the most of the fact that, whereas Louis XIV installed Madame de Montespan magnificently on his own floor, Louis XV chose rooms under the roof for Madame de Mailly? It has been done.[2] The comparison is meant to underline the decline of grandeur at Versailles in the fifty years of Louis XV. But grandeur is not the only form of beauty, and Louis XIV's monumentality, as Madame de Maintenon discovered, defied livability. The lowered ceilings, the human scale of the *petits appartements;* the light, bright, dancing beauty of the sculpted woodwork and paneled walls; the comfort and intimacy of the new rooms have their own appeal to those with a sense of domesticity and bourgeois privacy—if a sense of privacy, contrasted to the Sun King's overt style, must be called middle-class.

Until he was twenty-eight, Louis XV suffered the frigid grandeur of Louis XIV's great bedchamber, lighting the fire himself early mornings, as he half-pridefully, half-complainingly remarked to the Duc de Luynes, "to let those poor devils"—his lackeys—"sleep."³ Much later, more assertively, he had architect Gabriel install a second fireplace (with a lighter, mirrored mantelpiece characteristic of the Louis Quinze style). In the meantime he moved his bedroom next door to the State Council Room, then finally to the converted Billiard Room with its two windows facing south across the marble courtyard. A cluster of smaller rooms—bath, dining room, study—was arranged around an interior courtyard, the Cour des Cerfs. The dining room was new to Versailles—and France. Louis XIV had his table set for the usual public ritual in the Antichambre de l'Oeil-de-Boeuf.* Another touch of privacy was the *cabinet* accommodating the new *"chaise à l'anglaise,"* complete with faucets and valves, as well as the marquetry of Jean-Philippe Boulle; it replaced the *chaise percée,* the chamber pot, and the gentlemen thereof. And soon Versailles' other tenants were installing their own, somewhat improving palace sanitation.

Serving as a private staircase to the third- and fourth-floor *petits cabinets* and Louis' mistresses was—is—the intriguingly named Staircase of the Dogs (adjacent had been the room for the royal hounds). It shifted three times in four years as mistresses and their accommodations changed. The complex of rooms in this corner of the palace still confuses guides at Versailles; it is a three-story town house within a great château. Once, entering his bedroom, Louis XV was startled to find a cook in his shirt sleeves looking around in bewilderment: he had lost his way to the kitchen in the labyrinth of rooms and staircases.⁴ There were kitchens and dining rooms on every floor, workshops and even a distillery, bedrooms and libraries, and on the roof, hidden from below, a terrace with dovecotes and cages of birds, a summer dining room and a little park of trellises, fountains, and trees. The workshops were hobby shops; in 1740 Louis gave Madame de Mailly an ivory toothpick, "turned out by himself," and thirty years later an ivory clock to Marie Antoinette.⁵

Arranging an apartment above his own for Madame de Mailly, Louis went through a curious, transparent pretense that it was meant for the Marquis de Meuse. Appropriately the marquis thanked him,

---

* Named for the round *oeil-de-boeuf* (bull's-eye) window admitting light from the Cour de la Reine; here courtiers crowded every morning and night waiting their *entrées* to the royal bedchamber of Louis XIV for the formal *levers* and *couchers* of the King.

saying how pleased he would be to be so near the King. Louis (coldly): "But I'm closing the passage to my apartment." They discussed the apartment; it would contain "a small *antichambre*, a second, larger one as a dining room, a pretty bedroom, a study, a pantry, a kitchen and two dressing rooms. The King, continuing the conversation, to the Marquis de Meuse: 'Your bedroom will be furnished: you will have a bed, but you won't sleep in it; you will have a *chaise percée*, but you won't use it.'" The conversation is recorded in the Duc de Luynes' memoirs. La Châteauroux, who refused to occupy the apartment of her predecessor, had another, vaster (ten-room) apartment with a splendid view of the gardens, and her sister Adélaïde an eleven-room apartment in the attic above the *grands appartements* (albeit of small, attic rooms).[6]

In the *grands appartements,* Louis' approach was self-effacing; he had inherited the artisans and style of Louis XIV and here respected them. The Salon d'Hercule, which he completed, is indistinguishable in its grandeur from the other great, stately rooms, and is today the entry to them. Its remodeling (it was initially a chapel) was begun by Robert de Cotte under Louis XIV in 1712 and finished by Jacques V Gabriel, Mansart's cousin, in 1736—the *ancien régime* still had a sense of endless time. For his work in marble, Claude Tarlé received fifty thousand livres, Antoine Vassé 9230 livres for his work in bronze. But it is the names of Jacques Verbeckt, sculptor in wood and stucco, and François Lemoine, artist and teacher of Boucher, which the Room of Hercules commemorates. Perhaps the finest painting in the palace is the latter's immense (60 by 56 feet) ceiling portraying *The Apotheosis of Hercules.* It eclipsed Le Brun, marking the victory of the colorists; it rivaled the spacious Veronese painting, *Christ at the House of Simon the Pharisee,* presented the Sun King by the Venetian Republic and framed in a wall of the Salon d'Hercule. Lemoine was clearly inspired by it and consciously competed with it. When the magnificent ceiling was finished—142 figures in a single, unbroken composition—Louis XV was so impressed he named Lemoine first painter to the king on the spot—which did not keep the depressed, psychotic artist from killing himself a year later at forty-nine, stabbing himself nine times with his *épée.*

In Le Nôtre's gardens the great effort was simply maintenance, though Louis XV's reign is also marked by the completion of Neptune's Basin in the north end of the park. But the park and the gardens were too small for the King's passion for the outdoors and hunting. He would exhaust several packs of dogs in a single day. (When he didn't hunt, the Court said, "Today the King does nothing." In 1738, one pack of royal hounds ran down 110 stags, a second ninety-eight.) As for his huntsmen . . .

"One day," recounts Dufort de Cheverny, the *introducteur des ambassadeurs*, "the hunting was particularly rough. Two stags had been killed. Dogs, horses and men were dead tired. The King, in that husky voice which would set him apart from a hundred thousand men, called to Lansmate.* 'Lansmate,' he said, 'are the hounds tired?' 'Yes, Sire, they are just about done for.' 'And the horses?' 'Indeed, they are!' 'Nevertheless,' said the King, 'I will be hunting again the day after tomorrow.' Lansmate was silent. 'Did you hear me, Lansmate? I'll be hunting the day after tomorrow.' 'Yes, Sire, I heard you the first time, but what gets me,' he added in an aside as he rejoined the pack, 'is that he always asks whether the dogs or the horses are tired, but never the men!' This was said in a voice loud enough for the King to hear every word."[7]

At Court, there was more *laisser faire, laisser aller* than in the time of Louis XIV, but his great-grandson was no less inquisitive about his courtiers' lives. Every Sunday he had a personal report from his police chief, with passages from their correspondence read to him. Boredom seems to have led him to the practice, for he never made political use of it; however, his cynicism about human motives and behavior was "confirmed." To his minister, Choiseul: "The thievings in my household are enormous, but there is no remedy. Too many powerful people are involved. But calm yourself: the evil is incurable."[8] Of a new minister: "He has spread out his wares like the others, promising all sorts of good things, none of which will take place. He doesn't know *ce pays-ci*"—this country here, this strange land of Versailles—"but he will discover it."[9]

Ce pays-ci was the way those inside described Versailles—a country with its own customs within the country of France—and those outside felt the same way and resented it. However, the courtiers were freer under Louis XV and, following his youthful example, were more often in Paris. In March 1737, for instance, the King spent an incognito evening at the Opéra and a night with the city's *demoiselles de petite vertu*, returning to Versailles at six in the morning. (One

---

* His huntsman, properly spelled Lasmartres.

might note that Louis XV introduced the new custom of an unfixed
hour for the public *lever:* he told his valet when he wished it to take
place.)

At the palace, stakes replaced stags, gambling was as heavy as
ever—the Queen and her dowdy entourage played a *démodé
cavagnole* with dice—the gowns heavier than ever, with great hoop
skirts embroidered with flowers and weighted with precious stones, the
bodices lightened by lace. It was the Court of a handsome King who increasingly liked handsome women—once free of the Nesle family—who
even preoccupied himself with the first day of his daughter Adélaïde's
rouge. He compensated for his own coolness toward the people with
dazzling public fêtes and displays, and the state rooms of Versailles
were more open to vistors than under Louis XIV. Barbier came just
to look at the young King, he records, and found him *très beau;*
on another occasion to admire the fireworks on the Dauphin's birth
("the road back to Paris was an unbroken line of carriages").[10]
Pickpockets, too, penetrated as far as the Grande Galerie, as Louis
XV belatedly noticed after he had lost his watch, and the Salon de la
Paix in the Queen's corner, where some of the ladies gambling missed
their snuffboxes. In the park, lengths of lead pipe were regularly pinched
from the fountains and resold not only by the palace pages but by the
park guards. Stalls, with or without permission, were set up at the gates
and pressed, inside the courtyards, to the palace walls. Within, merchants
following the Court spread their silks for sale in the *galeries* on the
ground floor.

Traffic in the corridors had protocol and precedence, with some aid
from the ushers, as its policemen. Almost as hierarchical and complicated as the question of who sat on a *tabouret,* who in a *fauteuil*—
when and where—were the usages of the *chaises à porteurs,* the sedan
chairs—where and how far they might go. A princess of the blood,
for instance, visiting the Queen, would have to descend in the Salle
des Gardes, but the Daughters of France (that is, of the King) might
be carried to the *antichambre,* which was two rooms closer. Visiting
their father, they might ride to the Oeil de Boeuf. At rush hours,
when courtiers hurried to the *lever* or *coucher,* the corridors were like
a Molière comedy with music by Mozart, valets and *porteurs* elbowing
the way for—even more obnoxious and status conscious than—their
masters.

The Queen, too, had her *petits cabinets*—her small rooms—behind the public ones; her bedchamber was hardly more private than the royal *chambre de parade*. She also had her *levers* and *couchers,* and in her bedroom were born the Daughters and Sons of France with the Court as witness. Throughout the poor Queen's life, the King embellished her bedchamber, at first out of affection, later perhaps, as other men bring flowers, out of infidelity. Today it remains one of the finest examples of Louis Quinze style: shellwork and garlands, soft, sinuous lines, the marriage of de Cotte, the two Gabriels, father and son, Boucher and Verbeckt. On the evenings Louis dined with the Queen, his mistress, as her *dame du palais* (imposed by him), often shared their company. When he retired, the lady-in-waiting would rise and ask permission of the Queen to do likewise—a request she could not deny, however humiliating. Once, when La Châteauroux joined them for a supper, Marie could not hide her "ill humor, and it was noticed."[11] That, too, was Louis Quinze style.

Casanova, as a young man, visited Versailles and described the Queen's style. "I saw the Queen," he says, and one believes him, "in a large *bonnet* and without rouge, looking old and devout."* She was sitting down, alone, at a table "set as if for twelve. Ten or twelve courtiers had placed themselves in a semi-circle before it, twelve paces distant and in the deepest silence, and I joined them.

"The Queen began to eat, looking at no one, her eyes fastened on her food. Finishing a dish, finding it particularly to her taste, she turned for more of it and in turning looked at the courtiers in attendance to see if there were one to whom she might address herself on the subject. She found one and called out, 'Monsieur de Lowendal.'

"I saw a handsome man, two inches taller than I, bow, step three paces forward, and reply, 'Madame?'

" 'I find the stew preferable to all others is the fricassee of chicken.'

" 'I am of the same opinion, Madame.'

"After that reply, which was given in the most serious of tones, the Queen continued eating and the Maréchal de Lowendal stepped three paces backward to his original position. The Queen, without another word, finished her dinner and retired to her chambers."[12]

Casanova was astonished and delighted to see the "famous warrior who had conquered Berg Op Zoom [in the War of the Austrian Succession] . . . obliged to discuss a chicken stew with the same tone of voice as if he were sentencing a man to death." And he

* Still in her forties.

promised himself a fine time that evening at his own dinner with friends retailing the story. (But only fellow foreigners—and very few Frenchmen—would have understood his astonishment.)

Servility in the King's corner was of another order, taking place outside the *petits appartements*. Once in, the courtier became the King's companion—and those out who wanted in thronged the door to the inner sanctum, waiting for it to open and let them enter. It occurred at least once a week, on the day of a hunt, when the King gave his sought-after supper parties, beginning at seven and lasting past midnight. "The King would open the door to his *cabinet particulier*," the Duc de Luynes tells us, "regard those presenting themselves at it, immediately close it and draw up a list. An usher then read out the names on the list and each entered and sat down to table." Those unnamed turned shamefaced away, to return a week later.

Regularly at the door was the Prince (later Duc) de Croÿ, a pushing but likeable young courtier who sometimes made the list (but more often didn't), each time talking about it in his journal—for which historians have been grateful. "The Maréchal de Saxe was there," he writes of his first night among the invited, "but having just supped he did not sit down at the table. Instead he walked about, picking at the food, since he was extremely *gourmand*."* (One thinks of the contrast of Lowendal *chez* the Queen.)

After two hours at the table, where eighteen sat closely together with their royal host, Croÿ continues, "the King went into the *petit salon*, where he made and poured the coffee himself, there being no servants in that room." The party sat down to three tables for some gambling; Croÿ looked on at the table with the King and his mistress. She "was very sleepy and pressing him to retire. Finally, at one o'clock, he rose and said quietly to her, I thought, and gaily, 'Come then, let's go to bed!" The ladies curtsied and withdrew, the King bowed and went into his *petits cabinets*." There were rooms behind rooms, Croÿ relates, where only the most intimate were admitted. "Then we went down Madame de Pompadour's staircase, around through the *grands appartements* to the public *coucher*, which took

---

* He was also a superb field officer, who, in the opinion of Frederick the Great, "could give lessons to any general in Europe." Born a German Protestant he became a French hero in the War of the Austrian Succession. He maneuvered women, wife and mistresses, with the same skill as his divisions—but with far less devotion.

place immediately. Thus passed my first supper in the *petits apparte-ments* of Versailles."[13]

The mistress of Croÿ's story was Madame de Pompadour, the stair-case, better known as the Staircase of the Dogs, was the one most often used. Later, when she moved to the ground floor, to *appartements* for-merly reserved for princes and princesses of the blood, a *"fauteuil volant,"* or "flying armchair," was installed to carry her by rope and pulley to the King.

Incredibly, at twenty-four, Jeanne-Antoinette Poisson, whose family name means *fish*, had climbed one of the world's steepest social ladders from one of its lowest rungs to become the Marquise de Pompadour, the King's mistress—and that of France.

Her mother was a beauty, her father a scoundrel who ran errands for the profiteering bankers, the Pâris brothers. They helped François Poisson up the first rung from a nondescript place on Rue de Cléry to a presentable house on Rue de Richelieu. But when Jeanne was only four, her father had to flee an accusation of fraud involving black-market wheat sold in Paris during a famine. The brothers Pâris were to blame, but their agent became the public target and barely es-caped to Germany. The house was seized, but the mother and child were succored, as Poisson had half-anticipated for his pretty wife, by a wealthy tax collector, Le Normant de Tournehem. And when Poisson returned, cleared, eight years later from exile, he teamed with the family protector, and at nineteen Jeanne was married to the latter's nephew, Le Normant d'Etioles.

Jeanne bore him two children. He loved her. She had money, a château, a suddenly famous salon with Voltaire performing. She was happy. "She often said," says Nancy Mitford, her most empathic biographer, "that she would never leave him—except, of course, for the King. This seems to have been a family joke, but it was more than a joke to Madame d'Etioles."[14]

At nine, a fortuneteller had predicted that Jeanne Poisson would become the King's mistress—and like Madame Bovary, Madame d'Etioles dreamed from that day of her nobler lover. But unlike Mad-ame Bovary, encouraged by her mother, she did something about it. Schooled to be the entertainer of a king born bored—she was early taught to dance, sing, act, and play musical instruments like a pro-fessional—she now learned to drive a phaeton, so she could follow the King on his hunts. There, in his favorite woods of Sénart, her pretty face soon haunted him. In February 1745, it was unmasked at a great Versailles ball celebrating the Dauphin's marriage to the Spanish Infanta.* Louis, too, unmasked and their love affair began, to end no less than twenty years later. In September, Madame d'Etioles was installed in the palace, at first in Madame de Mailly's old apartment, then in La Châteauroux's larger one. Monsieur d'Etioles was advised to accept it, not to behave "like a bourgeois." He was made a reluctant tax farmer, his wife the Marquise de Pompadour; he was "decent" about it, but he never spoke to her again. The marquise was presented to the Queen, who invited her to dinner in her corner of the palace. But the Dauphin called her Madame Whore.

The Court called her La Bourgeoise and was not easily won. But Madame de Pompadour had the wit, patience, and charm with which to succeed, as with the King. From his politics—except for foreign affairs, where he dealt a personal, secret hand—to his pleasures, she soon became his prime minister. But it was through dominating the second that she influenced, then dominated, the first. She did everything she could do to divert him, and what she couldn't do she arranged. Thus she organized the *théâtre des petits cabinets* with an elaborate décor by Perrot and Boucher. She performed in its *comédies* and sang in its *opéras* like a prima donna (which, indeed, she was), and persuaded even the Dauphin to take a part. Virtually the entire Court competed for roles; it was one way to ensure entry. There were seats for a dozen, and for very few more.† In the beginning the little theater was set in the Galerie de Mignard, which disappeared among the new *petits cabinets,* then, in an ingeniously mountable and dismountable framework, in the great well of the Ambassadors' Staircase, before that too was torn down for Madame Adélaïde's apartment.

La Pompadour's unpopularity, particularly with Parisians, seems to have begun with the success of her *petit théâtre,* which dramatized her *divertissements* for the King. Since few saw it, the entertainment was inflated into an extravaganza of expense and a costly diversion of the King from the business of being a king. It was untrue for the

---

* Who died the next year, and the *following* year a masked ball celebrated the Dauphin's marriage to Marie-Josèphe de Saxe.
† The Comte de Noailles himself, governor of Versailles, was not among the invited for the first show of the *petit théâtre,* Molière's *Tartuffe,* and left, humiliated, that day for Paris—"to console himself in the arms of his wife," Louis XV said to the Dauphin.

petit théâtre, but less so for Madame de Pompadour. In her twenty years at Versailles, it is estimated, she cost France 36,327,000 livres in addition to her yearly 33,000 livres for "household expenses."[15] But a great part of that fortune became the heritage of France (and the museums of the world): jewels, silver and gold work specially designed, collections of Meissen, Chinese and Japanese ceramics, exquisite buhlwork furniture, some of the most handsomely decorated houses of the land: Bellevue, Crécy, Ménars, the Hôtel d'Evreux (now Paris's presidential Elysée Palace)—many of which have since disappeared. On her death, it took two lawyers over a year to make an inventory of what she had left. "Few human beings since the world began can have owned so many beautiful things."[16]

But it was the artistic and artisanal direction and inspiration of Madame de Pompadour and her remarkably worthy brother, the Marquis de Marigny, the King's superintendent of buildings, that must be recorded along with the cost. The two were astonishingly in accord with the artists and writers of their day—"she was one of us!" (Voltaire)—and the vast sums decried went to a considerable extent to them. Madame de Pompadour commissioned work from Boucher, Vanloo, La Tour, Chardin, and a hundred lesser artists; her brother worked with sculptors and architects in perfect harmony. Her tact and understanding, unlimited for the King, extended to the artists and the literary. She understood their strengths and supported their weaknesses; she had an extraordinary tolerance for their eccentricities.

The most difficult—and most interesting*—was Maurice Quentin La Tour. He was as insolent as he was talented, as arrogant as he was gifted, the finest pastel portraitist of France, and he did not doubt it. Once, painting the King, he objected to the room selected. Light poured into it from all sides and La Tour complained it was like painting inside a lantern. "I myself chose this room," Louis said, "so that we might not be disturbed." "I did not know, Sire," said La Tour, "that you were not master in your own house." Painting the Dauphin, he tasked him with being misinformed about a certain affair. "You see," he said, "how easily people of your kind allow themselves to be taken in by swindlers." Invited to paint Madame de Pompadour, La Tour at first cannily refused. "Tell the lady," he said, "that I do not

* Among the artists. For the literary friends of Madame de Pompadour, the prize must go to Voltaire on both accounts.

H*

go out to paint." He went, of course; money, for La Tour, was almost always most convincing. When he arrived, he made himself comfortable, removing his gaiters, his wig and collar, unbuckling his boots. Then the door opened and the King entered. La Tour grumbled that no one was supposed to interrupt him when he worked. Louis left. La Tour then continued.[17]

François Boucher, less amusing in life, less interesting in painting, nonetheless floods the Versailles palace with his floral, bucolic paintings which, for many, spell Madame de Pompadour and the period. "Flesh-deep" has been the description of his nudes, and they need hold us no longer than their models him. His shepherdesses, as the *Mercure de France* commented in 1750, would be more at home on the Opéra stage than in the fields. Diderot dismissed his lack of life, his lack of *le naturel*. But his paintings seem to have pleased the King, and that may most have pleased La Pompadour. Hers, after all, and it is not meant deprecatingly, was a decorative taste and Boucher, all in all, save for his drawings, was a decorative painter. In fact, he was a *décorateur*, designing for all forms and media—from wool to porcelain, from furniture to tapestries. His paintings find their full value in their decorative settings. The architecture of Mansart and his successors, who made the transition from baroque to neoclassical without falling into rococo, easily, comfortably made a place for them.

Between Versailles and Paris, Madame de Pompadour established, encouraged, and inspired the porcelain factory of Sèvres—and once again the palace became the showcase of French manufacture. There was a yearly sale of its china in the King's *appartements*. Similarly furniture, fans and hairdos, boxes, cameos, and dresses—in brief, the objects of the daily life—responded to her influence. Madame de Pompadour made the minor arts of France its major industry.* Not even under the Sun King were they more radiant or more sought abroad.

But the King was bored.

* The Goncourt brothers crown her Queen of Rococo in their biography.

16. The King Is Bored, the Deer Park Is Born

She was the most complete, most cultivated of consorts.[1] She sang like David when the King fell into melancholy—which was frequently. He often spoke of sickness, operations, and death and liked to ask the old and the infirm where they planned to be buried. ("At your feet, Sire," one responded.) Once, passing a cemetery with Madame de Pompadour, he stopped the carriage and sent an equerry to inquire if there were a fresh grave. (There were three.) He would interrupt her in the midst of a gay tale and ask her to hurry up and finish it.[2]

For seven years Madame de Pompadour entertained the ultimately unentertainable Louis XV, and ultimately she failed: he became bored in her bed. She had, he complained, the cold-blooded temperament of a cold-water duck. Madame de Pompadour, the perfect companion, was a flawed hetaera. Sexuality, do what she would, was a chore. Tubercular from childhood, she was coughing blood. The inexhaustible King and his Court had exhausted her. To her physical failure she applied the known arts, including the play-acting of pleasure, and several of the false sciences and aphrodisiacal cures, which made her desperately ill. "My life," she confided to her *femme de chambre*, Madame du Hausset,* "is that of a Christian martyr, *le combat perpetuel.*" One day, she said, *la petite maréchale* (de Mirepoix)

---

* Her journal, from which we have quoted several times, was barely saved from the fire. The Marquis de Marigny, on the death of his sister, Madame de Pompadour, was about to burn it as inconsequential trivia when interrupted by a friend. Eventually the manuscript made its way to a collector in Scotland, where it was published. The manuscript itself has disappeared, but the memoirs based on it have been accepted by most historians as essentially authentic.

told her, "It is your staircase the King loves. He is accustomed to going up and down it. If he found another woman at the end of it, to whom he could chat about his hunts and his affairs, in three days it would be the same for him."

Madame de Pompadour's illness from one diet brought her maid to speak of it to her friend, the Duchesse de Brancas. "For days," Madame du Hausset told her, "Madame has had little but *chocolat à triple vanille,* flavored with amber, truffles, and celery soup." It was making her miserable and worse, she added, wretched to look at.

"So I've noticed," said the duchess, "and I'm going to talk to her about it."

Scolded by her friend, Madame de Pompadour was at first vexed, then burst into tears. (Madame du Hausset had left them together, closed the door, and taken her usual listening post behind it.) "My dear," she said, "I am terrified of losing the King by no longer pleasing him. You know how much importance men attach to certain things, and I, alas, am cold by nature. I thought I might repair the fault with a special diet to warm my blood. And this elixir," she said, showing it to her friend, "has been doing me a world of good, or at least I think so."

The Duchesse de Brancas smelled the concoction. *"Fi!"* she exclaimed, and threw it into the fire.

"I won't be treated like a child!" cried Madame de Pompadour, again bursting into tears. "You don't realize what happened last week. With the pretext that it was too hot, the King came and spent half the night on my sofa. He will soon tire of me and take someone else."

"But your diet won't prevent it," said her friend, "and it will kill you. Offer him more and more of your precious company, without putting him off, of course, at those certain moments. Let time work its charms. Habit will tie him to you forever." They embraced, the duchess pledged secrecy, the diet was abandoned.[3]

But the Deer Park was begun. ". . . that gorge of innocence and virtue in which were engulfed so many victims who, when they returned to society, brought with them depravity, debauchery and all the vices they naturally acquired from the infamous officials of such a place."*

* The passage is from Mouffle d'Angerville's *Private Life of Louis XV* and is quoted by Norman Mailer as preface to his own *Deer Park,* that amalgam, he adds, of all the Hollywoods that ever existed, if only in the heated imagination.

Legendary, "infamous," it still exists at Versailles—at No. 4, Rue Saint-Médéric, several hundred yards from the Orangerie. A third floor and a wing have been added to the *hôtel* known as Louis XV's Parc aux Cerfs (literally, Stag Park). The interior has been remodeled, but the garden seems the same. It is shabbily distinguished, shamelessly disappointing, too small for its myths. But it has become a historical compound of all the houses Louis XV had employed to lodge the young women who now served his pleasure. Even its name, Deer Park, evoking a nostalgic memory of Eden and sin, of lost innocence in a green shade, derives from a commonplace fact: the house on Rue St.-Médéric is located in that quarter of Versailles where once Louis XIII had raised stags for *his* favorite sport. The enclosed acres had long since been broken up under Louis XIV into *hôtels* and gardens for noblemen who had no place, or little room, at the palace: the entire quarter was called the Parc aux Cerfs. Nevertheless, even in its own time, the house on Rue St.-Médéric was specifically referred to as Louis XV's Deer Park with the attendant notion of evil in the grass, of a cloven-hoofed King chasing a bevy of does, bringing them one by one to the ground.

It is first mentioned in the early 1750's, when Louis was in his early forties. In March 1753, Barbier noted Paris rumors of a sixteen-year-old girl lodged at the Parc aux Cerfs "for the King's amusement." It was likely the house on Rue Saint-Médéric, though a bill of sale records it as purchased, by proxy, "for the use and profit of the King, the price paid for by His Majesty's funds," on November 25, 1755.[4] It could easily have been used by Louis before he decided to purchase it; or, as is most likely, Barbier's reference is to yet another house. The memoirs of the Marquis de Valfons speak of several.[5]

Thus it is uncertain exactly when the Deer Park began or how many houses Louis XV rented in that convenient quarter of Versailles before he bought one (or more). But we know it was not only the ennui of a jaded prince that had him fill his private bordellos with the very young and preferably the virginal. He feared disease ("with reason," says d'Argenson; a butcher's daughter had once infected him) and often had his police agents investigate Deer Park possibilities. Their reports are available to us. A young girl named Gerbois had written to the King a naïve declaration of love. Police Chief Berryer, routinely opening the King's correspondence, knew what to do about it. He put Inspecteur Meusnier on the case. Meusnier's report: "Fourteen to fifteen years old, well enough developed for her age, blue eyes, healthy color, white enough skin, dark chestnut hair, neither fat nor thin, little or no breasts . . . no lovers," but not for the King: cultivated by a woman agent, she had refused to co-operate.[6]

Before the Deer Park, says Michelet, those who would co-operate were brought directly to the palace and lodged in the attic. But they made so much noise in their rooms under the roof that they disturbed Madame de Pompadour. At first she thought of establishing a convent for them. Instead, Louis XV's *premier valet de chambre* and prime procurer arranged the house (or houses) in the Parc aux Cerfs.[7] The one we are certain of at No. 4, Rue St.-Médéric was modest enough—two floors, eight rooms—for Louis' "incognito" pleasures—and convenient enough—two steps from the palace, a gateway from the *hôtel* of his Household Guards—for quick, "unremarked" visits. In truth little touching Louis XV was either incognito or unremarked, but he seemed happier with the illusion of it.

The King came to his *grisettes* (in winter they were brought to him) as a Polish count related to the Queen, thus eligible for residence at the palace—or so he replied to teen-age questions. One girl, however, discovered his identity (she had gone through his pockets and found two letters addressed to His Majesty) and had become frantic when she heard of Damiens' attempted assassination.* She so bothered the King he avoided her. But she persisted, bursting into the room of a rival when he appeared, crying to him of her fears for his life, sufficiently crazy, in short, to have fallen in love with Louis XV, and she was put away for a time in a madhouse.[8]

The madame of Louis' house, Madame Bertrand, wife of an official in the War Office, was called "the abbess." She had a staff of two maids, a cook, a coachman, and a lackey. The girls were procured by Louis' valet, Lebel, or, as we have seen, by his police lieutenants, but once the King himself spotted a likely tenant on a state visit to Paris: twelve or thirteen years old, she had been standing with her parents as he passed. With a connoisseur's eye he described her appearance, her dress, the likely class of her parents to Lebel, who undertook a search for her. In less than a month she was found and arrangements made with her compliant parents. A two-year school-

* See Chapter 17.

ing followed, but when the time came to install her in the Parc aux Cerfs, she refused. A house in Auteuil had to be specially rented.[9]

Candidates usually passed through the *trébuchet,* or "bird trap"— as two ground-floor rooms in the northern wing were known—before going on to the Parc aux Cerfs. Generally they were lower-class girls, "who did their work with no fuss," says a rather approving Miss Mitford, "made no demands on him, had no influential relations or angry husbands, who did not insist upon their children being ennobled and who were content to retire with a modest dowry."[10] And Madame de Pompadour, ever aware of the ladies at Court jockeying for her position, was content with their lesser threat to it. So long as their little ways satisfied the King, complementing her superb companionship, there was no problem. "It is his heart I want," she said to Madame du Hausset, "and those ignorant little girls won't steal that from me."

In the two decades of the Deer Park's existence, more than one tried, but none came closer than its first occupant—Louise O'Murphy, daughter of an Irish cobbler in Paris. Casanova, in his memoirs, claims to have discovered her, a thirteen-year-old slattern on a mattress of straw, and to have had her painted nude, full-length on a divan. Louis XV, he says, saw the many-dimpled portrait and had its model not long afterward.* Art historians do not disdain the legend that Louise O'Murphy was Boucher's favorite model, her round, angelic parts exposed in many of his canvases—one, with her lying on a divan, exactly as described by Casanova. But there is no substance to Miss Mitford's tale (presumably based on Soulavie's anecdotal history of the period)[11] that the poor Queen was exposed "every day of her life" to the O'Murphy figure in a painting of the Holy Family in her private chapel. According to Inspecteur Meusnier's reports, *la petite Louison* had worked for a Madame Fleuret, "half dressmaker, half procuress," and it was in her shop that Lebel had found her, "had her washed and properly dressed" before bringing her to the King. She was to spend several years at the Deer Park (the house on Rue Saint Médéric may have been bought for her) and there was occasion between chores for posing. She may even have become Boucher's favorite subject. For a moment it seemed she might become Louis', as the papal nuncio wrote home, replacing Madame de Pompadour in the palace as resident mistress.

---

* For Casanova's full account, see Appendix III, p. 487.

She did not, but she was given wall-to-wall carpeting, lest, pregnant, she fall and hurt herself.

Madame de Pompadour was to outlast Louise O'Murphy, if not the Deer Park, and keep her place in the *petits appartements* until she died some ten years later. They were cruel years and it was a sad death, but nothing so cruel, sad, or unfair as the satirical epitaph that appeared in her lifetime: *"Here lies a woman who was twenty years a virgin, eight years a whore and ten years a pimp."* The numbers vary, but the Goncourts seem to credit the idea fully, accusing Pompadour of complicity in stocking the Deer Park as the best of compromises: "giving the King his freedom while having a hand in its direction." She presided over some of the pregnancies and several of the births, but she presided without jealousy—and she had no hand in Louise O'Murphy's downfall.

As the years passed, the habit of La Morphil (as the French call her) grew on Louis XV. Carelessly, however, provoked by a mischief-making lady of the Court, she trespassed, as Madame de Pompadour never did, on this secretive man's sensibilities. "How are you getting along with the old lady?" she had asked. Whether it was the Queen or Pompadour she meant, it did not matter. "Wretch," Louis cried, "who put you up to it?" Told, he banished the offender from Court, turned his back on La Morphil and never saw her again. But she did receive four hundred thousand livres, a tidy fortune, with which to find a respectable husband—an officer in the French Army. Their son, General Beaufranchet, was to order the drums to roll as Louis' grandson, Louis XVI, was beheaded.

Beaufranchet was not, as some believed, Louis XV's bastard, but the link to Louis XVI is irony enough, and the line from the Deer Park to the Revolution equally traceable. D'Angerville's *Private Life of Louis XV* appeared but eight years before the Bastille was taken. Published abroad, violent and exaggerated, it reflects the wrath of the time. Others at Court had houses for their *grisettes* in the environs of the palace; the Prince de Conti maintained a ballet dancer in a place near the Paris Opéra. But the infamy of Louis' was king-size. Not only was his Parc aux Cerfs "that gorge of innocence and virtue in which were engulfed so many victims," it was portrayed as an insatiable maw into which was poured the resources of a starving France.

"Independent of the injury which this abominable institution did to morals," wrote lawyer-chronicler d'Angerville (the passage taken from the original Dublin edition directly follows the one above), "it is dreadful to calculate the immense sums which it cost the State. In fact, who could sum up the expences of that series of agents of all kinds, both principal and subordinate, exerting themselves to discover the objects of their researches—to go and fetch them from the extremities of the kingdom—to bring them to the place of their destination—to get them cleaned—to dress—to perfume them—and, in a word, to supply them with all the means of seduction that art could imagine. Add to this, the sums given to those, who, not having the happiness to rouze the languid sensations of the Sultan, were not the less indemnified for their services, for their discretion, and especially for his contempt;—the reward due to those more fortunate nymphs, who gratified the temporary desires of the Monarch;—in a word, the sacred engagements entered into with other Sultans who shewed signs of fertility;—and we may judge that there was not any, one with another, who had not been a charge of a million, at least, to the public treasury. Let us only reckon that two in a week passed through this sink of infamy, that is to say, a thousand in ten years, and we shall have a capital of a thousand millions."[12]

In Soulavie's post-Revolutionary account, 1800 women passed through the Parc aux Cerfs. "We are all Louis XV's bastards!" people said. The figures are wild; Louis XV was in no sense the father of his country. There may never have been more than one or two at the house on Rue Saint Médéric at a time, and sometimes they stayed for months (La Morphil for several years). Pregnant, they were usually taken to another house on Avenue de Saint Cloud (on the other side of Versailles) and given ten thousand to one hundred thousand livres as a dowry for marriage in the provinces; the children born received a pension of ten thousand or more a year.[13] Some made surprisingly good marriages to wealthy men of the world who thought the Parc aux Cerfs an excellent school for wives, "where," says a 1793 account, "they learned that love was a game, like the *quadrille,* which one varied at will."[14]

But the very notion of the Deer Park was provocation enough. Jansenists prophesied heavenly fire falling on the Sodom of Versailles. "The French King will be assassinated," it was predicted in Europe's courts. "I know I will die," said Louis XV, "like Henry IV." And in 1757, when he was stabbed by Damiens at the bottom of the

Dogs' Staircase, the wound was viewed by the people as the punishment of an outraged God. Stories about the Deer Park, its "orgies," its conscripted virgins and "strange ceremonies," coincided with the singular disappearance of children from Paris streets. They were kidnaped, it was darkly said, for the colonies, the girls for the King's Deer Park, the very young for their blood, in which leprous aristocrats bathed themselves for a cure.

On one occasion, recorded in Barbier's *Journal,* a child was rumored abducted, a cry raised by its family, and an entire quarter brought to fury. Spying a police agent, the mob chased him through the streets until he took refuge with a *commissaire.* "They demanded he be turned over to them. . . . A guard shot one of them in the stomach. It put them into a rage. They stoned the house, broke down the carriage door, smashed all the windows. They even, it was said, went looking for arms." Cowed, the *commissaire* thrust his agent into the street. "He was dragged by the feet, his head in the gutter, to the house of Monsieur Berryer, Chief of Police." The mob was promised justice and was thus stalled until mounted police scattered it. A few months later three of the demonstrators were hanged. "But what is certain," Barbier pointedly comments, "is that none of the families was dishonored by those hung." There had been cries, the day of the riot, of "On to Versailles!" and rumors at Court that the Bastille had fallen.[15]

Louis XV now avoided Paris. "I do not see why," he said defensively, "I should go where people call me Herod." Driving to Compiègne, he took the new road specially laid out for him north of the capital, across the plain of Saint-Denis. It is still called the Chemin de la Révolte. It leads to the burial place of French kings. One might say it passed through the Parc aux Cerfs.

17. At the Bottom of the Staircase: Damiens

It was a bitterly cold winter. Snow covered the courtyard at Versailles. On January 5, 1757, a man who would be called tall for his time—he was five foot six inches—lurked in a recess at the bottom of the Dogs' Staircase. He was not alone. By five-thirty that afternoon a sizable crowd had collected in the gathering dusk. A short, thin man turned to him. *"Eh bien?"* he said. *"Eh bien?"* said Damiens, "I am waiting." *Like you,* he might have added.[1]

There was nothing unusual in their presence, though both were of the "people." Access to the grounds, even to the palace, of Versailles was never a great problem—except occasionally for the palace guards. One night they arrested a fourteen-year-old named Suzanne Lenoir, because *for three weeks* she had been soliciting courtiers in the palace corridors. On May 27, 1756, Françoise Brancourt, forty-nine, was arrested; she had been found sleeping on a palace staircase. It was not her first offense; a year before she had been reprimanded for "running about in the château."[2]

Courtiers, too, were in the crowd at the bottom of the staircase, their hands warmly thrust in muffs of fur. The Duc de Richelieu was warming his face with a forearm: to his eternal regret, for he missed what was about to happen.

Since early January the Court had been at the Trianon, where cold was more easily coped with than in the vast, drafty rooms of the Versailles palace. On January 5 the King had returned—it was but a ten-minute carriage ride from the Trianon—to spend the after-

noon with his daughter, Madame Victoire, who had been left behind
in bed with influenza when the Court changed palaces. The King's
carriage was waiting in the Marble Courtyard to take him back to
the Trianon. A footman stood at its door, preparing to open it for
its royal passenger. Two lines of horse guards pressed back the
curious. A full moon was obscured by clouds. At five forty-five,
when the King descended the staircase, it was almost as dark as
night. His way was lighted by flaring torches. He leaned on the
arm of his first equerry, Henri de Beringhen. He was preceded by
the Marquis de Montmirail, captain of the Swiss Guards, and followed by the Dauphin and the Duc d'Ayen. He reached the last
step. Out of the shadow of his recess Damiens darted, spinning one
guard to the left, another to the right. He put his left hand on the
shoulder of the King and struck him, slightly to the rear, between
the fourth and fifth ribs, with the three-inch blade of a pocketknife
held in his right hand, then slipped back between the same two
confused guards. No one seems to have seen the blow.

The King pitched forward, recovered. "Someone has struck me
with his fist!" he cried. He took a few steps toward his carriage,
felt his side, looked at his hand. It was covered with blood. "I've
been wounded!" There was more surprise than pain in Louis XV's
voice.

"What is that man doing with his hat on?" the Duc de Richelieu
was loudly asking at the same time. He had remarked Damiens.

"What do you mean," demanded a guard mechanically, "by keeping
your hat on in the presence of the King?"

"I always keep it on," said Damiens, "in the presence of kings."

"There," said Louis XV, pointing toward Damiens, "is the man
who did it! Arrest him, but do not kill him!" Twice he repeated
his admonition, and then, as if in wonderment, to himself: "Why
do they want to kill me? I have harmed no one."

The coach footman now cried, "The King is wounded!" The
courtiers pressed forward to carry him back up the stairs. "No,"
said the King, "I have enough strength to walk." Slowly he ascended
the staircase to his bedchamber. But the bed had no sheets and there
was no night shirt for the King: everything had been removed to
the Trianon. The King lay on the bare mattress in a delayed reaction.
He felt faint and feared death. More precisely, he feared hell-fire—
and he called frantically for a doctor and a confessor. The courtiers

rushed about in confusion. "Let the blood flow," some cried, "in case of poison." Again the King called for a confessor. One was found and brought from the village. Hastily Louis began the recital of his sins and asked for instant absolution, promising a full confession, should time be granted him. By now his first physician, Jean Sénac, had arrived and dressed the wound, but he did not dare probe it without the first surgeon's presence. The latter was at the Trianon, where, as every Wednesday, the Italian players were performing. Finally he arrived, examined the King, announced that the wound was superficial. But all thought of the possibility of poison. Twice the Duc d'Ayen sent to demand of Damiens, who was being held in the *salle des gardes* directly below the royal bedchamber, whether or not the pocketknife was poisoned. Each time Damiens replied that it was not, but the knife was tested on a dog and carefully placed on the mantelpiece of the Council Room, adjacent to the King's bedroom, now crowded with courtiers.

Fear of a generalized plot seized the Court. Damiens, within seconds of his capture, warned darkly of danger for the Dauphin and implied accessories in his crime. Guards were dispatched to reinforce those of the Dauphin and to stand in watch at every gate and palace entrance. Within twenty-four hours there were dozens of arrests and the frontiers were watched.

To the King's bed, in the meantime, had come the King's daughters, who, seeing the blood, fainted away. The Queen, making her way through the crowded antechamber, reached the King's bed, saw the blood, and was barely caught in time before she too collapsed to the floor.

"Madame," said the King, "I have been assassinated." And he turned solemnly to the Dauphin: "You were born more fortunate than I. Administer the kingdom with the wisdom God has given you. Make your people happy."

Publicly Louis XV apologized for his conduct, asking pardon of his children for the scandal he had caused them, of the Queen for the wrongs he had done her, and again sent for a confessor. His own was still unfound; an abbé was brought from the Commons. For an hour and a half the King confessed, and the first surgeon told the abbé to be done with it—he had a wound to dress and a patient to bleed. Louis, still convinced his last day had come, called for last rites. The holy oil arrived, but not the cardinal to administer it. Finally the King's own almoner arrived and, for the third time, the King confessed.

Poison was still feared, though Damiens' knife had had to penetrate a fur-lined coat, a velvet jerkin, and two shirts before reaching the skin. Even then, it was but a glancing cut; the King, however, was convinced that he was dying. "I shall not recover," he told those around his bed. With typical *brusquerie,* Lasmartres, the King's hunts- man, had pushed his way to the bed. "I am wounded," Louis said sadly. "Have the snivelers removed, Sire," said Lasmartres. "I would speak to you alone." The King made a sign to his daughters to retire. "Cough," Lasmartres commanded the King. "Spit into my hand." There was no blood in the spittle. He handed the King a chamber pot. "Piss," he said. There was no trace of blood in the urine. "Your wound, Sire," he said, "is a scratch. Neither your lungs nor your bladder has been touched." He uncovered his own chest. "Look," he said, pointing to his trench-deep scars, "thirty years ago! and I am still alive. In a day or two you and I will be running down a stag together." Thus was the King calmed, and he spent a quiet night.[3]

Madame de Pompadour had not. She had hurried back to the palace from the Trianon, but she had not dared go to the King's bed. She spent the night in her own apartment below, in tears. A few loyal friends—many had deserted her, believing that her days were as numbered as the King's—tried to comfort her. Among them was the good Dr. Quesnay, who brought her occasional, reassuring news from the King's bedside. But the courtiers, convinced she would soon be evicted by the outraged Queen and about-to-be-crowned Dau- phin, crowded into her apartment, which became "as open as a church, with all feeling free to enter it. They wanted to see what face she was putting on the situation. And Madame did nothing but weep and faint away."[4] La Pompadour's brother, the Marquis de Marigny, was advised by the Duc de Richelieu to absent himself for a while. Two of the King's teen-age *grisettes* were sent away, to the delight of the *dévots* of the Court, who had not had so much cause for rejoicing since the King's illness at Metz, where he had also once thought he was dying.

The Dauphin was now twenty-seven. On the morrow of Damiens' *attentat* he summoned the State Council and presided over it in his father's place, while his father's bedroom was black with doctors and clerics. For days, Louis XV brooded behind the drawn curtains of his bed. When his first surgeon assured him his wound was superficial, he replied, "It is deeper than you think, for it reaches my heart."

He had experienced a great fright and he had not recovered from it. "He was afraid he could no longer go out in public without risking his life, believed he would have to change even his private life and separate himself from the woman who had become so important to him. For a week he was plunged in melancholy and doubt behind the four curtains of his bed. . . . Not until the ninth day did the curtains part sufficiently for us to see him, and his expression seemed to say, 'Behold your King, whom a wretch would assassinate, but who is himself the most miserable of men in his kingdom.' "[5]

But the King finally rose from his bed and appeared in the Council Room when few were in it. He received ambassadors and the ladies of the Court, sitting in an armchair in his dressing gown, his right leg on a footstool. But he still sent no word to Madame de Pompadour.

A man she considered her friend, Machault d'Arnouville, keeper of the seals, came to counsel her to quit Versailles immediately, and intimated that such was the wish of the King. In fact, he had been urged to do so by her enemy, the Comte d'Argenson, minister of war.* Both had cast their lot with the Dauphin and the party of the *dévots,* in the conviction that theirs was the party of the future. Machault left La Pompadour trembling, her teeth chattering, and she told Madame du Hausset, her *femme de chambre,* to prepare her trunks and ready her carriages for departure. But as the preparations were being made, the little Maréchale de Mirepoix entered. "What is this, madame?" she asked in astonishment. "Why all these trunks?"

"Alas, my dear," said Madame de Pompadour sadly, "Monsieur de Machault says the King wishes me to leave."

"Your Garde des Sceaux is betraying you," said her friend, and she advised the marquise to do nothing until she was certain the King so desired. "Who leaves the table," she said, "loses the game."[6]

But from the King there was still no word.

It was two in the afternoon of the eleventh day. The King was walking desultorily about the Council Room, leaning on his stick. Most of the courtiers had gone off for dinner, and he motioned to

---

* Brother of the Marquis d'Argenson, whose memoirs we have frequently quoted and who was to die three weeks after Damiens' *attentat.*

the Dauphin and Dauphine that they too might leave. The Duchesse de Brancas made as if to follow. The King stopped her, asked for her coat, slung it around his shoulders, circled the Council Room one more time, then went through the door to his *petits appartements* and down the Dogs' Staircase.

Intrigued, Fontanieu, Champcenetz, and Dufort de Cheverny decided to forget about their own dinner for the moment and await the King's return. When he returned, Dufort de Cheverny tells us, between three and four o'clock, "he was no longer the same man. Instead of the sad, strained look, he appeared serene and untroubled. There was a smile on his lips and he chatted good-humoredly, a word for each of us, joking about the woman's coat wrapped around his shoulders. He left us saying he was off to dinner, and advised us to do likewise. . . . A single chat with the one person truly concerned about him had rid him of his melancholy, which had made him ill more than anything else."[7]

Madame de Pompadour, "the person truly concerned," had told the King that Damiens was simply a madman who had acted alone; that the King was still the Well Beloved of the people, who would gladly tear Damiens apart could they lay their hands on him; that the troublesome leaders of the Paris Parlement, far from having inspired his crime, would do the same. The following day the King went hunting. That night he supped with the marquise. Not long afterward, Machault and d'Argenson were dismissed from their posts and exiled from Versailles.

And Damiens?

When Louis had cried, "There is the man who did it!" three footmen and a guard had seized Damiens, roughly jerked his hands from his pockets to see if they held weapons, then took him to the Guards' Room on the ground floor of the palace. He was stripped, his hands were tied behind his back, his clothes—a dirty gray redingote, shabby pants, large black hat—were searched. Pinned in his hat was an enigmatic number "1," wherefore the first thoughts of a plot. His belongings included a small calf-bound book, *Instructions et prières chrétiennes,* a red tobacco pouch, two belt buckles, a corkscrew, three soiled collars, a yard of black ribbon, three combs, a battered wallet, a sack holding thirty-six louis d'or (second "proof" of a plot), and a black, horn-handled, two bladed pocketknife. The shorter blade matched the rent in the King's fur-lined coat.[8]

Messieurs d'Argenson and Machault had come at a run, the latter in such a fury he ordered fire tongs heated and applied to Damiens' feet. (They destroyed an Achilles' tendon and the feet were not to heal the rest of Damiens' life.) Was the knife poisoned? *No,* Damiens had said. Did he have accomplices? If he replied to that, he said ambiguously, "all would be finished." "But let the Dauphin beware," he added. Who were his accomplices? Damiens refused to name anyone. Enraged, Machault ordered the guards to heap fagots on the fire and throw Damiens into it.

The Marquis de Sourches, grand provost of France, who was charged with the security of the King and his Court, intervened. He countermanded the order and had Damiens removed to the Versailles jail. There, with Damiens in chains, the interrogation was continued. Why had he committed so sacrilegious an act as attempted regicide? "For religious reasons," he replied. What possibly could be the "religious reasons"? "Everyone in Paris was perishing and despite Parlement's remonstrances the King would listen to no one." And he asked his inquisitors whether it was not indeed true that "the entire kingdom is perishing." "If they had cut off the heads of four or five bishops," he said, "it—his *attentat*—would not have occurred."[9] Again and again he was asked about his accomplices. He went into silence (and later was to deny ever suggesting there were any, saying he had said so only to escape Machault's torture and gain some time).

So passed the first night. The next day, January 6, the Duc de Croÿ, like so many absent others, had hurried back to Versailles and joined the crowd of courtiers in the Oeil-de-Boeuf anteroom. D'Argenson, he was told, had been looking for him. Since Damiens was originally from Arras, capital of the province of Artois, and Croÿ was militarily responsible for the province, d'Argenson put him in charge of the Damiens investigation, particularly the search for possible accomplices. "I remarked," says Croÿ in his memoirs, "that I must therefore see the criminal. He approved the idea, praised me for it, and sent me to M. de Sourches. M. de Sourches was glad to hear of my charge and took me to the gaol where his men were conducting their interrogation of the prisoner. He had me see the criminal, who was not an unseemly man with deep-sunken eyes, an aquiline nose and a flush brought on by the fever of his burns. He was chained to his bed, ill, and complaining of M. de Machault's having needlessly ordered his burning.

"I asked if he were from Artois," Croÿ continues. " 'Until death!'

he said. 'The men of Artois are honest men and unafraid. The King does not have more worthy subjects!' For answers to further questions, he referred me to M. de Sourches. He spoke in a quiet voice and at first I was duped, thinking he was a man of quality—but not for long. As we left, he thanked us, saying he no longer had need of anything but God and a confessor. My final conclusion was that he was a fanatic, and nothing more." And on January 8, "in the dreadful freeze of a terrible winter," the Duc de Croÿ traveled to Arras and voyaged into Damiens' past.[10]*

Robert François Damiens was born in the hamlet of Thieuloy and the diocese of Arras on January 9, 1715, the eighth of ten children. His father was Pierre Joseph Damiens, a man who had so mismanaged his little farm he had lost it and become a farm laborer, then a prison guard. Questioned, he said his son Robert François had been fairly well behaved as a boy, was occasionally beaten, but only when he, the father, was moved to anger. Croÿ notes from other sources that the youth had been known as Robert the Devil and had been several times hung by his heels in punishment by his father.

On the death of his mother, Damiens, sixteen, was sent to live with his uncle. He did not take well to schooling and was apprenticed to a locksmith, who did not take well to him. He then served an apprenticeship under a cook in an abbey of Arras. Afterward he served as a valet for a succession of army officers. Unsuccessfully, it would seem, since he was next reported serving in the refectory of Paris' Jesuit Collège de Louis-le-Grand. Expelled, he nonetheless returned as the valet of one of the *pensionnaires* before he was definitively expelled—at about twenty-three—for insolence. According to his superiors, his fourteen or fifteen months of service were marked by sullenness, stubbornness, and impudence (this character report, of course, was ex post facto—that is, retrospectively made after his *attentat* against the King). About this time Damiens married Elizabeth Molerienne, a housemaid who was seven or eight years his senior. They had a son, who died early, and a daughter, who was still living, earning her living by coloring paper cutouts.

Damiens served many masters (some sixty in Paris, according to Croÿ, "of all kinds and conditions"). They generally agreed on his intelligence, the paradox of his tendency to withdraw within himself

* Giving us a rare account of an uncommon common man whose life would "touch" the King of France at Versailles.

and his desire to be noticed, his vanity, curiosity, and cantankerousness. "Stubborn in the pursuit of whatever he projected, bold in its execution, impudent and a liar, he himself was aware of the turbulence of his blood and sought to calm it [by having himself bled]. His face mirrored his character and he was above average height. His face was long, his look cheeky and sharp, his nose like the beak of a parrot, his mouth tightly drawn, and he had the habit of talking aloud to himself."[11]

He drank and was quarrelsome, said the Comte de Maridort, one of his masters, and was sent away for fighting with the other servants. On the other hand, Damiens claimed to have left because he was bored on the count's country estate in northwestern France.

Then a series of masters, the Duc de Croÿ thought, who were counselors of the Paris Parlement, proved crucial in his fate, for they formed his opinions and motivated his crime. The parliaments of France, one might recall—each of the thirteen major cities boasted one, that of Paris was predominant—were not so much legislative bodies as law courts, and their leaders were the more recent *noblesse de robe* (increasingly Jansenist) at odds with and in contrast to the more ancient *noblesse d'épée* (nobility of the sword), the King, the Court, and the Jesuits. They were, in reality, ennobled bourgeoisie, lawyers by profession ambitiously seeking to replace the clergy among the rulers of the land, men of money who resented the Church's favoring of the landed gentry and scorning interest as usury. Parlement was growing in popularity as the clergy's standing with the people declined. "They hardly dare show themselves in the streets of Paris," observed memorialist d'Argenson, "without being hooted. The minds of the people are turning to discontent and disobedience. Everything seems to be leading toward a great revolution in religion and government."[12]

In 1753, Louis XV remarked to the Duc de Gontaut: "Parlement and the Church are always at daggers drawn. They make me despair with their quarrels, but I detest *'les grandes robes'* the most. My clergy, on the whole, is attached and loyal to me, the others would like to hold me under their thumbs."

Gontaut: "They are nothing more than insignificant lawyers, who could not conceivably trouble the State."

Louis: "You do not know what they are capable of doing and

thinking. They are a gathering of republicans . . . Oh well, enough of that. At least things will last as they are for *my* lifetime."[13]

But in the meantime, the Archbishop of Paris zealously applied the papal bull *Unigenitus,* instructing the clergy to refuse all sacraments, such as extreme unction, for known Jansenists. In reply, the Paris Parlement ordered the arrest and imprisonment of all clerics who obeyed the archbishop. Louis intervened, condemning Parlement's interference in religious matters and commanding it to step aside. When Parlement paid no heed, he took action against its leaders.

Damiens was serving in the household of Bèze de Lys, a counselor of Parlement, when a musketeer arrived in the middle of the night with a *lettre de cachet* of the King sending Bèze de Lys to prison in a fortress. It was part of a general exile of Parlement's principal activists, and often during this governmental crisis, Damiens would slip away to the Palais de Justice to listen to the heated conversations in the corridors among parlementarians and their friends. If he had not gone there so often, he said in a rare moment of remorse (or was so reported having said), he might not have struck the King.

Throughout his torture and interrogations, Damiens spoke of his hatred for the archbishop because of the churchman's refusal of sacraments for the Jansenists and said "the idea [of an *attentat* against the King] had first occurred to him when he heard of that order. . . . He was further provoked when he heard of Parlement's going to Versailles and being greeted by the remark, 'Here come the monkeys!' and the King's making its members wait almost four hours for him, while he lingered at Bellevue"—the château of Madame de Pompadour a few miles from Versailles. Repeatedly Damiens asserted the archbishop's responsibility for everything. Never, he insisted, had he meant to kill the King. Had he so intended, he would have stabbed him more than once: he had had plenty of time to do it. He did what he did, he said, "so that God might 'touch' the King and move him to make amends and put things aright."[14]

Damiens had heard Dominique Gautier, the intendant of Bèze de Lys, remark one day in his presence that "all these troubles would be ended if only someone would 'touch' the King." And he told his inquisitors that he had formed his plan to do this "meritorious deed . . . when Parlement's leaders had been exiled and he saw three quarters of the people perishing from misery . . . for he saw the little regard of the King for the remonstrances of Parlement."

That, Damiens' inquisitors objected, could not have been his real reason, "since he had spent his time in the houses of the rich, where one could not possibly see the misery of the people. Moreover, such misery was past history."

Damiens: "He who was only for himself was good for nothing." Serving the rich, he nevertheless identified himself with the poor.

Shortly after his service *chez* Bèze de Lys, Damiens became a domestic in the household of Canon Cagne de Launay, a Sorbonne professor—and quit after hearing guests at dinner agree that "those people over there in Parlement were the world's worst rascals, because of their actions against the clergy, and if they were the masters of France, they would gladly bathe their hands in the blood of Parlement's chieftains."

The maid of another household recalled Damiens declaring to fellow domestics that "if Parlement favored it, he and his comrades would seize the Archbishop and remove him from Paris." Asked who these "comrades" might be, he replied, No one in particular and everyone in general. There would be no problem, he said, finding the men to undertake the task.

Henceforth Damiens ceased going to a confessor, fearing disclosure of his plan somehow to "touch" the King. He avoided seeing his wife, used false names, and told employers he was unmarried. The few times he met his wife, she testified, "he talked violently of his hatred for ecclesiastics" and his admiration for Parlement. (Damiens' entire family—wife, daughter, father, his brothers, and their wives—were imprisoned and questioned shortly after his own arrest, though initially he tried to hide the fact that he had any family. Why had he lied about them? he was asked. Because, he replied, they were completely innocent of his action.) He drank heavily, Damiens' wife said, and threw her money "as if she were a dog." And when he drank, "he was brutal to her as if she were a horse."

Damiens' next master was a former governor of India, who had just spent three years in the Bastille, presumably for some lese majesty. Damiens was to see him die from its effects. (The Bastille was no longer a place for pleasantries, as under Louis XIV.) The "master" who succeeded was in fact a mistress, in both senses of the term, since she was kept by the Marquis de Marigny, brother of La Pompadour (one explanation for her anxiety to reassure the King there was no plot and hasten an end to the *affaire*). Here, in the

household of Madame de Saintreuse, Damiens had become the butt of
the other domestics' jokes, and his mood hardened. Instead of a
servant's room, he chose an isolated corner of the attic. Finally,
Madame de Saintreuse testified, she sent him away, because she
thought he was mad. If, indeed, he was, she had contributed to
his madness: it amused her to play sorceress and she had "read
the palm of his hand," predicting that it would be his destiny "to be
torn apart alive." And one day it further amused her to empty
a basket of firewood down a flight of stairs and order Damiens to
descend and pick up the scattered kindling. It was a "sure sign,"
she said, "that he would also be burned alive." She and her chambermaid, Damiens said, had thus cast a spell over him.

Several masters later, in July 1756, Damiens served in the house
of Jean Michel, a bookseller. The latter had absented himself one
day, returned, and discovered the following day that Damiens, who
was nowhere to be found, had stolen 240 louis d'or from a wardrobe
in his bedroom. Domestic thefts were punished by torture and hanging,
and Damiens had fled Paris for Arras. He took shelter with an aunt
he had not seen for approximately fourteen years, then with his
brother Antoine, whom he had not seen for twenty-five. He told
them nothing of his theft, but in a burst of generosity he bought
his brother 292 livres' worth of wool, so that he might work it at
home. His brother's place lacking conveniences—it seems to have
been without furniture—Damiens lodged with a sister he had—we are
told—*never* seen.

On July 11, Damiens visited his father, "jeered" at the piety of
his niece and his brother, both apparently Jansenist. Saying he had lost
his knife, he bought a black, horn-handled pocketknife for himself and
his brother. Damiens also bought his brother six table knives and dishes,
and a dress for his niece, explaining that he had won the money in a lottery. They were astonished—and puzzled by his bounty. But not for
long. On the thirteenth, a letter arrived from the second brother, Louis,
a domestic in Paris, which told them of Damiens' theft.

Terror-stricken, the family begged Damiens to return the money
and to return to God. Damiens bought arsenic, dissolved it in water,
drank the mixture, and promptly vomited it. He told his family he
did not fear death so much as dishonor for the family. They urged
him to see a priest. He replied that he would take a trip to Dunkirk
to walk along the sea and reflect. They gave him several volumes

of piety, among them *Instructions et prières chrétiennes,* and he told them of Madame de Saintreuse's prediction, bitterly railing against her as a witch.

On July 23, Damiens, his brother, and his sister traveled to Dunkirk, where he bought the former a few secondhand clothes and several small gifts. They were to tell the investigators of his distracted air, the way he ground his teeth in fury, though no word of what he was thinking escaped his lips. When they returned to Arras, they learned that the police were looking for him, and Damiens fled to west Flanders under a false name. There, one day in a tavern, where he had a room, he was bled, but he tore the bandage from the incision with the intention—his investigators concluded—of bleeding to death. (Suicide, in the eyes of the Church, was even more sacrilegious than regicide and one more indication, for the authorities, of his "madness.") However, he did not die: the bleeding apparently stopped by normal coagulation, since no vital vein or artery was concerned.

Damiens changed his lodging, shared a room with a man called Playoust, and talked so loudly to himself at night that his roommate could not sleep. To overcome his own insomnia, Damiens brewed a "poppy-tea." At the Tête d'Or, Playoust would further recall, Damiens sat drinking and brooding and one night dictated a letter to his companion for the Marquis de Marigny, complaining of the fortune predicted him by the marquis' mistress. But the letter, if written, was never sent. The two shared a room in another lodginghouse, where Damiens suddenly talked of Parlement, and late one night rose from his bed and descended barefoot to the cellar. Brought back by Playoust, he shouted that his roommate, too, was a sorcerer, and became so menacing Playoust threatened him with a club. Not long afterward, Damiens decided to leave Flanders and return to France. "I will return and I will die," he said to Playoust, "and the greatest of the earth will also die and you will hear people talk of me."

He returned in the fall. In November 1756 he was in Arras, changing his lodging three times. At the Lion d'Or, he had himself bled—"to calm his blood"—explaining that he had not slept for four days. He asked the surgeon for something to make him sleep; he received three grains of opium, which had no effect. He met Nicholas Breuvart, a former *portier* at the Jesuit school in Paris, and hinted at the plan forming in his mind: "All is lost," he told him, "the country is collapsing. I am lost. 'They' have something against me, but people will hear of me." And to a distant cousin on December 23: "My poor wife is lost, my daughter is done for!" The cousin told of his trembling lips and drawn look. Toward the end of December, he heard of the King's *lit de justice*, aimed at forcing Parlement to respect the papal *Unigenitus*; he heard of it from royal officials in the provinces who added to his indignation by saying that it would be a good thing to cut off a few heads in Parlement. On the eve of the New Year, 1757, Damiens arrived in Paris.

He sent word to his brother Louis to meet him discreetly in a tavern. When they met, his brother warned him that the police were still looking for him and he should leave Paris. Damiens replied that Parlement's action against the King—ceasing all judicial functions as a form of protest—had brought him to the capital and would keep him there. Reluctantly his brother told him where he might find his wife—she was serving as a cook in a Paris household—and when they separated, immediately went off to warn her of Damiens' arrival, but failed to find her at home. Sometime later Damiens arrived, and fearfully she installed him in her room, hiding him until January 3. Here he had a visit from his daughter, who brought a friend of his wife, both urging him to quit Paris and hide from the police by joining a military regiment.

On January 3, at eight in the evening, Damiens left the room with his wife and daughter, said farewell to them in a beer tavern on Rue Saint-Martin. He was off, he said, to join a regiment and "serve in the islands." At eleven he bought a seat in a public coach, popularly called the *pot de chambre*, whose destination was Versailles. He spent the time between eight and eleven, he initially told his inquisitors, with a prostitute; under torture, he said he had spent them sleeping at an inn owned by an acquaintance, who had awakened him in time for the coach to Versailles.

At two and a half hours past midnight, Damiens arrived in Versailles and passed the night in the porter's lodge of the coach station. Between six and seven of the morning of January 4 he took a room in an inn on Rue de Satory, declaring he was a merchant named Lefevre. He drank a half bottle of wine, ate some bread, and went to sleep until two in the afternoon. He rose, dressed, and spent the afternoon (all this according to his testimony) walking idly in

11. Molière

12. *Madame de Maintenon with her niece*

13. La Palatine

14. Racine

15. *Marie Thérèse of Austria* (*Louis XIV's wife*)

16. The Regent, Philippe d'Orléans

17. *Marie Adélaïde of Savoy*

18. *Louis XV*

the gardens and courtyards of the palace. He returned to his lodging at eleven that evening. He asked for chicken and was told that there was none. He became angry, according to the innkeeper, and cried, "This damned Versailles! You can't do anything or have anything you want! Here the King is off to the Trianon until Saturday!" He had some mutton and went to his room.

The next morning—January 5, 1757—Damiens asked the innkeeper (a woman) to fetch him a surgeon; he wished to be bled. She did nothing about it. She thought he was joking, she explained to his investigators, and besides it was bitter cold. "Had she done what I asked," Damiens said in prison, "I might not have struck the King"—or so he was reported to have said. At ten Damiens left the inn and ate something at a local tavern. He spent part of the afternoon pacing the snow-covered courtyard of the palace. By five he was stationed in the recess at the bottom of the Dogs' Staircase. François Bonnemant, a guard, noticed him there, but thought nothing of it, since he was one of a number waiting for the King to descend. A small, thin man had said to him, the guard testified, *"Eh bien?"* And Damiens had replied, *"Eh bien,* I am waiting."

At five forty-five, the King had descended the staircase. . . .

After the preliminary interrogations in the prison of Versailles, Damiens was taken to the Conciergerie in Paris, France's Tower of London. He had hoped for the Bastille: prisoners more often emerged from it alive. The transfer, for security reasons, was made at night (the possibility of a plot was never eradicated from the official mind). There were three coaches in the cortege. A man then suspected of being Damiens' accomplice, because he had been a fellow domestic at the Jesuit school and had been seen with him at Arras, was in one carriage; Damiens, in chains, his burned feet wrapped in sheepskins was in another; a court clerk with all the evidence and documentation was in the third. The cortege was heavily guarded by men on foot and horse with a mounted constabulary preceding it, ordering all doors and windows along the route closed and shuttered, and warning the curious away, lest they be shot. Thus, at the gate of the Versailles prison itself, two of the Dauphin's own stableboys were fired upon for pressing too close.

Arriving at the Conciergerie at two in the morning of January 18, Damiens was interned in the Montgomery Tower and guarded by a

I

hundred men. Here Ravaillac, the assassin of Henry IV, had been kept before he was executed. Damiens, who, according to d'Argenson, had attempted to kill himself in prison "by twisting *les parties génitales*," was so chained to the bed and floor he could scarcely lift his hands to his mouth. Whenever he was moved from his cell, he was carried in a cocoonlike hammock, designed to prevent his dashing his head against the walls. Four sergeants of the French guard were permanently in his cell, relieved at four-hour intervals. There were guards on the floors immediately above and below his cell. Parlement's own surgeon and his assistant visited Damiens three times daily and tested the food brought him specially from Versailles by an officer of the King's kitchen—precautions aimed at keeping him from being poisoned by others in the "conspiracy," who might fear his talking under torture.

The Duc de Croÿ, completing his investigation after rounding up witnesses and sending them on to Paris, noted in his journal that, as usual, the sophisticates in the salons of Paris talked knowingly of a "plot" involving higher-ups among the Jesuits or in Parlement— or even among both, though they themselves were in conflict. The very night of Damiens' *attentat,* in anticipation the president of the Paris Parlement, René Charles de Maupeou, had immediately hurried to Versailles and spent the night in the Oeil de Boeuf antechamber, as so many, waiting vainly to be admitted to the King's bedside. Other members of Parlement hastily met at four in the morning and drew up a letter testifying to their undying affection for Louis XV. Two days later the entire Parlement charged its president humbly to beseech the King authority to conduct the investigation, i.e., torture, and trial of Damiens. It was not granted until a week later, thanks to the persuasion of La Pompadour, who thought to ease the King's mind of all thoughts of a parliamentary plot. Nevertheless, sixteen counselors considered the most rebellious in Parlement were exiled from Paris by royal *lettres de cachet.*

Damiens underwent eight *interrogatoires* lasting six to seven hours each. Five were held in the Montgomery Tower, but it was so malodorous,* the rest took place in the Chambre de la Tournelle. Here, on March 12, the Duc de Croÿ saw Damiens for the first time since Versailles. He found him dressed in the same dirty-gray redingote, strapped to an armchair by heavy leather thongs. His burned, swollen

---

* To an officer of the guard, who held his nose when he entered Damiens' cell, Damiens said, "Did you expect the boudoir of a pretty woman?"

feet were stretched out on a *tabouret*. "I found him," says Croÿ, "thin-
ner, dejected, his eyes sunken but less than before, because his cheeks
had so fallen in. His eye was less quick, his complexion more pale, but
his lips no longer twitched . . . that movement had been transferred to
the fingers of his right hand."

Finally, on March 26, Damiens appeared in the Grand Chambre
of Parlement for his "trial." Five princes of the blood, twenty peers
of the realm, twelve presidents of Parlement, seven *conseillers d'honneur,* and eighteen other notables questioned, judged, and sentenced
him. Recognizing several he had served in various households at the
table, he spoke to them directly. *"Quelle audace!"* they murmured.
The calm with which he answered their questions, notes Croÿ, surprised all but the duke; and, for Croÿ, Damiens established beyond
possible doubt his sole responsibility for his crime. "Only one as crazy
as he," concludes the duke, "could have doubted it."

Sentence was delivered that evening and signed by President
Maupeou. Damiens was condemned to the same torture and death as
Ravaillac, the assassin of Henry IV, though Louis XV, unlike Henry
IV, had not died. The house of his birth was to be razed to the
ground and no other ever to be built on the site. His family was to be
exiled from France forever, its name changed and forgotten.

Execution was on Monday, March 28, 1757. Damiens was taken
from his cell at six in the morning for his last session in the chamber
of tortures. On bended knee he heard the sentence; he bowed his
head and remarked, "It will be a hard day." No sign of fear or
repentance was reported. Not long before he had assured Parlement's
surgeon that he would see to it personally that the surgeon was well
placed for the execution. At seven, he was bound hand and foot with
rings of iron. He complimented one of the officers of the guard on his
fine gold snuffbox. Again he was questioned about his act. He repeated before President Maupeou and two counselors that he had
been provoked to it by the archbishop's treatment of the Jansenists,
by the King's treatment of Parlement, and by his own wish to "touch"
the King and bring him to his senses, but not once did he express
hatred for him.

Damiens' inquisitors proceeded with the torture of the boot—the
methodical crushing of his legs. Medical experts consulted by Parlement had advised it as the best way to prolong his torture with the
least risk of provoking a premature death. Slowly the cords around the

wooden "boots" were tightened. Damiens cried out and seemed to faint. The doctors and surgeons at hand said he was simulating. Revived, he asked for wine in the water offered him. "I will need it," he said. For two and a quarter hours the torture of the boot continued, then was stopped, lest he die after all. A confessor was brought to the chamber; afterward Damiens was taken to the prison chapel and exhorted by the prison priest to confess for the last time whatever he had hidden. There were intermittent chants during which Damiens beat time with his left hand, its fingers convulsively jerking.

At two in the afternoon Damiens, a torch in one hand, was tied to a straw-covered tumbrel. The execution procession, with an executioner and two praying priests beside him, left for the Place de Grève. Guards preceded the procession and followed it, pressing back the crowds along the route, alert for any signs of riot. The procession stopped before the great western portal of Notre Dame cathedral, and Damiens, released, descended from his tumbrel, knelt before the closed door, "and asked pardon . . . for his most detestable act of parricide." The procession resumed. It arrived at the Place de Grève, the great square in front of the Hôtel de Ville. Damiens was taken inside and confronted by the city magistrates. And again he was interrogated; and again he replied that he had had no accomplices, his wife and his daughter were completely innocent of his action. As he answered, a crucifix was held before him to kiss. After three quarters of an hour Damiens was brought back to the square, but not everything was quite ready for the execution of his sentence—and the chief executioner would spend several days in prison as a result.

For a week the preparations had been going on. A place for the execution itself, thirty-three meters square, had been fenced off by a wall of planks and pointed stakes, and within it, a scaffold three and a half feet above the ground. Here Damiens was stripped, and "it was remarked how carefully he regarded every part of his body, then turned unmoved to face the great crowd."[15] From seven in the morning—it was now five in the afternoon—the square had been filling with people. The roofs of the surrounding houses to the tops of the chimneys were covered with spectators. Windows overlooking the square had been rented for as much as one hundred livres d'or, men and women of the Court, city, and provinces were early in their places, lorgnettes in the ladies' hands. Among them, in a mezzanine window, accompanied by two women and a man, was Casanova. One more intrepidly curious had even penetrated the fenced-off area around the scaffold, his presence interfering with the last-minute preparations of the sixteen black-hooded executioners, one from as far away as Lyons. As they gathered angrily about him, ordering him to leave, an executioner recognized the amateur and called to the others, "Messieurs, make room for M. de la Condamine, he is a connoisseur!"

Damiens was stretched out on the scaffold, a pile of straw for a pillow; his right hand, closed around the handle of the pocketknife that had "touched" the King, was chained to an iron bar. Bands of iron circled his neck and shoulders, stomach and thighs. The execution began.

An executioner poured burning sulfur on Damiens' right hand. He cried out once, then fell silent, watching the sulfur burn into the flesh. Then the executioner from Orléans approached and dexterously plucked bits of flesh from Damiens' legs, thighs, arms, and chest with a pair of sharp iron pincers. Damiens screamed, then ceased when the pincers stopped. He raised his head and regarded the bits of flesh. The executioner from Lyons dipped a giant spoon into a boiling mixture of resin, sulfur, wax, lead, and oil and poured spoonfuls into the open wounds, avoiding those in the chest—it was not yet time for Damiens to die.

The quartering began. Ropes were tied to Damiens' arms, legs, and thighs, cutting into his wounds, evoking new screams, but "he continued to look on with singular curiosity."[16] The four young, vigorous horses that had drawn his tumbrel were now hitched to the ropes tied to his limbs and whipped to a sudden start. Sixty times they surged forward under the whips, but each time they failed to detach a single member of Damiens' body. For an hour they strained, then two more horses were added, one to each leg. Still conscious, Damiens looked on. When the men whipping the horses began to curse, he bade them refrain from blasphemy. He said he held nothing against them and asked the two priests to recite prayers for him. But for an hour more, as the six horses strained, his screams were heard above the cries of the crowd. Horrified, one of the priests covered his face, the other, on Damiens' request, gave him a "kiss of peace" on his forehead.*

Night was falling. An end had to be put to the spectacle. Samson, the Paris executioner, under the advice of the surgeons present and by

* For the contrasting views of Damiens' torture by Casanova and our own Nancy Mitford, the reader is invited to turn to Note 17, p. 503.[17]

authorization of the city elders, drew a knife from his pocket and expertly cut the muscles and tendons of Damiens' thighs so that the six horses, after five or six lunges, succeeded in tearing his lower limbs from his body and trailed them along the ground. Then the Paris executioner did similarly for the upper limbs, and the two horses, on the fourth lunge, tore the arms free and trailed them on the ground as the great crowd applauded the horses.

Damiens was not yet dead. His torso was seen still heaving with his breath, his lips seemed to be trying to say something. Then trunk and limbs were thrown onto a bonfire inside the enclosure. The torture had taken two hours and a quarter, the burning another four hours. When the last bit of flesh was reduced to ashes, the ashes were thrown to the winds and scattered.

That night, Louis XV was told how the ladies of the Court had enjoyed the spectacle, one of them heard crying, "Oh, the poor horses, how I pity them!" as they were whipped to superhuman effort.

"Fi!" said Louis XV, *"les vilaines!"*—Oh, the naughty women.

The last comment on Damiens, however, has not been made. Most remarkable in his martyrdom, according to Dr. Adnès, was "a self-control, a grandeur of the soul, no less, that the most atrocious torture man has ever experienced could not break down." His analysis has contributed to the writer's own conclusion that Damiens was a politically motivated Raskolnikov who, literally singlehanded, took on what he considered a historic mission.*

* For a more extensive discussion, see Note 18, p. 504.[18]

18. Voltaire, the Man Who Made It
Diderot, the Man Who Didn't

In the reaction of 1757, a royal ordinance read: "Anyone convicted of composing, ordering or printing works intended to attack religion, inflame spirits, assail royal authority or disturb the order and tranquillity of the realm will be put to death."

Few, actually, were threatened with death. From 1750 to 1763, during the critical years of Madame de Pompadour's patronage, the chief censor was Chrétien-Guillaume de Malesherbes, who was himself a cultivated humanist who had written on the freedom of the press.[1] Writers, said his booklet, were for France "what the orators had been for Rome and Athens," and he who read only what had been expressly authorized by the crown "would be behind his contemporaries by almost a century." Malesherbes favored the *philosophes*—Voltaire, Diderot, Helvétius—by granting "tacit permission" when the *"privilège du roi,"* direct royal approval, was difficult or impossible. Yet, writers were in and out of prison; flogging, nine years in the galleys or the pillory was the penalty risked in buying or selling such works as Voltaire's *Dictionnaire philosophique*.

Voltaire's own first taste of the Bastille, as we have noted, came at the age of twenty-three. But he returned from there to the Regency court with *Oedipus*, winning applause and an allowance. He was *embastillé* a second time, when he was thirty-one. In the meantime he had accrued money, thanks to the Pâris brothers and the war-profiteering contracts they had awarded him, the death of his father, and his own astute investments: he would cross France when he heard of a real estate possibility.* And he had accrued fame and its concomitants: enemies, particularly among the clergy. He was frequently in trouble with the Church, sheltering with his "adorable dukes," Sully or Richelieu, visiting the brothers d'Argenson, schoolboy friends. Voltaire's school had been Louis-le-Grand; typically, the Jesuits had trained the Church's sharpest critic. He had a dancing wit and dined out frequently on it. He was a slim, elegant snob, and remained one, but he had an unbridable tongue, and it saved him, if not from himself, at least for us. His long poem, the historical *Henriade,* officially disapproved, was "secretly" printed in Rouen; it circulated from hand to hand in the salons and was translated into seven languages. Crown Prince Frederick of Prussia said he preferred it to the *Odyssey,* flattering its author.[2] Recounting religious crimes through the ages with the Massacre of St. Bartholomew as its point of departure, Voltaire's epic was unpopular with the Crown and distasteful to the Church, but the young writer, because of his wit and talent, was received at Court by Louis XV and presented a purse of 1500 livres by the young Queen. He became the intimate of courtiers, his teasing, lifetime desire, but he was irrepressible in their presence, which proved his saving grace.

One night in December 1725, at the Comédie Française, Voltaire was sitting with Adrienne Lecouvreur, the most famous actress of her day and likely a former mistress. Entering her box, jealously looking for a quarrel, came the Chevalier de Rohan-Chabot. "Monsieur de Voltaire? Monsieur Arouet?" he sniffed. "What really *is* your name?" "Voltaire," came the reply, "the first of my line, as you are the last of yours." The nobleman raised his cane, the writer put his hand on his sword, the actress wisely fainted between them, arresting the action.[3]

Several days later Voltaire was dining with the Duc de Sully when a message was brought in saying someone wished to see him outside. Voltaire rose and exited. Two carriages were drawn up on the street. He approached the first, put his foot on the step—and was fallen upon and cudgeled by ruffians. From the second carriage, the Chevalier de Rohan-Chabot cried to them: "Be careful of his head, something good may come out of it!" "Oh, the gracious Seigneur!" was heard from the crowd of the curious. In pain and fury Voltaire made his way back to his ducal host. He asked Sully to accompany

* One should make money, Voltaire believed, in order to write, not write in order to make money.

him to the local *commissaire* to lodge a complaint against Rohan. He was blandly refused. The other guests were equally glacial. For them, as for Sully, a Rohan counted more than a Voltaire. It was a lesson for a commoner who would call noblemen his friends. Voltaire appealed to the Duc de Bourbon. "Monseigneur," he said, "I ask for justice. "Monsieur," said the duke, "You have just received it." Madame de Prie, his mistress, offered sympathy but no more. Disenchanted, Voltaire quit the upper levels for the lower depths, went slumming, brooded, retired to the suburbs, and practiced swordsmanship. He reappeared at Versailles and was rumored seeking a duel with Rohan, though duels had long since become punishable by the Crown. Rohan, contemptuously or cautiously, avoided Voltaire, and, possibly to the relief of both, Voltaire ended, for the second time, in the Bastille, a case of preventive arrest. He was treated well, but he detested, and was always to dread, imprisonment. He sought and received release from the Bastille in exchange for a promise to reside in what he hoped was a freer England.

It was an unusually sunny day in May 1726 when Voltaire sailed up the Thames to London, met en route by gaily decorated barges and boats. They were not, however, in his honor, but to greet the King. Nevertheless, when he landed, the festive air, the pink-cheeked women, and open-faced men in the street convinced Voltaire that he had indeed arrived in the land of free men. His personal sense of good fortune was brief: his letter of credit for twenty thousand francs found the banker against whom it was to be drawn in bankruptcy. "That damned Portuguese Jew!" he exploded in a letter to his friend Thieriot in a racist outburst that would often mark his writing. A London merchant whom he had met in France came to his rescue and George I generously sent him a hundred guineas.[4]

Everywhere, or so he would recall the remainder of his life, he encountered a generosity of spirit, a tolerance for eccentricity and free thought which made England ever after his reference for the meaning of freedom itself. He resided there for almost three years, learning English well enough to write it in more than adequate, witty verse. He schooled himself in the physics of Newton—arriving in time for his funeral—and the empiricism of Locke, met Pope, Gay, Swift, and Congreve, and missed Paris and French life. English manners were impeccable, but the climate was unendurable, the food uneatable. He would forever needle the French with the finer state of England, but when he was finally permitted to return to France, he was never to return to England. It had been not only his finishing school, but the basis of his financial independence. He had published a new version of the *Henriade* in London with a dedication to the Queen, three editions of which sold for a handsome total of 150,000 francs, in turn judiciously invested on the Continent. One of Voltaire's first ventures in Paris was to snatch up *all* the tickets in a lottery, on the advice of a mathematical friend, and win at a smart profit. (It is scarcely believable, though a matter of record, that Voltaire had to sue in order to collect.[5])

Plays, unplayable now, made Voltaire's reputation; his books and pamphlets, sources of his troubles, provide the elements of his immortality. Belatedly, he published twenty-four letters written from England to Thieriot, appearing in London in 1733 as *Letters Concerning the English Nation.* Their publication in France, since the *privilège du roi* was not forthcoming, was something else, but again they were "secretly" printed in Rouen. The first four letters admiringly quote the English Quakers, in a Voltairean version. On war (with the French monarchy clearly in mind): "Our God, who bade us love our enemies . . . surely does not want us to cross the sea to cut the throats of our brothers merely because murderers dressed in red, with hats two feet high, recruit citizens while making a noise with two [drum]sticks on the stretched skin of an ass." Further (with the Church as a target): "An Englishman, like a free man, goes to heaven by whatever route he chooses," with the right to "profess, unmolested, whatever religion he chooses." This was the substance of other letters, in which Voltaire challengingly proposed Newton in the place of Descartes as a philosophical *maître à penser* and elevated, with Locke, human experience above divine revelation as the source of knowledge.

More personal was the criticism of Pascal's *Pensées* that was somehow appended to a pirated edition of the *Letters Concerning the English Nation.* The root cause of man's unhappiness, according to Pascal in a famous passage, was his "not knowing how to remain in repose in his chamber." To this Voltaire replied, anticipating existentialism and exposing the restless energy that fueled his own prodigious production,* "Man is born for action as fire tends upward

---

* There are forty-four volumes of Voltaire's work in English, well over twice that in French, and in addition 102 volumes of his correspondence edited by Theodore Besterman.

and the stone downward. Not to be occupied [*engagé?*]* and not to exist are one and the same thing for man."[6]

The *Letters* were among the first salvos of the Enlightenment, engaging Church and Crown in almost openly declared war. Reading them, Lafayette would remark, had made him a republican before he was ten. The royal response to Voltaire's *lettres* was the inevitable *lettre de cachet*. As copies were publicly burned by the state executioner and the printer went to the Bastille, Voltaire fled beyond the border to Lorraine, and there worked his way back, if not yet to favor, to a conditional pardon. The conditions: disavowal of authorship and residence at a safe distance from Paris. Better than prison, wrote Voltaire to a friend in justification of his recantation, was to say, "Pascal is always right. . . . [and] the Holy Inquisition a triumph of humanity and tolerance."[7] It was the rule of the game, perfectly understood by the readers of the *Letters Concerning the English Nation*. And so Voltaire settled for ten intermittent years at Cirey, in the château of Madame du Châtelet, his mistress and companion in letters, and her complaisant husband, the marquis. The château in Champagne was made comfortable for him and he added a wing for his own use—all at his own expense.

They had met, Voltaire and Emilie (the Marquise du Châtelet), a year previous; he was thirty-eight, she twenty-six. Their liaison, which lasted sixteen years, is one of the most famous in French literature, and it has been eloquently sung.[8] Voltaire began his own memoirs with their meeting. "In 1733," he wrote, "I found a young woman who thought as I did and who decided to spend several years in the country cultivating her mind." She was a prodigy, possibly, as Voltaire considered her, a genius. She early learned Latin and Italian, English and higher mathematics; she married at nineteen, gave her husband three children, gambled at Court, survived two lovers, one of them the Duc de Richelieu. She was tall and commanding, which seems to have suited Voltaire, and when she talked Newton and Locke, calculus and Latin poetry, he decided he loved her. "How fortunate," he told her, "that I can admire her whom I love!"

At Cirey they pursued their work, each in his and her own wing, the marquis considerately off to war. They met, during the day, in the laboratory and the dining room. In the evening they often per-

* Voltaired used the word *employé*, but Jean-Paul Sartre's precedence can here be found.

formed in a little theater, preferably Voltaire's plays, with their guests in minor roles. Science was now the only way to truth, and Emilie hid Voltaire's unfinished manuscript on the *Siècle de Louis XIV,* directing him back to his studies. But such single-mindedness was not for Voltaire, and as Emilie worked on her translation of Newton's *Principia,* he worked on his Jeanne d'Arc, *La Pucelle d'Orléans.* Satire, not science, was his forte. His pen flowed at Cirey, his plays flourished in Paris, it was time for another run-in with the authorities. A lesser poem, *Le Mondain* (The Worldly Man), was the proffered occasion. It was nothing more than a worldly view of Adam and Eve in the Garden of Eden; its suppression tells us a great deal about the state of the Church, its narrowness and power. The Book of Genesis was not thus to be trifled with, and the price was to be another sojourn in the Bastille, if a *letter de cachet* caught up with Voltaire. Advised of its imminence, he packed up and left Cirey for Brussels and Holland. He stayed abroad three months, outlasting the storm, then returned to Cirey and some bad moments with Emilie. He was nervous under criticism, and he was now receiving it, intolerant to all satires except his own. When Desfontaines' scathing *La Voltairomanie* appeared, in reaction to Voltaire's own libelous attack, Voltaire sought police action to suppress it. And both, such was the absurdity of the time, had to disclaim their own works.

When business took the Châtelets to Brussels, Voltaire went with them—his was a better head for affairs than theirs. But a letter from Frederick, now King of Prussia, took Voltaire to Germany—without Emilie. Frederick the Great, a cultivated young monarch, had invited him; possessive and homosexual, he had carefully excluded Voltaire's mistress. And as Emilie fretted in Brussels, Frederick perched on the edge of Voltaire's bed, the latter priding himself on his intimacy with a man who commanded an army of one hundred thousand men—he, Voltaire, the public antimilitarist. Shrewdly, Emilie went down to the French Court at Fontainebleau to work for an invitation for Voltaire to Versailles. His return, however, was relatively brief: next year he was back in Prussia. But with a flattering, secret mission: to discover Frederick's military intentions in the War of the Austrian Succession and return him, thanks to Voltaire's influence, to the French side.

Thus Voltaire played diplomat in Potsdam, as well as court philosopher. He curried favor with Cardinal Fleury and Versailles, while simultaneously engaging in an ambiguous intimacy with the Prussian monarch. It was a double game that Voltaire played badly, if only because Frederick, one of the time's most gifted men, easily and amusedly saw through it. Soon Voltaire was back once more with Emilie, but there was no return to the former ardor. Always more spirit than flesh, the one willing, the other ailing (at will), Voltaire's friendship nevertheless never failed, even as his capacity as a lover, never great, flagged. So, at least, it appeared to Emilie, who philosophically accepted and endured it. "I loved for two," she said in a moving letter.[9] In truth, Voltaire would be soon enough "sighing like an idiot" at the knees of his plump widowed niece, Louise Denis, with whom he may already have been intimate. (His letters to her are the bawdiest in the Besterman collection.) Meanwhile, too, Voltaire continued his pursuit of honors at the French Court and a seat in the French Academy. He had always been, he told the influential Abbé de Bernis, a true Catholic and his work, rightly read, orthodoxly religious. It was a Tartuffe ploy that failed him at first, but Voltaire plugged on and finally made it.

The idyl at Cirey, except for a summer interim, was virtually over. In 1744, Emilie and Voltaire moved to Paris. It was that much closer to Versailles. The Dauphin was to marry the Spanish Infanta; Voltaire, in celebration, was to write an opera with Rameau, *La Princesse de Navarre*. The difficult, imperious Rameau,* for his part, thought the libretto of least importance, had it touched up and returned to Voltaire (working again at Cirey) for changes. Counting on the opera's success for his own at Court, Voltaire obliged, then, nervously ill, left for Versailles for the rehearsals. Finally, on February 23, 1745, the work which had brought on so much fever was performed. Few heard it in the hubbub. The colorful crowd glittered and chattered in the improvised theater of the royal manège at Versailles, and the Dauphine, presumably prepared for her response by her Jesuit tutors, glowered at Voltaire's "lack of grandeur."[10] But the King pronounced himself pleased. Voltaire had reached his goal— Versailles (and pharisaically told his friends he felt at Court, "like an atheist at church"). Several weeks before, he had written the comptroller of finances about the position of historian to the King, Racine's former post, and offered to do the job for a petty four hundred

---

* Who had had his own difficulties. He was past fifty when his opera, *Les Indes galantes,* was performed at Versailles, and it was the singers, not he, who won the applause. His music was "too complicated, too modern."

livres. Louis XV, who was never small in such matters, named
Voltaire to the office at the full rate of two thousand livres a year.
(Voltaire's income, at this time, from books, plays, rents, loans, investments, and annuities may have been *forty times that*.[11]) He was
now, in his own words, "a fifty-year-old court clown," with a room
at the palace that was "the most stinking hole in Versailles."* He
belittled what he had long sought, what he sought belittled him.
Fortunately not for too long. He was to be a greater man, with his
own court in Ferney, but for that he must once again be in flight.

In the meantime his friend, Madame d'Etioles, had become Madame
de Pompadour; there was his job as royal historian and his first opportunity to perform it with a poem on the bloody, pyrrhic victory at Fontenoy
against the British. D'Argenson, who had experienced it, wrote to him of
its butchery. Voltaire, in three days, turned it into an ode of 350 lines;
in ten days there were five editions selling over one hundred thousand
copies. No gazette, said Lord Chesterfield, listed more names of the living, wounded, and dead. Those mentioned entered national glory; those
unmentioned made it in the next edition. The King was pleased.
Voltaire, the poet, may not have been; the opportunist was. He
followed the official effort with another, a festival opera titled, *Le
Temple de la gloire,* showing Trajan, a transparent Louis XV, returning triumphant from the battlefield. After it was performed, that
night at the King's table Voltaire loudly asked Richelieu, "Is Trajan
pleased?" Trajan, this time, was not. Louis XV had his faults, but
he was not a fool. Flattery was not an open door to him. He was
cool to Voltaire the rest of the evening.

Madame de Pompadour, however, proffered Voltaire the friendship
refused him by the King, and things seemed to go fairly well, even
his campaign for the elusive seat in the French Academy. (Voltaire
wanted to net all honors; none was too small. He became, at his
request and with Pompadour's support, a gentleman of the King's
bedchamber, and eventually sold it for a large sum, though it didn't
cost him a sou.) For his seat in the Academy, Voltaire went all out
soliciting Rome's aid. He asked Pope Benedict XIV to accept dedication of his play, *Mahomet,* to him, though the play, a denunciation of the Moslem faith, was in fact a veiled attack on the Church,
and so playgoers received it. Pope Benedict, a man of letters and

* Odors from the public toilets and the Prince de Conti's kitchen wafted into it
from below.

humor, chose to allow the dedication and sent his apostolic benediction. He also sent a large medal of himself which Voltaire had variously sought through several envoys, each unknowing of the other's mission. "With the utmost respect and gratitude," Voltaire wrote Benedict, "I kiss your sacred feet."[12] With Madame de Pompadour and now the Pope on his side, the King could no longer hold out, and Voltaire had his seat in the Académie Française. But his flowing cup, carelessly held, spilled over.

Voltaire had neither the discretion nor ultimately the patience for the life of a courtier. Worse, in a position of some power, he showed a lamentable lack of humanity, not to speak of largeness. When well-deserved parodies of his Fontenoy poem appeared, he was furious; when he was exposed to satire, instead of rising above it, he sank leadenly below, using his palace position to take out *lettres de cachet* against his critics. In one case, the police mistakenly dragged off the elderly father, rather than the "guilty" son, and Voltaire was condemned by the public. He consoled himself with the idea that, in any event, he was about to die. Voltaire was "about to die" most of his life and finally succeeded in his eighty-fourth year. His downfall at Court, however, had a more trivial cause. "Here I am at Fontainebleau," he tells us in a letter, "and every evening I firmly resolve to rise in the morning for the *lever* of the King"—as required of a gentlemen of the King's bedchamber—"and every morning I remain in my dressing gown working on *Sémiramis*." Even that might have been forgiven; Louis XV was not Louis XIV. But one unforgettable night, the unforgivable occurred. As usual, Emilie was gambling; as usual, she was losing: this time at the Queen's table, as she sat with the lordliest of the land. She lost the four hundred louis she had on her. She lost the two hundred louis Voltaire had on him. He muttered to her to stop; she paid no heed; he sent a lackey to an *homme d'affaires* to borrow two hundred more, at an exorbitant interest. A friend, when that was gone, loaned another hundred and eighty. Lost. Emilie continued to gamble, on credit. And lost. One hundred and three thousand louis in all. Voltaire could no longer restrain himself. "Can't you see," he cried in English, "that you are playing with cheats!"[13]

The shock and outrage on several faces made Voltaire realize his blunder. Cheating at cards, as the Duc de Luynes recounts in his *Mémoires*, was common, but unmentionable, at the French Court, even in English. The pair fled that night for Paris in the first available post chaise. It broke down on the way; they had no money for repairs. Fortunately a traveler recognized them and loaned them money. They continued, but decided to avoid Paris; it offered too much danger. They stopped at a farm. Voltaire sent a message to the Duchesse du Maine, still living at Sceaux. Would she receive and hide them? She would, gladly. The thought of intrigue and scandal delighted the old rascal. For several months they hid out in her château, Voltaire writing *Zadig* and other little tales for the titillation of the duchess, reading them to her at two in the morning, when he slipped down from his hiding place to her bedroom for dinner. Once again the storm passed, Emilie paid her gambling debts, and the pair appeared publicly. Cautiously at first, on the stage of Sceaux's little theater. Then distantly, across the frontier, at the Court of ex-King Stanislas in Lunéville.

In Versailles, Madame de Pompadour faithfully performed Voltaire's play, *L'Enfant prodigue,* but Voltaire was not invited. He was *persona non grata.* In Lorraine, Emilie took a lover, Saint-Lambert, and became pregnant with his child. The three journeyed to Cirey, where they were joined by a fourth, Emilie's husband, the marquis. He was dined and wined, and bedded with his wife, and subsequently told he would, for the fourth time, be a father. However, at forty-three, the marquise sadly felt she would not survive the birth of her child. Concerned, as the time approached, Voltaire and Saint-Lambert took her to Lunéville and Stanislas' court for better care. And there Emilie died, her child not long afterward.

For months Frederick the Great had been pressing Voltaire to stay with him at Potsdam. There was little now retaining Voltaire— his niece, Madame Louise Denis "of the adorable buttocks," was to follow him—so he went north.

We need not follow him to Prussia—it is too far from our scene, and Louise, too, thought it better to remain in France—though he spent the better part of three years in Potsdam. The years ended badly and shabbily, and Voltaire was to end at last, with Louise, where he belonged—in his own "court" at Ferney, a short step from the Swiss border, should the French censor press too closely.

Voltaire was not quite nineteen when Denis Diderot was born in 1713, the son of a decent, charitable cutler who told Denis he preferred the soft, comfortable "pillow of religion and the laws" to the hard, if "excellent pillow of reason."[14] And Denis Diderot's was indeed the harder life, harder than his father's, harder by far, but also by choice, than Voltaire's. *His* entrance to Versailles was by way of the backstairs to the entresol of Dr. Quesnay, Madame de Pompadour's friend and physician. Here, in the little suite overlooking a gloomy, interior courtyard, *philosophes* and physiocrats would congregate—d'Alembert, Buffon, Mirabeau *père,* Helvétius, Turgot, and Diderot. They were, for the most part, deists, that is, they believed in God (they said), but not in religion (i.e., the Church). They were reformists rather than revolutionaries, but they undoubtedly paved the way for the coming upheaval. Better, they set the air dancing with the possibility of change, the physiocrats questioning the feudal ownership and cultivation of the land, the *philosophes* questioning everything—Church, crown, and social system. Why the Church with such special emphasis? It was, in part, because the *philosophes,* too, were system makers and moralists, intellectuals turning on their teachers in a brother-enemy French dialogue that continues down to our own day. But there was a more important social reason, special to that time: the Church was the second power in the land with a conspicuous stake in the *status quo* and with privileges second to none. It was a state within the State. Its princes were generally noblemen by birth made bishops and archbishops by royal appointment. More than the *intendants,* they were the visible, omnipresent—for they were effective in every parish—government of France. At the same time, they were the luxurious absentee owners of its land. Six out of seven monasteries richly benefited absentee abbots, covered vast acres—perhaps one fifth of France—included thousands of serfs—twelve thousand for instance, in that of Saint-Claude in the Jura—and held out longest against any reforms of serfdom.[15] Bishops boasted great, untaxable incomes in many thousands of livres, the Church was an untaxable sanctuary of one third of the nation's wealth. Its clergy dominated, educated, and indoctrinated the young by state order, self-interest, and fiat. Even the idea of educational reform was an attack on the Church.

Yet—or rather, therefore—the Revolution and its prerevolutionary leaders emerged from that dominion. Diderot himself was destined for the priesthood and studied, as so many of the Church's opponents, at the Jesuit *collège* in Paris, Louis-le-Grand. But he dropped his calling about the same time he picked up his master's degree, age nineteen. He became, for a decade, a lawyer's apprentice, a tutor, a ghost writer of priestly sermons, a precarious scribbler hacking for a bookseller. He fell in love, sought his father's help in marriage, failed to get it, married anyway. Four children came, three died, Diderot eked out a living translating from English, resumed his café life, and played chess. His first serious work, *Pensées philosophiques,* coincided with his first mistress and the financing that required; it was quickly followed by *Les Bijoux indiscrets,* a ribald, better-selling novel. Montaigne and Bacon, Hobbes and Locke informed his writing; the *Pensées* was initially attributed to Voltaire. "Enlarge and liberate God!" it cried, and it was burned by the public executioner on the *place* where Damiens would be torn apart. Diderot had arrived: The fifty louis he received went to clothe his mistress. As for *Les Bijoux,* it is still being "discovered" and republished, more than ten editions in the past twenty years. Diderot himself made 1200 livres from the first edition—and virtually nothing from the scientific papers that he was publishing at the same time.[16]

In June 1749, Diderot's *Lettre sur les aveugles* (Letter on the Blind) moved him to the front rank of the *philosophes.* Design in the universe, once claimed as proof of divine intervention, was now asserted to be the result of survival by adaptation (anticipating Darwin). A sense of right and wrong—or morality—was not derived from God, but from the senses and their experience, and so, too, was the idea of a supreme being. "If you want me to believe in God," says the subject of the *Letter,* the blind English mathematician, Saunderson, "you must make me touch him."[17] Diderot had taken a giant's step from deism to unambiguous atheism.

Voltaire to the author: "Perhaps I am mistaken, but in his [Saunderson's] place, I should have recognized a very intelligent Being, who had given me so many supplements to sight."

Diderot to Voltaire: "It is very important not to mistake hemlock for parsley, but not at all important whether or not you believe in God. The world, said Montaigne, is a ball that He has abandoned to the philosophers to bat around."[18]

And *philosophes,* Diderot might have added, for the authorities "to bat around." A *lettre de cachet* sent him to the fortress prison of Vincennes as he was preparing for the century's major work—the *Encyclopédie.* He took with him to prison the book he happened to have in his pocket, Milton's *Paradise Lost;* he was allowed nothing else (he was not Richelieu, or even Voltaire, and Vincennes was not the

Bastille). His wife pleaded with Police Lieutenant Berryer to have him released, so he might provide for his needy family; his publishers, who wanted to get on with the *Encyclopédie,* had more effect. But Diderot spent three months at Vincennes—with visits from his wife, his co-editor, his mistress and Jean-Jacques Rousseau (who walked the ten miles to and from Paris), before he was freed.

Two years before, bookseller Le Breton and three other publishers had approached Diderot about doing a French edition of Chambers' English *Cyclopedia, or Universal Dictionary of Arts and Sciences.* Diderot accepted—at 144 livres a month—and asked Jean d'Alembert, a foundling who had become a *philosophe* and scientific authority, to be responsible for the material on mathematics (he was, in the beginning, to do much more). Adapting Chambers' work for France, Diderot conceived a vaster plan: an entirely new encyclopedia which would embody the dispersed, uncollected, and experimental research, discoveries, and knowledge that had been accumulating throughout the Enlightenment. Somehow his publishers obtained the formal *privilège du roi* (a year before Diderot's troubles with his *Lettre sur les aveugles*), and work began in earnest after his release from prison. Subscriptions were solicited even as articles were commissioned, and a prospectus of eight thousand copies went out in November 1750 to a potential clientele. The immense growth of knowledge, it stated, made an alphabetical encyclopedia not only indispensable but obligatory: knowledge unshared was socially useless. The response was gratifying and in a small way revolutionary: subscriptions were found largely among the upper bourgeoisie, who were increasingly replacing King and aristocrat as literary patrons. A new era in literature began with the first volume of Diderot's *Encyclopédie, ou dictionnaire raisonné des sciences, des arts, et des métiers,* which appeared seven months after the prospectus had been sent out and contained 914 double-column, folio-size pages. Finished, there may be no comparable record of a writer's devotion, at the cost of prison, poverty, and exhaustion, to the extension of knowledge.

Troubles began with Volume II, as usual with the Church; criticisms were not yet leveled at the monarchy, but rather at dogmatic ignorance. Pressure was exerted on the otherwise lethargic and *laissez faire* Louis XV by the Archbishop of Paris. Appeals to Malesherbes, d'Argenson, and Madame de Pompadour achieved a compromising "tacit permission" to publish further volumes, providing there was prior censorship by three clerics. And subscribers rose from 3100 with Volume III to 4200 with Volume IV.[19] D'Alembert weakened; Diderot chose to fight on against censorship, but dissembled his attacks on the Church. Safely from Switzerland Voltaire wrote on *Élégance, Éloquence,* and *Esprit,* Diderot on the idea of *Encyclopédie* itself. The *encyclopédiste,* he wrote, works not only toward the enlightenment of his contemporaries, but for the sake of posterity—so that "our ancestors, becoming better informed, may become at the same time more virtuous and happy, and we may not die without having deserved well of the human race." Posterity, said Diderot, was for the philosopher what the "beyond" was for the religious man.

The fateful year of 1757 brought its warning of death for subversive writers and another crisis for the *Encyclopédie.* D'Alembert had praised Geneva over Paris in such a fashion (asserting that Swiss Calvinists had rejected the divinity of Jesus Christ) that he was as roundly condemned by the pastors of Geneva as by the Archbishop of Paris. In Versailles the King heard a sermon denouncing the *Encyclopédie.* Intimidated by threats of prison, d'Alembert resigned as co-editor. Diderot carried on alone, and the *Encyclopédie, mirabile dictu,* was brought to a completion.

Perhaps it was Catherine the Great's generous offer to the harassed Diderot to patronize the last volumes of his encyclopedia in St. Petersburg, or Frederick the Great's similar proposal for Potsdam, which prodded Louis XV, not to be outdone, to allow their publishing in Paris. Perhaps it was Madame de Pompadour's persuasion; as the Goncourts relate and Voltaire himself believed (there was also the rumor, a publisher's dream, that she had contributed the article on *Rouge*). Publication and sales of the *Encyclopédie* had been officially stopped for some time. There was a gay, intimate supper party at the Trianon, the story goes, when the Duc de la Vallière, chatting of hunting, suddenly wondered what, after all, gunpowder was made of. Here they were always shooting, or being shot at, without the faintest idea of what was happening to them. La Pompadour at this point recognized an opportunity and rose to it. "Yes," she said, "and what about face powder? If only, sire," she turned to the King, "you had not impounded the *Encyclopédie,* we might have found out in a glance." Louis then had the volume carried from his own library, one of the best in France, and for the remainder of the evening the ladies and gentlemen of his Court were dipping into the entries on gunpowder, face powder, and, of course, rouge and the like. And Diderot was formally permitted to bring out Volumes VIII to XVII, saving the honor of France.[20]

There was, however, a shattering anticlimax. Diderot discovered that his own publisher, Le Breton, had been subjecting him to censorship. He had been laboring on the proofs of the final volume, ten hours a day for a month, as he had on every volume. He had endured everything to ensure the encyclopedia's completeness, then, one day, referring, almost by chance, to a printed article in a previous volume, he discovered to his absolute horror that it had been cut. For years Le Breton had been deleting passages he considered *too* provocative for the Church or for Parlement. Furious, disheartened, Diderot accused Le Breton of having betrayed the men "who had devoted their time, their talents, their vigils," their very lives, in the interest of truth and the enlightenment of their fellow men.[21] Le Breton confessed to it, tried to justify his action as a necessary compromise. Neither Diderot nor posterity has forgiven him, though the *Encyclopédie* remains essentially intact, marred as much by the fear of censorship as by Le Breton's mutilation, the limitations of its own time and conceptions, however overleaping the insights and goals. And no one was more aware of it than Diderot. "One should only ask of me," he wrote in his *Pensées philosophiques,* "that I seek the truth, not that I find it."

Diderot also wrote, "Ideas are my trollops!"[22] And he relished in them as if they literally were, writing swiftly in the heat of their discovery, playing them against each other in lively dialogues, his characters taking his ideas to opposing extremes.* Truth was in the search for it, the mind of man was immortality enough and reason the philosopher's grace. Diderot dealt with everything and illuminated it: from the manufacture of pins to the making of steel, from the criticism of art and acting to a new ways of farming. He wrote what might be considered the first proletarian novel, *Jacques le fataliste et son maître,* and the first French middle-class drama, *Le Fils naturel.* Goethe translated *Le Neveu de Rameau,* the Romantic movement took inspiration from it. Diderot had a limited appreciation of democracy (he thought the propertied should replace the titled privileged in the hierarchy of power), but he did not believe, as did Voltaire, that an enlightened monarchy was the answer (he decried Frederick the Great as a tyrant, declaring a ruler should be responsible to his subjects and receive his authority from

---

* Marx called his novel, *Le Neveu de Rameau,* "a dialectical masterpiece."

them). Yet in his old age he had a vision of anarchocommunism as the future ideal, convinced "that there cannot be any real happiness for mankind except in a social state in which there would be no king, no magistrate, no priest, no laws, no thine or mine, no ownership of property, no vices or virtues."[23]

Diderot received no post at Versailles, no seat in the French Academy. He was generous and good-humored; he helped a young writer finish a satire of his own work, so the youth might make money from it. Unlike Voltaire, he would never pursue even his enemies with a *lettre de cachet* or police action. When he himself was desperate for money, for his daughter's dowry, he put up his library for sale. Catherine the Great, hearing of it, had it bought by an agent, then left it in Paris with Diderot as her "librarian" on a yearly salary. In gratitude, Diderot spent a few months in St. Petersburg, but he argued freedom and even democracy with his benefactress. He could not be bought. He returned to Paris in 1774 and continued to write his fugitive pieces for the next (and last) ten years. When he heard that a Dutch publisher was collecting his work for a complete edition, he reacted "with peals of laughter" that his "trollops" should find such a respectable home. Diderot died on July 30, 1784, six years after Voltaire and Rousseau, and the fifth anniversary of his death was celebrated, almost to the day, by the storming of the Bastille.

Rousseau, who had quarreled so bitterly with the *philosophes,* compared Diderot to Plato and Aristotle in his *Confessions,* and praised him for his universality. Carlyle and Michelet called him Promethean —the supreme genius of an age of genius.[24] "Voltaire," the Goncourts concluded, "was the last spirit of old France; Diderot was the first genius of new France."[25]

19. Arrivals and Departures
Enter Madame du Barry, Exit Louis XV

Louis XV, in the fifty years of his reign, lost the Bourbons their crown* and France, in the Seven Years' War, its colonies.

France was better off without either.

There had been eight years of peace since the inconclusive War of the Austrian Succession. It was 1756, time for the Seven Years' War. Prussia, under Frederick the Great, had made its entry as a central power in Europe (and has not been dislodged since). Louis XV, whose domestic policy was marked by lethargy, moved with some energy against Frederick the Great. Perhaps in compensatory imitation of Louis XIV, he even conducted a secret, *second* ministry of foreign affairs, of which, he fondly believed, his official foreign ministers were completely ignorant.[1] For three decades he employed secret agents, engaging in a vast, coded correspondence with them. Sometimes their activities were in accord with the official policy, often they were not. But they coincided in one result: a *renversement des alliances,* a reversal of traditional alliances. The Treaty of Versailles of May 1756 found Habsburgs and Bourbons—France and Austria, ordinarily the cats and dogs of Europe—in military alliance against Frederick's Prussia. Frederick, however, whose spies were as competent as Louis', when indeed they were not the same, had anticipated it by his own alliance with England the previous January. According to its terms, Prussia was to dominate the Continent as England, thanks to its fleet, would extend its empire at the expense of France in America and

* "I found it in the mud," says Napoleon, "picked it up and put it on."

India. Frederick struck first in the Seven Years' War in *blitzkrieg* fashion, aiming to knock out his enemies one by one—France, Austria, and Saxony—before they joined battle with him on three fronts. In August 1756 he marched his superbly disciplined army into Saxony (whose elector was the Polish king). He took Dresden and the following spring drove on to Prague. Typically, as the war opened, Louis XV hesitated, and Frederick had pressed a tardy courtship on Madame de Pompadour, promising her a principality once he had won it from Austria. Contemptuously she forwarded his letter to Vienna: she had not forgotten his cutting remark about her as Cotillon IV—Petticoat (Mistress) IV of Louis XV—and she regarded *him,* rather than the Habsburgs, as Public Enemy I of France. Maria Theresa of Austria had additionally softened Madame de Pompadour with a gift of gems worth 77,728 livres. Russia and Sweden were also drawn in on Austria's side—Spain much later—and Frederick found himself virtually alone in Europe, since England preferred fighting on the seas and in the colonies.

There was no greater military strategist on the field than Frederick—we have Napoleon's word for it—but the opposing forces were overwhelming in number, and the Prussians fell by the thousands. Sick with depression, Frederick contemplated killing himself: he was to carry a vial of poison with him to the end of the war.[2] Despairingly he wrote to his "dear sister" Wilhelmina, who wrote to Voltaire. "The affairs of Europe," wrote Voltaire to Frederick, "are never long on the same basis, and it is the duty of a man like you to hold himself in readiness for events."[3] Courage and patience, counseled the French writer to the enemy of France, and the combination of courage, superior tactics, and the blundering of his opponents brought Frederick respite and eventually the peace of stalemate. At the crucial battle of Rossbach, west of Leipzig, Frederick's army, reduced to twenty-one thousand men, faced a force twice that number. But a sudden Prussian cavalry charge scattered their ranks as Prussian artillery pounded them, and the enemy lost fourteen to Frederick's one. In France the *philosophes* greeted Frederick's victory against the French Army as if it were their own against French reaction.[4] Defeat, however, followed victory, then victory, once again, defeat, Frederick quick-marching his men on occasion twenty-two miles a day to strike unexpectedly, then slip away like a fox. Many times he was hopelessly outnumbered, but rarely outmaneuvered. However, there was a limit to even the greatest military genius, embattled as Prussia was on three fronts without outside support, and as the years passed mutual exhaustion was the outcome on the Continent.

Overseas, on the other hand, England under William Pitt the Elder was to go from victory to victory in its battles with the French for their colonies. The French fleet destroyed early in the war, the door to Canada was opened wide for English troops. At Quebec, on the Plains of Abraham, James Wolfe met and defeated the Marquis de Montcalm, both dying from their wounds. Canada became British. Meanwhile Robert Clive had taken India from the French in the battle of Plassey.

The nineteenth century was to be more critical of these losses than Louis XV's eighteenth.* "Men should stay where they are," Montesquieu had written in *Lettres persanes*. "Transported elsewhere, they become ill. . . . Empires might be compared to a tree whose branches, spread too far, drain all the juices from the trunk and provide nothing but shade." Voltaire repeatedly scorned colonial policy: "We Europeans discovered America only to devastate it and cover it with blood"; "Canada is a country covered with snow and ice eight months of the year and inhabitated by bears, beavers and barbarians"; "France can be happy without Quebec"; and so on. The *Encyclopédie* too dismissed Canada—in twelve lines. Diderot invited "the wicked and ambitious men" despoiling foreign lands to decamp immediately; and Rousseau decried the demoralization and massacre of "the noble savage."[5]

Consequently, Louis XV was not faulted for his failure to defend Canada or India from the British, but for his ineptitude in Europe and at home. And even then the fullness of his folly was not known until a century after his death, when his bizarre, secretive conduct of foreign affairs through secret agents was uncovered.[6] Not even Madame de Pompadour was privy to it, though she suspected it. The vast correspondence involved was kept in a locked secretary, the key to it on the King's person. This much she knew, and one night in 1763, as she supped with Louis XV, Madame de Pompadour played Mata Hari. A letter to one of Louis' oddest agents, the

---

* It is not until our own time, two centuries later, that the equation of colonies with prosperity, or even power, has been questioned. Louis may not have been wrong in seeking a European rather than a world role, but rather in going about it so ineffectively.

Chevalier d'Eon, from his Versailles contact, a man named Tercier, recounts the strange story:

"The King sent for me this morning [writes Tercier]. I found him very pale and agitated. He told me in a strained voice that the secret of our correspondence had been violated. Having supped alone with Madame de Pompadour a few days before, he fell asleep after a slight excess, of which he believes she was not completely innocent. Taking advantage of his dozing, she took the key to the *secrétaire* which His Majesty keeps locked, and discovered your relations with the Comte de Broglie."[7]

Tercier and Broglie were the men at Court—Tercier officially in the foreign ministry—through whom Louis dispatched his secret instructions to his private agents. (The Duc de Choiseul, then foreign minister, *pretended* an ignorance that was real in the case of the Abbé de Bernis, his predecessor.) The King had two obsessions, which he was pursuing: placing a French prince on the Polish throne and plotting an invasion of England. His instructions and intrigues were aimed single-mindedly at those goals, the one unrealizable, the other almost unbelievable. But one of the most peculiar aspects of this most peculiar man was the type of agent in whom he put his trust. The Chevalier d'Eon de Beaumont, a protégé of the Prince de Conti, had been sent to Russia at the age of twenty-eight *apparently*—there is still some dispute about it—dressed as a woman. The official mission of the French ambassador, to whom he, or she, was attached, was to win Russia away from England; the secret mission of Louis' agent was to win support for a French candidate to the Polish throne and try to arrange the marriage of the Russian Empress and the Prince de Conti. When Conti declined in favor at Versailles, that part of the plan was dropped. After failure of his mission in Russia, d'Eon fought briefly in the Rhineland campaign and then showed up in England, at the French Embassy, toward the close of the Seven Years' War as minister plenipotentiary, presumably to discuss terms of a possible peace. Secretly he worked on a plan for invading England. It was a high moment for d'Eon, who made the most of it, until his embroglio with the Comte de Guerchy, who had been sent over as the new ambassador and was unacquainted with d'Eon's "importance." Ordered home by Choiseul, who preferred being ignorant of it as well, d'Eon refused to obey on the grounds that the order had not been signed by the King. Concerned by the growing arrogance and increasing indiscretion of d'Eon, Louis XV instructed Tercier to "send him money, and keep him there, but above all, no more problems." But d'Eon brashly published his account of his quarrel with Guerchy in London and thus gave Louis real cause for concern that he might even publish the letters exchanged with the King. Rumors unleashed by agents of Guerchy ran freely in England that the Chevalier d'Eon was in fact a woman in dragoon's clothing. To add to the mystery, Broglie's secretary, sent to London, returned to Versailles with the information that d'Eon "himself" had confirmed that "he" was indeed a woman—and so the King was told. Toward the end of "his" career, after an interval in France, d'Eon was to return to England and spend his last twenty years in blatantly female dress. And there "he" died in 1810 at the age of eighty-three.*

An even more peculiar personnage played a role in Louis XV's shadow foreign ministry: the Comte de Saint-Germain. Born, no one is sure when, died, no one is more certain when (he claimed an elixir of immortality), the count was early introduced at Versailles by the Maréchal de Belle-Isle as the child of the latter's late years. Saint-Germain was a scientist, a chemist, a linguist, says Casanova, a man as pleasant to men as he was agreeable to women. He was dark of complexion and darker of eye. He gave women potions for their skin and "transmuted" silver into gold for men, though Casanova, who witnessed one of his own coins so transformed, suspected sleight-of-hand rather than alchemy.[9] He was a doctor and miracle healer, but when he was called upon to cure the dying Duchesse de Châteauroux, the Comte de Saint-Germain protested that it was too late, subsequently lost his prestige and left Versailles, confident he would return again in a more favorable climate. And so he did—after a passage in England, where he was briefly in prison as a Jacobite spy, and another to India, where he was a protégé of Clive. He returned to Versailles (it was then Casanova met him) and became an intimate of Louis XV and Madame de Pompadour. He had won the King by taking a flawed diamond worth six thousand francs and bringing it (or another) back without a flaw and with a value of ten thousand francs. Discreetly, however, he declined Madame de Pom-

* An autopsy performed by a British surgeon and published in the London *Times* should have, but hasn't, settled the question of d'Eon's true sex: it states unequivocally that the surgeon found "the male organs in every respect perfectly formed."[8]

padour's request for his elixir of immortality for the King—and Dr. Quesnay was quite alone at Versailles in considering him a quack for even claiming he possessed one.[10] The age of enlightenment was still one of superstition and the willing suspension of disbelief.

One day, as Saint-Germain attended Madame de Pompadour at her *toilette,* she turned to him and asked, "What sort of a man was François I? A king I could have loved?"

"He was indeed a lovable man," said Saint-Germain, and then spoke of the French king, who had died two centuries earlier, as if he had just left him. "It is a pity he was so fiery. I wanted to give him some advice that might have been of some assistance, but he closed his ears to it, as, unfortunately, is the practice of princes at critical moments."

Madame de Pompadour: "Was the Court of François I attractive?"

Saint-Germain: "Very, but that of his grandchildren surpassed it." And he spoke familiarly of Mary Queen of Scots and Marguerite de Valois. "Theirs was one of enchantment, and it was a pleasure to hear them recite their verses."

Madame de Pompadour (laughing): "You seem to have known them all!"

Saint-Germain: "I have a good memory, Madame, and I have read a great deal. But sometimes it amuses me not to make people believe, but in letting them believe, that I have lived for ages."

Madame de Pompadour: "But you never do tell us your age. The Comtesse de Gergy claims to have met you in Venice fifty years ago, looking no younger than you look today." (He looked fifty, Madame du Hausset tells us.)

Saint-Germain: "It is true, madame, that a long time ago I knew the countess."

Madame de Pompadour: "Then you must now be more than a hundred!"

Saint-Germain: "It is not impossible."

And he laughed.[11]

Impressed by the Comte de Saint-Germain, the King sent him on a secret mission to Holland to help arrange peace talks with the British on neutral territory. Choiseul, who was more war-minded, got wind of it, undercut Saint-Germain's standing at The Hague by referring to him publicly as *"ce fils de juif"*—this son of a Jew—and had him warned of expulsion to France and prison. Unsupported by Louis,

Saint-Germain fled to London, then on to Russia, and out of our story.*

The end of the Seven Years' War led, less than a year later, to the end of what Voltaire called "a dream."†

For eight years, commencing when she was thirty-five, Madame de Pompadour had been coughing and spitting blood. Her health, never good at its best, rapidly worsened, and those who knew her were shocked by her appearance. She suffered from insomnia and wept in her solitude. It was the shabby years of the Deer Park, and with some penitence the King talked to her of building a little house in the Trianon gardens. Designed by Gabriel, it was to be known as the Petit Trianon. Together they studied the plans, together they watched the terraces and walls rise. It had the excellence of her taste, the balance and poise of her aesthetic judgment. It is a jewel of a *pavillon,* a classic cube to perfection, but it was to be enjoyed by another: the mistress who would succeed her. She probably had no illusions. It is most likely she who had remarked, *"Après moi, le déluge."*[12]

The ceremonial opening of Gabriel's Place Louis XV—eventually Place de la Concorde—was the occasion for Madame de Pompadour's last public appearance in Paris—and it was accompanied by Parisian jeers. They were to be expected. When the huge equestrian statue of the King had been previously dragged to the great square, mocking cries had come from onlookers: *"Il est ici comme à Versailles, sans coeur et sans entrailles"*—here he is, as at Versailles, without a heart and without bowels (feelings).

The last illness of Madame de Pompadour found her with the King at Choisy. She was coughing incessantly, her poor, inflamed lungs filled with liquid, and the King, in considerate violation of all custom, took her back to Versailles with him so that she might die there like royalty. She was told that there was no hope, and even the Dauphin admired the courage with which she responded. Calmly

---

* To die about 1780, after initiating Cagliostro into the society of Freemasons (according to Cagliostro's memoirs), in Schleswig-Holstein, though several ladies of the French Court insist that they saw him in 1789 in Paris, very much alive, nourishing the fable of his immortality.

† One might also report here the suppression, if not the end, of the Society of Jesuits in France in 1764. It had become too powerful. Nor was this unique to France. The Society of Jesuits had been suppressed in Portugal five years earlier and was to be in Spain three years later.

she made out her will with legacies for her servants, ministers, and the King (to whom she left her Paris *hôtel,* later to become the presidential Elysée Palace). Patiently she sat upright in her chair: she could not breathe lying down. And reluctantly she accepted a priest to hear her ultimate confession, for absolution depended on her no longer seeing the King. Sadly he went up the staircase from her bedroom for the last time. The priest further told her she must send for her husband and ask *his* forgiveness. It was done, but d'Etioles declined coming, saying he was too ill. The next day Madame de Pompadour took leave of Choiseul, Gontaut, and Soubise, who had been faithfully by her side. "The end is coming now," she said to them, "leave me to my soul, my women and the priest." And when the priest, too, seemed about to leave, she said, "One moment, monsieur le curé, we will leave the house together," and died—age forty-two.[13] Hastily her corpse was removed from the palace. From a window the Duchesse de Praslin saw the body on a stretcher, a sheet outlining the form of a woman. She sent to ask who it might be and learned it was the late marquise, on her way to a nearby dwelling, there to await her funeral.

On her request, Madame de Pompadour was to be buried in the Capucines convent on Place Vendôme, and the day came for the ceremony. It was six in the evening and a strong winter wind was blowing. The shutters of the King's apartments had been closed, as if to close out the sight of her cortege leaving Versailles. Louis XV, however, took Champlost, his *valet de chambre,* by the arm and went out on the balcony. There he watched the funeral train as it wound down the Avenue de Paris. In the wind and cold he watched it the length of the avenue, then turned and stepped back into his apartments. Two tears streaked his cheeks. "That," he said to Champlost, "is the only tribute I can pay her."[14]*

There were several more deaths, but not yet that of the King. The Dauphin, his only son, died, but not before fathering the next three kings of France. ("I die," he said, "without having enjoyed

---

* There was Voltaire's as well: "I mourn her out of gratitude. . . . She had *justesse* in her mind and justice in her heart, and all this is not to be met with every day. It is the end of a dream."

But there was also Diderot's dismissal, expressing the popular feeling of the time: "So what remains of this woman who cost us so much in men and in money, left us without honor and without energy, and who overthrew the whole political system of Europe? . . . A handful of dust."

anything and without having done good to anyone."[15]) Then the Dauphine passed away in 1767 and the Queen, the half-forgotten Marie Leszczynska, sixty-five, was not long in following. Louis himself was fifty-eight. Would he now be content with the parade of teenagers through his Deer Park and an occasional affair with a lady of the Court? Or would there be a formal successor to Madame de Pompadour? Courtiers and ministers were more than curious: they were concerned. Madame de Pompadour had been Louis' *de facto* prime minister, as well as his resident mistress. Her replacement as *maîtresse en titre,* if there were to be one, could affect the balance of ministerial powers.

That Louis was lonely in the vastness of Versailles was all too evident to the Court. He lacked for the companionship of one who "loved him for himself" without asking for love in return, who amused and entertained him with spirit and served him with discretion. In short, he missed Madame de Pompadour. The first candidate for the vacancy appears to have been the Duchesse de Gramont, sister (and choice) of the Duc de Choiseul. She was tall, commanding, and crisp. She might have been a sixth Nesle sister, but Louis showed no desire to return to his youth. The second candidate was the Comtesse d'Esparbès, who had been a friend of Madame de Pompadour— which had not kept her from falling into the King's bed while her friend was still alive. She was loving, in fact too loving, as Chamfort reports in a dialogue between the countess and the King.

The King: "It seems you have slept with all my subjects."

The countess: "Oh, Sire!"

"You had the Duc de Choiseul."

"He has such an air of power!"

"And the Duc de Richelieu."

"He has such *esprit!*"

"And Monville?"

"He has such handsome legs!"

The King: "Well then, what about the Duc d'Aumont, who has nothing at all?"

The Countess: "Ah, Sire, he is so attached to Your Majesty!"[16]

But she proved too indiscreet about her intimacy with the King, announcing in advance that she would soon have the title and privileges of the residing mistress. It was that rather than her promiscuity which doomed her chances. And the King continued to look for a companion.

He could scarcely have looked lower.

Madame du Barry was born Jeanne Bécu in August 1743, daughter of Anne Bécu, dressmaker. Jeanne's father, according to the parish register of Vaucouleurs, was "unknown," though fingers pointed at a local monk, Brother Angel.[17] Three and a half years later, Anne Bécu gave birth to a second illegitimate child, and this time the scandal drove her with both children to Paris for a living. There she found work and within two years a husband and a rich friend. The rich friend, taken by Jeanne's pretty ways, paid for her education at a convent. The prettiness became precocious beauty, as, fifteen, Jeanne returned home. She was apprenticed to a hairdresser, whose infatuation with Jeanne led to her being sent away by his mother. She went on to a wealthy widow as a *demoiselle de compagnie,* was courted by not only the lady's two sons, but by one of their wives. She resisted the latter, succumbed to the former, and was dismissed as before by the mother.[18] Fate took her to a fashion house, where she modeled clothes and very soon became "known," as a contemporary notes, "by the *grands amateurs* of the capital."[19] She was tall, blond, oval-faced and freckled, "with a bosom with which women are not counseled to risk comparison."[20] Was she a prostitute? The pamphlets of the period say she was, but she appears on no police lists as such, though police reports were now being made on her activities. From the age of seventeen to twenty her known lovers included a wealthy silk merchant, an abbé, a colonel, an official, and a financier.[21] Then fate brought her Jean du Barry, who was to bring her, with a few detours, to Louis XV.

Jean du Barry called himself a count, though the title belonged to his older brother. He had married in the provinces and left his wife there, gambled and wenched in Paris. Nicknamed the Roué, he paid his way by procuring women and not least among those he served was the oldest among *roués,* the Duc de Richelieu. Du Barry was briefly in the diplomatic service and quickly dismissed. He, too, was under police surveillance and a report was made that Jeanne Bécu, also known as Vaubernier, was now installed in his house and was being made available at a price.[22] Overworked (the report continued), she had taken the fifty louis she had received from the Duc de Richelieu and set herself up in her own apartment, but within three months she was back with du Barry, calling herself countess. Du Barry provided a good table and women, and his "countess" a lively salon, to which dukes, marshals, and bankers came slumming. Madame du Barry became skilled in light conversation, flattering listening, and the varied arts of pleasure for the jaded. Looking like a debauched angel, she was ready for an aging, debauched king.

It is not certain how Madame du Barry, not quite twenty-five, met Louis XV shortly after—it may even have been before—the Queen's death. One version has them meeting in the corridors of Versailles; it was not hard to arrange: people, as we have so often noted, had ready access to them. Catching sight of her, the King may well have dispatched Lebel with the well-exercised mission of fetching her to the *petits apartements* via the valet's "bird trap." It was probably not, as another version has it, the Duc de Richelieu who had arranged it, though, approached, he might have put in a good word for "Comtesse" du Barry (and have her beholden to him thereafter). In any event, we know the King was not disappointed. On the contrary, she stirred him as no woman, not even the young Madame de Pompadour. "She is the only woman in France," he confided to Richelieu, "who has found the way to make me forget I am nearing sixty." And to the Duc d'Ayen he disclosed that he experienced with her "a sensual pleasure of an entirely new sort."[23] Court cynics commented that this was because Louis XV had never patronized a really professional brothel. However, for the privilege of paying visits to the royal family, of riding in the royal carriages, and being present at royal receptions, in brief, for the formal privileges of the Court, Madame du Barry would first have to be formally presented at Court, that is, to the King. But before that the lowly Madame du Barry must be made a lady—a married lady. Unmarried, a mistress might become a Madame de Maintenon with the pretensions of a full queen.

The trappings—carriage, money, clothes, jewelry—were advanced by Jean du Barry as an investment with guaranteed returns. The marriage, too, was arranged by the Roué—to his own brother, a retired naval officer, the Chevalier Guillaume du Barry, living unremarked in the country. Guillaume accepted, came to Paris, was married on September 1, 1768, and returned that night, alone, to the country, richer by a dowry of thirty-five thousand livres and a royal pension of five thousand a year. Lebel, in the meantime, had died and La du Barry was installed temporarily in his "bird trap" below the King's bedroom. She was now *maîtresse* in residence, but not yet in title. First

K

there was to be the formal presentation of Madame du Barry at Court by a lady of the Court—if one could be found to perform it.

Several were discreetly approached; each found an excuse for declining. Presenting Madame du Barry meant certain offense to the Duc de Choiseul, Mesdames (the King's daughters), and the archbishop (talks were in progress with Vienna about marrying Louis XV to an Austrian princess, the eldest daughter of Maria Theresa). For a time the Baronne de Montmorency seemed a possibility, but she asked too much. Finally Richelieu turned up with the Comtesse de Béarn, who was widowed, in debt, and a recent arrival at Court. The King agreed to pay her debts and provide for her sons. Presentation day was set for January 25, 1769. The Comtesse de Béarn meanwhile saw palace doors closed in her face, and lost her nerve. Judiciously she sprained an ankle and asked for the ceremony to be postponed, indefinitely. But the King persisted and, despite a hunting accident, fixed a new date for April 22. That day the countess appeared as scheduled, but not Madame du Barry. Arm in a sling, the King watched for her arrival at the Marble Courtyard. It was long delayed: her headdress was taking longer than planned. Impatiently Louis talked of calling everything off, but at last du Barry appeared for a presentation the most colorful in the history of the palace. Splendid (if not virginal) in white, blazing with jewelry that cost the King (that is, France) a small fortune,* Madame du Barry glided through the great Galerie des Glaces on the arm of Richelieu, stopped before the King, gracefully kicked back her train, curtsied thrice, and sat down to power, privilege, and the giving of pleasure. Her beauty had conquered all, even the young Dauphin, Louis' grandson, whose own tastes ran heavily to hunting.[24] As for the King, his visits to the Deer Park slackened and he closed it not too long afterward.

La du Barry had conquered all, that is, but the Duc de Choiseul, Mesdames, the archbishop, and their party. Choiseul's resistance to her had not been reduced, his war with her remained open—and his replacement by one of *her* party, the Duc d'Aiguillon, Richelieu's nephew, openly advanced. So openly that Choiseul brought it up with the King, who wrote in reply (mixing private and public affairs in a manner that would have scandalized the Sun King): "How can you imagine that Aiguillon could replace you? What good could

* Altogether du Barry drained the French treasury of 6,000,375 livres in four years.

he do, hated as he is? You manage my affairs well and I am pleased with you. But beware of your entourage and busybodies. You know Madame du Barry. She is pretty, she satisfies me, that should be enough. She feels no hatred for you; she is aware of your ability and wishes you no harm. The outburst against her has been terrible and largely undeserved. Is it desired I take a woman of birth? If the Archduchess [of Austria] were to my taste, I would marry her with great pleasure, but I should like to see and know her first. The fair sex will always trouble me, but you will never see me with a Mme de Maintenon. I believe that will be enough for this time."[25]

The King arranged a meeting between Choiseul and du Barry, but it was to no avail; the abyss between them was too deep, and du Barry deepened it. "The lady no longer hides her hatred," wrote a lady at Court (Madame du Deffand) to Horace Walpole, the English writer and statesman who frequently visited the French Court. "Choiseul is subjected to her pinpricks, for instance, exclusion from the little suppers in the private apartments, and when they are partners at whist, she makes faces and pettishly shrugs her shoulders."[26]

Moodily the duke thought of resigning but was restrained by his strong-minded sister. Dismissal by the King was not immediately in the offing. Choiseul had gained the confidence of Austria and Spain. France could not afford a possible offense to either. It was one reason Louis toyed with the idea of marrying a daughter of Maria Theresa (but went no further than commissioning a portrait). The idea itself did not die. Talks begun at the end of the Seven Years' War continued between Choiseul and the Austrian ambassador, revolving around Marie Antoinette, the Empress' youngest daughter, and Louis' grandson, the new Dauphin. Negotiations reached such a point that on Marie Antoinette's thirteenth birthday her mother sent to Paris for a French tutor and a French hairdresser.

And in 1770, when Marie Antoinette was not quite fifteen, nor Louis-Auguste, the Dauphin, sixteen, they were married by proxy. The papal nuncio officiated; the bride's brother represented the bridegroom. They were to be the monarchy's star-crossed couple, soon enough to hold the center of the Versailles stage.

Louis-Auguste, however, was as removed from Romeo as from his grandfather. He had a plumpness that would give way to stoutness. He had a passion for carpentry, working at an anvil and hunting; he kept a diary in which he meticulously recorded each slaughtered piece, though by this he is not to be thought either cruel or even unkind. He was studious, nearsighted, clumsy, and taciturn, noted at Court for his appetite and capacity for sleep.

Marie Antoinette was not, of course, the figure of legend she has become. In fact, she was an unknown for the French Court. Her portraits showed her as a young, pert blonde with too high a forehead, too long a nose and too large a chin; she was, after all, a Habsburg. Reports from her French tutor, the Abbé de Vermond, were read—or rumored—with interest and some disappointment. "A bit of laziness," he wrote the Austrian ambassador, Mercy-Argenteau, "and a great deal of giddiness have made my instruction difficult." However, he added, "she has a good memory." He was charmed by her graceful figure, her carriage, and hoped she might grow a bit taller, as befitted a future queen. He was alarmed by her indolence and willful ignorance (she disliked reading), but wrote of a slumbering intelligence. "I came in the end," he concluded, "to recognize that she would only learn so long as she was being amused."[27]

The Empress, her mother, was even more aware of it and almost despaired at the thought of her frivolous child at the French Court (one can almost hear the sighs as she wrote Mercy the first of many letters). Two months before Marie Antoinette's departure, she had her daughter sleep with her in her bedroom, so that they might have long, intimate talks about her new life and the intricacies of an intriguing Court. "May Your Majesty be good enough to guide her," she wrote Louis XV. "She is full of good will, but at her age I beg indulgence for any mistake." And as her daughter prepared to depart, Maria Theresa told her, "You will find a tender father who, if you desire it, will also be your friend. Love him, obey him, try to anticipate his thoughts as much as you can. It is this father, this friend, who is the only consolation for my grief, my hope that you will follow my advice to await his counsel in everything. Of the Dauphin, I say nothing. The wife is subject to her husband in everything, and she should have no other occupation than to please him and do his will. The only true happiness on earth is a happy marriage. Everything depends on the woman."[28]

Thus burdened, the fourteen-year-old bride made her way to France in a cavalcade of 340 horses and a carriage sent her by the King.

At Compiègne the King himself, a handsome, tired sixty, met the little princess with the royal family—Mesdames (his three elderly daughters) and his three grandsons, including the Dauphin. The Duc de Choiseul had gone in advance to greet her. Arriving, Marie Antoinette kneeled before the King. He raised her to her feet, kissed her with the affection of a father and the keenness of a connoisseur, and presented her to the tall (five foot ten), awkward, and tongue-tied Dauphin, and to Mesdames, her aunts. The same day Louis XV wrote his grandson in Madrid how touched he was by the Austrian princess, how she had enraptured the entire royal family, and he nostalgically referred to her as *"my* Duchesse de Bourgogne," the teen-age Princess of Savoy who had been his mother.[29]

As the augmented cavalcade slowly made its way to Versailles, Madame du Barry awaited it at the edge of the Bois de Boulogne in the Château de la Muette. Was it conceivable, the Austrian ambassador wrote his empress, that the King would impose his mistress, for her *first* formal gathering, on this important occasion? It was indeed, and she sat next to the King at supper on the evening of the arrival. Innocently the Dauphine asked her lady-in-waiting, the Comtesse de Noailles, who might the beautiful lady be, and what her role. "Her role?" repeated the embarrassed countess. "To amuse the King." "Then I shall be her rival!" said Marie Antoinette gaily.[30] Mesdames, however, would not be long in describing the du Barry role in less euphemistic terms.

At Versailles the second, more significant, wedding ceremony took place in the royal chapel with the Archbishop of Rheims consecrating the wedding, blessing the thirteen ritual gold pieces and the wedding ring, the great organ playing, a great crowd watching, a greater crowd outside, waiting. Half of Paris was in the park. But the fireworks promised that night were rained out in the afternoon, and damply the masses flowed homeward.* In the palace itself, however, the festivities continued with gambling in the Grande Galerie, supper in the newly finished Opéra of Jacques-Ange Gabriel, the King's architect

---

* Four days later in Paris, fireworks celebrating the marriage set fire to scaffolding in the Place Louis XV and in the hysteria that followed 132 people were crushed to death. Marie Antoinette, who had witnessed some of it, sadly returned to Versailles. At Versailles the previous four days were given over to a series of fêtes—ballets, balls, and entertainments, Lully's *Persée* and Racine's *Athalie*—in the new, beautiful Opéra of Gabriel. "How do you find my entertainments?" Louis XV had asked his *contrôleur général des finances.* "I find them, Sire," he responded, *"impayables!"* In 1769 he had reported His Majesty's finances "in a state of terrifying collapse, expenditure exceeding revenue by fifty million francs . . . with urgent liabilities of eighty millions."

and the finest of the age. Here in the north wing of the palace, in a theater of jewel-box splendor, a temporary floor had been laid extending the very deep stage across the banked seats. Chandeliers with a myriad of candles glistened in the encircling mirrors. And in the midst was a great table for twenty-two of the royal household. From the galleries and parterre hundreds upon hundreds looked on— five to six thousand had been invited to the festivities. (Madame du Barry, this time, supped alone with her entourage in her new, gold-and-white apartments directly above the King's.) And eighty musicians played.[31]

Marie Antoinette sat fascinated, a bit intimidated, vastly entertained. Louis-Auguste ate on unheedingly. "Don't overload your stomach tonight," cautioned the King. "Why not?" the Dauphin asked. "I always sleep better after I have supped well." The King did not insist.[32]

At the *coucher* it was the King who ceremoniously tendered the nightshirt to the bridegroom, already nodding to sleep, and the Duchesse de Chartres, in another bedchamber, the nightgown to the bride. Formalities concluded, the couple joined, the four-poster curtains were drawn about them. The next day the Dauphin wrote in his diary, *"Rien"*—nothing. Normally it meant, "No hunting today." This time it signaled the first of seven years of *"Rien."*[33]

Youngsters of fourteen and fifteen, the royal couple may—or may not—have been conscious of the "failure" of their wedding night. And the fact may be belabored in romantic biographies, such as Stefan Zweig's. "During these seven years of [Louis-Auguste's] impotence," he writes, "the characters of the King and Queen were warped, each in its own fashion—with political results which would be unintelligible had we no knowledge of the prime cause. The fate of this one marriage was intertwined with the fate of the world."[34] Well, of one world. But as the years passed and Marie Antoinette was taunted unjustly with sterility, it could not but have left its mark. Knowing the fault was not hers, but rather that of her husband, she must have experienced frustrations, temptations and have displayed occasional flaunting scorn.

Marie Antoinette wrote her mother about it; her mother consulted a Court physician and then wrote Louis XV about it. He was not unaware of some problem—"the Dauphin," he once commented to Mercy, the Austrian ambassador—"is not a man like the others."

And *his* Court physician, after examining Louis-Auguste, found the
cause was not psychological, but physiological: phimosis. The prepuce of the penis was too tight: sexual excitement for the Dauphin
meant sharp pain. The royal heir to the Most Christian King needed
a circumcision.[35] Five years after their marriage, Marie Antoinette
tried to persuade the Dauphin to it (as a letter to her mother tells us),
but it was another two years before he consented to it.

However, that was three years after the death of Louis XV and
a number of intervening affairs. Affairs that involved Marie Antoinette in her first, and perhaps only, difficulty with the King. The
earliest of her letters to Maria Theresa, written shortly after her arrival
in France, presages it. "The King," she wrote, "has a thousand kind-
nesses for me and I love him dearly, but his weakness for Madame du
Barry—the most stupid and impertinent creature imaginable—is pitiful.
She has joined our play every evening. Twice she sat next to me, but she
did not speak to me, nor I to her, though I addressed her when it was
unavoidable."[36] Very soon both Mercy and the King, made unhappy
by an outraged Madame du Barry, were complaining to the young
Dauphine that she was publicly humiliating the person closest to the
King by scorning to speak to her at all. And for almost two years
Marie Antoinette had held out—despite Louis' entreaties and her
mother's orders—until the war of silence between the women was ended
by nine grudging words.

The reconciliation had been arranged for New Year's Day 1772.
The ladies of the Court, as was the custom, filed past the royal family,
expressing their seasonal greetings. They came in order of precedence,
and among them was Madame du Barry. She was accompanied by
the Duchesse d'Aiguillon, wife of the new foreign minister, who
extended her good wishes to Marie Antoinette and moved on. It
was Madame du Barry's turn. She moved up and waited. There
was complete silence as *all* waited and watched. Inclining her head
in the general direction of Madame du Barry, Marie Antoinette said,
"Il y a bien du monde aujourd'hui à Versailles"—there are quite
a few people today at Versailles. Soon after, still furious for having
yielded, the little Austrian told Mercy, "I followed your advice, and
here is the Dauphin"—who remained speechless—"to bear witness.
I have spoken once, but that is as far as I will go. Never again will
that woman hear the sound of my voice."[37]

It was not entirely mock warfare between two women. The relations between France and Austria were becoming involved. And at home, by snubbing Madame du Barry, Marie Antoinette had publicly cast her lot with Choiseul and her spinster aunts. It was the losing side, however, and Marie Antoinette's nine-word gesture to Choiseul's chief opponent, Madame du Barry, was the price for it.

For some time Louis XV had also tried to reconcile the Duc de Choiseul and his mistress, but that reconciliation as well never came off, though more than nine words were exchanged between them. Finally, a year before Marie Antoinette's capitulation, the King sent his minister notice of dismissal and exile. "I command my cousin the Duc de Choiseul," he wrote, "to place his resignation in the hands of the Duc de la Vrillière, and to retire to Chanteloup to await my further orders." News of his disgrace reached Paris about the same time as Choiseul himself, who had gone to the capital to pick up his wife before going on to his country estate. The streets near his Paris town house were crowded with people and lined with carriages, and he was cheered when he made an appearance. The demonstration was as much defiance to the King and his mistress as a tribute to the duke, who was moved to tears by it. When he retired to Chanteloup, "half the Court abandoned Versailles to render him a visit."[38] The old regime had seen nothing quite like it, but Louis XV would not, or could not, do anything about it.

Two men fell heir to Choiseul's power: the Duc d'Aiguillon, as foreign minister, and Maupeou, an elderly lawyer who once presided over the Paris Parlement, as chancellor. On the shoulders of Maupeou was placed the long-standing problem of the Parlements and their challenge to the Crown. "It is in my person that sovereign power resides," Louis had pronounced. "The Courts derive their power from myself alone. To me alone belongs the legislative power. If the Parlements continue the scandalous spectacle of a challenge to my sovereign power, I shall feel compelled to employ the authority received from God in order to preserve my peoples from the tragic consequences of such enterprises."[39] But the Parlements persisted in their remonstrances against the King's measures, and Maupeou was summoned to deal with them, particularly the Paris Parlement. He proceeded to do so, in the process calling on Voltaire at Ferney to help him influence public opinion. Voltaire proved more than willing. He wanted his monarchy enlightened, not replaced by the rule of parliamentary lawyers,* and he responded with a pseudonymous work published in Amsterdam. "Better," he wrote, "to be ruled by a great lion than by two hundred rats of their kind!"[40] It had its effect.

When the Paris Parlement, supported by all the other Parlements of France, met the King in headlong conflict over the Duc d'Aiguillon's imposition of taxes in Brittany, where he was governor, the King disbanded all Parlements and exiled their members. In a *lit de justice* at Versailles, Louis XV created a Supreme Tribunal, to be called the Maupeou Parlement, and six Superior Councils for the provinces. Simultaneously he abolished the venality, or purchase, of public offices: magistrates were henceforth to be replaced by royal appointment, not by sale to the highest bidder. The changes, which could have been significant, were to last as long as Louis XV. But no longer.

The last years of the Adonis-King were spent, one might say, in an amorous calm before the storm. Twenty times a day he ascended the staircase behind a hidden door in his library to the apartments of Madame du Barry. He was probably as happy as his natural melancholy permitted. Once, hunting, he inquired about the death of a peasant he had somehow remarked. "Of what did he die?" he asked. "Of hunger," came the answer, and Louis XV rode off. The smell of death was strong those days. Lugubriously the Abbé de Beauvais had spoken in the Lenten sermons of 1774 at the royal chapel of Versailles, pointing to the premature deaths of the King's own parents and on Easter day he solemnly warned, "Within forty days, sire, Nineveh will be destroyed!"[41]

Within thirty days the King had come down with fever. Too weak to continue his hunt, he had returned to the Petit Trianon, where he frequently took refuge with Madame du Barry. "It is at Versailles," his first surgeon told him, "that one must be ill," and he was driven, in his dressing gown, to the palace. The Court physicians examined him, consulted, and, not knowing what to do, bled him. The fever did not abate. In a few days the fatal spots appeared: the King had smallpox. The contagion was so great that fifty of the palace came down with the plague, and ten died of it. As a precaution, the Dauphin

---

* Often more reactionary than the Crown, the Parlements proved more Catholic than the Jesuits in their persecution of the Huguenots and as zealous in their suppression of dissident writers. The most famous *affaire* of the century was the *affaire Calas,* in which Voltaire, at considerable personal cost, successfully rehabilitated a Huguenot family of that name in opposition to the Parlement of Toulouse.

and the Dauphine kept to their apartments, Louis-Auguste on the ground floor, Marie Antoinette above him in the apartments formerly the Queen's. In "fear and cowardice" the King lay dying, the grand master of the royal wardrobe, the Duc de La Rochefoucauld-Liancourt, tells us in his day-to-day account.[42] The King's doctors had not dared tell him the truth, but he had read it in their faces.

The time had come for confession and extreme unction, which meant, as at Metz, the sending away of his mistress. Reluctantly Louis XV summoned Madame du Barry; gently he told her to leave Versailles. Scarcely had her carriage quit the courtyard for Rueil and the Aiguillon château, when Louis sent his valet for her. "She has left, sire," said the valet. "Ah," murmured the King, "already . . ."[43]

Courtiers crowded the Oeil-de-Boeuf antechamber. The sickroom was avoided. A great stench filled it from the King's suppurating sores, though the windows and doors were kept constantly open. And there were great crowds in the courtyards. The dying of a king in an absolute monarchy often spells crisis and sometimes a major change. The last days of Louis XV contained signs of both, and there may have been some in the crowds who suspected he would be the last of his line to die at Versailles. Was there, too, a sense of a dying order? In apocalyptic prose and near perfect hindsight, Carlyle would write, "Alas, much more lies sick than poor Louis; not the French King only, but the French Kingship; this too, after long rough tear and wear, is breaking down. The world is all so changed; so much that seemed vigorous has sunk decrepit, so much that was not is beginning to be!—Borne over the Atlantic, to the closing ear of Louis, King by the Grace of God, what sounds are these; muffled ominous, new in our centuries? Boston Harbour is black with unexpected Tea: behold a Pennsylvanian Congress gather; and ere long, on Bunker Hill, DEMOCRACY announcing, in rifle-volleys and death-winged, under her Star Banner, to the tune of Yankee-doodle-doo, that she is born, and, whirlwind-like, will envelop the whole world!"[44]

But the storm that would break after America's had been gathering long before in France.

A lighted taper had been placed in the window of the King's bedroom, to be extinguished at his death. One by one the tapers guttered low and were replaced. Then, at three-fifteen in the afternoon of May 10, 1774, the last taper was snuffed out. "At that signal," says Madame Campan, "a terrible noise, absolutely like thunder was heard." It was a stampede of the courtiers rushing from the Oeil-de-Boeuf through the Grand Galerie to salute the new King and Queen. "By this strange noise Marie Antoinette and her husband knew their time had come to rule, and with tears in their eyes the young couple fell instinctively to their knees and cried, 'Dear Lord, guide us, protect us, we are too young to rule!' "[45]

"What a burden, at my age!" another courtier has Louis-Auguste, now Louis XVI, exclaiming. "And they have taught me nothing!"[46]

20. Marie Antoinette and Louis XVI
Too Young, Too Little, Too Late

Did Louis XVI and Marie Antoinette actually fall to their knees when Louis XV died, as Madame Campan's memoirs tell us? It can be doubted—and has been—on the rather solid grounds that the little Austrian was too lightheaded and too eager for the unleashed freedom of being Queen, and that Louis XVI, for his part, was "cold-blooded as a fish."[1] Marie Antoinette, we know, did confide her pleasure to her mother immediately afterwards in the thoughtful way "Providence had arranged for me, the youngest of your children, to be Queen of the finest realm in Europe."[2] But then she *might* have fallen to her knees, in the light of an onlooking Court's expectancy, since Louis XVI had most likely dropped to his own. There is no contradiction between lightheadedness and play acting. As for Louis, he had, after all, been raised in piety by his religious father and was to consult God most of his abbreviated life before making any major decision. Providence and Marie Antoinette—the order is not certain: the voice of the little Austrian may have been the louder—were to be his greatest influences. Nearsighted but not permitted glasses—it would have marred the public image of a King—tubercular and shunted aside in his youth for his older brother before he died, outshown and out-performed by his younger brothers, the Comtes de Provence and d'Artois, Louis-Auguste had turned to God, hunting, and locksmiths, taking shelter in his hobby shops under the eaves. Asked, as the Dauphin, what he would like to be known when King, he had replied, "Louis le Sévère."[3]

And, legend has it, he once took over from a peasant and plowed a remarkably straight furrow.

The young Queen was not long in putting aside the lady-in-waiting of her apprenticeship years, the Comtesse de Noailles, whom she scornfully greeted as Madame l'Étiquette. Even as the Dauphine, she had begun to form a young court of her own favorites with small theatricals and balls in her apartments, evenings in Paris, and sleigh rides in the winter. When she became Queen, her first chore was to receive long lines of black-robed ladies mourning Louis XV, and she did not dissimulate her distaste for these "high-collared ancients of another century," all but referring to them as the Ancien Régime. Predictably the ancient duchesses took offense, vowing to quit the Court and never more set foot in it. "Let them go," said Marie Antoinette. "I do not know how any woman past thirty dares appear at Court!"[4]* And many, calling her *"la petite moqueuse,"* left. Concerned, Mercy dispatched a courier to Maria Theresa, who warned her daughter about her conduct. "To please five or six young ladies or cavaliers," she wrote, "you are losing all the others."[5] Marie Antoinette shrugged and continued, joining her equally bored, still younger brother-in-law, the Comte d'Artois, in a variety of adventures and escapades in Paris and at the palace, dancing, flirting, and running up gambling debts. (Meanwhile, the secret corridor running from the King's apartments in the north wing to her own in the south, passing under the state rooms, led only to the frustrations already mentioned: *rien,* nothing involving the State, such as an heir, was forthcoming.) And Marie Antoinette played Queen in her own increasingly criticized Kingless fashion with an early, misleading triumph. In the famous battle between the *gluckistes* and the *piccinistes,* begun when she was yet Dauphine, she imposed Gluck over Piccini at the Paris Opéra— German music over the prevailing French-Italian mode—and it gave her a taste for ordering things that would endure.

But in the wake of the eternal optimism of an older king's death and the emergence of a new young sovereign, someone wrote *Resurrexit* on the statue of Henry IV.[6] (And not too long afterward, the same was to be written on the statue of Louis XV, as disenchantment followed.[7]) Replying to Marie Antoinette's letter on the kindness of

---

* One might as well record at this point that Marie Antoinette in all probability never said, "Let them eat cake"—that is, *brioche,* her morning biscuit of pastry dough—during a bread famine devastating France.

God in making her Queen of France, her mother had advised caution. Above all, she had warned, "do not change anything. Let matters go on as they are. Otherwise chaos and Court intrigue will become too much for you both." And to her son, Joseph II, the Empress had sadly commented, "I am very sorry that the King and Queen are such novices; six years more would have been better for them. I fear this is the end of your sister's peaceful and happy days."[8]

Cautious, apathetic, or paralyzed by "the universe that would shortly fall upon me," nineteen-year-old Louis XVI changed nothing at first and hoped that matters would indeed go on as they were. Conscientiously he shut himself up in his *cabinet* and studied the royal dossiers, but he also tinkered with locks in his attic workshops and spied comings and goings across the Marble Courtyard with his telescope. He worked by day, rising three hours before his formal *lever* at eleven-thirty in the Grande Chambre. The Queen played by night. They seemed to meet only in passing. But even then Marie Antoinette made the meetings political. Louis knew little of the men who were governing and less of those who might replace them. Aware of Louis' weaknesses, beholden to Choiseul as the forger of the French-Austrian alliance, if not her own marriage, the eighteen-year-old Queen pressed for the duke's recall to Court and power.

It was not the only pressure on the bewildered King. The emptiness of the treasury was a greater one: France faced bankruptcy. The richest, most populated (24,500,000) country of Europe was its most mismanaged. Annual revenue of the French government was 213,-500,000 francs, annual expenditure 235,000,000 francs. The contrast between the possessors and the possessed, the privileged handful and the depressed masses, was a willful invitation to disaster. The youth and weakness of Louis XVI invited more traditional dangers: the ambitious Orléans branch of the royal family saw opportunities in Choiseul's return to government and the King's own brother, Monsieur, the Comte de Provence, had early made the Palais Royal a center of intrigue and rival power. Were Louis to die childless, and each passing day seemed to indicate the probability, Tartuffe (as Louis called his brother) would inherit the crown.*

Refusing the Duc de Choiseul and simultaneously reaching for the security of the past, the young King sent for the Comte de Maurepas, seventy-three-year-old Phélypeaux, who had been deposed

* And eventually did, as Louis XVIII.

by Madame de Pompadour two decades before. "I will be your man," Maurepas told him, "and only yours,"[9] and gratefully Louis let him form a new ministry. The Maupeou parlements were dismissed, along with Maupeou, and the banished parlements reassembled. The Comte de Vergennes became foreign minister. More importantly, Baron Turgot became finance minister. When one recalls his relations with the *philosophes,* his articles in the *Encyclopédie* advocating a physiocratic freedom of enterprise, his belief in reason, tolerance and progress, one can understand the dismay of the *dévots* at Court and the stirring of hope among the newer merchants, still unrepresented in either the government or the parlements.[10] (Many older, incrusted merchants had long since been ennobled by purchase of offices and titles.) "I give myself not to the King," said Turgot to Louis XVI, "but to the *honnête* [honorable] man"[11]—for such was the opinion of the newly crowned King. And when Louis XVI and Marie Antoinette appeared in Paris in the late summer of 1774, there were still signs of enthusiasm in the streets. Maurepas even put a suggestion box outside the palace gate at Versailles for communications to the King. (There were so many, it was soon taken away.[12])

Rapidly Turgot initiated reforms. Since expenditures grossly exceeded revenues, he ordered cuts in expenditures—a move greatly unpopular among those affected. ("What," said the King, when Turgot resisted paying a *pension* to someone, probably on the urging of the Queen, "what possibly are a mere thousand écus a year?" "Sire," said Turgot, "they are the taxation of a village." And the King acquiesced, perhaps as reluctantly as the Queen.[13]) As an encouragement to farmers, the finance minister ordered freedom of the grain trade—but there was a series of bad harvests, the price of bread rose, and riots occurred even at Versailles. Louis XVI forbade firing on the rioters and ordered the price of bread reduced. The rioting continued, the order was rescinded. Turgot imported foreign wheat, prices fell, but two rioters were hung in the Place de Grève; and the King, it was said, and it may well have been true, grieved.

As for the Queen, in a few months she had squandered much of the good will advanced with such pathetic eagerness by the underprivileged whenever change seems in the air. But the first attacks came from the *anciens* of the Court. "Little Queen of twenty," read one pamphlet inspired by the Duc d'Aiguillon and the du Barry clan, incidentally aging her by two years, "who treat the ancients so badly, you will be sent back across the border someday." It was the Duc d'Aiguillon, however, who was sent away by Louis, on the insistence of the Queen, and the Duc de Choiseul returned to Court from his estate. But not to a ministry. "Monsieur le Duc," said the King briefly, when they were brought, as if by chance, together, "you have lost much of your hair since last I saw you"[14]—and that was all. Choiseul was not to be part of the new government and became, instead, a leader of the opposition.

Carelessly Marie Antoinette had described to Count Rosenberg, who had just returned to Vienna from a visit to Versailles, how she had tricked the King into seeing Choiseul. "You will never imagine how cleverly I managed it," she wrote the old count. "I told him that I had a fancy to see Monsieur de Choiseul, but could not quite decide on the day. I did it so well the poor man arranged the most convenient hour for me to see the duke"—and fell into the trap by "happening" to meet Choiseul when he came.[15]

"The poor man"—*"le pauvre homme"*—to describe the King.

The shocked Viennese courtier showed Marie Antoinette's letter to a horrified Maria Theresa. "What a manner," she hastily wrote Mercy, "what a way of thinking! It confirms my worst fears. She is racing to her ruin." The Empress and Joseph II (who shared the throne with his mother) chided Marie Antoinette for her attitude, comparing her to a Pompadour and a du Barry in her conduct and trickery. Indeed, Joseph's first letter had been so strong the Empress had her son rewrite it.

And in truth, Marie Antoinette was in the process of achieving the impossible: the legitimate Queen, she was reducing herself to the position of one who had succeeded in a long line of mistresses. Her predecessor, in the public eye, would be, at best, Madame de Pompadour, at worst, du Barry. Unfortunately the King, in his faithfulness, would be of no assistance. He adored her, she despised him, "there are moments when uxoriousness is a deadly sin"[16]—or, as Mirabeau *fils* would say, she was "the only man" in her family.[17]

The men in Marie Antoinette's life, on the other hand, began, lightly enough, with her younger brother-in-law, the Comte d'Artois. (The young Swedish count, Axel von Fersen, appeared in passing at a masked ball in Paris and will reappear more significantly much later.) D'Artois' historic contribution to France was horse racing, *à l'anglaise,* and dashingly he took the Queen to the track at Sablons in his *diable,* a two-wheeled open carriage. It was not a popular spectacle and the King, in a rare move, ordered the stand specially built for the Queen removed. In the Queen's entourage, too, were the Comtes d'Adhémar and de Vaudreuil, and there was a Hungarian nobleman named Esterházy, for whom Marie Antoinette found an expensive regiment and the best available winter quarters (going directly to the minister of war about it). There was also the exceptional, civilized Prince de Ligne, neither self-seeking nor self-profiting, who deemed life ideal when one was everywhere a foreigner, as he, "an Austrian in France and a Frenchman in Austria." He had a dispassionate respect for Marie Antoinette. "We adored her," he would reminisce, "without dreaming of loving her."[18] Her companions were as young as she, for the most part, or only slightly older. But the most insinuatingly influential was the Baron de Besenval, a man in his mid-fifties. It was not the assurance of his maturity that won her, but his quality of being unfailingly entertaining."

It was the women in Marie Antoinette's life, however, who proved fatal during the early impressionable years of public opinion. The first of the Queen's favorites was the Princesse de Lamballe, "pretty from a distance,"[19] modest and innocent enough to create no scandal. Twenty-one, she was already two years a widow. Her ducal husband had died of syphilis, after recounting to her all details of how he had acquired it—a tale of debauchery from which she was never quite to recover.[20] Pale, frail, and subject to fainting, she was taken under Marie Antoinette's wing and made superintendent of the Queen's household, at a yearly salary of 150,000 livres—from which Turgot was not quickly to recover. Nevertheless that experience was as nothing compared to the voracity of the Comtesse de Polignac and her family. She was twenty-six in 1775, wife of an army colonel in straitened circumstances. Marie Antoinette first remarked her at a Court ball, was struck by her "celestial figure . . . her angelic face"[21] and inquired about her. That evening she asked why she had never seen her before. She had not the means, the countess replied, to be often at Court. Here, at last, the young Queen sighed, was the purity essential for true friendship, and she had the King provide the means: 400,000 livres to pay off the family debts, 800,000 livres as a dowry for the countess's daughter, an embassy and allowance for her father, a dukedom and estate for her husband—in all, an average of 500,000 livres a year for the first four years (as Mercy informed Maria Theresa).[22] Few mistresses had ever cost the crown more—in every sense. The Princesse de Lamballe, complained Marie Antoinette's new favorite, bursting prettily into tears, was horribly jealous of her. Marie Antoinette consoled the countess, put her arm around her celestial waist, and they walked to a bosky part of the park.[23] Was it the "unnatural love" attributed promptly by a score of pamphlets? There was, Marie Antoinette wrote her mother, a veritable "epidemic" of them, "liberally ascribing to me two tastes, one for women, the other for men." The ingenuousness of the disclaimer seems genuine enough, and one tends to dismiss the pamphlets as scurrilous, as well as the pornographic prints and cartoons that began to spread.

Should one make little more of dresses called *plaisirs indiscrets, soupirs étouffés* (stifled sighs), or *désir masqué,* worn by Marie Antoinette but two months after Louis XV's death, when her mourning robes were so quickly put away?[24] The Duchesse de Chartres had introduced the young Queen to Rose Bertin, the Paris *modiste* on Rue Saint-Honoré, and several mornings a week she would arrive at the palace with a retinue of *midinettes* carrying great packages for Her Majesty. There were at least 150 gowns to choose for the year, one more costly and extravagant than the other. And the colors? One season it was "flea brown" (as the King, who arrived during a fitting, saw fit to call it) and no lady was seen at Court without it. Another time it was ash blond (the color of Marie Antoinette's hair), and without a blush even brunettes *à la mode* wore it. Every morning— or shortly before noon—Marie Antoinette had the task of choosing the four or five ensembles for the day, and the maids of her maids held large folio volumes of the fabrics of her gowns before her. A pin stuck here, a pin stuck there in the swatches, and the selections were made.[25] They were made for fashionable ladies from Paris to St. Petersburg as well. But from Vienna, Maria Theresa sent back a portrait of Marie Antoinette in full regalia and wanted to know whether she was seeing the Queen of France or an actress dressed for the stage.

The height of flamboyancy, however, was reached in the hairdress. Here Monsieur Léonard, *coiffeur* of the Queen, was King. He fashioned entire gardens, preferably English (they allowed for more fantasy), and landscaped them in Marie Antoinette's highly piled, stiffly pomaded hair. But his *tour de force* may have been a four-masted frigate in full sail for a lady of the Court. There were coiffures in homage to Gluck, to Peace, to Inoculation, with great plumes planted among them. So high did they reach, feathers and all, carriages and doorways had to be altered and the ceilings of theater boxes were arched to accommodate them.[26] "They tell me," wrote Maria Theresa frigidly from Vienna, "that your hairdresses rise as much as three feet from your forehead, not to mention the plumes and ribbons." But *everyone,* replied Marie Antoinette, was wearing them.

The height of extravagance, on the other hand, was reached in Marie Antoinette's penchant verging on mania for jewelry, particularly diamonds. It was a passion cultivated by Böhmer and Bassenge, two dealers in de luxe jewelry, originally from Germany. When the generosity of the King was insufficient, they extended "generous" credit terms and repurchased trinkets the Queen tired of—at half the purchase price.[27] In 1774, when still a teen-age Queen, she bought from Böhmer and associate jewels worth 360,000 livres.[28] In 1775, she paid 200,000 francs for a girandole of diamonds and 250,000 livres for a bracelet. Her mother, hearing of it from Mercy, complained. "I would not have thought," Marie Antoinette wrote to Vienna, "that anyone would have bothered you about such bagatelles." The same year Böhmer tempted her with a pair of chandelier earrings priced at 30,000 livres. Again Mercy alerted Vienna: "Although the King, on various occasions, has given the Queen more than 100,000 écus' worth of diamonds during the past year, and although Her Majesty already had a prodigious collection, nevertheless she determined to acquire these chandelier earrings from Böhmer. I did not conceal from Her Majesty that under present economic conditions it would have been wiser to avoid such a tremendous expenditure, but she could not resist—although she handled it carefully, keeping her purchase from the King."[29] The subsequent purchase of even more costly bracelets was also concealed from the King. Rather, Marie Antoinette turned in some "tired" jewelry and made a token down payment for them, then, unable to pay the balance, appealed to the King, who paid for the bracelets from his personal account, though it took years.* Again Maria Theresa responded: "For your own good, I cannot keep silent. Do not risk losing, by such frivolities, the esteem you won in the

---

* Poor Louis kept his own petty cash accounts down to the smallest coin, carefully noting such items as his laundry, butcher, wine and hobby shop bills ("to Gamin [his locksmith] for files and steel, 22 1. 7 s."). Until 1778 he allowed himself 18,000 livres a month and only twice that thereafter.— *Comptes de Louis XVI,* Paris, 1909.

beginning. The King has a reputation for moderation and economy, so it will be upon you that all blame will fall. I hope I do not live to see such a change effect itself in the opinion of your people."

The hope was already vain. "Marie Antoinette preferred the title of Queen of Fashion," a contemporary witness tells us, "to that of Queen of France."[30] And imitation of the Queen, her dress, her mania for jewelry, had become an inflammatory—almost household —problem. There were cries from Frenchmen that if she continued to set so extravagant a fashion "she would bankrupt the women [that is, the men] of France."[31]

In debt, the Queen gambled. Gambling, she doubled her debts. The new game was faro, and it drew professional cardsharps even to the Queen's table. Either she didn't know or she didn't care. "I am terrified of being bored," she had said to Mercy, and gambling was the antidote and the poison, a century-old contagion at Court which each Louis had tried to control, Louis XVI least successfully. There were card tables in the minuscule *chambres* of the King's pages, in the *antichambre* of the Queen's apartments, in the rooms of every apartment on every floor of the palace.[32] Stakes varied according to one's rank and often ran higher. At the Queen's table they were astronomical, and the King was to hear of it when the Queen's debts brought her to him. Occasionally he looked on. Preferably the sight was kept from him. Warned of his approach across the State rooms, players quickly cleared the tables of cards and money; he had formally forbidden faro. When he retired, usually at eleven, the gambling resumed. Once, at least, the clock had been advanced an hour to hasten his departure, and the Court regaled itself at "the poor man's" expense.[33]

But intrusion was always possible, and increasingly Marie Antoinette withdrew with her intimates to the Petit Trianon at the edge of the park. There the King went "by invitation only," an agreement that was only half jest. In her early search for privacy at the palace, she had arranged, as Louis XV, *cabinets* and *petits appartements* behind her more public rooms. They were cunningly disposed, charming but cramped around a sunless interior court (with the exception of the serene, gold-and-white *grand cabinet intérieur*), a wall's thickness from the noisy Salle des Gardes, the Grand Salon, and Grande Chambre, where two doors hidden behind tapestries allowed the Queen to slip away to her *petits appartements*. They were to be redone endlessly under Richard Mique, the royal architect who had succeeded Gabriel, with orders and counterorders adding to the considerable, but unconsidered, costs. Green silk tapestries were replaced by gilded woodwork, one décor, furnishings and hangings, by another, as if they were so many gowns. Capriciously the Queen wanted to turn Le Brun's Salon de la Paix into a theater, a project saved only (ironically) by the Revolution.* *Le style Marie Antoinette* (it is her style, her age, though historically it is called Louis XVI) was cluttered with tassels, rosettes, draperies, valances and braid, on everything was imprinted, incised, or molded the pattern of flowers. Furniture, however, was never more beautiful (was it her ordering?): light and elegant, legs straight, delicate and tapering.

Light—sunlight—became an obsession for Marie Antoinette. The *petits appartements,* overlooking an interior court, were too obscure; her *grands appartements,* exposed to the south, were too public. Only the Petit Trianon might offer her what she sought: sun, privacy, and flowers. At the great palace, too, etiquette ruled, though Madame l'Étiquette did not, and even the Queen was its prisoner. Complaining of dust on her bed, for instance, to her *garçon de chambre,* she was reproachfully told that the Queen's bed, when she was not in it, was furniture, and thus dusting it the province of the *premier valet de chambre tapissier.* Was her *dame d'honneur* or *première femme de chambre* not immediately available, when she thirsted? Then the Queen could not drink, for she might not fetch her own glass of water. And when finally the drink arrived, it was well warmed by its protocolar passage from hand to proper hand. At the Petit Trianon Marie Antoinette was not the Queen, but the Antonia of her childhood in the Schönbrunn Palace of Vienna, where life was homely and cheerful (and all too bourgeois, Goethe found). At the Petit Trianon, when she entered the salon, whoever was playing at the pianoforte continued playing, the ladies did not cease their embroidering, nor the men their billiards or backgammon. And the dress was relaxingly informal.[35]

Conceived for Madame de Pompadour, occupied by Madame du Barry, the rooms of the Petit Trianon are haunted by Marie Antoinette. It is hers as the Grande Galerie is the Sun King's, the great park Le Nôtre's, and the world within a world at the palace Louis XV's. When did it become hers? During the first days of June 1774, according to

* Versailles' historian Pierre Verlet: "One often hears how fatal the Revolution was for Versailles. Here one would hurry its arrival."[34]

Mercy-Argenteau, when she already felt the need for its refuge. "Madame," the King gallantly remarked (or is so quoted), "this lovely site has always been the residence of the favorites of the King. It should therefore be yours."[36] Perhaps the gesture was as much to purge the Petit Trianon of the du Barry presence* as to grace it with Marie Antoinette's, and the King gave the young Queen a symbolic key to her kingdom, encrusted with 531 diamonds.[37]

The Petit Trianon could be the secondary residence of a country nobleman, romantic in feeling, classic in form, as jewel-like as the little hunting lodge which was the first Versailles abode for the Bourbons. And, as Louis XIII's *pavillon* had no room for the Queen, so the Petit Trianon's bedroom with its small single bed seems never to have accommodated the bulky Louis XVI.[38] On the ground floor from the garden side—or second floor from the sunken entry court—are an anteroom and a dining room, a billiard room which was once Louis XV's dining room (with a table that could rise through the floor from below, completely set for each course, eliminating intruding servants), a salon, the Queen's boudoir and bedroom, *cabinets* and dressing rooms. That was all, though it did not prevent a pamphleteer from describing the Petit Trianon as "tapestried with diamonds."[39] A library had been planned, presumably for appearance's sake. "Except for a few novels," Besenval reveals, "the Queen never opened a book."[40] And except for a few favorites, tucked in rooms under the flat roof, there were no accommodations for anyone but the Queen and her servants. It was as exclusive a domain as any in the history of the French crown, and deeply resented by the excluded of the Court.

Allergic to Louis XIV's grandeur, Marie Antoinette was similarly antipathetic to Le Nôtre's. One of her first acts was the complete transformation of the grounds beyond the small formal garden.†

---

* Madame du Barry was banished on the death of Louis XV to the abbey of Pont-aux-Dames, near Meaux, by order of Louis XVI. The year following Marie Antoinette interceded in her behalf and she was allowed to reside at Louveciennes, near Paris, and given a pension.

† There was a huge, salutary transplantation of trees in the great park at the same time by Louis XVI. "Nature," wrote Rousseau, launching the romantic garden, "never plants in a straight line,"[41] and rarely was the natural so artificially created as by Marie Antoinette. One can still wander by a brook, lake, and stream, up and down a dale, past a charming belvedere and pavilion and a small temple of love, where a stone cupid fashions his bow from the club of Hercules (in a satisfying copy of Bouchardon's original statue). A contemporary account may fill in what almost two centuries of time have removed or changed.

"To [the] Trianon," notes the English farmer and traveler Arthur Young in his diary on October 23, 1787, "to view the Queen's *Jardin Anglois*. . . . It contains about 100 acres, disposed in the taste of what we read of in books of Chinese gardening, whence it is supposed the English style was taken. There is more . . . effort than nature, more expence than taste. It is not easy to conceive any thing that art can introduce in a garden that is not here; woods, walks, temples, and even villages. There are parts of the design very pretty, and well executed. The only fault is too much crowding; which has led to another, that of cutting the lawn by too many gravel walks. . . . But the glory of La Petite Trianon is the exotic trees and shrubs. The world has been successfully rifled to decorate it. Here are curious and beautiful ones to please the eye of ignorance; and to exercise the memory of science. Of the buildings, the temple of love is truly elegant."[42]

The "villages" referred to by the English traveler are the famous Hameau, or Hamlet, a fantasy of Marie Antoinette's last years at Versailles (1782–89). Wandering paths lead to what is left: thatched cottages and a little mill reflected in the pond and stream, play farmhouses that once sheltered the families of a farmer, gardener, and keeper and their laundered, beribboned livestock. (The Queen had sent to Switzerland for a billy goat, requesting that it be "nice and white and inoffensive.") And though Marie Antoinette may not literally have played milkmaid herself, as myth would have it,[43] the Hameau was part of her love for the theater and is best viewed as a vast theatrical set. Cracks were painted in the woodwork, as if they were the work of time, and the outsides of the cottages were carefully "weathered," as if by affectionate elements.[44] Within the Queen's cottage, where there is now so little, there once was luxury, and nearby were a boudoir and a *billard* in cottages by themselves.

Though in reality only a mile or so from the great palace, the grounds and life at the Petit Trianon and its Hameau seemed to the Prince de Ligne, "a hundred leagues from the Court, where one could breathe the air of happiness and freedom."[45] And Marie Antoinette completed her world with an exquisite little theater, which she had constructed in a cluster of trees near the small Trianon. Its colonnaded entrance alone indicates something other than a nondescript, farmlike building, leaving one unprepared for the sudden, glorious revelation of a blue-and-gold auditorium and stage, gilded balconies and papiermâché sculpture, dressing rooms for the Queen and visiting *comédiens,* and a tiny suite for the architect, Mique. It is Gabriel's opera-theater in miniature, and as such was criticized as one more needless expense on the part of Marie Antoinette. She herself performed —with no conspicuous talent—along with her intimates, particularly the Comte d'Artois, in light, generally trivial comedy. And the door to the theater was closed to all but the King, Monsieur, and the princesses of the blood, when it was inaugurated. Later, to fill the seats and create the feeling of a public, the Queen's *femmes de chambre,* her equerries, the officers of her guard, and their families were permitted entrance—but not members of the Court. (Mercy himself was allowed to look on from behind a grill on the second balcony, and sent a conscientious report of the innocence of it all to the Empress Mother.) The ladies and noblemen of the Court, needless to say, added the new restriction to their mounting resentment.

Worse, at the palace itself there was no longer a sense of high excitement or even welcome, the mystical aura of being "close to the King" which had made the Court of Louis XIV. Versailles was ceasing to be the center of France, and the older nobility was leaving it for the country and their estates, without the encouragement, but without the former *discouragement,* of the King. "Only on Sundays," says the Duc de Lévis, "might those provided with proper introductions see Their Majesties for a few minutes." But such was the "ungracious reception, they preferred to stay at home." Versailles was becoming "a provincial town, which one visited with reluctance and left with alacrity."[46] King and Queen were withdrawing into their own private (and crumbling) worlds, Marie Antoinette to her "little Schönbrunn" or "little Vienna," as those excluded called it,[47] Louis XVI to his hobby rooms and the palace attic. He had a map room, an artillery room (with models of cannons, pistols, and guns), a carpentry shop, *a galerie d'électricité* (Benjamin Franklin's experiments had crossed the ocean), libraries (which he really used). But above all, under the roof, were his locksmith shop and forge, where he worked regularly with his favorite locksmith, François Gamin—and would come down to Marie Antoinette's parties (and scoldings) with forge-blackened hands. (One might note the other key to his character in the fact that he installed his chief minister, Maurepas, in the former rooms of Louis XV's mistresses. *He* would have no mistresses.[48])

Were the scoldings of Marie Antoinette her only interferences in royal affairs, French history, at least in its telling, would be quite different. To what extent she hastened the Revolution by hurrying the end of Turgot, it is fruitless to speculate. Having survived the "Grain War," Turgot had pressed on, urging stricter control of profiteering tax farmers and further reductions in royal expenditures. Comfort and support came not from Maurepas, but from Malesherbes, a new member of the King's Household, who added a note of caution. Each new reform, he warned, created new enemies for Turgot; too many at one time would prove fatal. To this the impatient forty-eight-year-old minister replied: "The needs of the people are enormous, and in my family we die of gout at fifty."[49]* Implementing his impatience, disregarding Malesherbes' advice, Turgot swiftly initiated a series of reforms: increased freedom for the grain trade, the easing of taxation on the peasants, the abolition of guilds and their restrictions on the growth of a skilled labor force, and, most controversial of all, abolition of the *corvée*—two weeks of forced, unpaid labor by the peasants on the roads, bridges, and highways of France. And Turgot put these astonishing words of the royal edict "in the mouth of the King himself" (Tocqueville):

"Except for a small number of provinces, almost all the roads of the Kingdom have been built by the poorest of our subjects. Thus the entire weight has fallen on those who have nothing but their hands and a very secondary interest in the roads. Those really interested are the landowners, nearly all of them privileged individuals, whose property increases in value by the establishment of these roads. Compelling the poor man alone to maintain them, forcing him to give his time and toil without pay, one deprives him of his only means to escape poverty and hunger, in order to make him work for the profit of the rich."[50]

The series of reform edicts was promulgated in January 1776. In February, Parlement, which had so often declared itself the defender of the people against the Crown, sided with the feudally privileged against the people and refused to register Turgot's reforms; it even called abolition of the *corvée* an unacceptable violation of sacred feudal rights. Angrily Turgot retorted that by so doing the Parlement of Paris, like all others, had exposed itself as being composed, not of the people, but "of the wealthy . . . and of the noble, since their offices carry nobility." The remark was part of a message to the King, and Turgot added that since "the people have no voice in the *parlements*," His Majesty, after properly listening to the latter, "must judge

---

* He would lose power at forty-nine and die of gout at fifty-four.

for himself, that is, judge in favor of the people, for this class is the most unhappy," the most in need of the King's support.[51]

In March, Louis XVI summoned the Paris Parlement to a *lit de justice* at Versailles, compelling it to register Turgot's edicts, and "parades of workingmen [in Paris] celebrated Turgot's victory."[52]

In May, Louis XVI dismissed Turgot, and Marie Antoinette celebrated.

The pressures had proved too much for the weak twenty-two-year-old King. As Malesherbes had predicted, they had accumulated with crushing effect in the wake of Turgot's compulsive reforms. And Malesherbes himself, in anticipation of the inevitable, offered his resignation to the King. "You are a fortunate man," Louis said to him tiredly. "Would that I could resign my post."[53]

Turgot had offended every significant circle of power. "He finds himself," the Swedish ambassador had reported two months before the end, "facing a most formidable league composed of all *les grands* of the French Kingdom, all the parlements, all the great financiers [he had borrowed money from abroad, spurning their higher rates of interest], all the ladies of the Court and all the *dévots* [he was essentially a *philosophe*]."[54] The ambassador, in his dispatch, either did not deem it politic or thought it superfluous to mention that high in the league of Turgot's opposition was the First Lady of the Court, Marie Antoinette. She was probably crucial in forcing the King's hand. She had always resented Turgot's attempt to curb her expenditures; when he joined Vergennes in asking the King to recall the Comte de Guines from the French embassy in London, despite Guines' known membership in the Queen's entourage of untouchables, she complained to the King and finally won Turgot's dismissal.

Maurepas, too, who had his own grievances against Turgot, had added his voice. Reflectively, sensing the end, Turgot had returned to his estates and from there sent the King a forthright letter, warning him of the "weakness that brought to the block the head of Charles I [of England]." "You are deemed weak, Sire," he wrote bluntly, ". . . nevertheless I have seen you, on occasion . . . exhibit genuine courage." Show it once again, he urged, before it was too late.[55]

Louis XVI did not even reply to Turgot's letter. As if to underline his act, the day he signed the order for Turgot's dismissal, he made the Comte de Guines a duke. The Queen's circle rejoiced and Turgot's successor reinstated the *corvée*. The reform movement was over before it really began.

There was more petulance than politics in the behavior of Marie Antoinette (and it is not the hindsight of history to remark it, for none was more aware than the aging Empress in Vienna, who wrote vainly to her daughter about it). Once, during the difficult month of April 1776, the young Queen had just returned from the Paris Opéra and the King had asked her whether "she had received her usual huzzas." Sullenly she had made no reply and Louis had understood. "Apparently, madame," he said, "you had not had enough cheers." "I should have liked to have seen you there, sire," she retorted, "with your St. Germain [Minister of War] and your Turgot. You would have been rudely hissed."[56] Such stories were becoming current, and the Queen's irritability is more understandable when one realizes they were coupled with popular taunts about the Queen's "sterility."

"When, in 1777," Madame Campan, her first *femme de chambre*, reveals, "the son of the Comte d'Artois was born, the market women and fishwives, who asserted their right to crowd the palace at times of royal birth, followed the Queen to the very door of her apartments, shouting in the roughest and most vulgar terms that it was up to her, and not to her sister-in-law, to provide heirs to the French Crown. Hurriedly the Queen closed her door on these vicious hags and closed herself in her bedroom with me to weep over her sad state."[57] And to her mother Marie Antoinette wrote quite pathetically of the pains she suffered "at thus seeing an heir to the throne who was not my own child."

However, she was soon herself, complaining of the "coldness" of the King and turning more recklessly than ever to unbridled spending, borrowing, gambling, and horse racing. It was the period of Mercy's most worrying letters to Maria Theresa, full of foreboding details, including an account of the forgery of the Queen's name by a lady of the Court as the guarantee for a loan. And Maria Theresa encouraged her son, Joseph II, to make his long-delayed trip to France to see what he could do at Versailles.

Joseph II was a man of philosophic pretensions and political ambitions with a fondness for giving advice. The two-month visit, April–May 1777, would give him the occasion to exercise all three aspects: he would scold his younger sister about her behavior (she was fourteen years younger), counsel his younger brother-in-law, the French King (who was thirteen years younger), and seek to bind France to Austria in a tighter personal alliance, thanks to the impression he planned to make. At home, Joseph II carefully cultivated the image of a modest ruler more concerned about his people than appearances, and he arrived at Versailles as the simply cloaked Count von Falkenstein (an incognito known and announced well in advance), insisting on staying in a lodging house rather than in the palace.

There was a good deal of protocolar fuss on the part of the princes of the blood as to who should first visit whom, they an "ordinary Count," or he them. With Louis XVI, however, whose modesty and simplicity were painfully real, there was no such problem. He welcomed his brother-in-law sincerely and they got along well. (Joseph II found Louis XVI "weak, but not a fool," as he wrote his brother Leopold,[58] and probably not the "imbecile" Frederick the Great, for his own purposes, claimed to have heard from Joseph in a letter.) The encounter with the Queen was also as an older brother, and Joseph reportedly greeted her: "Were you not my sister and I not married, I would gladly ask you to marry me."[59] Whatever the greeting, he relieved Marie Antoinette of enough of her initial anxiety (she had received a sufficiency of critical letters from him over the years) for her to repeat her chagrin at the birth of a son to the Comte d'Artois and the continuing coldness of the King. He promised to speak to the King about it, and did, encouraging him to undergo the small operation ending his "coldness." Joseph did it, as if casually, between trips of conspicuous modesty to hospitals, barracks, arsenals, manufactories, and the Opéra. Gratefully Marie Antoinette organized a splendid fête for him at the Petit Trianon, but mistakenly took him to the palace apartment of her dear friend, the Duchesse de Guéménée, for an evening of faro. Roundly he condemned the duchess's apartment as a "veritable gambling den" and the people at her tables as inexcusably "ill behaved."[60] He reproached his sister for the company she kept and the direspect she invited. She promised to make amends—after his departure.

In departing Joseph II left behind him some thirty pages of moral directions. Question after rhetorical question—she was, despite everything, the Queen of France and not to be commanded—pointed to the right path. What will happen, he warned to begin with, what will become of you, if you continue to waste your time, for you no longer have the excuse of being a child? An unhappy woman, he replied for her, and a still unhappier Queen. As for the King, do you honestly respond to his timid advances? "When he caresses you, when he speaks to you, do you not rather show boredom and even disgust?" How then can you expect a man of his cold temperament to love you? Do you keep silent about his faults and impose silence on those around you? "Have you thought of the effect of your liaisons and intimacies upon the public, if they are formed with people who are unworthy of it, since it will seem that you are participating and authorizing their vices?" Do you honestly believe you are not recognized at the masked Opéra balls? Do you not know they have an evil reputation? "Why, then, do you continue to go there?" Why do you associate with libertines and loose women? Think of the King left alone all night at Versailles while you mix with the canaille of Paris. And Joseph II concludes: "I tremble for your happiness, for in the long run things can not go on as now. . . . The revolution will be a cruel one, and may be of your own making."[61]

Words, words, words? Marie Antoinette did not appreciatively change her ways, certainly not her direction. The change, if any, that occurred resulted from Joseph's words with the King.

The surgical operation he advised—mentioned by Marie Antoinette in a letter to her mother, January 1776, as promised her even then by the King—was finally performed in June or July 1777, shortly after Joseph's departure.* By the end of the year, the Queen could "confide" to Madame Campan that at last she had become, "in the true sense of the phrase, Queen of France."[63] It confirmed what she had written several months earlier (August 30) to her mother: "More than a week ago, my marriage was completely consummated."[64] The Spanish ambassador, in a report to Madrid, set the date as August 25, which allows that close observer of the King's activities a few additional days to catch up. He had the information, he wrote, separately from Maurepas and Vergennes. The King, he adds, told his maiden aunts, "I find the pleasure very great, and I regret that so long a time had passed without my being able to enjoy it."[65]

But soon Marie Antoinette was again complaining to Maria Theresa of Louis' coldness, though Mercy had another explanation for the failure of pregnancy, despite the successful operation: if Her Majesty played all night, he suggested, and His Majesty worked all day, there

---

* The letter is among the correspondence frequently referred to. The operation is still disputed by such historians as Bernard Faÿ, and I have reserved discussion of it on page 509. Here one might note that Mr. Faÿ believes the story of the King's operation was falsely put out by the Queen and her party.[62]

was hardly a moment for their being fruitfully together. Nevertheless, pregnancy was fairly certain by spring and Marie Antoinette had a happy complaint, for a change, to make to the King. "Sire," she said that summer, "one of your subjects has been so disrespectful as to kick me in the stomach."[66] He paused, then laughed, and embraced her. And Mercy, ever alert to Austria's interests, urged her to make use of her "new situation" (as he wrote to Maria Theresa) to bring France militarily to the side of her brother in his sudden occupation of Bavaria; but here Louis proved less compliant (war with England over America, begun in earnest by mid-1778, was already one war too many).*

In the fall and winter of 1778, the ladies and gentlemen of the Court, and not a few of the people of Paris, were full of the Queen's pregnancy and their expectancy of a Dauphin. Bells rang, masses were celebrated, prayers were said, as birth pains began on the night of December 18. And early the next morning after a long night's labor, a mob of the curious literally piled into the Queen's bedroom. Never was the custom of a publicly witnessed birth in the royal family so enthusiastically observed—an "enthusiasm" explained by the Queen's exclusiveness perhaps and the opportunity of those normally excluded to enjoy the pain and humiliation of her lying-in as a public spectacle.

"With a wise precaution," Madame Campan describes the scene, "the King had huge, tapestried screens tied together with ropes and placed around Her Majesty's bed. Without that precaution they would surely have been overturned and fallen on her. It was no longer possible to move in the bedroom, which overflowed with so mixed a crowd that one might think one were in a public square. Two individuals from Savoy climbed onto the furniture the better to see the Queen on her bed, which was specially arranged for the delivery in front of the fireplace." Thus, for hours the great crowd pressed around the bed, the air hot with their breath, and a half hour before noon, the baby was born. Suffocating, "the blood rising to her head," the Queen seemed to lose consciousness. " 'Air,' cried the *accoucheur,* 'hot water! Her Majesty must be bled!' The windows had been tightly sealed. The King opened them with a blow." The Queen was bled; she recovered con-

---

* And when Voltaire, in his eighty-fourth year, came that spring to Paris, pious, Catholic Louis XVI refused Marie Antionette's fitful request that he be received at Versailles. Hurt, Voltaire had to be content with the extraordinary triumph at the Comédie Française, when an entire audience rose and he was crowned with laurel leaves. Two months later he was dead.

sciousness. "The *valets de chambre* and the ushers took those who were in no hurry to leave by the collar, in order to clear the bedroom."[67]

The baby born was a girl. Twenty-one guns were fired in salute, and not the hundred and one had there been a Dauphin. Monsieur and the Comte d'Artois were comforted: they were still heirs to the throne. But the King, too was relieved: he knew he could have a child, and the next one could be a boy. From Vienna, Maria Theresa wrote Marie Antoinette: "We must have a Dauphin."

Lightly the Queen promised to do her best. Lightheadedly she did not. She continued going to masked balls at the Opéra, despite their "evil reputation" and its effect on hers. Nor was her name helped when Paris heard that, in bed with measles at the Petit Trianon, she insisted on four cavaliers, and not the customary *femmes de chambre,* sitting in attendance: Coigny, Guines, Esterházy, and Besenval. Was her infatuation with the handsome young Swedish count, Axel von Fersen, as she, twenty-four in 1779, as well known outside as inside the Court? No matter for the moment. He left in 1780 for America, to fight alongside the rebels as aide-de-camp of General Rochambeau. He would return.

The year of Fersen's departure, Maria Theresa died. And as she lay dying, she blessed her children at her bedside, tears springing to her eyes when she mentioned the absent Marie Antoinette.

The Dauphin was born the following year. And this time—the King saw to it—the Queen's lying-in was for a very few of the Court, and the birth was a relatively easy one. The hundred and one guns thundered, Monsieur and the Comte d'Artois may have participated in the gay fêtes at Versailles, but they did not celebrate.* The Marquis de Lafayette, on the other hand, hero of the day just back from the war in America, warmly saluted the Queen before the people of Paris.

One by one the guilds sent delegations to Versailles (a more convincing mark of feudal custom, one must admit, than a measure of the Crown's popularity). Each delegation, proceeded by musicians, came with the tools of its trade. The chimney sweeps carried a mock

---

* Monsieur neither "showed" nor "pretended" joy at the news. As for the Comte d'Artois, when his young son, the Duc d'Angoulême, after seeing the little Dauphin in his crib, said to him, "How tiny is my cousin!," he wryly replied, "The day will come, my son, when you will find him big enough." Gambling, dancing, going to horse races and masked balls with the Queen was one thing, the throne of France was another.[68]

chimney with their smallest chimney sweep perched upon it. The butchers came with their fattest ox, the pastry makers with their richest pastry. The locksmiths brought a cunning lock that, finally opened by the King, sprang from its midst the figure of a tiny Dauphin.[69]

And the gravediggers brought a little coffin.

19. Madame de Pompadour

20. *Madame du Barry*

21. Marie Leszczynska (Louis XV's wife)

22. *Voltaire*

23. *Diderot*

24. Louis XVI

25. *Marie Antoinette and her children, c. 1787*

26. *The Dauphin, son of Louis XVI and Marie Antoinette*

27. *Lafayette*

21. Three Friends for Benjamin Franklin

It's a strange story, the French aristocrats who befriended the American revolt, and three vignettes might serve as a background for the most famous of its representatives, Benjamin Franklin, shortly to arrive from the New World.

FOREIGN MINISTER VERGENNES

Charles Gravier, Comte de Vergennes, son of a parliamentarian, nephew of a diplomat, has his own uncommon story. After years in the diplomatic service, he had been recalled by Choiseul as French ambassador to Turkey in 1768 for having contracted marriage "without the sanction or even knowledge of the King"[1] with a woman below his birth and rank. Moreover, before marrying Madame Testa, widow of a Constantinople doctor, he had had two children with her. He was in retirement at his country estate in Burgundy when, in 1771, the Comte de Broglie proposed to Louis XV that Vergennes be sent to Sweden as French ambassador. In the margin of Broglie's proposal, the King himself wrote, "I do not approve the choice of M. de Vergennes, but I accept it, since you are so insistent. However, I forbid his taking that *vilaine* wife with him."[2] And when, in 1774, Maurepas proposed elevating the capable Comte de Vergennes to foreign minister, and Louis XVI agreed, the problem of Vergennes' formal presentation at Court arose, that is, of his *vilaine* wife, whom

L

custom required be presented with him. The anti-Vergennes cabala tried to persuade the Queen to refuse to receive her, forcing Vergennes to resign. Marie Antoinette consulted her mother in Vienna, who turned to her own foreign minister and chancellor, Kaunitz, "whose view was favorable, and so Madame de Vergennes was received."[3]

There are several ironies in the story. Despite the crushing difficulties, the Vergennes marriage, in the opinion of the Goncourts, was "one of the finest, most exceptional examples of love and happiness in the 18th century."[4] A second irony is the fact that the Austrian chancellor had helped promote the man who would most limit the effectiveness of the French-Austrian alliance, particularly during the clash between Joseph II and Frederick of Prussia over the Austrian occupation of Bavaria. Of more concern for France, Vergennes believed, was the opportunity offered by a Britain mired in a war with America. "Perhaps without striking a blow," he had noted in July 1775, France together with Spain could reduce British power and retake its "place of superiority" in Europe.[5]

Before befriending Franklin in their mutual interest, Vergennes would discover the uses of Beaumarchais.

BEAUMARCHAIS, PLAYWRIGHT AND ADVENTURER

He was born Pierre Augustin Caron, son of a watchmaker, in Paris in 1732. He was precocious, shrewd, passionately fond of music, and ambitious. At twenty-one he invented a new escapement which allowed him to make a watch so small it could be set in a ring. He was summoned to court, Louis XV ordered a watch-ring for Madame de Pompadour, and Caron called himself "watchmaker to the king."[6] Trim, comely, and with careful dash, he became a handsome, familiar figure at Versailles and bought the office of a "controller of the royal pantry" from its holder, the elderly Monsieur Franquet, who was persuaded to it by his young wife. When Franquet died a year later, Caron married his young widow. When *she* died a year later, her property went to her first husband's family, but the name of one of the estates, Beaumarchais, had already been added to Caron's own—and he was now Pierre Caron de Beaumarchais. A favor— through the King's unmarried daughters—to the most famous banker of the day, Pâris-Duverney, brought him stocks worth sixty thousand livres, and Beaumarchais was launched, à la Voltaire, on a career of successful speculations.* At thirty-two, he went down to Spain to force a Spanish gentleman and minor dignitary (José Clavigo y Fajardo) to marry his twice-promised older sister. He failed after a series of hilarious efforts, his sister found another lover, and Beaumarchais wrote his first play, *Eugénie*, partly based on his Spanish experience. (Goethe wrote a better one, made it a tragedy, and called it *Clavigo*.) Beaumarchais would triumphantly return to the Spanish scene six years later with the unforgettable Figaro in *Le Barbier de Séville*.

His banker friend, Duverney, died in 1770. That part of his testament acknowledging a debt of fifteen thousand francs to Beaumarchais was contested as a forgery by Duverney's heir, and the matter was referred to the Paris Parlement. Beaumarchais, meantime, was in prison because of a quarrel with the Duc de Chaulnes over an actress. Released to plead his cause, he bought his way to one of the judges by way of the judge's wife and was accused of bribery. Eventually it was Beaumarchais versus the Maupeou Parlement, a cause he won in popular opinion by a series of brilliant memoirs, much admired by Voltaire, but lost before the Parlement, and again he went to jail. A month later he was released as a secret agent of Louis XV, sent to England on a special mission: the destruction of all copies of a pamphlet denigrating Madame du Barry. He succeeded, and not long after it was Louis XVI who sent him back to London to prevent the publication of a scandalous pamphlet about Marie Antoinette. He bought off the author, who left for Germany with what Beaumarchais suspected was a second manuscript copy. He pursued him, seized the copy, and made his way back to France by way of Vienna, where he was temporarily imprisoned as a spy.

And now it was Vergennes who sent Beaumarchais to London. Impressed by his adroit handling of delicate missions, the foreign minister dispatched him on two more. The first was to persuade the androgynous Chevalier d'Eon not to publish some of his secret correspondence with Louis XV, particularly concerning the mad "in-

---

* His success, inevitably, was envied. One day, as he emerged from the apartments of Louis XV's daughters, a marquis tried to recall him to his proper place. "Eh, you!" he cried. "I understand you were recently some sort of watchmaker." "In effect, monsieur," said Beaumarchais. "I have a watch with me," said the marquis, "that needs repairing." "I have lost my hand," said Beaumarchais, "and have become quite clumsy." Disdainfully the courtier pressed the watch on him. Beaumarchais pretended to examine it, then let it drop crashing to the floor. "You see, monsieur," he said, "I told you I had become too clumsy."[7]

vasion plan." After purchasing d'Eon's silence, Beaumarchais proceeded
with the far more important second mission. It was April 1775.
Beaumarchais was to scout around and confidentially report on the
smoldering relations between England and her American colonies.
His reports from London, enthusiastically predicting the success of the
American revolt and growing dissension in England, were forwarded
by Vergennes directly to Louis XVI as an important part of his own
campaign to persuade the King to aid the rebellion. By February
1776, Beaumarchais was boldly advocating sending guns and powder to the embattled Americans, by whatever means, to bring about
a British defeat.[8] And in April, Vergennes wrote to Beaumarchais:
"We will secretly give you one million livres. We will try to obtain
an equal sum from Spain [subsequently obtained]. With these two
millions you will establish a commercial firm, and at your risk and
peril you will supply the Americans with arms, munitions, equipment,
and all other things that they will need to maintain the war. Our
arsenal will deliver to you arms and munitions, but you will either
replace them or pay for them. You will not demand money from
the Americans, since they have none, but you will ask in return
for the produce of their soil, which we will help you sell in this country."[9]

By May, France had recognized America's rights as a belligerent,
which greatly encouraged Congress's declaration of independence.
By the time of Silas Deane's arrival, the fictitious firm of Roderigue
Hortalez and Company had been set up by Beaumarchais to camouflage
French aid to America. A fleet of cargo ships soon began to carry arms
and gunpowder to Les Insurgents, as the French called the American
forces, the arrangements made by Deane and Beaumarchais.

A nineteen-year-old French nobleman would make his own arrangements.[10]

THE MARQUIS DE LAFAYETTE

Marie-Joseph-Paul-Yves-Roch-Gilbert du Motier, Marquis de Lafayette, was born in the provincial château of Chavaniac in Auvergne,
on September 6, 1757. Before he was two, his father, a twenty-seven-
year-old colonel in the French Grenadiers, was killed at Minden
in the Seven Years' War, "by a ball from an English battery, commanded
by a certain General Phillips. By a strange coincidence," his son

relates in a letter, "twenty-two years later [shortly before the battle of Yorktown] two of our cannon opened fire on the English headquarters at Petersburg, on the Appomattox in Virginia, and one of the balls passed through the house in which General Phillips was lying sick. He was killed outright."[11] In fact, General Phillips died from his illness somewhat later.[12] But the coincidence is strange enough; and the death of his father by an English cannon ball fed young Lafayette's dream of vengeance.

Since his mother spent most of her time at Court in Versailles, the young boy was raised by his grandmother and two aunts in the small Auvergne château. There was a pension of six hundred livres a year from his father's death, and not a great deal more. At thirteen, he lost his mother, shortly afterward a maternal uncle, who left him an enormous fortune of 120,000 livres a year—and Lafayette entered the Black Musketeers, taking the first step toward his dream. "At fourteen," he recalls, "I received news that my grand-father had arranged for me to marry Mlle [Adrienne] de Noailles, the second daughter of the Duc d'Ayen, who was then only twelve years of age."[13] The marriage was deferred for two more years. The young bride, fourteen and a half, adored her young husband, sixteen and a half, soon became pregnant, but soon afterward had a miscarriage.

Young Lafayette, thanks to his in-laws, the Noailleses, quickly became part of Marie Antoinette's own entourage—a circle in which a faithful husband was a figure of fun, whatever his age, however recent his marriage. And if the young marquis was a risible figure, it was not because of his fidelity, but rather his provinciality, his awkward dancing in the Queen's quadrille. The courtiers gladly spent his money and laughed at his manners. Tall, shy, sandy-haired, long-nosed, young Lafayette tried to redeem himself by paying court to the Comtesse Aglaé d'Hunolstein, the married, acknowledged mistress of the Duc de Chartres, son and heir of the Duc d'Orléans. With the flirt of a shrug, she turned him down, and Lafayette, a failure at Court, further dreamed of winning glory on some battlefield distant from Versailles.

He was not alone. The first shots at Bunker Hill fired other young noblemen with thoughts of glory and action against the British. At sixteen, thanks again to his father-in-law, Lafayette had become a regimental captain; now, nearing eighteen, he restlessly talked to Adrienne, fifteen and pregnant for the second time, of going to

America. And he talked to his friends, the young Vicomte de Noailles, the more dashing son-in-law of the Duc d'Ayen, and to the Comte de Ségur, both yearning for the same adventure. In December 1775, Adrienne gave birth to a daughter. Throughout 1776 her husband and his two friends plotted their departure. It was a time when scores of young officers were besieging the house of Silas Deane, volunteering for service with Washington. "Had I ten ships here," Deane wrote home, "I could fill them all with passengers for America."[14] In fact Deane was not doing too badly: Congress had authorized him to contract with French officers for a rank and pay one grade superior to their own, and it attracted many of them.

Ardently Lafayette, Ségur, and Noailles laid their plans, and rumors reached beyond their families to royal ears. If *they,* young noblemen so close to the Crown, were allowed to join the American rebels, the British would certainly suspect collusion on the part of the French King, and Louis XVI was not yet convinced that France should risk an open break and hostilities with England. He let his displeasure be known; family and royal pressures proved sufficient to dissuade Ségur and Noailles, but not Lafayette. On December 7, 1776, when Adrienne, seventeen, was pregnant for the third time, Lafayette, nineteen, signed on with Silas Deane for service in the American army as a major general. (Lafayette's family, his noble example, Deane pleaded with Congress, made his appointment at such an exalted rank most advisable. When Lafayette offered to serve without pay, Congress, after his arrival, found it possible to accord it.) The commitment was kept secret from the Duc d'Ayen who in any event was unprepared for Lafayette's persistence. (He had once urged Ségur to do something about his son-in-law's "apathy.") "Judge of their astonishment," the Comte de Ségur would write in his memoirs, "when they suddenly learned that this prudent young man of nineteen, so seemingly cold and easy-going, was on fire for glory and danger to such an extent that he proposed to cross the ocean and take up arms in the cause of American freedom!"[15]

In the cause of American freedom? Eventually. Not immediately. Gouverneur Morris to General Washington, January 22, 1790: "He [Lafayette] left America, you know, when his education was but half finished."[16]

But the problem in 1776 was how to get Lafayette to America. An idea occurred to the secretary of the Comte de Broglie, now curiously entangled in American affairs. (He thought of himself as future commander-in-chief of American forces and, as Lafayette's commander at Metz, had been in close, encouraging contact with his young officer.) Why not have the rich marquis buy a boat, unknown to either his family or to British spies? The secretary proposed the idea to Lafayette, who jumped at the thought. The French government got wind of the plan; Broglie thought it shrewd to throw everyone off the scent by sending Lafayette to England first. The young marquis, however, was delayed by Marie Antoinette's Mardi Gras ball. He danced at the Queen's affair from five to nine, supped, then went on with Her Majesty and her party to another at the Paris Opéra and did not get to bed before six in the morning.[17] A few days later the young nobleman went to London—and was presented to George III by his uncle, the Marquis de Noailles, French ambassador. He wrote a long letter to his father-in-law, explaining what he planned to do, but he did not send it. Instead, Lafayette returned to France secretly to arrange for the purchase of the boat. He could not resist contacting Ségur and Noailles but kept his return from his wife. Then Lafayette and Johann Kalb, a middle-aged professional soldier of Bavarian origin, left for Bordeaux and the boat. After a delaying contretemps involving a courier sent from Versailles with a letter from the King to stop Lafayette's departure, they sailed with other French officers via a Spanish port for America.

And thus, early in 1777, "Lafayette stepped out of insignificance into fame."[18]

It was certainly not the case of Benjamin Franklin, who had arrived not long before from America.

22. A "Quaker" at the Court of Versailles

For the French, he was a combination of Voltaire and Rousseau, science, freethinking, wit, warmth, and humanity, and the new republic he represented was the promise of a new age, a new order. He had shared (though less than they thought) in the drafting of the Declaration of Independence, its ringing assertion "that all men are created equal, that they are endowed by their Creator with certain unalienable Rights, that among these are Life, Liberty and the pursuit of Happiness. That to secure these rights, Governments are instituted among Men, deriving their just powers from the consent of the governed. That whenever any Form of Government becomes destructive of these ends, it is the Right of the People to alter or to abolish it, and to institute new Government, laying its foundation on such principles . . ."

But how could a monarch who would be absolute, as Louis XIV and Louis XV, or his ministers and his Court, receive such a representative of a people that had not only dared to declare its independence from a monarchical Britain but the universal right of revolution?*

Benjamin Franklin was a month from his seventy-first birthday when he landed with the illegitimate son of his illegitimate son, fifteen-year-old William Temple, and another grandson, the seven-year-old Benjamin Franklin Bache, legitimate son of his legitimate daughter, on the French coast on December 3, 1776. He had been in France

---

* Asked by a lady at Court what he thought of the American cause, Joseph II crustily replied, "Madame, it is my profession to be a royalist."[1]

ten years before, already well known for his writings and his experiments in electricity. He had visited Versailles, even attended a
supper of the King, Louis XV, "who spoke to us very graciously and
very amiably."[2] He had met Dr. Quesnay and the elder Mirabeau in
the former's entresol apartment at the palace, had become part of the
circle of physiocrats, written home about his findings, and afterward
maintained an enormous correspondence with them. This time Franklin had come as a commissioner elected by the Continental Congress,
along with Arthur Lee, who was in London, and Silas Deane, already
in Paris, to represent America in France.

A cold wind had driven the armed sloop *Reprisal* for four weeks
and two days. Franklin and his two grandsons had been seasick. He
had also been liverish and troubled with boils, living "chiefly on salt
beef, the fowls being too hard for my teeth."[3] Nevertheless he
studied the course and took the temperature of the Gulf Stream. Preparing for a new adventure, he had tossed his wig into the ocean and
put on a cap of beaver: he would play the complete American. And
so he landed at night in Quiberon Bay on the coast of Brittany. From
there he traveled by calash and cabriolet to Paris, but he stopped a
fortnight at Nantes to test the political temperature of France with
letters to Deane and French friends. The attitude was warm among the
people, officially cool at Court. Discretion was counseled the better part
of diplomacy, and discreetly Franklin paused at Versailles, before continuing on to Paris, for a private conversation with Foreign Minister
Vergennes.[4]

Through the veiled language of diplomacy and a first meeting were
discernible the first glimmerings of friendship. But neither Vergennes
nor the young French king was ready for an open break with
Britain (whose ambassador, Lord Stormont, already had reason to
suspect French complicity in the American rebellion). So Vergennes
advised Franklin to mask his moves, to put out that he had come to
France for his health and the education of his grandchildren, and to
make his visits to Versailles most circumspectly.

If duplicity was required, Franklin flexibly agreed, duplicity it would
be. He had come for French aid when American fortunes were at
their lowest. The only card Franklin had to play, and consequently
played, was the fact that without French aid America faced defeat
and France a lost opportunity. That assistance, Vergennes assured him,
would be forthcoming. Indeed it was being sent (as Franklin well

knew) through the dummy company organized by Beaumarchais and secretly financed by Versailles.[5]

Discreetly, too, money was advanced to Franklin by Vergennes to establish himself initially in Paris, then in Passy. Here, in a village now part of Paris, in the wing of a handsome house belonging to Le Ray de Chaumont, an influential friend of the American cause, on a hill overlooking the Seine, in which he taught William Temple how to swim, Franklin was to live happily for more than *eight years*. No American was ever more popular. For days Paris buzzed with his coming, women wearing their hair in a bouffant *coiffure à la Franklin,* a high curly mass in imitation of his beaver. Parisians were delighted with his simplicity, his unembroidered brown suit, his unbewigged Roman head. They called him a Quaker, and wisely Franklin did not disabuse them. The Quakers, for the French, were a quaint, "primitive" sect quite like the early Christians, appealing in their innocence— a general opinion of the Americans. Whenever he appeared on the streets, crowds followed him, and Vergennes was early obliged to instruct the police to forbid all talk about the "Quaker" and Les Insurgents in the cafés, so as to avoid unduly provoking the British ambassador.

Few men were better known than Franklin, even before his arrival. He was one of eight foreign members of the prestigious royal Académie des Sciences. Three editions of his scientific writings had appeared, impressing the Voltaireans. His *Poor Richard's Almanack* would go through eight editions in French in three years, delighting the Rousseauians. "Franklin's reputation," the very critical John Adams would write after experiencing it on the Continent, "was more universal than that of Leibnitz or Newton, Frederick or Voltaire; and his character more esteemed and beloved than all of them. . . . If a collection could be made of all the gazettes of Europe, for the latter half of the eighteenth century, a greater number of panegyrical paragraphs upon *le grand Franklin* would appear, it is believed, than upon any other man that ever lived."[6] Famous families sought him out: the La Rochefoucaulds, the Noailleses, the Lafayettes. The young Duc de La Rochefoucauld would serve as his secretary, translating the constitutions of the American states, and the young Marquis de Lafayette, as we have seen, depart to fight alongside Washington. If Franklin were to be reproached, it would be for the latter.

But Lafayette himself was unreproached at Versailles, and least of

all for having left behind a very young, very pregnant wife. Rather
the ladies saluted his daring. "It's undoubtedly an act of folly," wrote
Madame du Deffand to Horace Walpole, "but one which does him
no dishonor and which, on the contrary, is characterized by courage
and the desire for glory. People praise him more than they blame
him."[7] Including, it seems, the Queen. The Duc d'Ayen was dis-
comfited by his son-in-law's flaunting of the King and the embarrassment of his brother, the Marquis de Noailles (who had just presented
to the British King a nephew about to join His Majesty's rebels). As
for Adrienne, she had a second daughter on July 1. Soon after, her
first daughter died, and it was three months before she heard from her
husband. Nevertheless she remained his devoted defender, refusing
all family criticism.

Within a year, however, the criticism ceased. Even the Duc d'Ayen
took pride in Lafayette's exploits: a few months after his arrival, he
won Washington's admiration at the Battle of Brandywine when he
fought on, though wounded.

But the war itself was going very badly for Washington. Howe was
pressing him strongly, and he had to retreat. It did not greatly help in
France, that fall of 1777, when Franklin replied to news of Howe's
taking Philadelphia, capital of the fledgling republic, that "Philadelphia
has taken Howe, ça ira—all will be well."[8]* It was difficult enough
to secure aid from Versailles; such news made it more difficult, and
the King further resisted an open alliance with a rebellion in retreat.
Moreover, even a minister such as Turgot, a *philosophe* who was
Franklin's friend, had counseled, before his disgrace, against it, on the
prophetic grounds that all Europe's colonies were destined in the long
run to gain their independence, with or without French aid, and French
finances were more urgently needed for internal reforms. When
Jacques Necker, a Protestant banker born in Geneva, took Turgot's
place,† the bankruptcy facing the French treasury made loans to
America seem the height of folly, and so he indicated to Louis XVI.

* *"Ça ira"* became the French Revolution's first theme song: *It will go, all will
be well.*
† As a Protestant, Necker was not immediately granted the full title of finance
minister or admitted to the Royal Council. He had arrived by a combination
of intrigue and criticism of Turgot's policies with a banker's conception of
finances: to increase funds primarily by borrowing rather than by increasing
production and consequently taxes.

Vergennes, nonetheless, managed a loan of a million livres to Franklin before 1778, and millions more thereafter.[9]

The turning point came in December 1777. Driving directly to Franklin's courtyard in Passy, a young Bostonian, Jonathan Loring Austin, arrived bearing good news from America: General Burgoyne and his entire army had surrendered at Saratoga! Beaumarchais, who was visiting Franklin, leaped into his carriage and ordered his coachman to whip the horses to Paris. On the road, the carriage overturned, Beaumarchais tumbled out and badly hurt his right arm. But he made it to Paris, and the King was informed at Versailles.[10]

Vergennes, sensing the time had come to act, pressed more insistently for a treaty of alliance with America. He was opposed by Necker but supported by Maurepas, and reluctantly Louis XVI consented. On February 6, 1778, the French government signed two treaties (the second was secret) with the three commissioners of "the United States of America" (Franklin, Deane, and Lee). The first established relations of trade and aid; the second provided for joint military assistance should England declare war on France as a consequence of the first, until a mutually satisfactory peace and American independence had been won.[11]

And on March 20, 1778, in a ceremony marking the end of an epoch, hastened by the ceremony itself, the French monarchy in full panoply received the representatives of a democratic America.

For the signing on February 6, Franklin had sentimentally put on an old blue coat, and Silas Deane had asked him why. Franklin: "To give it a little revenge. I wore this coat on the day Wedderburn abused me at Whitehall."[12]* For the presentation at the French Court on March 20, Franklin was to be equally dramatic. He appeared at the palace of Versailles "without wig or sword, in brown velvet, white hose, his hair hanging loose, his spectacles on his nose, a white hat under his arm"[13]—the quintessence of republican simplicity when he met the resplendent great-great-great-grandson of the Sun King. The symbolism was not lost on the cheering crowds in the courtyard as the carriages of Franklin, Deane, Arthur Lee, and two other Americans—Lee's brother William and Ralph Izard—drew up at the royal gate. (The four others were in prescribed Court dress, in striking contrast to Franklin.) It was not, as we shall shortly see, lost on the Duc de Croÿ inside the palace.

---

* In 1774, at the end of his stay in England as the agent of Connecticut's grievances.

In accordance with protocol for diplomatic presentations, the Americans proceeded to Vergennes, who led them to the palace, up the marble stairs, through the Grande Galerie and its two rows of bowing ladies and gentlemen, courtiers, bishops, and diplomats to the King's apartments. The great doors swung open, the major of the Swiss Guards stepped forward and announced, "The Ambassadors of the Thirteen United Provinces!"[14]

"There, in the Oeil-de-Boeuf antechamber," writes the Duc de Croÿ, "was the famous Franklin, with the two other deputies of America, surrounded by a plentiful crowd which was struck by the importance of the spectacle. The picturesque figure of the old man with his odd spectacles and bald head, his air of the patriarch and founder of a nation joined to his fame as the inventor of electricity, the legislator of the Thirteen United Provinces, and the knowledgeable scientist, added to the beauty of the tableau.

"With M. de Vergennes at their head, the deputies of America entered the Royal chamber. His Majesty rose from his prayer-stool and adopted a Royal stance. M. de Vergennes presented M. Franklin, M. Deane and M. Lee, and two other Americans. The King was the first to speak and he spoke with more care and grace than I had ever heard from him. 'Pray assure Congress,' he said, 'of my friendship. I hope this will be for the good of both our nations.'

"Very nobly M. Franklin thanked the King in the name of America and replied: 'Your Majesty can depend on the gratitude of Congress and its loyalty to its engagements.' Then M. de Vergennes added: 'It is certain, Sire, that these gentlemen could not have conducted themselves more wisely or with more discretion in your kingdom.' "[15]

The Americans then went on to a sumptuous dinner with Vergennes and later to the gaming rooms of the Queen, who looked up from her cards, welcomed Franklin, and was charmed by him. And the Duc de Croÿ marvels in his memoirs at the scene he had just witnessed at the palace. It meant, for him, "an implacable war" with Britain, "and perhaps the creation of a country vaster than our own which could one day subjugate Europe." In the Oeil-de-Boeuf, "knowing Franklin," he continues, "I had gone to him and said, 'It could only be one who discovered electricity who could electrify the two ends of the earth.' (He did not say, he adds, " 'enflame' them!") And Croÿ concludes: "One can not hide the bad side of all this. What an example to substitute Franklin, the rebel and chief of rebellion, for the ambassador of the King of England on the very day of [the latter's] departure, to recognize rebels before they are even independent, and to be the first to recognize them!"[16]

But all was not exemplary among the rebellion's own men. A neurotic suspicion nagged Arthur Lee, the patrician from Virginia, that Deane was pocketing money in his dealings with Beaumarchais, that Franklin was criminally careless in his accounts, and the delegation itself was infested with spies. Here, unfortunately, there was substance for Lee's suspicions. Franklin's own secretary (whom Lee did *not* suspect) was a spy, but more damaging, Dr. Edward Bancroft of Massachusetts, whom Franklin held to be a friend, as well as a confidential secretary, and had housed with himself at Passy, was eventually to be exposed as a spy in the pay of the British since December 1776. Every week he would send copies of Franklin's important letters and anything else of possible significance—news of ship movements to and from America, notes of diplomatic and other conversations—through a messenger of the British ambassador to the British prime minister in England. He would write his reports in invisible ink, deposit them in a sealed bottle in the hole of a tree on the south terrace of the Tuileries, and every Tuesday evening at half-past nine, they would be picked up by the courier of Lord Stormont and make their way from Paris to Lord North in London.[17]

Lee did pass on his suspicions about Bancroft, but Franklin replied with massive indifference. He knew, he said, that he was surrounded by spies (though he did not believe his good friend Bancroft one of them) and thought the best response was to ignore it, since he could do little about it. To be forthright and honest in all his dealings with either the British or the French, he explained, would be the best policy; let spies report his words, diplomats, by their very profession, would never believe them.[18] And in fact, George III was so suspicious of anything that did not accord with his own opinions he discounted virtually all reports, especially those of his own spies.

Less palatable, or easily answered, were Lee's denunciations of Deane and Franklin, which went regularly to Congress with some effect. The accusations against Deane would lead to his recall and replacement by John Adams,* those brought against Franklin were soon rejected by Congress and finally provoked from that patient man

---

* But would be recognized as largely invalid by Congress, when, fifty years after Silas Deane died in poverty, it voted $37,000 to his heirs.

a memorable reply. "I hate disputes," Franklin wrote Lee, then in Madrid soliciting Spanish aid with maddening unsuccess, "I am old, cannot have long to live, have much to do, and no time for altercation. If I have often received and borne your magisterial snubbings and rebukes without reply, ascribe it to the right causes, my concern for the honor and success of our mission, which would be hurt by quarreling, my love of peace, my respect for your qualities, and my pity of your sick mind, which is forever tormenting itself with its jealousies, suspicions, and fancies that others mean you ill, wrong you, or fail in respect to you. If you do not cure yourself of this temper, it will lead to insanity."[19] And Lee would be recalled by Congress shortly after Silas Deane's departure.

Their replacement by John Jay and John Adams, however, created another problem for Franklin. Neither had any great affection for him, and each had less for the French. They were austere, harsh, puritanical men of rectitude, with more than their share of self-righteousness.[20] After his first semi-investigatory trip to Paris in 1778, John Adams called Franklin "indolent" in a letter to his cousin, Samuel Adams. "He loves his ease," he wrote, "hates to offend, and seldom gives any opinion till obliged to do it." He found Franklin "overwhelmed with a correspondence from all quarters . . . with unmeaning visits from Multitudes of People, chiefly from the Vanity of having it to say that they have seen him . . . There are so many private families, Ladies, and gentlemen that he visits so often,—and they are so fond of him, that he cannot well avoid it,— and so much intercourse with Academicians, that all these things together keep his mind in a state of dissipation."[21]

We owe to Adams, as well, a description of Franklin and Voltaire meeting as fellow members of the Académie des Sciences. Adams recounts it as if it were their first meeting, although Franklin had taken his grandson, William Temple, two months before to the old French writer, shortly after he had arrived in Paris. They had talked in English. Deeply moved, Franklin had asked Voltaire's blessing for his grandson. Equally moved, Voltaire blessed Temple in the name of "God and Liberty"—and all present wept.[22]

John Adams to his diary, April 27, 1778:

"Voltaire and Franklin were both present [at a session of the academy], and there presently arose a general cry that M. Voltaire and M. Franklin should be introduced to each other. This was done, and they bowed and spoke to each other. This was no satisfaction; there must be something more. Neither of our philosophers seemed to divine what was wished or expected; they, however, took each other by the hand. But this was not enough; the clamor continued, until the explanation came out. *'Il faut s'embrasser, à la française.'* The two aged actors upon this great theatre of philosophy and frivolity .embraced each other, by hugging one another in their arms, and kissing each other's cheeks; and then the tumult subsided, and the cry immediately spread through the whole kingdom, and I suppose, all over Europe, *'Qu'il était charmant de voir embrasser Solon et Sophocle!'* "[23]

Adams, an intelligent man, was not too long in discovering that Franklin, in his fashion, so vastly different from his own—he thought Franklin and Lee both "lived extravagantly for republicans"[24]—was nevertheless of immeasurable value to the republic. In his salute to Franklin's reputation as "more universal than that of Leibnitz or Newton, Frederick or Voltaire," he was generously and perceptively to add, "His name was familiar to government and people, to kings, courtiers, nobility, clergy and philosophers, as well as to plebeians, to such a degree that there was scarcely a peasant or a citizen, a *valet de chambre,* coachman or footman, a lady's chambermaid or scullion in the kitchen who was not familiar with it and who did not consider him a friend of human kind. . . . When they spoke of him, they seemed to think he was to restore the golden age. . . . His plans and his example were to abolish monarchy, aristocracy, and hierarchy throughout the world."[25]

And monarchical France was to finance him! How blind could the French King have been? Rather, how nearsighted. Humbling Britain was as far as he could see. Louis XVI was not oblivious of the rebel in the patriarchal figure of Franklin, but the rebellion itself was distant, and he expressed his own distaste with what can only be called a royal practical joke.

The cult of Franklin had reached the embarrassment of idolatry. The American's image and likeness were everywhere: stamped on snuffboxes, enclosed in rings, worn in medallions. "The numbers sold," Franklin himself wrote his daughter, Sarah Bache, "are incredible. These, with the pictures, busts and prints . . . have made your father's face as well known as that of the moon."[26] At the close of a long, colorful account of Franklin's popularity, Madame Campan relates the "little-known" story of Louis XVI's response:

"I was present [she writes] at one of those fêtes, where the prettiest of some three hundred women was chosen to place a crown of laurel on the white head of the American philosopher and two kisses on his aged cheeks. Even in the palace of Versailles, at the display of Sèvres porcelain, medallions of Franklin were sold under the very eyes of the King with the legend, *Eripuit caelo fulmen, sceptrumque tyrannis.**

"The King never expressed himself on an enthusiasm which he doubtless disapproved of. But when the Comtesse Diane [de Polignac], who thought herself a woman of *esprit,* manifested a similar ardor for the fad enveloping the delegate of America, a little-known *plaisanterie* of the King allowed us to know what he privately thought. He ordered the manufactory at Sèvres to make him a chamber pot with the image so in vogue [Franklin's] at its bottom, together with the famous legend; and he had it sent for New Year's to the Comtesse Diane."[27]

It was a savory joke that must have amused Franklin, no foreigner to ribaldry, if he heard of it. Certainly there was no amusement in playing mendicant friar at the French Court. As he wrote to John Adams, October 2, 1780, "I have long been humiliated with the idea of running from court to court begging for money and friendships, which are the more withheld the more eagerly they are solicited, and would perhaps have been offered if they had not been asked."† And again, on February 12, 1782, when he revealed that he was "quite sick of my Gibeonite office: that of drawing water for the whole congregation of Israel."[29] Drafts from everywhere in Europe for American purchases came to him in Passy for payment and as America's paper currency fell to nothing, Franklin drew an incredible forty-five million livres in all from an exhausted French treasury. (The loan would be repaid in full by 1802—well after the French Revolution it had so largely contributed to.)

Bothered by goùt (a ceremony at Versailles once laid him up for a week), Franklin sought his pleasures closer to home in Passy. He

---

* Turgot's widely quoted phrase in tribute to Franklin: "He wrested the thunder from the sky and the scepter from the tyrants."

† One day, when a lady exclaimed at the wonderful show of courage America was presenting the world, Franklin replied that it was indeed a beautiful spectacle, but unfortunately the spectators did not pay to see it.[28]

had a comfortable household of nine servants and a wine cellar of about a thousand bottles, much of it *vin rouge ordinaire* (most of which was for the servants). Neither the house, cellar, nor servants were excessive. Despite Adams' remarked disapproval, "he lived more plainly than any other ambassador in Paris."[30] And, with due consideration of his age, as fully.

Nearby was the pretty Madame Brillon de Jouy, wife of a treasury official. She was in her thirties, Franklin in his seventies. She sat in his lap, kissed him, and called him "Papa." "Somebody," Franklin wrote home, "gave it out that I lov'd Ladies; and then everybody presented me their Ladies (or the Ladies presented themselves) to be embraced, that is, to have their Necks kissed. For as to kissing of Lips or Cheeks, it is not the Mode here; the first is reckon'd rude, and the other may rub off the Paint."[31] Madame Brillon played the pianoforte, Franklin played the harmonica (he had invented it). They chatted and they played chess—once until after midnight, as Madame Brillon sat in her bath (coyly covered).

Slightly farther away was Madame Helvétius, widow of the famous *philosophe*. She lived in an adjacent village, in a little park on the edge of the Bois de Boulogne, with two daughters, pigeons, chickens, cats, and dogs, and Franklin called her Notre Dame d'Auteuil. She was in her sixties, with enough beauty lingering for a younger Turgot and an older Franklin both to pay her court, both of them seriously. Yet Franklin, at least, with a sense of humor. Once, when Madame Helvétius invited him to spend the day with her, he replied that he had already spent so many days with her it was time to spend a night. "Come this evening, then," she sent back. "I am waiting," he returned, "until the nights are longer!"[32]

Seventy-four, Franklin proposed marriage to Madame Helvétius, sixty-five. Gently she reproached him. She was, she said, faithful to her dear departed, doctor-philosopher husband. Franklin persisted. He composed, on his little printing press, the "Descent to Hell" for her reading. It recounted his own descent to the nether region and his encounter there in hell with her dear departed husband. Monsieur Helvétius, he discovered, was happily remarried and to none other than Franklin's own dear departed wife. And Franklin reproached wife Deborah for her infidelity. But the dear departed Deborah had replied: "I was your wife for almost half a century. Be content with that." And Franklin concluded his fable, addressing Madame

Helvétius: "Here I am"—alive on earth, as you. "Let us have our revenge!"[33]

The widow deemed Franklin serious enough to discuss his proposal with Turgot, her suitor since his youth. Turgot told her that if she were to marry Franklin she would most likely lose her salon. And, as many a French lady in elevated society, she finally turned down the American so that she might retain her French friends. She also, of course —there is no contradiction—kept Franklin as a very close friend. Indeed, Abigail Adams, wife of John Adams, was scandalized in 1784 by seeing her holding Franklin's hand during dinner—and his obviously liking it—while her other arm hung casually over the back of John Adams' chair.[34]

Unlike many men, Franklin really liked women, and not only, in his youth and manhood, for sensual reasons, or in his old age, for more remotely sensual ones, but simply for their presence. "We [philosophers]," he wrote Madame Helvétius, "find in your sweet society that charming benevolence, that amiable attention to oblige, that disposition to please and be pleased, which we do not always find in the society of one another. It springs from you; it has its influence on us all, and in your company we are not only pleased with you but better pleased with one another and with ourselves."[35]

Again, like not many Americans, Franklin really liked the French, their civilization, their virtues and flaws ("They have some frivolities, but they are harmless"), as Adams, for another, did not. "There is everything here," Adams wrote his wife Abigail, "that can inform understanding or refine the taste, and indeed, one would think, that would purify the heart. Yet it must be remembered there is everything here, too, which can seduce, betray, deceive, deprave, corrupt and debauch it."[36] The attitudes, inevitably, were reciprocated. The French liked Franklin and disliked Adams. The latter's bluntness ("he made a virtue of tactlessness"[37]) deeply offended Vergennes, who was having his own difficulties with Necker and the King. It might even have defeated the American mission had the French minister, who refused to deal further with Adams, not returned once more to Franklin. "This Court," Franklin cautioned Congress, "is to be treated with decency and delicacy. . . . Mr. Adams, on the other hand . . . seems to think a little apparent stoutness and greater air of independence and boldness in our demands will procure us more ample assistance."[38] At first Adams blamed Franklin for his failure, accusing him of subservience to France and its interests. Eventually, however, he realized the remarkably warm relationship between Franklin and the French was to America's own greater interest.

In the salon of Madame du Deffand, Franklin had passed his initial test among the wittiest and testiest of French wits and aristocrats, as he had completely won over the academicians at the French Academy and the courtiers at the French Court. Not even Marie Antoinette was more frequently sought as a model by sculptors and painters (he finally referred them to busts and portraits for copying). As a Mason from Philadelphia, he was welcomed into the Nine Sisters' Lodge of Paris, and when it was threatened with closure,* he was quickly elected grand master, and it was spared. *Poor Richard's Almanack* in French became the poor man's catechism, future spokesmen for the poor sought to contact him: Marat, the younger Mirabeau, a young lawyer named Robespierre. He also had an exchange with a Dr. Guillotin, whose name has an even more sanguinary association with the rapidly approaching Revolution. The lightning rod on Franklin's house in Passy, considered a blasphemy by the clergy, had begun to appear in many places. A suit brought against the installation of one in the provinces (by pious, frightened neighbors) was the occasion for Robespierre to send a copy of his unsuccessful plea in its defense to its inventor, Benjamin Franklin, in homage. Marat, a science student, had written Franklin about the nature of fire, and Mirabeau *fils,* son of his physiocratic friend, the marquis, had incorporated many of Franklin's own paragraphs (with his encouragement) in a pamphlet denouncing hereditary privileges, which he published in London.[39]

But it was the example of Franklin himself, the man who had made his way by initiative rather than privilege, that was to prove the most revolutionary. He became not only the symbol but the promise of a new order, the dying age of inherited privilege giving way to the new age of merit and accomplishment. Condorcet would very shortly point to it in his *De l'influence de la révolution d'Amérique sur l'Europe,* 1786.[40] A story involving Marie Antoinette indicates how general it may have become. "The Queen, struck by Franklin's modest

---

* French Freemasonry was more political than social, unlike the society in America. French Masons were freethinkers and *philosophes* in active opposition to the Church and absolutism, hopefully working for a constitutional monarchy. Danton, Desmoulins, and Condorcet, for example, were among their number.

and simple demeanor, had asked a courtier what his occupation had been before being made ambassador. 'Overseer of a printing-house,' was the answer.* Another, overhearing it, remarked, 'In France he could never have risen to be higher than a bookseller.' Philosopher Marie-Charles-Joseph Pougens tells the same story, except that it is a duke who refers disdainfully to Franklin's occupation in America, and a man of letters who replies sardonically, 'Too bad that he was not born in France; he would have been able with your protection to become one of the thirty-six printers in Paris.'"[41]

There is, however, the matter of the American Revolution, which has a historic priority in our present chapter, and which occupied—if it did not preoccupy—our first expatriate hero. (Franklin did think of permanently settling in France, and proposed the same to William Temple in an attempt to marry his grandson to Madame Brillon's daughter, but both proposals fell to the ground.)

And there was, that rarer thing, France's first expatriate hero. In February 1779, Lafayette returned with the glory he had sought, a hero at last in his own country at twenty-one. And he came back with a plan approved by Washington for the conquest of Canada, as well as with papers from Congress commissioning Franklin as sole American plenipotentiary at the French Court. At Versailles, Franklin presented his papers, Lafayette his plan; the reception was cordial for the first, discouraging for the second.

But the Comtesse Aglaé d'Hunolstein was now happy to see Lafayette (as, of course, was his wife) and he was made lieutenant-commander of the Royal Dragoons. Soon he was calling Franklin "my good friend" and hunting with the King, and no one laughed any longer at Lafayette when he chose to dance in the Queen's quadrille. More germane to our story, his plan for the conquest of Canada was reshaped into a plan for the harassment of the coast of Britain, with 1500 to 2000 men under him on vessels commanded by another sudden hero, the successful raider Captain John Paul Jones. Franklin had already thought well of the idea and Lafayette took John Paul Jones to Versailles for Vergennes' support. The French minister, however, though he did not reveal it to either Franklin or Lafayette, favored Broglie's old scheme for a direct invasion of Britain and considered the proposed plan a diversion of effort and men. Lafayette was sent off to join his regiment, then recalled to Versailles when

* Franklin's own favorite description of himself was, "Benjamin Franklin, Printer."

the invasion plan was nearer completion and the invasion fleet was gathering near Le Havre. It was an ill-fated venture that did little more than hoist anchor. An epidemic ravaged the crew, the fleet was dispersed, the plan "postponed."

Lafayette fretted from the inactivity and found life at Court more distasteful than ever. French nobles, he complained to his "fellow American," Benjamin Franklin, "have no notions of equality among men, they want to govern, they have too much to lose."[42] More and more he felt his place was in America at the side of Washington. In March 1780, he returned to it. More significantly, Rochambeau, with a strong force of six thousand French troops, was sent as well. A year and a half later, in a combined attack—the forces of Virginia under Lafayette, the French forces under Rochambeau,* the bulk of the American army under Washington—Cornwallis was driven back to Yorktown, cut off from the sea by the French fleet under de Grasse, and forced to surrender. The British defeat at Yorktown, October 19, 1781, signaled the beginning of the end, and Lafayette, commended by Washington, came back to France under the assumption that he would be useful in the negotiations for a general peace.

He was not. Even Franklin was suspected by Congress of being pro-French. As early as February 1780, John Adams, who had been back and forth, had returned to Europe for secret discussions with the British—as secret from Franklin as from the French, despite the provisions of the Franco-American treaty of alliance. Not too disturbed when he had inklings of it, Franklin wrote his friend David Hartley in England that if Congress had "entrusted to others rather than to me the negotiations for peace, when such shall be on foot, as has been reported, it is perhaps because they have heard of a very singular opinion of mine, that there hardly ever existed such a thing as a bad peace or a good war; and that I might therefore easily be induced to make improper concessions."[43]†

In fact, Franklin never inclined toward the slightest compromise or concession. He even went along with John Jay, who, with himself, John Adams, Jefferson (kept in America), and Henry Laurens (captured en route by the British) were commissioned by Congress in 1781 to arrange peace with England, when Jay insisted on nego-

* Including Fersen as his aide-de-camp.
† Throughout the war, Franklin maintained a correspondence with his good friends in England, always stipulating the essential condition for peace: recognition of the independence of the United States.

tiating the terms without keeping the French informed. Jay and
Adams had outvoted Franklin in deciding deliberately to break their
instructions from Congress, requiring them "to make the most candid
confidential communications on all subjects to the ministers of our generous ally, the King of France; to undertake nothing in the negotiations for peace or truce without their knowledge or concurrence;
and ultimately to govern yourself by their advice and opinion."[44]
By this time Spain had joined the war against Britain, after a secret
agreement with France aimed at regaining Gibraltar at the war's end,
and was engaged in its own private negotiations with the British
directed toward preventing American expansion to the east bank of
the Mississippi and beyond West Florida (both territories in Spanish
possession). All this was suspected, if not known, and both Jay
and John Adams firmly believed that France was too committed
to Spain to be trusted during tight negotiations with England's envoys. Vergennes, it might be noted, had also been putting out feelers
in London.*

Thus, finally, when the peace treaty was ready for signature between
the British and the American delegates—that is, the proposed draft
of the most important clauses—and Franklin was emburdened with
the delicate task of informing Vergennes—which he did during his
usual Tuesday meeting at Versailles—the French statesman was sufficiently sophisticated, and knowing, to remark dryly to his American
friend, "You had not been particularly civil to the King."[46] Then,
in one of the cleverest letters in diplomatic history, Franklin disarmed Vergennes by suggesting the British would be only too happy
if France openly rebuked America because it had not been consulted.
"The English," he wrote, knowing his letter would reach the French
King, "I just now learn, flatter themselves they have already divided
us. But I hope this little misunderstanding will therefore be kept a
secret and they will find themselves totally mistaken."[47] And the
first 600,000 livres of a new French loan of 6,000,000 livres were
secured for the United States. The war itself came virtually to its

* Diplomats, it scarcely needs noting, act in their own nation's interests first,
and inform their allies afterward, except when informing an ally is considered in
their nation's interest—which simply closes the self-centered circle.

In 1785, when John Adams became the American Ambassador to the
Court of St. James's and was presented to George III, the latter intimated
his awareness of Adams' lack of confidence in the French government. Adams
acknowledged it, replying, "I must avow to Your Majesty that I have no
attachment but to my own country."[45]

end at Versailles, on January 20, 1783, when England, France, Spain, and America signed the preliminary draft of the peace treaty in Vergennes' offices.* When the final treaty was signed in the fall, Franklin wrote Josiah Quincy, "May we never see another war! For in my opinion there never was a good war or a bad peace"[48]—a sentiment one forgives Franklin's repeating.

Franklin had several times petitioned Congress for his recall (particularly during Lee's wildest denunciations). Now, aging rapidly, plagued by gout, stone and bladder—and with peace achieved, Franklin petitioned it again. And again his petition was refused: he was to remain for two more years. He didn't seem greatly to regret it. Never given to diplomatic routine, he dealt less than ever with it, devoting himself to science (incidentally perfecting his stove and fashioning himself the first bifocals), his wide correspondence, the essays and tales he called *Bagatelles,* which he printed on his Passy press, and, of course, his ladies. On August 27, 1783, he witnessed Paris' first balloon ascension at the Champ-de-Mars. What good, a skeptic had asked, are such things? "What good," Franklin had replied, with a *bon mot* that swept the Continent, "is a new-born baby?"[49] But he also less shrewdly predicted that balloons would make future wars impossible, "convincing sovereigns of [war's] folly . . . since it will be impractical for the most potent of them to guard his dominion" against balloon-borne troops.[50] On September 19, Joseph Montgolfier, together with his brother the first among balloonists, put on a demonstration in the great courtyard of the palace at Versailles. King, Queen, and Court sat decorously looking on, as if at a Molière spectacle, ringed by dignitaries, diplomats (Franklin most likely among them), and an immense crowd. Air was heated under a huge, gaily painted balloon, and in eleven minutes it was inflated, rising about 1500 feet and landing eight minutes later two miles away. The first air travelers in history were a sheep, a cock, and a duck, uninjured in the descent except for the cock, which had been kicked in the wing by the sheep.[51]

Less historic, if equally flighty, was the Mesmer *affaire,* which Franklin was formally invited to investigate. Franz Mesmer, an Austrian "doctor," had established a curious clinic at Place Vendôme, to which the sick came by the thousands for expensive cures by "animal magnet-

---

* The street running along the ancient Foreign Ministry building at Versailles is commemoratively called Rue de l'Indépendance-Américaine.

ism." His consulting rooms were dimly lighted and hung with mirrors. The sick sat "mesmerized" around a vat of chemicals, iron filings, and crushed glass, holding hands or joined by a cord, maintaining an unbroken circuit. Dressed as a magician, Mesmer glided among them to the sound of soft music, making mysterious passes. There were more convulsions than cures, but enough cures for the French government to offer Mesmer a yearly sum for his "secret." He held out for more money (and a château). The government appointed a committee of academicians, with Franklin, Guillotin, and Lavoisier among its scientific members, to investigate Mesmer's claims.* Since Franklin was too indisposed to travel to Paris, the committee came to him in Passy and held one of its most important experiments in his garden. Mesmer's assistant, Dr. Deslon, who was also first physician to the Comte d'Artois, had "magnetized" an apricot tree, announcing that it would profoundly affect anyone touching it. He stood at a distance as a twelve-year-old boy was led blindfolded toward four trees, none of them magnetized or anywhere near the apricot tree. "At the first tree, the boy perspired and coughed. At the second he felt a pain and stupor in his head. At the third he complained of an increasing headache and said he was getting closer to the magnetic tree, though he was further from it than ever. At the fourth tree he fainted."[53]

"Imagination," said the report, with Franklin first among its signers, "is the principle. . . . Persons who thought they were magnetized felt pain, warmth and great heat, when they were not touched, and when no sign had been used. With some subjects, of very excitable nervous temperament, we produced convulsions, and what are known as crises." A second report stated: "Decisive experiments have demonstrated that imagination apart from magnetism produces convulsions, and that magnetism without imagination produces nothing. . . . The animal magnetic fluid . . . is non-existent."[54] Women, said a secret report, were especially susceptible to men such as Mesmer; in their case, the sensations experienced were at least in part erotic, and

---

* Lafayette was one of Mesmer's rich and influential sponsors. Before leaving France in 1784 on a visit to Washington, he had gone to Versailles to take leave of Louis XVI. "What will Washington think," the King had remarked to him, "when he learns that you have become the first apothecary's boy of Mesmer?" Lafayette was neither moved nor amused. He took a letter from Mesmer to Washington with him, which Washington simply acknowledged. Jefferson called Mesmer a "maniac."[52]

therefore his methods objectionable. Denounced as a fraud, Mesmer eventually left France, taking his fortune with him.

Finally it was time for Franklin to return home. Seventy-eight and ill, he left Passy on July 12, 1784, part way on a litter sent to him by the King, an adoring procession following, two weeping ladies left behind. From Le Havre he wrote (in flawed French) to Madame Helvétius: *"Je ne suis sur d'être heureux in Amérique; mais il faut que je m'y rende. Il me semble que les choses sont mal arrangés dans ce bas monde, quand je vais que les êtres si faites pour être heureux ensemble sont obligés à se separer."*[55]* On the voyage home, Franklin again studied the course of and took the temperature of the Gulf Stream.

Franklin himself was followed at Versailles by Thomas Jefferson, who has described for us *that* experience:

"The succession of Dr. Franklin at the Court of France was an excellent school of humility. On being presented to anyone, as the minister of America, the commonplace question used in such cases was, 'C'est vous, Monsieur, qui remplace [sic] le Docteur Franklin?' 'It is you, sir, who replace Dr. Franklin?' I generally answered him, 'No one can replace him, sir. I am only his successor.' "[56]

When Franklin died in Philadelphia at eighty-four, on April 17, 1790, and news of it reached Paris, Mirabeau rose and addressed the revolutionary National Assembly. "Too long," he said, "have political ministries taken formal note of the death of those who were great only in their funeral elegies. Too long has the etiquette of courts prescribed hypocritical mourning. Nations should wear mourning only for their benefactors. The representatives of nations should recommend none but the heroes of humanity for homage. . . .

"I propose that it be decreed that the National Assembly for three days wear mourning for Benjamin Franklin."[57]

Mirabeau's proposal was seconded by Lafayette and La Rochefoucauld; it passed by acclamation. And the journeymen printers of Paris met to mourn Franklin's death as if one of their own.

---

* "I am not sure I will be happy in America, but I must return. It seems to me that things are arranged badly here below, when I see how those made to be happy together are obliged to separate."

23. The Curtain Falls

We left the Queen, as Alexander Dumas might say, in the fall of 1781 with the birth of the Dauphin. And now we must bridge the great gap between the Quaker simplicity of Franklin and the famous trial and *affaire* of the Queen's four-million-dollar necklace—a trial from which, Napoleon would note, "we must date the Queen's own death."[1]

The year had begun with Louis XVI beholden to the Swiss banker who had become his finance minister for the masterful borrowings which alone kept the Crown afloat. That would have been vexing enough, but Necker compounded the injury by publishing a prideful *Compte rendu au roi*—an Accounting to the King—which sold as a little blue book in thousands of copies. It brushed a bright, self-congratulatory picture (leaving out military expenditures and the huge national debt), thus winning a large public while it lost most of the courtiers (with its exposure of the Court's extravagant practices and loosely awarded allowances). Even the sensible Vergennes joined Necker's enemies, writing the King in his turn a *Mémoire sur le Compte rendu,* which accused the Swiss banker of a "Genevese-Protestant plan" for upsetting the established French order and creating a fiscal Fronde.[2]

Necker's vanity and the various parlements (offended by his proposal to replace them with provincial assemblies) combined with Maurepas and other ministers to bring Necker down from his high post—though he left it with the public convinced that only his financial wizardry might yet save France from catastrophe. He was replaced by the affable, ineffective Joly de Fleury; and Louis XVI, as if released, bought Marie Antoinette a *rivière* of diamonds from Böhmer that cost 750,000 livres. On a quick six-day visit, Joseph II, the Austrian Emperor, advised his sister, the French Queen, to keep her head cool and "her heart Austrian."[3] He had his own expansionist plans for 1781, which involved the Franco-Austrian alliance, despite French involvement—one is tempted to say, entanglement—in America's war with Britain. Then, as the year closed, there was the new Dauphin at Versailles, a new Opéra for Paris, the victory at Yorktown, and the passing of Maurepas in his eighty-first year (and the King sighed that he no longer heard his minister's comforting footsteps overhead at the palace).

In May 1782, the dwarfish son of Catherine the Great visited Versailles as the Comte du Nord, paused in Lyons, where he heard the ladies exclaim, "How ugly he is!," which led him to remark, "At last, a country that does not flatter me. I would be happy to remain here."[4]* In June, the Queen danced with Lafayette, in the fall, Franklin, Jay, and Adams discussed peace terms with the British, in time informed the French, and in January 1783 signed them. Joly de Fleury, who had lasted a few years as finance minister was replaced by d'Ormesson, who was to last a few months and be replaced by Calonne, whose four years would be marked by "his astounding system of falsification."[5]

But in the brief meantime, in June 1783, Swedish Count Axel von Fersen had returned to France, its Court, and his Queen. We had left *him,* the reader might recall, leaving Marie Antoinette three years before with remarkable restraint for America and its war. The Queen's feelings—beyond rumor, idle gossip, or the tittle-tattle of contemporary memoirs—were made the subject of a careful official dispatch from the Swedish ambassador to his King:

"I have to report to Your Majesty [he wrote] that young Fersen is so much in the Queen's good graces that this has roused suspicion in certain quarters. I must admit that I myself believe she has a fondness for him. The signs I have seen are too plain for any doubt on the subject to remain in my mind. Young Count Fersen has, in these circumstances, behaved in the most exemplary way, not only in respect to his modesty and his reserve, but also in that

* He returned to Russia, tsardom, and assassination.

he has made up his mind to go to America. He has put an end to all danger by his departure; and it cannot but be admitted that to have withstood such a temptation signifies he is endowed with a resolution hardly to be expected at his age.

"During the last days before he left, the Queen could not keep her eyes off him, and when she looked at him, they were filled with tears. I would ask Your Majesty to be good enough to keep this matter to himself and to Senator Fersen. When the favorites at court heard of the Count's intended departure, they were delighted, and the Duchess of Fitz-James said to him: 'What, Sir, are you leaving your conquest in the lurch?'—'Had I made one, I should not leave it in the lurch. I am going away because I wish to, and without any regrets.' I think Your Majesty will admit that this reply indicates a prudence and power of self-restraint beyond the man's years. Moreover, the Queen now shows much more self-control and prudence than of yore."[6]

But it was three years since Marie Antoinette had seen Fersen, and when he walked into her gilded salon, though announced, she started at her harp, and abruptly stopped playing. Their intimacy resumed, probably intensified. Fersen had paid court to several ladies, had had an affair or two, had even dallied with the idea of marriage to a Miss Leijel, a young English lady, then to Mademoiselle Necker, the Swiss banker's rich, intelligent, and homely daughter. Miss Leijel married and Mademoiselle Necker would become the Baronne de Staël. Fersen's affections, if not his interests, were elsewhere. "I am really glad," he wrote his sister Sophia, "that Miss Leijel is married. They won't talk to me about *her* any more, nor, I hope, of any other, since I have made up my mind. I have decided never to marry. It would be too unnatural. . . . I cannot belong to the one woman to whom I should like to belong, and who alone truly loves me, so I will belong to no other."[7]

To keep Fersen close to her, Marie Antoinette arranged the purchase of a French regiment, the Royal Suédois, for him to command (and herself wrote Gustavus III about the arrangement). A miscarriage of the Queen, a long trip through Germany and Italy with his King interrupted their intimacy. Then, on the way back to Sweden, Fersen and an incognito Gustavus stopped off at Versailles. Louis XVI, hunting at Rambouillet, was told of the visit; he rushed back and dressed so hurriedly he put on one shoe with a silver heel, the other with a red one. "Have you dressed for a masquerade?" the Queen bantered him when he arrived.[8]* The stopover lasted six weeks, joyously celebrated with Trianon entertainment. "We are swimming in *fêtes, plaisirs* and *divertissements*," Fersen wrote his father.[9] The Queen, transformed, became almost beautiful, "as if by a miracle."[10] Then Axel returned to Sweden with the royal suite, not to return to France until the birth of Marie Antoinette's second son—a son, said many, of which he was the father.[11]† And when the Queen visited Paris shortly thereafter, the reception was frigid—"not a single cry greeted her," Fersen wrote the Swedish King. Back in Versailles, she broke into tears. "What have I done to them?" she cried. "What have I done to them?"[13]

But she soon recovered, and as Fersen went off to join his regiment, Marie Antoinette began rehearsals for what would be, though she could not know it, her last performance in the Trianon theater, as Rosine, in Beaumarchais' *Le Barbier de Séville.*

There was even a fatality in her choice of comedy. Beaumarchais had made somewhat of a fool of Louis XVI the year before with his *Le Mariage de Figaro,* which continued the now fabulous career of the Seville barber. From 1781 until 1784, though accepted by the Comédie Française, it had awaited production at the royal theater. Louis XVI had read it—or rather, had it read to him—and was properly shocked. Beaumarchais' *Figaro,* even more than his *Barbier,* mocked all his received values. "It is detestable," he exclaimed. "It must never be performed! To allow it would be the same as destroying the Bastille. This man ridicules everything that should be respected in government."[14]

Indeed, Figaro, the barber who would be a playwright and has become a nobleman's major-domo, derides nobility and decries the system that produced it. "What is it to be a courtier?" he is asked. "To receive, to take, to ask," he replies. Addressing the grandees of France (via Spain), he says scornfully: "What have you done for

---

* The French King, Mercy wrote Joseph II, "no longer has any standing in State affairs; he brings to them little intelligence and less knowledge."

† A popular song had already condemned her:

Veux-tu connaître	Would you know
Un cocu, un bâtard, une catin?	A cuckold, a bastard, a whore?
Voyez le Roi, la Reine,	See the King, the Queen,
Et Monsieur le Dauphin.	And Monsieur the Dauphin.[12]

so much good fortune? You gave yourselves the trouble to be born, and nothing more; for the rest, you are simply ordinary!"[15]

To get around the King's interdiction, Beaumarchais read scenes of his play in the salons of the privileged. Vastly amused—truly, satire is a mirror in which one sees only the face of one's neighbor—his aristocratic listeners protested to Louis XVI that, really, he *must* allow its production. And finally, after being promised cuts in the most objectionable passages, the King yielded. Opening night on April 27, 1784, found noblemen and women fighting commoners for places, with windows and doors giving way under the pressure for seats. "What do you foresee for this evening?" Louis XVI had nervously asked one of his ministers. "Sire," came the reply, "I hope it fails." "So do I," said the King.[16] But Beaumarchais' *Figaro,* applauded by its own targets, was a wild success; its production, as Louis XVI had anticipated, was "the Revolution already in action" (Napoleon).[17]

And now the Queen of France, in the spring of 1785, was rehearsing Beaumarchais' *Barbier de Séville* for her little gold and white theater at the Trianon with the Comte d'Artois, the King's brother and a future King of France, in the role of Figaro, the mocker of aristocracy! Irresponsibility, shared by an entire ruling class, may never have reached giddier heights, or provoked a more rapid fall. The performance was set for the middle of August, but the curtain would begin to come down before *that* performance with the *affaire du collier de la Reine,* the story of the Queen's necklace, a historical occurrence more incredible than the Dumas novel based upon it, an intrigue more complicated than any Beaumarchais comedy, with a plot as Machiavellian as any in *The Prince.*

But Marie Antoinette was too busy with *Le Barbier de Séville* to pay attention to Court jeweler Böhmer, when he handed her a letter on July 12, 1785. She was between Mass and a rehearsal, and she could give him only a few minutes. She read the letter after he had gone.

"I was reading in the library [writes Madame Campan], when the Queen came in with that letter, saying that since I was so good at solving the puzzles in the *Mercure de France,* I might try solving the one that fool Böhmer had just given her. Such were her very words.

"Böhmer's letter had some expression about how happy he would be to see her 'in possession of the finest diamonds in Europe' and his fond hope that she 'would not forget him.' She read it aloud, commenting that she could see in it only proof of the man's madness, since she couldn't remotely understand what he meant by complimenting her on the beauty of her diamonds or by praying her not to forget him.

"Then Her Majesty held the letter to the flame of a candle which was kept burning for the sealing of letters. 'It is not worth keeping,' she said. But she would regret having destroyed that enigmatic message."[18]

That "enigmatic message" was the key to Marie Antoinette's fate and characteristically she threw it away. Böhmer's letter read:*

"Madame,

"We are at the very height of happiness at the thought that we have again been able to show our zeal and respect for Your Majesty's orders by devotedly submitting to the latest terms proposed to us, and we have infinite satisfaction in the thought that the most beautiful diamond jewelry in the world will serve the greatest and best of Queens."

Did Marie Antoinette suspect that Böhmer was referring to the famous diamond necklace originally designed for Madame du Barry (as so many she had procured from Böhmer and Bassenge)? Twice it had been offered to her, and twice it had been refused, each time more regretfully. The first time was in 1778, on the birth of her child, Madame Royale. "Dazzled, the French King determined to present it to his Queen [Catherine the Great heard from her Paris correspondent]. . . . But Her Majesty renounced the glorious jewel with the well-known phrase, 'At that price, we have less need of a necklace than a ship of the line.' "[19]

It may be the only favorable anecdote about Marie Antoinette before her fall—and is dismissed by even Madame Campan in her memoirs as actually not in the Queen's nature: the phrase was in fact expressed "by *His* Majesty rather than *Her* Majesty."

A second time, in 1781, Böhmer had returned to Versailles with the necklace, after having made a vain tour of Europe's courts in search of another client. The occasion had been the birth of the Dauphin. Tempted, reports Madame Campan, the Queen suggested to the King

---

* He had, of course, kept a copy, happily for historians.

that he *might* consider buying it as a future wedding gift for one of his children, but "the King replied that he would not consider so great an expenditure for something which could not be of benefit for years to come."[20]

The spectacular necklace, denuded of historical significance, would still have rated a historical. Magnificently composed of 647 diamonds weighing a total of 2842 carats, it encircled the neck and decorated bared shoulders and breasts with ropes, festoons, tassels, and pendants of great brilliance. The incredible bauble was offered by Böhmer and Bassenge, with varying, "generous" terms, for sixteen hundred thousand livres.* Even Louis XV might have hesitated buying it for Madame du Barry. For years the royal jewelers had been putting the stones together, rummaging the world for matching diamonds, running into debt, mortgaging their showrooms, their residences, "even Mme Böhmer's cherished country place."[21] It explains, in part, Böhmer's desperation and behavior when, after the King's refusal, he finally was received by the Queen a few months later. Madame Campan:

"Böhmer threw himself to his knees, clasped his hands as in prayer, wept and exclaimed, 'Madame, I am ruined and disgraced if you persist in refusing my necklace. I do not even want to survive such a misfortune. I will go directly from hence to the river and throw myself into it!'" The Queen told him to rise, never to mention the necklace to her again and coldly advised Böhmer to parcel the necklace, sell its diamonds separately, "'and then you won't need to drown yourself!'"[22]

The Queen, continues Madame Campan, heard no more of the necklace from Böhmer, until the "enigmatic message" of July 1785, which had so puzzled her. On the third of the following August, Madame Campan "chanced" to meet Böhmer at her country place in Crespy, where he was a Sunday dinner guest of her father-in-law. Madame Campan:

"Böhmer arrived and, extremely uneasy at having received no reply from the Queen, asked whether she had not given me a message for him. I replied that she had given me none, because she had no further commissions for him, and I faithfully repeated all she had instructed me to say [that the Queen would nevermore buy a single carat from him].

* To duplicate it in 1972, the French society of jewelers informs the author, one would have to be prepared to spend over £1,600,000.

M

" 'But the answer to my letter?' he asked. 'To whom must I turn for the answer?'

" 'To no one,' I told him. 'Her Majesty burned your letter without ever being able to understand it.'

"Oh, Madame,' cried Böhmer, 'that isn't possible! The Queen knows very well there is money due me!'

" 'Money, Monsieur Böhmer? We completely settled the Queen's account with you a long time ago.'

" 'Madame, are you not in her confidence? A man can not be said to have been paid in full, when he is owed over fifteen hundred thousand francs and who is being ruined because he is not being paid!'

" 'Have you lost your mind?' I asked. 'For what object could the Queen possibly owe you such an exorbitant sum?'

" 'For my diamond necklace, Madame,' replied Böhmer coldly.

" 'What?' I exclaimed. 'Again that necklace with which you have vainly tormented the Queen for so many years? But you told me yourself that you had sold it in Constantinople.'

" 'It was the Queen who had me instructed to make that reply to anyone who asked questions,' the wretched imbecile said. And then he told me that the Queen had wanted the necklace after all and had sent Monseigneur the Cardinal de Rohan to purchase it for her.

" 'You are mistaken!' I exclaimed. 'The Queen has not addressed a single word to the Cardinal de Rohan since his return from Vienna [ten years before]. There is no man at Court who is in such disfavor.'

" '*You* are mistaken, Madame,' said Böhmer. 'She sees him so much in private that it was to His Eminence she gave the thirty thousand francs which were paid to me as the first instalment for the necklace. In the Cardinal's very presence, she took the money for it from the little Sèvres porcelain desk by the fireplace in her boudoir.'

" 'And was the Cardinal de Rohan the one who told you that?'

" 'Yes, Madame, the Cardinal himself.'

" 'Oh!' I cried. 'What a detestable plot!'

" 'In truth, Madame, I am beginning to be very alarmed myself, for His Eminence assured me that the Queen would wear the necklace on Whit Sunday. But I have not yet seen her wearing it, and it was that which decided me to write the letter to Her Majesty.'

"He then asked me what I thought he should do. Whereupon I advised him to go directly to Versailles instead of returning to Paris, and ask an audience with the Baron de Breteuil, who, as head of the

King's Household, was in charge of the Crown jewels, and above all to be very careful. . . .

"But instead of following my advice, he went to the Cardinal in Paris. . . .

"After Böhmer had departed, I wanted to follow him and go to the Queen at the Trianon. My father-in-law [an official secretary at Versailles] prevented me, telling me it was best to leave the infernal *affaire* to the Baron de Breteuil to manage."[23]

In effect, in a time-immemorial manner, Monsieur Campan had advised his daughter-in-law, *Don't get involved!*

And the Cardinal de Rohan, when Böhmer anxiously reported Madame Campan's response to him, simply assured him she was obviously not in the Queen's confidence. And the intriguing "Comtesse" de La Motte [the plot thickens: we shall shortly attempt to clarify it] counseled the frantic jewelers to ask the Cardinal himself to pay for the necklace from his enormous fortune, and to take the *affaire* no further. She had, as we shall see, her own reasons for the counsel. Böhmer, however, went instead to the Queen once more, throwing himself at her feet and appealing for her mercy because of his— and his partner's—complete innocence, and he revealed all they knew of the mysterious business.

And so Madame Campan found the Queen, after Böhmer had left, in a state of fury and desperation: "The very thought that anyone could have believed that she would have confided in a man like the Cardinal, that she would have entrusted him to deal with a tradesman without the King's knowledge, for something which she had refused to accept from the King himself . . .

" 'When the Roman purple and the title of Prince are used to cloak a common money-grabber,' " she cried to her lady-in-waiting, " 'a cheat who dares compromise the wife of his sovereign, then France and all Europe should learn of it!' "[24]

Böhmer and Bassenge were instructed to draw up a memorandum containing all they knew about the diamond necklace *affaire* and the Cardinal's connection with it. Consulted, the Abbé de Vermond and the Baron de Breteuil, both of whom shared Marie Antoinette's intense dislike for the Cardinal de Rohan, encouraged the Queen in her insistence on the King's taking public action against him.

Breteuil's brooding hatred for the Prince Louis de Rohan dated from the time he was precipitously replaced by him as French ambassador to the Court of Vienna. Previously Rohan had been the Bishop of Strasbourg who had greeted Marie Antoinette as a bride on her way to Versailles. His apparent membership in the du Barry party, however, antagonized the young Dauphine, and before he took his post in Vienna, she wrote the Empress, her mother, "He belongs to a great house, but he conducts himself like a gay army officer rather than a churchman."[25] It was an odd rebuke from Marie Antoinette. Soon, in return, she was to hear of Rohan's telling the Empress of her own irresponsible conduct at the French Court—and her abiding hostility to him was reinforced. Then the Empress was scandalized by the Prince de Rohan's luxurious equipage and gallant, unchurchmanlike ways, his stable of fifty horses and his liveried guards, and she feared, as she wrote Mercy, "for my ladies! Young and old, pretty or ugly, they are all under his spell!" And she feared, too, for her son, Joseph II, "who loves to chatter with Rohan, listen to his indiscreet gossip and little tales."[26] Repeatedly she wrote her daughter to press for Rohan's recall before he further "corrupted my nobility." But the Rohans were too powerful and the Dauphine's influence too limited. His recall had to await her becoming Queen. When he returned from Vienna for the coronation of Louis XVI, she kept him in suspense about his return to the Austrian Court (where he had left his personal secretary, the Abbé Georgel,* in provisional charge). Finally Rohan was replaced by his predecessor, the Baron de Breteuil (who was coldly received by the disappointed Court of Vienna, adding to *his* hostility for Rohan). So great was the power of his family, however, Rohan was made grand almoner of France (as promised by Louis XVI) with control over the vast alms of the King, and eventually Cardinal, Archbishop of Strasbourg, General Administrator of the Sorbonne, member of the French Academy, and abbot of St. Vaast, Noirmoutiers, and Chaise-Dieu, with annual revenues of some "two and a half millions of livres. Yet the Cardinal was restless and unhappy until he should be reinstated in favor at Court and had appeased the animosity which Marie Antoinette felt against him."[27] He even dreamed of becoming, once that favor had been regained, cardinal-minister of France à la Richelieu and Mazarin.

Abbé Georgel, in his memoirs (as most of the participants, he was to write his own account of the famous *affaire*):

---

* "The shrewd, foxy Jesuit, who [would know] more about the diamond necklace *affaire* than anyone else in the world"—Madame Campan.

"Having risen so high—despite opposition from a powerful Queen— he must needs fly higher, and so he opened the gulf into which we shall see him plunge. His fall from favor at Court was the unending scourge of his life."[28]

The gulf unconsciously opened by the Cardinal in his blind efforts to scramble back into favor was suddenly revealed to him on August 15, 1785. It was Assumption Day, one of the holiest of the year, when the Cardinal Prince de Rohan, as titular head of the French Church, was to celebrate High Mass in the Royal Chapel in the presence of the King and the Queen, the royal family, the Court, and France's most distinguished notables, who had carriaged to Versailles especially for the occasion. It was the day chosen by the Baron de Breteuil, in charge of the King's guards, for bringing his enemy, the Cardinal de Rohan, humbly to his knees, not in prayer, but in public disgrace, and without further ado.

The King, more "kindly" (Georgel), thought the accused Cardinal might at least be allowed to reply to the memorandum written, on royal instructions, by Böhmer and Bassenge, containing a chronology of the Cardinal's involvement in the necklace scandal. With this in mind, Louis XVI summoned Miromesnil, his minister of justice (Garde des Sceaux), and Vergennes for their opinions. They were shown the jewelers' memorandum, heard the Queen and Breteuil speak for immediate action against the Cardinal, then counseled that the Cardinal, too, might be heard privately.

As the Court and the great throng of visitors crowded the Grande Galerie waiting for the royal procession to pass on its way to the chapel, Cardinal de Rohan was called from among them to the King's study. There he was astonished to find the King, the Queen, and the three highest ranking ministers of the land, solemnly assembled, waiting for him. Madame Campan, who had it from the Queen, describes the dramatic scene:

"The King asked the Cardinal, 'Is it true that you purchased the diamonds from Böhmer?'

" 'Yes, Sire.'

" 'What have you done with them?'

" 'I thought they had been delivered to the Queen.'

" 'Who charged you to make the purchase?'

" 'A lady named the Comtesse de La Motte-Valois, who gave me a letter from the Queen. I thought I was pleasing Her Majesty by undertaking the commission for her.'

"Here the Queen interrupted the Cardinal, exclaiming, 'How, Sir, could you have believed that I would select *you*, to whom I have not spoken for eight years, to conduct this negotiation for me, and with such a woman as an intermediary?'

" 'I now realize,' he replied, 'that I have been cruelly deceived. I will pay for the necklace. My great desire to please Your Majesty blinded me. I did not suspect trickery, and I am deeply sorry for it.'

"The Cardinal then took a small portfolio from his pocket containing the letter from the Queen to Madame de La Motte supposedly commissioning him to act for Her Majesty.

"The King read the letter, then, holding it up to the Cardinal, exclaimed, 'This is neither written, nor signed by the Queen! How could a prince of the House of Rohan, a Grand Almoner of France, have believed that the Queen would sign herself "Marie Antoinette of France"? Everyone knows that queens sign only by their baptismal name. . . . But now, Monsieur,' the King continued, 'explain this enigma to me. I do not wish to find you guilty. I had rather you could justify your conduct. Explain the meaning of your dealings with Böhmer, your letters and pledges to him.'

"Visibly paling, the Cardinal leaned against the table for support. 'Sire,' he said, 'I am too confused to answer Your Majesty in a way that—' [he stopped helplessly].

" 'Try to compose yourself, Monsieur le Cardinal, and go into my cabinet. There you will find paper, pens and ink. Write down what you have to tell me.'

"The Cardinal went into the King's cabinet and returned in a quarter of an hour with a written statement as confused as his verbal answers had been. Whereupon, the King said to him, 'Withdraw, Sir.' "[29]* And the Cardinal left the room.

Mixing tears and anger, the Queen demanded justice. Embarrassed, Miromesnil and Vergennes held their tongues while Breteuil hotly demanded the arrest of the Cardinal on the spot. The King, "moved by the Queen's tears,"[31] gave the orders for it.

The grand almoner, the Cardinal Prince de Rohan, was walking slowly down the Grande Galerie, waiting for the King, the Queen, and

* The King is also said to have remarked, "Now I must do my duty as becomes a King and a husband."[30]

the royal family to join him in the procession. Suddenly, he heard the Baron de Breteuil cry out behind him, "Arrest the Cardinal!" Stunned, the great crowd looked on in amazement. The expression on the Cardinal's face froze; Breteuil's beamed with triumph. Two officers of the guard closed around the Cardinal. With unexpected presence of mind, Rohan bent, as if to adjust his garter, scribbled a note screened by his red cardinal's cap to his secretary, Abbé Georgel, and managed to slip it to his valet. At a full gallop, the valet rode for Paris and the Cardinal's residence. When he arrived, his horse, led to the stable, fell dead.

Abbé Georgel: "I was in my apartment. The valet, horror on his face, rushed in to me, saying, 'All is lost! The Prince has been arrested!' He fell in a faint to the floor, letting fall the note he was to deliver to me."[32]

The Cardinal's note instructed the abbé to destroy all the gilt-edged letters presumably written by the Queen, which he would find in the study in a red leather portfolio. The abbé followed instructions. That night Prince de Rohan, Cardinal of the French Church, scion and flower of one of the noblest families of France, was taken to the Bastille. After an unexplained interval of three days, Madame de La Motte-Valois, too, was taken to the fortress prison.

Shown her room, the "Comtesse" sharply asked her jailer whether the prison's governor expected her to sleep on the "miserable pad" furnishing a corner. Without waiting for a reply, she demanded a bed "at least as good as that provided the Cardinal." She continues (in *her* account of the *affaire*): "Soon after, I saw my jailer return with excellent linen sheets, decent bed curtains and a deep, soft, feather bed." But her room, she complained, still had "no tapestries, no rugs, no pictures."[33]

The brazen aplomb, the effrontery, sets the tone, even if it does not wholly prepare one for the story of a master-mistress of intrigue who could have been a great minister or playwright.

Madame de La Motte, she herself tells us, was a self-made woman born of the lowest and highest orders of France. Her mother had been a servant maid, her father the impoverished Baron de Saint-Rémy, an elder son in the house she was serving. But their offspring could trace her ancestry back five generations through her father to a French king, Henry II of the House of Valois. The French King had given his mistress, the Baronne de Saint-Rémy, a son, whom he legitimized—and the royal archives, searched so often by her biographers, indisputably establish Jeanne de Saint-Rémy de Valois, the future Madame de La Motte-Valois, as their descendant.³⁴

By then, however, the family of Saint-Rémy had descended a long way. "He was weak," Madame de La Motte says of her father, "lazy and a slave to his ardor for his faithless wife." Reduced to want, her father was easily persuaded by her mother to pull up his roots in Champagne and replant them closer to Versailles. Where better to pursue their fortunes by reminding "the Bourbon King of his obligations to his Valois cousins"? So they walked and begged most of their way from Bar-sur-Aube to Paris, some 135 miles distant, little Jeanne and her older brother, Jacques, her father, and her mother. She and her mother would enter a roadside tavern, unroll a copy of the family arms, sob, tell their story, and beg for money. Reaching a Paris suburb, they were befriended by a parish priest, who undertook to press their claim with the King's ministers. Another daughter was born, her father died, her mother took a lover, and Jeanne, six years old, was set to begging again with her baby sister on her back. "Take pity," she would plead, "on two little orphans descended from one of your greatest kings!"³⁵

It was effective with the people, less so with the police. Two years later Jeanne was adding for the benefit of the Marquise de Boulainvilliers, who happened by on the Passy road in a splendid coach, "Pity two poor orphans, Madame, who lost their father and were abandoned by their mother!" The marquise listened to their tale, checked their story of Valois blood, and then took them in hand, sending them both to a seminary. The sister died, Jeanne quickly matured. Barely in her teens, she caught the marquis' eye, but (she writes) escaped his lecherous hands and worked as a modiste, serving men (on her own) as well as women (for her *patronne*).

The years passed. Brother Jacques, who had been briefly a bootblack, had blossomed, as a Valois, in the navy and in 1775 had even been presented to the new King. (Contemporary newspapers carried the account.) He, Jeanne, and another sister, Marianne (who had been abandoned as a foundling back in Champagne), were each granted a small pension of eight hundred francs a year as Valois descendants. Recognition, however, brought with it expenditures beyond their incomes, and in 1779 Jeanne and her sister decided to return to their "ancestral acres" at Bar-sur-Aube, so as to make the most of their few francs and new status. Comte Beugnot, a bright young lawyer who would become Jeanne's lover,* describes the twenty-three-year-old adventuress at this time:

"She was not what one could strictly call a beauty. She was of average height, but svelte and well proportioned. She had expressive blue eyes under dark, well-arched brows. Her face was rather elongated, her mouth wide, her teeth splendid and, as so often with her type, her smile was enchanting. She had nice hands and tiny feet. Her complexion was exceptionally fair. As for her bosom, nature, beginning well, had capriciously arrested her work when only half done, leaving the beholder regretting the missing half."[36]

One might immediately note that another lover, Rétaux de Villette, would find Jeanne's bosom more than adequate, indeed, "all that men most admire: snow white, firm, nicely separated—peaks of perfection!"[37] And one might add that the story of Versailles, its lives and loves, reveals, if nothing else, that from Louise de la Vallière to Marie Antoinette and Madame de La Motte, Frenchmen, unlike Anglo-Saxons, frequently have no objection, if indeed they do not favor, small-breasted women who have spirit and "enchanting smiles." Such was sufficiently the case of Nicolas de La Motte, a cavalry officer, whom Jeanne met in Bar-sur-Aube and married, one month before she gave birth to shortly lived twins. As limited in means as his friend and fellow officer Rétaux de Villette, La Motte lived on credit, his officer's pittance, and a small sum from his uncle. But he now called himself "Comte" and Jeanne "Comtesse," and history has tended to drop the quotation marks. Rétaux soon shared their fortunes and Jeanne's bed ("I loved her to distraction"), eventually becoming the odd couple's personal secretary (he had a greater gift for penmanship than for the poetry to which he pretended). La Motte's commanding officer fell foolishly in love with La Motte's wife; La Motte resigned his commission and the La Mottes cast about for ways to increase their diminished incomes. (Their marriage, she would recall, proved "a union of drought with famine.")

Perhaps it was the Marquise de Boulainvilliers who introduced the Comtesse de La Motte to Cardinal-Prince Louis de Rohan at his château near Strasbourg. In any event, it was a fateful meeting, in Carlyle's phrase, of "these preappointed two." Jeanne also seems to

---

* And an important official under Napoleon, Louis XVIII, and Charles X.

M*

have met there "Count Cagliostro," the Italian mountebank who had fascinated and fastened himself to the Cardinal. The acquaintance deepened between the countess and the Cardinal (in his vulnerable fifties) in Paris, to which the La Mottes, and later Rétaux, removed, to be closer, one is tempted to write, to their prey. And in exchange for the Cardinal's favors, including thousands of francs from the King's alms, the countess, Rétaux de Villette tells us, gave the Cardinal hers.[38]

They soon had reason to hope each would give the other much more, creating the perfect situation for an almost perfect crime— or rather, the perfect confidence game. The countess initially hoped the Cardinal would help her suit for a larger pension at Court. In turn, the Cardinal urged her to go directly to the Queen, explaining his own difficulty there, and soon hoped the countess would be his advocate at the Queen's side.

Abbé Georgel: "In confessing, however, that he himself was unable to help the Comtesse secure an audience with Her Majesty, the Cardinal confided too much, going so far as to depict his consuming grief at having incurred the hostility of the Queen. Her enmity, he said, was the constant torment of even his brightest hours." In fact, the Queen's attitude and the Cardinal's reaction were well known to all at Court. But the abbé continues: "This unwise revelation to Madame de La Motte proved the spark for the most devastating scheme, an intrigue unequalled in the history of man's folly."[39]

The first step in the countess's scheme was to convince the Cardinal, who was all too willing to be gulled, that she had indeed reached the Queen and had even become her intimate. And if the Cardinal's gullibility seems too great for credibility (as it is for some chroniclers, thus their accusation of his complicity), one might point out that the countess' creditors, a more suspicious lot, were taken in by the same stories of intimacy she now proceeded to spread about. Access to the palace, as we have seen so often, could hardly have been more easily arranged, particularly for one of acknowledged Valois descent, whose husband, by this time, was among the officers of the Comte d'Artois' own bodyguards. Several times the two schemers staged fainting spells for Jeanne in the palace's anterooms, once in the Grande Galerie, through which the Queen was expected to pass. They did succeed in getting the King's pension raised for Jeanne from eight hundred to fifteen hundred francs, but familiarity with the Queen—as the La Mottes asserted to all who would listen, hinting at midnight dalliances at the Petit Trianon—was (beyond most doubt) never remotely achieved.

However, wanting to believe, the Cardinal believed, especially when Madame de La Motte began to show him notes to "dear Cousin Valois" from the Queen on gilt-edged Trianon stationery (penned by the versatile Villette). Nor, she told him, had she forgotten her good friend, the Cardinal, when talking to the Queen. She had been authorized, she said, to let him know that the Queen would graciously accept a letter of apology from him, explaining his previous, unaccountable behavior. (Why not, the countess obviously plotted, bait the trap with a convincing correspondence with the Queen—she and Rétaux replying to the Cardinal's letters?)

Abbé Georgel: "This news seemed to signal to the Cardinal the dawn of a new day." And soon the apology, "written in his own hand," was entrusted to the countess for the Queen. "A few days later she brought back a reply on small, gilt-edged notepaper, upon which Marie Antoinette, whose handwriting a clever forger had sought to imitate, had supposedly written: 'I have read your letter. I am pleased that I no longer need consider you guilty. I can not yet grant you the audience you ask for, but as soon as circumstances allow one, I shall let you know. Above all, be discreet.' These few words gave the Cardinal indescribable satisfaction. Thereafter, the Comtesse de La Motte appeared in his eyes like a guardian angel, opening the road to happiness. . . . Thus letters and replies rapidly succeeded one another."[40]

And led to the next step: a "letter from the Queen" requesting sixty thousand livres for charitable purposes, remitted, of course, through "dear Comtesse de La Motte-Valois." The money "received," a letter of thanks followed. So did a conspicuous rise in the living standard of the La Motte household, explained to the Cardinal as proof of the Queen's loving interest and bounty!

The countess presented further proof of her intimacy with the Queen. Frequently, she told the Cardinal, she had secret nocturnal rendezvous with Her Majesty at the Petit Trianon, and occasionally she would tell him of them in advance, so he might station himself in the gardens outside the gate and see for himself her comings and goings. (She had ingratiated herself with the concierge at the Trianon, who lent her a hand in the deception.)

Abbé Georgel: "One night, when she knew the Grand Almoner

was watching for her exit, she had Villette, her principal accomplice, escort her out of the Trianon gate and somewhat beyond, then turn back, as if to return to the palace. It was a bright moonlit night, the Prince, disguised, met Madame de La Motte as had been arranged and asked her the name of her escort. She told him it was Desclaux, the Queen's confidential *valet de chambre*."[41]

By this time Madame de La Motte was well entrenched in the clique of the Cardinal's confidants, among whom Cagliostro played oracle, predicting the highest office in France for the Cardinal, thanks to the newly won friendship of the Queen. The countess, in other words, "played them all for fools" (Georgel). And she managed 120,000 more livres from the Grand Almoner "for the Queen's charities," which again went no further than her own households in Paris and at Bar-sur-Aube.

In midsummer 1784 the countess staged a scene of such perfection it still has some French historians convinced—as Michelet, for example —that it could only have been achieved with the Queen's complicity. Involved was an impersonation à la Beaumarchais that would have delighted Marie Antoinette and have been completely in her manner.

As the *pièce de résistance*, Madame de La Motte had promised the overjoyed Cardinal a midnight rendezvous with the Queen herself. The site, to begin with, had to be credible. Accordingly she shrewdly chose the Bosquet de la Reine, the Queen's own grove, known also as the Grove of Venus, below the great staircase of the Orangerie. Here rumor—or fact—had Marie Antoinette habitually strolling in the early hours of the morning with one or the other of her favorites, though Madame Campan insists the Queen never left the upper terrace. She adds, however, in her memoirs, that "most probably it was these moonlight promenades which inspired the impersonation plot that would so delude the Cardinal de Rohan."[42] And months later in the Bastille, the Cardinal persisted to Abbé Georgel: "My eyes and ears could not thus have deceived me. It was the *Queen* whom I saw and to whom I spoke in the Versailles gardens!"[43]

The "Queen" the Cardinal saw was a professional lady of the streets, Mademoiselle d'Oliva, procured for the part by the Comte de La Motte and coached for her role by the countess. The Queen herself, Oliva was reassured, would be close by, in hiding, enjoying the harmless prank.

On the day of the scheduled rendezvous, August 11, 1784, Madame de La Motte personally dressed Mademoiselle d'Oliva in clothes similar to the Queen's—a white muslin gown and a wide-brimmed hat—and that night took her, together with husband La Motte, to the Grove of Venus in the Versailles park. She pressed a rose and a letter in her hand and gave her final instructions: "You are to hand this flower, along with the letter, to the great lord who will join you here, but you are to speak only these words, 'You know what this means!' Now, remember that the Queen is close by, watching and listening. She is over there, just behind us, not ten steps away."[44]

Meantime, the Prince de Rohan was making his way from the terrace in the dark night down to the darker shades of the Queen's Grove. Dimly he made out the familiar white muslin gown; moved, he dropped to his knees before it and kissed its hem. The disguised Oliva gave him the rose, delivered her one line, but in her nervousness forgot the letter. As the Cardinal stammered his thanks, murmuring eternal gratitude, he heard footsteps and an urgent whisper from Madame de La Motte: "Come away quickly, Madame and the Comtesse d'Artois are approaching!" The noises offstage were most likely Villette's and La Motte's. The Cardinal, delirious with joy (he would have a box specially made for the precious rose), hurried away as the Queen's impersonator was taken back to her lodgings.[45]

Henceforth Madame de La Motte, for the Cardinal, was beyond suspicion and all was set for the final dupery: his purchase, presumably for the Queen, of the famous diamond necklace.

Whether the countess had heard of the necklace and had asked to see it, or Böhmer, hearing of the Queen's new confidante, had asked to see *her,* we cannot be sure. But, as 1784 drew to a close, the Saxon jeweler, desperately in debt, found his way to the La Motte household on Rue Neuve St. Gilles. He opened a great leather case and Madame de La Motte found herself, she tells us, "gazing at that superb, unique necklace." If she succeeded where he had failed, in persuading the Queen to buy it, she would have, Böhmer said ingratiatingly, not only his undying appreciation, but a handsome commission. Was it instantly that the thought flashed in her mind of not merely pocketing the commission, but the necklace as well? No matter. Soon enough a bold scheme for snaring the Cardinal occurred to her: she would tell him that the Queen was heartsick at the idea that she might never possess the fabulous jewel and was now prepared to acquire it without the King's knowledge, plan-

ning to surprise him with it after paying for the necklace in in-
stallments out of her own purse. However, to assure secrecy, and
as a sign and proof of her confidence in him (Madame de La Motte
would add), Her Majesty would like His Eminence to arrange the
transaction with the jewelers *in his name.*

To set the final plot in motion, the countess first had Rétaux
de Villette forge a letter from the Queen informing the Cardinal that
she was about to entrust a secret matter to him, about which the
countess would speak to him. Queried, the countess told the Cardinal
of the "Queen's desire." She received the expected enthusiastic response
and advised Böhmer and Bassenge that shortly "a very great, and
a very rich, nobleman would look at their necklace and probably
buy it" (Georgel).

On January 24, 1785, the Cardinal called on Böhmer and Bassenge
in their deluxe showrooms on the Place Vendôme. On the twenty-ninth
he proposed the conditions for the purchase of the necklace, after receiving "a note from the Queen" approving the terms he had arranged:
an initial payment of 400,000 livres at the end of six months, three
additional payments of a similar sum at six-month intervals. The jewelers
signed the contract, but, on an impulse, the Cardinal hesitated. After all,
a huge sum was involved. Might there not be some indication of the
Queen's own commitment? Nothing could be simpler for the La Motte-
Villette combine. Back on a copy of the contract, in the Cardinal's own
hand, came the Queen's "Approved" in the margin and "Marie Antoinette of France" as the signature.

And here the chronicler must balk. The Queen never signed any
document other than by her given name, never adding "of France,"
since she was "of Austria." Strangely the Cardinal, who should have
known it (and admitted his carelessness afterward), did not observe
this obvious blunder. Nor did he seem to realize—any more than
the La Mottes—that had the Queen actually signed the contract,
even if only a copy for the Cardinal's keeping, she risked defeating
her own alleged purpose of secrecy in having him purchase the necklace *in his name,* thus avoiding the use of her own.* However,
everything conspired against the Cardinal's better judgment: his blind-
ing ambition, indisputable "proof" of the countess's intimacy with the
Queen, his own midnight rendezvous with Her Majesty, Cagliostro's

* This is one of the more contradictory elements in the diamond necklace
puzzle which seems to have escaped its historians.

prophecy by candlelight that his negotiation for the necklace would be crowned with success and win him the realm's supreme office.

On February 1, the jewelers delivered the diamond necklace to the Cardinal, and they too were strangely oblivious to the error in the Queen's "signature," when he showed them, in violation of the Queen's "desired secrecy," his copy of the contract. That evening, the necklace was taken to the countess's apartment, where, in the words of Abbé Georgel, she had prepared "a veritable stage and performance."

Abbé Georgel: "The Cardinal, at the prearranged hour, made his way at twilight on February 1 to Madame de La Motte's, followed by his confidential *valet de chambre,* who carried the leather jewel case. Arriving at the door, the Cardinal dismissed his valet. Alone, the leather case in his hands, he entered with the trusting faith of a sacrificial lamb.

"The setting consisted of a room with an alcove, which contained a small cabinet behind a glass-paneled door. The talented *comédienne* showed her spectator to a seat in the cabinet.

"All is obscured by the half-light of a tiny lamp. A door opens. A voice cries out:

"'In the name of the Queen!'

"Madame de La Motte advances respectfully, takes the jewel case from the Cardinal's hands and tenders it to 'Her Majesty's messenger.'

"And thus was the necklace transferred.

"The Prince, the mute and hidden spectator, thought he recognized the messenger. Madame de La Motte 'confirmed' that it was the Queen's confidential valet at the Trianon [whom he had seen one moonlit night]. He had a similar stature and wore the Queen's livery."[46]

A few days later two jewelers reported to the Paris police that a certain Rétaux de Villette had approached them with several diamonds at a suspiciously low price. Brought in for questioning, Villette invoked the name of the King's own cousin, the Comtesse de La Motte-Valois, as having commissioned him to sell them for her—and the investigation was dropped. Madame de La Motte, taking warning, sent off her husband with the bulk of the jewels from the now broken-up necklace, to London and its merchants. She reserved only a few for her own use, in new settings, as bracelets, earrings, and rings. Why did she not simply take flight with him and enjoy her fortune in safety abroad? She seems to have thought she might have her cake and eat it, quite safely in Bar-sur-Aube, queening it, as it were, in the very place she had spent an impoverished youth. Rich and successful, one does not return to the scene of one's crimes so much as to the site of one's previous humiliations. And she returned with two dozen cartloads of fine furniture, with liveried servants and splendid carriages, paid by means of the letters of credit brought back from London by her husband. *Should* anything go amiss, she counted on the Cardinal's preferring to pay for the necklace *sub rosa* rather than expose himself as the century's greatest dupe.*

The grand intriguer did not count on Böhmer and Bassenge going, in their great concern, directly to the Queen.

The concern, in fact, was first motivated by the Cardinal. As the days passed and became months and the Queen, when she appeared, failed to wear the necklace, doubt began to assail him. It became critical as August 1, the day specified for the initial payment by the Queen, approached. Anxiously, he asked Madame de La Motte for an explanation. She replied that the Queen, on second thought, considered the price too high, had a little problem raising the 400,000 livres and wondered if the Cardinal would not gratify her by borrowing the sum for her. Rohan sought the loan from a banker named Saint-James, who, more skeptical than he about the Queen's engagement, hesitated. Rohan then went to the jewelers, saying the Queen desired more favorable terms, would they reconsider them? Agreement was reached, presumably with the Queen's approval, and it was at this point that the grateful jewelers wrote Her Majesty "of their infinite satisfaction in the thought that the most beautiful diamond jewelry in the world will serve the greatest and the best of Queens." It was that "enigmatic message" which the Queen had carelessly held to a candle, leading to the frenzy of Böhmer and Bassenge when they received no reply.

Disregarding the advice of Madame de La Motte that they deal *only* with the Cardinal, who could pay them, if there were any problem, from his own vast revenues, Böhmer went finally to the Queen, as we have seen, exposing the diamond plot with the result that now the Cardinal and the countess were in the Bastille.

Meanwhile Marie Antoinette went on with her last rehearsals for

---

* Cardinal de Rohan, in a statement to a royal commission: "She relied on the fact that she had implicated me so deeply that I would never dare speak out. And she was right. I would not have. I would have preferred to pay for the necklace and keep silent . . . while she enjoyed her ill-gotten gains. . . ."[47]

Le Barbier de Séville in her little theater at the Petit Trianon, though the curtain had begun to fall on her little world.

Had the Cardinal prince possessed half as much common sense as vanity, had Louis XVI been more of a king and less of a husband, had Vergennes, rather than Breteuil, had his way, the diamond necklace *affaire* might have been adjudicated behind closed doors, the jewelers discreetly paid by a chastised Cardinal, Madame de La Motte exiled or imprisoned with a *lettre de cachet,* and a scandal that eventually cost the Queen more than a crown might have been avoided. But Marie Antoinette, stung by the abuse she received in public, was resolved, as she wrote her brother, "to clarify the whole wretched business [and clear her name] before the eyes of the entire world."[48] She who had scorned public opinion would now appeal to it—a dangerous precedent—and foolishly the King agreed. He gave the Cardinal the choice between throwing himself upon the mercy of the Crown or presenting himself before the judges of the Paris Parlement. Consulting his family and cousins, the Cardinal chose Parlement, *already in conflict with the Crown.*

What a spectacle it would prove for the people: the country's noblest clergyman, an adventuress, countess and Valois, the Queen of France herself, involved in a great diamond conspiracy! Surely there was already too much smoke for there to be no fire. The trial itself confirmed the stories, libels and slanders about a loose-moraled, licentious Queen and Court. Even Count von Fersen did not believe Marie Antoinette completely innocent, and one can easily imagine what others, less charitably inclined, were saying, if *he* could write his King, as on September 9, 1785: "The tales about the Cardinal, especially in the provinces, are fantastic. Most people seem to think that the necklace transaction and the forgery of the Queen's name are not the real reasons for his imprisonment; instead they attribute it to secret political motives, which is certainly not the case.

"In Paris the most popular theory is that it was all an intrigue between the Queen and the Cardinal; that she pretended to dislike him, the better to conceal their little game; that actually he was very much in her good graces and that she did commission him to arrange the necklace purchase for her; that the King finally heard about it and made a scene, whereupon she feigned to faint away, claiming the excuse of pregnancy. . . ."[49] (Fersen was unshocked; it was not a sentimental age.)

The Cardinal's powerful kinsmen—Rohan, Condé, Soubise, Marsan —took as a personal rebuke the palace arrest of one of their own. The clergy, high and low, cried aloud to Rome of its outrage. The King's brothers did not conceal their delight and "Mesdames, his aunts, criticized the King, their nephew" (Madame Campan), as the people reveled in the disclosure of Versailles' discomforts.

Every major capital in Europe dispatched correspondents to Paris, for not only a cardinal, but a French queen, if not the French monarchy, was on open trial. And the opposition that was forming, including the King's own brothers, would discover, to its astonishment, in the denouement of the diamond necklace trial, its own growing strength.

Speeches and pleas for the defense, in the peculiar practice of the time, were published and snapped up as soon as they appeared; couriers raced them by diplomatic pouch to the insatiable of Europe's courts. The Cardinal, absolving the Queen, accused the countess of the entire conspiracy; the countess, absolving the Queen, accused the Cardinal of *his* duplicity; and all were convinced of a royal cover-up, which further infuriated Marie Antoinette's enemies and, paradoxically, further implicated her in the public's eye. The Cardinal and Cagliostro, said the countess, had used her to acquire the diamonds for themselves. What could be more absurd, she cried, than that a Cardinal-Prince de Rohan should look to her, an obscure countess who had never even been presented at Court, to intercede for him with the Queen? That he, the King's own grand almoner, should ask her, a lowly countess, to arrange a midnight rendezvous with Her Majesty, his own sovereign! True, she lived in luxury, but that was easily explained: the Cardinal knew how to take care of his mistresses. And "the tide of public opinion flowed strongly in Madame de La Motte's direction" (Abbé Georgel), until the arrest and confessions of Mademoiselle d'Oliva and Rétaux de Villette (picked up in Geneva) redirected it in the Cardinal's favor.* Dramatically, accused confronted accused, denunciation followed denunciation as Madame de La Motte and Villette fell out, until finally, on May 31, 1786, sixty-two magistrates of the Paris Parlement prepared to render their judgment.

Public curiosity, as Count Mercy reported to Vienna, was "at a

---

* Monsieur de La Motte, throughout the trial, had remained in hiding in London, where he had fled on his wife's arrest.

fever pitch." Tens of thousands crowded the great square outside the Palais de Justice and spilled across the Seine to the Right Bank. Mounted guards patrolled the square, neighboring bridges and streets. Inside the Palais, packed, buzzing galeries looked down on the proceedings in the Grand' Chambre, while below nineteen members of the Rohan, Soubise, Guéménée and Lorraine houses, dressed in mourning black, were formidably ranged in the first two rows, silently reminding Parlement's judges of where their own interests lay.

For more than a week the magistrates had listened to the long reading of the investigatory transcripts and had heard the accused make their final defense pleas. Meticulously gowned, Madame de La Motte had sat on the *sellette* (stool) before them, as composed as if she were on a *bergère* in her own comfortable salon. Where, she had asked, were the letters, the written evidence against her? They had never been produced, she replied with effect. As soon as she had left the Grand' Chambre, the *sellette* had been removed and the Cardinal Prince de Rohan brought and bowed into an armchair. Dressed in robes of deep violet, the blue ribbon of the Royal Order of the Holy Ghost across his chest, a bishop's cross hanging from a golden chain around his neck, he had declaimed that his only guilt was his overwhelming desire to regain the good graces of Her Majesty, his Queen. Mademoiselle d'Oliva had followed the Cardinal after a brief delay. Her dress touchingly disheveled, she explained that she had been nursing her newborn child, charming judges and spectators. Then a gold-embroidered Cagliostro had testified, protesting that he was a noble but innocent voyager, healer of those wounded by slander, and, smiling wanly, the judges dismissed him.

And now they sat, on May 31, to render their final judgments. The King, they had been warned by the prosecutor, demanded at least a public apology by the Cardinal for the "criminal presumption" that Her Majesty would accord him a secret rendezvous. The Queen—in other words—must be kept sacredly unsubject to any court's inquiry or jurisdiction: the Cardinal acquitted, Marie Antoinette's own trial, seven and a half years hence, in the same Palais de Justice, would have its precedent.

After a passionate eighteen-hour session, by the vote of a narrow majority, the Cardinal Prince de Rohan was acquitted of *all* charges against him.

It was their last judgment. Cagliostro had previously been totally ex-
onerated, Oliva lightly spanked with a reprimand for having dared im-
personate the Queen, and Rétaux de Villette banished for life from the
kingdom of France. Only the La Mottes in a sense paid the price of the
diamond necklace affair,* and even then not in full. Monsieur de La
Motte was sentenced *in absentia* to the galleys for life, but never served
a fraction of his sentence. Madame de La Motte was condemned to be
flogged, branded, and imprisoned in the Salpêtrière for the rest of her
days (and we shall soon see what happened to *her*).

But to write "only the La Mottes paid the price" is to forget
Marie Antoinette, even for the moment.

Madame Campan: "As soon as I heard the verdict, I went to the
Queen. I found her alone and weeping in her study.

"'Come,' she said to me, 'cry with your sovereign, who has been
so grievously insulted and victimized by cabals and injustice. The
schemer whose aim was to destroy me, to get his clutches on some
golden coin by abusing my name and forging my signature, has just
been acquitted without even a reprimand!'"[51]

And the King came, too, to offer his condolences, though he was
equally in line to receive them:

When the sentences were announced from the steps of the Palais
de Justice, *"Vive le cardinal!"* rang from the crowd, a cry echoed
from the masses on the Right Bank. There was no customary *"Vive le
Roi!"*

"The members of Parlement, as they leave the hall," says Cagliostro
in the historic present of his memoirs, "are surrounded by jubilant
crowds who applaud them, press their hands, strew their path with
flowers. A universal rejoicing resounds through the corridors of the
Palais de Justice, out and into the streets of Paris. The Cardinal,
clad in the Roman purple, is released in response to the vociferous
demands of the populace and is escorted by them to the gates of his
Palais-Cardinal [in fact, to the Bastille, for his last night]. They share
his triumph as they shared his tribulations." And Cagliostro, when he
reached his own home after being released at midnight, discovered

---

* It was the Cardinal, however, who undertook payments to the jewelers for
the missing necklace (some of whose stones are still being worn by two
noblewomen of England) until his death. Afterward, the Rohans claim, they
made the final payments by the end of the nineteenth century as a matter of
family honor.[50]

thousands there (he says), waiting to carry him from his carriage "into the very arms of my wife."[52]

With a *lettre de cachet,* Louis XVI banished the Cardinal, stripped of his office as grand almoner, to his Abbey of La Chaise-Dieu; with another, he banished Cagliostro from France. But unlike Louis XIV, he did not dare disband Parlement for its lese majesty. And that, too, was noted.

And Madame de La Motte?

At dawn on June 19, she was dragged screaming and kicking to a scaffold in the courtyard of the Palais de Justice. A great crowd looked on: people stood on roofs, filled every window space. She was heard crying obscenities against the Cardinal and Parlement, but when she began to include the Queen, "she was gagged" (Georgel). She struggled between her executioners and in her struggles, instead of just her shoulder, her breast was bared, and a V for *voleuse* (*thief,* though some would say it was for Valois) was burned into it. She writhed, she fainted, unconscious she was carried to the Salpêtrière prison—and public sympathy swiftly turned to flow once more in her direction.

Parlement now joined the Queen in unpopularity for its imprisonment of Madame de La Motte. It became fashionable to visit the "poor martyred countess," as did even the Princesse de Lamballe. The Duchesse d'Orléans organized a collection for her benefit; more importantly, the Duc d'Orléans (most likely) organized her escape. From London she could serve his purposes by "exposing" the Queen's part in the diamond necklace scandal. And a series of *mémoires,* signed by the Comtesse de La Motte-Valois, were published, accusing Marie Antoinette of having ordered and received the necklace from the Cardinal, of having sacrificed her "cousin" on the altar of Parlement, despite their more than intimate relationship, not to speak (as La Motte did) of the Queen's "love affair," as Dauphine, with the Prince de Rohan. Thus was launched the period of the most scabrous pamphlets about the "secret life," the *"fureurs utérines,"* of the French Queen.[53]

Madame de La Motte had escaped. Marie Antoinette had not.

"With the end of the diamond necklace trial," writes Madame Campan sadly, "the fortune-laden years of the Queen's life came to an end. Farewell forever to those peaceful days at the Trianon, to the gay fêtes glittering with the splendor, the sparkling wit, the exquisite taste of the French Court. Farewell above all to respect and reverence for the throne."[54]

ACT THREE

24. The Curtain Also Rises

"Pause, if you please," wrote Michelet, "and regard this miserable people huddled on the earth, this Job," who would rise in wrath and put an end to the *ancien régime*.[1]

"The French bourgeoisie," counters Jean Jaurès, most respected of French Socialists, "had become conscious of its strength, its wealth, its rights, its vast potential for expansion. . . . It is not from the depths of misery that the Revolution rose."[2]

It was generations in the making, says Tocqueville, "this Revolution which abolished those political institutions which we commonly call feudal," yet it came with violence and was "completely unforeseen."[3]

Strange. It was so visible. And it was more than once foretold.

For instance, the Marquis d'Argenson, in December 1751: "A philosophic breeze of freedom and anti-monarchical sentiment is blowing. It affects the mind and we know how opinion governs the world. Perhaps this form of government has already taken shape in minds, to be implemented at the first opportunity. Perhaps the revolution will be made with less opposition than one expects. There would be no need for a prince and no enthusiasm for religion. All the Orders [Estates] are dissatisfied. The military, dismissed directly the war was over, is treated with harshness and injustice, the clergy reviled and mocked, the Parlements and other corporations, the provinces, the common people overburdened and wretched, the financiers triumphant. All this is inflammable material. A riot can easily turn into a revolt and the revolt into a revolution in which real tribunes of the people would be chosen, and committees and communes, and where the King and the Ministers would be deprived of their undue power to do harm."[4]

And a year or so later: "The race of great lords must be destroyed completely. By great lords I understand those who have dignities, property, tithes, offices and functions, and who, without deserts and without necessarily being adults, are none the less great, and for this reason often worthless."[5]

Arthur Young, in 1788: "Nantes is *enflammé* in the cause of liberty, as any town in France can be. . . . The American revolution has laid the foundation of another* in France, if the government does not take care of itself." Since 1787 the English agronomist had been traveling in France, noting its miseries, listening to its discontents. In Paris he heard people openly discussing the imminence of the Crown's bankruptcy, resulting civil war and overthrowal of the government. Near Payrac, he met "many beggars. . . . All the country, girls and women, are without shoes or stockings, and the ploughmen at their work have neither sabots nor feet to their stockings. This is a poverty that strikes at the root of national prosperity. . . .† It reminded me of the misery of Ireland."[6]

Almost everywhere, Arthur Young met the visible, explosive force at the base of France's pyramid and the bourgeoisie that would guide that force. For the French middle class knew what it was about.

Joseph Barnave, lawyer, product of the industrial life of the Dauphiné province, future deputy and orator of the Third Estate, wrote fifty-six years before Marx: "The rule of the aristocracy lasts so long as the people of agriculture continue to be ignorant and unskilled and land wealth to be the only wealth. . . . As soon as trade and skills become more common and create a new form of wealth for the laboring [i.e., middle] class, a political revolution is inevitable: *a new distribution of wealth leads to a new distribution of power.* As the ownership of land has elevated the aristocracy, so the ownership of industries raises the people [i.e., the bourgeoisie], and they win *their* freedom." (Emphasis mine.[7])

"Thus," says Jaurès of Barnave's insights, "the revolutionary

* And of a vastly different kind.
† It was the poverty *within the prosperity* that was most striking, and though sometimes put on by peasants—and others—to put off the tax collector, it was profoundly real.

bourgeoisie had an admirably realistic and penetrating sense of its force, of the economic and historic movement it represented."[8]

But in the meantime the curtain is still rising, the Bastille is yet to fall and the Estates General to be convoked, as royalty's last resort.

First of the three estates was the Church. Second was the nobility. The Third was virtually everybody else, as "the most famous and powerful pamphlet in all history"[9]—*Qu'est-ce que le Tiers état?*, by the remarkable Abbé Emmanuel-Joseph Sieyès—was boldly to proclaim in January 1789.

"The plan of this pamphlet," it begins, "is simplicity itself. We have three questions to ask ourselves:

"1. What is the Third Estate? (*Qu'est-ce que le Tiers état?*) Everything.

"2. What has it been, until now, in the political order? Nothing.

"3. What does it ask? To become something."[10]

More than twenty-five million of France's twenty-six million souls, Sieyès continues, belong to the Third Estate. It is thus no less than the nation itself.

In effect, the First and Second Estates formed a single privileged caste. In 1789, the eighteen archbishops, 118 bishops, 8000 canons, and several thousand of the monks and nuns of the greater abbeys were *all* nobility. In 1730, under Louis XV, half of the bishops were of bourgeois origin (as Bossuet, for instance, in the time of Louis XIV). Under the Sun King, nobles of ancient lineage were never ministers; under Louis XV and Louis XVI, they were; in 1789, *all* ministers were of noble families. An edict of 1781 limited officers' ranks to those who could prove a background of four noble grandparents.[11] In the face of an economically rising bourgeoisie, the nobles had recaptured and closed off the commanding societal heights; friction, resentment, and a final conflict between the privileged and the otherwise powerful were clearly pursuing their now classical course.

Meanwhile, the seigneurs were suddenly reasserting the oldest feudal rights in a moment of economic crisis, bad crops, and general hardship. They were the lords of the land—nobles, high clergymen, the King's own—and of the *métayers,* the sharecroppers, who toiled for them. Less than 2 per cent of the population,[12] they possessed well over half of the arable land. Peasant proprietors divided what remained in such small holdings they ordinarily had to hire themselves out as laborers on larger estates. And even their little plots—"no land without a seigneur"[13]—were subject to feudal strictures.

Some of the peasant farms, Arthur Young observed, were so tiny they held a single fruit tree, and others, several chestnuts "yielding the food of the poor." But the smallest parcel was all the more precious. "Give a man the secure possession of a bleak rock," the English traveler also observed, "and he will turn it into a garden."[14]

But the possession was not that secure and it was the peasant as small landowner who found feudalism most onerous, and for whom Church and *seigneurie* were synonymous. Tocqueville: "The Church inspired such furious hatred, not because its clergy claimed to arrange the affairs of the beyond, but because they were landowners, seigneurs, collectors of tithes, administrators in this world; not because the Church could not find a place in the world about to be made, but because it occupied the most privileged, the most powerful place in the old society about to be reduced to powder."[15]

It was the Church as a pillar of the feudal system that would suffer from the peasants it exploited and the merchants it obstructed. Credit, the lifeblood of trade, it regarded as usurious, and the life of a tradesman, forbidden French noblemen,* unlike the English practice, it loftily scorned. Exempt from taxation, the Church *granted* perhaps twelve million livres a year to the Crown, but collected ten times that much in tithes, most of which left the parish. Its wealth has been estimated at four billion livres, three billions of it in land.[16] When Louis XVI freed the serfs on lands belonging to the Crown, many of the richest abbeys refused to follow.

By 1789, 95 per cent of the peasants had ceased to be serfs (the remainder were mostly on Church land).[17] They had either bought their freedom or fled their servitude. But they were still not free from the grinding anachronisms of the feudal system, confusedly varying from region to region. Though the *corvée* might be waived for a payment in most of France, in many places the peasant did three or more days of forced labor on roads, bridges, and waterways every year for seigneurial benefit. Wolves still roamed the countryside, killing the peasant's few sheep; wild animals came in from the woods to destroy up to one tenth of his crops. But he could not own a gun or shoot them, even on his own land: they were game reserved for the nobleman's

---

* But they could, and did, enter more "noble" trades, such as shipbuilding, mining, chemical industries, and overseas trade.

sport, and the seigneur rode freely across the peasant's fields and over his harvests. The King spent more feeding the wild boar and deer he would hunt near Versailles than he did for the poor in the entire Paris region.[18]*

Where the peasant had grazed his cow on common ground, increasingly he found the seigneur's newly fenced-off enclosure. Had he some wheat to grind, he had to pay for it in the seigneur's mill and might take it to no other, though closer or cheaper. So with the lord's bake ovens and wine presses—and only the lord, for a payment, might allow him to fish on the ponds or in the streams. He paid a fee for selling his small produce at the market place prescribed for him; he paid a fee at river crossings; he paid a fee for marriage, baptism, and burial; he paid a fee for the few possessions he left his family. There was the tithe to the Church (even for Protestants)[20] and taxes to the State we might recall: the *taille,* the *vingtième,* or twentieth, the *aides,* or excise taxes on such items as wine and soap, the *gabelle,* or forced purchase of overpriced government salt, and assessments by the tax farmers (collecting at a great profit on sums advanced to the government).

And these were taxes and assessments, the people well knew, largely unpaid or entirely avoided by the privileged, because, though rich, they were too powerful! It was easier for the Crown, when hard pressed, to demand more of commoners by way of an increased *taille* than to impose new taxes or collect old ones from the Church and the nobility.[21] As a consequence, members of the Third Estate had barely half their income left after tithes and taxes,[22] the peasants, who bulked largest among them, barely half their production.[23] A contemporary cartoon of a peasant bearing a nobleman and a clergyman on his back was, in truth, painful fact. And Necker, writing on the importance of religious attitudes in times of crisis, made this point: "The deeper taxation drives people into dejection and misery the more indispensable is the religious education they receive."[24] But no other instruction: it was preferable—"necessitous," said Necker—that the people be kept ignorant.[25] Illiteracy among workers and peasants, however, did not mean blindness or stupidity, as the privileged often ignorantly, and fatally, believed.

But it is needless in our time to belabor the facts of feudal life,

* "What a country," cried a pamphlet early in 1789, "that takes better care of its wild game than of its people!"[19]

except to revive a sense of the period's outrage and the people's accumulating wrath. Indeed, we have touched on the same ground in an opening chapter, though it was a century and a half earlier, and an age had passed: it was no longer one of resignation, and new forces, a new class, had come into play.

It is the humiliation and restraints placed on the bourgeoisie which call for emphasis, because relatively so unfamiliar. Not simply such cumbersome problems as some forty tolls to be paid the government or the local seigneur for a boat carrying cargo from Southern France to Paris,[26] or even the galling slights and insolences of a parasitical nobility, degrading or unforgettable as they were.* There was even worse. Witness the almost incredible testimony of Pierre Dupont† de Nemours, the respected physiocrat and bourgeois who eventually moved with his family to America. It is recorded in the *cahier de doléances* (grievance book) drawn up by Dupont in his capacity as elector of the Third Estate of Nemours, in preparation for the historic meeting of the Estates General in spring 1789 (which will have our full attention). He writes of Nemours' leather industry, particularly the taxation to which leather was subject: "15 percent of the total value of the product or over 50 percent of the profit." *That* Dupont finds exorbitant enough, but he protests the arbitrary system of establishing the value of the product on the basis of its measurements and the inhuman penalty for those accused of fraud. Leather, he points out, "shrinks with dryness and expands with humidity, thus no measurement stamped on the product may be accurate after a few months and unintentional 'fraud' may be too easily accused the manufacturer." Nevertheless, he continues, the penalty is such that it means "the galleys for men and the public whip for their wives and daughters! As if these innocents could go against their father's or husband's will or could denounce their husbands or fathers without betraying all the virtues of their sex! What legislation is it that would create such victims or fiscal spies in a man's own home!" Moreoever, Dupont effectively adds, even the government's records establish "the decline by half in the production of leather in the twenty-nine years since such legislation has been enforced."[27]

---

* The youthful Barnave would never forget—or forgive—the removal of his mother from a seat at the theater of Grenoble, so that a "gentleman of quality" might sit down.
† Sometimes spelled Du Pont.

Thus to provoke the productive class of the kingdom, to threaten its men, in the Age of Enlightenment, with the galleys and their wives with the whip, was a monarchical madness attesting to the intolerable medievalism persisting in the French order. And this at a time when the industrial revolution (one might repeat, *revolution*) was at last beginning to take place in France. The spinning jenny had crossed the Channel, textile factories were springing up in Lyons, Rouen, Mulhouse, Troyes. Coke furnaces were going up in Lorraine, remarkably efficient mines were going into the ground, and in 1789 thirty-eight soap factories or workshops could be counted in Marseilles alone.[28] Shipbuilding and the traffic of slaves flourished at Nantes; the freedom its rich merchants would soon demand would be . . . *for their slave trade*. Overseas commerce was booming. Paris was becoming a great complex of industries—tanning, textile, furniture, building, and politics—with a population of six hundred thousand, of whom three hundred thousand were workers, artisans, and shopkeepers. Work began *before* dawn and lasted after dusk with wages varying from ten sous a day for a woman or child (the day's bread for the average family cost fifteen sous) to 40 to 50 sous a day for a skilled male. Workers' unions were considered a conspiracy against society and punished as a crime.[29]

The population of France had expanded from about nineteen millions at the beginning of the eighteenth century to about twenty-six millions on the eve of the Revolution; and those who had survived birth might now expect to live to the age of twenty-nine instead of twenty-one. Those who had passed their first birthday might reach their forty-fifth. England, among a few other countries, had done better, but France was still the most populated of Europe, offering the greatest number of consumers (and, in a crisis, of unemployed).[30] So production rose and with it prices—an average of 65 per cent from 1726 to 1789—especially of bread—reaching a high of 150 per cent in July of 1789. Profits doubled, wages did not: they rose by 22 per cent, and bread alone, in Paris, now took over 80 per cent of the workers' wages. Firewood rose 91 per cent, wine 14 per cent, thus winegrowers, the most powerful group among the agricultural, were doubly struck by the low prices of what they sold and the high prices of what they bought.[31]

In short, the eighteenth was a century of prosperity—in customary terms of production and profit—with intermittent then suddenly terminal crises. And with a background of shattering contrasts. As an

Italian diplomat wrote home, 90 per cent of the French population was dying of hunger, 10 per cent of indigestion.[32] His percentages may have been too generous. Witness Chamfort, the lapidary critic of the age, writing to a lordly gentleman of Louis XVI's Court, on December 15, 1788: "What is it really all about? The case of 24 million men versus 700,000 of the privileged. . . . Can't you see that an order of such monstrosity must be changed, or we will all, clergy, nobility and Third Estate, perish together?"[33]

After fifty years of the greatest rise in production and expectations, there was an abrupt slowing down. During fifteen years of Louis XVI's reign, just about everything that could happen to a country happened in France: droughts, floods, too little wheat, too much wine, the decimation by disease of farm stock, the draining of the treasury by mismanagement and the American war, idled industries, unemployment—all peaking in the years 1788 and 1789, with the price of bread significantly at its height on the day the Bastille fell.

The sequence of the last ten years indicates the crescendo of economic tension. In 1778 and 1785, droughts that brought an abundant grape harvest and a decline in the price of wine led to bad wheat crops, the death of sheep and cattle, and sharp rises in the price of bread and meat. Consumption shrank, industries suffered, factories closed. In 1786, Finance Minister Calonne, inopportunely yielding to the physiocratic thesis that agriculture was all, concluded the Eden-Rayneval accord with Britain, exchanging French grain and wine against British cloth and hardware. Result: some alleviation for winegrowers but a sharper rise in the price of bread and the number of industrially unemployed. In 1787 there were floods; in 1788 drought, hail, and destructive thunderstorms; that is, two years of disastrous harvests. The winter of 1788–89 recalled the great freeze of 1709 in its intensity: rivers were icebound, boats and mill wheels blocked. There were grain riots, growing, roving bands of the hungry and desperate, pillaging by the unemployed.[34]

And these were the years the Crown, Church, and seigneur, because of their straitened circumstances, demanded the most of peasants and merchants, experiencing their own hardest times—after a half century of comparatively freer expansion and well-being. Never did the feudal system seem more unbearable or a more explosive social mixture await the occasion of a spark.

Were the French privileged too blind, too callously accustomed to the calamity of others, too cynical or fatalistic, to see or attempt to modify their own fate? They were not unique in Europe, and there is still something disturbingly contemporary in the attitude described by Gouverneur Morris in his diary. Conservative, rather pro-monarchy, the American had landed at Le Havre in January 1789 as an agent for American tobacco interests, and was shortly writing: "Not long since I saw a [French] gentleman of my acquaintance weep at an air of an opera, who had heard a beggar clatter his crutches in pursuit of him for the length of a street without turning round to look at him." And Morris adds: " 'Tis true there is a difference in the music."[35]

And we might add that there were four million beggars in France in 1789[36] and a hundred thousand families in terrible need in Paris,[37] whose members would shortly be clattering pikes, rather than crutches, in similar streets in pursuit of similar French gentlemen.

There were many warnings, but they were disregarded. There were even explosions, but they were contained—and if for a time, why not forever?

There were food riots in Rouen, Reims, Poitiers, Dijon, Versailles, and Paris; again and again in Paris in 1788 and 1789. And briefly in 1768 rioters had taken over Rouen. It was too much, too soon—but not for too long.

"Take care," Mirabeau would warn the nobility, "do not despise those who produce everything, those who to prove their power have but to remain immobile."[38]

In 1774, in the region of Lyons, forty thousand workers quit their machines at Saint-Etienne. In Lyons itself the strike movement was followed by more thousands of silk workers. Confidently the factory owners waited for hunger to drive them back. Instead, many took their families and left Lyons for Switzerland and Italy. They were met at the borders by armed troops, and forcibly returned. They had not even the right to work for other French manufacturers in other French towns. They rose in revolt and seized municipal power in Lyons. For days they were the masters of the city, obliging owner after owner to sign contracts incorporating such innovations as sick benefits and pay for the injured. But the owners were biding their time until the troops had come. Then workers were beaten, contracts were broken, two leaders were hung, work was resumed. The wrath of the workers was now turned against the government, and in the clash between middle class and King fifteen years later, it would be used by the middle class to good account.

But in 1786, three years before *that* clash, the silk workers struck again, and new leaders drew up new demands. "The worker," their statement read, "can not live on the wages of a forced [*sic*] eighteen hours of work a day." Further: "When silk workers are regarded as nothing more than machines for the making of silk, inhumanly reduced to indifferent abstractions, they are not even treated as well as domestic animals. For even these are given enough to live on to produce."[39]

The silk strike extended to other industries and became generalized in Lyons. The hatmakers demanded an increase of eight sous for their twelve-hour day, the stoneworkers demanded wages more often than every three or four months. En masse, the striking workers withdrew from Lyons to nearby Charpennes, refusing to return until all were satisfied. The city authorities gave way on increases in wages, ordered work resumed, forbade any assembly of more than *three* workers, and called on a battalion of royal artillery (one of whose officers was a young lieutenant named Bonaparte). The workers were fired upon, many killed, three hung, and the rest rounded up and herded back to their machines.

These were not the proletariat of our time, Jaurès points out. Their leaders were usually master-workers, or even small entrepreneurs, frequently working at home, often with their own tools, and in constant if clandestine contact with each other. The scene at Lyons, he continues, was significant and prophetic, but generally both workers and owners were in conflict with the regime and the feudal order. Their own clash would be reserved for a later century, when power, troops, State, and government would belong to the bourgeoisie.

In the eighteenth century, it was the *peasant* who was the alienated, isolated, illiterate, and humiliated man, subject to the indignities and injustices of those who cannot even read the rights they sign away with a cross instead of their names. They were the nonpersons of their time. In view of the foot soldier's lot, for instance, it was considered "too cruel to conscript any but those of the lowest class"— that is, the peasant, "who was also constantly subject to arrest for some infraction of the *corvée* or service in the militia, for begging, police offenses and a thousand other petty infractions."[40]

People, even for the *philosophes,* began with the bourgeois. Voltaire grandly advocated education of "the people," but for his estate at

Ferney, he wanted "ignoramuses to drive and harness my ploughs."[41] When one thus describes at least 80 per cent of one's country, and adds 18 per cent more of working- and middle-class discontent, one is describing the slumbering volcano which was France.

For the times had ripened. Discontent was everywhere. The conjuncture of economic crises, famine and Enlightenment, explosive forces, knowledgeable leaders, and a floundering ruling class (Lenin's conditions for a revolutionary situation) could have only one outcome.

But it was still to be played out.

"Through what crevice," as Carlyle asks, "will the main explosion carry itself?"[42]

25. The Calling of the Clan

Heavy with child—she was eight months' pregnant—and the weight of the necklace judgment, Marie Antoinette wept for two days, then dried her eyes and "tranquilly" resumed, for all the world, playing milkmaid by proxy in her far corner of the Versailles gardens.[1]

Eighteen days after exiling the Cardinal de Rohan to *his* refuge, the far from uncomfortable Abbey of La Chaise-Dieu, Louis XVI went on an unaccustomed trip to the renovated, newly fortified port of Cherbourg, for a "bath" (as the French say) "in the *foule*"—the popular mass. He badly needed it, and happily he wrote back to Marie Antoinette that he was hearing that rare cry, *"Vive le Roi! Long live the King!"* (to which he replied, *"Vive mon peuple! Long live my people!"*)[2] "You will be pleased with me, I hope," he wrote in one of his daily letters, "because I don't believe I raised my voice against anyone even once."[3] And "graciously," as he awaited a change of horses at Houdan, he allowed a peasant woman to "embrace" him.[4]

But as Louis wended homeward a week later, the rare cry of *"Vive le Roi!"* became rarer. "I note," he sighed, "that I am approaching Versailles."[5]

On July 9, 1786, a second princess was born to Louis and Marie Antoinette, named Sophie, and buried eleven months later. The Dauphin, too, was sickly and rickety, but her second son, Marie Antoinette wrote brother Joseph II defiantly, was a "real peasant's child."[6] She herself, a Court page would recall, was walking with a kind of "defensive dignity."[7] The pastoral Hamlet adjacent to the Petit Trianon was now more retreat than play-acting, though one was obviously part of the other. The slim waist had thickened[8] as the abundant hair had thinned, and Marie Antoinette, when she had turned thirty, had told Mademoiselle Bertin she would no longer wear feathers or flowers.[9]

But the expenditures had continued, the passion for jewelry (was it compensation?) had remained unabated, and Calonne, the finance minister, generally pandered to all the Queen's requests.* A year before the necklace *affaire,* six million livres were found for the purchase of the palace at Saint-Cloud from the Duc d'Orléans, as a gift from Louis to Marie Antoinette. The scandalized public called her "Madame Déficit." In the Paris Parlement, Duval d'Eprémesnil cried, "It is immoral, and bad policy, for French palaces to be owned by the Queen"[11]—read: *l'Autrichienne,* the Austrian. For Marie Antoinette was also widely, if falsely, suspected of having secretly sent her brother, Joseph II, one hundred million livres over a period of three years.[12] True, even Calonne had hesitated at the purchase of the Saint-Cloud palace, but the Queen had icily told him, "If I do not have it, I will forbid your presence before me, and your presence at Madame de Polignac, whenever I am there."[13] She had her palace, but she was not pleased with his hesitancy. She felt, moreover, that she might never have undergone the necklace ordeal had he been more "understanding" about her desire for jewels, and she never forgave him for it.[14] As a conciliatory gesture, Calonne offered the ailing Dauphin a little carriage, three feet high, drawn by eight Siberian ponies, three feet tall, complete with equerry, coachman, and footmen, each three feet in height.[15]

Of such was the Court—and treasurer—of Versailles of Louis XVI.

Charles Alexandre de Calonne was more banker than financier, but even more courtier than banker. As Necker, he borrowed heavily, but it was primarily to maintain the Court's appearances. Publicly he borrowed 100,000,000 livres in 1784 and 125,000,000 in 1785; secretly, 354,000,000 from 1784 to 1786; in three years, more than 800,000,000![16] Privately, he accepted the *pot-de-vin* (traditional gratuity) of 300,000 livres from the tax farmers, previously declined

* "How was I to know the poor state of the treasury?" Marie Antoinette would query at a later day. "When I asked for 50,000 livres, I was brought 100,000!"[10]

by Turgot and Necker.[17] His looseness with royal revenues, which he disbursed among the royal family and its favorites, greatly lowered his prestige among France's bankers. When Necker attacked his practices with a pamphlet in 1785, Calonne's credit rating dropped to virtual zero. The Parlement of Paris, suspicious of his public accounting, urged that it be checked by the King—the least likely of public accountants. Parlement was proving more and more reluctant to register Calonne's measures; in 1786, it flatly refused to accept his reminting of the money, calling the reduction of its content "hidden taxation."[18]

With bankers refusing new loans, Parlement refusing new taxes, Calonne was driven to the consideration of basic reforms. On August 20, 1786, he brought the King his *Précis d'un plan d'amélioration des finances.* The treasury that summer was in deficit for 100,000,000 livres and half next year's revenue had already been spent. Calonne's *Plan* spoke of a situation "where the richest class was taxed the least." It proposed extending taxation to all orders, replacing the *vingtième* by a land tax on all estates, "with no exceptions." Further the proposed reforms included abolition everywhere of the *corvée,* reduction of the *taille,* suppression of interior custom tolls, freedom of the grain trade, establishment of provincial assemblies. It was "pure Necker," said the King. (Actually it was pure Turgot.) "Parlement will never agree."[19] Read further, suggested Calonne. His plan counseled the calling together of France's privileged à la Henry IV—an *Assemblée des Notables,* last summoned (and entirely dominated) by Richelieu in 1626.

Flattered by the comparison with Henry IV, Louis XVI consulted his two other principal ministers, Vergennes and Miromesnil. The former was initially hesitant, preferring a traditional *lit de justice* imposing the royal will on Parlement, but finally lent his support after Calonne argued that the common sense of the Notables, faced with the catastrophic state of the treasury and consequently of the regime, would persuade them to go along with the vital reforms. More duplicitly, Miromesnil agreed. Calonne then implored the Queen's support. It was not forthcoming. The calling of the clan was postponed. The Crown's finances became more desperate. Calonne, looking for new sources of revenue, even considered taking over the butcher shops of Paris and making them a State monopoly.[20] Finally, the Assembly of Notables was convoked by the King for January 24, 1787. The day after the decision, Louis told Calonne, "I did not sleep last night. But it was from pleasure."[21]

If true, the pleasure was premature.

The Notables began to arrive at Versailles early in January, twenty-two of the most notable, among them Lafayette, lodging at the palace. But they did not meet before February 22, 1787, in the Hôtel des Menus Plaisirs du Roi, several hundred yards east of the palace, on Avenue de Paris. Their assembly was delayed by Calonne's falling ill. The sickness was genuine but suspected of being a delaying maneuver. Nevertheless, when it was reported that Calonne was spitting blood, the gruesome witticism went the rounds, "His or the State's?" More importantly, the death of Vergennes occurred on February 13, further delaying the opening. (Louis XVI's journal for that date notes, "Nothing"—no hunting—"death of M. de Vergennes at three this morning."[22]) The month's delay and the death of Vergennes would add to Calonne's malaise.

As the Notables awaited the assembly's opening, they heard themselves mocked in theaters and Paris salons, by the public, press, and clubs, for the role of puppet and cuckold predestined for them. A satirical cartoon circulated caricaturing Calonne as a monkey in chef's clothing, addressing an assembly of meek, farmyard fowl. "My good friends," says the monkey from his raised platform, "I have brought you together to hear from you with what sauce you would like to be eaten." "But we don't want to be eaten," says a cock. "You are wandering from the subject before us," says the monkey.[23] The satire was devastating, and one can understand the temper of the Notables, whatever their intentions when they had come to Versailles or their limited sense of enlightened self-sacrifice, as they filled the days with Court gossip and fretted their evenings in derisive salons. Nor did Calonne improve their mood by presenting them with memoranda of the reforms to be consented to, rather than discussed, barely a few days before they met.*

Their irritation is the more understandable when one considers their eminence and composition. Mistakenly, Calonne had allowed his own rival, Loménie de Brienne, Archbishop of Toulouse and, not incidently, a favorite of the Queen, to choose the fourteen prelates

---

* Prepared principally by Dupont de Nemours, who had also assisted Turgot and would be one of the Assembly's secretaries, and by Charles Maurice de Talleyrand, not quite thirty-three, nor yet a bishop.

among the Notables, but he had counted on the seven princes of the blood, thirty-six *grands seigneurs,* thirteen intendants and *conseillers d'état,* and dozens of provincial and municipal officials (most of the latter his own men) to countervail Brienne's fellow prelates and the thirty-three magistrates of the thirteen parlements. One hundred and forty-four, they were all among the most privileged, all but an insignificant three or four titled.[24]

At the opening session, the King spoke for less than two minutes ("I have assembled you to acquaint you with my projects"), Calonne spoke an hour and six minutes, eloquently and seductively ("too much so"—Talleyrand[25]). But he exposed the parlous state of the treasury and indicated that taxing the untaxed was the only escape from bankruptcy. The deficit, he declared, was eighty million livres. In fact, it was larger, but the figure he revealed astonished the Assembly; the Notables had read Necker's comforting little bluebook demonstrating the contrary. "To borrow," Calonne continued, "would be to aggravate the evil. . . . What then must be done to fill the huge deficit and find the desired equilibrium? Put an end to tax abuses! Yes, gentlemen, it is in tax reform that the State can find the funds it needs to reestablish order in its finances. It is in the elimination of tax abuses alone that the State might meet its needs."[26] And Calonne put forward the proposed reforms—outlined in his *Plan*—adding pique to the proposed reduction of their privileged tax status by presenting the reforms as the King's own, and thus virtual *faits accomplis.*[27]

As a result, instead of proceeding directly to a discussion of the reforms, the Notables protested the manner in which they were being imposed upon them; the lords of the land, they were not being treated as "free men"—and there was more righteousness than irony in their complaint.

Believing the princes of the blood beholden to him for his generosity and to the King by family loyalty, Calonne arranged for each to preside over one of the seven committees into which the Assembly was divided.*

* He was as much in error about their gratitude as about their common sense, and the seven committees, or commissions, were soon lightly called in order: the Committee of *Esprit,* headed by Monsieur, the Committee of Gaiety (Artois), the Committee of Folly (Orléans), the Committee of Falsity (Condé), the Committee of Nullity (Bourbon), the Committee of Frankness (Conti) and the Committee of Sadness (Penthièvre). Lacking was an eighth Committee of Confidence."[28]

Only Artois favored Calonne among the princes of the blood, but even in his committee one heard the effective gadfly criticism of Lafayette, who remarked on Calonne's past mismanagement. Monsieur's committee, for another, found the proposal of provincial assemblies "unconstitutional [*sic*], dangerous and useless"[29]—the self-contradictions didn't seem to bother the King's brother. But the others were only too happy to follow the lead of one so "close" to the King. The Duc d'Orléans, the King's cousin, declared that the proposed provincial assemblies would cost him at least 300,000 livres a year. With an annual income of 7,500,000 livres, he explained, "I pay what I want to the Intendants. The provincial administrators would have me pay much more."[30]

On March 2, Calonne met with the presiding prince of the blood and five members of each committee before Monsieur and his group. For five hours he defended his position cleverly and well but unsuccessfully. No sauce he had prepared proved appetizing to those who were convinced, like the barnyard animals of the caricature, that they were being readied for a royal plucking. Calonne now announced the Crown's deficit as 113,000,000 livres, and not 80,000,00, as previously declared. Immediately details were demanded of him as to *how*—and *why*—*his* treasury had arrived at such a condition, but Calonne refused to furnish the data on the grounds of royal secrecy. "I have given the King the necessary information," he replied, adding that the treasury, after all, was the King's.[31]* Surely, said Calonne, *no one* would contest the right of the King to impose his wishes in this regard. "That one," replied the Archbishop of Narbonne, "is I." "And I another," said the Archbishop of Arles.[33]

Archbishop Dillon of Narbonne, one of the leaders of the Assembly, led the Church attack on Calonne's reforms. "Monsieur de Calonne," he said, "would like to bleed France further, and he is asking the Notables whether he should bleed her in the foot, in the arm, or in the jugular."[34] Monseigneur de Boisgelin expressed *his* princely contempt of Calonne, in a widely read letter to the Comtesse de Gramont, as "a bourgeois and a financier who well knows he is despised by his audience as one who is looking for naught but money."[35]

And the Duc d'Orléans, to show his disdainful disinterest in the

---

* The Comte d'Artois, not long before, had told the Paris Parlement that the King was not required to adjust his expenditures according to his revenues, but rather vice versa.[32]

Assembly's procedures, left his committee and went hunting, running down a stag near the Bastille "in the faubourg of Saint-Antoine, under the scandalized eyes of the Parisians."[36]

Having lost his audience, Calonne appealed over the heads of the Notables to the people. (Public opinion now was an acknowledged force.) Through a pamphlet he hoped to find understanding and support at least among those whom his reforms would most benefit, but oddly he found neither. He had created what in our time would be called a credibility gap: people believed he was covering up his own failures with demagoguery. Orators in the clubs and the Paris cafés, particularly those around Orléans' Palais Royal, denounced him as a thieving speculator who freely dipped his own hand in the Crown's treasury.[37]

The Notables, in turn, riposted. Monsieur's committee expressed shock at "the break in the invisible link of obedience joining the people to the great of the kingdom." Bourbon's group: "An infraction of the monarchical State itself."[38] And they presented their own case in a public pamphlet. "There was no sacrifice," it protested, "they had not offered to alleviate the weight of taxation on the people. . . . Unfortunately" they were being refused the information on which to base their recommendations for tax reforms, of which, moreover, they had not been absolutely convinced by Calonne and concerning which there was much more study to be done.[39] In d'Artois' commission, Lafayette called for an immediate investigation of tax frauds and stock speculations. He was applauded, but no investigation was initiated; Calonne himself was too deeply involved.[40]

The opposition to Calonne became overpowering. (Chamfort: "They had left him in peace when he set fire [to the ship of State] and punished him only when he sounded the alarm."[41]) Necker, accused of having falsified the royal treasury report, asked the King for the right of rebuttal before the Notables. He was refused, but he sent each of them a self-defending memorandum confounding, if not refuting, Calonne's disclosures, and he too presented his case to the public in a pamphlet. Loménie de Brienne, positioning himself for the battle of Calonne's succession, criticized Necker, his only serious rival, for overheating public opinion—and Necker, for a time, was exiled twenty leagues from the capital by the King.[42] And *"tout Paris* [all Paris society]," writes Madame de Staël, his daughter, "visited M. Necker during the twenty-four hours allowed him to pack for his departure."[43]

Meanwhile Miromesnil had been stealthily undermining Calonne's position with the King, soliciting a memorandum from Joly de Fleury on the question as to who was right about the disputed deficit, Necker or Calonne. Necker, Fleury had replied, and Miromesnil passed on his reply to the King. Troubled, Louis XVI passed it on to Calonne, who urbanely tried to pass it off. Miromesnil persisted. "One can see what Calonne is seeking to do," he wrote the King, "to oppose you to the bishops, to the nobles, to the magistrates, to your own ministers. And he is making an appeal to public opinion which can have dangerous consequences."[44] More troubled than ever, his confidence in Calonne sapped, Louis XVI was seen weeping on April 2, and heard to murmur, "If only Vergennes were alive. He would have gotten me out of this wretched business."[45]

Feeling the ground slipping from under his feet, Calonne had gone to the Queen and offered personally to render her a daily account of happenings at the Assembly of Notables. Frostily, she had refused his gesture. Sensing the end (almost from the beginning), Calonne had once asked Louis whether he might not be sacrificed to the Church and nobility as Turgot had been. "Fear nothing," Louis had reassured him, "I was a child then. Now I am a man."[46]

On April 8, 1787, Calonne was dismissed.

He had asked for Miromesnil's head and received it, then asked for that of Breteuil, friend and favorite of Marie Antoinette, and was handed his own. Several months later, when the Paris Parlement opened charges against him for malpractice in office, Calonne fled to England.[47]

The candidates for Calonne's succession were Necker and Loménie de Brienne, but Louis XVI declared he wanted *"ni Neckerville, ni Prêtraille"*—neither Neckership, nor Priesthood.[48] He disliked Necker for being smug, Protestant, and a banker, and six years before, when Loménie de Brienne had been recommended for the archbishopric of Paris, Louis had objected, "We should at least have an Archbishop of Paris who believes in God."[49] (Brienne, then, one might remind the reader, was Archbishop of Toulouse.) Thus, for a brief interim, the obscure Bouvard de Fourqueux controlled the finances of France, and government bonds fell at the exchange.[50] Pressed by the Queen to name Brienne, the King resisted—for all of ten days—then summoned the archbishop to the post of finance minister. And government bonds rose at the exchange.[51] Briefly. With this act, Louis XVI semiabdicated responsibility for the daily conduct of the government to Marie Antoinette and her minister.*

Loménie de Brienne was likely the deist, if not atheist, Louis XVI believed him to be.[53] Admiringly the *philosophes* hailed the Archbishop of Toulouse as the "antimonk" and welcomed him to power as another Turgot. Brilliant and ambitious, Brienne was a period mixture of wit, intelligence, charm, and self-interest. It was he who would have the King recall Necker from suburban exile. And it was he who would exchange his diocese of Toulouse for that of Sens, because Sens brought in more revenue. But he would also turn over his salary as finance minister to the treasury and his sixty thousand livres a year from the Abbey of Saint-Ouen to the poor.[54] Enthusiastically Lafayette wrote his good friend, George Washington, of Brienne's "ability and honesty," expressing the hopes held by the *philosophes* for a "man who was enlightened and liberal."[55] The other Notables, however, among whom Brienne had so recently sat, reacted differently when he who had opposed Calonne in the Assembly now took over Calonne's program and proposed it as his own. He trimmed its measures accordingly. They didn't like the land tax? Brienne cut it in half.[56] But even half measures found them unco-operative. Disillusioned, he counseled the King to dismiss the Assembly of Notables.

Before the clan dispersed, however, an impulsive intervention of Lafayette and a more considered suggestion of the Assembly's President d'Aligre were to mark, in inverse order, climactic turning points in the last act of Versailles' greatness.

Lafayette, on hearing the order for dismissal: "His Majesty should convoke a truly National Assembly."

Comte d'Artois: "What, Sir, you ask the convocation of the Estates General?"

Lafayette: "Yes, monseigneur, and even more than that." And Loménie de Brienne, Lafayette recalls in his memoirs, was shocked that his young friend entertained notions of a "really representative Government!"[57]

Lafayette, in reality, was projecting future events in his memoirs, which

---

* In this connection, Marie Antoinette told Madame Campan a strange story (if we are to believe the anecdote related in memoirs published well after the Revolution). "After I had commenced attending the private council meetings of the King," says the Queen, "I heard, as I traversed the Oeil-de-Boeuf, one of the Chapel musicians say loudly so that I might hear every word: 'A Queen who does her duty should stay in her apartments and embroider.' "[52]

N*

recount the story. The shock of Brienne and the Comte d'Artois came rather from the fact that the Estates General had not met since 1614— 173 years previously—though its meeting had been suggested on several occasions since. It was not a representative *government,* but rather an assembly representative of the *nation* (a notion, to be sure, revolutionary enough)—a gathering of deputies of the three estates or orders.* Largely appointive originally, it became entirely elective in the last third of the sixteenth century. In the process of elections, sometimes held in several stages, the electors of each order drew up a *cahier de doléances* (statement of grievances) eventually combined in general *cahiers* for presentation to the King, who responded to them in the Royal Council. It was early established that only the Estates General might authorize new taxation, a power lost in the seventeenth century, but not forgotten in the eighteenth.† Thus, since Louis XIV, the Estates General had become a historical memory, a nostalgic reference point, and if occasionally it was suggested as a possible recourse, as in the time of Louis XV, the very thought of it was hastily thrust aside by the King.[58]

And now the Marquis de Lafayette was proposing that it be summoned as a "truly National Assembly," which the Assembly of Notables, the meeting of the clan, was clearly not. Here indeed were the seeds of a representative government, and Loménie de Brienne was not alone in his reaction. The Notables, too, recoiled almost to a man before the Pandora box Lafayette proposed opening. It was, therefore, not idly suggested by President d'Aligre, during the closing session of May 25, that perhaps Parlement might now take up the problems unsolved by the Assembly of Notables. Nor was the suggestion idly taken up by the minister of finance.

What Calonne had tried to avoid Brienne would give a last try. Members of the Parlement of Paris, he reasoned, were among the privileged of the land. They were nobles, and none but the titled, at this time, might enter their ranks.[59] They were a part—a cantankerous part—of the clan, but possibly, just possibly exposed to the imminent collapse of a monarchical system on which their own privileges

---

* First summoned by Philip IV in 1302, when the Third Estate was but an intimidated fraction. He had called on it for aid and counsel in his struggle against the Pope.
† When last the Estates General met in 1614 (the twenty-fifth meeting in its entire history), in the wake of disturbances following Henry IV's assassination, its members quarreled among themselves and their assembly was dissolved.

depended, they might join the King and his minister and sensibly register the tax measures that alone might save them all. So Brienne gambled, encouraged by d'Aligre, counting as well on the traditional *lit de justice,* the royal way for overriding a rebellious Parlement, should it be required. It had been favored by the late Vergennes. Perhaps rightly. It had not failed Louis XIV or Louis XV. Why should it fail Louis XVI?

An anecdote might anticipate Parlement's response.

Louis XVI to the Duc de Richelieu, who was nearing ninety· "You have seen, it seems, three centuries."

Richelieu: "Not quite, Sire. Rather three reigns."

Louis: "What, then, do you think of them?"

Richelieu: "Under Louis XIV, Sire, no one dared say a word. Under Louis XV, one spoke in a whisper. Under Your Majesty, one speaks out loud."[60]

26. The Overexposure of Parlement

Too late—it might be engraved as her epitaph—Marie Antoinette, as a gesture to her minister, Loménie de Brienne, cut down on her stable, table, and dresses. She sent off Mademoiselle Bertin, suspended work at Saint-Cloud, suppressed masked balls, substituted billiards for faro.[1] And Louis momentarily reduced his hunts, dismissed his grand falconer, combined the Great Stable with the Small—but let the Duc de Coigny keep his allowances as grand equerry, because he had made a scene—and sold off several of the royal residences, such as La Muette and Choisy.[2]

One hundred and seventy-three gentlemen-servants and similar charges were eliminated in the Queen's household alone. The endebted Duc de Polignac was embittered by the loss of his fifty thousand (incidental) livres a year; the Baron de Besenval was more outspoken. "Madame," he complained to the Queen, "how dreadful to live in a country where one isn't sure from one day to the next what one possesses. Such things occur only in Turkey!"[3]

It was too little, as it was too late. The emptiness of the State treasury was cavernous, and the household economies of even a "Madame Demi-déficit"—if one might be allowed the lèse-majesté—did not begin to refill it. Moreover, few of the royal economies were to last very long. Brienne nonetheless hoped they might impress Parlement, his predecessors having tried the opposite tactic: borrowing heavily to lend the Crown and the Court the appearances of prosperity and thus the country of solvency. It was a policy that proved both unconvincing and provocative.

At first it seemed that Brienne might win his gamble. Currying popular favor, Parlement quickly registered freedom of the grain trade, abolition of the *corvée,* and even the project—prepared by Dupont—for provincial assemblies. But it balked completely at the tax on all properties. *That* brought reform too close to home. As for the stamp tax on official, commercial, and other public papers, which Brienne had unsuccessfully submitted to the Notables, he had no more success with the members of Parlement. Delightedly they pointed out its precedent in the American colonies, where the British Stamp Act of 1765 led to riots in Boston and New York and eventually open revolt.

In the course of one debate, the Abbé Sabatier wittily remarked that the government was constantly referring to its deplorable *état des finances,* state of finances, when it should really be calling for the *États Généraux,* the Estates General. And so, wrote Madame de Staël, "a play on words became a political force."[4] She thought it the first time the Estates General had been evoked. Rather, the notion launched by Lafayette had, at this point, become a parlementary ploy. Thus, on July 20, 1787, Parlement sent Louis XVI a statement declaring that "the Nation, represented by the Estates General, alone has the right of granting the King subsidies, whose need must be proved to it."[5] For the gowned nobles of Parlement, the Estates General was still a feudal body dominated by the first and second estates, among whom they would sit should it be summoned. Few actually thought it would be; loudly proposing that it be called was a legalistic device for indefinitely postponing tax reforms touching on their privileged exemption. For Parisians, however, Parlement's declaration that "the Nation, represented by the Estates General," and therefore the people, "alone had certain sovereign rights," struck an immediate popular response, and they demonstrated their enthusiasm in the streets, cafés, and clubs.[6]

On August 6, Louis XVI summoned Parlement to Versailles for a *lit de justice* and ordered the stamp and land taxes formally registered. It was the hottest day of the year, and "during the proceedings the King slept and snored."[7]* The following day, back home in the Palais de Justice, Parlement declared the forced registration null and

---

* Mercy to Joseph II, at this time: "The King is becoming very obese. Returns from the hunt are followed by meals of such immoderation that they bring on lapses of reason and a kind of lassitude that is very awkward for those involved. The Queen is almost alone in unconcern; she is feared and respected by her husband."[8]

void. On the thirteenth, as a crowd of twenty thousand Parisians filled the streets and the Palais corridors, discussion of the King's tax edicts was resumed. Heatedly Duval d'Eprémesnil denounced their imposition as "contrary to the rights of the Nation."[9] Again a meeting of the Estates General was demanded, and on the fourteenth, a royal *lettre de cachet* was delivered to each magistrate, exiling the entire Parlement to a château in Troyes, one hundred miles southeast of Paris.*

And Paris exploded, as if in rehearsal for the revolution. Lawyers and jurists took the exile of Parlement, whose primary function was that of a high court of justice, as a personal affront. They poured into the streets, particularly the younger clerks among them, joined by the youth of other social groups, many of the working class. One day's record of arrests, for instance, lists an apprentice woodworker, a mattress stuffer, a shoemaker, the employee of an *entrepreneur de spectacles,* the son of an usher at the Châtelet prison, all of them youths between fourteen and seventeen years of age.[11] Crowds chased police through the streets, closed shops, entered courtrooms and mocked their procedures, burned royal edicts of the King and royalist pamphlets, hurled insults at the French guards, paraded with posters (one of which read, "In a week, either Parlement or fire!").[12] Merchants took fright, implored Brienne to restore law and order. In response, he closed the political clubs, asked the merchants and factory owners to keep their young clerks, workers, and apprentices home. Troops cleared the Palais de Justice, the street guard was doubled, some order re-established. Finally Parlement was recalled to Paris, and it returned in public triumph. There were bonfires of celebration in the streets; Calonne, Breteuil, and the Duchesse de Polignac—but not yet Marie Antoinette—were burned in effigy. Cries were raised for the calling of "the Nation's representatives," the Estates General.[13]

There was still the appalling deficit.

Brienne borrowed twelve million livres from the municipality of Paris. It was the proverbial drop in the bucket. He proposed a tax loan of 120,000,000 livres to the reassembled Parlement, promising the convocation of the Estates General in five years, if it were accepted. It was refused. On November 11, the King ordered a royal session to force registration of the measure. Unmoved, Parlement listened to a succession

---

* "Take care," said Augeard, secretary to the Queen, to Lamoignon, who had replaced Miromesnil. "You are not opening a battle with Parlement, but unleashing a civil war!"[10]

of the King's ministers. Then the Duc d'Orléans rose and "stammered a protest" at the King's presence.[14] "S-Sire," he said, "it is illegal. This is not a *lit de justice.*"* Taken by surprise, the King too, stammered, "It's all the same to me . . . you are the master here . . . No! It is legal because I wish it!"[15] And he commanded that the five-year tax loan be registered. The members of Parlement obeyed, but as soon as the King had departed, they declared the registration nullified. The next day Louis XVI exiled the Duc d'Orléans to his château at Villers-Cotterets, and *lettres de cachet* sent two of the parlementary leaders to fortress prisons.

One might, however, record one blow for freedom. As 1788 began, French Protestants once again received a measure of civil equality. Their children were now regarded as legitimate; they could practice most professions, but they were still excluded from the judiciary, the government (with notable exceptions, such as Necker), and the teaching profession. The new tolerance coincided with the rather abashed French reception of refugee Dutch Calvinists, Holland having been abandoned by its ally, France, during an invasion by Prussia. The new edict of tolerance also served as an invitation to French Huguenots to return to the homeland with "their industry . . . machines . . . and above all capital."[17] In fairness to Brienne and the King, it should also be pointed out that the edict was *not* popular with the majority of the French people.[18]

Dramatically, hoping to impress Parlement with the desperate state of French finances, Brienne published the figures for the royal deficit: 160,000,000 livres. It made Parlement feel all the more powerful, particularly since the bankers of France were refusing any loans without Parlement's sanction. It was becoming clear that henceforth loans to the State must be secured by more than the Crown's lofty promise of future repayment, that is, by nothing less than established State revenue. Parlement, however, representing the nobility, would have none of the *first* step, that is, tax reforms eliminating the privileged exemptions of the First and Second Estates, richest, untapped sources of State revenue. Moreover, it boldly published a declaration that France was a hereditary monarchy, subject to laws registered (approved) by Parlement.[19] The declaration, accepted by the Crown,

---

* Talleyrand: "There is nothing in the entire history of the monarchy to equal it. Princes of the blood have been seen, sword in hand, resisting the power of the King. But no one has witnessed them attempting to put constitutional limits to his authority."[16]

would have meant the end of absolute monarchy and the beginning of constitutional reign. One might call it a move toward an English, as distinguished from the great French, revolution.

But the French monarchy would have no part of it. The King ordered the arrest of the two most active leaders of Parlement's opposition, Duval d'Eprémesnil and Goislard de Montsabert. Between ten and eleven on the night of May 5, the Marquis d'Agoult led a squad of the French Guard, through a massed, jeering crowd, into the Palais de Justice and demanded the two parlementary leaders. He was met by the Duc de Luynes and the withering remark, *"Monsieur l'Officier,* you are not properly dressed for executing the orders of the King. You are not wearing your gorget." Embarrassed, the Marquis d'Agoult fumbled for it in his pocket and adjusted it nervously around his neck.[20] His embarrassment was not ended. He was obliged to ask that the two men he was to arrest be pointed out to him, since he didn't know them. And as he looked about in bewilderment, the members of Parlement cried, "We are all d'Eprémesnil and Montsabert! You must take us all!" D'Agoult, uncertain as to what he should do, left the hall. That night a deputation of Parlement hurried to Versailles for an audience with the King, but he refused to receive it, and its members returned at dawn. At eleven in the morning of May 6, d'Agoult returned for d'Eprémesnil and Montsabert, who surrendered themselves and were led off to prison. But as they left, the crowds outside the Palais de Justice cheered them as heroes.[21]

The Parlement of Paris was suspended, as well as the twelve other parlements in the provinces, which had taken up resistance to the Crown with even greater energy. A Plenary Court was established to replace the Parlement of Paris, and other courts were appointed to function in the provinces. Churchmen and nobles protested the suspension of Parlement. An assembly of high clergy condemned the royal act as illegal, reduced the Church's contribution to the Crown from the usual 12,000,000 livres a year to 1,800,000, and demanded restoration of Parlement's traditional rights, or no further funds at all.[22] Since several of the provincial parlements continued to assemble, defying the royal ban, *lettres de cachet* were dispatched for their members. In the province of Dauphiné, ever the most rebellious, students, lawyers, clerks, and young workers harassed the soldiers delivering the sealed letters, seizing their muskets, in some cases, as they hesitated to shoot. In Rennes, capital of Brittany, soldiers were firing in the air and officers tendering their resignations rather than lead their men against the rioters.[23]

The most striking incident occurred at Grenoble, capital of Dauphiné, on June 7, 1788, a day that has gone down in history as the *Journée des Tuiles,* the Day of Tiles.[24]

It was Saturday and market day, and Grenoble was crowded with peasants and townspeople. It was the day the Duc de Clermont-Tonnerre, governor of the province, sent his troops to arrest members of Grenoble's Parlement. Angry groups gathered. Their leaders rang the church bells, calling the people to arms, and they came running with pikes, pitchforks, clubs, and paving stones. They closed and barred the city's gates. The market women massed in the courtyard of the Parlement's President, to prevent his being taken away. (He had already packed and ordered his carriage prepared for departure with the duke's men.) The most daring of Grenoble's citizens climbed the roofs and hurled tiles down on the heads of Clermont-Tonnerre's troops, while others attacked them from the streets. The attackers were held off by bayonets, the soldiers having received orders not to shoot. But a hatmaker was killed (Stendhal, as a boy, watched him stagger off, bleeding from a bayonet wound[25]) and furiously a great crowd swung toward Clermont-Tonnerre's headquarters. Hundreds of peasants who had responded to the church bells rushed to the city, climbed its walls, and joined the attackers, some fifteen thousand in all. The two regiments involved were kept in check (one refused to take any action) as Clermont-Tonnerre negotiated with the rebels and the more compliant members of Parlement. Finally, five days later, by agreement, the latter discreetly left Grenoble, obeying the King's orders. The refractory regiment was removed to Briançon, but no punishment was attempted against the people of Grenoble. Their day of revolt was triumph and history.[26]

And it was the province of Dauphiné that took the next historic measure, summoning its ancient Estates General with the Third Estate's representatives equaling the sum of the two other orders. Moreover, voting was by individual representative rather than by order or estate, thus the First and Second Estates could not automatically predominate two to one as in the past. The meeting of the province's Estates General, forbidden by the Crown to assemble at Grenoble, was held some miles distant under the leadership of two young lawyers, Jean Joseph Mounier and Joseph Barnave. Here five hundred deputies drew up a series of demands: re-establishment of Parlement's right to register all new laws, the end of *lettres de cachet,* the immediate summoning of a national Estates General—and the solemn pledge to submit to no new taxation until it was summoned. A pattern was set for all France to follow.[27]

New forces were in evidence, a new party was called for, and it was formed. Feeling its way in 1787, the Parti National, the party whose followers called themselves *nationalistes* and *patriotes,* was fairly well organized by the end of 1788. The way to it had been paved by the "Republic of Letters"—by Fénelon, Montesquieu, Malesherbes, Turgot and Franklin, Diderot, Rousseau, and Voltaire. Its key members were the Committee of Thirty, including Condorcet, the Duc de la Roche-foucauld-Liancourt, Talleyrand, Dupont de Nemours, the Duc d'Aiguillon, the Duc de Luynes, the Abbé Louis, Mirabeau *fils,* Lafayette, and the Abbé Sieyès.[28] None favored or spoke for a republic; generally England was taken as the model; and as one man they called for a meeting of the "Nation"—that is, the Estates General. They organized protests, wrote, published, or inspired pamphlets spurring public opinion, and were often behind violent demonstrations. Their opponents called them the *enragés,* the wild ones,* a term referring to the postilions who drove the lead horses of the fast carriages at a full gallop between Versailles and Paris, making the round trip in three hours.[29] (The eight-horse, twenty-passenger public *carabas* required six and a half hours simply to go one way.[30]) For the older men of the *ancien régime,* the *patriotes* were for the most part young men in a hurry.† With reference to England, Holland, and America, however, they were historically in retard. (Fundamentally conservative and traditional, the character of France, and its consequence, has been that, when it catches up, it is with a bang.) But there was another reproach, to be heard in every social revolution since: privileged sons of the privileged were turning against their privileged fathers.

A close friend of Lafayette, a colonel under Rochambeau in the Amer-

---

* Such is the vitality of tradition in France, the term was applied to the *gauchistes,* or extremists, among the student rebels during the near-revolution of May 1968.

† "Should one," asks a contemporary French historian, "reinterpret the French Revolution in terms of a conflict between the generations?"[31]

Tocqueville asserted it earlier: "It was a time of youth, enthusiasm and pride, of generous, sincere passions, whose memory, despite its errors, men will forever cherish."[32]

ican rebellion, a counselor of Napoleon later in life, the Comte de Ségur would recall the gallantry of those younger days with the remorse, not necessarily the wisdom, of an older man regretting the actions of his youth. "As for us," his memoirs read, "the young French nobility, with neither regret for the past nor anxiety for the future, we walked gaily on a carpet of flowers concealing an abyss. Laughing scoffers at traditional forms, at the feudal pride of our fathers and their feudal ways, all that was ancient seemed burdensome and ridiculous. We felt the weight of ancient doctrines. . . . Liberty, whatever the language it took, pleased us with its audacity, equality with its new convention. One takes pleasure in descending, so long as one believes one might climb back at will. Without reflecting, we simultaneously enjoyed our patrician advantages and the appeal of a plebian philosophy. Thus, though it was our own privileges, the remains of our ancient powers, which were being mined under our feet, the war game pleased us. We did not see the dangers: we applauded the spectacle. . . . We laughed at the cries of alarm which came from the old Court, the thunderings of the Church against the spirit of innovation. We cheered republican scenes in our theaters, the speeches of the *philosophes* in our academies, the daring works of our men of letters."[33]

The flower-covered abyss, however, was not dug by the forces of change; they simply discovered and eventually crossed it. One class's abyss, one might say, was the occasion for another class's bridge. The abyss, in its most banal form, was the deficit in the monarchy's finances. (Actually, it was the treasury's reflection of the great gap between the economically productive and the socially powerful, between taxed commercial and industrial income and untaxed land wealth.) Bankers refusing to loan the Crown money in the classical manner, nobles and clergy totally unco-operative, as in the Assembly of Notables, the monarchy felt impelled to call the Estates General together. There was no other recourse for tax reform and needed revenues.

However, it was almost two centuries, as we have already noted, since the Estates General had last met; and Louis XVI's exploratory edict of July 5, 1788, was an extraordinary appeal for "all scholars and informed persons of the Kingdom" to send the government "all information and memoranda" touching on the Estates General, incorporating suggestions on its organization and procedures.[34] It was an astonishing admission of the monarchy's bewilderment as it stood before the abyss. In effect the edict put an end to censorship, unloosing a flow of pamphlets that would become a flood. In the words of a memorialist of the period: "A field without limits opened for a freedom without restraint."[35]

Royal power was withering away. Louis XVI inspired pity and contempt rather than fear or hate. He knew it, he was sad, and he was seen to weep. Marie Antoinette was offering confused advice at the Royal Council. Not even the royal family was loyal (and there may be naïveté in the notion it ever is or was). Monsieur, the King's brother, was an open pretender to the throne. The Duc d'Orléans, the King's cousin, was an open enemy. The pastime of the Court was intrigue, Brienne was the convenient target. "The King," he was discovering, "was not displaying the cordiality and ease he usually showed me."[36]

As August 1788 began, Brienne was to make another disagreeable discovery: there were only 400,000 livres in the royal treasury, or enough "for one quarter of one day's expenses in running the State."[37] There could no longer be any delay. On August 8, Brienne had the King summon the Estates General for an assembly in Versailles on May 1, 1789. In the meantime Brienne appropriated emergency funds for victims of the winter freeze, savings of the Hôtel des Invalides and other hospitals, the operating funds of the Opéra and Comédie Française, in order to keep the government functioning. On August 16 he declared virtual bankruptcy: all payments by the government would be suspended for six weeks. Public emotion ran high; bankers' emotions ran higher. Brienne did not last the six weeks. He was dismissed on August 25. The day after his departure, Marie Antoinette sent for Necker and sounded him out in the privacy of her apartments. Somewhat reassured, she had the King name Necker as Brienne's successor. "I tremble," she wrote Mercy with a new, frightened modesty, "that it is I who recalled him. It is my fate to bring bad luck."[38] But government bonds quickly rose 30 per cent at the exchange.

Necker, the "miracle man," had returned. "Be comforted," he told a crowd waiting for his appearance in the Versailles courtyard, after a crucial audience with the King, "I remain." The crowd wept, and he wept.[39] Said Louis XVI to Necker: "It is years since I have known such a moment of happiness." Necker to the King: "In a short time, Sire, you will never have to say that again. All will be well."[40]

Only too happy to give credit to the Necker myth, bankers loaned the Crown seventy-five million livres, to which Necker, firmest believer in the Necker myth, added two millions of his own. It was not enough. Necker had the King recall the Paris Parlement. He further modified the tax reforms, but Parlement refused to register them. Moreover, as the question of representation and voting procedures for the Estates General agitated all France, the Parlement of Paris suddenly dropped its popular pose and ranged itself publicly on the side of the privileged. Each estate, it declared, should have the same number of representatives and voting should be by estate, thus ensuring the dominance of the first two orders over the third. Exposed as the spokesman for the privileged, alongside whom it was now openly aligned, Parlement became a mockery for the people. The resolutions of the Grenoble Estates General had become the popular goal: "doubling" the deputies of the Third Estate, so that they equaled the sum of the other two, and voting "by head" rather than by separate estate to give the "doubling" its full effectiveness.

Nothing less would satisfy the people* and soon Parlement would fade from French history, to disappear completely with the opening of the Estates General.

And as one says farewell to a Parlement that was never a parliament, for it would have nothing to do with a House of Commons, one might add a last comment on the last appearance of that other clan meeting, the Assembly of Notables, fruitlessly called a second time by Necker. On its closing day of December 12, 1788, the Comte d'Artois and the Prince de Condé penned a protest to the King about the impending "new system"—that is, the calling of a national Estates General—and besought him "not to sacrifice and humiliate that brave and ancient nobility which has spilled so much blood for the country."

"Was the blood of the people, then," ex-Jesuit Cerutti asked, "water?"[41]

---

* Typically, Louis XVI, yielding to Necker, granted the doubling of the Third Estate, but left undecided the controversial question of how the Estates General would vote.

27. Enter Mirabeau

Honoré-Gabriel Victor Riqueti, Comte de Mirabeau, "was the first great figure opening the era of revolutions"[1]—an era that has not yet closed and may well prove permanent.

We have touched on the Mirabeaus, father and son. It was a line that began in the sixteenth century, when Jean Riqueti, a wealthy Marseilles merchant, married into an old noble French family and bought the estate, title, and château of Mirabeau, between Aix-en-Provence and Marseilles. A descendant received Louis XIV in 1660, and the title, in 1685, became that of a marquis.[2] Jean Riqueti's great-great-grandson, Jean-Antoine Riqueti—our Mirabeau's grandfather—stamped the character of the line. At Cassano, in 1705, he defended a bridge in the face of Prince Eugène's troops. A ball shattered his right arm, another tore his throat. He fell, the enemy rode over his body. But he survived to wear his right arm in a sling of black silk and his neck in a collar of silver. He was forty. He married. He had seven children, one of them Victor, Mirabeau's father, the redoubtable marquis. They were raised in iron discipline and dread.

Victor Riqueti was early described by his friend Vauvenargues as "ardent and melancholy, prouder, more restless and changeable than the sea, sovereignly insatiable for pleasure, knowledge and glory." And at twenty-five the marquis admitted to the same friend that "immorality for him was a second nature."[3] He bought the estate of Bignon, some seventy-five miles southeast of Paris, and at twenty-eight married for money. His father, who had died when he was twenty-two, had left him a very modest sixteen thousand livres a year. He married, sight unseen, Marie de Vassan, a widowed heiress of seventeen, who proved neither bright nor pretty and would bring him no money. She had no appealing trait, indeed she was irritable and slatternly, but she bore the marquis eleven children in eleven years, five of them surviving infancy.

The Marquis de Mirabeau wrote several unremarked pamphlets, then struck fire with his *Ami des hommes,* Friend of Mankind, which became his sobriquet and to which has always been added his son's qualification, "but not of his wife and children." He may have been, as his son would write, one of the age's greatest hypocrites. A *philosophe* advocating freedom of the individual, he had five *lettres de cachet* issued against his son, Honoré-Gabriel, and forty-five more against the rest of the family. He wrote warmly about educating daughters at home but sent his three daughters to convent schools. A pamphlet he wrote in 1760, denouncing tax farmers as parasites, led the marquis to imprisonment in the Château de Vincennes for nine days (his friend Dr. Quesnay persuaded Madame de Pompadour to intercede for him); he would have his son imprisoned in the same dungeon for three and a half years. In 1762 he charged his wife with adultery, discharged her to her mother in Limousin, and then installed his mistress nearby. The Friend of Mankind wrote that "coercive measures are those most likely to produce a contrary effect" and beat his son Honoré systematically and often.

The first child born to the marquis died at three from accidentally drinking his father's ink. The second child was a daughter who would become a mental invalid. A second daughter, Caroline, "normal to the point of vulgarity,"[4] would have eighteen children as the Marquise de Saillant. The fifth child and oldest son, Honoré-Gabriel, was born on March 9, 1749, with a twisted ankle, a tied tongue, a supernaturally large head, and two teeth, forewarning of a ferocious appetite for life. The ankle would soon straighten, the tongue untie, but the head would remain leonine, the appetite fierce. "He beats his nurse," wrote the marquis to his younger brother, known as the Bailli. At three, Honoré had smallpox; his mother had been opposed to inoculation,* and she

---

* The period was still before Jenner and vaccination. The prevention of smallpox was by inoculation with a mild form of the disease. Louis XV, uninoculated, would die of smallpox, though he had insisted on Marie Antoinette's inoculation before she left Vienna for Versailles.

applied an eyewash to his sores which would deepen the pitted scars. "Your nephew," wrote the marquis to the Bailli, "is as ugly as Satan." Honoré did not simply sense it; he heard it from his father. "You are all Vassan [your mother]," said the marquis, rejecting his son, unforgivably born without the handsomeness of a Mirabeau. In 1752, a third daughter, Louise, was born and survived to marry the mad Marquis de Cabris; her father would not allow her to meet him before the marriage. In 1754, a second son, Boniface, was born and became his father's favorite—"all Mirabeau," said the marquis—and survived to become an obese alcoholic known as "Barrel" Mirabeau.

Having suffered the iron discipline of his father, the marquis submitted Honoré to the same, adding visible distaste at the sight of his son. At thirteen Honoré saw his parents separate and his father's mistress installed. Soon after he discovered sexual pleasure and would endlessly seek it. He went from a male tutor at home to an ex-Captain de Sigrais in Versailles for further instruction. The ex-captain, who liked Honoré, wrote his father: "His ways have already forced me to dismiss two maids." The wife of the ex-captain: "One flees at the sight of him, then stops to listen when he speaks."[5] After a few months the marquis sent his son on to a school in Paris kept by Abbé Choquard. He sent him, as to Versailles, with the humiliation of another name, "Pierre-Buffière" (after an estate of his mother in Limousin), because Honoré hadn't "earned" the right to be called Mirabeau. At Choquard the young lad quickly won over the students, among them two young Scottish noblemen named Elliot, and eventually the abbé. In the three years at the school he learned ancient and modern languages, shone at mathematics, resounded in music—his voice would be his medium— read Locke, and regained the name of Mirabeau, though his father persisted in regarding him as "all Vassan."

At eighteen Honoré was attached to a cavalry regiment at Saintes. Within a year, gambling debts and a girl in town (possibly the colonel's) had Honoré off to Paris without leave. For punishment, the Friend of Mankind toyed with the idea of sending his son to the Dutch colonies (a form of slow death), then reconsidered and had a *lettre de cachet* encage him instead on the island citadel of Ré, off the coast of Brittany. "Pierre-Buffière" once again, Honoré persuaded his keeper to help him have the *lettre de cachet* revoked, so he might join a military expedition to Corsica. He landed there the year of Bonaparte's birth, fought well, re-earned his father's respect when he returned with a manuscript on the history of Corsica, most of it plagiarized from a local priest.

Twenty-one, Honoré stayed with his uncle, the Bailli, who was managing the estate and château of Mirabeau, near Aix, for his older brother, the marquis. The reception was cordial. "I found him ugly, but not unpleasant," the Bailli wrote his brother. "Behind the pitted face there is something fine, gracious and dignified. . . . If he doesn't become worse than Nero, he will be better than Marcus Aurelius, for I don't believe I've ever met so much brilliance of mind." Later: "He is either the biggest humbug in the world, or the man in Europe best suited to become a general on land or sea, a minister, chancellor or Pope, whichever he wishes." After seven months, the marquis agreed to receive his son, was surprised to discover the same qualities and disconcerted by his volcanic energy (he would call him "the Hurricane"). To his brother, the Bailli: "What the devil is one to do with this hot-blooded exuberance? What land is big enough for him? I can think of no one he would be fit to marry except the Empress of Russia." In the meantime he once again permitted "Pierre-Buffière" to become Honoré-Gabriel Riqueti, Comte de Mirabeau.

The marquis had need of his son to help him acquire the estate of his late mother-in-law (for which he had married a Vassan to begin with) and to run his own ill-managed estate at Bignon, where he was having troubles with his peasants. Obediently Honoré went to see his mother about the heritage, she fired a pistol at him, according to his own account, written eight years later ("objective truthfulness about his own affairs was not one of his virtues"[6]), then they talked. He failed to move her (in fact, he was no more devoted to his father's cause than to his mother's; as each of them, he was most devoted to his own). He did better with his father's peasants. The marquis, in retrospect: "He had the terrible gift of familiarity which enabled him to turn the great around his little finger and which appealed to the small as well."* The familiarity and energy soon fatigued the marquis, however, and he dispatched Honoré back to his brother in Provence to look after his troublesome peasants there.

Mirabeau (as we shall now refer to him) looked after his own interests as well. He wooed, compromised, and married eighteen-year-old Emilie de Marignane, tiny, swarthy, and plain, but one of the

---

* But Honoré is also reported to have beaten one peasant with his cane.[7]

richest heiresses of Provence. She had been half promised to another, and the Marquis de Marignane would have none of Mirabeau, but he had bribed his way into the Hôtel de Marignane via a housemaid, left his carriage conspicuously outside during the night with Emilie, and appeared at her window in shirt sleeves and shorts.[8] The wedding that followed took place on June 23, 1772, but neither Mirabeau's father nor his mother bothered to attend.

Bride and groom resided in the Château de Mirabeau, entertained lavishly, and ran up a debt of 180,000 livres (the bride had brought a disappointing 3000 livres a year from her father). Told that his son was selling off his wife's jewelry and, worse, the château furniture, the marquis obtained a *lettre de cachet* ordering Honoré to the Provençal town of Manosque and depriving him of his civil rights (as well as removing him from his creditors). Here in the house of the Gassaud family, Mirabeau discovered that Emilie was deceiving him with a son of the house, a young musketeer; having been deceiving her regularly, however, he forgave her magnanimously—*after* requiring Emilie to write the musketeer a compromising letter of rupture, which Mirabeau had returned for his own keeping.

Restlessly, rashly, Mirabeau broke the royal order to remain in Manosque by visiting his sister Louise, the Marquise de Cabris, in Grasse. Married to a man increasingly manic, Louise was going about openly with her lover, and she wore a man's clothes. Chancing on one of her sharper, aristocratic critics, Mirabeau (twenty-five) thrashed the nobleman (fifty) with the latter's own parasol and was sued for attempted assassination. This time, to get him further out of his and harm's way, the marquis had his son interned in the Château d'If, on an island off Marseilles.

It was at Manosque that Mirabeau wrote his first serious work, an *Essai sur le despotisme,* which would be his first entry into history—other than that of libertinage. A monarch's power, he had written, recalling Rousseau's social contract, should not reside in absolutism, but in justly earned popularity. It is this Mirabeau one follows to the Château d'If, and thereafter. Pleased with the separation, Emilie remained behind with the son born the previous year, and her exchange of letters with Honoré became more and more embittered. "You are a monster," Mirabeau finally wrote, "farewell forever," and he took the canteen keeper's wife. "She was the only woman at If," he would later write his father, "who looked like a woman, and I was twenty-six." The

cantinière, complaining of beatings by her husband, fled the island
with his money and a letter from Mirabeau to sister Louise. The
canteen keeper named Mirabeau as his wife's seducer, and the marquis
had his son removed to the fortress of Joux, near Pontarlier and the
Swiss border. And here he met Sophie de Monnier.

She was twenty, the second wife of the Marquis de Monnier,
who was seventy. Mirabeau was moved, "troubled"—"I was dreadfully
afraid of love"—and may have avoided Sophie for several weeks.
Sophie, too, was "troubled." She felt the force and was repulsed by
the figure: the huge head, the woolly hair, the pitted face, large nose,
thin lips. But he had hands that women, sensing them, call beautiful,
and when he talked, Sophie stopped her flight and listened. We
know that Mirabeau wrote Emilie, asking her to join him, and that
Emilie, enjoying other men's company, replied with a cold note. That restraint to that extent removed, Mirabeau fell in love with Sophie. They
became lovers, and the talk of Pontarlier. As a further indiscretion,
Mirabeau had crossed the border and published his essay on despotism
in Switzerland. It was anonymous, but he became known as the author,
as having again broken a royal order to remain put, and Saint-Mauris,
who was responsible for him, restricted him to the fortress of Joux.
Granted four days of leave before the restriction, Mirabeau spent part
of them in a closet adjoining Sophie's bedroom. Returning to it one
day, he was caught by the servants and taken to her husband. He
was dropping by, he explained, to see them both.

Sophie suggested her going to Dijon to visit her family until the
gossip came to an end. Monsieur de Monnier complacently agreed.
Mirabeau, however, by prearrangement, followed her, and the scandal
reached Versailles. The entire affair, involving several noble families,
was now tossed into Malesherbes' liberal lap with Mirabeau's mother,
the marquise, writing the minister for her son's freedom, his father,
the marquis, writing for his imprisonment. Malesherbes, if one is
to believe Mirabeau, simply counseled him to leave the country—and
he slipped across the Swiss border. Meanwhile Sophie had returned to
Pontarlier and was being threatened with a convent should she cor-
respond with Mirabeau. She countered by threatening to kill herself—
"Gabriel [Honoré] or death"—and twice tried to escape. Finally, after a
hare-and-hounds chase involving government police, two private sleuths
hired by the marquis, and the help of Mirabeau's breeches-wearing sister Louise and her lover, Sophie joined Gabriel in Switzerland.[9] The

flight continued, however, to Holland, where they spent eight happy months.

They lived frugally over a tailor shop in Amsterdam. Mirabeau did hack work for a publisher, translating English books for a louis a day. But he also wrote on his own—notably a defense of the American revolt and an attack on the English use of Hessian mercenaries—while Sophie earned money giving Italian lessons. He worked from six in the morning until nine in the evening, and then, he has written, "an hour's music relaxed me, and my adorable companion made my life beautiful. She who had been raised in luxury was never so gay, so courageous, so considerate, so calm and tender as in poverty. She made my extracts; she worked, read, painted, corrected my proofs. Her even-tempered sweetness, her unfailing sensitivity were in full flower."[10]

Was there, as well, a compulsion for self-destruction in Mirabeau? He wrote and published a work calling the Friend of Mankind a philosophical hypocrite, "the worst of husbands, the harshest and most profligate of fathers," an agricultural theorist "who could not tell wheat from rye." And his father, who had looked on his son's flight to Holland with some benevolence, now regarded his son, even in exile, as a menace. To add to the marquis' displeasure, Mirabeau had lately corresponded with the marquise, helping her with her suit for separation of "body and property" from his father. So, joining forces with poor Monsieur de Monnier, the marquis succeeded in having Sophie and his son extradited from Holland (the arresting officer, des Bruguières, barely prevented Sophie from poisoning herself). In Pontarlier, a conviction of rape and abduction had been secured against Mirabeau *in absentia,* with a sentence of death. Sophie had been convicted of adultery and sentenced to branding and imprisonment as a prostitute. Two months' pregnant, she had her sentence changed to confinement in a house of correction. As for Mirabeau: on June 8, 1777, he was taken to the château-dungeon of Vincennes by order of his father's *lettre de cachet;* with the death sentence still suspended over him, he was imprisoned, as the marquis requested, "for life."

His cell was in the outer, western wall of the dungeon, ten feet square, dimly lit by a small, barred opening that caught only the last rays of the setting sun. When, after many months, he was finally allowed books, he so strained his eyes reading, he wrote Sophie, that he saw "through torrents of black spots."[11] As always with those with whom he had long, close contact, Mirabeau won over his prison commandant and officers, Rougemont and Boucher, and Police Lieutenant Le Noir. Early in his imprisonment, des Bruguières, now a friend, carried his clandestine letters to Sophie; later they were authorized. He was permitted paper and pens, as well as books, and he devoured masses of reading matter, stocking his prodigious memory. When a daughter was born to Sophie (mother and child were transferred to a convent at Gien), Mirabeau wrote a French grammar for her future use. He wrote pornography to make money to buy books; he wrote pornography to Sophie out of the frustration of his prison life. But Mirabeau also wrote *Des lettres de cachet et des prisons d'état,* eventually published; Louis XVI would read it and, publicly shamed, empty the Vincennes dungeon of its prisoners in 1784. "Without a constitution," said Mirabeau, "we are slaves." Freedom of the person, for him, was the essential freedom, and he wrote ministers, even the monarch, for his own or, failing that, a public trial. To Sophie he penned this reverie: "If only we were living in Boston. You would be at peace and I would be useful and appreciated, and our daughter would be an American!" To Le Noir, he spoke bitterly of his father: "The tender-hearted Friend of Mankind, whose soul, too lofty to stoop to vulgar affections, disdains his family and loves only the human race." And to his father, after suffering a summer of hemorrhages, Mirabeau wrote of the "horrible mutilation" of his existence, and cried: "I can no longer endure this life, my father, I cannot! Let me see the sun, let me breathe a freer air, let me see the faces of my own kind!"[12]

Only the death of Mirabeau's five-year-old son, whom he had not seen since infancy, would aid Mirabeau with his father. The marquis did not want the name of Mirabeau to die. He had, said the Bailli, *"postéromanie"*—a mania for posterity—and his other son, the beau Boniface, was now "Barrel" Mirabeau, the alcoholic. So the marquis sent his friend Dupont (later de Nemours) as an envoy to his son in prison. Emilie alone, Dupont advised Mirabeau, could arrange for his liberation with the marquis. Humbly he wrote her; so did Sophie, pleading for her lover. (His freedom, she wrote Mirabeau, counted most for her, even if it meant his returning to his wife; shortly after, their own little girl, Sophie-Gabrielle, died.) The marquis raised the price of freedom: his son must also take his side against the marquise. To all this Mirabeau acquiesced, and on

December 13, 1780—after three and a half years in his dungeon cell—*a lettre de cachet* released him to his father.*

"On behalf of the King [read the sealed letter]

the *sieur comte de Mirabeau* is ordered to betake himself to such places as his father shall appoint to him, His Majesty forbidding the said *sieur comte de Mirabeau* to depart thereform on any pretext whatsoever, and this until further order on his part, under pain of disobedience.
Versailles, the 13th of December, 1780

[Signed]
LOUIS

The Comte de Mirabeau was thirty-one. Such were the *lettres de cachet* a Frenchman could obtain against a less influential, less powerful brother, wife, son, or enemy.

"Naked as a worm" (in his father's delicate phrase), Mirabeau emerged from Vincennes—not as a Mirabeau, but as Monsieur Honoré. He was met by Dupont and his brother-in-law, the Marquis du Saillant; he lodged with Boucher, his "good angel" in prison. Dutifully he helped his father with his legal affair, but his mother won her suit: the Paris Parlement awarded her separation of "body and property." However, the marquis was impressed by the man his son had become. (They had met briefly at the office of the family lawyer, turned quickly away from each other, though they had not met for almost nine years.) "He has the vision," the Bailli heard unexpectedly from the marquis, "of an eagle"—the powerful sweep one begins to recognize in his writings.

Pursuing his own affairs, Mirabeau sent Emilie a letter proposing they re-establish life together—then disappeared for eight days. He spent five of them with Sophie in her convent at Gien; she had managed to get a key to its gates for him, and he slipped in to join her. It was their last time together, and sadly she sensed it. Four years apart had been too much; four days after he left, she wrote him, *"Adieu!"* Mirabeau now went down to Pontarlier, "to get his head back on his shoulders again," as his father advised him. (The death sentence still hung over him for the rape and abduction of Sophie.) Voluntarily

* Old Maurepas, before he died, wryly remarked that "there ought to be a special secretary of state for purely Mirabeau family affairs."[13]

he constituted himself prisoner, then pleaded his case. "Rape and abduction" having taken place abroad, they could not be proved in France. Mirabeau's sentence was voided, Sophie's reduced; a year later her husband died, and she was free.*

Mirabeau and his father came uneasily together. "He is a magpie of all men of wit," wrote the marquis to his brother, ". . . he has a mirror instead of a soul in which everything is reflected, then immediately erased." Several times, during a conversation, he would pull out his watch and say of his son's contribution that so many hours just previously he himself had made the same remark.[14] Nonetheless he pressed Mirabeau to go down to Provence to arrange matters with Emilie, so that the "noble race" of Mirabeau might continue.

He went down to Aix (where "everyone fled me as if I were the Anti-Christ"), wrote to Emilie and her father, was turned away (letters to Emilie came back unopened), and boldly decided to bring suit for her return. His appearance at court was the revelation of a public orator: his plea left half the spectators—his father-in-law the Marquis de Marignane possibly among them—in tears. He won, but the Marignanes appealed the decision to a higher court, the Parlement of Aix. In anticipation, Mirabeau published a *mémoire* containing the once affectionate letters of his wife. In rejoinder, the Marignanes published an account which included the marquis' most derogatory letters about his son ("a thorough scoundrel who should be removed from the memory of man").

On May 2, 1783 the Grande Chambre of the Aix Parlement was packed to its doors; even the windows were filled. From 8:15 A.M. until 1:00 P.M. Mirabeau spoke, addressing the magistrates, and beyond them, the great crowd. Eloquently he replied to the attack on his personal life, decrying the use of his father's letters as a crime against the Friend of Mankind "in the old age of his genius." In the lower court he had successfully asked that his wife provisionally live in a convent, rather than with her father. And now, he asked the magistrates of Aix with rich irony, is she to remain in the house of that well-known "Epicurean"? If so, his voice rose, "we shall see

* She moved into a little house near the Gien convent and served the poor. Eventually she met a former cavalry captain who asked her to marry him. She finally accepted. He died before they could wed; she killed herself the next day— September 9, 1789. Mirabeau, informed of it at the National Assembly, turned pale, rose from his seat, and was not seen for two days.

her, as we have already seen her, enjoying the company of men without her father, in social circles without her father, at public spectacles without her father, entertaining the friends of an unmarried man [the Comte de Galliflet, her known lover], performing on the private stage of that man's house!" *That,* he paused, would *really* be her home, if she remained in her father's house, rather than in her husband's or in a convent.

True, Mirabeau continued, he had not lived a blameless life, but he had paid for it many times over and would now gladly redeem himself, whereas the "virtuous Madame de Mirabeau . . ." He took from his pocket the letter he had preserved from Emilie to her lover, Musketeer de Gassaud, and read it to the judges. "And that man," he roared, "spent the winter in the house of Monsieur de Marignane, in the apartment destined for me when I was to live with Madame de Mirabeau!" But all that, he quietly added, could and would be forgiven by a man who acknowledged that he himself was not without a fault and wished, above all, to have his wife rejoin him.

At the end of the five hours' plea, the crowd of enraptured onlookers burst into applause. With difficulty the Marignane lawyers replied. Ultimately Mirabeau lost—in the face of so many demonstrated mutual infidelities, the magistrates ordered separation maintained—but a new public figure had been born during the procedures, a new eloquence heard. For the people of Aix, Mirabeau had become the man who had stood up alone against the local seigneur, the count cast out by his own kind who had become, by his stand, a champion of the people, a spokesman for the Third Estate.

"He has turned all men in his favor," the marquis wrote his brother. But after the sentence, he again refused to receive his son, returning the *lettre de cachet* to the authorities and disowning him. Mirabeau sued and won a small allowance of three thousand livres a year. He borrowed heavily, resumed life luxuriously, met Henriette de Nehra— a young, pretty, and intelligent blonde—and took her to England. It was the year Mirabeau also met Talleyrand, Benjamin Franklin, and Chamfort,* and had antagonized Miromesnil, wherefore the sudden

---

* Marie Antoinette to the famous writer of maxims and epigrams: "Do you realize, Monsieur de Chamfort, you have pleased everybody here at Versailles, not, I should say, because of your *esprit,* but despite it?"

Chamfort: "The reason is quite simple. At Versailles I am content to learn many things I already know from people who do not know them."[15]

28. *Petit Trianon*

29. *"House of the Queen" — Marie Antoinette — in the Hameau, or
Hamlet, of Versailles*

30. The Hall of Mirrors

31. The Oeil-de-Boeuf antechamber or waiting room of the Court

32. Bedchamber of Marie Antoinette (two paintings of the Queen visible)

33. *Comtesse de la Motte*

34. *Cardinal de Rohan*

35. *Mirabeau*

36. Duc d'Orléans

trip to England. He took with him, as well as Henriette and an adopted two-year-old boy, Coco (Lucas de Montigny, his biographer and most likely his son), a manuscript of Franklin, which we have mentioned earlier. He was to incorporate it in a pamphlet of his own, published in London, *Considérations sur l'ordre de Cincinnatus,* a condemnation of hereditary privileges to which Chamfort, too, contributed. But writing was not (it never was) his only activity during his months in England. Thanks to his Choquard schoolmates, the Elliot brothers, he met the leading Whig members of Parliament, and it was Gilbert Elliot, first Earl of Minto, with whom he stayed at Bath (Henriette and Coco remaining discreetly behind in London).

Gilbert Elliot to brother Hugh, on Mirabeau at this time: "I found him as ardent a friend as I left him, and as little altered as possible by twenty years of life, of which six have been consumed in prison. . . . He is very much ripened in his abilities, which are really considerable, and has acquired a great store of knowledge. . . . Mirabeau is as overbearing in his conversation, as awkward in his graces, as ugly and misshapen in face and person, as dirty in his dress, and withal as perfectly *suffisant* [satisfying] as we remember him twenty years ago in school. I loved him however, then, and so did you. . . . I brought him with me the other day to Bath, where he made hasty love to Harriet [Gilbert's sister-in-law], whom he had little doubt of subduing in a week, and where he so totally silenced my John Bull wife, who understands a Frenchman no better than a Molly housemaid, where he so scared my little boy by caressing him, and so completely disposed of me from breakfast to supper, and so astonished all our friends, that I could hardly keep the peace in his favour; and if he had not been called unexpectedly to town this morning, I am sure my wife's endurance, for I cannot call it civility, would not have held out another day."[16]

Back in Paris, after Henriette had sounded out the safety of his return, Mirabeau rapidly brought out five publications in less than five months ("he had as always a host of collaborators"[17]). The first two favored Calonne, evoking the accusation that Calonne had paid for them—an accusation soon refuted by the publications that followed, which criticized the finance minister. And Mirabeau, on the advice of Talleyrand, took himself to Berlin in December 1785, to offer his services to Frederick the Great. On the way, between

o

Toul and Verdun, his carriage was shot at, according to Henriette, and in Frankfurt he had a fleeting affair ("a pretty face, a woman's advance," she recognized, "would set him on fire," and she resigned herself to it, so long as she felt "sure of his heart"[18]).

In Berlin, Mirabeau was twice received by the aging, dying Prussian monarch, warming himself before the fireplace, but his offer of services was not taken up, and he returned to Paris—to the *affaire* of the Queen's necklace and a reconciled Calonne. He was soon back again in Berlin, this time on a secret mission for the French government; in six months he dispatched seventy long reports to Talleyrand for Calonne, Vergennes, and the King. "We are completely satisfied with your reports," Talleyrand wrote him. "It is repeated to me daily. The King reads them with a great deal of interest. M. de Calonne thanks you for your exactitude and the care with which you prepare them."[19] Thus, going to Germany, Mirabeau entered French public life on an official level—for a brief time.

While in Germany, Mirabeau published a remarkable plea for Jewish civil rights and collected material (most of it, on a *third* trip, from a Prussian major) for an eventual, four-volume history of the Prussian monarchy. But a diplomatic career, despite his admired reports, did not open for him, nor, he felt, were three hundred louis sufficient recompense for six months' efforts. Returning to France early in 1787, Mirabeau wrote a pamphlet denouncing stock-jobbing which clearly involved Calonne, though he was unnamed. The pamphlet created a sensation; the time had found its man. Lafayette quoted it at the Assembly of Notables. "The King read it and remarked sorrowfully . . . [on its] truth."[20] A month after its appearance, Calonne was dismissed. Almost distantly Mirabeau looked on at the failure of the Assembly of Notables, defended the rights but not the privileges of the parlements, then pressed strongly and openly for a meeting of the Estates General.

If it were not called soon, Mirabeau wrote a minister, the monarchy risked a revolution. "I ask," his letter read, "if you have well calculated the convulsive force of hunger added to the spirit of despair. I ask who will dare answer for the consequences, for the personal safety of all those who surround the throne, of the King himself?"

When finally the Estates General was summoned and elections for it ordered, Mirabeau was ready. His long period of preparation—and probation—was over.* "I have recognized his genius," the marquis wrote his brother. "His unique capacity for untiring work, his complete lack of self-doubt, his natural hauteur, all joined to what is called *esprit,* have made him a personage in finance, public writing, and above all modern politics."

On January 15, 1789, Mirabeau went down to Aix and sat with the nobles of the Second Estate as the forthcoming Estates General was discussed. In the parade of all three estates of Provence, however, before the beginning of their separate local sessions, Mirabeau had significantly walked between the ranks of the Second and Third Estates, as if the last of the nobles and first of the commoners. Indeed, the latter received him warmly, recalling his performance against the Marignanes, while the reception by his peers could not have been colder. All three estates, he told the nobles, should vote as one body. Almost as a body, the Second Estate rejected the proposal and proceeded to find grounds for rejecting Mirabeau himself: he possessed no fief in Provence. Well then, he would present himself as a candidate of the people, of the Third Estate. "If I am not a noble," he wrote his father, "I shall be a commoner. I must get into the Estates General!"

Three days before his expulsion from the nobility, Mirabeau thundered: "I was, I am, I will be unto death the man of public freedom, the man of the constitution. Woe to the privileged orders! It is better to be one of the people than one of the nobles, for privileges come to an end, whereas the people are eternal!"

But before campaigning in Aix for election by the Third Estate, Mirabeau made a quick trip to Paris to arrange a few private matters. On his return he was struck by the signs of his popularity: church bells rang, crowds lined his route. Twelve miles out of Aix men began unhitching his horses, so they might draw his carriage themselves. He stopped them. "Man," he said, "is not made to bear the burden of another man. You have already borne too much."[21] At Aix that night there were fireworks and torchlight parades. He was hailed as the father of his country and a deputation marched to the Hôtel de Marignane, demanding Madame la Comtesse. When Emilie appeared,

* Typically, however, it was compromised at the last minute by the publication of his *Histoire secrète de la cour de Berlin,* exposing his secret reports to Versailles. The book was burned by the public executioner; its author by then was safely campaigning in Provence.

Earlier, we might also note here, Mirabeau's liaison with the possessive wife of his Paris bookseller brought an end to his years with Henriette.

she heard a loud cry that the race of Mirabeau was "too good to die!"[22] She listened, she smiled, she now took an interest in her husband's prospering career.

To multiply his chances of "getting into the Estates General," scheduled for May in Versailles, Mirabeau also presented his candidature at Marseilles, twenty miles distant. As for general procedures: clergy and noblemen of the First and Second Estates elected their representatives directly. For the Third Estate, elections were in two, three, or more stages. Every French male above twenty-five who was on any tax list, virtually all but domestics and itinerants, was permitted to vote. Commoners voted for electors who in turn chose the deputies who would represent their *baillage,* or district, in the Estates General. In some *baillages,* such as Paris, the procedure was more complicated, involving balloting by guild and corporation. But it was a remarkable election, freer and more universal than many held since.[23]

All three estates, at various stages of the electoral process, drew up *cahiers de doléances,* which constituted not only a list of grievances to be presented to the King, but in final form instructions for their delegates to Versailles. The temper of the Third Estate at Aix, for instance, is reflected in its *cahier,* one of the thousands that have been preserved and in whose preparation Mirabeau took an active part. Voting at the Estates General, it stated, should be by individual, not by order, and its list of reforms included: freedom of the press, abolition of *lettres de cachet,* election of bishops (instead of appointment by the Crown), suppression of the venality or sale of offices, elimination of feudal abuses, trial by jury, better education for *both* sexes.[24] It was not uncharacteristic of the nation as a whole, many of the *cahiers* of the Third Estate including religious tolerance, some even marriage for priests. None were antimonarchical.[25] As Mirabeau, the country was still monarchist: the fight was with feudalism.* Here the *cahier* of the region containing the Château de Mirabeau is doubly relevant:

"If the Community of Mirabeau [it reads] could not flatter itself for having as its seigneurs the Riqueti, such as the Friend of Mankind, and such as the Comte de Mirabeau, the Friend of the People, whose

---

* By summoning the Estates General, Louis XVI had aroused *"la grande espérance"*—the great hope—among the people of imminent changes and reforms, seemingly placing himself on the side of the people against the privileged, of the Third Estate against the first and second.

name will always be dear to the Provençal nation and especially to this Community, which will never forget that he alone in his order pled the cause of the Third Estate and had the firmness and courage to defend it against the usurpation and tyranny of the first two orders, it would not lift its voice to demand that the Estates General abolish feudal rights bearing heavily on its inhabitants, since the benevolence of the Friend of Mankind and the Friend of the People would suffice for that; but it is a question of a general regeneration and to this the Community adds its voice and will expose the vexations to which seigneurial rights have exposed the people of the country." As for the seigneurs of the Church, the *cahier* continues: "Of all the abuses existing in France, the most burdensome for the people, the most crushing for the poor, are the immense wealth, idleness, tax exemptions and outrageous luxury of the high clergy."[26]

The marquis was now a sick old man, in retirement near Paris, and he would die in July. There was no question of his candidacy, but Mirabeau had sought his approval, if not his blessing, in posing his own at Aix. Soon his standing in Marseilles would receive its test.

The great winter had also struck the south: olive and orange trees froze, crops were ruined, bread was scarce, its price prohibitive. "It is as if the Exterminating Angel had smitten man throughout the kingdom," Mirabeau wrote his father. "Everywhere I see men dying of cold and hunger." Rioting broke out in Manosque, Toulon, Marseilles. His troops overwhelmed, Duc de Caraman, commandant of Provence, called on Mirabeau for aid, and he responded, riding down to Marseilles. There the bourgeois youth had formed a militia and named it Mirabeau in honor of their idol. Gladly they accepted his command. Calmly, capably, Mirabeau restored order, appeasing the rioters with a promise of change. "The King," he told them, "will hear of this." When riots broke out in Aix and left dead and wounded in the streets, Caraman again called on Mirabeau, and he galloped back to perform the same feat. From horseback he addressed and calmed the crowds, a patriarchal figure riding from street to street adjuring patience and promise of change when the Estates General would at last assemble.

Several days later Mirabeau was elected deputy by both Third Estates of Aix and Marseilles. At Aix he had led the list of those elected; at Marseilles, where the *grande bourgeoisie* was more reserved in its attitude toward him, he was fourth. On April 7, 1789,

Mirabeau chose to go to Versailles as a deputy of Aix. Before leaving, he went down to Marseilles to thank those who had voted for him. He was given a hero's send-off: a torchlight parade of young men on horseback. At Aix, he tried to leave more discreetly, arranging his departure late at night. But a great crowd waited outside his house and followed him as he left; and there was a crowd at every post where he stopped for a change of horses on his way to Paris and Versailles.

The Comte de Mirabeau, forty, rejected by his class, would now enter the most historical, possibly honorable, undoubtedly climactic period of his—and Versailles'—complex life; and he would enter it as a representative of the roused middle class.

28.   The Men in Black Make the Scene

They were kept waiting in the palace's Salon d'Hercule on Saturday, May 2. The King received representatives of the clerical First Estate at eleven in the morning, then the noblesse of the Second Estate at one. Tired, bored, he had lunched, rested, then summoned the somberly dressed commoners of the Third Estate. Singly they were admitted to his bedroom through the double-paneled door, only half-opened for them, though both panels had swung wide for the privileged orders when they had been received in the King's study. Thus the bourgeoisie was early shown its "place," and it was not soon to forget the demonstration.[1] (Many of its members would visit the Petit Trianon, convinced that several rooms had been cunningly hidden from them, particularly the salon "tapestried with diamonds."[2])

That the Estates General met at all in Versailles was an earlier, more costly mistake of Louis XVI. For hours his Council had discussed the meeting place. Marie Antoinette had wanted it forty or fifty leagues further from Paris than Versailles, so it would be that much further removed from the "immense population" of the turbulent capital.[3] Necker had initially opted for Paris itself, "feeling sure of his influence and popularity" among the Parisians, "but it was the King who decided for Versailles, for the frivolous motif that there would be less inconvenience for his hunting and comfort."[4] So recalls the Comte de Saint-Priest, who was in charge of the King's security. In fact, the population of Versailles (perhaps sixty thousand) would prove turbulent enough.

On the morning of May 4, and during the night before, half Paris poured into Versailles for the magnificent procession—monarchy's last.[5] The sun shone, the avenues were splendid with tapestries and pennants hanging from balconies on both sides of the route. People crowded the streets, cluttered the rooftops. The Dauphin looked on from the terrace of the Small Stables, elegant women were at every window. At ten the King, Queen, royal family, princes of the blood left the palace in their carriages for Versailles' Church of Notre Dame. Here the procession of the Estates General was to begin; here they descended—and awkwardly joined the Nation.

Five hundred and fifty-odd deputies of the Third Estate (those from Paris, not yet elected, would arrive several weeks later), dressed in the prescribed—and resented—black coats, black stockings, black three-cornered hats, preceded the other orders. Behind them were the noblesse wearing gold-trimmed capes, white-plumed hats and ceremonial swords, and behind *them,* cardinals in scarlet vestments, bishops in white cassocks, separated—on their request—from the lower clergy by a hastily rearranged group of the King's musicians. Following the Archbishop of Paris, who carried the Holy Sacrament under a sheltering baldachin, came the King. Indeed, in that procession the people of France were seeing their last four kings: Louis XVI and his two brothers, the Comtes de Provence and d'Artois, who would be Louis XVIII* and Charles X, and the sixteen-year-old son of the Duc d'Orléans, who—two revolutions later—would be crowned as Louis Philippe. As for the Duc d'Orléans, he had to be persuaded by the master of ceremonies, the harassed, twenty-seven-year-old Marquis de Dreux-Brézé, sent by the King, to return to the princes of the blood from the ranks of the Third Estate, where he had taken his place—to the crowd's applause. All carried candles, except the King's falconers, who had birds on their wrists.

"It was a very imposing—and a very new—spectacle for the French," writes Madame de Staël, her eyes, as so many others, searching for a famous figure. Tall, massive, lion-headed, it was not difficult to find. "Once catching sight of it," continues Necker's daughter, describing Honoré-Gabriel Mirabeau, "it was difficult to tear oneself away from it. His enormous mane distinguished him immediately from all the others. One might say, as of Samson, that his strength seemed to depend on it.

* "Louis XVII" would never reach the throne.

Even his ugliness contributed to his impression of power, and his entire figure gave one a sense of the rough force that would make him a tribune of the people. No other name but his was as yet celebrated among all six hundred deputies of the Third Estate."[6]

Past the Place d'Armes wound the procession on its way to the Church of Saint-Louis, and as it passed, the loudest cheers were for the men in black with a "Long live the King!" on the sight of Louis XVI. But as Marie Antoinette followed, silence followed her, save for a sudden, taunting cry, "Long live the Duc d'Orléans!" She turned pale, faltered, and seemed about to faint. "It was feared that the procession might have to be brought to a halt. But the Queen recovered, with a swift regret that she had shown signs of weakness."[7] Her face hardened. She continued. For Gouverneur Morris, who had driven from Paris that dawn to watch the procession, she seemed to say, with visible contempt, "For the present I submit, but I shall have my time."[8] In the Church of Saint-Louis, after Mass, she suffered a sermon by Bishop de la Fare, who berated those close to the King who lived in "barbarous" luxury at the expense of the people, and she returned to the palace so furious "she broke her diamond bracelet."[9]

"Ces Français indignes!" she exclaimed to Madame Adélaïde. "Those unworthy French!"

"Dites indignés, Madame," said the King's aunt. "Say, rather, those *indignant* French."[10]

The day following, at the opening session of the Estates General, the frigid reception Marie Antionette received, as she sat next to the King, made matters no more palatable.

The historic meetings would take place in the Salle des Menus Plaisirs,* the reconverted storehouse for the King's minor playthings—tennis rackets, musical instruments, theater and festival sets. (The Grands Plaisirs involved the King's hunts.) The late, fated Assembly of Notables had also met here, and the *salle* on the ground floor had been hurriedly prepared for the vaster assembly of the Estates General. The great hall, over 120 by 60 feet in its central area, could now accommodate 1200 deputies and 2000 spectators (sitting between and behind Ionic columns and in the galler-

---

* A dilapidated wing with a weatherworn commemorative plaque remains standing on the Avenue de Paris of today's Versailles.

O*

ies).[11]* Dr. Guillotin, arriving late in May, along with the Abbé
Sieyès and other Paris deputies, would improve the ventilation (as
he would the headman's ax). The lighting, however, needed no improvement: filtering down through a white taffeta ceiling, it flattered women,
who dressed smartly for the Salles des Menus Plaisirs. "Gods!" exclaimed Morris, "what a theater this is for a first-rate character!"

Thus for Mirabeau? An audience, it is said, is a woman, and all conquests—private or public—may have much in common.

From eight in the morning of May 5 the deputies arrived, but the
men of the Third Estate had to wait in a hangar, while the privileged
were shown to their seats—a procedure of three long hours of anti-
quated protocol. Confusedly the young Marquis de Dreux-Brézé
applied, or tried to apply, the forms of 1614, as the only precedent he
could draw upon. The Duc d'Orléans, however, once again upset him
by bowing the priest of his *baillage* of Villers-Cotterets before him, and
cheers rose from the public benches. Finally clergy and nobility found
their places to the right and left of the hall. The men in black, when
eventually seated, were massed in the center, facing the purple velvet
dais with its throne for the King and armchair for the Queen, stools
for the royal family and folding chair for the grand chamberlain.
Gouverneur Morris: "An old man who refused to dress in the costume
prescribed for the Tiers [Third Estate], and who appears in his
farmer's habit, receives a long loud plaudit." When Mirabeau made
his solo entrance, "a strong, low [disapproving] murmur filled the
hall"; when he sat down, deputies on all sides drew away from him,
leaving him alone "in an empty space," soon filled by the press of
other deputies.[12] His reputation, repelling as it intrigued, had preceded him.

When joined by the twenty Paris deputies, there would be a total
of 578 representing the Third Estate, the bulk of whose seats had
been captured by the urban bourgeoisie: 200 lawyers, 150 merchants.

* A few nobles and prelates lodged at the palace. Some had their own Versailles
hôtel, or town house, or stayed with their families or friends, as Lafayette
at the Hôtel de Noailles. (When the Notables met, he had lodged at the
palace, since there were fewer of them.) Others of a lower estate found rooms
in the dozens of boardinghouses and new-style hotels that sprang up as
Versailles grew, or also stayed with friends. They lunched at the early hour of
ten-thirty where they lodged or in the numerous cabarets, cafés, or restaurants.
Sanitation measures, never the best at Versailles, were makeshift, outdoor latrines
—and the meetings in the Salle des Menus Plaisirs would be long and unin-
terrupted.

bankers, industrialists, and landowners. Among them were Mounier, Barnave and Robespierre, scientists, such as astronomer Bailly, writers and economists, such as Volney and Dupont de Nemours, a Protestant pastor, Rabaut Saint-Étienne, and those who had belonged to the privileged orders, the Comte de Mirabeau and the Abbé Sieyès—the system builder who would sit wrapped largely in impressive silence. Of the 291 ecclesiastics of the First Estate, over 200, significantly, were lowly parish priests, committed by their *cahiers* to a large measure of reform. A majority in the electing Church assemblies, they had stubbornly elected their own, and would be pivotal in the coming crisis. So, too, would be the some fifty liberal aristocrats—*patriotes,* such as Lafayette, La Rochefoucauld, Condorcet, Noailles, Liancourt—among the 270 of the Second Estate.[13]

Huzzas greeted the King on his entry, silence the Queen. *"Voilà la victime,"* whispered Mirabeau to his neighbor.[14] Less clinical, more moved, Gouverneur Morris writes: "The Queen weeps or seems to weep, but not one voice is heard to wish her well. I would certainly raise my voice if I were a Frenchman; but I have no right to express a sentiment, and in vain solicit those who are near me to do it."

Carefully the King read the short speech he had twice rewritten and "often rehearsed."[15] He spoke frankly of the Crown's "immense debt," brought about by the "costly but honorable" American war, promised economy at Court, mentioned the sacrifices the first two orders are prepared [*sic*] to make, and hoped for the best for "my people."[16] Deputies in the center cheered, the public wept. Necker followed.

For three hours the finance minister filled the air with statistics, from which emerged the total of 56,150,000 livres as the royal deficit. It was, in actuality, three times as great, and Necker's characteristic sleight-of-hand defeated his own ends. Members of the Estates General listened to him in amazement. Why call them together if the government debt could be so easily met, as Necker insisted in his exposé, by simply "extending the sale of snuff to Brittany?"[17] Additionally and irreparably, the Third Estate was angered by Necker's warning that any insistence on voting by individual rather than by order would risk dissolution of the Estates General.

The next morning each order assembled in its own chamber. That is, the first two orders retired to smaller rooms, specially arranged for them, while the Third Estate remained in the general assembly hall, since none other had been prepared. Thus an architectural economy became a political *faux pas.* The Third Estate occupied the Nation's meeting place, replete with galleries and benches for an increasingly vigorous public. It already considered itself, in terms of Sieyès' powerful pamphlet, more than 95 per cent of the nation; it would wait until the other orders, or their wavering deputies, duly recognized it and joined it in a national assembly.

The first days passed in this fashion. Verification of each deputy's credentials, said the Third Estate, must be done jointly. Regarding the proposal as a fatal precedent, the privileged orders refused, though a sizable minority of each, particularly of the clergy, was inclined to go along. There was a stalemate wittily described by Dumouriez in a popular broadsheet: "How will they vote in order to decide how they will vote? By order to decide they will vote by head? By head to decide they will vote by order?"[18] In the meantime, trusting in the gravitational force of its greater number, the growing impatience of public opinion, and the pressure of the Crown's needs, the Third Estate called itself the Commons *à l'anglaise,* and waited.

Deputy Delaville Le Roulx in a letter dated May 12: "We have managed to meet every day and do nothing. This apparent inertia has become the best conduct we could possibly adopt. We occupy the national chamber. The privileged orders know, and cannot ignore, that we are waiting for them there."[19]

In the national chamber, two days later, Le Chapelier, member of the Breton Club which would one day merge with the radical Jacobin Club, proposed the following motion: "That the Commons recognizes only those deputies whose credentials are verified in common, to which verification the other two orders are invited."[20] The privileged were properly outraged, more by the British appellation, the Commons, boldly asserting a new order of magnitude for the Third Estate, than by the invitation, which they summarily (with significant exceptions) rejected.

These were not lost days for the deputies of the Commons. They had much to learn about the democratic process of partisan debate, about the very organization of parliamentary life. "Typically French," Mirabeau writes in his *Journal des États Généraux,* "all want to be heard before they even listen." But such, he adds, is the nature of the first beginnings of democratic assembly. "You have begun with chaos," he addresses his fellow deputies, "but the world itself, did it begin in any other way?"[21] Nevertheless, he had the rules of English parliamentary order printed and distributed.

Speedily enough the more revolutionary deputies would group to the left of the speaker, the more conservative on the right (and so *left* and *right* have come down to our day with their political connotations). More monarchist than many on the left, Mirabeau would identify with and seat himself among them. During May, aware of the suspicion that surrounded him, he bided his time, but he would be ready when it came. His entire past had prepared him for the rough-and-tumble of politics. His prodigious memory had made him a "walking encyclopedia," his "stentorian" voice would make him heard even from his seat against the babble and acoustical shortcomings of the great *salle*.[22] Prison had been his school, as for so many political leaders, the occasion for reading, study, solitude, and reflection. His pamphleteering had taught him clarity, his experiences a sense of the moment, of seizing an opportunity, of expressing himself lucidly, and thinking ahead, even while standing on the Tribune and addressing the deputies.

Though he spoke little in the opening days, Mirabeau was heard through his *Journal*. Quickly suppressed by the Royal Council, it was as quickly replaced by his *Lettres du comte de Mirabeau à ses commettants*. How could the government prevent a deputy's reports to his constituents, even if published as open letters? And Mirabeau formed a small secretariat of informed men about him, devoted and capable, contributing to his speeches and his writings.[23] He called it his *atelier,* or workshop, anticipating the modern statesman's personal staff. And like Churchill (though the comparison must not be pressed), he became the great Commoner. To those irritated by Mounier's reference to him as the Comte de Mirabeau, he replied: "I attach so little importance to my title that I offer it to whoever will have it. My proudest title is that of representative of a great province."[24]

So ended May with the Commons stoically awaiting deputies from the other orders to join them in the Salle des Menus Plaisirs. And at the palace meanwhile the King and Queen awaited the death of the Dauphin. Rickets had bent his back, sickness had hollowed his cheeks; he could not walk without support. Twice he had sent away the Duchesse de Polignac, complaining of her strong perfumes.[25] On June 4 he died. Custom obliged the King and Queen to leave his poor body to others at Meudon. Custom did not oblige the mourning monarch to receive a deputation of insistent deputies. But he did, remarking bitterly: "Are there, then, no fathers in the Third Estate?"[26]

One can understand his bitterness; but he did not understand those fathering a new order, and *that* would be fatal.

As bankruptcy haunted the monarchy, famine haunted the land. The Great Hope in the King and the Estates General had turned into agitated unease at the deadlock in Versailles. Public opinion, that new deciding force, stirred—and was stirred—throughout France. Witness Arthur Young's diary for June 9, 1789:

"The business going forward at present in the pamphlet shops of Paris is incredible. I went to the Palais Royal* to see what new things were published, and to procure a catalogue of all. Every hour produces something new. Thirteen came out today, sixteen yesterday, and ninety-two last week. . . . One can hardly squeeze from the door to the counter. . . . This spirit of reading political tracts, they say, spreads into the provinces, so that all the presses of France are equally employed. Nineteen-twentieths of these productions are in favor of liberty, and commonly violent against the clergy and nobility. . . . Is it not wonderful, that while the press teems with the most leveling and even seditious principles, that if put in execution would overturn the monarchy, nothing in reply appears, and not the least step is taken by the court to restrain this extreme licentiousness of publication. . . ? But the coffeehouses in the Palais Royal present yet more singular and astonishing spectacles; they are not only crowded within, but other expectant crowds are at the doors and windows, listening *à gorge déployée* to certain orators, who from chairs or tables harangue each his little audience: the eagerness with which they are heard, and the thunder of applause they receive for every sentiment of more than common hardiness or violence against the present government, cannot easily be imagined."

On June 10, Young notes more ominously:

"The want of bread is terrible: accounts arrive every moment from the provinces of riots."[27]

And on June 10 in Versailles, the Abbé Sieyès proposed to the Commons that it put an end to the deadlock by formally inviting representatives of the other orders to join them, that the Commons

---

* To the scandal of the Court, the Duc d'Orléans had added several wings to his Paris residence, housing, at a profit, not only pamphlet shops, but cafés, boutiques, rented apartments and rooms for political clubs, and the like. See below, p. 424.

consider those refusing as no longer deputies and consequently proceed without them in the name of the Nation. Two weeks earlier, aware of the disarray between the upper and lower clergy, Mirabeau had appealed to the latter, "as ministers of the God of Peace, to range themselves on the side of reason, justice and truth, and join the other deputies in the common hall."[28]

Finally, on the thirteenth, three priests from Poitou crossed over and were emotionally embraced. On the fourteenth there were six more; within four days, sixteen in all. Though the liberals among the aristocrats had not yet moved, the Third Estate now considered itself the Nation and discussed an appropriate name. Meticulously Sieyès proposed "The Assembly of Known and Verified Representatives of the French Nation." Mirabeau would shorten it to "Representatives of the French People." The shiver among the bourgeoisie at the word *people* was visible and quickly made audible. Their protests brought an impassioned defense from Mirabeau. "Can't you see," he cried, "that you need the name of the people to show them we have linked our fate to theirs?"[29] But he experienced one of his rare parliamentary defeats. Finally, after two days of debate, the members voted for the "National Assembly." Eighty-nine, fearing dissolution and arrest, voted against it. From the Third Estate to the Commons to the National Assembly was nothing less than a political revolution, and the great majority in favor, as well as those opposed, knew it.

The middle class had arrived: the men in black had triumphed. Or had they? Would Louis XVI wisely comply, accept a constitutional monarchy, rather than risk losing all, support the representatives of "his people" against the privileged, and thus save the Crown? One knows the outcome, but it had to be played out.

The men in black were still monarchist. They wanted political power, but within the monarchy. Compromising, they decreed that existing taxes, "despite their illegality," should continue to be paid until the current Assembly was dissolved; that taxes thereafter be only those authorized by the succeeding, properly constituted Assembly; and that the current body prepare a constitution.[30] (Two days later the clergy voted, 149 to 137, to join the men of the Third Estate.)

Exasperated, the noblesse resisted and together with the princes of the Church pressed the King to dissolve the Estates General.[31] Necker cautioned otherwise. "Resign yourself, Sire," he counseled, "to an English constitution. Anticipating the wishes of your nation, you will

graciously accord it today what it may force from you tomorrow."[32]
At the Royal Council, Louis' minister warned of bankruptcy and
collapse if the privileged orders would not yield. The other ministers
(all nobles) protested the end of *all* order (that is, theirs) if the
Third Estate were permitted to act as if it were the nation. During
a long evening session, a note from Marie Antoinette took Louis
from the Council meeting, suspending it. The next day two princes
of the blood and two magistrates (both *noblesse de robe*) joined the
resumed discussions, advocating maintenance of the ancient order and
trust in the military. Thus was the King led in the direction in which
he was already inclined. ("I will never abandon my nobility or my
authority," he had reassured the Duc de Montmorency-Luxembourg.
"You can count on that."[33]) He decided to oppose the Third Estate
and impose the Crown's will in a *séance royale* at the Salle des Menus
Plaisirs. Necker tendered his resignation. The King, apprehensive of
the public reaction, turned it down.

Arthur Young, Saturday, June 20:

"News! News! Everyone stares at what everyone might have expected.
A message from the King to the presidents of the three orders, that he
should meet them on Monday [it would be Tuesday, June 23]; and
under pretense of preparing the hall for the *séance royale,* the French
guards were placed with bayonets to prevent any of such deputies
entering the room. The circumstances of doing this ill-judged act of
violence have been as ill-advised as the act itself. Mons. Bailly
[President of the National Assembly] received no other notice of it
than a letter from the Marquis de Brézé, and the deputies met at the
door of the hall, without knowing that it was shut. Thus the seeds of
disgust were sown wantonly in the manner of doing a thing. . . .
The Palais Royal was in a flame."[34]

Arriving at the Menus Plaisirs, the deputies indeed found workmen
and troops in their meeting hall, the workmen "preparing" it for the
royal session, the troops protecting it from their assembly. They hesitated, their tempers rose. Some wanted to push on immediately for
Paris and assemble there. It was Dr. Guillotin who suggested the
historic alternative: moving to the nearby Jeu de Paume, a covered
tennis court, where the Sun King had played.* And here in a bare,
black-walled, high-windowed setting, the deputies held their meeting

---

* It still stands, a remarkably neglected, "sainted slum" (André Chenier), on a
little Versailles street of the same name.

and took the still-resounding oath "never to separate, and to reassemble wherever circumstances might require, until the Constitution of the kingdom is solidly established on firm foundations." Refusing an armchair, Bailly stood with the other deputies as they swore and, all but one, signed the oath.[35]

A crowd outside heard them. So did the Duc des Cars, who hurried to the Comte d'Artois with the news. Conjointly they hastened to the King, exhorting instant dispersion of the rebellious deputies. Louis temporized; there was still the royal session in three days. The Comte d'Artois let it be known that he intended to play tennis, and the Jeu de Paume would no longer be available for the Third Estate.[36] Its deputies moved on to the Church of Saint-Louis, where they were reinforced by the first two of the liberal noblesse and the 149 of the clergy previously mentioned. In Paris crowds swarmed in the gardens of the Palais Royal and swore to defend the National Assembly. In Versailles crowds harassed noblemen and prelates who risked the streets and obliged the Archbishop of Paris to promise to join the Assembly before they let him pass.[37]

The public benches had been removed for the royal session of June 23, and troops surrounded the Menus Plaisirs. Deputies of the Third Estate stood in the rain, waiting outside a rear entrance, as those of the first two orders were ushered to their places through the front doors by the plumed Marquis de Dreux-Brézé. "They fumed and fretted," says Bailly, "and spoke of leaving."[38] But they entered, and they would remain. In grim, damp silence they greeted the King. (Necker had stayed away and Marie Antoinette would regard his failure to accompany the King "as treason or criminal cowardice."[39]) Royal reproaches were followed by a series of decrees, read by a secretary of state: Null and void was the Third Estate's declaration that it constituted a National Assembly. Meetings of all three orders might be held in common, but nothing "touching on the ancient and constitutional rights of the orders . . . on feudal and seigneurial property, rights and honorific prerogatives of the first two orders" might be considered jointly. Taxation would be equalized, but only if the privileged orders consented to it. Then Louis resumed his speech, threatening dissolution should the Third Estate dissent:

"If you abandon me in this great enterprise, I alone will work for the good of my people and alone will consider myself their representative."

And he closed with this command:

"I order you, Messieurs, to separate at once and return tomorrow, each of you to the chamber of your respective order."[40]

The King left the hall. Most of the nobility and part of the clergy followed. The men of the Third Estate remained in their seats. After a short time, the young Marquis de Dreux-Brézé returned to the *salle*. "Messieurs," he said, "you have heard the orders of the King."

Bailly, presiding on the tribune: "I do not believe it is for the nation assembled to receive orders."

Sieyès to the Assembly: "We have sworn to reestablish the rights of the French people. You are today what you were yesterday."

Mirabeau rose to the great occasion. "You, Sir," he thundered from the floor to the King's master of ceremonies, "have neither a place, voice nor right to speak in our Assembly. . . . Go tell those who have sent you* that we are here by the will of the people and will not leave except by force of bayonets!"[42] The exact wording will never be known, but so it has been recited by generations of French school children, and the deputies remained in their places.

Bailly would remark in his memoirs that Mirabeau's were unnecessary heroics, since no one spoke of bayonets. But soon enough soldiers would be on their way, if not immediately (according to one account), then within very few days. The first version has troops arriving shortly after Dreux-Brézé's ignominious departure and discovering their passage to the meeting hall blocked by a number of liberal nobles—Lafayette, La Rochefoucauld, Liancourt, the two Crillons, several others—drawn swords in their hands.[43] (Two days later, forty-seven nobles, highest among them the Duc d'Orléans, would take seats alongside the men of the Third Estate.†) A second version has the King dissuaded by the liberal nobles from dispatching troops, then exasperatedly remarking, "*Foutre*, let them stay then."[44]

But the threat of *lettres de cachet* and imprisonment was unlifted, and Mirabeau, who knew more about both than most men, warned of the danger and urged a motion declaring the deputies immune from arrest. Bailly opposed the motion, since inviolability of the deputies was "already taken for granted." Mirabeau: "You do not

* "Go tell your master . . ." Victor Hugo has Mirabeau say, with an antimonarchist violence that was never his.[41]

† But not yet Lafayette, who awaited a change of instructions from his Auvergne district permitting him to sit with the Third Estate.

know what you are exposing yourself to! If the motion is not voted, sixty deputies, and you the first among them, will be arrested tonight." The motion was carried, 493 to 34.[45]

It was not the motion, however, or the liberal nobles that restrained Louis XVI from sending a regiment into the Salle des Menus Plaisirs, but rather the thinness of his forces measured against the crowds massed in the streets of Versailles—and the mood of his French troops. On the very eve of the royal session, Louis had been persuaded by the Court Party—Artois, the Polignacs, the Queen, *et al.*—"to dismiss Necker and to overawe the National Assembly by a display of military force."[46] But the crowds had got wind of the plot and thousands thronged the courtyards of the palace, shouting for Necker to remain. French guards under the command of the Prince de Conti were given the order to fire. They had refused.

Blithely after the royal session, however, nobles among the deputies had followed the King to the palace. First they went to the Comte d'Artois, whose idea it had been, and congratulated him. They then proceeded to the Comte de Provence, who was not available to them, and went on to the Queen. Marie Antoinette received them in the game room, holding her little daughter by the hand and the little Dauphin on her arm. They celebrated their "triumph," but the noise of the crowds in the courtyard and beyond, news of a delegation of the Third Estate with Necker, interrupted their celebration. Anxiously the Queen sent for the King's minister and pressed him to put aside any thought of resigning. He acceded. He returned to his residence on foot, making his way slowly through the great crowds. "Yes," he assured them, "I am remaining." And Versailles, observed the Marquis de Ferrières, "resounded with cries of *'Vive M. Necker!'* "[47]

A half day's march away, there were other, greater crowds. Arthur Young, on June 24: "The ferment at Paris is beyond conception; 10,000 people have been all this day in the Palais Royal; a full detail of yesterday's proceedings was brought this morning, and read by many apparent leaders of little parties, with comments, to the people. . . . The constant meetings there are carried to a degree of licentiousness, and fury of liberty, that is scarcely credible."[48]

Scarcely as credible is the story of the Palais Royal's high-born resident: the King's own cousin, the great grandson of the former Regent of France, the first prince of the blood—the Duc d'Orléans.

29. The Prince and—Incidentally—the People

Henri d'Orléans, Comte de Paris, descendant of Louis-Philippe I (1773–1850), is the Bourbon pretender to the throne of France, this year of Our Lord, 1972. The father of Louis-Philippe I, as we have mentioned several times, was Louis-Philippe-Joseph, Duc d'Orléans—he who would be honored with the revolutionary title of Citizen Philippe-Égalité by the Commune of Paris and would vote the death of his cousin, Louis XVI, in 1793.

Perhaps it was this act of regicide on the part of the first prince of the blood, perhaps it was simply because, chronologically, it occurred early in his life, but all accounts of the Duc d'Orléans seem to begin with the story of a young rake and the first quotation is that of a prostitute in a brothel he frequented: "The Prince was extremely crude, without any delicacy and swore like a wagon driver." The description occurs in a police report.[1] One so close to the Crown was closely watched, not so much for his own safety, as for an accounting to Louis XV. Nor were his contemporaries scandalized; it was conduct quite proper "for his age and fortune."[2]

That fortune would soon be the greatest in France.

At twenty-two, Philippe married his sixteen-year-old cousin, the daughter of the melancholic Duc de Penthièvre—grandson of Louis XIV and Madame de Montespan and among the richest men of Europe. The Orléans wealth was enormous enough; the combination, in ambitious hands, could be dangerous, and Louis XV, initially, withheld his consent. One can understand his hesitation. When the Duc d'Orléans eventually came into possession of both heritages, his estates would cover over ten thousand square miles, or one twentieth of all France (most of it a gift of the Sun King to his brother Philippe I d'Orléans) and his income, as much as nine million livres in a good year (including allowances from Louis XVI), would be three times that of the Comte de Provence and seven times that of the Comte d'Artois (the King's own brothers).[3]

However, Louis XV finally consented to the marriage. For him the illegitimacy of the Penthièvre line removed the Orléans heirs that much further from the throne.[4]

The first child was born dead, but the truth was kept from the young duchess. She was told it had died after an emergency baptism. Suspiciously she asked to see the gazettes reporting the event. A copy was specially printed for her with a false account. Eventually there would be three sons, including the future Louis-Philippe I, and twin daughters. The duke, meantime, resumed his life as a rake. He took the Comtesse de Genlis as his mistress, had an arm tattooed —twice—in her honor, made her in later years the governess of his twin daughters and, contrary to custom, of his sons when they had reached the age of a male tutor. For *this,* he had to have the King's permission. With indifferent disdain, Louis XVI told him, "I have a Dauphin, the Comte d'Artois has children, do what you want"[5]—in other words, *your* children will never rule. And the Court laughed at the "governor" of Philippe's sons.*

Historically, traditionally, the Orléans branch of the Bourbons has produced shadow kings with shadow courts, alternatives to the reigning monarch. Somewhat in line with the tradition, in 1771 Philippe had been made the grand master of the masons, and those convinced of an Orléanist plot have made overmuch of the fact. At the age of twenty-four, Philippe was still pleasure bent, and had been chosen primarily for his wealth and family influence. His first real venture into the open was on the sea, in pursuit of his father-in-law's Grand Admiralty. His sole qualification, brought duly to the notice of the new King, Louis XVI, who wrote him a congratulatory note about it, was that he had survived a sea voyage (hugging the coast of Spain) without becoming seasick. Given the command of a squadron of vessels, Philippe joined Admiral Comte d'Orvilliers' fleet in the

---

* Louis-Philippe I to Victor Hugo, apropos the Comtesse de Genlis as his tutor: "I was cowardly as a child, even afraid of mice, but she made a man of me."[6]

424 *Versailles*

Battle of Ushant against the British. At a critical moment, flags were run up the mast of the admiral's ship, signaling Philippe to attack. He did not. Ignorance of the naval code? Cowardice? The former, said the admiral diplomatically. The latter, said the Comte d'Artois, who wanted the Grand Admiralty reserved for one of his sons.

Philippe now turned his back to the sea and sought glory on the land. In compensation for the end of his "naval career," he was named Colonel-General of the Hussars, a largely honorific post. When he wanted to join French forces leaving for America, he was stopped by a letter from Marie Antoinette. The King, she told him, did not want him to depart, and she was writing to spare him "the more severe form of royal Command."[7] And Philippe now turned his back on a Court that mocked him, and began his break with the Crown.

In 1781 he received the Palais Royal as his own residence, in 1785—on the death of his father—the title of Duc d'Orléans. In the interim years he vastly changed the aspect of Richelieu's former palace and grounds, in a venture frankly speculative. He opened most of the great gardens to the public and framed them on three sides with handsome, long row, commercial housing. There were arcades and galleries, cafés (the famous Foy and Caveau), shops, restaurants and billiard rooms. Above, on the second floor, were clubs and gaming rooms and some fashionable apartments; on the third floor, more apartments. There were concert halls, a theater, and a circus; spectacles were daily and until midnight the Palais Royal was as lively as Venice's San Marco. It became the capital's "pleasure capital,"[8] accommodating the common people as well as "the most sprightly and brilliant of Paris society."[9]

The King to Philippe: "So, my dear cousin, now that you are opening a shop, we shall not see you except on Sunday?"[10]

Louis XVI was masking a graver complaint. The Palais Royal was offering France a pole other than Versailles, and in the hard winter of 1783–84 it had open fires—and firewood—for the poor.[11] The Orléans prince was becoming too popular.

Even Philippe's *anglomanie* had its popular side; England was regarded as the land of free men (but by Louis XVI as the land that had beheaded its King). Several times a year the duke crossed the Channel, each time requiring Versailles' reluctant permission. In 1785 nevertheless he was thrice in London. He commissioned a portrait by Joshua Reynolds (showing him remarkably like Louis XVI:

more blotched in complexion but as round-faced, Roman-nosed, and prematurely heavy), became a friend of the Prince of Wales (whose mistress, Grace Dalrymple Elliott, soon became his), and attended the House of Commons. "Were I English," he told its members, "I would be happy to sit among you. I admire a government whose authority derives from the will of the people"—words that shortly reached the people of France.[12]

To Philippe's *anglomanie* must be added his fascination with hot-air balloons. (He had helped finance the Montgolfier brothers.) He was not alone. A popular quatrain satirically sang that as England had proudly built an empire by controlling the sea, France had light-headedly taken to the air.[13] In 1784 Philippe had a huge balloon made, the *Caroline*, to take him on the first flight across the Channel. A test flight was made from Saint-Cloud. Two thousand carriages had brought spectators to see it. Swiftly the *Caroline* rose with balloonists and the duke aboard—and landed a league away.[14] The Court laughed. The Parisians, too, irresistibly drawn to ridicule, mocked the prince, but their raillery was different: the duke was *their* prince. Montjoie, editor of the ultra-Royalist *L'Ami du Roi,* recognized the difference if the Court did not:

"The Parisians [he wrote], seeing him always among them, meeting him at all their spectacles, all their gatherings, on all their public promenades, knowing he liked to be with the multitude, cherished and covered him with their applause; he was, so to speak, the only one of our princes they set eyes upon."[15]

Perhaps the Duc d'Orléans wandered into politics on his way else-where—out of pique with his younger cousin, the King. One recalls his first public opposition, in November 1787, at the Parlement of Paris, when he rose, stuttering with the shyness that always overcame him when he rose to speak, and challenged the King's imposing his will without a formal *lit de justice.* He was applauded as he left the Palais de Justice; his carriage was unhitched and drawn by the people to the Palais Royal. To his confidant, Brissot, however, he is said to have said: "Don't think I challenged the King to serve a people I despise or a group of no concern to me. I was simply indignant that anyone could treat me so insolently."[16]

Or is this the retrospective belittling of a future regicide? The outrage at being exiled to his château at Villers-Cotterets, as winter began, may well have been personal until five months' brooding made it political. At the Assembly of Notables, the duke had played a notably bored role, and when the Estates General was announced, he wagered one hundred louis that it would not even abolish the *lettres de cachet.*[17] Was the change affected by the entrance into his life of an ex-artillery officer, Pierre Choderlos de Laclos, who arrived late in 1788, recommended by brother Masons? Forty-seven years old, Laclos was already famous for his one novel, *Les Liaisons dangereuses,* an acid treatment of aristocratic amorality that may have brought on his retirement from the artillery.[18] Typical of many talented, ambitious Frenchmen of his time, he found his way upward blocked by the privileged. But he could—and did—become the *Eminence Grise* of someone like the Duc d'Orléans. With his advent as the prince's secretary, the Palais Royal became the opposition's center. Laclos created a political salon and the creed of a liberal Orléanism. He persuaded the duke to use his immense wealth during the great winter, daily distributing thousands of loaves of bread to the starving, winning him the popular title, "Protector of the People." During the elections for the Estates General, Laclos drew up a model *cahier de doléances* not only for Philippe's many estates but for most of France. It was one of the most liberal of the instructional pamphlets, including an antimonarchical sentiment few followed and an emphasis on individual rights of particular interest to Philippe.[19]

The Duc d'Orléans, elected as a deputy of the Second Estate in Paris and at Villers-Cotterets, chose to represent the latter. He wanted to take part in the Estates General, he said, so that when individual freedom was discussed he might raise his voice in its favor and ensure that "when I feel like going to London, Rome or Peking, nothing will prevent me."[20]

Ten days before the Estates General opened, however, part of laboring Paris exploded, incidentally involving the Duc d'Orléans. On April 23, a wallpaper manufacturer named Réveillon, a liberal elector of the Third Estate who paid his 350 workers twenty-five sous a day, or five above the average, presumably regretted in a speech that a worker's family could no longer live on fifteen sous a day. Rumor seems to have transformed his words into a statement that workers should be reduced to that wage, at a time when the four-pound loaf of bread had risen to an impossible fourteen and one half sous. There was a lull, then the storm broke on April 27. The five to six hundred who met in protest near the Bastille in the working-class district of Faubourg Saint-Antoine swelled to three thousand in the march to the Place de Grève before the Hôtel de Ville.[21] French guards kept them, on the return, from Réveillon's home and factory. The following day thousands more were recruited from surrounding factories and from the docks along the Seine. There were demonstrations all that day, closing shops and blocking traffic. The carriage of the Duc d'Orléans, however, on its way to the Vincennes horse races, was cheered and allowed to pass, after the duke had stopped, descended, and told the crowd, "Keep calm, my friends, keep calm, we are close to happiness."[22]

From six to late that evening there was conflict. The workers attacked the French guards who were defending Réveillon's house, and were fired upon. "In spite of the massacre . . . the crowds stood firm and fought back with shouts of *'Liberté . . . nous ne céderons pas* [we will not give in].' Others shouted, *'Vive le Tiers état!'* and even *'Vive le Roi! Vive M. Necker!'* "[23] Additional troops finally subdued them, after they had broken through several hundred French guards and into Réveillon's house. The highest estimate of the dead was 900; officially there were twenty-five dead and twenty-two wounded. On April 29, a blanketmaker and a worker were hung in the Place de Grève; three weeks later a woman scrivener was hung at the Porte Saint-Antoine.[24] Their crime: participation in a riot.

There was talk of a "clerical plot" and an "Orléanist conspiracy," including the bribing of rioters with "Orléanist gold." No proof was ever presented for either suspicion, but the "fact" of the Duc d'Orléans' involvement in all subsequent Paris crowd action became common currency at the Court. The twelve carefully wrapped francs reported by Montjoie to have been paid the rioters and discovered on the wounded were a royalist myth; none were actually found by the police on those taken prisoner. There was no need of a plot or a conspiracy to explain the working-class explosion. Food shops alone were broken into, besides the houses of Réveillon and another manufacturer, also rumored to have spoken for the reduction of workers' wages. "All the evidence, in fact," says Rudé's scholarly study, "points to hunger as the main motive force behind the disturbances."[25]

That the Prince played to the crowd is equally evident. It was visible at the Versailles procession of the Estates General, when the master of ceremonies had to be sent by the King to order Philippe from the ranks of the Third Estate back to those of his own order.

On the following day, at the opening session, however, he resolutely sat with the deputies of Villers-Cotterets, rather than with the princes of the blood, despite the King's rebuke. And on June 25 he too crossed over, leading the forty-six liberal nobles who joined the commoners and lower clergy in the National Assembly.

The Duc d'Orléans was at the height of his popularity with the people and the men of the Third Estate. But the fatal, paralyzing shyness he felt in public would bring him literally to a faint whenever he tried to read the speeches Laclos had written for him. And he turned down the presidency of the Assembly when a large majority offered it to him. "I am not up to it," he said—truthfully.[26]

Several times, before and after, Mirabeau conversed privately with the Duc d'Orléans at the Versailles *hôtel* of the Comte de La Marck. He probed him for his intentions and each time left him less convinced of his capacities. The Duc d'Orléans, so admirably placed as the first prince of the blood to become an alternate monarch, Mirabeau concluded, "was nothing but a eunuch, who had the desire, but not the potency."[27]

It is doubtful the Duc d'Orléans had even the desire. At most, he played host to the revolutionary party—or parties—at the Palais Royal. When the day of the great explosion came, he would be away on a fishing party with his English mistress.

30. The Day a World Ended

Much has been written of the bumbling good intentions of Louis XVI, little of his duplicity. On June 27, four days after the fiasco of the royal session, he did a seeming about-face, summoning the first two estates to join the Third at the Salle des Menus Plaisirs. It looked like a revolution by consent—the peaceful transition from an absolute to a constitutional monarchy. Versailles crowds flocked to the palace courtyard, cheering the King, the Queen, and Necker. In Paris that night there were illuminations and bonfires. But secretly Louis had signed marching orders for six regiments—mostly Swiss and German—moving them from outlying districts to Versailles and the environs of Paris.[1] A week later more border troops were enjoined, some thirty thousand in all, to ring Versailles and Paris by July 13.[2]* The plan: dissolution of the Assembly and the crushing of Paris's expected reaction.

The King's Council had thought it best for the prelates and nobility to sit with the Third Estate and temper its actions until enough troops had converged to disperse its deputies and contain the fury of the crowds. His personal safety, Louis wrote the nobility, depended on their obedience. He did not think it wise to explain why, nor did most of the nobility have the wit to see a counterrevolution in the making. *"Messieurs,"* cried the Marquis de Saint-Simon, "the King says his life is in danger. Let us race to the palace and form

---

* The marching orders are still on file in the archives of the French War Ministry at the Château of Vincennes.

a rampart with our bodies!"[3] Actually the body sought was a loyal army corps.

On June 30, there was a new urgency. Eight hundred Parisians had forced the Abbaye prison, releasing fourteen French guards who had been jailed for insubordination—they had declared their refusal to fire on the people. There was no resistance. "The soldiers on guard," Gouverneur Morris noted, "unfixed their bayonets and joined the assailants."[4] "The released guardsmen," wrote the Marquis de Ferrières, a deputy of the Second Estate, in a letter to his wife, "accompanied by a great multitude, were carried in triumph to the Palais Royal, where they were placed under the safekeeping of the Nation"[5]—in one of the duke's rented apartments.

Disquieting to the crowds of Paris—and the deputies at Versailles —were reports of the regiments on the march. On July 1, Jean-Paul Marat warned in his journal, *L'Ami du Peuple,* of approaching government bayonets, provoked civil war, and dissolution of the Assembly. There was little secrecy left to the royal plot.

By the first week of July, thousands of foreign troops under the Maréchal de Broglie were camping in Le Nôtre's gardens at Versailles and twice as many under the Baron de Besenval in the Champ-de-Mars on the left bank of the Seine. Deputies, fearful of arrest, were sleeping in the Assembly hall or with friends, and on July 8, Mirabeau, in a memorable speech, attacked the King's counselors (rather than the King). "Have these men studied," he asked, "how, in the history of peoples, revolutions begin and how they are carried out? Have they observed by what fatal chain of circumstances the wisest of men are driven beyond all limits of moderation, and by what terrible impulsion an enraged people is precipitated into excesses, whose very thought would have made them shudder?"[6]

The following day Mirabeau helped draft a motion adjuring the King to remove his troops from Versailles and the capital. Louis was in no haste to reply. However, the report of eighty artillerymen breaking out of their barracks at the Hôtel des Invalides on July 10 and being "publicly fêted in the Palais Royal and the Champs Élysées"[7] speeded his response and counterplan. That night several of the Court Party met secretly with the King at the palace.[8] The next day, July 11, Louis replied to the deputies, assuring them he intended no drastic measures, but later the same day he dismissed Necker, replacing him by the Baron de Breteuil, the Queen's favorite, and installing Maréchal de Broglie as minister of war.* The counter-revolution was in full swing.

Though Necker was ordered to leave France quietly and without informing anyone, his dismissal became known in Versailles that evening, and deputies met anxiously in the Menus Plaisirs the following Sunday morning at seven. Communications were cut with the capital, but news reached Paris before noon.[10] Bankers and financiers were likely the first to hear of Necker's downfall, seeing in it "bankruptcy for the State and the certain loss of their own fortunes," and they determined to close the exchange on Monday, July 13.[11]

As the news spread to the people that Sunday, angry crowds gathered in the Palais Royal gardens, grouping themselves around impromptu orators. The most impassioned was Camille Desmoulins, a radical lawyer of twenty-nine. He had leaped onto a table outside the Café de Foy. "Citizens!" he shouted. "You know that the Nation demanded that Necker be retained in office, and that now he has been driven from it. Can they defy you so insolently? After this they will dare anything, and for tonight they are plotting and perhaps preparing a Saint Bartholomew's Eve for patriots! . . . The Germans in the Champ-de-Mars will enter Paris and butcher its inhabitants!" Drawing his pistol, he cried, "To arms! Let us take as our cockade† the color green, the color of hope!"[13] And revolutionary myth has Desmoulins plucking a leaf to pin to his hat, before jumping from the café table, followed by a crowd that imitatively stripped the trees in the Palais Royal gardens for their own cockades, echoing, "To arms! To arms!" as it swept out into the streets.

Crowds flowed in all directions. A group of three thousand stopped the Sunday-afternoon performance at the Opéra, as other theaters were closed in sign of mourning for the national catastrophe of Necker's dismissal.[14] Five to six thousand demonstrated on the boulevards, carrying wax busts of Necker and the Duc d'Orléans (taken from a shop museum) and brandishing black flags as another sign

---

* "He [the King]," wrote Thomas Jefferson, America's ambassador, to John Jay, July 19, 1789, "was now completely in the hands of men, the principal among whom had been noted through their lives for the Turkish despotism of their characters."[9]

† A knot or rosette of ribbon worn on the hat as an identifying badge or part of a uniform. The royal color was white, those of Paris blue and red, by coincidence the same colors as the Duc d'Orléans'. And where was the supposed master-intriguer at this time? On that fishing excursion, previously noted, outside Paris with his English mistress, Grace Dalrymple Elliott.[12]

of mourning. At Place Vendôme they clashed with a detachment of dragoons, overwhelming them. The Prince de Lambesc, commanding the Royal Allemand (German) regiment of cavalry, came to his men's rescue and fell back with them to the Place Louis XV (now Place de la Concorde). Crowds followed, filling the Place and the Tuileries gardens and the terraces overlooking the Place.[15]

While Lambesc's cavalry was trying to break up the crowds with flat saber charges, *à la prussienne,* rumors of a popular massacre reached the French guards, who left their barracks on the run and joined the Parisian stone throwers.* Meanwhile the Parisians fanned out in search of arms, ransacking gunshops and harness shops (for belts and shoulder straps), returning in greater numbers and force. Together with the French guards, they were too many for the royal German troops (whose hearts were demonstrably not in the fighting), and the latter fell back at midnight.[17]

During the night and the following day, forty of Paris's fifty-four customs posts were emptied of their provisions and put to flame. More than the symbol, they were the reality of the feudalism walling in the city. They belonged to the tax farmers. They were the detested *barrières,* whose exactions raised the price of wine, firewood, eggs, livestock, and wheat, resented by shopkeeper, merchant, housewife, and poor alike. Records and shelters were burned, but neighboring buildings were protected and looters warned off or punished.[18] And during the night, too, the search for defensive arms went on.

At seven the next morning, July 13, having returned the night before from his fishing party at Raincy, the Duc d'Orléans rose in haste to be at the King's *lever* in Versailles, so that he might remove the inevitable suspicion that he had had a guiding hand in the Paris uprising. He joined the small group in the royal bedchamber. As first prince of the blood and thus ranking nobleman present, he handed the King the royal shirt.

Louis XVI, crisply: "What do you want?"

Philippe: "I come to receive Your Majesty's commands."

The King, with great harshness: "I want nothing of *you.* Return from whence you came."

---

* Thomas Jefferson, in a letter to John Jay: "The horse charged, but the advantageous position of the people and the shower of stones [from the terraces], obliged them to retire, and even to quit the field altogether, leaving one of their number on the ground. The Swiss in their rear were observed never to stir."[16]

The duke, who was "very much hurt and very angry," went to the Assembly and returned to Paris that night.*

All day the deputies sat in uneasy session at the Salle des Menus Plaisirs in Versailles. A delegation of their members headed by President Bailly had gone the few hundred yards to the palace and had been ushered in to the King. They expressed the "profound regrets of the Nation" at Necker's dismissal, the request that the King's troops be withdrawn from Paris and order be assured by a *milice bourgeoise,* or civic guard, as in other cities. Confident in the ultimate restoration of order by his own forces, Louis replied shortly that other cities might set up an internal guard, but not the capital. And he forbade the Assembly's sending a delegation to Paris.[20] The deputies withdrew to their hall and waited, though they did not—could not—know exactly what for. The action was now in Paris.

Inspirational center for the action was the Palais Royal, for its control, the Hôtel de Ville. The 407 electors of the Third Estate had never dispersed. They met sporadically at the Hôtel de Ville, seat of the municipal government, and had a large room to themselves. And at dawn on Monday, July 13, they met to the sound of tocsins and cannon summoning citizens to the defense of their city. The electors formed a Permanent Committee and created their own force, the *milice bourgeoise* of Paris, with the dual purpose of defending the capital from the regiments converging on it and maintaining order on its streets. Initially composed of two hundred, then rapidly within the same day, eight hundred propertied or properly—i.e., employer —certified men from each of Paris's sixty districts, the citizens' militia became an organized patrolling force of some forty-eight thousand.[21] Irregulars were to be disarmed, looters and pillagers restrained or punished on the spot. The Permanent Committee became the effective government of Paris, but with conservative caution its bourgeois members asked Jacques de Flesselles, Prévôt des Marchands (roughly the Crown's Mayor of Paris), to act at their head. Desmoulins' green cockade was discarded—green was not only the color of Necker's livery, but also that of the Comte d'Artois—for the blue-red cockade of Paris, which was now pinned to the hats of the bourgeoisie and their militiamen.

Monday was marked by the emptying of prisons and customs

---

* We owe the account to Mistress Elliott, who had urged the action on her lover and heard of its result on his return.[19]

houses and the search for arms. Two prisons for criminals were deliberately skirted; indeed, a revolt at one, the Châtelet, brought a citizens' patrol to suppress it.[22] Stores from the customs houses were taken to the markets of Les Halles or piled in great heaps in the Place de Grève outside the Hôtel de Ville. But the search for weapons was not meeting with much success. The Royal Arsenal, the Parisians were quick to discover, had transferred its ball and powder to the "impregnable" Bastille. But there was the royal warehouse on the Place Louis XV, and they broke into it, finding nothing but museum pieces—a sword of Henry IV, a small, silver-chased cannon presented to Louis XIV by the Siamese King—which they nevertheless confiscated.

Back the crowds came to the Hôtel de Ville, demanding guns from a disinclined Flesselles. He distributed 360 muskets, promising more from a gun manufacturer, which he said were already on their way. When the cases arrived, they were immediately opened. They were filled with old rags. The crowds cried, "Treachery!" Flesselles sent them to the monastery of Chartreux with a signed order for its arms. It had none. The crowds returned more angry than before and redoubled their cries of "Treachery!" Flesselles told them he was sending a delegation to Besenval and to Sombreuil, governor of the Hôtel des Invalides, formally requesting weapons for the city of Paris (to defend it from Besenval's men!).

The delegation arrived late Monday. It was told instructions were awaited from Versailles. None came. Besenval, later, in his memoirs: "Versailles forgot me in this cruel situation and persisted in regarding 300,000 rebels as nothing but a demonstration of rowdies, and the Revolution as a riot."[23] Besenval knew the delegates would return and with them the less restrainable crowds. He ordered twenty men to work over the thirty-two thousand muskets that night in the Invalides stockrooms, stripping them of their hammers, so that they would be unusable. But the soldiers, sympathetic to the rebels, worked with such deliberate slowness scarcely two dozen were so rendered.

The same night of July 13–14, the Permanent Committee requested Paris residents to keep lights burning in the lower floors of their houses, illuminating the streets for the citizen patrols, which by evening (an Englishman wrote home) "almost exclusively occupied the streets."[24] Flesselles, however, did not venture outside the Hôtel de Ville.

Tuesday, July 14, 1789[25]:

The great fear was a royal attack. Paris' moves, thus far, were defensive. At two in the morning, a man brought the alarming rumor to the Hôtel de Ville that fifteen thousand government troops were on their way through the neighboring Faubourg Saint-Antoine and "all was lost." It was untrue, but the Permanent Committee alerted its French guards and had barricades erected in the surrounding area.[26] During the morning, reports arrived of foreign troops with horse-drawn artillery at the city gates, planning "a blockade of Paris and perhaps even bringing the horrors of war to its interior."[27] Meantime crowds arrived bringing, or asking for, bread, wine, muskets, flour, and powder.

Thousands were already demonstrating on the esplanade of the Hôtel des Invalides when the delegate of the bourgeoisie arrived for the reply to the request for arms. The Marquis de Sombreuil received him, saying no instructions had yet been received from Versailles. The clamor of the crowds, grown to at least ten thousand, and possibly four times as many, brought Sombreuil himself to the Invalides gate to explain his dilemma. The gate opened and did not close. A crowd swarmed through it and seized the Invalides' stored arms.

Thomas Jefferson: "It was remarkable, that not only the Invalides [soldiers] themselves made no opposition, but that a body of five thousand foreign troops, encamped within four hundred yards [in the Champ-de-Mars], never stirred."[28]

What Jefferson seems not to have known (his letter to Jay was written only five days later) is the astonishing, crucial fact of July 14. At ten that morning, Besenval had assembled his commanding officers in preparation for the expected assault on the Invalides, despite lack of instructions from Broglie in Versailles.* Besenval, to his consternation, was informed by his field officers that "their men would not march," that is, fight.[29]

Parisians now had perhaps thirty-two thousand muskets, twelve cannons, and a mortar from the Invalides' armaments, but little ball and powder. The cry became, "On to the Bastille!"

The Bastille, however, was not the Hôtel des Invalides. It was an eight-tower fortress with walls one hundred feet high and thirty feet thick. Two walled forecourts had to be traversed before the fortress-prison itself—main gate, drawbridge, and moat—could even be ap-

---

* Who, in turn, had none from Louis XVI. The King had prepared for a day of hunting, which did not come off because of the Paris disturbances. His journal, consequently, contains a single-word entry for July 14: "Nothing."

proached. It loomed, a symbol of absolutism so bleak "it could have cast a shadow on darkest midnight," on the eastern edge of working-class Faubourg Saint-Antoine. That would be one of its problems. Access and support would have had to pass through these rebellious streets. There were even shops leaning against the walls of the forecourts.[30] Most important, there was gunpowder in the Bastille's cellars; the prisoners were incidental.

The fortress's governor was the frightened, incompetent Marquis de Launey. For days he had been pleading for reinforcements for his eighty-two French soliders. "No one," he was told, "would dream of taking the Bastille."[31] On July 7 nonetheless, a detachment of thirty Swiss guards under Lieutenant de Flue was ordered to the Bastille garrison. The Swiss lieutenant found his new commander anxious, "irresolute" and "so terror-stricken that he mistook tree shadows during the night for the enemy and for that kept us on the alert all night."[32]

Windows had been boarded up, cannons mounted on the towers, and wagonloads of old iron and paving stones taken to the tops of the crenelated walls. Launey had prepared for a feudal siege, but neglected to stock more than two days of food. The cannons pointing down along the streets toward the Hôtel de Ville, less than a mile away, brought the first delegation of bourgeoisie. They requested that the cannons be withdrawn. They were invited to lunch.

By the time the delegation had come, a crowd had collected before the Bastille's outer court. Many had been there all night, most of them from the quarter. Woodworkers, locksmiths, cobblers, stonemasons, porters, wine merchants—two thirds of them were artisans and journeymen, some were unemployed—954 would be honored as "the victors of the Bastille."[33]

Time passed. The crowd stirred impatiently. It saw the cannons being pulled back from the towers and spontaneously believed they were being loaded for firing. Men raced to the local district headquarters (in a church). A second delegation was sent from here to the Bastille's governor. Its members met the first delegation emerging from its lunch. The second delegation was shown the withdrawn cannon, unloaded. Its spokesman, lawyer Thuriot de La Rozière, boldly pressed Launey to open the Bastille to the *milice bourgeoise*. The French soldiers were inclined to agree, the Swiss were not. Launey, having seen the dense crowd from his towers, refused. Thuriot and the delegation left, jeered by the crowds, whose cry now was, "Down with the Bastille!"[34]

The mood and pitch had sharply risen. More than gunpowder was at stake as noon came and went.

Thuriot continued to the Hôtel de Ville, where he made his report. A third delegation was on its way back to the Bastille, when it heard another kind of report: the boom of cannon. Two men had climbed the outer wall via the roof of an abutting perfume shop and jumped into the forecourt (enclosing the governor's own residence and garden). Others quickly followed, seized axes and maces, and cut the chains lowering a drawbridge. One man was killed, another wounded in the drawbridge's fall. The gates were smashed, men swept across the drawbridge into the forecourt—and came to the great moat, wall, and principal gate of the fortress. It was at this time that the cannon had thundered from the towers, its defenders ultimately claiming it was in response to musket fire.[35] But the cry of the crowd was, "Treachery!" It did not know that the drawbridge had been brought down by its own men. It believed that Launey had ordered it lowered, enticing them into a trap.

Launey made a gesture. The crowd thought it conciliatory and lowered its arms. Another salvo, however, greeted the men grouped in the forecourt, and twenty lay dead or wounded. Some now sought flight, others vengeance. The crowd arriving made retreat as difficult as making a stand. It was the first truly bloody encounter of the three days. Dead and wounded were carried to the Hôtel de Ville. Those in the forecourt hugged the walls and sought shelter in the corners. Two cartloads of hay were dragged to the edge of the moat and set on fire. The smoke hid the assailants from the fortress, but their musket fire was feeble and ineffective against its walls.

Yet another delegation came from the Hôtel de Ville. Launey (who had lost his head, monarchist Rivarol would write, long before it would be cut off) ordered the delegation fired on, though it waved several white handkerchiefs—and men fell on both sides of the bourgeois truce seekers. And they too returned to the Hôtel de Ville to report the failure of a mission, when they met the column of French guards which would strikingly reverse the order of the day.

These soldiers had been stationed in the defense of the Hôtel de Ville, their passions mounting with the sight of the dead and wounded and the sound of the Bastille's cannon. They double-marched toward the fortress under the leadership of Pierre-Auguste Hulin, a tall career officer, followed by an armed crowd and above all four cannons and the mortar seized at the Invalides that morning. At the Bastille they met another column, under Second Lieutenant Elie. Their arrival presented Launey with a professionally directed assault. The smoking carts were dragged away so that the cannons might bear directly on the Bastille's main gate and drawbridge. Elie and several volunteers succeeded under fire in removing the carts, but two men were killed in the action. The cannons, however, finally had a clear field of fire.

Was it the cannon of the French guards, the pleas of his own French soldiers, the hopelessness of receiving reinforcements, or the dismaying sight of streets black with people all the way to the Hôtel de Ville, which brought Launey to seek a negotiated surrender? It was four in the afternoon. It would take another hour. In the meantime, Launey himself hysterically threw down paving stones at his assailants and seems to have made the mock heroic gesture of going to the powder room with a burning torch, threatening to blow up the Bastille, himself, and his men before being prevented by his subordinate French officers.[36] Finally, on his orders, two men waved *his* white handkerchiefs as a sign of *capitulation,* or conditional surrender. And this time it was *they* who were fired on by the furious crowd in the courtyard, no longer in the mood for any conditions.

Then Launey wrote a note and gave it to his Swiss lieutenant, de Flue, for transmittal, somehow, to his besiegers. The note read: "We have twenty thousand pounds of powder, we will blow up the garrison and the entire quarter, if you do not accept our *capitulation.* From the Bastille, 5 in the evening, 14 July 1789, Launey."

De Flue took Launey's note, thrust it through a firing hole in the main gate and waved it. Between the besiegers and the note, however, was the great moat. A dozen boards were fetched in haste from a local carpentry shop. The longest was slid its full but inadequate length across the gap. Several men anchored it on the near end with their weight. A cobbler named Bezier inched along the plank toward the brandished note, fell, and fractured his elbow. Elie immediately followed and made it. He returned with the note and handed it to Hulin.

From inside the Bastille, the besieged heard the cries: "No *capitulation!* Down with the drawbridges!" De Flue: "I waited for the Governor to keep his word and blow up the fortress. Instead, I was astonished to see four French soldiers approach the drawbridges [foot and carriage] and lower them. The mob rushed across and disarmed us in an instant."[37]

Seven prisoners were liberated. They were as incidental at the end as in the beginning.

The Bastille had fallen, and with it a world.

The dead and wounded were almost wholly among the people of Paris—ninety-eight dead, seventy-three wounded—fewer than in the Réveillon riots. There were virtually no casualties among the besieged— one French soldier dead, three wounded, none among the Swiss. Lieutenant de Flue was taken with the others to the Hôtel de Ville; he offered to join in the defense of Paris and was paraded the same day to the Palais Royal in joyful triumph. Flesselles, when he left the Hôtel de Ville on foot for the Palais Royal, was shot by an unknown and his head cut off. Governor de Launey suffered a similar fate. Despite the protective efforts of Hulin and Elie, he did not reach the Hôtel de Ville alive. He had become the symbol of treachery, the sacrificial victim of the Bastille dead and the *ancien régime's* torments. He was beaten and stabbed, his head cut off and stuck on a pike. Almost all the envoys of Paris—Russian, Neapolitan, Sardinian, Portuguese, and Venetian, among others—wrote of Launey's "treachery" at the Bastille in their dispatches as a matter of fact.[38] The coolest—and most politic—comment may indeed have been Louis XVI's to an apologetic Bailly, two days later: "He deserved his fate."[39]*

For July 14, however, there still stands the King's monumental entry in his diary for the day—"Nothing"—though he was *not* kept uninformed.

---

* Would Louis as well?

Tocqueville: ". . . a great number of the practises employed by the Revolution had their precedents and examples in the treatment of the people during the last two centuries of the monarchy." Also: ". . . the Revolution, though prepared by the most civilized classes of the nation, was executed by the least educated and the most unruly . . . and if one considers what they endured under the *ancien régime*, one can easily understand how they would now behave."[40]

Babeuf, French revolutionist: "Judicial torments of every kind, quartering of the condemned, torture, the wheel, stake and whip, gallows and hangmen multiplying everywhere, all have accustomed us to the worst. Our masters, instead of civilizing us, have rendered us barbarian, for that is what they are themselves. They are harvesting—and they will continue to harvest—what they have sown." "Had not Paris discovered [and foiled] the terrible plot [to return it to slavery]," Babeuf wrote in an earlier passage of this letter to his wife, July 1789, "an even more dreadful crime would have taken place"—the crushing of Paris by the royal troops.[41]

Late in the afternoon, the Vicomte de Noailles had arrived in Versailles and brought the National Assembly news of the assault on the Invalides and the siege of the Bastille. Immediately a delegation was sent to the palace to see the King, urging withdrawal of the royal troops. He replied with a noncommittal note.

While the deputies were still at the palace, two electors arrived from the Hôtel de Ville and told the Assembly of the dead and wounded at the Bastille and of Launey's "perfidy." Hearing it, the Assembly called "on God and men to bring vengeance upon the head of the guilty man"[42] and sent a second delegation to the King, led by the Archbishop of Paris. Again Louis turned the deputies away, saying he was pained by their account of Paris' troubles, "but it was impossible to believe they were caused by the orders given to the troops."[43] Either the King's confidence in Besenval's men remained unshaken, or he believed Paris was experiencing but one more riot, no more serious than in April. Or both. In his memoirs, Besenval would remark that "no one wished [or dared] to tell the King the whole truth about that fatal day, so that he had only bits and pieces of information, leaving him in uncertainty."[44]

Did revelation come that night? There is the story told by the Comte de La Rochefoucauld-Liancourt that his father, the Duc de Liancourt, woke the King during the night to acquaint him with the grave happenings in Paris. "Is it a revolt?" asked the King. "No, Sire," replied the duke. "It is a revolution."[45]

More likely it was the morning of July 15, at the King's *lever,* that the Duc de Liancourt related the events of July 14, impressing even Louis XVI with his recital of the deaths of Launey and Flesselles, if not with the full significance of the fall of the Bastille. One consequence, in any event, was Louis' sanctioning Besenval's withdrawal of his regiments back toward Versailles, bivouacking them at Sèvres and Saint-Cloud (where many would desert).[46]

The night before, the Comte d'Artois and the Polignacs had descended from the palace to the Orangerie, where German regiments were encamped, and gaily cheered as the soldiers danced on the terrace.[47] The Bastille fallen (though they may have been unaware of it), their behavior was the height of folly, and the following morning, July 15, Mirabeau told a delegation about to leave for an audience with the King: "Tell him of the hordes of foreigners investing us who received the visit of princes, princesses, *favoris* and *favorites,* of their embraces and exhortations . . . as the Germans drunkenly sang of the enslavement of France and the destruction of the National Assembly."[48]

Before the delegation had departed, however, the Duc de Liancourt arrived to say the King himself was coming with his brothers to the Assembly's meeting hall. When the deputies cheered, Mirabeau sharply advised their withholding their cheers until they had heard what Louis had to say. "The silence of the people," he said, "is a lesson for kings."[49] In fact, Louis announced neither the dismissal of Breteuil nor the recalling of Necker, though he did say he had ordered troops removed from Paris and Versailles. For the first time, however, the King referred to the "National Assembly,"[50] his dependence on it, and his being "at one with the Nation."[51]

It was enough. The deputies rose, cheered, and jubilantly surrounded the King as he left with his brothers on foot for the palace, slowly making his way through the Versailles crowds which were crying with relief and joy, *"Vive le Roi!"* as they followed him to the palace.

Hearing their cries, Marie Antoinette came to the balcony, hand in hand with the Dauphin and his ten-year-old sister. A number of the royal family joined them, and finally the King, responding to "a thousand cries of love which brought him out to hear the blessings of the people."[52] The following morning, the King would hold a virtual council of war and that evening the first flight of the nobles from Versailles would begin.

In the meantime, after the King's speech of conciliation to the Assembly, Bailly and a deputation sped to Paris and the Hôtel de Ville, where Lafayette read to a crowd what the King had promised. By acclamation Lafayette was declared commanding general of the *milice bourgeoise* (soon the National Guard) and Bailly, Mayor of Paris (the old title of Prévôt des Marchands was hooted down). Paris celebrated, but there were still cries for Necker's recall.

The latter was one of the considerations of Louis' Council, meeting the morning of July 16, with the Queen and the King's brothers joining the ministers. Another was the possibility of resistance and royal attack; a third, moving the Court to Metz and the protection of its border troops. Resistance, Maréchal de Broglie, as minister of war, reported, had to be ruled out—even the Swiss and German regiments were refusing to march. As for removing the Court elsewhere, he could not guarantee the security of the countryside through which the Court would have to pass. (In 1792, Louis XVI would confide to Fersen: "I realize I missed the moment [for flight], which would never come again. It was on July 14."[53])

There remained the recall of Necker and the marking of time until the royal troops were again a dependable force. But the Comte d'Artois and the Queen's most conspicuous favorites preferred marking that time on the other side of the French frontier. With his wife and his mistress, the King's brother fled that very night to Flanders. At the same time, or soon after, the Polignacs, the Prince de Condé, the Duc de Bourbon, Vaudreuil, Breteuil and others, even the Abbé de Vermond, departed, leaving Marie Antoinette unconscionably alone—with Louis. But as they left and news of Necker's recall became known, government bonds rose at the exchange.

The recalling of Necker, relayed to the National Assembly, spurred a further demand by the people and bourgeoisie of Paris: the consecration of their victory at the Bastille by the presence of the King himself at the Hôtel de Ville. They were convinced that Versailles kept the King from healthy contact with the people in an isolation of conspiring courtiers, a suspicion so strong, the British ambassador wrote London, that "no less than 50,000 armed men" were prepared to leave for Versailles to bring Louis XVI to Paris, "by force if necessary."[54] And Marie Antoinette, hearing the same rumor, had Madame Campan pack all her diamonds in a huge chest and hurriedly burned "a great quantity of papers."[55]

But Louis, still temporizing, yielded to popular pressure. "Tomorrow," the Queen told her lady-in-waiting, "the King is going to the Hôtel de Ville. It was not he who decided. . . . The future will tell us whether the right choice was made."[56]

On the morrow, July 17, Louis left for Paris. The Queen wept: "They will not let him come back!" And she prepared a speech to deliver to the deputies of the National Assembly, should there be a need: *"Messieurs,* I have come to present you the wife and family of your sovereign. Do not allow them to separate here on earth those who were joined by heaven." Louis, too, had feared that he might be held in Paris, or assassinated en route. After prayers and confession in the morning, he had named his remaining brother, the Comte de Provence, Lieutenant General of the Kingdom, "in case he should not return."[57]

Thus, in a spirit of gloom, with a few officers of his household, a few bodyguards and an escort of thirty-two deputies, drawn by lot, the King and his cortege proceeded at a funereal pace to the Chaillot gate of Paris—a journey of four hours. Here he was met by Paris's new municipal council and its mayor, Bailly. "Here," Bailly greeted Louis XVI, "the people have reconquered their King, as Henry IV reconquered his people."[58] It was a phrase that would not please Marie Antoinette.

Slowly the augmented cortege continued its way the length of Paris to the Hôtel de Ville. "The King's carriage," writes Jefferson, "was in the center, on each side of it [deputies of] the States General, in two rank, afoot, and at their head the Marquis de La Fayette, as Commander in Chief, on horseback, and *Bourgeois* guards before and behind. About sixty thousand citizens of all forms and colors, armed with the muskets of the Bastille and Invalides, as far as they would go, the rest with pistols, swords, pikes, pruning-hooks, scythes, etc., lined all the streets through which the procession passed, and, with the crowds of people in the streets, doors, and windows, saluted them everywhere with cries of *'Vive la Nation'*; but not a single *'Vive le Roy'* was heard. The King stopped at the Hôtel de Ville. There Monsieur Bailly presented and put into his hat the popular cockade"— the red and blue of Paris, to which Lafayette that day would add the white of the Bourbons—"and addressed him. The King being unprepared and unable to answer, Bailly went to him, gathered from him some scraps of sentences, and made out an answer, which he delivered to the audience as from the King. On their return, the popular cries were *'Vive le Roy et la Nation.'* He was conducted by a *Garde Bourgeoise* to his palace at Versailles, and thus concluded such an *amende honorable,* as no sovereign ever made, and no people ever received."[59]*

And so, late that night, Louis XVI was back in his palace at Versailles, somewhat to his surprise and greatly to his relief.

Marie Antoinette, it is said, leaped into his arms and wept, and then, it is also said, recoiled, when she caught sight of the cockade of the Revolution in his hat, saying smartly, "I did not know that I had married a commoner."[60]

---

* See Note 59, p. 523, as well, for the continuation of Jefferson's letter to John Jay, dated July 19, 1789. It describes Paris's return to 'normality' and concludes with an observation on the remarkable discipline and relative non-violence of the three revolutionary days of July 12, 13 and 14, 1789.

P*

31. The History of Man Begins

"One might be permitted to hope," said Mirabeau, when the King had invited his prelates and nobility to join the Third Estate on June 27, 1789, "that now the history of man begins."[1] Was it not, rather, with the fall of the Bastille or the Declaration of the Rights of Man, six weeks later?*

The inveterate English traveler Arthur Young was not in Paris when the fortress-prison fell, but in Metz, and was not to hear of it before July 20 in Strasbourg. Fortunately, since he vividly describes the French countryside, preparing one for the Great Fear that succeeded the Great Hope. He rebrushes La Bruyère's famous portrait of the French peasant—more particularly, of his wife. Or should one say, à la Carlyle, the "drudge's drudge," drawing a moral line from Marie Antoinette, last seen scorning her husband as a commoner, to the "poor woman" Arthur Young met in Champagne on July 12, 1789, as he walked on foot up a long hill, breathing his mare?

"The poor woman," Arthur Young writes, "complained of the times, and that it was a sad country." Asked her reasons, "she said her husband had but a morsel of land, one cow, and a poor little horse, yet they had a *franchar* [forty-two pounds] of wheat, and three

---

* Recalling, at the same time, that shortly before the Revolution of 1848, Habsburg General Windischgrätz could still cynically remark, "Man begins with the Baron." We know that for most of the deputies of the National Assembly of Mirabeau's time man began with the bourgeois.

chickens, to pay as a quit-rent to one Seigneur; and four *franchar* of oats, one chicken and 1s. to pay to another, besides very heavy tailles and other taxes. She had seven children, and the cow's milk helped to make the soup. But why, instead of a horse, do not you keep another cow? Oh, her husband could not carry his produce as well without a horse; and asses are little used in the country. It was said, at present, that *something was to be done by some great folks for such poor ones, but she did not know who nor how,* but God send us better, *car les tailles & les droits nous ecrasent* [because the taxes and dues are crushing us].

"This woman, at no great distance, might have been taken for sixty or seventy, her figure was so bent, and her face so furrowed and hardened by labour,—but she said she was only twenty-eight. An Englishman who has not travelled, cannot imagine the figure made by infinitely the greater part of the countrywomen in France; it speaks, at the first sight, hard and severe labour: I am inclined to think, that they work harder than the men, and this, united with the more miserable labour of bringing a new race of slaves into the world, destroys absolutely all symmetry of person and every feminine appearance. To what are we to attribute this difference in the manners of the lower people in the two kingdoms? To GOVERNMENT."[2]

Claiming a bit much for the government of George III, our English traveler looked on while Strasbourg's Hôtel de Ville was being stormed, after news of the Bastille had reached its citizens. "I remarked," he writes, "several common soldiers, with their white cockades, among the plunderers, and instigating the mob even in sight of the officers of the detachment. There were amongst them people so decently dressed, that I regarded them with no small surprize:—they destroyed all the public archives; the streets for some way around strewed with papers; this has been a wanton mischief; for it will be the ruin of many families unconnected with the magistrates."[3]

It was not quite "wanton mischief," but rather the destruction of royal tax lists and feudal records, to be followed, generally, by the rapid formation of a controlling *milice bourgeoise* and Permanent Committee in imitation of Paris. In fact, it was the pre-Jacobin moment when France became a loosened web of fairly independent municipalities defying or ignoring the authority of Versailles. The King's intendants flinched or fled; royal power further withered away.[4]

But even as taxes went uncollected, feudal dues unpaid, fears grew of an aristocratic plot and counter-revolution. Borders were watched, roads surveyed, carriages searched, the *grands personnages* trying to reach the frontiers held up and reluctantly allowed to go on. Simultaneously at the frontiers themselves, stories spread of French nobility already returning with troops recruited from concerned, sympathetic ruling cousins, for the French Revolution was a frontierless royal family affair. At four one morning, a rumor swept Limousin that the Comte d'Artois was advancing from Bordeaux with an army of sixteen thousand men, slaughtering all those resisting their passage to Versailles and restoration of the old order. In the east, there were fears of Germans and Austrians marching to Marie Antoinette's rescue; in Dauphiné, of a Savoyard invasion[5]; in the west, of an English attack on the port of Brest (requiring the British ambassador formally to deny it).[6] And in Paris, the retired bookseller Hardy wrote in his journal for July 17 of "the infernal plot of infiltrating during the night fifteen, thirty thousand men into the capital, backed by brigands,"[7] even as the national cockade was being pinned to Louis XVI's hat.

Patiently—or almost—the peasants had awaited the promised change. Had not the King recognized the need when he summoned the Estates General, creating the Great Hope expressed by Arthur Young's peasant woman? Now the Bastille had fallen. Paris had celebrated; the cities had revolted. But for the peasants, the feudal burden remained unlifted, the system intact, the seigneur in place. Hunger was the reality, and there were more food riots in July than ever before. "One tenth of the rural population, at least, went begging from farm to farm asking for a morsel of bread or a *liard*"—a half farthing.[8]* Unemployed thousands roamed the land looking for work. But the rumored numbers of "brigands" pillaging farms and villages were ten times as great, and the rumors' universality still mystifies historians.

A cloud of dust raised by a courier would bring a sound of alarm from the church bell. Women and children fled as their men armed themselves with scythes, pitchforks, clubs and the few muskets. Their sortie found no brigands, but their own appearance would bring panic to the neighboring village—and so it went, creating the Great Fear throughout France. The "brigands" were in the pay of the aristo-

---

* In times of relative plenty, wheat was not stored, but rather exported abroad where it would fetch higher prices. When harvests were bad, as in 1788, there were no stocks to draw upon.

crats, the peasants said, and several times Arthur Young was arrested on suspicion of being a foreign agent of the Queen. The "brigands," said the aristocrats, were in the pay of the bourgeoisie, provoking peasant revolt.

Panic fed on panic in spreading waves. Most significantly, the peasants, armed to meet "brigands," soon ceased pursuing a phantom enemy and turned toward a real one: the seigneur. They stormed his château as if it were their local Bastille, seizing the papers, documents, and ancient parchments indebting them to him, and making bonfires of them in the village square.[9] "It was not collective madness; it was the people's justice."[10] Often they marched in columns to the château to the sound of fife and drum, many youths among them. Arriving, they would ask for bread and wine, or more boldly for eggs and ham. Or they might roast the seigneur's hated pigeons (like their owner, pigeons had a free range of the sown fields, and only the seigneur had the right to a dovecote). If the seigneur signed away his rights, all might be well, and the column of peasants marched home. If he did not, he might be hung and his château burned down (as in the case of absentees)—some sixty châteaus in July.[11] So, too, were stormed the great abbeys, monasteries, and manor houses, increasingly peasant committees and militia clashing with bourgeois landowners and bourgeois militia.

And there was alarm at Versailles, not least of all in the Salle des Menus Plaisirs, and not only among the nobles. Here, too, was a Great Fear: of the *possédants* losing all.

At first the bourgeois deputies, in their majority, considered a decree condemning the peasant revolt and taking measures for suppressing it. But the risk of losing their popular support restrained them, and they conceived another strategy, "cleverly employing a liberal nobleman, the Duc d'Aiguillon, one of the largest landowners of the Kingdom."[12]

Few dates are more frequently referred to in France than the "Night of August 4" in Versailles. It commemorates the voluntary renunciation of their rights by the nobility, the ending of the feudal order by the generous action of the privileged themselves. In fact, as one closes in on the spectacle while all France seems aflame, something else emerges: how little was "voluntary" or "generous" on that famous night, and what horrors it actually exposed.

Le Chapelier, a founder of the radical Breton Club, was the Assembly's presiding officer. At a meeting of the group (a Breton deputy named Coroller would reveal in a letter) "it was decided that a proclamation would be made putting an end to pillage in the country, the burning of manor houses and châteaus, and the proscription of the great and noble. . . . Several very rich seigneurs of our Assembly, whom we had convinced for the sake of the credibility of such a proclamation that it must first be preceded by a thorough renunciation of tax exemption and feudal rights by the privileged themselves, were prepared to follow our direction."[13]

The renunciation was set for the night of August 4, the Duc d'Aiguillon was to make the first move.

At 8 P.M. President Le Chapelier opened the Assembly's session with a preliminary statement on the necessity of re-establishing public order. Precipitously the Vicomte de Noailles asked for the floor and received it. He was the penniless youngest son of one of France's richest families, for whom, it would be quickly said, the renunciation of privileges would be at the least personal cost.*

Public order, said the Viscount, could be re-established only if the causes of public revolt were removed. To achieve this purpose, he proposed to the Assembly "that taxes be paid by all individuals of the kingdom according to their revenues, that all public charges should in the future be borne equally by all, that all feudal obligations be redeemable by the payment of fixed sums of money . . . [but] that the *corvée,* mortmain and other personal servitudes be abolished without indemnity."[14]

Thus, to look a gift horse in its noble mouth, a distinction was neatly made between "personal servitudes," which could be abolished forthwith, and other "feudal obligations," which, bringing in revenue, might be considered property rights, redeemable only by an appropriate and not inconsiderable sum few, if any, peasants could pay.† Considering the great fear that all might yet go up in the smoke of burning châteaus, parchment privileges, and dues, one can more easily understand the applause that followed the young viscount's speech.

---

* Whether, as most thought, it was pique that another should precede him, or he had also been part of the Breton Club meeting and plan, in either case, or both, the Vicomte de Noailles was first to engage in the famous night of renunciations.

† In fact, debts deriving from the redemption of these obligations, never paid by the peasants, were simply declared null and void by the Jacobin Convention of July 1793.[15]

Better part than all, especially if compensation accompanied "renunciation."

The Duc d'Aiguillon now rose, thanked Noailles "for being my faithful interpreter," but more carefully spelled out the proposal that "feudal dues" be considered "property rights" and as carefully avoided specifying privileges to be renounced, even those of personal servitude.[16] Nevertheless, a deputy of the Third Estate congratulated both noblemen for their "glorious" gesture, to be succeeded by another—the country-dressed cloth merchant with the Breton name of Le Guen de Kerengal—who was to stun his audience as he still stuns the reader.*

"Gentlemen," he said, addressing the nobility, "you might have prevented the burning of your châteaus, if you had been quicker in declaring that the terrible obligations they contained, which have tormented the people for centuries, would be nullified. . . . The people, impatient for justice, tired of oppression, are impulsively destroying those claims upon them, which are monuments to the barbarism of our ancestors. Let us be just, Gentlemen, let those claims which outrage not only decency, but humanity itself, be brought before us . . . those claims which humiliate men by requiring them to be harnessed to carts like animals . . . which oblige them to agitate the ponds at night so that the frogs will not disturb the sleep of their *voluptueux seigneurs!*"

The Breton merchant's speech was long, cries interrupted it, according to the *Courier de Provence,* which added that "vassals agitated the waters [only] when the seigneur's lady was in labor, delivering her from the importunate noise of the frogs."[17]

Horror was to follow baroque humor when Lapoule, a lawyer from Besançon, took the floor. "He spoke of mortmain," reports the *Courier de Provence,* "of the obligation imposed on some vassals to suckle the dogs of the seigneur, of that dreadful right, undoubtedly relegated long ago to the dusty past of our barbarous ancestors, by which the seigneur was authorized, in certain cantons, to have two of his vassals disemboweled on his return from the hunt, so that he might refresh his feet in their warm bodies."[18]

Again cries of indignation interrupted the speaker, together with

* Neither the Abbé Sieyès nor Mirabeau (at a family reunion following his father's death), Bailly nor Lafayette (both busy in Paris) were at the historic night session.

shouts for proof.* But the shock gave a new momentum to the proceedings, despite Dupont de Nemours' appeal for judicious calm. The Duc du Châtelet, colonel of the French Guards during the Réveillon riots and target of public opprobrium, called loudly (hoping to catch Paris' ear) for immediate suppression of feudal servitudes and for redemption of all others. He personally renounced feudal rights, he said, in the name of the new spirit of "public freedom which will establish itself never to disappear from our great country." His renunciation scene precipitated a pell-mell succession of others, as nobles almost fought for the privilege of being next to renounce their privileges. Were there gestures of real generosity among them? It seems possible, but it need not be the explanation. All knew every statement would be published and circulated, every opponent at the Assembly put on lists of the suspect, their estates exposed to the reaction of an aroused public.†

It was an hour to midnight. The session must be continued, decided President Le Chapelier after some hesitation, in order to give the clergy a chance to be heard, else "they would be extremely mortified."

By now most of the prelates had left, but not all. The Bishop of Nancy picked up Le Chapelier's "invitation" and added his voice in favor of the redemption of feudal obligations. The Bishop of Chartres nobly advocated the abolition of hunting rights. Not to be outdone, nobles called for the abolition of Church tithes. Each generously gave away the other's privileges.[20] But lower clergymen also renounced their own special fees for saying Mass, and noblemen, serfdom on their own estates. By midnight there was even gaiety (some whispered, "hysteria") mixed with the seriousness, and a multitude of proposals tumbled from the tribune: cities, too, should surrender special rights and privileges, all titles should be abolished, the venality of public offices ended, local parlements and corporations suppressed, and, with the latter, distinctions between masters, journeymen, and apprentices; a medal should be struck commemorating the night and

---

* Furnished by Patrick Kessel in his excellent book on the Night of August 4 (see Note 13) and by J. A. Dulaure in *Esquisses historiques des principaux événements de la révolution française* (Paris, 1823–25, 5 vols.) The right of disembowling two peasants had, indeed, fallen into desuetude, but the right still legally existed and redemptory payment required in some instances for its nonapplication.

† ". . . fear of losing all alone led to the forever memorable night of August 4."[19]

the King, as a climax, proclaimed "Restorer of French freedom"—which was done by acclamation, the deputies standing.

It was two-thirty in the morning of August 5. The session was suspended. The deputies retired, not sure exactly what they had done, or whether what they had done was law. Some spent the rest of the night, or the next few days, writing their constituents, hoping thereby to commit the Assembly to its declarations and put a quietus to peasant revolt.

Meanwhile that night, a thousand paces from the Salle des Menus Plaisirs, where the *ancien régime* was being oratorically buried, a ball was held in the apartments of the Queen. More soberly the King, on August 5, wrote the Archbishop of Arles: "I will never consent to despoil my clergy and my nobility. . . . I will never sanction the decrees that despoil them. . . . Monsieur the Archbishop, submit only to the decrees of a Divine Providence, as do I in refusing to submit to the folly that has overcome the orders."[21]

The Assembly resumed its session at noon the same day—and many who had been so noble the night before regretted their "drunkenness" and reconsidered their "renunciations." When the minutes of the night session were read, they protested "extension" or "distortion" of their words,[22] the necessity of re-examining all "decrees" with "cooler heads."[23] Even Mirabeau, when he returned to the Assembly, remarked (according to Dumont): "That is the French for you. They spend a month disputing every syllable and then in one night upset the ancient monarchical order."[24] Nonetheless, Mirabeau would write (in the *Courier de Provence* of August 10) that the intentions of that memorable night and the majority's subsequent efforts to write them into law were well aimed at "giving the people a down payment on happiness and tempering their anxiety by the prompt enjoyment of the first fruits of freedom."

And slowly some calm returned to the country as news of the Night of August 4 and the Assembly's efforts reached the people.

Despite the dragging feet, despite the conservatism encouraged by the Crown and the remorse of those who forgot their fears as the Great Fear seemed to subside, there were enough among the nobles and more than enough among the bourgeoisie and clergy to complete the decrees, article by article, initiated on August 4, for submission to the King by August 11. Indeed the very fact that they were to be submitted to Louis XVI sufficed for many to lend their names to the decrees, since they had little doubt he would never sanction them as the law of the kingdom.

"The National Assembly," began the first article, "destroys in its entirety the feudal regime." Not yet if it meant approval first by the feudal King. But the refusal would not be direct. The fall of the Bastille was still alive in everyone's mind, not least of all Louis'.

At noon on August 13, members of the Assembly came to the palace to present the King the decrees. They were met at the gate by the grand master of ceremonies and conducted to the Grande Galerie. They stood as the King sat on a raised platform in the great mirrored hall. "It was a beautiful ceremony," the Marquis de Ferrières wrote his wife the next day, "but the feelings of the greatest number were those of sadness . . . in seeing a lawyer from Rennes, Le Chapelier, our *président,* prescribe orders to Louis XVI, commanding him to sanction decrees which despoil him of his most precious prerogatives . . . and this in the great gallery where Louis XIV, his ancestor, once sumptuously displayed all his splendor and power."[25]

Louis XVI was surely as conscious of it, but his reply to Le Chapelier did not reveal it. For the title of "Restorer of French freedom," the beleaguered monarch even expressed his *"reconnaissance"* (gratefulness), a word that rarely, if ever, graced the Sun King's lips, even in worship. And so deputies, courtiers, royal family, and King went to the royal chapel for a *Te Deum*—that is, in Ferrières' bitter phrase, for Louis XVI "to thank God that he was no longer King."[26]

And the deputies of the National Assembly, having decreed the feudal regime destroyed in its entirety, now felt the imperative necessity of building the new order on a constitutional basis. As early as July 9, 1789, Mounier had proposed a Declaration of Rights as the preamble for a constitution that was still to be written. Two days later, Lafayette, aided by his friend Thomas Jefferson, submitted a short draft echoing the American Declaration of Independence and the Declaration of Rights of Virginia. "Nature," it read, "has made all men free and equal . . . with inalienable and imprescriptible rights, such as freedom of opinion, the care of one's own honor and life, the right of property. . . ."[27]

On the same day (July 11), Jefferson wrote to Tom Paine, then in London, praising the deputies of the National Assembly for "having shown through every stage of [their] transactions a coolness, wisdom, and resolution to set fire to the four corners of the kingdom, and to perish with it themselves, rather than relinquish an iota from their plan of a total change of government. . . ." Optimistically he added that "the mass of the nation, the mass of the clergy, and the army are with them: they have prostrated the old government, and are now beginning to build one from the foundation."[28]*

It would prove as difficult, and almost as long a process, as the drafting of the American Constitution, further complicated by a persisting monarchy. But in the meantime there was the preliminary Declaration of Rights, which most of the *cahiers de doléances* had demanded, even those of the nobility and clergy, who also sought *their* freedom from the Crown. A committee of five was formed on August 12. To Mirabeau, as *rapporteur,* was entrusted the bulk of the writing, though he opposed Mounier's proposal that the declaration precede the writing of the constitution itself somewhat as putting the cart before the horse.[30]

And it is something of a miracle that by August 26 the Declaration of the Rights of Man and the Citizen was adopted and approved by the Assembly; that the first constitutional step toward a democratic France was taken at the very gates of that great palace of Versailles, which was not only the stage, but the symbol, of absolute power.

"Death certificate of the *ancien régime,*" as French historian Alphonse Aulard termed it,[31] the Declaration of the Rights of Man was also the birth certificate of a new order that would radiate from Versailles with a new kind of splendor. For here were proclaimed the rights of man, not simply the Frenchman, a new order for humanity, not simply France.†

"All men," declares Article 1, "are born and remain free and equal in their rights. All social distinctions are based solely on social usefulness." "These rights," says Article 2, "are liberty, property, security and resistance to oppression." The articles continue: "The

---

* Returning shortly to America, reinforced by his French experience, Jefferson roundly supported a Bill of Rights for the American Constitution. Clearly in his debates with Hamilton, soon to follow, he had brought back more than the taste for French wine and cuisine which teased Patrick Henry into his humorous remark before a popular audience that Jefferson had "abjured his native victuals."[29]

† Indeed the revolution's leaders considered changing the name of Versailles to that of Cradle of Liberty.

principle of all sovereignty resides essentially in the Nation"—not the King. "Liberty consists in being able to do anything that does not injure others. . . ." "No man can be accused, arrested or detained except in cases determined by the law. . . ." "Every man [is] presumed innocent until he is declared guilty. . . ." "No one ought to be disturbed on account of his opinions, even religious. . . ." And Article 11, which might be considered Mirabeau's personal victory: "The free communication of ideas and opinions is one of the most precious rights of man. . . ."

If not ideal—civic equality was still incomplete for Jews, Protestants, and actors, and unknown for women—if not quite the realization of even the *philosophe's* limited dream, the seventeen articles of the Declaration of the Rights of Man* would do for their time, and for decades thereafter.

It was a time of beginnings, a period of some political innocence, "distinguished above all," as Michelet says, "by a singular faith in the power of ideas, firmly believing that truth became invincible immediately upon being formulated as law."[32] A period of political innocence not altogether past.

However, as the other historic August decrees (despite the paradox), the Declaration of the Rights of Man was submitted to Louis XVI for his approval. He temporized, he dallied, he did not quite refuse to sign the decrees and the declaration—and he thereby sealed the fate of Versailles.

* Complete in Appendix IV, pp. 489–91.

32. Adieu Versailles

Louis XVI did not lack for encouragement. Throughout August and September, constitutional debates stiffened his attitude, if they did not strengthen his hand. Nobles, prelates, and conservatives in the Assembly rallied around Mounier in opposition to the *patriotes*. To put a brake to the Revolution, they pressed for a second, upper chamber of lords, to be named by the King, and the royal prerogative of an absolute veto.

After succeeding several times to the fortnightly presidency of the Assembly, the *monarchiens* (sometimes called the *anglomanes*) had hopes of consolidating a majority. No less than the King, they failed to count the voices of the people.

Even the least observant might have noted the chair porters at the doors of the Hôtel des Menus Plaisirs "in the greatest agitation over the question of the King's veto."[1] Within, the Abbé Sieyès was saying, "An absolute or suspensive veto is nothing but a *lettre de cachet* against the popular will."[2] With remarkable speed, the Versailles debates were related in Paris to the crowds at the Palais Royal and the Hôtel de Ville's Place de Grève. And the sixty districts of Paris responded with a defiant warning: "The veto does not belong to a single man, but to twenty-five million citizens."[3]

More than one in the capital spoke as Academician Dussault, official of the Paris Commune, to Tax Farmer General Augeard, August 26. "This business," said Dussault in the Tuileries gardens, "will be settled only when the King lives in that château." He indicated the Tuileries Palace. "We made a great mistake in July when we did not keep him there. The residence of a king should be in his capital."

Augeard: "You are right, but who, among the Estates, can oblige him to make it his residence?"

Replying, Dussault gave voice to the feeling of Paris: "When it is for the good of all, he should be compelled—and it will come to that."[4]

Marginal was the August discussion of the State deficit. Necker had foundered in negotiations for a loan of thirty million francs to the Crown: the French bankers would have little of it. Necker himself had had few illusions when he received the King's letter of recall. "So I return," he had written his brother from Switzerland, "but as a victim of the esteem which honors me, for, I fear, I shall be reentering the abyss."[5]

Fruitless, too, were Lafayette's efforts at a compromise between the *monarchiens* and the *patriotes*. The meeting he arranged in the home of Thomas Jefferson lasted from shortly after noon until evening, but it brought neither party nearer the other. Mirabeau, a monarchist, though far from Mounier's *monarchiens,* kept some distance, as well, from Barnave and Robespierre. He also hoped to play a moderating role, and might have, had he lived beyond the next thirty months, or had not Paris, once again, taken the play from all hands.

On Mounier's election to the Assembly presidency, there was a tentative move in that direction. At the Palais Royal's Café de Foy, the *patriotes* met, Desmoulins among them, and talked violently of going to Versailles en masse to demonstrate against any form of a royal veto. Fifteen thousand men, they said, would march on Versailles to punish those deputies who favored it and "to petition the King and the Dauphin to live in the Louvre, where they would live in security."[6] Two hundred set off that night, led by the impulsive Marquis de Saint-Huruge, but they were stopped on Lafayette's orders by the National Guard. *Patrouillotisme* still held *patriotisme* in check.

The token march of August 30 barely reached beyond the Palais Royal gardens, but it shook the monarchist party at Versailles. A committee of thirty-two went to the palace, saw Necker, and proposed moving the Assembly to Soissons or Compiègne. Necker convoked the Royal Council for that evening. Tired from his hunt, the King arrived. The meeting went on until midnight; the ministers favored the Assembly's transfer, and therefore the Court's, to a site farther from Paris. The King meanwhile slept, or feigned to sleep—"out of timidity or fear of his usual weakness in such discussions"—woke to say No, and ended the discussions. His "was a passive courage, a kind of shame at the idea of leaving Versailles."[7]

To everything Louis XVI brought an attitude of lethargic negativity, to which Necker, whose prestige was daily lowering, brought no positive alternative. Even a compromise worked out with the *patriotes* went for naught. On September 11, a *suspensive* veto was approved by the Assembly with the understanding from the minister that the King in return would sign the August decrees and the Rights of Man. Only the day before the Assembly had overwhelmingly voted against a second chamber, 89 to 849, evidencing the declining influence of the *monarchiens*. Nevertheless, Louis XVI did not fulfill his promise, further discrediting his supporters. Instead, on September 14, he signed marching orders for the Flanders regiment of 1050 men, moving it from Douai to Versailles.

The regiment would not reach Versailles before September 23. To gain time, the King again delayed consideration of the August measures. When he did reply, it was with deliberate obscurity and avoidance of direct refusal. The day after, September 19, an impatient Assembly sent a deputation to insist on the King's immediate proclamation of the August decrees. On the twentieth, a communication from the King (written by Necker) was so skillfully worded it evoked applause from many in the Assembly: it promised *publication,* not *proclamation,* of the Assembly's measures. The printing was accordingly ordered, but the sheets, on royal instructions, never left the royal printery.[8]

News of the Flanders regiment approaching Versailles reached Paris against a background of hunger, rising anger, and bread riots. Though the harvest of 1789 had been good, flour was not arriving in Paris. Bread was lacking, bakeries were guarded, waiting lines endless. "Workers," writes the Marquis de Ferrières, "would queue an entire day for a 4-lb loaf . . . and frequently return without it to their hungry families."[9]

The public workshops of Montmartre were closed in mid-August, spilling out eighteen thousand unemployed, many of them sent back to their native provinces.[10] There were too many unemployed already in Paris, and there were protest meetings at the Palais Royal. Shouting for bread, women demonstrated on the Place de Grève and stormed the bakeries. The food riots were not limited to the capital. On September 13, there was an outburst at Versailles. "The King was brought along [with the troops] *'pour calmer les esprits.'* Several people were injured and twenty-one arrested, of whom three were hanged ten days later."[11] And on September 14, one might recall, the King sent for his Flanders regiment.

On September 15, Joseph Pergaud, military pensioner, was arrested at the Hôtel de Ville for declaring the King must be brought to Paris, and he for one volunteered to go to Versailles to help fetch him.[12] The same day Lafayette informed the Comte de Saint-Priest, minister of the King's household, that former French guards under his command, recently at Versailles, were speaking loudly of returning and replacing the aristocratic Gardes du Corps (Bodyguards) now at the palace.[13] They were echoing Desmoulins, Danton, and Marat, who were demanding the monarch's recall to the capital.

Bread and better times, the Parisians believed, would accompany the King to Paris, where, removed from the cabals of Versailles, he would also find safety and salvation.

For Louis, however, safety—if not salvation—was in the arrival, at last, of the Flanders regiment. Marie Antoinette seems to have had the same illusion. On September 29, she gave an honor flag to each company of the reinforced palace guard. On the thirtieth, the flags were blessed in the Church of Notre Dame. On October 1, the officers of the royal Gardes du Corps invited the officers of the Flanders regiment to the fateful banquet,* held by permission of a grateful royalty, in the grand Opéra theater of the palace.

Two hundred and ten officers sat around the enormous U-shaped table on the deep, extended stage.[15] Eating—and drinking—began at three in the afternoon. Regimental trumpets accompanied the toasts. At dessert time, the royal family appeared in its loge on the balcony. Marie Antoinette had come, as counseled,[16] bringing the Dauphin and the King, still spurred and booted from the hunt. Spotting them, the officers burst into cries of *Vive le Roi! Vive la Reine! Vive le Dauphin!* and joyfully beckoned them to descend to the banquet. They did. The men stood and drank toasts to the King, the Queen, and the Dauphin, but deliberately not to the Nation.[17] An officer led the

---

* "In a time of fermentation," Mirabeau would very shortly write of it, "nothing is unimportant, nothing is insignificant in itself."[14]

little boy on a tour atop the long U-shaped table. There were more cheers, more toasts, the regimental band played *O Richard! O mon Roi!* There were manly tears as the men sang *Oh Richard, oh my King, the universe is abandoning thee!* and they drew their swords and swore eternal fidelity to the French king, whose own eyes teared. Reluctantly—it was a long time since it had enjoyed such an evening* —the royal family retired. Gallantly, the officers escorted the Queen to her apartments. Then all descended to the Marble Courtyard, gathered under the King's windows, and called for him. He chose not to appear, but officers and soldiers sang, danced, and drank some more, while outside the gates a great crowd looked on. And the following evening—four hundred bottles of wine had been left over[19]—there was another banquet.

Did the officers drunkenly trample the red, white, and blue cockade at their dinner the first evening? Marie Antoinette would deny it at her trial, saying, How could they trample "something the King himself wore?"[20] But that was the account in the *Courier de Versailles,* which described the officers' banquet as a drunken, political orgy, arousing a tempest when it was picked up by the press of Paris. "All citizens," wrote Marat in his *Ami du Peuple,* "should assemble in arms . . . each district should withdraw its cannon from the Hôtel de Ville." The districts went into permanent session. The Cordeliers Club, presided over by Danton, sent a delegation to Lafayette, urging him to go to the King and insist on the recall of the Flanders regiment. The Paris Commune declared "the red, white, and blue cockade the sole authorized for citizens,"[21] expressly forbidding the King's white and the Queen's Austrian-black ribbons.

Excited, Sunday crowds gathered at the Palais Royal on October 4; many respectably dressed women among them were heard saying that the Queen was responsible but "on the morrow they would take things into hand themselves and set them aright."[22] Members of the National Guard mingled sympathetically with the crowds; Desmoulins, from a café table, repeated his call for the people of Paris to fetch the King back to his capital. Once more the Paris stage was set for an insurrection.

Set by the Duc d'Orléans' money? "True or not," says Necker's daughter, Madame de Staël, "one must have no conception at all of the Revolution to imagine that this money, even if it were used, had

* "I was enchanted with Thursday!" said Marie Antoinette repeatedly.[18]

the slightest influence. An entire people is not stirred into motion by such means. The great mistake of the Court has always been to see in a few incidental facts the cause of an entire nation's feelings."[23]

Hunger was too remote from Court life for its members, even distantly, to understand its moving power. But on Monday morning, October 5, Carlyle writes with little hyperbole, "maternity awakes, to hear children weeping for bread," and in turn cries for justice.[24] A young woman took a drum from an unresisting guardsman and beat it through the streets of the central markets, assembling the women. Great numbers gathered in other quarters to the sound of church bells, and the groups converged at about 9:00 A.M. on the Place de Grève. A delegation, "mostly young, dressed in white, well coiffed and powdered,"[25] told the commune officials in the Hôtel de Ville of their determination to march on Versailles. They received no encouragement. Meantime a group had forced its way through another door in search of arms, with some success. Another group of women had gone looking for Stanislas Maillard, a leader of the "victors of the Bastille." He had been among the Bastille demolition workers that morning. Finding Maillard, they persuaded him to be their leader.

By early afternoon the women's march on Versailles—with some men among them—began. Their ranks swelled as they swept along the quais, through the Tuileries gardens, and massed in pouring rain on the Place Louis XV. They had picked up two cannon at the Châtelet and two dray horses for them, and the legendary Théroigne de Méricourt, the *Amazone de la liberté*,[26] may well have been astride one as, six or seven thousand strong, the women followed the Seine along the right bank to the bridge at Sèvres,* crossed it, and went on, eventually, to Versailles.

Rumors of a march had reached Mirabeau, sitting in the Assembly at the Salle des Menus Plaisirs. That morning the deputies had discussed another of the King's long, veiled, unpromising letters on the August decrees and the Rights of Man. A deputy had seized the occasion to denounce the "orgy" at the palace on the night of October 1. A deputy on the right had demanded proof that there had indeed been an "orgy" and desecration of the tricolor cockade as alleged. Mirabeau had replied that he could easily furnish the evidence, but first the Assembly should declare "only the King inviolable from

---

* Maintained in wood since the time of Louis XIV, so it might be easily destroyed in the event of a popular march on Versailles, the women of Paris found the Pont de Sèvres intact.[27]

arrest," clearly implying that the Queen then would take the consequences.[28] Soon after, learning of the agitation in Paris, Mirabeau had gone up to the tribune.

"Monsieur le Président," he said in a low voice to Mounier, "40,000 men are marching on us from Paris. Hurry up the debate, suspend the session, say you are going to the palace."

"I never hurry a discussion," said Mounier. "I find they are too often hurried."

"But the 40,000 men?" asked Mirabeau.

"So much the better," said Mounier. "They have but to kill us all—all of us, you hear me—and the Nation's affairs will go all the better."

"It's a pretty speech," said Mirabeau, and he returned to his seat.[29]

The story is Mounier's, a recollection in part, at least, of what was to occur.

Since morning, in Paris, thousands of the National Guard, summoned by the church bells of their districts, had assembled on the Place de Grève. Fitfully they had helped establish some order, but there were cries among them of "On to Versailles!" Toward noon, a committee of former French guards mounted the steps of the Hôtel de Ville and sought Lafayette.

"Mon Général," said their spokesman, "we are delegated by the six companies of grenadiers. We do not think you are a traitor, but we think the government is betraying you, and it is time that it end. We cannot turn our bayonets against women crying for bread. The people are miserable, the source of evil is at Versailles. We must go and bring the King to Paris. We must exterminate the Flanders regiment and the Gardes du Corps, who trampled on the National cockade. If the King is too weak to wear his Crown, let him lay it aside. You will name a Council of Regency, and all will be better."

The eloquence and *sang-froid* of the grenadier "astonished all who listened to him." His comrades were proud of their spokesman. "Let him speak," they told Lafayette when he attempted to interrupt. "He speaks well." And when Lafayette, with less eloquence, tried to dissuade them, they replied, "It is useless to convince us. All our comrades think the same way and even if you convince us, you will not change *them.*"[30]

Lafayette nevertheless went outside to the square and addressed his National Guardsmen from the steps of the Hôtel de Ville. "To Versailles!" was their response to his appeal to "duty." He mounted his white charger, moved among them on the Place de Grève, and continued his efforts to dissuade them. "To Versailles!" they repeated. It was a long, wet afternoon of vain efforts too by Mayor Bailly and, again and again, by Lafayette. Tempers had risen with the departure of the women. The uglier, angrier "*À la Lanterne!* To the lamppost!" was now heard, and a cord was made ready.[31] There had been more than one hanging on the Place de Grève by Paris crowds since July 14.

Late in the afternoon, Lafayette decided he could resist no longer. Remaining on the square, he sent an aide-de-camp inside the Hôtel de Ville to inform the commune's officials. A letter returned not only authorizing, but ordering, Lafayette to lead his troops to Versailles. The alternative was loss of all control. At six, still mounted on his charger, Lafayette placed himself at the head of fifteen thousand men of the National Guard and slowly led them in the rain out of Paris. Fifteen thousand "volunteers," armed with pikes, muskets, and miscellaneous weapons, followed. It was night when they reached the Pont de Sèvres. Lafayette crossed it, as if it were his Rubicon. He was thirty-two.

At ten the morning of October 5, the King had gone hunting in the woods of Meudon. Later that morning Marie Antoinette had walked to the Petit Trianon and to a grotto in her beloved Hameau. Neither went with a premonition that it might be for the last time. There was a feeling of euphoria at Court since the night of the officers' banquet. Had a courtier taken a few steps from the palace and discreetly sat at the Café Américain the evening before, he would have heard the *Versaillais* talk about the cartridges they were preparing "for the Gardes du Corps."[32]

However, the alert would come soon enough—early in the afternoon. The Comte de Saint-Priest, alarmed by a report from Paris, sent an equerry with an urgent note to the King and a page with another for the Queen. Louis was still hunting. Marie Antoinette was alone on a stone bench in the grotto when she saw the page running toward her. She hurried out to meet him, read Saint-Priest's note, and hastened to the palace. Two thousand were already in the state rooms, the men with their hats clapped under their arms, their swords at their sides, the women crowding to the windows, especially in the Salon d'Hercule, so they might see what was happening outside.[33] It was at this moment, or soon afterward, that Fersen, who had by-passed the marching women, "sprang from the saddle and ran hot-foot up the marble staircase," to be near his endangered Queen.[34] Less urgently Louis arrived and joined his Council. (His diary would record his disappointment in the day's hunting with a comment, "interrupted by events.")

The women of Paris had not yet reached the Pont de Sèvres, but no one at the King's Council proposed destroying the wooden bridge. Saint-Priest advised sending the royal family to Rambouillet while the King led his most faithful troops to Sèvres and there impressed the marchers with his royal presence. Necker said he saw no harm in the approaching women. Louis hesitated. He consulted Marie Antoinette, who opposed the move to Rambouillet, since it would separate them. He still could not make up his mind.[35]

Meantime defense measures were taken. The Flanders regiment was ordered to the Place d'Armes, the three-hundred-odd Gardes du Corps were stationed in the courtyard. "Gates which had not turned on their hinges since Louis XIV were closed for the first time."[36] Versailles' own National Guard, under the Comte d'Estaing, when "called upon, began to murmur that it would not fire on the people of Paris."[37]

In the palace, confusion—and the Council meeting—continued. The captain of the Gardes du Corps asked for orders. "Come, come," said the King. "Against women? You must be joking." The Comte de Saint-Priest now recommended the withdrawal of the entire royal family to Rambouillet, where they could safely be within a few hours. Louis hesitated. "Sire," said Saint-Priest, "if you are taken tomorrow to Paris, you will lose your crown." A sigh, a tentative decision: they would leave for Rambouillet. "Pack your things," said the Queen to her entourage. "We are leaving in half an hour. Hurry!" She soon informed them that all had been changed: they were staying.[38] The decision, or indecision, was no longer the King's. The royal carriages for the flight had been turned back at the Orangerie gate by the crowds and guardsmen of Versailles. And the women of Paris had arrived.

Cold, drenched, hoarse, their muddied skirts hitched up, they came down the Avenue de Paris. Red-coated Théroigne de Méricourt had galloped in before them from Sèvres, preparing the Versailles crowds for their coming. *"Vive nos Parisiennes!"* cried the people along the avenue.[39] Maillard halted his marchers in front of the Hôtel des Menus Plaisirs and asked to be heard by the National Assembly. Fifteen were permitted entry with their chief, but many more penetrated by way of the back doors, filling the galleries and seating themselves among the deputies.

The people, said Maillard, lack bread and have come to Versailles for it, and to punish those who have desecrated the tricolor. Then, taking the Queen's cockade from his pocket, he dramatically ripped the black ribbon to shreds. Demurs rose from the deputies on the right. We are all brothers, we are all citizens, Maillard cried, if anyone here feels dishonored, he should be expelled from the Assembly! The majority protested its brotherhood. It is bread we want! women shouted from the floor and from the galleries. And several held up moldy chunks of bread, saying they would make "the Austrian" swallow them. There were a few cries for "Mother Mirabeau,"[40] but Mirabeau did not come forward. Finally it was decided that a deputation should go to the palace to acquaint the King with the gravity of the situation and press him for immediate, unconditional acceptance of the Rights of Man and the August decrees.

Mounier and Guillotin were among the deputies of the delegation. When they left the Menus Plaisirs assembly hall, many of the women followed, insisting on going with them to the King. The rain was still falling, day was stretching into night. They crossed the Place d'Armes through the crowds and past the soldiers, who were surrounded by women. With Théroigne de Méricourt conspicuous among them in her redingote of red silk, the women were flirting, joking, and threatening the men of the Flanders regiment.[41] And the men held out their guns to show the Parisians they were uncharged.[42] Few, in fact, had cartridges. At the gates of the palace, as the delegation drew up, there were more women, brandishing pikes at the King's Gardes du Corps.

Twelve women went up the Staircase of the Queen with Mounier and the other deputies, through the dazzle of aristocrats to the King. Five were allowed entry to the King's chamber, where he received the delegation. It may have been Louis' first encounter with Dr. Guillotin. Seventeen-year-old Louison Chabry, a sculptor's helper, was the women's spokesman. She asked Louis for bread for the people of Paris. He promised all the bread that could be found. She faltered and began to faint. She was brought wine "in a great goblet of gold," and smelling spirits.⁴³ Leaving, she asked Louis if she might not kiss his hand. She merited better than that, the King said, and kissed her on both cheeks. The delegation (without Mounier) returned to the women waiting outside the palace. They recounted their success and were greeted with jeers and accusations of having sold out, and were told to go back and get the King's promise in writing. They returned with Dr. Guillotin and obtained it. They redescended and soon departed for Paris—Louison Chabry, Maillard, and some forty women —in carriages of the Court and with the King's promise of bread for Paris' officials.⁴⁴*

Mounier had remained in the palace to wait for the King's signing of the August measures. His wait was long, as Louis consulted for more than an hour with his Council. Then Louis ceded and signed. Tired and triumphant, Mounier made his way back to the Assembly hall. There he found many women but few deputies. To these few he announced the Assembly's victory. "We knew," the women responded, "that we could make him sign!"⁴⁵ Annoyed, Mounier had the absent deputies summoned by drum to a night session.

At the palace in the meantime, tension mounted. During the evening, a Versailles guardsman had become embroiled with one of the King's bodyguards. An officer of the Gardes du Corps, the Marquis de Savonnières, swung his horse toward the guardsman to arrest him and was brought to a halt by a musket bullet in his arm fired by a fellow guardsman. An entire contingent of the Versailles National Guard now threatened the King's men. From the palace came orders for the royal Gardes du Corps to withdraw. "With enthusiasm,"⁴⁶ it obeyed, marching under a hail of stones to its quarters in several of Versailles' government buildings. Further threatened, the bodyguards eventually bivouacked at the Trianon. And inside the palace, the Comte de Saint-Priest again counseled flight to Rambouillet. "A fugitive king! A fugitive king!" Louis repeated to himself.⁴⁷ He ordered the carriages prepared for another attempt, then countermanded his order. "Only the Queen showed character," says the Marquise de La Tour du Pin, "as the others paced the length and breadth of the rooms at the palace without exchanging a word."⁴⁸

At ten that night, Lafayette had sent word to the palace from Sèvres of his approach—inspiring Saint-Priest's counsel of flight—

* So ending Maillard's "leading role" in the "Orléanist conspiracy."

and had received a reply that "the King saw his approach with pleasure, and had just signed *his* [Lafayette's] Declaration of Rights." At midnight, Lafayette's memoirs continue, he arrived at Versailles, stopped his army before the Hôtel des Menus Plaisirs, addressed his troops, and "had them renew their civic oath of loyalty to the Nation, the law and the King."[49] He entered the Assembly, where the deputies had resumed their session, assured them he had come to protect both the Assembly and the King, took his leave, and marched his men down the avenue to the Place d'Armes.

Alone, except for several members of the Paris Commune, Lafayette presented himself at the palace gate. The Hundred Swiss now guarding the courtyard hesitated opening it to him. He saluted the *"brave régiment des gardes Suisses"* and the gate swung open. He went up the marble staircase, "found the apartments full of people," directed himself to the King's Council Room. As he traversed the Oeil-de-Boeuf, he heard a courtier loudly remark, "Ah! There goes Cromwell!"

"Monsieur," Lafayette replied, "Cromwell would not have come alone."[50] And to the King, surrounded by his Council and officers of his guard, he said, "I come, Sire, to offer you my head to save Your Majesty's. If my blood must flow, may it be in the service of my King, rather than by torchlight on the Place de Grève."[51]

Louis seemed somewhat reassured. Lafayette proposed that the palace be guarded from without by his men and from within by a detachment of the Gardes du Corps. The King agreed. There was, in fact, no other recourse. When Lafayette further proposed, as instructed by the Commune, that the King come and live in Paris, there was no answer. And Lafayette left to execute what had been agreed upon.

He posted his wet, weary men around the palace, bivouacked many in the churches and many more on the Place d'Armes. (The Flanders regiment had been withdrawn to the adjacent Great Stables and was already fraternizing with the Paris guardsmen.) He rode to the Assembly, suggested Mounier suspend the session, rode back to the palace, found the King asleep, did the rounds of his posted guards, retired to his headquarters at the Hôtel de Noailles, a hundred paces north of the palace's principal gate, had a bowl of soup, and, at four in the morning, flung himself on a bed. "He had been seventeen hours in the saddle, and his would be a well merited rest."[52] But because of what would very shortly happen, Lafayette would ever after be known in royalist circles as "General Morpheus."[53]

The women of Paris, too, slept where they might—some on the benches in the Menus Plaisirs, some with the men in the churches of St.-Louis, Notre Dame, and the Récollets—and some not at all. During the night, a nobleman had remarked a gate open near the Opéra courtyard. At three in the morning, he noted, it was still unlocked and guarded by a single Versailles militiaman.[54]

At dawn on October 6, the women—and men—who had not slept may have found that gate, or another, open. With pikes and improvised lances, they pushed past the yielding Paris guards and spread through the Court of Ministers to the terrace under the Queen's apartments. Their cries awakened her. She called to Madame Thibault, her first lady-in-waiting, and asked what the noise meant. Madame Thibault replied that it was only some of those women from Paris who couldn't find a place to sleep. Relieved, Marie Antoinette lay back in her bed.[55]

But the crowd grew and the cry was now, "To the Queen's apartments!" The Gardes du Corps took their positions in the Queen's wing. The gate of the royal court was forced, the Marble Courtyard overflowed. From a window in the palace, a Garde du Corps shot a young journeyman named Lhéritier. His body would lie in the courtyard, inspiring revenge. The marble staircase of the Queen was stormed, two Gardes du Corps died. Their heads would deck the pikes that killed them.

A brave man stood on the top steps of the marble staircase. "My friends," said Miomandre de Sainte-Marie to the crowd, "you love your King, yet you come to his very palace to disturb him!" He was badly beaten and barely snatched back into the Grande Salle des Gardes by his fellows in time. Its door was smashed down. The Gardes du Corps retreated to the Queen's smaller Salle des Gardes. It was broken into. A bodyguard braced himself before the far door, which led to the Queen's suite. He was knocked to the ground. Miomandre de Sainte-Marie took his place. He was struck down by a pike. He struggled to his feet, opened the door, cried across the large antechamber to a lady-in-waiting, "Madame, save the Queen!" Madame Auguié locked and bolted a second, smaller antechamber, and rushed into the Queen's bedroom. There she found Madame Thibault. They threw a mantle

Q

over Marie Antoinette's nightdress and took her through a hidden door behind her bed, through a small corridor, to the Oeil-de-Boeuf. Its door was closed. Guards had locked it to shut off the King's apartments. They beat on it, their voices were recognized, the door was opened. They race to the King's bedroom. Louis is not there. He had gone by the secret passageway under the Oeil-de-Boeuf to Marie Antoinette's bedroom. Told by the guards of her flight, he returned to his bedroom and found her. They were joined by the little Dauphin, brought by his governess, Madame de Tourzel. King and Queen together went for his older sister, Madame Royale, and brought her back to the King's bedroom. And all together—as the Gardes du Corps barricaded themselves in the Oeil-de-Boeuf—they waited.

First to arrive were the Paris grenadiers under Captain Gondran—in rescue. They who had pressed Lafayette to lead them to Versailles, so they might "exterminate" the King's men, now came to save them, if that meant saving the King. A crowd that got out of hand was not to the liking of *these* grenadiers, in any case. They drove through the throng to the Oeil-de-Boeuf, stopped those battering at its door, called out their friendly intentions to those inside, and embraced the Gardes du Corps as brother soldiers when they opened the door·to them. Simultaneously, roused from his sleep by the first shots, Lafayette had ordered the grenadiers of his command post at the Hôtel de Noailles to intervene at the palace.

"At the same time, hastening there," Lafayette writes, "I jumped on the first horse I found."[56] But in the short distance to the palace he also came upon several Gardes du Corps in the hands of an angry crowd crying vengeance for the fallen Lhéritier. "My friends," Lafayette called to grenadiers nearby, "I gave my word of honor to the King that no harm would come to his bodyguards. If you cause me to break my word of honor, I shall no longer be fit to be your general!"[57] His men cheered him, disengaged the Gardes du Corps, escorted them to safety in the Great Stables, and Lafayette rode on to the palace. Staircase, guards' rooms, and Queen's suite had been cleared by the time he arrived, but there were great crowds in the courtyards below, unappeased and still "turbulent."[58]

The King was in his Council Room, encircled by ministers and the most eminent of his noblemen—among them the Duc d'Orléans. The prince, it was being murmured in the Oeil-de-Boeuf, had been seen during the night distributing money to "those who had not slept."

In fact, he had ridden to Versailles that morning from Paris and had peacefully reached the Pont de Sèvres, an officer of the National Guard would testify, well after dawn.[59] But Marie Antoinette, when she saw him, had recoiled and withdrawn to the King's bedroom. Here the royal family had assembled—Monsieur and Madame, the King's elderly aunts, and his younger sister, Madame Elisabeth. Marie Antoinette stood in a corner, looking tristfully out the window; the Dauphin and Madame Royale—the little boy playing with his sister's hair—were at her side. She could see the crowds; all could hear their insistent cry: *"We want to see the King!"*

Phlegmatically Louis XVI obliged, stepping out on the balcony of the Sun King's Royal Chamber. *"Vive le Roi!"* greeted him and *"Vive la Nation!"*—as if King and Nation were now one. But there was still the arrogant "Austrian," and there were shouts for the Queen, "the Queen to the balcony!" Marie Antoinette, however, did not appear. It was a long, dangerous moment, for the shouts became menacing and might soon be followed by stones, musket fire, and another invasion of the palace. Finally Lafayette went to her.

"Madame," he asked, "what do you intend to do?"

"I know the fate that is awaiting me," Marie Antoinette replied, "but my duty is to die at the feet of the King with my children in my arms."

"Well, then, Madame," said Lafayette, "come with me."

"What, Sir, on that balcony? Have you not seen those threatening gestures they have been making?"

"Yes, Madame," he said, "let us go."[60]

With the Queen holding each child by the hand, they slowly walked through the Council Room to the royal bedchamber. As she entered, Madame de Staël remarked "her disarranged hair, her pallid face that maintained its dignity" as it showed what she feared "from the armed men who filled the Marble Courtyard."[61] Still holding her children by the hand, Marie Antoinette went out on the balcony. "No children!" the great crowd shouted. Defiantly, she thrust them back behind her and stood alone. The cries were no less antagonistic. Lafayette stepped forward and attempted to make himself heard. In vain. Then, with a gallant gesture, he took the Queen's hand and kissed it. "The multitude, struck by the gesture, spontaneously shouted, *'Vive le Général! Vive la Reine!'*

"The King, who had remained in the rear, came forward and

asked Lafayette in a grateful voice, 'And now what can you do for my faithful guards?'

" 'Bring me one,' said Lafayette. Which done, he pinned his own tricolor cockade on the King's bodyguard and embraced him, and the people cried *'Vivent les Gardes du Corps!' "*[62]

Meanwhile, the Queen, who had quietly withdrawn from the balcony, said with little illusion to Madame Necker (says Madame de Staël), "They will compel us nevertheless, the King and me, to go to Paris, with the heads of our Gardes du Corps preceding us on the ends of their pikes."[63]

Lafayette had kissed her hand, saving her life, and she never forgave him. The great Parisian crowds had cheered the gesture, but they had not forgotten what they had come for. Even as they cried, *"Vive le Roi!"* voices added, *"Le Roi à Paris!* The King to Paris!" It soon became a solid cry: *"The King to Paris!"*

There was no gesture now that could stifle it.

Louis consulted his ministers. It was but a formal gesture. Even the Comte de Saint-Priest counseled yielding to the unavoidable. And Louis yielded. Lafayette reappeared on the balcony and announced the King's decision. Notes were scribbled with the information and dropped from the palace windows. Cheers rose from the Marble Courtyard and spread beyond the gates to the Place d'Armes and the streets. The King was going to Paris. He would leave at one o'clock.

The men of the National Guard fired their muskets in celebration. The men of the National Assembly voted to follow the King to Paris.

"And so," says Madame Royale, daughter of Marie Antoinette and ten years old at the time, "each of us returned to our rooms to tidy up, for we were all"—all the women—"still in our night bonnets."[64]

The King cleared his desk, making a little packet of his private papers. The Queen distributed some of her things as gifts and took "only a chest of diamonds."[65] At one twenty-five the royal family descended the small staircase in the north wing, where Damiens had waited, "so it might not see the blood on the Queen's Staircase."[66]

"Try," said Louis XVI to the nobleman left in charge, as he climbed sadly and heavily into the carriage for Paris, "try to save my poor Versailles."[67]

He sat dejectedly in the back with Marie Antoinette. Facing them were the Dauphin, on the lap of his governess, and little Madame Royale. Crowded in the same carriage were the King's brother, the

Comte de Provence, and his sister, Madame Elisabeth, seated at the doors. Alongside, as the royal family left Versailles for the last time, rode Lafayette and the Comte d'Estaing.[68] They were preceded— followed and surrounded—by a singing, chanting people: "We are bringing the baker, the baker's wife and the baker's apprentice! They will bring us bread!"

Slowly, at a footpace, the great cortege moved down the Avenue de Paris, past the Hôtel des Menus Plaisirs. Deputies stood and watched as it passed, among them Mirabeau. But even before the cortege would reach Paris, the Hôtel de Ville, and night at the Tuileries palace:

". . . a terrible solitude already reigned at Versailles."[69]

And there was heard only the sound of the closing of doors and shutters which had not been closed since the days of the Sun King.

Q*

Epilogue Without Tears

The carriages were heavy that evening with brass-bound chests and trunks; the Court was departing for Paris or for its estates in the country. Some of the palace's furniture, carefully noted by caretakers, was hurriedly carted to the empty Tuileries—and would return to Versailles when replacements were arranged or copies made. The most precious pieces were inventoried and stored in the Royal Warehouse, against the day when the royal family, too, would return. And in 1790, the great paneled paintings on the ceiling of the Grande Galerie were retouched and rebrightened in anticipation of that time.[1] In the long, in fact, interminable, interim, one might pick up the loose ends in the lives of Versailles' last residents and tie them into the larger fabric of history.

"Paris is delighted to see you in the palace of our kings," Mayor Bailly said to an unmoved Marie Antoinette, "and hopes that the King and Your Majesty will be so good as to make it their habitual residence."[2] The Tuileries would not even be Their Majesties' last residence.

Mirabeau, who sincerely believed that the monarchy, once limited, was an anchor for France, had let it be known that he was ready to serve the royal cause. Marie Antoinette had replied with hauteur through La Marck, "I trust we will never be so unfortunate as to be reduced to the painful extreme of seeking help from Mirabeau."[3] Not long afterward the women of Paris descended on Versailles, the King and Queen were uneasily installed in the Tuileries, and the help of Mirabeau was no longer so disdained. The only other man of equal popularity who might have aided them was Lafayette, but the Queen regarded him as a second Cromwell, though it was Lafayette's insistence that sent the Duc d'Orléans "on a mission" to England to remove him from the troubled scene.

Daily in the Assembly, now meeting in the royal Manège, or Riding School, near the Tuileries, Mirabeau demonstrated his commitment to the retention of royal powers, and it soon became the subject of an extraordinary secret contract with the Crown. Mirabeau's debts (208,000 francs) were paid off; he was promised another million francs and a monthly allowance of six thousand more should his services prove satisfactory by the Assembly's end. Thus Mirabeau was paid by the monarchy, as later accused, but it was to put forward and defend his own ideas*—and the long letters of advice he now sent to Louis XVI, had they been followed, might have saved the King his crown. Louis, Mirabeau repeatedly wrote, should derive his power from the people—that is, the new bourgeoisie and its Assembly—and not assert ancient rights against them. Louis paid, but he did not listen. Mirabeau appealed to the Queen in a secret meeting at Saint-Cloud. She listened, but she had no faith in Mirabeau or in his ideas. And virtually the last words of Mirabeau would be, "I exposed myself to disaster, hoping to save the King and Queen. But they did not want to be saved."[5] Courageously Mirabeau defended the monarchy in the Assembly, but his motives were increasingly suspect; recklessly he spent the energy sapped by his early excesses, and in the spring of 1791 he died, age forty-two.

Attacks mounted in the Assembly against the monarchy. Those directed at himself Louis XVI could endure, those upon the Church he could not. Though he ratified the revolutionary Civil Constitution of the clergy, it was to gain time for a later counterrevolution. Louis could never have countenanced a state-controlled church, a salaried clergy, and popular election of priests and bishops. But he dissembled his feelings, and he agreed to a flight from Paris to join loyal troops under royalist General de Bouillé, eventually to be reinforced by an Austrian army.

The flight was organized by the Queen's devoted Axel von Fersen

* Madame de Staël: "Mirabeau, whether or not he received money from the Court, had determined to be the master, not the instrument, of the Court."[4]

and reached as far east as Varennes. But the spanking-new green
and white coach, drawn by six horses, and the undisguisable royal
family were too conspicuous, and the flight was arrested. Louis'
kingship was suspended and all were brought back. He continued to
sit formally on the throne and even declared war on Austria and
Prussia, as France's chief of state, though they were marching to his own
rescue. But the first French defeats brought Paris's crowds storming into
the Tuileries. They well knew where Louis' interests and loyalties lay.
He survived that encounter, but not the next. Brashly the Duke of
Brunswick, commanding general of the invading forces, threatened to
destroy Paris if the King and the royal family were not freed. He
thereby condemned them. The fury of Paris was all too predictable.
Lafayette could no longer contain his National Guards, much less
the capital's crowds. On August 10, 1792, the royal family sought
refuge with the National Assembly in the royal Manège.[6] The refuge
was temporary. The Temple prison would be the King's last residence,
the Conciergerie the Queen's. The guillotine would be their end.

And so, too, it would be for the Duc d'Orléans. Allowed to return
to France in July 1790, he voted death for the King in January 1793,
and was himself executed in November, three weeks after Marie
Antoinette. He had been compromised by his son's slipping away to
join the émigré army of the King's brothers abroad. In between time,
Lafayette, who had defended the royal family too often, was declared
a traitor to the Revolution by the National Assembly. He fled France
and spent the next five years in Prussian, then Austrian prisons, before
he was liberated by Napoleon.

Republican France did not know quite what to do with Versailles'
royal palace. In truth, neither the Revolution nor its heir, Napoleon,
had much time or thought for it, except as an annex of the Hôtel des
Invalides—a home for the mutilated of Napoleon's wars. Its demolition
would have been too costly and the new order needed money as much
as the old. Consequently, on the departure of Louis XVI and Marie
Antoinette, the Assembly decreed an auction of the palace's contents—
and aroused the opposition of the people of Versailles. A compromise
was effected. Paintings and the more irreplaceable objets d'art would
be removed to the museum newly created at the Louvre, and the rest
would be auctioned off. There were further protests. Paintings and
sculpture were retained at Versailles, on order of the later Convention,

but the auction proceeded. More than 1700 lots were sold in the courtyard of the Small Stables, and some of the palace's finest pieces of
furniture departed for foreign shores, particularly England. More
gravely, in 1796 the republic's needs drove it to emptying the former
Royal Warehouse of the most chosen items; its stored buhlwork and
porcelains were sold off to the highest bidders or presented to army
contractors in lieu of payments.[7]

Meanwhile, Versailles' Jacobin Club held its meetings in the palace's
Opéra, and Le Nôtre's park was preserved by the astuteness of
gardener Antoine Richard. He saved the parterres, when it was wildly
suggested they be plowed under, by planting them with vegetables
and fruit trees. A departmental Central School was established in
one wing of the palace, a library of royal and émigré collections in
another. The Royal Chapel became the nation's Temple, a Liberty
Tree was planted in the Marble Courtyard, and in 1799 the library
in the north wing was removed to make room for Napoleon's *invalides*.

Fontainebleau rather than Versailles was Napoleon's preference, fortunately for Versailles. His project for the transformation of the palace
into a summer residence would have meant a drastic remodeling of
the entire townside in neoclassical, neo-Roman style. The park would
have been denuded of its stone nymphs, which Napoleon found in bad
taste, to be replaced by what he considered better—panoramic walls
of masonry depicting capitals he had conquered and celebrated battles
he had fought.[8] Here, too, lack of money saved Versailles. Instead,
Napoleon concentrated on the Trianons—after dislodging the drink
merchants and their concessions. Briefly and fugitively—he was always
pressed for time—he dwelt in the Grand Trianon with Marie-Louise,
and his sister, Pauline Borghese, settled in the Petit Trianon.

More fugitive, for Versailles, was the return of the Comte de Provence and the Comte d'Artois as Louis XVIII and Charles X—a return,
that is, to Paris. Louis XVIII, in the Restoration aftermath of Napoleon's fall, would gladly have returned with his court to the palace
of his youth. But there was neither time nor (again) money for more
than a few needed restorations and the housing of a few needy
courtiers (who had to be told by the palace's governor not to hang
their wash out of the palace's windows). However, the pavilion of
architect Dufour was erected in the entry courtyard, re-establishing an
architectural balance with the existing pavilion of Gabriel. For Charles

X, who succeeded his brother, there is even less to be said. He went to Versailles twice—the first time, in August 1826, to the palace; the second time, in July 1830, when he stopped for a few hurried hours at the Trianon, on his flight from revolution to Rambouillet and exile.

And now another figure from Versailles' ancient past appeared—Louis-Philippe, son of the Duc d'Orléans, whose eighteen-year reign would have the greatest impact on the palace since Louis XVI. He who would be the "King of all the French" determined the palace itself would be transformed into the symbol of national union—in his own phrase, the Museum of all the Glories of France. Balzac, a Versailles resident, would bitingly describe the result, *"L'hôpital des gloires de la France."*

Carved woodwork, decorative panels, delicately chased bronze ornaments were ripped entire from the walls of the ground floor and south wing apartments—those of the Dauphin, Mesdames de Pompadour and Maintenon—and a hospital-gray paint applied to create the dreary, neutral background of yesterday's museum walls. "Whereas formerly," as Versailles historian Bernard Champigneulles has written, "when Louis XV and Louis XVI removed elements of the past, they replaced them with new beauties, this time they were replaced with a kind of nothingness."[9] Yet no contemporary critic lifted his voice against the desecration. Rather, the changes were praised as the modernization of the palace, and the new Galerie des Batailles (featuring wall-high paintings of French victories) was favorably compared with Louis XIV's Grande Galerie (luckily left unimproved). Outside, the Marble Courtyard was lowered to make access to the ground-floor rooms of the new museum easier. However, Louis-Philippe repaired the palace roof, restored the Petit Trianon and the Hamlet, and in 1848 stopped off at the Grand Trianon in his flight from revolution to exile in London, as Mr. Smith.

His successor, Louis-Napoleon ("the nephew"), also repaired roofs, as well as the ceiling of Louis XIV's Grande Chambre, entertained Queen Victoria with a palace ball and Ludwig II of Bavaria at the Trianon. Empress Eugénie identified herself with Marie Antoinette and brooded over her fate at the Petit Trianon. But in the prosperous mood of the Second Empire, neither she nor Napoleon III could have dreamed of the next phase in the life of Versailles.

Came the Franco-Prussian War, and the French hospital improvised on the ground floor of the palace became a German hospital, as the Prussians occupied Versailles and laid siege to Paris. And as the guns of Krupp pounded the starving capital, Count von Bismarck realized his life's goal—Wilhelm I of Prussia was proclaimed Emperor of the new German Empire in Versailles' Hall of Mirrors. The Sun King's palace was still the symbolic center of political Europe.

For several months Bismarck and Moltke, Wilhelm I, the Crown Prince and the Prussian Court had been installed at Versailles. Prussian troops had drilled in the Place d'Armes. The Prussian King and his entourage had exercised their horses in the *allées* of Le Notre's park. It was all incidental to the work of Bismarck, who for years had assiduously sought agreement for this day from the other German states. Only Ludwig II of Bavaria still held out. He would be put up at the Trianon, he was told. Finally he, too, assented. And on January 18, 1871, the Grande Galerie echoed with the strange foreign sounds of Prussian cannon and German cheers, as six hundred officers drew their sabers, saluted and hailed their emperor in the great hall.[10] (The French Emperor himself was captive in Prussia.)

There would be another day, as designedly chosen, for a second appearance of Germany's men in the same mirrored hall of the palace of Versailles. But a Third French Republic had first to spin much of its course.

That republic began badly, moving the newly elected National Assembly from Bordeaux, when the war ended, to Versailles *à la* Louis XIV, in order to keep a radicalized Paris at a distance. Then Paris exploded, and as the Commune took over the capital, the conservative Thiers government decamped hurriedly for Versailles. To the deputies already lodged in the palace, covering themselves as they slept with the curtains and drapes of the Grande Galerie, were now added the ministries which made do in the apartments and *petits appartements* of the Queen's wing. But it would not be for long. This time Versailles would march on Paris, and it would make the previous marches of Paris on Versailles, historians are in accord, look like innocent outings. By the first days of April 1871, Adolphe Thiers managed to scrape together sixty thousand troops at Versailles. By the end of the last "Bloody Week" of May, which still festers in the French mind, Thiers' *Versaillais* had executed, in "expiation," twenty-five thousand to thirty thousand Communards in Paris. No battle in the Franco-Prussian War had resulted in so many fallen. The Revolution's often invoked, often decried Reign of Terror had cost less than one tenth as many lives, though it extended over a year's time.[11]

Cautiously the Constitution of 1875 retained the National Assembly in Versailles. The Opéra became the seat of the Senate, the south wing was devoted to the Chamber of Deputies, the north wing to its committees and services, an assembly hall arranged between them. Four years later, however, all were in Paris, and it would be another forty years before Versailles re-entered history. But more importantly, a young curator with the sensitivity of a poet and the appreciation of a scholar came to the palace and began to return Versailles to itself. Book after inspired book by Pierre de Nolhac quickened public interest; room by neglected room he resurrected the palace. But there was more to be done than he could do. It had to await the end of two world wars, which history might yet join as one, if only because the treaty ending the first contributed to the second.

On June 28, 1919, in the Grande Galerie where Wilhelm I had been proclaimed Emperor of Germany at the expense of a prostrated France, the Allies signed the Treaty of Versailles, signaling this time, as French guns thundered outside, Germany's defeat.

Mayor of Montmartre during the siege of Paris, ancient Communard Georges Clemenceau brushed past the delegates around the huge horseshoe table, saving his first greeting for the French disabled he had invited to be present. From the Salon de la Guerre (by coincidence, the Salon of War) emerged the German Reich's two obscure plenipotentiaries, Dr. Mueller and Dr. Bell. There would be no equivalent of Bismarck or Moltke, King or Crown Prince of Prussia. Civilians would sign this peace treaty and later be accused of it. And they would sign first. Then Woodrow Wilson, professorial and clerical, and his associates, white-maned Lloyd George and old, tigerish Clemenceau and the French delegation (each looking like a national stereotype), then Greeks, Belgians, Poles, and lesser Allies including the Japanese and Argentines signed, until finally the man from Uruguay penned his name. A ceremony of forty-five minutes ended a war of fifty-two months and 8,538,315 dead. Afterwards, Clemenceau invited his Allied guests down into the gardens for a fountain display in the Basin of Neptune.[12]

Four years of war, however, had left gardens, palace, and Trianons in a parlous state. And it was the generosity of an ally, the legendary millions of John D. Rockefeller, Jr., "which stung the French state," says Curator Gérard Van der Kemp, "into competition for necessary restorations."[13] Twenty-seven acres of roof were kept from collapse. "The Orangerie was rebuilt, the park replanted, its groves entirely renewed." Some of the *grands appartements* were redecorated. But it was only the beginning, or rather eternal recommencing, of work that still awaited the end of World War II and a new period of reconstruction.

During the last half of General de Gaulle's ten-year reign, special efforts were taken at the Grand Trianon. It was remodeled and redecorated in the somewhat heavy Empire style of Napoleon's occupancy. It might have been more politically than aesthetically appropriate: the General had considered leaving the Élysée Palace for residence in the Trianon, occupying one wing—with an entourage frequently referred to as "the Court" and Madame de Gaulle as "Madame de Maintenant" (Madame of the Moment)—and visiting chiefs of state, while in France, the other.[14] Events, including a near-revolution in May 1968, retired de Gaulle instead to his own estate at Colombey-les-Deux-Eglises.

Thus Versailles and its Trianons are largely the public's—a public including tourists, more of whom visit the palace and the park than any other French monument or site, save the Eiffel Tower. Indeed Versailles has never been more beautiful or impressive since that day in October 1789 when Louis XVI and Marie Antoinette left it, never to return. For our time has a respect for the past that the past has never had. Well over fifty *salles* at the palace have been scrupulously restored to the life, time, and styles of Louis XIV, XV, and XVI. Millions now revisit the seventeenth century in the King's north wing and the eighteenth to the south of it. Walls are now covered with silk instead of sacking. The Grande Chambre of the Sun King is newly resplendent. The apartments of Marie Antoinette once again have some of the décor she lived with—a commode, a marble chimneypiece, a garlanded bedcover. More pieces from the auctions of the 1790's are expected to return in the 1970's, as those who have fallen heir to them restore them to their home in Versailles. The French budget for museum purchases still requires that kind of generosity.

For Versailles is above all a museum—without disparagement of Pompeii or the Acropolis, the greatest living museum of a vanished life on the face of our planet. It lives in the real sense that the experience of it, the pleasure and impact of it are here and now, when the hundreds of fountains play, fireworks fall from the sky, and the musical fanfares of Lully are heard.

It is specially true when one stands on that great terrace, as a young black American writer recently in search of his identity, and can say, "I am Louis XIV."

Q**

Appendices

The complete deposition of Abbé Guibourg, October 10, 1680, was presumably destroyed with the official files of the *affaire des poisons* on the order of Louis XIV. What remains are Police Lieutenant La Reynie's sketchy and in some spots obscure and disconnected notes:

"Incantation read at the Mass in Mesnil [Paris suburb]: "Astarte, Asmodeus, Princes of Friendship, I conjure you to accept the sacrifice of the child I am presenting you in exchange for what I ask—that the friendship of the King and Mgr le Dauphin for me continue and be honored by the Princes and Princesses of the Court, that nothing I ask of the King be denied my family and my servants."

"And it named the names of the King and those of Mme de Montespan which were in the incantation.

"He [Guibourg] had bought a baby for an *écu* which was sacrificed at this Mass and had been presented him by a grown-up girl and, having drawn blood from the baby whose throat he had pierced with a penknife, he poured it into the chalice, after which the baby was removed and taken to another place and its heart and entrails brought him for a second Mass to be used, Leroy and the gentleman told him, to make powders for the [King] and Mme de [Montespan]: the lady for whom he celebrated the Mass always wore her coif down, covering her face and half her breasts. He celebrated the second Mass in a hovel near the ramparts of Saint-Denis, over the same woman, with the same ritual, La Pelletier present. Celebrated the third Mass in Paris at La Voisin's, over the same person, perhaps eight or nine years ago, though afterwards he said thirteen or fourteen. Also declares that five years ago he said thirteen or fourteen. Also declares that five years ago he celebrated a similar Mass at La Voisin's over the same person, who he was always told was Mme de Montespan, for the same purposes, and La Laporte was present; and, after everything was finished, removing his coat from a chair, he found a piece of writing which seemed a copy of a pact, seeing it was on paper [and not a wafer], with these words:

"'I, . . . , daughter of . . . , ask the friendship of the King and Mgr le Dauphin, that it continue, that the Queen be sterile, that the King abandon her bed and table for me, that I obtain from him all I request for myself and my family, that my servants and domestics be agreeable in his eyes; that cherished and respected by the grands seigneurs I might be called to the councils of the King and know what takes place there, and that this friendship be doubled over the past, that the King abandon and no longer look at La Vallière, and that the Queen be repudiated so I may marry the King.'

"Leroy, Gouverneur des Pages de la Petite Écurie, was the first to propose that he work for Mme de Montespan; thinks there were others who were already working for her for the same purposes; had asked him for more than a year for the first Mass. There was a gentleman who conjointly solicited him for the same affair; was not able to find out his name; his lackey told him his name was Saint-Morisse; thinks he [the gentleman?] belonged to [the suite of?] Mgr the Archbishop [Mme de Montespan's uncle]; promised him fifty pistoles and a benefice of 2,000 livres. The first Mass he celebrated was at Leroy's in Mesnil, near Montlhéry.

"And, when he came to this point in his reading [sic], the paper was torn from his hands; he always left the wafer and infants' blood in the vessels brought him, the wafer cut into small pieces.

"At La Voisin's, dressed in an alb, stole and maniple, he had recited an incantation in the presence of La des Oeillets, who claimed to be making a spell for the [King] and who was accompanied by a man who had given him the incantation, and since it was necessary to have sperm of both sexes, des Oeillets, having her monthlies (*ayant ses mois*), was not able, but poured her menstrual blood into the chalice and the man who accompanied her, after going to the side of the bed with him, Guibourg, poured his sperm into the chalice. La des Oeillets and the man each added to it the powdered blood of a bat and flour to give a firmer body to the entire composition and after he had recited the incantation, he poured the mixture from the chalice into the little vessel that La des Oeillets or the man had brought."

From Mongrédien's *Madame de Montespan et l'Affaire des Poisons*, pp. 117–19.

This was not gossip, as so much of the period's memoirs, but the notes of Louis XIV's own conscientious police chief. One can imagine the King's reaction to these sordid stories about those so close to him.

Mademoiselle des Oeillets, brought before members of the band who had testified against her, was immediately recognized and named by them. It was the most damaging evidence against her and her mistress, Madame de Montespan.

APPENDIX II

"Here," wrote Madame de Maintenon to the Cardinal de Noailles, Archbishop of Paris, in December 1695, "is a letter written to the King two or three years ago. You must return it to me; it is well written. But such truths cannot change him. They can only irritate or discourage him. One must do neither the one nor the other, but rather lead him gently in the way we want him to go."

For years the Fénelon letter referred to was regarded as being doubtfully authentic, until a copy in his own hand turned up in 1825 at an auction. From Madame de Maintenon's note, it would seem she had intercepted it before it reached the King and kept it from him for the reason she offers the Cardinal. Nevertheless the letter of François de Salignac de la Mothe Fénelon, shortly to be named Archbishop of Cambrai, remains one of the most significant and moving documents of the period. For one thing, it undercuts the apologist's defense of Louis XIV's often ruthless pursuit of grandeur as a reflection of the "universal" amoral spirit of the time. For another, it is its own demonstration of another, more universal spirit, despite the time—the critical French spirit:

"Sire, he who takes the liberty of writing you this letter has no worldly interest. He writes it from neither disappointment, nor ambition, nor from a desire to mingle in great affairs. He loves you without being known by you; he sees God in your person. For all your power, you can give him nothing he desires, and there is no hurt he would not gladly suffer to make you recognize the truths necessary for your salvation. If he speaks strongly to you, do not be surprised; it is because truth is free and strong. You are not used to hearing it. People accustomed to being flattered easily mistake for disappointment, bitterness and exaggeration what is only pure truth. It would be a betrayal of truth not to show it to you in its entirety.

God is witness that he who speaks to you does it with a heart full of zeal, respect, fidelity and affection for everything that concerns your real interest.

"You were born, Sire, with a just and upright heart, but those who raised you gave you as the science for governing mistrust, jealousy, the distancing of virtue, the fear of all signal merit, a taste for servile and groveling men, haughtiness and attention only to your own interests.

"For about thirty years, your principal ministers have shaken and overturned all the ancient maxims of State in order to elevate your authority to new heights, an authority which became theirs because it was in their hands. No one any longer spoke of the State or its laws; they spoke only of the King and his good pleasure. They have pushed your revenues and your expenditures beyond any limit. They have praised you to the skies for having, they say, effaced the grandeur of all your predecessors combined, that is to say, for having empoverished all France in order to introduce a monstrous and incurable luxury at Court. They have sought to elevate you upon the ruins of every class in the State—as if you could be great by ruining all your subjects upon whom your greatness depends. It is true you have been jealous of authority, perhaps even too much in foreign affairs, but fundamentally each minister has been master throughout his administration. You thought to rule by limiting those who govern, but they have shown their power to the people, who have felt it to excess. They have been hard, haughty, unjust, violent and ill-willed. They have known no other rule in domestic or foreign negotiations but to threaten, crush or destroy anything that resisted them. They talked to you only to hide from you any merit that might diminish them. They have accustomed you continuously to receive extravagant praises to the point of idolatry which, for your own honor, you should have rejected with indignation. They have rendered your name odious and the entire French nation unbearable for your neighbors. They have retained none of our former allies, because they wanted only slaves. They have been the cause, for more than twenty years, of bloody wars. For instance, Sire, in 1672 they had your Majesty undertake the Dutch War for your glory and to punish the Dutch for their raillery. . . . I cite this particular war, because it was the source of all the others. Its motives were nothing but glory and vengeance, which can never make a war just; thus all the frontiers you have extended thanks to it are unjustly acquired because of it. It is true, Sire, that subsequent treaties of peace seem to cover and compensate this injustice, since they accord you the conquered areas; but an unjust war is no less unjust for being successful. Peace treaties signed by the defeated are not freely signed. They sign with a knife at their throat; they sign despite themselves to avoid worse losses; they sign as one gives up one's purse when the alternative is to die. Thus, Sire, you must go back to the origin of the Dutch War when you give an account of your conquests before God.

"It is needless to say they were necessary for your State: the good of others is never necessary for us. What is truly necessary is to practise an equitable justice. You should not even claim the right to retain forever certain conquered areas, because they serve to secure your frontiers. It is for you to find that security in good alliances, by your moderation, or in areas that can be fortified behind your frontiers. Finally, the need to watch over our security never gives us the right to seize the land of our neighbor. . . .

"Since that war, you have always sought to dictate the peace and impose its conditions instead of arranging them with equity and moderation. That is why no peace has endured. Your enemies, shamefully beaten down, thought only of rising and uniting against you. Should one be surprised? You have not even stayed within the terms of the peace treaty you so haughtily dictated. In the midst of peace you have made war and entered on prodigious conquests. . . . Such conduct has stirred and reunited all Europe against you. Even those who do not dare declare it openly wish impatiently for your weakening and your humiliation as the sole hope for the peace and freedom of all Christian nations. . . .

"Meanwhile your people, whom you should love as your own children and who have until now been so devoted to you, are dying of hunger. The cultivation of the land is almost abandoned; the towns and the countryside are being depopulated; all crafts and trades are languishing and can no longer support their workmen. All commerce has been crushed. You have consumed half the real strength of your State in order to defend vain conquests abroad. Instead of extracting money from your poor people, you should have succored and nourished them. All France is now a vast poor-house, desolate and without provision. The magistrates are exhausted and despised. The nobility, whose estates are all indebted, survive only by *lettres d'État* [royal letters allowing a moratorium]. . . . If the King, the people say, had the heart of a father for his people would he not find his glory in giving them bread and relief after all thei miseries rather than in holding on to a few territories at the frontier, whose possession is the cause of the present war? What can be your answer to that, Sire? Popular uprisings, so long unknown, are becoming frequent. Paris itself, so close to you, is not exempt. Its magistrates are forced to endure the insolence of rebels and secretly give them money to appease them, thus rewarding those who should be punished. You are reduced to the shameful and deplorable extremity of letting sedition go unpunished, and thus grow, or of ordering the inhuman massacre of people you have subjected to misery by wrenching from their mouths, by your war taxes, the bread they have strained to win by the sweat of their brow.

"But while they are without bread, you yourself are without money and you refuse to recognize the extremity to which you have been reduced. Because you have always been triumphant, you can not imagine it being otherwise. You are afraid to open your eyes; you are afraid to have them opened for you; you are afraid to see any part of your glory diminished. This glory which hardens your heart is dearer to you than the injustice done, than your own peace of mind, than the saving of your people, who die every day from the diseases of famine, dearer even than your own eternal salvation, which is so incompatible with this idol of glory.

"Such, Sire, is your condition. You live as if there were a fatal bandage over your eyes; you plume yourself with daily triumphs that decide nothing. . . . Everyone sees it, but none dare open your eyes to it. You will see it yourself, perhaps, too late. True courage consists in not flattering oneself, in standing firm on the basis of reality. You do not lend a willing ear, Sire, except to those who flatter you with vain hopes. Those you esteem to be the most solid are those you fear and avoid the most. You must go half way to meet the truth, since you are King, urge people to tell you the truth without softening it and encourage those who are too timid. On the contrary, you seek only to stay on the surface of things, but God will finally know how to lift the veil from your eyes and show you what you are trying not to see. For a long time His hand has been raised over you, but He is slow to strike, because He has pity on a prince who has been surrounded all his life by sycophants and because your enemies are also His. But He will know how to separate His just cause from yours, which is not just, how to humble you in order to convert you, for you will not be Christian except by humiliation. You do not love God; you do not even fear him, except with a slavish fear; it is Hell and not God that you fear. Your religion consists only in superstitions, in petty, superficial observances. . . . You love only your glory and your gain. You refer everything to yourself, as if you were the God of the earth and all else was created in order to be sacrificed for you. Actually it is God who has put you on this world, but only for your people. . . .

"One had hoped, Sire, that your Council would have saved you from so wrong a road, but your Council has neither the strength nor the force to pursue the common good. At least Mme de M[aintenon] and M. le D[uc] de B[eauvilliers] might have used the confidence you have in them to disabuse you, but their weakness and timidity dishonor them and scandalize everyone. France is in desperate straits; what are they waiting for to speak to you frankly—that all be lost? Do they fear displeasing you? Then they do not love you, for one must be ready to anger those one loves rather than flatter or betray them by one's silence. What good are they if they do not show you that you must return the lands that are not yours, prefer the good life of your people to a false glory, repair the wrongs you have done to the Church, think of becoming a true Christian before you are surprised by death. . . .

"You may ask, Sire, what it is they should say to you. It is this: they should say that you must humble yourself before the powerful hand of God, if you do not wish it to humble you; that you must sue for peace and expiate by that humility all the glory which you have made your idol; that you must reject the unjust counsels of political sycophants; and finally that to save the State you must restore as soon as possible to your enemies the conquests which you cannot, in any case, retain without injustice. Are you not too happy among all these misfortunes? May God put an end to all those successes which have blinded you and constrain you to make the restitutions necessary for your salvation . . .

"Sire, he who tells you these truths, far from being opposed to your interests, would give his life to see you as God would wish you to be, and prays without cease for you."

From François de la Mothe Fénelon's *Lettre à Louis XIV*, Paris, 1825.

APPENDIX III

Casanova was in his mid-twenties when, in the mid-1750s, he first made his way to Paris. Here he frequented the nobles and notables of the day, was made director of the state lotteries, and, in turn, made his fortune. Early in his visit, he met (he says) the famous Louise O'Murphy (whom he calls Helen) before she was installed in the Parc aux Cerfs as Louis XV's mistress. She was Irish, but he refers to her sister as Flemish and to herself as Greek (possibly in a slangy, pejorative sense).

I was at the St. Laurent fair with my friend, Patu, when the fancy took him to sup with a Flemish actress named Morphi, and he enlisted me in his caprice. The girl didn't appeal to me, but how can one refuse one's friend? I did what he wished. After supping with *la belle,* Patu wanted to spend the night, extending the pleasure, and not wanting to leave him, I asked for a couch that I might sleep upon.

La Morphi had a sister, a little slattern of about thirteen, who told me that if I gave her an *écu,* she would give me her bed. I agreed and found myself in a small room with a straw mattress laid across four boards.

"You call *that* a bed, my child?" I said.

"I have no other, sir," she said.

"It's not for me, and you will not have your *écu.*"

"You were going to undress, sir?"

"Of course."

"Oh, we have no sheets," she said.

"You sleep fully clothed then?" I said.

"Not at all," she said.

"*Eh bien,* go to bed as usual and I'll give you your *écu.*"

"What for?"

"Just to look at you."

"But nothing else," she said.

"Not the slightest thing," I said.

She lay down on the straw mattress and covered herself with remnants of an old curtain. Seeing such perfect beauty, I did not see the rags, but wanted to see more. I set about satisfying my curiosity, but she resisted. An *écu* of six francs made her more docile, and finding her flawless except for the dirt, I proceeded to wash her with my hands.

[Casanova merely admired the body, he insists, and spent two months and three hundred francs admiring it.]

I wanted to possess that magnificent body in a painting, so I had a German painter portray her, which he did divinely well for six *louis d'or*. The pose he had her take was delightful. She lay on her stomach, her arms and a breast on a pillow, her head half-turned to the viewer. The artist had painted her lower body with such art and realism that one could not have desired anything lovelier.

[Casanova had a copy made for his friend Patu] but the artist, summoned to Versailles, took it with other portraits, and Monsieur de Saint-Quintin found it so beautiful that he hurried to show it to the King. His most Christian Majesty, a great connoisseur of such things, wanted to see for himself whether the painter had been faithful to his model. If the original were as beautiful as the copy, the grandson of Saint Louis [sic] knew the use he would make of it.

M. de Saint-Quintin, the ever obliging friend of the King, was charged with the affair: such was his ministry at the palace. He asked the painter if the original might not be brought to Versailles. The artist, confident it could be arranged, promised to look into it. He subsequently came to me and told me of the proposition. Finding the situation delicious, I immediately imparted it to the older sister, who jumped with joy. She promptly washed her younger sister and two or three days later, having dressed her decently, went with her and the painter to Versailles. The valet of the King's minister of such pleasures, instructed by his master, met the two females and installed them in a *pavillon* of the park. Meanwhile the painter waited in an inn. A half hour later the King entered the *pavillon* alone, asked the young O'Morphi if she were Greek, took her portrait from his pocket, studied her and cried, "I've never seen anything so lifelike!" Soon afterwards he sat, took the little one on his knee, caressed her somewhat and having assured himself with his Royal hand that the fruit was unculled, kissed her.

O'Morphi looked at him closely, and laughed.

"Why are you laughing?" the King asked.

"Because you are the spitting image of the face on the *écu!*"

This naïveté brought a loud laugh from the King, and he asked her if she would like to stay at Versailles. "That depends on my sister," she said. And the sister hastened to tell the King nothing would make her happier. The King left them closed up in the *pavillon*. A quarter of an hour later Saint-Quintin came, took the little one to an apartment in the palace, leaving her in the charge of one of the women, and went with the older sister to rejoin the painter. The latter received fifty louis d'or for the portrait, La Morphi nothing. He only took down her address, assuring her she would hear from him. The next day she had a thousand louis d'or. . . .

The young and beautiful O'Morphi, as the King always called her, pleased the King more by her innocence and nice ways than by her beauty, the most perfect I have ever seen. He installed her in an apartment of his Parc aux Cerfs, the veritable harem of this voluptuous prince, where no one was permitted to go, except ladies presented at Court.

—Translated from the three-volume edition of
Casanova's *Mémoires*, published in Paris in 1923.

APPENDIX IV

DECLARATION OF THE RIGHTS OF MAN AND THE CITIZEN
Versailles—August 26, 1789

The representatives of the French people, constituted in National Assembly, believing that ignorance, omission or contempt for the rights of man are the sole causes of public misfortunes and the corruption of governments, have resolved to set forth, in a solemn Declaration, the natural, sacred and inalienable rights of man, so that this Declaration, constantly held up before the members of the social body, will unceasingly remind them of their rights and duties; so that all acts of the legislative and executive powers, subject at all times to comparison with the goal of every political institution, may thereby be the more respected; so that the complaints of citizens, based on simple and uncontestable principles, revolve always around the maintenance of the Constitution and the happiness of all.

Consequently, the National Assembly recognizes and declares, in the presence and under the auspices of the Supreme Being, the following Rights of Man and the Citizen.

Art. 1

All men are born and remain free and equal in their rights. All social distinctions are based solely on social usefulness.

Art. 2

The goal of every political association is the preservation of the natural and imprescriptible rights of man. These rights are liberty, property, security and resistance to oppression.

Art. 3

The principle of all sovereignty resides essentially in the Nation. No body, no individual can exercise any authority that does not derive from it.

Art. 4

Liberty consists in being able to do anything that does not injure others; accordingly, the exercise of the natural rights of each man has only those limits which secure the enjoyment of the same rights to other members of society. These limits can be determined only by law.

Art. 5

The law has the right to forbid only such actions as are injurious to society. All that is not forbidden by the law cannot be prohibited, and no one can be constrained to do what it does not order.

Art. 6

The law is the expression of the general will. All citizens have the right to take part personally, or through their representatives, in its formation. It must be the same for all, whether it protects or it punishes. All citizens, being equal in its eyes, are equally eligible for all dignities, situations and public employments, according to their capacity and without any distinction other than that of their virtues and talents.

Art. 7

No man can be accused, arrested or detained except in cases determined by the law, and according to the forms it has prescribed. Those who solicit, expedite or execute, or have executed, arbitrary orders should be punished, but every citizen called or seized by virtue of the law, must obey instantly; he renders himself guilty by his resistance.

Art. 8

The law ought to establish only penalties which are strictly and obviously necessary, and no one can be punished except in virtue of a law established and promulgated prior to the offense and legally applied.

Art. 9

Every man being presumed innocent until he is found guilty, if it is judged indispensable that he be arrested, all unnecessary rigor in the seizure of his person should be severely repressed by the law.

Art. 10

No one ought to be disturbed on account of his opinions, even religious, provided that their manifestation does not disturb the public order established by law.

Art. 11

The free communication of ideas and opinions is one of the most precious rights of man; every citizen then can freely speak, write and publish, subject to responsibility for the abuse of this freedom in cases determined by law.

Art. 12

The guaranty of the rights of man and the citizen requires a public force; this force is thus instituted for the benefit of all and not for the particular use of those to whom it is entrusted.

Art. 13

For the maintenance of the public force and for the cost of its administration, a general tax is indispensable: it ought to be equally attributed among all citizens according to their ability to pay.

Art. 14

All citizens have the right to establish by themselves or through their representatives the need of public taxation, freely to consent to it, oversee its use and determine its allotment, basis, collection and duration.

Art. 15

Society has the right to demand an accounting of every public agent of its administration.

Art. 16

Every society in which the guaranty of rights is not assured, or the separation of powers determined, has no Constitution.

Art. 17

Property being a sacred and inviolable right, no one can be deprived of it unless a legally established public necessity obviously demands it under the condition of a just and prior indemnity.

Notes and Bibliography

1. THE WOMANLESS BIRTH OF VERSAILLES

1. Principal sources:
   Griffet, Henri. *Histoire du règne de Louis XIII.* Paris, 1758. 3 vols.
   Vaunois, Louis. *Vie de Louis XIII.* Paris, 1961.
   Le Vassor, Michel. *Histoire du règne de Louis XIII.* Amsterdam, 1701–11. 10 vols.
   Also contemporary memoirs, particularly:
   Bassompierre, François de, Maréchal. *Mémoires.* Cologne, 1665. 3 vols.
   Dubois (   ), *Valet de chambre* of Louis XIII. *Mémoires.* Michaud and Poujoulat edition. Paris, 1836.
   La Porte, Pierre de. *Mémoires.* Geneva, 1755.
   Montglat, François de Paule de Clermont, Marquis de. *Mémoires.* Amsterdam, 1727. 4 vols.
   Motteville, Françoise Bertault, Madame de. *Mémoires.* Amsterdam, 1723. 5 vols.
2. Guérard, Albert. *France: a short history.* London, 1947.
3. Vaunois, *op. cit.*
4. Composed from sources in Note 1, above.
5. Montglat, *op. cit.*
6. Available in mss. at the Bibliothèque Nationale in Paris. There is also an abridged, slightly bowdlerized version in print: Héroard, Jean. *Journal du roi, 1601–28.* Paris, 1868. 2 vols.
7. Franklin, Alfred. *La Cour de France et l'assassinat du maréchal d'Ancre.* Paris, 1913.
8. Epton, Nina. *Love and the French.* London, 1959.
9. Vaunois, *op. cit.*
10. Héroard, *op. cit.*
11. Vaunois, *op. cit.* Source for what follows.
12. Le Roi, Joseph-Adrien. *Louis XIII et Versailles.* Versailles, 1849.
13. Espée de Sélincourt, Jacques. *Le Parfait Chasseur.* Paris, 1683.

14. Herbert, Edward, Baron. *The Life of Edward Lord Herbert of Cherbury*. London, 1847.

15. Baschet, Armand. *Le Roi chez la reine ou histoire secrète du marriage de Louis XIII et d'Anne d'Autriche*. Paris, 1866. Source for the scene that follows.

16. Héroard, *op. cit.*

17. Baschet, *op. cit.*

18. Tallemant des Réaux, Gédéon. *Historiettes*. Paris, 1932–34. 8 vols. Tallemant was a collector of court anecdotes, generally scandalous, which he published for friends in 1657.

19. Nolhac, Pierre de. *La Création de Versailles*. Versailles, 1901.

20. Bassompierre, *op. cit.*

21. Erlanger, Philippe. *Richelieu*. Paris, 1967.

22. Erlanger, Philippe. *Louis XIII*. Paris, 1946.

23. Marie, Alfred. *Naissance de Versailles*. Paris, 1968. 2 vols. Most documented work in progress on the palace of Versailles.

24. Nolhac, *op. cit.*

25. Motteville, *op. cit.*

26. Griffet, *op. cit.*

27. Haucour, Louis d'. *Conspiration de Cinq-Mars*. Paris, 1902.
    Vigny, Alfred de. *Cinq-Mars*. Paris, 1882. 2 vols.

28. Erlanger, *Louis XIII*.

29. Motteville, *op. cit.*

30. Erlanger, *op. cit.*

31. Bernard, Charles. *Histoire du roy Louis XIII*. Paris, 1646.

2. THE MAKING OF A SUN KING

1. The story is repeated by the memorialists of the period (see Montglat) and used, if not certified, by historians.

2. Lewis, Walter Hamilton. *Louis XIV*. London, 1959.

3. Motteville, Françoise Bertault, Madame de. *Mémoires*. Amsterdam, 1723. 5 vols.

4. Carré, Henri. *L'Enfance et la première jeunesse de Louis XIV*. Paris, 1944.

5. *Ibid.*

6. Lavisse, Ernest. *Histoire de France*. Paris, 1903–11. 9 vols.

7. Mitford, Nancy. *The Sun King*. New York, 1966.

8. Cf. Professor John B. Wolf's "Formation of a King," *French Historical Studies*, Raleigh, North Carolina, Vol. 1, no. 1, 1958.

9. Wolf, John B. *Louis XIV*. New York, 1968.

10. Elizabeth Charlotte of Bavaria, Duchesse d'Orléans. *Briefe*. Stuttgart, 1843.

11. Voltaire, François-Marie Arouet de. *Le Siècle de Louis XIV*. Many editions.

12. Carré, *op. cit.*

13. La Porte, Pierre de. *Mémoires*. Geneva, 1755.

14. Carré, *op. cit.*

15. Saint-Simon, Louis de Rouvroy, Duc de. *Mémoires*. Paris, 1879–1930. 43 vols. Boislisle edition. Saint-Simon entered Court life in the last years of Louis XIV's reign, thought himself unjustly passed over in his brief military career and his status as duke subordinated to that of the King's legitimized

bastards. His bitter portrait of Louis XIV as monstrously egoistic persists down through the centuries, though his account contains falsifications. Nevertheless, his memoirs are indispensable, his portraitures unequaled.

16. Louis XIV. *Oeuvres*. Paris, 1806. 6 vols.
17. Péréfixe, Hardouin de. *L'Histoire du roy Henri le grand*. Paris, 1661.
18. Desmarets de Saint-Sorlin, Jean. *Les Jeux de cartes des roys de France*. Paris, 1664.
19. Lewis, *op. cit.*
20. See Note 8, above.
21. Erlanger, Philippe. *Monsieur, frère de Louis XIV*. Paris, 1953.
22. Dubois (   ). *Mémoires*. Paris, 1836.
23. Retz, Jean-François Paul de Gondi, Cardinal de. *Mémoires*. Amsterdam, 1717. 3 vols.
24. *Ibid.*
25. Lorris, Pierre Georges. *La Fronde*. Paris, 1961.
26. Mazarin, Jules, Cardinal. *Lettres du Cardinal Mazarin pendant son ministère*. Paris, 1872–1906. 9 vols.
27. Montpensier, Anne-Marie-Louise-Henriette d'Orléans, Duchesse de, called La Grande Mademoiselle. *Mémoires*. Paris, 1728. 6 vols.
28. Lorris, *op. cit.*
29. La Porte, *op. cit.*
30. Loménie de Brienne, Henri-Auguste, Comte de. *Mémoires*. Amsterdam, 1719. 3 vols.
31. Carré, *op. cit.*
32. Dubois, *op. cit.*
33. Lavisse, *op. cit.*
34. Chéruel, Adolphe. *Histoire de France sous le ministère de Mazarin*. Paris, 1882. 3 vols.
35. Cf. J. Robiquet's *Louis XIV et la faculté* (preface by Dr. T. de Martel). Lyons, Laboratoires Ciba, 1936.
36. Vallot, Antoine, d'Aquin and Fagon. *Journal de la santé du roi Louis XIV, 1647–1711*. Paris, 1862.
37. Lewis, Walter Hamilton. *The Splendid Century*. New York, 1953.
38. Elizabeth Charlotte of Bavaria, *op. cit.*
39. Lavisse, *op. cit.*
40. Mazarin, *op. cit.*
41. Erlanger, Philippe. *Louis XIV*. Paris, 1965.
42. Loménie de Brienne, *op. cit.*
43. Gramont, Antoine III, Duc de, Maréchal. *Mémoires*. Paris, 1716. 2 vols.
44. Carré, *op. cit.*
45. Lacour-Gayet, Georges. *L'Education politique de Louis XIV*. Paris, 1898.
46. Lavisse, *op. cit.*

3. PYRAMIDS AND EARLY PLEASURES

1. Lavisse, Ernest. *Histoire de France*. Paris, 1903–11. 9 vols.
2. Principal sources:
   Goubert, Pierre. *Louis XIV et vingt millions de français*. Paris, 1966.

Labrousse, Ernest, *et al. Histoire économique et sociale de la France, 1661–1789*. Paris, 1970. Vol. 2.

Mandrou, Robert. *La France aux XVIIè et XVIIIè siècles*. Paris, 1967.

Sée, Henri. *Histoire économique de la France*. Paris, 1939–41. 2 vols.

3. Voltaire. *Le Siècle de Louis XIV*.

4. Goubert, *op. cit.*

5. Sévigné, Marie de Rabutin-Chantal, Marquise de. *Lettres*. Many editions. See also, Note on Money, p. vi.

6. Louis XIV. *Oeuvres*. Paris, 1806. 6 vols.

7. Lewis, Walter Hamilton. *The Splendid Century*. New York, 1953.

8. Elizabeth Charlotte of Bavaria, Duchesse d'Orléans. *Briefe*. Stuttgart, 1843.

9. Goubert, *op. cit.*

10. Lavisse, *op. cit.*

11. Bussy-Rabutin, Roger de Rabutin, Comte de. *Histoire amoureuse des Gaules, suivi de la France galante*. 2 vols. Sainte-Beuve edition. Paris, 1868.

12. Motteville, Françoise Bertault, Madame de. *Mémoires*. Amsterdam, 1723. 5 vols.

13. La Fayette, Marie-Madeleine Pioche de la Vergne, Comtesse de. *Histoire de Mme. Henriette d'Angleterre*. Michaud and Poujoulat edition. Paris, 1839.

14. Sévigné, *op. cit.*

15. La Fare, Charles-Auguste, Marquis de. *Mémoires*. Paris, 1838.

16. Sainte-Beuve, Charles-Augustin. *Galerie de portraits historiques*. Paris, 1883.

4. A DAY IN AUGUST

1. Principal sources:
   Chatelain, Urbain-Victor. *Le Surintendant Nicolas Fouquet*. Paris, 1905.
   Lair, Jules-Auguste. *Nicolas Fouquet*. Paris, 1890. 2 vols.
   Mongrédien, Georges. *L'Affaire Fouquet*. Paris, 1956.

2. Voltaire. *Le siècle de Louis XIV*.

3. Sainte-Beuve, Charles-Augustin. *Galerie de portraits historiques*. Paris, 1883.

4. Lavisse, Ernest. *Histoire de France*. Paris, 1903–11. 9 vols.

5. *Ibid.*

6. Colbert, Jean-Baptiste. *Lettres, instructions, et mémoires*. Paris, 1861–82. 10 vols.

7. Chatelain, *op. cit.*

8. Lair, *op. cit.*

9. Ziegler, Gilette. *Les Coulisses de Versailles*. Paris, 1963. 2 vols.

10. Colbert, *op. cit.*

11. Sainte-Beuve, *op. cit.*

12. Hautecoeur, Louis. *Histoire de l'architecture classique en France. Le règne de Louis XIV*. Paris, 1948. 2 vols.

13. Mongrédien, *op. cit.*

14. La Fontaine, Jean de. *Le Songe de Vaux*. In many editions of his *Oeuvres*.

15. Corpechot, Lucien. *Parcs et jardins de France. Les Jardins de l'intelligence*. Paris, 1937.

16. Fox, Helen Morgenthau. *André Le Nôtre, Garden Architect to Kings.* London, 1963.
17. Sévigné, Marquise de. *Lettres.*
18. Cronin, Vincent. *Louis XIV.* London, 1964.
19. La Fontaine, Jean de. *Oeuvres.* Paris, 1883–92. Letter to Mauxroix, August 22, 1661.
20. Mongrédien, *op. cit.*
21. Louis XIV. *Oeuvres.* Paris, 1806. 6 vols.
22. Jouin, Henry. *Charles Le Brun et les arts sous Louis XIV.* Paris, 1889.

5. THE FAIRY TALE OF A FAIRYLAND

1. Principal sources:

   Corpechot, Lucien. *Parcs et jardins de France. Les Jardins de l'intelligence.* Paris, 1937.

   Fox, Helen Morgenthau. *André Le Nôtre, Garden Architect to Kings.* London, 1963.

   Ganay, Ernest de. *André Le Nostre, 1613–1700.* Paris, 1962.

   Guiffrey, Jules-Joseph. *André Le Nostre.* Paris, 1913.
2. Colbert. *Lettres, instructions, et mémoires.*
3. Saint-Simon. *Mémoires.*
4. Louis XIV. *Oeuvres.*
5. Fox, *op. cit.*
6. Colbert, *op. cit.*
7. Guiffrey, Jules-Joseph, ed. *Comptes des bâtiments du roi, 1644–1715.* Paris, 1881–1901. 5 vols.
8. Sévigné, Marquise de. *Lettres.*
9. From *L'Adduction des eaux de Versailles,* a paper in the author's possession delivered as a speech ca. 1950 by Monsieur de Burfevant, chief engineer and director of water services at Versailles.
10. Verlet, Pierre. *Versailles.* Paris, 1961.
11. Saint-Simon, *op. cit.*
12. Perrault, Charles. *Des Hommes illustres.* Paris, 1696–1700.
13. Mollet, Claude. *Théâtre des plans et jardinages.* Paris, 1652.
14. Caemmerer, Hans Paul. *A Manual on the Origin and Development of Washington.* Washington, 1939.
15. Corpechot, *op. cit.*
16. The scenario following in fable style is based on nephew Claude Desgots' account, *L'Abrégé de la vie de Le Nostre,* printed in P. Desmolets' *Mémoires de littérature et d'histoire.* Paris, 1726. Saint-Simon's version is less dependable.
17. Tallemant des Réaux, Gédéon. *Historiettes.* Paris, 1932–34. 8 vols.
18. Lister, Martin. *A Journey to Paris in the Year 1698.* Reprinted in Pinkertown's *Voyages.* London, 1809, vol. 4.
19. Le Nôtre's testament is published in the *Bulletin de la société de l'histoire de l'Art français,* 1911.
20. Saint-Simon, *op. cit.*

6. THE REMAKING OF A PALACE

1. Colbert, Jean-Baptiste. *Lettres, instructions, et mémoires.* Paris, 1861–82. 10 vols.
2. Guiffrey, Jules-Joseph, ed. *Comptes des bâtiments du roi, 1644–1715.* Paris, 1881–1901. 5 vols.
3. Marie, Alfred. *Naissance de Versailles.* Paris, 1968. 2 vols.
4. Colbert, *op. cit.*
5. Motteville, Françoise Bertault, Madame de. *Mémoires.* Amsterdam, 1723. 5 vols.
6. Laprade, Albert. *François d'Orbay, architecte de Louis XIV.* Paris, 1960.
7. Perrault, Charles. *Mémoires de ma vie.* Paris, 1909.
8. Wren, Christopher. *Parentalia, or Memories of the Family of the Wrens.* London, 1750.
9. Laprade, *op. cit.*
10. Guiffrey, *op. cit.*
11. Montpensier, Anne-Marie-Louise-Henriette d'Orléans, Duchesse de, called La Grande Mademoiselle. *Mémoires.* Paris, 1728. 6 vols.
12. Ménestrier, Claude-François. *La Devise du roy, justifiée.* Paris, 1679.
13. Scudéry, Madeleine de. *La Promenade de Versailles.* Paris, 1969.
14. Félibien, André. *Relation de la feste de Versailles du 18 juillet 1668.* Paris, 1668.
15. Bussy-Rabutin, Roger de Rabutin, Comte de. *Histoire amoureuse des Gaules.* Paris, 1868. 2 vols.
16. Carré, Henri. *Mademoiselle de La Vallière.* Paris, 1938.
17. Félibien, André. *Les Divertissements de Versailles donnés par le roi au retour de la conqueste de la Franche-Comté, en l'année 1674.* Paris, 1674.

7. THE ENTERTAINERS

1. Edwards, Henry S. *Idols of the French stage.* London, 1889, 2 vols.
   Other principal sources:
   Brisson, Pierre. *Molière.* Paris, 1942.
   Jurgens, Madeleine, and Maxfield-Miller, Elizabeth. *Cent ans de recherches sur Molière, sur sa famille et sur les comédiens de sa troupe.* Paris, 1963.
   Mantzius, Karl. *Molière, les théâtres, le public et les comédiens de son temps.* Paris, 1908. Translated from Danish.
   Mongrédien, Georges. *La Vie privée de Molière.* Paris, 1950.
   And, of course, Molière's works.
2. From the preface by La Grange to Molière's *Oeuvres*, Paris, 1682. (See also footnote on p. 93.)
3. Voltaire. *La Vie de Molière.* Amsterdam, 1739.
4. Palmer, John L. *Molière: His Life and Works.* London, 1930.
5. Somaize, Antoine Baudeau. *Le Dictionnaire des précieuses.* Paris, 1856.
6. Bordonove, Georges. *Molière, génial et familier.* Paris, 1967.
7. Brossette, Claude. *Correspondance de Boileau-Despréaux et Brossette.* Paris, 1857.

8. Las Cases, Emmanuel-Auguste, Marquis de. *Mémorial de Sainte-Hélène*. Paris 1823. 8 vols.

9. *Lettres de Racine et mémoires sur sa vie* . . . Lausanne, 1747. 2 vols. The memoirs from which this story is taken are by Louis Racine, the playwright's son. See Vol. 2.

10. Prunières, Henry. *La Vie illustre et libertine de Jean-Baptiste Lully*. Paris, 1929.

11. Grimarest, Jean-Leonor. *La Vie de M. de Molière*. Paris, 1705. Grimarest had the account directly from Baron.

12. See Note 9, above.

8. THE BUILDER AND THE DECORATOR

1. Lambert, Claude-François, Abbé. *Histoire littéraire du règne de Louis XIV* . . . Paris, 1751. 3 vols.

2. Blondel, Jacques-François. *Architecture française*. Paris, 1752–56. 4 vols.

3. Bourget, Pierre, and Cattaui, Georges. *Jules Hardouin Mansart*. Paris, 1960.

4. Ormesson, Olivier Le Fèvre d'. *Journal*. Paris, 1860–61. 2 vols.

5. Verlet, Pierre. *Versailles*. Paris, 1961.

6. Levron, Jacques. *Versailles, ville royale*. Paris, 1964.

7. Guiffrey, Jules, ed. *Comptes des bâtiments du roi sous le règne de Louis XIV*. Paris, 1881–1901. 5 vols.

   Hautecoeur, Louis. *Histoire de l'architecture classique en France. Le règne de Louis XIV*. Paris, 1948. 2 vols.

   Blomfield, Reginald. *A History of French Architecture from the Death of Mazarin till the Death of Louis XV*. London, 1921. 2 vols.

   Verlet, *op. cit.*

8. From the Penguin edition. *Rilke's Selected Poems*. London, 1964. Translated by J. B. Leishman.

9. Blunt, Anthony. *Art and Architecture in France, 1500 to 1700*. London, 1953.

10. Jouin, Henry. *Charles Le Brun et les arts sous Louis XIV*. Paris, 1889.

11. Félibien, André. *Description du château de Versailles, de ses peintures, et d'autres ouvrages faits pour le roi*. Paris, 1696.

9. THE POISONED YEARS

1. Lavisse, Ernest. *Histoire de France*. Paris, 1903–11. 9 vols.

2. Goubert, Pierre. *Louis XIV et vingt millions de français*. Paris, 1966.

3. Voltaire. Le *Siècle de Louis XIV*.

4. Lavisse, *op. cit.*

5. Mongrédien, Georges. *Madame de Montespan et l'affaire des poisons*. Paris, 1953.

   Mossiker, Frances. *The Affair of the Poisons*. New York, 1969.

6. Primi Visconti, Giovanni Battista. *Mémoires sur la cour de Louis XIV*. Paris, 1909.

7. Maintenon, Françoise d'Aubigné, Marquise de. *Correspondance générale*. Paris, 1865–66. 5 vols.

8. Scarron, Paul. *Oeuvres*. Paris, 1786. 7 vols. See Vol 1.
9. Choisy, François-Timoléon, Abbé de. *Mémoires*. Utrecht, 1727. 2 vols.
10. Lionne, Hugues de. *Lettres inédites*. Valence, 1877.
11. Saint-Maurice, Thomas-François, Marquis de. *Lettres sur la cour de Louis XIV*. Paris, 1911–12.
12. La Reynie, Gabriel-Nicolas. *Lettres et notes*, in mss. at the Bibliothèque Nationale of Paris. Most pertinent items may be found in Mongrédien, *op. cit.*, and Mossiker, *op. cit.*
13. Mongrédien, *op. cit.*

10. A TWILIGHT OF MAINTENON

1. Langlois, Marcel. *Madame de Maintenon*. Paris, 1932.
2. Macaulay, Thomas Babington. *History of England*. Many editions.
3. Cordelier, Jean. *Madame de Maintenon, une femme au grand siècle*. Paris, 1955.
4. Hébert, François. *Mémoires du curé de Versailles, 1686–1704*. Paris, 1927
5. Voltaire. *Le Siècle de Louis XIV*.
6. Levron, Jacques, *Les Courtisans*. Paris, 1960.
7. La Bruyère, Jean de. *Les Caractères*. Many editions.
8. Hébert, François, *op. cit.*
9. Choisy, François-Timoléon, Abbé de. *Mémoires*. Utrecht, 1727. 2 vols.
10. Languet de Gergy, Archbishop Jean Joseph. *Mémoires sur Mme de Maintenon*. Paris, 1863.
11. Voltaire, *op. cit.*
12. Le Vassor (?), Michel. *Les Soupirs de la France esclave*. Amsterdam, 1689.
13. Fénelon, François, de la Mothe. *Lettre à Louis XIV*. Paris, 1825.
14. Lewis, W. H. *The Sunset of the Splendid Century*. New York, 1963.

11. AN INTERLUDE OF LOVE

1. Carré, Henri. *La Duchesse de Bourgogne*. Paris, 1934.
2. Louis XIV. *Lettres à Mme de Maintenon*. Paris, 1822.
3. Dunoyer, Anne-Marguerite Petit. *Lettres historiques et galantes de deux dames de condition, dont l'une était à Paris et l'autre en province*. Cologne, 1713.
4. Mitford, Nancy. *The Sun King*. New York, 1966. See two chapters on Saint-Cyr.
5. Fénelon, François de la Mothe. *Dialogues des morts* in *Oeuvres choisies*. Various editions published by Hachette.

12. THE DEATH OF A KING

1. Villars, Louis Claude. *Mémoires*. Paris, 1904.
2. Buvat, Jean. *Journal de la régence*. Paris, 1865.

3. Anthoine, Jean and François. *Journal de la mort de Louis XIV.* Paris, 1880.
4. Voltaire. *Le Siècle de Louis XIV.*

13. BETWEEN PALACES AND PLEASURES

1. Marais, Mathieu. *Journal et mémoires . . . sur la régence et le règne de Louis XV.* Paris, 1863–68. 4 vols.
2. Lewis, W. H. *The Sunset of the Splendid Century.* New York, 1963.
3. Marais, *op. cit.*
4. Duclos, Charles Pinot. *Mémoires secrets sur le règne de Louis XIV, la régence et le règne de Louis XV.* Paris, 1864. 2 vols.
5. Erlanger, Phillippe. *Le Régent.* Paris, 1938.
6. Saint-Simon. Louis de Rouvroy, Duc de. *Mémoires.*
7. Erlanger, *op. cit.*
8. *Ibid.*
9. Saint-Gelais, Louis-François Dubois de. *Histoire journalière de Paris.* Paris, 1717. 2 vols.
10. Saint-Simon, *op. cit.*
11. Storcksburg, Jakob Staehlin von. *Orginalanekdoten von Peter dem Grossen.* Leipzig, 1785.
12. Saint-Simon. *op. cit.*
13. Richelieu, Louis-François-Armand de Vignerot du Plessis. *Mémoires authentiques.* Paris, 1918.
    Vie privée. Paris, 1791. 3 vols.
14. Saint-Simon, *op. cit.*
15. Ercole, Lucienne. *Gay Court Life. France in the Eighteenth Century.* New York, 1932.
16. Richelieu, *op. cit.*
17. Besenval, Baron Pierre-Victor de. *Mémoires.* Paris, 1805.
18. *Ibid.*
19. Champion, Pierre. *Notes critiques sur les vies anciennes d'Antoine Watteau.* Paris, 1921.
20. Goncourt, Edmond and Jules de. *L'Art du dix-huitieme siècle.* Paris, 1860. Vol. 1.
21. Guérard, Albert. *France.* London, 1947.
22. Méthivier, Hubert. *Le Siècle de Louis XV.* Paris, 1966.
23. Gramont, Sanche de. *Epitaph for Kings.* New York, 1967.
24. Saint-Simon, *op. cit.*
25. Barbier, Edmond-Jean-François. *Journal historique et anecdotique du règne de Louis XV.* Paris, 1847. 4 vols.
26. Erlanger, *op. cit.*

14. THE UNMAKING OF A MONARCH

1. Argenson, René-Louis de Voyer, Marquis d'. *Journal et mémoires.* Paris, 1859–1867.

2. Barbier, Edmond-Jean-François. *Journal historique et anecdotique du règne de Louis XV*. Paris, 1847. 4 vols.

3. Marais, Mathieu. *Journal et mémoires* . . . Paris, 1863–68. 4 vols.

4. Elizabeth Charlotte of Bavaria, Duchesse d'Orléans. *Briefe*. Stuttgart, 1843.

5. Saint-Simon. *Mémoires*.

6. Duclos, Charles Pinot. *Mémoires secrets sur le règne de Louis XIV* . . . Paris, 1864. 2 vols.

7. Levron, Jacques. *La Vie quotidienne à la cour de Versailles aux XVIIè et XVIIIè siècles*. Paris, 1965.

8. Barbier, *op. cit.*

9. From the journal of the King's page, the Marquis de Calvière; see Edmond and Jules de Goncourt, *Portraits intimes*. Paris, 1857–58.

10. Barbier, *op. cit.*

11. Hénault, Charles (President of Parlement). *Mémoires*. Paris, 1911.

12. Duclos, *op. cit.*

13. Gooch, George Peabody. *Louis XV: The Monarchy in Decline*. London, 1956.

14. Guizot, François. *L'Histoire de France*. Many editions.

15. Gaxotte, Pierre. *Le Siècle de Louis XV*. Paris, 1933.

16. Ziegler, Gilette. *Les Coulisses de Versailles. Louis XV et sa cour*. Paris, 1965.

17. Narbonne, Pierre. *Journal des règnes de Louis XIV et de Louis XV*. Versailles, 1886.

18. Gaxotte, *op. cit.*

19. Brancas, Marie-Angélique, Duchesse de. *Mémoires. Suivis de sa correspondance avec Mme de Châteauroux*. Paris, 1890.

20. D'Argenson, *op. cit.*

21. Villars, Louis-Hector, Maréchal de. *Mémoires*. Paris, 1892.

22. Gaxotte, *op. cit.*

23. *Ibid.*

24. Boucher, Philippe, Abbé. *Lettres* . . . *sur les miracles* . . . *de M. de Paris*. Paris, 1732
    Barbier, *op. cit.*

25. D'Argenson, *op. cit.*

26. Proyart, Liévin, Abbé. *Vie de la reine de France, Marie Lecksinska*. Bruxelles, 1794.

27. Villars, *op. cit.*

28. Durant, Will and Ariel. *The Age of Voltaire*. New York, 1965.

29. D'Argenson, *op. cit.*

30. Dufort, Jean-Nicolas, Comte de Cheverny. *Mémoires sur les règnes de Louis XV et Louis XVI et sur la Révolution*. Paris, 1866. 2 vols.

31. Goncourt, Edmond and Jules. *Madame de Pompadour*. Many editions.
    ———. *Les Maîtresses de Louis XV*. Paris, 1860. 2 vols.

32. Maurepas, Jean Phelypeaux, Comte de. *Mémoires*. Paris, 1791. 3 vols.

33. Ziegler, *op. cit.*

34. Levron, Jacques. *Louis, le Bien-Aimé*. Paris, 1965.

35. Luynes, Charles-Philippe d'Albert, Duc de. *Mémoires sur la cour de Louis XV*. Paris, 1860. 17 vols.

36. Châteauroux, Marie-Anne, Duchesse de. *Correspondance*. Paris, 1806.

37. Marville, Claude-Henri Feydeau de (police lieutenant). *Lettres au Ministre Maurepas*. Paris, 1896–1905. 3 vols.

38. Brancas, *op. cit.*
39. *Ibid.*

15. WORLDS WITHIN WORLDS

1. Nolhac, Pierre de. *Le Château de Versailles sous Louis XV.* Paris, 1898.
2. Verlet, Pierre. *Versailles.* Paris, 1961.
3. Luynes, Charles-Philippe d'Albert, Duc de. *Mémoires sur la cour de Louis XV.* Paris, 1860. 17 vols.
4. Hausset, Madame du (*femme de chambre* of Madame de Pompadour). *Mémoires.* Paris, 1891.
5. Gaxotte, Pierre. *Le Siècle de Louis XV.* Paris, 1933.
6. Nolhac, *op. cit.*
7. Dufort, Jean-Nicolas Comte de Cheverny. *Mémoires sur les règnes de Louis XV et Louis XVI.* Paris, 1886. 2 vols.
8. Choiseul, Etienne-François, Duc de. *Mémoires.* Paris, 1904.
9. Hausset, *op. cit.*
10. Barbier, Edmond-Jean-François. *Journal historique et anecdotique du règne de Louis XV.* Paris, 1847. 4 vols.
11. Luynes, *op. cit.*
12. Casanova di Seingalt, Giacomo Girolamo. *Mémoires.* Several editions.
13. Croÿ, Emmanuel, Duc de. *Mémoires sur les cours de Louis XV et Louis XVI.* Paris, 1891.
    Anecdote in: *Journal inédit.* Paris, 1906–07. 4 vols.
14. Mitford, Nancy. *Madame de Pompadour.* London, 1954.
15. Taine, Hippolyte-Adolphe. *L'Ancien régime.* Paris, 1876.
16. Mitford, *op. cit.*
17. Goncourt, Edmond and Jules de. *L'art du dix-huitième siècle.* Paris, 1859–75.

16. THE KING IS BORED, THE DEER PARK IS BORN

1. Goncourt, Edmond and Jules de. *Madame de Pompadour.* Many editions.
2. Hausset, Madame du. *Mémoires.* Paris, 1891.
3. *Ibid.*
4. Le Roi, Dr. Joseph-Adrien. *Histoire de Versailles, de ses rues, places et avenues* . . . Versailles, 1868. 2 vols.
5. Valfons, Charles de Mathei, Marquis de. *Souvenirs.* Paris, 1860.
6. Quentin, Henri. *Un Policier homme de lettres: L'Inspecteur Meusnier (1748–1757).* Paris, 1892.
7. Michelet, Jules. *Histoire de France.* Many editions.
8. Hausset, *op. cit.*
9. Campan, Jeanne-Louise. *Mémoires sur la vie privée de Marie-Antoinette* . . . *suivis de souvenirs et anecdotes historiques sur les règnes de Louis XIV, de Louis XV et de Louis XVI.* Paris, 1822. 3 vols.
10. Mitford, Nancy. *Madame de Pompadour.* London, 1954.
11. Soulavie Jean-Louis. *Mémoires historiques et anecdotiques de la cour de la Marquise de Pompadour.* Paris, 1802.

12. Argerville, Moufle d'. *The Private Life of Louis XV*. Dublin, 1781. 4 vols.
————. *Vie privée de Louis XV*. London, 1788. 4 vols.
13. Goncourt, Edmond and Jules, *op. cit.*
14. Manuel, Louis-Pierre. *La Police de Paris dévoilée*. Paris, 1793.
15. Barbier, Edmond-Jean-François. *Journal historique* . . . Paris, 1847. 4 vols.
See also: Meyrac, Albert. *Louis XV, sés maîtresses, le Parc aux Cerfs*. Paris, 1914. 2 vols.

17. AT THE BOTTOM OF THE STAIRCASE: DAMIENS

1. This scene, as most of the chapter, has been reconstructed from the slightly varying accounts in the memoirs and documents of the time, particularly the following:
Pièces originales et procedures du procès fait a Robert-François Damiens, tant en la Prevote de l'Hotel qu'en la Cour de Parlement. Paris, chez Pierre-Guillaume Simon, Imprimeur du Parlement, 1757. (An invaluable record of the torture, trial, interrogations, and execution of Damiens.)
Duc de Croÿ. *Journal inédit*. Paris, 1906–07. 4 vols. (The duke was entrusted with the investigation of Damiens, his family, his acquaintances, his possible accomplices.)
Memoirs and journals of Mesdames Campan and du Hausset, and Messieurs Dufort de Cheverny, Luynes, Valfons, Barbier, Cardinal de Bernis, *et al*.
A fine summary in André Bouton's *Damiens le régicide*, accompanied by Dr. André Adnès' *Damiens et la psychiatrie médico-légale*, both published as an extract from the *Bulletin de la Société d'Agriculture, Sciences et Arts de la Sarthe*. Le Mans, 1955.
2. Decaux. Alain. *La Belle histoire de Versailles*, Paris, 1954.
3. Campan, Jeanne-Louise. *Mémoires* . . . Paris, 1822.
4. Hausset, Madame du. *Mémoires*. Paris, 1891.
5. Dufort, Jean Nicolas. *Mémoires* . . . Paris, 1886.
6. Hausset, Madame du, *op. cit.*
7. Dufort, Jean Nicolas, *op. cit.*
8. *Pièces originales*, etc. (see 1, above).
9. These and other statements are quoted *indirectly*, for the most part, in *Pièces originales*, etc.
10. Croÿ, Duc de, *op. cit.* (see 1, above).
11. *Pièces originales*, etc.
12. Argenson, René-Louis, Marquis d'. *Journal et mémoires*. Paris, 1859–67. 9 vols.
13. Hausset, *op. cit.*
14. *Pièces originales*, etc. (subsequent quotations are from this source).
15. *Ibid.*
16. *Ibid.*
17. Casanova, in his *Mémoires*: "We had the constancy to remain for the four [sic] hours of this horrible spectacle. The torture of Damiens is too well known for me to speak of it, firstly because the accounting would take too long and secondly because such horrors outrage nature. Damiens was a fanatic who, believing he was doing a good deed which would

win him divine approval, tried to assassinate Louis XV, and though, in fact, he only administered a scratch, he was torn apart as if his crime had been consummated. During the torture of this victim of the Jesuits [sic], I had to turn my eyes away and cover my ears when I heard his terrible screams, even when only half his body was left."

Miss Nancy Mitford, in her *Madame de Pompadour:* "The King was so accessible that it would be easy to kill him at any time, inside as well as outside his palace, and this made it necessary to deter would-be assassins; torture was supposed to be a deterrent. Pain was regarded with a different eye from ours. Everybody, sooner or later, was obliged to endure horrid pain. There were no anaesthetics, the doctors applied their brutal remedies and conducted their primitive operations on fully conscious patients. Cardinal Dubois, for instance, must have suffered quite as much during the operation of which he died the next day, as Damiens on the scaffold; and they did not put him out of his misery when it was over [sic]. Women suffered dreadfully in childbirth; people with cancer had to bear it unalleviated until it killed them."

Several comments: Natural childbirth, in view of today's re-evaluation of it, is not necessarily "dreadful." Secondly, opium, as we know from the Damiens story, was available not only for sufferers from cancer but even from insomnia. Thirdly, Miss Mitford's "pain was regarded with a different eye from ours" strikes an odd note when one reads Casanova, a contemporary, saying he had to turn *his* eye away from Damiens' torture. As for the way Damiens was "put out of his misery when it was over," unlike poor Cardinal Dubois, no comment seems necessary, but rather suggests the reader continue the Damiens story to its bitter end.

18. The case of Damiens continues to intrigue psychiatrists as well as historians. Opinions are perforce based on the memoirs and accounts of the period, such as those of the Duc de Croÿ, who was in charge of the investigation. Was he simply trying to reassure the King, as Madame de Pompadour clearly preferred, that there was no plot and therefore none involving Parlement, or was he, as well (as I believe he was), sincerely convinced after his investigations that Damiens had indeed acted on his own? As for Damiens' being a "madman" or a "religious fanatic" (they seem to be the same in rationalistic, Cartesian France, even of that period), the evidence offered is secondhand, even in such "records" as the *Pièces originales,* from which we have necessarily quoted extensively. That collection of reports, testimonies, and *summaries* of testimonies, printed the same year as Damiens' *attentat* (1757), would, as its writers and publisher well knew, have no closer reader than the King himself. There are no harsh words about the King, even as quoted from the mouth of Damiens. The report inculpates Damiens as it exculpates Parlement, which controlled not only Damiens' trial and interrogations, but the report itself.

Was, then, Damiens an irresponsible "madman," or was he, thirty-two years before his time, a French revolutionary—or, as seems most likely, a man with a touch of both? Even this compromise may be an evasion— simply defining as mad anyone who attempts an assassination, whether he be a Ravaillac, Oswald, or Sirhan Sirhan. In Damiens' case there are as well accounts of very odd behavior. But in *his* case, at least, there is a strong doubt that he really meant to kill; it seems he really meant only to "touch" the King and bring him back to his senses. Moreover, if killing on one's own or as part of a conspiratorial group is a kind of madness, how should one regard the respectable generals involved in the bomb plot against Hitler? If the character of the victim becomes a justification for the killing of him, particularly when it involves a threat to society, a case can be made for Damiens and against Louis XV, whose conduct of France, as well as his personal conduct (witness his Deer Park of teen-age *grisettes,* a private bordello of young girls), was in large measure responsible for the French Revolution, which occurred not long after his death.

Understandably, the Duc de Croÿ, too, skirted the question by calling Damiens a "fanatic, and that is all." More recently, J. Lévy-Valensi in a paper before the XVIè Congrès de Médecine Légale de Langue Française suggests that Damiens was "a paranoiac with an obsessive preoccupation," but refuses to conclude about his sense of "responsibility." He situates him between Ravaillac, a schizophrenic, and Charlotte Corday, murderess of Murat, a *"passionnelle pure."* (See Alexandre Besson's *Damiens, étude de psycho-pathologie historique, thèse de doctorat en médecine,* Paris, 1930; and J. Lévy-Valensi's *Annales de médecine légale,* 1931, pp. 193–285.) For Dr. Adnès (see Note 1, above) Damiens' behavior was that of a *"déséquilibré"* who was more or less *"insociable"* until his act of stabbing the King. "But thereafter Damiens demonstrated a self-control, a grandeur of the soul, no less, that the most atrocious torture man has ever experienced could not break down." And Dr. Adnès quotes the Duc de Croÿ on Damiens' last hours. Croÿ: "Finally [Damiens] recalled a parliamentary official [Lautier] who, for four years before, had talked in his presence in a household where he was serving of a fright the King once had,* remarking that it would be a meritorious deed to give him another, so that he might return to better ways. He, Damiens, having heard this, was so struck by it that from that moment on, he was tormented by the idea of striking the King so as to return him to his senses and, feeling he had the courage in himself to do the deed, had resolved to sacrifice himself to it. That, in effect, was his plan, a project stimulated by the inconsidered remarks he had heard in Paris which the turbulence of his own blood had multiplied leading him to the execution of it. *There* is the whole truth of the affair."

For Dr. Adnès, Damiens' character is more akin to that of Charlotte Corday, the *"passionnelle pure,"* than to that of the generally acknowledged schizophrenic who was Ravaillac. Judging from the available evidence, however twisted to make Damiens appear mad, I tend strongly to a similar conclusion. Damiens, I believe, was a politically motivated, tormented man who undertook what he considered a historic mission. One's sympathies finally depend upon one's own attitude toward Louis XV and, ultimately, the Revolution.

* At Metz?

18.   VOLTAIRE, THE MAN WHO MADE IT; DIDEROT, THE MAN WHO DIDN'T

1. Malesherbes, Chrétien-Guillaume de .Lamoignon de. *Mémoire sur la liberté de la presse.* Paris, 1814.

2. Frederick II, called the Great, King of Prussia. *Mémoires*. Paris, 1866. 2 vols. (Written in French).
   For the best single-volume biography of Voltaire, see Besterman, Theodore. *Voltaire*. New York, 1969.
3. Orieux, Jean. *Voltaire ou la royauté de l'esprit*. Paris, 1966.
4. Durant, Will and Ariel. *The Age of Voltaire*. New York, 1965.
5. Desnoiresterres, Gustave. *Voltaire et la société française au xviiiè siècle*. Paris, 1871–76. 8 vols.
6. Voltaire, François-Marie Arouet de. *Letters Concerning the English Nation*. London, 1733.
7. Parton, James. *Life of Voltaire*. London, 1881. 2 vols.
8. Mitford, Nancy. *Voltaire in Love*. London, 1957.
9. Brandes, Georg. *Voltaire*. New York, 1930. 2 vols.
10. Orieux, *op. cit.*
11. Parton, *op. cit.*
12. Voltaire, François-Marie Arouet de. *Oeuvres complètes*. Paris, 1828–34. 97 vols.
    ———. *Works*. New York, 1927. 44 vols.
13. Orieux, *op. cit.*
14. Crocker, Lester G. *The Embattled Philosopher: Life of Denis Diderot*. East Lansing, Mich., 1954. Quoted in Durant's *Age of Voltaire*.
15. Taine, Hippolyte-Adolphe. *Les Origines de la France contemporaine*. Paris, 1876–94. 6 vols.
    Tocqueville, Alexis de. *L'Ancien régime et la Révolution*. Paris, 1856.
16. Wilson, Arthur M. *Diderot: the Testing Years, 1713–59*. New York, 1957.
17. Diderot, Denis. *Oeuvres complètes*. Paris, 1875–77. 20 vols.
18. Crocker, *op. cit.*
19. Durant, *op. cit.*
20. Goncourt, Edmond and Jules. *Madame de Pompadour*. Many eds.
21. Grimm, Friedrich Melchior. *Correspondance littéraire, philosophique, et critique, par Grimm, Diderot, Raynal, Meister, et al.* Paris, 1877–82. 16 vols.
22. Guyot, Charly. *Diderot par lui-même*. Paris, 1967.
23. Diderot, *op. cit.*
24. Guyot, *op. cit.*
25. Goncourt, Edmond and Jules de. *Journal*. Paris, 1887–96. 9 vols.

19.   ARRIVALS AND DEPARTURES: ENTER MADAME DU BARRY, EXIT LOUIS XV

1. Broglie, Charles-François, Comte de. *Correspondance secrète du Comte de Broglie avec Louis XV, 1756–1774*. Paris, 1956.
   Broglie, Charles-Jacques, Duc de. *Le Secret du Roi, correspondance secrète de Louis XV avec ses agents diplomatiques, 1752–1774*. Paris, 1878. 2 vols.
   Georgel, Jean-François, Abbé. *Mémoires pour servir à l'histoire des événements de la fin du XVIIIe siècle*. Paris, 1817–18. 6 vols.
2. Carlyle, Thomas. *History of Friedrich II, called Frederick the Great*. London, 1858–65. 6 vols.

3. Brandes, Georg. *Voltaire.* New York, 1930. 2 vols.

4. Michelet, Jules. *Histoire de France.* Many editions.

5. Gaxotte, Pierre. *Le Siècle de Louis XV.* Paris, 1933.

6. Broglie, Duc de, *op. cit.*

7. Eon de Beaumont, Charles Geneviève, Chevalier d'. *Mémoires.* Paris, 1836. 2 vols.

———. *Lettres, mémoires et négociations particuliers du Chevalier d'Eon.* London, 1764.

8. Homberg, Octave, and Jousselin, Fernand. *Un Aventurier au XVIIIe siècle, le Chevalier d'Eon.* Paris, 1904.

9. Casanova di Seingalt, Giacomo Girolamo. *Mémoires.* Several editions.

10. Hausset, Madame du. *Mémoires.* Paris, 1891.

11. *Ibid.*

12. Goncourt, Edmond and Jules. *Madame de Pompadour.* Many eds.

13. Mitford, Nancy. *Madame de Pompadour.* London, 1954.

14. Dufort, Jean-Nicolas, Comte de Cheverny. *Mémoires sur les règnes de Louis XV et Louis XVI.* Paris, 1886. 2 vols.

15. Walpole, Horace. *Letters.* London, 1840. 6 vols.

16. Chamfort, Sebastien-Roch-Nicolas. *Pensées, maximes, anecdotes et dialogues.* Paris, 1860.

17. Ziegler, Gilette. *Les Coulisses de Versailles. Louis XV et sa cour.* Paris, 1965.

18. Saint-André, Claude. *La Vie de Mme du Barry.* Paris, 1930.

19. Levron, Jacques. *Louis le Bien-Aimé.* Paris, 1965.

20. Ligne, Charles-Joseph, Prince de. *Mémoires et mélanges historiques et littéraires.* Paris, 1827–29. 6 vols.

21. Castries, René de la Croix, Duc de. *Madame du Barry.* Paris, 1967.

22. Marais, Mathieu. *Journal et mémoires . . . sur la régence et le règne de Louis XV.* Paris, 1863–68. 4 vols.

23. Castries, *op. cit.*

24. Loomis, Stanley. *Du Barry.* Philadelphia, 1959.

25. Gooch, George Peabody. *Louis XV: The Monarchy in Decline.* London, 1956.

26. Deffand, Marie, Marquise du. *Lettres de la Marquise du Deffand à Horace Walpole . . . 1766 à 1780.* Paris, 1812. 4 vols.

27. Nolhac, Pierre de. *Marie-Antoinette, Dauphine.* Paris, 1929.

28. Maria Theresa, Empress of Austria. *Correspondance secrète entre Marie-Thérèse et le comte de Mercy-Argenteau, avec les lettres de Marie-Thérèse et de Marie-Antoinette.* Paris, 1874. 3 vols.

———. *Maria-Theresia und Marie Antoinette, ihr Briefwechsel während der Jahre 1770–1780.* Paris, 1865.

29. Louis XV. *Lettres de Louis XV à son petit-fils l'infant Ferdinand de Parme.* Paris, 1938.

30. Webster, Nesta H. *Louis XVI and Marie Antoinette: Before the Revolution.* London, 1936.

31. Verlet, Pierre. *Versailles.* Paris, 1961.

32. Levron, *op. cit.*

33. Castelot, André. *Marie-Antoinette.* Paris, 1962.

34. Zweig, Stefan. *Marie Antoinette: the Portrait of an Average Woman.* New York, 1933.

35. *Ibid.*

R

36. Maria Theresa (see Note 28 above).
37. La Rocheterie, Maxime de. *Histoire de Marie-Antoinette.* Paris, 1890. 2 vols.
38. Gleichen, Carl Heinrich von, Baron. *Souvenirs.* Paris, 1868.
39. Gooch, *op. cit.*
40. Voltaire, François-Marie Arouet de. *Histoire du parlement de Paris.* Amsterdam, 1769. 2 vols.
41. Ziegler, *op. cit.*
42. La Rochefoucauld-Liancourt, François, Duc de. *Relation inédite de la dernière maladie de Louis XV.* Paris, 1846.
43. Dufort, *op. cit.*
44. Carlyle, Thomas. *The French Revolution.* Many editions.
45. Campan, Jeanne Louise. *Mémoires . . .* Paris, 1822. 3 vols.
46. Provence, Comte de. *Réflexions historiques sur Marie-Antoinette,* published in the *Revue des Deux Mondes.* July 15, 1904.

20. MARIE ANTOINETTE AND LOUIS XVI
TOO YOUNG, TOO LITTLE, TOO LATE

1. Zweig, Stefan. *Marie Antoinette: the Portrait of an Average Woman.* New York, 1933.
2. Maria Theresa, Empress of Austria. *Correspondance secrète entre Marie-Thérèse et le Comte de Mercy-Argenteau, avec les lettres de Marie-Thérèse et de Marie-Antoinette.* Paris, 1874. 3 vols.
3. Faÿ, Bernard. *Louis XVI ou la fin d'un monde.* Paris, 1955.
4. Levron, Jacques. *La Vie quotidienne à la cour de Versailles aux xviiè et xviiiè siècles.* Paris, 1965.
5. Maria Theresa, *op. cit.*
6. Walpole, Horace. *Letters.* London, 1840. 6 vols.
7. Faÿ, *op. cit.*
8. Webster, Nesta H. *Louis XVI and Marie Antoinette: Before the Revolution.* London, 1936.
9. Véri, Abbé de. *Journal.* Paris, 1928. 2 vols.
10. Faure, Edgar. *La Disgrâce de Turgot.* Paris, 1961.
11. Say, Léon. *Turgot.* Paris, 1887.
12. Faÿ, *op. cit.*
13. Yonge, Charles Duke. *The Life of Marie Antoinette.* London, 1877.
14. La Rocheterie, Maxime de. *Histoire de Marie-Antoinette.* Paris, 1890. 2 vols.
15. Maria Theresa, *op. cit.*
16. Guérard, Albert. *France, a Short History.* London, 1947.
17. Lavisse, Ernest. *Histoire de France.* Paris, 1903–11. 9 vols.
18. Ligne, Charles-Joseph, Prince de. *Mémoires et mélanges historiques et littéraires.* Paris, 1827–29. 6 vols.
19. Castelot, André. *Marie-Antoinette.* Paris, 1962.
20. Durant, Will and Ariel. *Rousseau and Revolution.* New York, 1967.
21. Lévis, Gaston, Duc de. *Souvenirs et portraits, 1780–1789.* Paris, 1813.
22. Maria Theresa, *op. cit.*
23. Campan, Jeanne Louise. *Mémoires . . .* Paris, 1822. 3 vols.
24. Castelot, *op. cit.*

25. Campan, *op. cit.*
26. *Ibid.*
27. Zweig, *op. cit.*
28. Campan, *op. cit.*
29. Mossiker, Frances. *The Queen's Necklace.* New York, 1961.
30. La Rocheterie, *op. cit.*
31. Campan, *op. cit.*
32. Levron, *op. cit.*
33. Castelot, *op. cit.*
34. Verlet, Pierre. *Versailles.* Paris, 1961.
35. Morris, Gouverneur. *Diary and Letters.* New York, 1888. 2 vols.
36. Nolhac, Pierre de. *La Reine Marie-Antoinette.* Many editions.
37. Verlet, *op. cit.*
38. Nolhac, *op. cit.*
39. Faÿ, *op. cit.*
40. Besenval, Pierre-Victor, Baron de. *Mémoires.* Paris, 1805. 3 vols.
41. Rousseau, Jean-Jacques. *La nouvelle Héloïse.* Many editions.
42. Young, Arthur. *Travels in France During the Years 1787, 1788, 1789.* London, 1792.
43. Nolhac, *op. cit.*
44. Goncourt, Edmond and Jules de. *Histoire de Marie-Antoinette.* Paris, 1858.
45. Ligne, *op. cit.*
46. Lévis, *op. cit.*
47. Campan, *op. cit.*
48. Verlet, *op. cit.*
49. Say, *op. cit.*
50. Tocqueville, Alexis de. *L'Ancien régime et la révolution.* Many editions.
51. Say, *op. cit.*
52. Durant, *op. cit.*
53. Faÿ, *op. cit.*
54. Geffroy, Auguste. *Gustave III et la cour de France.* Paris, 1867. 2 vols.
55. Lavisse, *op. cit.*
56. Bachaumont, Louis Petit de. *Marie-Antoinette, Louis XVI et la famille royale.* Paris, 1866.
57. Campan, *op. cit.*
58. Marie Antoinette. *Marie Antoinette, Joseph II und Leopold II. Ihr briefwechsel.* Leipzig-Paris, 1866.
59. La Rocheterie, *op. cit.*
60. Maria Theresa, *op. cit.*
61. Marie Antoinette, *op. cit.*
62. Faÿ, *op. cit.* The author, monarchist, Catholic, and traditionalist, scorns the notion of the King's operation or even the need of it. "Rumor [of the operation]," writes Monsieur Faÿ, "rose from the entourage of the Queen, 1772 to 1777, was picked up by the [contemporary] *Nouvelles à la Main,* and has been repeated ever since by a succession of historians." He checked every date mentioned for the operation (he continues) against the King's journal and found that the King noted he had been hunting that very day, or shortly thereafter, though "the operation, if it had taken place, would have restricted him to his bedroom for twelve to fifteen days." He also quotes a letter from Joseph II to his brother, Leopold II, in

which the Emperor states, "Louis had very good erections, would introduce his member, which remained without moving for perhaps two minutes, then would withdraw it without discharging and say good night, remarking good humoredly that he did it solely from a sense of duty, since he had no pleasure in it." It was the Queen, says Monsieur Faÿ, who turned Louis off, and he refers to various memoirs and ambassadorial reports (other than the Spanish ambassador's) as asserting no evidence of an operation.

In partial reply, one might remark that Joseph II's description of Louis' dutiful performance does not contradict the possibility of phimosis, which allows for *painful* erections but, pleasureless, inhibits completion. Dr. Jean Torlais, in turn, considers Monsieur Faÿ's medical argument that approximately two weeks of convalescence would have had to follow an operation for phimosis (see Torlais' *Louis XVI—a-t-il été opéré?*—an extract from *Aesculape*, January 1956). "The operation practised in those days," he points out, "did not require the stitching described by M. Faÿ," and thus did not necessitate "prolonged rest. . . . Rather, surgeons practised a simple incision [a perpendicular cut] of the prepuce," a minor operation allowing for a minimum of time for recovery, permitting discretion, relative secrecy, and quickly resumed activity by the King. Dr. Torlais believes the evidence indicates Louis XVI's operation "probably early in June, 1777."

63. Campan, *op. cit.*
64. Maria Theresa, *op. cit.*
65. Zweig, *op. cit.*
66. La Rocheterie, *op. cit.*
67. Campan, *op. cit.*
68. Geffroy, *op. cit.*
69. Bachaumont, Louis Petit de. *Mémoires secrets pour servir à l'histoire de la république des lettres en France depuis 1762 jusqu'à nos jours . . .* London, 1777–89. 36 vols.

21.   THREE FRIENDS FOR BENJAMIN FRANKLIN

1. Bonneville de Marsangy, Louis. *Le Chevalier de Vergennes, son ambassade à Constantinople.* Paris, 1894. 2 vols.
2. Bonneville de Marsangy, Louis. *Le Comte de Vergennes, son ambassade en Suède, 1771–1774.* Paris, 1898.
3. Geoffroy, Auguste. *Gustave III et la cour de France.* Paris, 1867. 2 vols.
4. Goncourt, Edmond and Jules. *La Femme au dix-huitième siècle.* Paris, 1862.
5. Meng, John J. *The Comte de Vergennes. European Phases of His American Diplomacy, 1774–1780.* Washington, 1932.
6. Loménie, Louis de. *Beaumarchais et son temps.* Paris, 1856. 2 vols.
7. Thomasset, René. *Beaumarchais, écrivain et aventurier.* Paris, 1966.
8. Loménie, *op. cit.*
9. Durant, Will and Ariel. *Rousseau and Revolution.* New York, 1967.
10. Gottschalk, Louis. *Lafayette Joins the American Army.* Chicago, 1937.
11. Maurois, André. *Adrienne, ou la vie de Mme. de La Fayette,* Paris, 1961.
12. Gottschalk, Louis. *Lafayette and the Close of the American Revolution.* Chicago, 1942.
13. Maurois, *op. cit.*

14. Lecky, William. *A History of England in the Eighteenth Century.* London, 1878–90. 8 vols.
15. Ségur, Louis Philippe de, Comte de. *Mémoires, ou souvenirs et anecdotes.* Paris, 1824–26. 3 vols.
16. Morris, Gouverneur. *A Diary of the French Revolution* . . . Boston, 1939. 2 vols.
17. Mercy to Maria Theresa in Maria Theresa, *Correspondance secrète* . . . Paris, 1874. 3 vols.
18. Gottschalk, Louis. *Lafayette Joins the American Army.*

22. A "QUAKER" AT THE COURT OF VERSAILLES

1. Du Coudray, Alexandre J. L. *Anecdotes intéressantes et historiques de l'illustre voyageur* [Joseph II, Emperor of Austria], *pendant son séjour à Paris.* Leipzig, 1777.
2. Hale, Edward E., and Hale, Jr., Edward E. *Franklin in France.* Boston, 1887. 2 vols.
3. Franklin, Benjamin. *Writings* (Albert Henry Smyth, ed.) New York, 1907. 10 vols.
4. Faÿ, Bernard. *Franklin, the Apostle of Modern Times.* Boston, 1929. (First published in English.)
5. Chambrun, Charles de. *A l'Ecole d'un diplomate. Vergennes, etc.* Paris, 1946.
6. Van Doren, Carl. *Benjamin Franklin.* New York, 1938.
7. Du Deffand, Marie, Marquise. *Correspondance complète* . . . Paris, 1865. 2 vols.
8. Walpole, Horace. *Letters.* London, 1840. 6 vols.
9. Durant, *op. cit.*
10. Bachaumont, Louis Petit de. *Mémoires secrets* . . . London, 1777–89. 36 vols.
11. Doniol, Henri. *Histoire de la participation de la France à l'établissement des Etats-Unis d'Amérique.* Paris, 1886–99. 5 vols.
12. Lee, Richard Henry, the Younger. *Life of Arthur Lee* . . . Boston, 1829. 2 vols.
13. Du Deffand, *op. cit.*
14. Scene at Versailles based on Croÿ's *Journal,* Madame du Deffand's letters, and a Danish diplomat's eyewitness account in Faÿ's *Franklin.*
15. Croÿ, Duc de. *Journal inédit. Paris,* 1906–07. 4 vols.
16. *Ibid.*
17. Van Doren, *op. cit.*
18. *Ibid.*
19. Franklin, *op. cit.*
20. Bowen, Catherine. *John Adams and the American Revolution.* Boston, 1951. Jay, William. *Life of J. Jay* . . . New York, 1833. 2 vols.
21. Hale, *op. cit.*
22. Faÿ, *op. cit.*
23. Adams, John. *Works.* Boston, 1856. 10 vols.
24. Van Doren, *op. cit.*
25. *Ibid.*
26. Gramont, Sanche de. *Epitaph for Kings.* New York, 1967.
27. Campan, Jeanne Louise. *Mémoires* . . . Paris, 1822. 3 vols.

28. Grimm, Friedrich Melchior. *Correspondance littéraire* . . . Paris, 1877–82. 16 vols.
29. Franklin, *op. cit.*
30. Van Doren, *op. cit.*
31. Franklin, *op. cit.* (Original spelling is here preserved.)
32. Faÿ, *op. cit.*
33. Franklin, *op. cit.*
34. Van Doren, *op. cit.*
35. Franklin, *op. cit.*
36. Gramont, *op. cit.*
37. *Ibid.*
38. Franklin, *op. cit.*
39. Van Doren, *op. cit.*
40. Condorcet, Jean Antoine Nicolas de Caritat, Marquis de. *Oeuvres.* Paris, 1804. 21 vols.
41. Aldridge, Alfred. *Franklin and His French Contemporaries.* New York, 1957.
42. Gottschalk, *op. cit.*
43. Van Doren, *op. cit.*
44. *Encyclopaedia Britannica,* 11th edition.
45. *Ibid.*
46. Hale, *op. cit.*
47. Franklin, *op. cit.*
48. *Ibid.*
49. Grimm, *op. cit.*
50. Franklin, *op. cit.*
51. Fonvielle, Wilfred de. *Histoire de la navigation aérienne.* Paris, 1907.
52. Hale, *op. cit.*
53. Van Doren, *op. cit.*
54. *Ibid.*
55. Franklin, *op. cit.*
56. Jefferson, Thomas. *Writings. New York,* 1853–54. 9 vols.
57. Mirabeau, Honoré-Gabriel, Comte de. *Discours* . . . *dans la séance du 11 juin, sur la mort de Benjamin Francklin* [sic]. Paris, 1790.

23. THE CURTAIN FALLS

1. Mossiker, Frances. *The Queen's Necklace.* New York, 1961. Contains almost everything relevant to the *affaire,* translated from the original documents, memoirs, defense pleas, and trial procedures. Also recommended:
   Campardon, Émile. *Marie-Antoinette et le procès du collier.* Paris, 1863.
   Hastier, Louis, *La Vérité sur l'affaire du collier.* Paris, 1955.
2. Chambrun, Charles de. *A l'École d'un diplomate.* Paris, 1946.
3. Faÿ, Bernard. *Louis XVI ou la fin d'un monde.* Paris, 1955.
4. *Ibid.*
5. *Encyclopaedia Britannica,* 11th edition.
6. Zweig, Stefan. *Marie Antoinette.* New York, 1933.
7. Söderhjelm, Alma, ed. *Fersen et Marie-Antoinette.* Paris, 1830.
8. Castelot, André. *Marie-Antoinette.* Paris, 1962.

9. Söderhjhelm, *op. cit.*
10. Oberkirch, Henriette-Louise, Baronne d'. *Mémoires.* Paris, 1853. 2 vols.
11. Kunstler, Charles. *Fersen et son secret.* Paris, 1947.
12. Faÿ, *op. cit.*
13. Bachaumont, Louis-Petit de. *Mémoires secrets . . .* London, 1777–89. 36 vols.
14. Loménie, Louis de. *Beaumarchais et son temps.* Paris, 1856. 2 vols.
15. Beaumarchais, Pierre Augustin Caron de. *Le Mariage de Figaro.* Many editions.
16. Valmy-Baysse, Jean. *Naissance et vie de la Comédie-Française.* Paris, 1845.
17. *Ibid.*
18. Campan, Jeanne Louise. *Mémoires . . .* Paris, 1822.
19. Mossiker, *op. cit.*
20. Campan, *op. cit.*
21. Mossiker, *op. cit.*
22. Campan, *op. cit.*
23. *Ibid.*
24. *Ibid.*
25. Maria Theresa, Empress of Austria. *Correspondance secrète . . .* Paris, 1874. 3 vols.
26. *Ibid.*
27. *Encyclopaedia Britannica,* 11th edition.
28. Georgel, Jean François, Abbé. *Mémoires.* Paris, 1817–18. 6 vols.
29. Campan, *op. cit.*
30. Letter from Marie Antoinette to Joseph II. See Marie Antoinette. *Lettres.* Edited by Maxime de La Rocheterie. Paris, 1895–96. 2 vols.
31. Georgel, *op. cit.*
32. *Ibid.*
33. La Motte, Jeanne de Saint-Rémy de Valois, Comtesse de. *Mémoires justificatifs.* London, 1788. See also other variant editions. Our story of her life is assembled from these sources.
34. Documented in Mossiker, *op. cit.*
35. La Motte, *op. cit.*
36. Beugnot, Jacques-Claude, Comte. *Mémoires.* Paris, 1866. 2 vols.
37. Rétaux de Villette, Louis-Marc-Antoine. *Mémoire historique des intrigues de la cour.* Venice, 1790.
38. *Ibid.*
39. Georgel, *op. cit.*
40. *Ibid.*
41. *Ibid.*
42. Campan, *op. cit.*
43. Mossiker, *op. cit.* See note 53, below.
44. From memoirs of Mademoiselle d'Oliva, as quoted in Mossiker, *op. cit.*
45. Zweig, *op. cit.*
46. Georgel, *op. cit.*
47. Mossiker, *op. cit.*
48. Marie Antoinette, *op. cit.*
49. Mossiker, *op. cit.*
50. *Ibid.*
51. Campan, *op. cit.*
52. Mossiker, *op. cit.*

53. While the *affaire* was still being probed, Marie Antoinette wrote Count
Mercy that she was determined to "permit no mention of the midnight
rendezvous, the terrace [sic] incident." This is taken by some historians as
proof of the Queen's involvement, even if only mischievous, in this aspect
of the diamond necklace puzzle. However, the fact that she mistakenly calls
it the "terrace" rather than the "grove" incident indicates a matter more of
hearsay on her part than of actual participation. Further, Marie Antoinette
wanted virtually *no* mention of herself in the proceedings, least of all
anything adding to the libel surrounding her name, and in this largely
succeeded (neither the Cardinal, nor the countess, accused her of *any* part
in the diamond conspiracy during the trial).
54. Campan, *op. cit.*

24. THE CURTAIN ALSO RISES

1. Michelet, Jules. *Histoire de la révolution française.* Paris, 1847–53. 7 vols.
2. Jaurès, Jean. *Histoire socialiste* (1789–1900). Paris, n.d. 10 vols.
3. Tocqueville, Alexis de. *L'Ancien régime et la révolution.* J. P. Mayer edition. Paris, 1952–53. 2 vols.
4. Gooch, George Peabody. *Louis XV.* London, 1956.
5. Durant, Will and Ariel. *Rousseau and Revolution.* New York, 1967.
6. Young, Arthur. *Travels During the Years 1787, 1788, 1789 . . . [in] the Kingdom of France.* London, 1792.
7. Barnave, Antoine Pierre Joseph Marie. *Oeuvres.* Paris, 1843. 4 vols.
8. Jaurès, *op. cit.*
9. Durant, *op. cit.*
10. Sieyès, Emmanuel-Joseph, Abbé. *Qu'est-ce que le tiers état?* n.p., 1789.
11. Egret, Jean. *La Pré-révolution française, 1787–1788.* Paris, 1962.
12. Goubert, Pierre. *L'Ancien régime.* Paris, 1969.
13. Behrens, C. B. A. *The ancien régime.* Paris, 1967.
14. Young, *op. cit.*
15. Tocqueville, *op. cit.*
16. Taine, Hippolyte-Adolphe. *Les Origines de la France contemporaine . . . La révolution.* Paris, 1878. 3 vols.
    Sée, Henri. *La France économique et sociale au xviiiè siècle.* Paris, 1925.
17. Soboul, Albert. *La France à la veille de la révolution.* Paris, 1960.
18. Boucher de La Richarderie, Gilles. *Essai sur les capitaineries royales et autres, et sur les maux incroyables qui en résultent . . .* n.p., 1789.
19. Kessel, Patrick. *La Nuit du 4 août 1789.* Paris, 1969.
20. Goubert, *op. cit.*
21. Tocqueville, *op. cit.*
22. Taine, *op. cit.*
23. Mandrou, Robert. *La France aux xviiè et xviiiè siècles.* Paris, 1967.
24. *Ibid.*
25. Goubert, *op. cit.*
26. Taine, *op. cit.*
27. Jaurès, *op. cit.*
28. *Ibid.*

29. Lefebvre, Georges. *La Révolution française.* Paris, 1963.

30. Labrousse, Camille-Ernest. *La Crise de l'économie française à la fin de l'ancien régime et au début de la révolution.* Paris, 1943.

31. Soboul, Albert. *La Révolution française, 1789–1799.* Paris, 1948.
Labrousse, Camille-Ernest. *Esquisse du mouvement des prix et des revenus en France au xviiiè siècle* . . . Paris, 1933. 2 vols.

32. Gramont, Sanche de. *Epitaph for Kings.* New York, 1967.

33. Chamfort, Sébastien-Roch-Nicolas. *Oeuvres.* Paris, 1808. 2 vols.

34. Labrousse, C. E. *La Crise de l'économie française* . . .

35. Morris, Gouverneur. *Diary and Letters.* New York, 1888. 2 vols.

36. Lefebvre, Georges. *La Grande peur de 1789.* Paris, 1957.

37. Taine, *op. cit.*

38. Jaurès, *op. cit.*

39. *Ibid.*

40. Tocqueville, *op. cit.*

41. Gramont, *op. cit.*

42. Carlyle, Thomas. *The French Revolution.* Many editions.

25. THE CALLING OF THE CLAN

1. Mercy-Argenteau, Florimond-Claude Comte de. *Correspondance secrète du comte de Mercy-Argenteau avec l'empereur Joseph II et le prince de Kaunitz.* Paris, 1889–91. 2 vols.

2. Bachaumont, Louis-Petit de. *Mémoires secrets pour servir à l'histoire de la république des lettres en France, depuis 1762 jusqu'à nos jours.* London, 1777–89. 36 vols.

3. Grimm, Friedrich Melchior. *Correspondance littéraire, philosophique, et critique, par Grimm, Diderot, Raynal, Meister, et al.* Paris, 1877–82. 16 vols.

4. Boufflers, Stanislas-Jean de, Chevalier de Malte. *Correspondance inédite de la Comtesse de Sabran et du Chevalier de Boufflers, 1778–88.* Paris, 1875.

5. Castelot, André. *Marie-Antoinette.* Paris, 1962.

6. Marie Antoinette. *Marie Antoinette, Joseph II und Leopold II. Ihr briefwechsel.* Leipzig-Paris, 1866.

7. La Rocheterie, Maxime de. *Histoire de Marie-Antoinette.* Paris, 1890. 2 vols.

8. Eloffe (   ) Madame (dressmaker to Marie Antoinette). *Modes et usages au temps de Marie-Antoinette. Livre journal.* Paris, 1885. 2 vols.

9. La Rocheterie, *op. cit.*

10. Castelot, *op. cit.*

11. Campan, Jeanne Louise. *Mémoires* . . . Paris, 1822. 3 vols.

12. Bachaumont, *op. cit.*

13. La Rocheterie, *op. cit.*

14. Campan, *op. cit.*

15. Bachaumont, *op. cit.*

16. Lavisse, Ernest. *Histoire de France.* Paris, 1903–11. 9 vols.

17. Lacour-Gayet, Robert. *Calonne.* Paris, 1963.

18. Lavisse, *op. cit.*

19. Lacour-Gayet, *op. cit.*

R*

20. Métra, François. *Correspondance secrète, politique et littéraire.* London, 1787–90. 18 vols.
21. Lavisse, *op. cit.*
22. Lacour-Gayet, *op. cit.*
23. *Journées mémorables de la révolution française: 1787–89.* Paris, 1826.
24. Egret, Jean. *La Pré-révolution française, 1787–88.* Paris, 1962.
25. Talleyrand-Périgord, Charles-Maurice, Duc de. *Mémoires.* Paris, 1891–92. 5 vols.
26. Lavisse, *op. cit.*
27. Droz, Joseph. *Histoire du règne de Louis XVI pendant les années ou l'on pouvait prévenir ou diriger la révolution française.* Paris, 1858. 3 vols.
28. Staël-Holstein, Eric Magnus, Baron de. *Correspondance diplomatique.* Paris, 1881.
29. Faÿ, Bernard. *Louis XVI.* Paris, 1955.
30. Lacour-Gayet, *op. cit.*
31. Lavisse, *op. cit.*
32. *Ibid.*
33. Droz, *op. cit.*
34. Lavisse, *op. cit.*
35. *Revue historique,* 1902–03. Vols. 79–80.
36. Talleyrand, *op. cit.*
37. Jolly, Pierre. *Calonne.* Paris, 1949.
38. Lacour-Gayet, *op. cit.*
39. Lavisse, *op. cit.*
40. Egret, Jean. *Lafayette à la première assemblée des notables,* in *Annales historiques de la révolution française,* 1952.
41. Chamfort, Sébastien-Roch-Nicolas. *Oeuvres.* Paris, 1808. 2 vols.
42. Droz, *op. cit.*
43. Staël-Holstein, Anne-Louise-Germaine Necker, Baronne de. *Considérations sur les principaux éléments de la révolution française.* Paris, 1818. 3 vols.
44. Loménie de Brienne, Etienne-Charles de. *Mémoires.* Versailles, 1789.
45. *Ibid.*
46. Lacour-Gayet, *op. cit.*
47. Jolly, *op. cit.*
48. Faÿ, *op. cit.*
49. Lévis, Gaston, Duc de. *Souvenirs et portraits, 1780–89.* Paris, 1813.
50. *Gazette de Leyde,* 1787.
51. *Ibid.*
52. Campan, *op. cit.*
53. Cf. Sainte-Beuve, Charles-Augustin. *Causeries du lundi.* Paris, 1872. Vol. XV. Article on Voltaire and Rousseau.
54. Lavisse, *op. cit.*
55. Quoted with distaste in Faÿ, *op. cit.*
56. Droz, *op. cit.*
57. Lafayette, Marie-Joseph-Gilbert du Motier, Marquis de. *Mémoires.* Brussells, 1837–38. 6 vols.
58. Picot, Georges. *Histoire des états généraux . . .* Paris, 1872. 4 vols.
59. Goubert, Pierre. *L'Ancien régime.* Paris, 1969.
60. Nougaret, Pierre-Jean-Baptiste. *Anecdotes du règne de Louis XVI.* Paris, 1780.

26. THE OVEREXPOSURE OF PARLEMENT

1. La Rocheterie, Maxime de. *Histoire de Marie-Antoinette*. Paris, 1890. 2 vols.
2. Castelot, André. *Marie-Antoinette*. Paris, 1962.
   Verlet, Pierre. *Versailles*. Paris, 1961.
3. Besenval, Pierre-Victor, Baron de. *Mémoires*. Paris, 1805. 3 vols.
4. Staël-Holstein, Anne-Louise-Germaine Necker, Baronne de. *Considérations sur les principaux éléments de la révolution française*. Paris, 1818. 3 vols.
5. Flammermont, Jules. *Remonstrances du parlement de Paris au xviiiè siècle*. Paris, 1888–98. 3 vols.
6. Lavisse, Ernest. *Histoire de France*. Paris, 1903–11. 9 vols.
7. Target, Guy-Jean-Baptiste. *Un Avocat du xviiiè siècle . . . Journal de Target*. Paris, 1893.
8. Mercy-Argenteau, Florimond-Claude Comte de. *Correspondance secrète du Comte de Mercy-Argenteau avec l'Empereur Joseph II et le Prince de Kaunitz*. Paris, 1889–91. 2 vols.
9. Faÿ, Bernard. *Louis XVI*. Paris, 1955.
10. Augeard, Jacques-Mathieu. *Mémoires secrets*. Paris, 1866.
11. Egret, Jean. *La Pré-révolution française, 1787–88*. Paris, 1962.
12. Lavisse, *op. cit.*
13. Target, *op. cit.*
14. Egret, *op. cit.*
15. Sallier-Chaumont de La Roche, Guy-Marie. *Annales françaises . . . 1774 à 1789*. Paris, 1813.
16. Talleyrand-Périgord, Charles-Maurice, Duc de. *Mémoires*. Paris, 1891–92. 5 vols.
17. Egret, *op. cit.*
18. Mallet du Pan, Jacques. *Mémoires et correspondance*. Paris, 1851. 2 vols.
19. Faÿ, *op. cit.*
20. Egret, *op. cit.*
21. Lacretelle, Charles. *Dix années d'épreuves pendant la révolution*. Paris, 1842.
   "We are all d'Eprémesnil and Montsabert!" was a cry that echoed in May 1968, when students chanted in unison, apropos one of their government-banished leaders, Cohn-Bendit, "We are all German Jews!"
22. Lefebvre, Georges. *La Révolution française*. Paris, 1963.
23. Lavisse, *op. cit.*
24. Egret, Jean. *Le Parlement du Dauphiné . . .* Grenoble, 1942.
25. Stendhal, Henri Beyle. *Vie de Henri Brulard*. Paris, 1890.
26. Egret, *op. cit.*
27. Egret, Jean. *La Révolution des notables, Mounier et les monarchiens, 1789*. Paris, 1950.
28. Lavisse, *op. cit.*
29. Mercier, Louis-Sébastien. *Tableau de Paris*. Hamburg, 1781. 2 vols.
30. Oberkirch, Henriette-Louise, Baronne d'. *Mémoires*. Paris, 1853. 2 vols.
31. Goubert, Pierre. *L'Ancien régime*. Paris, 1969.
32. Tocqueville, Alexis de. *L'Ancien régime . . .* Paris, 1952–53. 2 vols.
33. Ségur, Louis-Philippe Comte de. *Mémoires . . .* Paris, 1824–26. 3 vols.
34. Lavisse, *op. cit.*
35. Wéber, Joseph. *Mémoires*. London, 1804–09. 3 vols.
36. Loménie de Brienne, Etienne Charles. *Mémoires*. Versailles, 1789.

37. Dupont de Nemours, Pierre-Samuel. *Discours prononcé à l'assemblée nationale sur les banques en général.* Paris, 1789.
38. Louis XVI. *Louis XVI, Marie-Antoinette et Madame Elizabeth, lettres et documents inédits.* Paris, 1864–73. 6 vols.
39. Michelet, Jules. *Histoire de la révolution française.* Paris, 1847–53. 7 vols.
40. Lavisse, *op. cit.*
41. *Ibid.*

27. ENTER MIRABEAU

1. Sainte-Beuve, Charles-Augustin. *Causeries du lundi.* Paris, 1872. Vol. IV.
2. Sources of specific events and quotations will be indicated *exceptionally* in this chapter on Mirabeau, since most of the abundant material on his life is reported and repeated in the following principal works and sources consulted:
   Mirabeau, Honoré-Gabriel Riqueti, Comte de. *Oeuvres.* Paris, 1826–27. 9 vols. Contains almost all the separate works referred to, such as the *Essai sur le despotisme, Lettres de cachet,* etc.
   ———. *Erotika biblion.* Paris, 1910. An edition with introduction and notes by Guillaume Apollinaire.
   ———. *Correspondance entre le Comte de Mirabeau et le Comte de La Marck.* Paris, 1851. 3 vols. Invaluable for its revelation of Mirabeau's political astuteness.
   Lucas de Montigny, Jean-Marie-Nicolas. *Mémoires biographiques, littéraires et politiques de Mirabeau, écrits par lui-même, par son père, son oncle et son fils adoptif.* Paris, 1834–35. 8 vols. The author was Mirabeau's adopted, and most likely illegitimate, son. Useful but not unbiased.
   Loménie, Louis and Charles. *Les Mirabeau . . .* Paris, 1879–91. 5 vols. Most complete biographical study.
   Barthou, Louis. *Mirabeau.* Paris, 1913. Exists in English as well. Best single volume.
   Vallentin, Antonina. *Mirabeau.* Paris, 1946–47. 2 vols.
   Scudder, Evarts S. *Mirabeau.* London, 1935.
   Welch, Oliver J. G. *Mirabeau: A Study of a Democratic Monarchist.* London, 1951.
3. Barthou, *op. cit.*
4. Vallentin, *op. cit.*
5. Scudder, *op. cit.*
6. Welch, *op. cit.*
7. Loménie, *op. cit.*
8. Meunier, Dauphin. *La Comtesse de Mirabeau.* Paris, 1908.
9. Cotton, Paul. *Sophie de Monnier et Mirabeau, d'après leur correspondance secrète édite.* Paris, 1903.
10. Lucas de Montigny, *op. cit.*
11. Mirabeau. *Lettres à Sophie* in collected *Oeuvres.* See Note 2, above.
12. *Ibid.*
13. Welch, *op. cit.*
14. Loménie, *op. cit.*
15. Vallentin, *op. cit.*

16. Kynynmound, Emma Eleanor, Countess of Minto. *A Memoir of the Right Honourable Hugh Elliot.* Edinburgh, 1868.
17. Scudder, *op. cit.*
18. Barthou, *op. cit.*
19. Vallentin, *op. cit.*
20. Welch, *op. cit.*
21. Chevallier, Jean-Jacques. *Mirabeau: un grand destin manqué.* Paris, 1947.
22. Meunier, *op. cit.*
23. *The New Cambridge Modern History.* Cambridge, 1965. Vol. VIII.
24. Loménie, *op. cit.*
25. Hyslop, Beatrice Fry. *A Guide to the General Cahiers of 1789 with the Texts of Unedited* [i.e. unpublished] *Cahiers.* New York, 1936.
Goubert, Pierre. *1789: les français ont la parole . . . Cahiers de doléances des états généraux.* Paris, 1964.
26. Loménie, *op. cit.*

28. THE MEN IN BLACK MAKE THE SCENE

1. *Journées mémorables de la révolution française: 1787–89.* Paris, 1826.
2. Campan, Jeanne-Louise. *Mémoires . . .* Paris, 1822. 3 vols.
3. *Ibid.*
4. Saint-Priest, François-Emmanuel, Comte de. *Mémoires.* Paris, 1929. 2 vols.
5. Principal sources for the procession scene:
Campan, *op. cit.*
Ferrières, Charles-Élie, Marquis de. *Mémoires.* Paris, 1821. 3 vols.
Franch d'Hézecques, Félix, Comte de. *Souvenirs d'un page de la cour de Louis XVI.* Paris, 1873.
Morris, Gouverneur. *Diary and letters.* New York, 1888. 2 vols.
Staël-Holstein, Anne-Louise-Germaine Necker, Baronne de. *Considérations sur les principaux éléments de la révolution française.* Paris, 1818. 3 vols.
Wéber, Joseph. *Mémoires.* London, 1804–09. 3 vols.
6. Staël, *op. cit.*
7. Campan, *op. cit.*
8. Morris, *op. cit.*
9. Castelot, André. *Marie-Antoinette.* Paris, 1962.
10. Morris, *op. cit.* Quotations of Morris hereafter are assumed from this source.
11. *Mercure de France,* May 16, 1789.
12. La Tour du Pin Gouvernet, Henriette-Lucie, Marquise de. *Journal d'une femme de cinquante ans, 1778–1815.* Paris, 1907–11. 4 vols.
13. Soboul, Albert. *1789: L'An un de la liberté.* Paris, 1950.
14. Zweig, Stefan. *Marie Antoinette.* New York, 1932.
15. Campan, *op. cit.*
16. Faÿ, Bernard. *Louis XVI.* Paris, 1955.
17. Castelot, *op. cit.*
18. Dumouriez, Charles-François. *La Vie et les mémoires du Général Dumouriez.* Paris, 1822–23. 4 vols.
19. Kessel, Patrick. *La Nuit de 4 août 1789.* Paris, 1969.
20. Lefebvre, Georges. *Recueil de documents relatifs aux séances des états généraux de 1789.* Paris, 1962.

21. Vallentin, Antonina. *Mirabeau*. Paris, 1946–47. 2 vols.
22. Young, Arthur. *Travels During the Years 1787, 1788, 1789* . . . [*in*] *the Kingdom of France*. London, 1792.
23. Dumont, Étienne-Pierre-Louis. *Souvenirs sur Mirabeau et sur les deux premières assemblées législatives*. Paris, 1832.
24. Lucet de Montignez. *Almanach du centenaire de 1789* . . . Paris, 1888.
25. Campan, *op. cit.*
26. Wéber, *op. cit.*
27. Young, *op. cit.*
28. Buchez, Philippe-Joseph-Benjamin, and Roux, Pierre-Célestin. *Histoire parlementaire de la révolution française*. Paris, 1834–38. 40 vols.
29. *Ibid.*
30. Soboul, *op. cit.*
31. Brette, Armand. *Recueil de documents relatifs à la convocation des états généraux de 1789*. Paris, 1894–1915. 4 vols.
32. Staël, *op. cit.*
33. Faÿ, *op. cit.*
34. Young, *op. cit.*
35. Bailly, Jean-Sylvain. *Mémoires d'un témoin de la révolution*. Paris, 1804. 3 vols.
36. Ferrières, *op. cit.*
37. Brette, *op. cit.*
38. Bailly, *op. cit.*
39. Campan, *op. cit.*
40. Soboul, *op. cit.*
41. Hugo, Victor. *Étude sur Mirabeau*. Paris, 1834.
42. Lefebvre, *op. cit.*
43. Mathiez, Albert. *Les Grandes journées de la constituante, 1789–91*. Paris, 1913.
44. Lefebvre, *op. cit.*
45. Vallentin, *op. cit.*
46. Rudé, George. *The Crowd in the French Revolution*. Oxford, 1959.
47. Ferrières, *op. cit.*
48. Young, *op. cit.*

29. THE PRINCE AND—INCIDENTALLY—THE PEOPLE

1. Manuel, Louis-Pierre. *La Police de Paris dévoilée*. Paris, 1793.
   Talleyrand-Périgord, Charles-Maurice, Duc de. *Mémoires*. Paris, 1891–92. 5 vols. For Talleyrand, the Duc d'Orléans was "the pail into which the Revolution's garbage had been thrown."
   See also, Crétineau-Joly, Jacques Augustin. *Histoire de Louis-Philippe d'Orléans et de l'orléanisme*. Paris, 1862–63. 2 vols.
2. Castelot, André. *Philippe-Égalité, le prince rouge*. Paris, 1950.
3. Hyslop, Beatrice. *L'Apanage de Philippe-Égalité, duc d'Orléans*. Paris, 1965.
4. Britsch, Amédée. *La Jeunesse de Philippe-Égalité, 1747–1785*. Paris, 1926.
5. Castelot, *op. cit.*
6. Hugo, Victor. *Choses vues*. Paris, 1887.
7. Britsch, *op. cit.*

8. Mercier, Louis-Sébastien. *Tableau de Paris*. Amsterdam, 1782–88. 12 vols.
9. Genlis, Stéphanie-Félicité, Comtesse de. *Mémoires*. Paris, 1825. 10 vols.
10. Castelot, *op. cit.*
11. Métra, François. *Correspondance secrète, politique, et littéraire*. London, 1787–90. 18 vols.
12. Britsch, *op. cit.*
    Elliott, Grace Dalrymple. *Journal of My Life During the French Revolution*. London, 1859.
13. Britsch, *op. cit.*
14. Bachaumont, Louis-Petit de. *Mémoires secrets . . .* London, 1777–89. 36 vols.
15. Montjoie, Félix-Louis, called Galart de. *Histoire de la conjuration de Louis-Philippe-Joseph d'Orléans . . .* Paris, 1796. 3 vols.
16. Castelot, *op. cit.*
17. *Ibid.*
18. Dard, Emile. *Un Acteur caché du drame révolutionnaire, le général Choderlos de Laclos . . .* Paris, 1905.
19. Hyslop, Beatrice Fry. *A Guide to the General Cahiers of 1789 . . .* New York, 1936.
20. Castelot, *op. cit.*
21. Jaurès, Jean. *Histoire socialiste (1789–1900)*. Paris, n.d. 10 vols.
22. Godechot, Jacques. *La Prise de la Bastille: 14 juillet 1789*. Paris, 1965.
23. Rudé, George. *The Crowd in the French Revolution*. Oxford, 1959.
24. *Ibid.*
25. *Ibid.*
26. Castelot, *op. cit.*
27. Vallentin, Antonina. *Mirabeau*. Paris, 1946–47. 2 vols.

30. THE DAY A WORLD ENDED

1. Lavisse, Ernest. *Histoire de France contemporaine*. Paris, 1921–22. 10 vols.
2. Godechot, Jacques. *La Prise de la Bastille: 14 juillet 1789*. Paris, 1965.
3. Ferrières, Charles Élie, Marquis de. *Mémoires*. Paris, 1821. 3 vols.
4. Morris, Gouverneur. *Diary and Letters*. New York, 1888. 2 vols.
5. Martin, Gaston. *Le 14 juillet 1789*. Paris, 1939.
6. Vallentin, Antonina. *Mirabeau*. Paris, 1946–47. 2 vols.
7. Rudé, George. *The Crowd in the French Revolution*. Oxford, 1959.
8. Martin, *op. cit.*
9. Jefferson, Thomas. *Memoir, correspondence and miscellanies*. Boston, 1830. 4 vols.
10. Flammermont, Jules. *La Journée du 14 juillet 1789. Fragments des mémoires inédits de L. G. Pitra, électeur de Paris en 1789*. Paris, 1892.
11. Lavisse, *op. cit.*
12. Elliott, Grace Dalrymple. *Journal of My Life During the French Revolution*. London, 1859.
13. Desmoulins, Camille. *Oeuvres*. Claretie edition. Paris, 1874. 2 vols.
14. Rudé, *op. cit.*
15. Godechot, *op. cit.*
16. Jefferson, *op. cit.*
17. Godechot, *op. cit.*

18. Rudé, *op. cit.*
19. Elliott, *op. cit.*
20. Godechot, *op. cit.*
21. *Procès-verbal des séances et délibérations de l'assemblée générale des électeurs de Paris réunis à l'Hôtel de Ville, le 14 juillet 1789* . . . Paris, 1790. 3 vols.
22. Godechot, *op. cit.*
23. Besenval, Pierre-Victor, Baron de. *Mémoires.* Paris, 1805. 3 vols.
24. Rigby, Edward. *Dr. Rigby's Letters from France . . . in 1789.* London, 1880.
25. Principal sources for July 14, 1789, other than those specifically referred to:
    Précis exact de la prise de la Bastille, rédigé sous les yeux des principaux acteurs qui ont joué un rôle dans cette même expédition. Paris (?), 1789.
    Humbert, Jean Baptiste. *Journée de Jean-Baptiste Humbert, horloger, qui le premier a monté sur les tours de la Bastille.* Paris, 1789.
    Béraud, Henri. *Le 14 juillet.* Paris, 1929.
    Mathiez, Albert. *Les Grandes journées de la constituante, 1789–91.* Paris, 1913.
    ————. *Les Capitalistes et la prise de la Bastille,* in *Annales historiques de la révolution française.* 1926, vol. 3.
    Michaud, Jean. *Les Etats généraux et le 14 juillet 1789.* Paris, 1960.
    Mistler, Jean. *Le 14 juillet.* Paris, 1963.
26. Godechot, *op. cit.*
27. See Note 21.
28. Jefferson, *op. cit.*
29. Flammermont, *op. cit.*
30. Bournon, Fernand. *Histoire générale de Paris. La Bastille* . . . Paris, 1893.
31. Flammermont, *op. cit.*
32. Letter of Lieutenant de Flue to his brother, in Flammermont, *op. cit.*
33. Durieux, Joseph. *Les Vainqueurs de la Bastille.* Paris, 1911.
34. Godechot, *op. cit.*
35. *La Bastille dévoilée.* Paris, 1789. Accounts by the besieged.
36. *Ibid.*
37. See Note 32.
38. Flammermont, *op. cit.*
39. Bailly, Jean-Sylvain. *Mémoires* . . . Paris, 1804. 3 vols.
40. Tocqueville, Alexis de. *L'Ancien régime* . . . Paris, 1952–53. 2 vols.
41. Babeuf, François-Noël, called Gracchus. *Pages choisies.* Paris, 1935.
42. Mirabeau, Honoré-Gabriel, Comte de. *Lettre à ses commettants.* Paris, 1789.
43. Legg, Leopold G. Wickham. *Select Documents Illustrative of the History of the French Revolution. The Constituent Assembly.* Oxford, 1905. 2 vols. Documents are in French.
44. Besenval, *op. cit.*
45. La Rochefoucauld-Liancourt, Frédéric-Gaëtan, Comte de. *Vie du duc de La Rochefoucauld-Liancourt.* Paris, 1827.
46. Godechot, *op. cit.*
47. Ferrières, *op. cit.*
48. Barthou, Louis. *Mirabeau.* Paris, 1913.
49. Vallentin, *op. cit.*
50. Bailly, *op. cit.*
51. Paroy, Jean-Philippe, Marquis de. *Mémoires.* Paris, 1895.

52. Ferrières, *op. cit.*
53. Fersen, Hans Axel von, Count. *Le Comte de Fersen et la cour de France.* Edited by R. M. de Klinckowström. Paris, 1877–78. 2 vols.
54. Flammermont, Jules. *Relations inédites de la prise de la Bastille par le duc de Dorset, ambassadeur d'Angleterre en France* . . . Paris, 1885.
55. Campan, Jeanne-Louise. *Mémoires* . . . Paris, 1822. 3 vols.
56. *Ibid.*
57. Castelot, André. *Marie-Antoinette.* Paris, 1962.
58. Bailly, *op. cit.*
59. Jefferson, *op. cit.* Continuation of letter to John Jay, July 19, 1789:

"Letters written by his [Louis XVI's] own hand to the Marquis de La Fayette remove the scruples of his position [as Commanding General of the National Guard]. Tranquillity is now restored to the capital: the shops are again opened; the people resuming their labors, and if the want of bread does not disturb our peace, we may hope a continuance of it. The demolition of the Bastille is going on, and the *Milice Bourgeoise* organizing and training. The ancient police of the city is abolished by the authority of the people, the introduction of the King's troops will probably be proscribed, and a watch or city guards substituted, which shall depend on the city alone. The whole country must pass successively through it, and happy if they get through it as soon and as well as Paris has done.

"I went yesterday to Versailles to satisfy myself what had passed there; for nothing can be believed but what one sees, or has from an eye-witness. They believe there still, that three thousand people have fallen victims to the tumults of Paris. Mr. Short [Embassy assistant] and myself have been every day among them, in order to be sure of what was passing. We cannot find, with certainty, that any body has been killed but the three before mentioned [Flesselles, the governor, and lieutenant governor of the Bastille], and those who fell in the assault or defence of the Bastille. How many of the garrison were killed, nobody pretends to have ever heard. Of the assailants, accounts vary from six to six hundred. The most general belief is, that there fell about thirty. There have been many reports of instantaneous executions by the mob, on such of their body as they caught in acts of theft or robbery. Some of these may perhaps be true. There was a severity of honesty observed, of which no example has been known. Bags of money offered on various occasions through fear or guilt, have been uniformly refused by the mobs. The churches are now occupied in singing '*De profundis*' and '*Requiems,*' 'for the repose of the souls of the brave and valiant citizens who have sealed with their blood the liberty of the nation.' "

The rest of the long letter is of less interest.
60. Castelot, *op. cit.*

31. THE HISTORY OF MAN BEGINS

1. Vallentin, Antonina. *Mirabeau.* Paris, 1946–47. 2 vols.
2. Young, Arthur. *Travels* . . . [in] *the Kingdom of France.* London, 1792.
3. *Ibid.*
4. Soboul, Albert. *1789: L'an un de la liberté.* Paris, 1950.
5. Conrad, Pierre. *La Peur en Dauphiné* (*juillet–août 1789*).

6. Lavisse, Ernest. *Histoire de France contemporaine.* Paris, 1921–22. 10 vols.
7. Hardy, Siméon-Prosper. *Mes loisirs, ou journal d'événemens tels qu'ils parviennent à ma connaissance.* Manuscript of eight volumes in the Bibliothèque Nationale. Fonds français, 6680–87. Covers 1764 to October 1789.
8. Lefebvre, Georges. *La Grande peur de 1789.* Paris, 1932.
9. Soboul, *op. cit.*
10. Lefebvre, *op. cit.*
11. Elizabeth de France, Madame. *Correspondance . . . publiée par F. Feuillet de Conches.* Paris, 1868.
12. Soboul, *op. cit.*
13. Kessel, Patrick. *La Nuit du 4 août 1789.* Paris, 1969.
14. *Procès-verbal de l'assemblée des communes et de l'assemblée nationale.* Paris, 1789–91. 75 vols. Minutes of the National Assembly's meetings.
15. *Cambridge Modern History.* Cambridge, 1902–11. 13 vols.
16. Unless otherwise indicated, quotations of deputies at the August 4 session of the National Assembly may be found in sources cited in Notes 13 and 14 above.
17. *Courier de Provence*, No. 23.
18. *Ibid.*
19. Granié, Pierre. *Histoire de l'assemblée constituante de France.* Paris, 1797.
20. Droz, Joseph. *Histoire du règne de Louis XVI . . .* Paris, 1858. 3 vols.
21. Buchez, Philippe-Joseph-Benjamin, and Roux, Pierre-Célestin. *Histoire parlementaire de la révolution française.* Paris, 1834–38. 40 vols.
22. Gauville, Louis-Henri-Charles, Baron de. *Journal.* Paris, 1864.
23. Kessel, *op. cit.*
24. Dumont, Etienne-Pierre-Louis. *Souvenirs sur Mirabeau . . .* Paris, 1832.
25. Ferrières, Charles-Elie, Marquis de. *Correspondance inédite (1789–91).* Paris, 1932.
26. *Ibid.*
27. Lafayette, Marie-Joseph-Gilbert du Motier, Marquis de. *Mémoires . . .* Paris, 1837–38. 6 vols.
28. Jefferson, Thomas. *Memoir, Correspondence and Miscellanies.* Boston, 1830. 4 vols.
29. *Encyclopaedia Britannica,* 11th edition.
30. Barthou, Louis. *Mirabeau.* Paris, 1913.
31. Aulard, François-Alphonse. *Histoire politique de la révolution française.* Paris, 1901.
32. Michelet, Jules. *Histoire de la révolution française.* Paris, 1847–53. 7 vols.

32. ADIEU VERSAILLES

1. Malouet, Pierre-Victor. Baron. *Mémoires.* Paris, 1868. 2 vols.
2. *Procès-verbal de l'assemblée des communes et de l'assemblée nationale.* Paris, 1789–91. 75 vols.
3. Soboul, Albert. *La Révolution française, 1789–99.* Paris, 1948.
4. Augeard, Jacques-Mathieu. *Mémoires secrets.* Paris, 1866.
5. Necker, Jacques. *Histoire de la révolution française.* Paris, 1821. 4 vols.
6. Lavisse, Ernest. *Histoire de France contemporaine.* Paris, 1921–22. 10 vols.
7. Malouet, *op. cit.*

8. Lavisse, *op. cit.*

9. Ferrières, Charles-Élie, Marquis de. *Mémoires.* Paris, 1821. 3 vols.

10. Bailly, Jean-Sylvain. *Mémoires* . . . Paris, 1804. 3 vols.
    Jaurès, Jean. *Histoire socialiste (1789–1900).* Paris, n.d. 10 vols.

11. Rudé, George. *The Crowd in the French Revolution.* Oxford, 1959.

12. *Ibid.*

13. Lafayette, Marie-Joseph-Gilbert du Motier, Marquis de. *Mémoires* . . . Paris, 1837–38. 6 vols.

14. *Courier de Provence.*

15. Principal sources for the banquet scene, other than those specifically cited:
    Battifol, Louis. *Les Journées des 5 et 6 octobre 1789 à Versailles.* Versailles, 1891.
    La Rocheterie, Maxime de. *Les 5 et 6 octobre.* Paris, 1874.
    Leclercq, Henri, Dom. *Les Journées d'octobre et la fin de l'année 1789.* Paris, 1924.
    Mazé, Jules. *Louis XVI et Marie-Antoinette. Les journées révolutionnaires d'octobre 1789.* Paris, 1939.

16. Campan, Jeanne-Louise. *Mémoires* . . . Paris, 1822. 3 vols.

17. Mathiez, Albert. *Étude critique sur les journées des 5 et 6 octobre 1789.* Paris, 1899.

18. Le Roi, Joseph-Adrien. *Récit des journées des 5 et 6 octobre 1789 à Versailles.* Versailles, 1867.

19. La Rocheterie, Maxime de. *Histoire de Marie-Antoinette.* Paris, 1890. 2 vols.

20. Castelot, André. *Le Procès de Marie-Antoinette.* Paris, 1965.

21. Lavisse, *op. cit.*

22. *Procédure criminelle instruite au Châtelet de Paris sur la dénonciation des faits arrivés à Versailles dans la journée du 6 octobre 1789.* Paris, 1790. This is a major if prejudiced source for the events of October 4, 5, and 6, 1789. Most of the 388 witnesses heard at the Châtelet inquiry, and quoted in the *Procédure criminelle* . . . , are clearly as tendentious as the inquiry itself. (See Rudé's *The Crowd in the French Revolution.*)

23. Staël-Holstein, Anne-Louise-Germaine Necker, Baronne de. *Considérations sur les principaux éléments de la révolution française.* Paris, 1818. 3 vols.

24. Carlyle, Thomas. *The French Revolution.* Many editions.

25. Ferrières, *op. cit.*

26. Goncourt, Edmond and Jules. *Portraits intimes du xviiie siècle.* Paris, 1857–58. 2 vols.

27. Leclercq, *op. cit.*

28. Barthou, Louis. *Mirabeau.* Paris, 1913.

29. Mounier, Jean-Joseph. *Appel au tribunal de l'opinion publique* . . . Geneva, 1790.

30. Ferrières, *op. cit.*

31. Lavisse, *op. cit.*

32. Mathiez, *op. cit.*

33. La Tour du Pin Gouvernet, Henriette-Lucie, Marquise de. *Journal d'une femme de cinquante ans, 1778–1815.* Paris, 1907–11. 4 vols.

34. Zweig, Stefan. *Marie Antoinette.* New York, 1933.

35. Saint-Priest, François-Emmanuel, Comte de. *Mémoires.* Paris, 1929. 2 vols.

36. La Tour du Pin Gouvernet, *op. cit.*

37. *Ibid.*
38. Weber, Joseph. *Mémoires.* Paris, 1822. 2 vols.
39. Bailly, *op. cit.*
40. Ferrières, *op. cit.*
41. Bertrand de Molleville, Antoine-François *Histoire de la révolution de France.* Paris, 1801–03. 14 vols.
42. Ferrières, *op. cit.*
43. Louison Chabry's testimony at the Châtelet inquiry. See Note 22, above.
44. La Rocheterie, *op. cit.,* Note 15, above.
45. Ferrières, *op. cit.*
46. La Rocheterie, *op. cit.*
47. La Tour du Pin Gouvernet, *op. cit.*
48. *Ibid.*
49. Lafayette, *op. cit.*
50. *Ibid.*
51. La Tour du Pin Govervet, *op. cit.*
52. Le Roi, *op. cit.*
53. Rivarol, Antoine, Comte de. *Journal politique-national.* Versailles, 1789.
54. Ferrières, *op. cit.*
55. Principal sources for October 5 and 6 have been indicated throughout this chapter from Note 1 to Note 69. See particularly Notes 15 and 22.
56. Lafayette, *op. cit.*
57. Ferrières, *op. cit.*
58. Lafayette, *op. cit.*
59. Testimony given at the Châtelet inquiry. The Duc d'Orléans' own convincing account of his presence in Paris from October 3 to early morning, October 6, may be found in the following:
    Orléans, Louis-Philippe-Joseph, Duc d'. *Exposé de la conduite de M. le duc d'Orléans dans la révolution de France. Rédigé par lui-même à Londres.* Paris, 1791.
60. Lafayette, *op. cit.*
61. Staël-Holstein, *op. cit.*
62. Lafayette, *op. cit.*
63. Staël-Holstein, *op. cit.*
64. Marie-Thérèse Charlotte de France, Duchesse d'Angoulême. *Récits de trois jeunes prisonnières* . . . Paris, 1910. The Duchesse d'Angoulême is better known as Madame Royale.
65. Campan, *op. cit.*
66. Marie-Thérèse Charlotte de France, *op. cit.*
67. La Tour du Pin Gouvernet, *op. cit.*
68. Tourzel, Louise-Élisabeth, Duchesse de. *Mémoires.* Paris, 1883. 2 vols. Madame de Tourzel was the Dauphin's governess.
69. La Tour du Pin Gouvernet, *op. cit.*

EPILOGUE WITHOUT TEARS

1. On departure scene at Versailles and aftermath, see Verlet, Pierre. *Versailles.* Paris, 1961. Also, Champigneulle, Bernard. *Versailles dans l'art et l'histoire.* Paris, 1954.

2. Zweig, Stefan. *Marie Antoinette.* New York, 1933.

3. Barthou, Louis. *Mirabeau.* Paris, 1913.

4. Staël-Holstein, Anne-Louise-Germaine Necker, Baronne de. *Considérations sur . . . la révolution française.* Paris, 1818. 3 vols.

5. Vallentin, Antonina. *Mirabeau.* Paris, 1946–47. 2 vols.

6. Reinhard, Marcel. *La Chute de la royauté, 10 août 1792.* Paris, 1969.

7. Van der Kemp, Gérard, and Levron, Jacques. *Versailles, Trianons.* Paris, 1957.

8. Las Cases, Emmanuel-Auguste, Marquis de. *Mémorial de Sainte-Hélène.* Paris, 1823. 8 vols.
   On Napoleon, see Lefebvre, Georges. *Napoléon.* Paris, 1965. Fifth, enlarged edition.

9. Champigneulle, *op. cit.*

10. Howard, Michael E. *The Franco-Prussian War. The German Invasion of France, 1870–1871.* London, 1961.

11. Horne, Alistair. *The Fall of Paris. The Siege and the Commune, 1870–71.* New York, 1965.
    Lefebvre, Henri. *La Proclamation de la commune, 26 mars 1871.* Paris, 1965.

12. Nicolson, Harold G. *Peacemaking, 1919.* London, 1933.

13. Van der Kemp, *op. cit.*

14. Viansson-Ponté, Pierre. *The King and His Court.* New York, 1964. (Translated from French. Original title: *Les Gaullistes.*)

Index